Rethinking Estate and Gift Taxation

Rethinking Estate and Gift Taxation

William G. Gale
James R. Hines Jr.
Joel Slemrod
Editors

BROOKINGS INSTITUTION PRESS
Washington, D.C.

Copyright © 2001
THE BROOKINGS INSTITUTION
1775 Massachusetts Avenue, N.W.
Washington, D.C. 20036
www.brookings.edu

Library of Congress Cataloging-in-Publication data

Rethinking estate and gift taxation / William G. Gale, James R. Hines Jr.,
Joel Slemrod, editors.
    p. cm.
Includes index.
   ISBN 0-8157-0069-5 (paper : alk. paper)
   1. Inheritance and transfer tax—Law and legislation—United States.
2. Gifts—Taxation—Law and legislation—United States. 3. Inheritance
and transfer tax—United States. 4. Gifts—Taxation—United States.
5. Tax planning—United States. I. Gale, William G. II. Hines, James R., Jr.
III. Slemrod, Joel. IV. Title.
   KF6572 .R48 2001   2001002137
   343.7305'3—dc21

9 8 7 6 5 4 3 2 1

The paper used in this publication meets minimum requirements of the
American National Standard for Information Sciences—Permanence of Paper
for Printed Library Materials: ANSI Z39.48-1992.

Typeset in Adobe Garamond

Composition by Circle Graphics
Columbia, Maryland

Printed by R. R. Donnelley and Sons
Harrisonburg, VA

ℬ THE BROOKINGS INSTITUTION

The Brookings Institution is an independent organization devoted to nonpartisan research, education, and publication in economics, government, foreign policy, and the social sciences generally. Its principal purposes are to aid in the development of sound public policies and to promote public understanding of issues of national importance.

The Institution was founded on December 8, 1927, to merge the activities of the Institute for Government Research, founded in 1916, the Institute of Economics, founded in 1922, and the Robert Brookings Graduate School of Economics and Government, founded in 1924.

The general administration of the Institution is the responsibility of a Board of Trustees charged with safeguarding the independence of the staff and fostering the most favorable conditions for scientific research and publication. The immediate direction of the policies, program, and staff is vested in the president, assisted by an advisory committee of the officers and staff.

In publishing a study, the Institution presents it as a competent treatment of a subject worthy of public consideration. The interpretations or conclusions in such publications are those of the author or authors and do not necessarily reflect the views of the other staff members, officers, or trustees of the Brookings Institution.

Foreword

AFTER ENDURING years of relative neglect, the estate tax has recently jumped to center stage in American politics. With the election of President George W. Bush, who campaigned in favor of eliminating the tax, some change in the estate tax—whether abolition or at least reform—has become highly likely.

The estate tax evokes strong emotional responses. Some consider it the fairest tax, because it is levied only on the wealthiest households. Others believe it the embodiment of everything that is wrong with tax policy. Critics call it unfair, inefficient, complicated, and immoral.

Despite the fierce debate, hard knowledge about the estate tax and its effects is sparse—partly because the relevant behaviors can span a lifetime and may be difficult to track, and partly because little is known about the very wealthiest families who pay the majority of estate taxes. These families may well have different motives for wealth accumulation and giving of transfers than other households do.

In fact, resolution of a whole series of difficult economic issues could usefully inform the debate. On May 4 and 5, 2000, the Office of Tax Policy Research at the University of Michigan Business School and the Brookings Institution convened a conference to examine numerous features of the estate tax. The goal was not to stake out a position but rather to develop a body of research that could help citizens and policymakers to make more informed judgments on the best course for policy.

Conference participants heard papers on the history of the tax and the economic characteristics of the decedents whose estates owed taxes; the methods and extent of (legal) avoidance and (illegal) evasion of estate taxes; the optimal taxation of estates and gifts; the impact of estate taxes on saving and capital formation, charitable contributions, and gift giving; and the distributional effects of policy alternatives to the estate tax. This volume contains revised versions of those papers, formal comments on them, and an introductory survey by William G. Gale and Joel Slemrod. These papers paint a subtle and varied picture of the estate tax and its impacts that does not clearly yield to any of the extreme or simplistic views prevalent.

The conference would not have occurred without the tireless efforts and good cheer of Mary Ceccanese of the Office of Tax Policy Research at the University of Michigan Business School. At Brookings, Catherine McLoughlin provided essential assistance in running the conference and shepherding the volume to completion. Theresa Walker and Tanjam Jacobson edited the volume, Debra Hevenstone verified the chapters, and Samara Potter provided research assistance. Carlotta Ribar proofread the book, and James M. Diggins prepared the index.

The views expressed in this volume are those of the authors and should not be ascribed to the authors' employers, funders, or affiliations, or the trustees, officers, or other staff of the Brookings Institution.

MICHAEL H. ARMACOST
President

April 2001
Washington, D.C.

Contents

1   *Overview*   1
WILLIAM G. GALE AND JOEL SLEMROD

2   *Elements of Federal Estate Taxation*   65
BARRY W. JOHNSON, JACOB M. MIKOW, AND
MARTHA BRITTON ELLER
Comment by C. Eugene Steuerle   108

3   *Avoiding Federal Wealth Transfer Taxes*   113
RICHARD SCHMALBECK
Comment by Jane Gravelle   159

4   *A Framework for Assessing Estate and Gift Taxation*   164
LOUIS KAPLOW
Comment by Pierre Pestieau   205

5   *Do Estate Taxes Reduce Saving?*   216
WILLIAM G. GALE AND MARIA G. PEROZEK
Comment by Roger H. Gordon   248

6   *Inequality and Wealth Accumulation: Eliminating the
Federal Gift and Estate Tax*   258
JOHN LAITNER
Comment by Douglas Holtz-Eakin   293

7 *The Impact of the Estate Tax on Wealth Accumulation and
   Avoidance Behavior*   299
   WOJCIECH KOPCZUK AND JOEL SLEMROD
   Comment by Alan J. Auerbach   344

8 *Charitable Giving in Life and at Death*   350
   DAVID JOULFAIAN
   Comment by James R. Hines Jr.   370

9 *Noncompliance with the Federal Estate Tax*   375
   MARTHA BRITTON ELLER, BRIAN ERARD,
   AND CHIH-CHIN HO
   Comment by Kathleen McGarry   411

10 *The Distributional Burden of Taxing Estates and
   Unrealized Capital Gains at Death*   422
   JAMES M. POTERBA AND SCOTT WEISBENNER
   Comment by Leonard Burman   450

11 *Elderly Asset Management and Health*   457
   JONATHAN S. FEINSTEIN AND CHIH-CHIN HO
   Comment by Jonathan Skinner   499

   Contributors   505

   Index   507

Rethinking Estate and Gift Taxation

WILLIAM G. GALE
JOEL SLEMROD

1 | Overview

THE IDEA OF making death a taxable event infuriates many
people. Winston Churchill called estate taxes an attempt
to tax dead people rather than the living.[1] Steve Forbes campaigned in favor
of "no taxation without respiration."[2] Equally striking remarks come from
tax experts. Lawyer Edward McCaffery has equated estate taxation with
grave robbery, while economist Bruce Bartlett points out that a key plank in
the Communist Manifesto was the abolition of inheritance rights.[3]

Opponents claim that the estate tax is imposed at a time—death—that is
at best illogical and at worst morally repugnant. They argue that the tax
impairs economic growth, destroys small businesses and family farms, encourages spendthrift behavior, generates huge compliance costs, and leads to

We thank Ben Harris, Pete Kimball, and Samara Potter for outstanding research assistance. We
gratefully acknowledge helpful comments from Henry Aaron, Alan Auerbach, Thomas Barthold,
Al Davis, Jane Gravelle, David Joulfaian, John Laitner, Andrew Lyon, Olivia Mitchell, James Morgan,
Richard Schmalbeck, Jonathan Skinner, Jay Soled, Dennis Ventry, and Jennifer Wahl.

1. Churchill (1906).

2. This line is contained in the Steve Forbes 2000 National Online Headquarters website and
was often uttered by Forbes on the campaign trail. It is, though, apparently not original to him. See
also Lisa Anderson and Michael Tackett, "5 GOP Contenders Try Hard to Be No. 2," *Chicago Tri-
bune*, October 29, 1999.

3. McCaffery (1999); Bruce Bartlett, "The End of the Estate Tax?" *Tax Notes*, July 7, 1997,
pp. 105–10.

1

ingenious avoidance strategies. As an inefficient, inequitable, and complex levy, the "death tax" is thought to violate every norm of good tax policy.

Supporters find the criticisms overstated or wrong. They note that the tax is only levied on the estates of about 2 percent of Americans who die—and only on those with substantial estates. They believe that a highly progressive tax that patches loopholes, helps provide equality of opportunity, reduces the concentration of wealth, and encourages charitable giving cannot be all bad.

These debates have increased in intensity and frequency in recent years, in part because of the stock market boom, the aging of the population, the budget surplus, and intensive lobbying. In 1999 and 2000, both Houses of Congress passed legislation to abolish the estate tax but could not override presidential vetoes. Additional legislation seems very likely in the near future.

It may seem remarkable that a tax that generated only about 1.5 percent of federal revenues in 1999 could be the subject of such heated dispute. But the estate tax is controversial precisely because it raises a number of interesting choices for policymakers, as well as intriguing issues for researchers. Besides its association with the rich and the dead—two never-ending sources of fascination—the estate tax epitomizes, in extreme form, the pervasive trade-off between equity and efficiency in the design of government policy. The tax also raises issues as private as the nature of relationships between parents and their children and as politically sensitive as the definition and implementation of equal opportunity.

In light of these factors, the Office of Tax Policy Research at the University of Michigan Business School and the Brookings Institution convened a conference on May 4-5, 2000, attended by leading economists and lawyers. The conference revolved around ten papers that addressed particular features of the U.S. estate and gift tax. This volume brings together those papers and formal comments by discussants.

The purpose of this introductory chapter is to help frame the estate tax debate and to interpret and integrate existing research on the tax. First the chapter provides background on the features of the estate and gift tax, characteristics of recent estate tax returns, the evolution of transfer taxes in the U.S., and the role of such taxes in other countries.

Then existing models and evidence on why people give intergenerational transfers are reviewed. Because estate and gift taxes place burdens on transfers of wealth, the impact and appropriate role of the taxes will depend in part on people's motives for transfers. There are many plausible motives for giving, and the empirical literature has not successfully distinguished among them. Uncertainty about transfer motives makes analysis of estate taxes more difficult but also opens a number of intriguing possibilities discussed in the following pages.

We examine the incidence and equity of transfer taxes. Transfer taxes are highly progressive if they are borne by transfer donors or recipients. It appears unlikely that much of the burden of the tax is passed on to other agents. The estate tax serves as a backstop to the income tax, taxing components of income—such as unrealized capital gains—that otherwise go untaxed.

Transfer taxes raise difficult issues of horizontal equity. Among donors with the same wealth, the taxes discriminate on the basis of how resources are spent, violating the notion that those with equal means should pay equal taxes. But among recipients with the same (preinheritance) wealth, transfer taxes reduce the inequality of inheritances and thus reduce horizontal inequity and unequal opportunity. Another issue is whether taxing at death is fair. While death may be unpleasant to contemplate, there are good administrative, equity, and efficiency reasons to impose taxes at death, and the asserted costs appear to be overblown. Moreover, to the extent that it really is a problem, taxation at death could be avoided by replacing the estate tax with equally progressive taxes imposed during life.

This chapter also examines efficiency issues. Standard optimal tax theory shows that alternative uses of labor income should be taxed at different rates only to the extent that the goods consumed are more or less complementary to leisure, which is untaxed. Consumption and bequests represent two uses of labor income, with the estate tax taxing placing heavier taxation on bequests than on consumption. On pure efficiency grounds, this would be optimal if and only if bequests were more complementary to leisure than lifetime consumption is. Two other factors also suggest a possible role for estate taxes in an optimal tax system. First, optimal systems trade off equity and efficiency. If the income tax cannot generate as progressive a tax burden distribution, relative to its efficiency cost, as society would prefer—because, for example, of the treatment of capital gains—there is a potential role for an estate tax. Second, standard optimal tax theory does not incorporate motives for transfers. The efficiency effects of transfer taxes depend in sensitive and surprising ways on the motives for transfers.

We discuss administrative aspects of the estate tax. Estimates of taxpayers' costs of complying with the estate tax and their ability to reduce their estate tax liability—through legal or illegal means—are often overstated. To the extent that it does occur, tax avoidance may reduce the effective marginal tax rate imposed by transfer taxes.

The effects of transfer taxes on saving, labor supply, and entrepreneurship are also examined. From a theoretical perspective, these effects should depend on why people give transfers. There is little reliable empirical evidence that transfer taxes have substantially reduced any of these factors, although historically the level of taxable estates does vary inversely with the level of estate taxation. There are compelling reasons to believe that the supposed deleterious effects on small businesses have been dramatically overstated.

Finally, the chapter examines a variety of other behavioral responses. Transfer taxes have measurable effects on the timing and level of inter vivos gifts, charitable contributions, and capital gains realizations. We review policy options, including abolishing transfer taxes, replacing current taxes with an inheritance tax, reforming the structure of existing transfer taxes, and we offer a brief conclusion.

An Overview of Transfer Taxes

Federal law imposes an integrated set of taxes on estates, gifts, and generation-skipping transfers.[4] By law, the executor of an estate must file a federal estate tax return within nine months of the death of a U.S. citizen or resident if the gross estate exceeds a threshold that in 2000 was set at $675,000.[5]

The gross estate includes all of the decedents' assets, his or her share of jointly owned assets, and life insurance proceeds from policies owned by the decedent. The gross estate also includes gifts made by the decedent in excess of an annual exemption that is currently set at $10,000 per donee per year and is indexed for inflation. The estate may also include other property over which the decedent had control, wealth transfers made during life that were revocable or provided for less than full consideration, and qualified terminable interest property.[6]

Typically, assets are valued at fair market value. But closely held businesses are allowed to value real property assets at their "use value" rather than their highest alternative market-oriented value. The maximum allowed reduction

4. See Joint Committee on Taxation (1998) for a summary of current law and legislative history of transfer taxes. States may also impose estate, inheritance, or gift taxes. The laws that govern how and to whom property may pass are the exclusive domain of the states. For example, many states provide a surviving spouse and minor children with some protection against disinheritance. In cases of intestacy, state laws provide a structure to guide succession.

5. This threshold is scheduled to rise over the next several years, along with the "effective exemption" described below and in table 1-5.

6. Qualified terminable interest property (QTIP) is created when the estate of the first spouse to die receives an estate tax deduction for a wealth transfer that provides the surviving spouse an income interest only and provides the remainder interest to someone else. When the second spouse dies, the QTIP is included in his/her estate.

in value was $770,000 for estates of decedents who died in 2000 and is in-dexed for inflation. In addition, it is often possible to discount asset value when such assets are not readily marketable or the taxpayer's ownership does not correlate with control. The estate is usually valued as of the date of death but alternatively may be valued six months after the death if the value of the gross estate and the estate tax liability decline during this period.[7]

The estate tax provides unlimited deductions for transfers to a surviving spouse and contributions to charitable organizations. Deductions are also allowed for debts owed by the estate, funeral expenses, and administrative and legal fees associated with the estate. Interests in certain qualified family businesses were also allowed an extra deduction of up to $625,000 in 2000 for the value of the business being transferred.[8]

After determining net estate—gross estate less deductions—the statutory tax rate is applied. Statutory marginal tax rates are given in table 1-1. Formally, the statutory tax schedule applies an 18 percent rate to the first $10,000 of life-time transfers, with the rate rising to 37 percent on transfers above $675,000, and rising in several stages to 55 percent on taxable transfers above $3 million.

For several reasons, however, effective tax rates differ from the statutory schedule. First, although the lowest formal tax rate is 18 percent, the low-est rate that any taxable return faces is 37 percent owing to the "applicable credit amount." As of 2000, this credit amount is set at $220,550, which pro-vides an effective exemption of the first $675,000 of transfers given during life and at death, above and beyond the $10,000 per recipient annual gift exemption and the other exclusions, deductions, and asset adjustments noted.

Another credit is given for state inheritance and estate taxes (but not for state gift taxes). The credit rate is based on the "adjusted taxable estate," which is the federal taxable estate less $60,000, and the allowable credit ranges from zero to 16 percent of the base. Thus, the credit for state taxes can reduce the maximum effective federal statutory tax rate to 39 percent for the largest estates. Most states now levy so-called soak-up taxes that exactly mirror the credit limit, so that the state transfer taxes shift revenue from the federal to the state treasuries without adding to the total tax burden on the estate.

Additional credits are allowed for gift taxes previously paid and for estate taxes that were previously paid on inherited wealth.[9] Finally, a 5 percentage

---

7. See chapter 3 by Richard Schmalbeck in this volume. If the six-month alternative valuation date is used, assets that were liquidated in the interim are valued at their sale price.

8. The value of this deduction, plus the effective exemption created by the unified credit and discussed below, cannot exceed $1.3 million.

9. The latter is phased out over ten years, in two-year intervals, from the date the wealth was in-herited, and is intended to reduce the extent of (double) taxation of recently inherited wealth.

Table 1-1. *Federal Unified Estate and Gift Tax Rates, 2000*

Taxable estate and gifts (dollars)	Statutory marginal tax rate (percent)
0 up to 10,000	18
10,000 up to 20,000	20
20,000 up to 40,000	22
40,000 up to 60,000	24
60,000 up to 80,000	26
80,000 up to 100,000	28
100,000 up to 150,000	30
150,000 up to 250,000	32
250,000 up to 500,000	34
500,000 up to 750,000	37
750,000 up to 1,000,000	39
1,000,000 up to 1,250,000	41
1,250,000 up to 1,500,000	43
1,500,000 up to 2,000,000	45
2,000,000 up to 2,500,000	49
2,500,000 up to 3,000,000	53
3,000,000 and over	55

Source: Internal Revenue Service (1999).

point surtax raises the effective marginal estate tax rate to 60 percent on taxable estate between $10 million and $17,184,000.[10]

By law, payment is due within nine months of the decedent's death, although a six-month filing extension may be obtained. However, the actual timing of the tax payment can be flexible, as the law provides for ex post spreading out of tax payments over fourteen years for closely held family businesses.[11]

To reduce tax avoidance under the estate tax, the federal gift tax imposes burdens on transfers between living persons that exceed the annual gift ex-

10. The surtax phases out the "benefit" of having lower marginal estate tax rates on the first $10 million in taxable estate. Before 1998, the surtax applied to estates of even higher value and took back the benefit of the unified credit as well. Due to a drafting error in the 1997 tax act, this part of the surtax was removed and has not been reinstated.

11. Moreover, in the presence of a well-functioning market for life insurance, a one-time estate tax liability at an uncertain future date can be transformed into a series of annual premium payments. In this context, it is interesting to note that the original estate tax law passed in 1916 contained a provision allowing for prepayment of estate tax liability with a 5 percent discount per year. This provision was eliminated by the Revenue Act of 1918.

emption noted above. Although the estate and gift taxes are said to be unified, there are some important distinctions between the taxation of gifts and estates. Gifts are taxed on a tax-exclusive basis while estates are taxed on a tax-inclusive basis. This provides a sizable tax advantage to giving gifts rather than bequests.[12]

However, there is also a tax disincentive for inter vivos gifts. When an appreciated asset is transferred as part of an estate, the asset's basis is "stepped up" (that is, made equal) to the market value at the time of death, thus exempting from future income taxation the appreciation during the decedent's lifetime. In contrast, if the asset is given inter vivos, the donor's cost basis (often, but not always, the original purchase price) is "carried over" as the asset's basis. In this case, if the recipient sells the asset, capital gains that accrued before the gift was made would be taxed under the income tax.

Federal law also imposes a tax on generation-skipping transfers (GSTs). Under the estate and gift tax, a family that transferred resources over more than one generation (for example, from grandparent to grandchild) at a time could in principle reduce the number of times the wealth was subject to tax over a given period and could greatly reduce its transfer tax liabilities. To close this avoidance mechanism, generation-skipping transfers in excess of $1 million per donor generate a separate tax, at rates up to 55 percent, above and beyond any applicable estate and gift tax. The GST tax raises virtually no gross revenue but does appear to successfully close the loophole noted above.[13]

Characteristics of Estate Tax Returns, 1998

Evidence on the gross estate, deductions, and tax payments from estate tax returns filed in 1998 can help shed light on several issues. Table 1-2 provides information on estate tax returns and gross estate. Roughly 98,000 returns were filed in 1998. The number of returns in 1998 amounted to 4.3 percent

12. Formally, if the marginal estate tax rate is e, the effective marginal gift tax is $e/(1+e)$. For example, suppose the applicable estate tax rate is 50 percent and consider the implications of giving a gift or a bequest that costs the donor $15,000, including taxes. If the funds are given as an inter vivos transfer, the recipient would receive $10,000 and the donor would pay gift tax of $5,000 (50 percent of $10,000). If the funds are given as a bequest, the recipient would receive only $7,500, and the estate would owe $7,500 in taxes (50 percent of $15,000). Thus, in this example, the estate tax is 50 percent of the gross-of-tax bequest; the gift tax is 50 percent of the net-of-tax gift but only 33 percent of gross-of-tax gift by the donor.

13. Schmalbeck, chap. 3, in this volume.

Table 1-2. *Number of Estate Tax Returns and Aggregate Estate Value, 1998*

		Gross estate size (millions of dollars)					
Type of return	All	0.6 under 1.0	1.0 under 2.5	2.5 under 5.0	5.0 under 10.0	10.0 under 20.0	20.0 and over
All							
Number of returns	97,868	49,705	36,419	7,689	2,665	944	446
Aggregate estate value (thousands of dollars)	173,817,135	38,335,193	53,419,415	26,340,377	18,138,696	12,991,370	24,592,085
Taxable							
Number of returns	47,483	20,106	19,846	4,633	1,836	688	374
Aggregate estate value (thousands of dollars)	103,020,298	16,340,412	29,144,527	16,022,285	12,600,670	9,515,756	19,396,648
Nontaxable							
Number of returns	50,385	29,600	16,572	3,057	828	256	72
Aggregate estate value (thousands of dollars)	70,796,838	21,994,781	24,274,889	10,318,091	5,538,026	3,475,613	5,195,437

Source: Internal Revenue Service (2000a).

of the number of adult deaths (age 20 or higher) in the United States in 1997.[14] Total gross estate among 1998 returns equaled $173 billion, less than 0.5 percent of privately held net worth.[15]

The size distribution of gross estates is highly skewed. The 89 percent of returns with gross estate below $2.5 million accounted for 53 percent of total gross estates. The 4.1 percent of estates valued in excess of $5 million accounted for 32 percent of gross estate value. Taxable returns—that is, returns that paid positive taxes—accounted for 49 percent of all returns and 59 percent of total gross estates.

Table 1-3 reports on the composition of gross assets in estates. Personal residence and other real estate accounts for about 19 percent of gross estates, stocks (other than closely held), bonds, and cash account for 61 percent, and small businesses (closely held stock, limited partnerships, and other non-corporate business assets) account for 8 percent. Farm assets account for 0.5 percent of all gross assets in taxable estates. This figure excludes farm real estate, which accounted for 2.6 percent of gross estates.[16]

The composition of estates varies by estate size. Among estates with gross assets below $1.0 million, small business assets account for 2.2 percent of gross estate, stocks account for 21 percent, and cash accounts for 19 percent. Among estates in excess of $20 million, closely held businesses account for 21 percent, stocks account for 43 percent, and cash accounts for under 5 percent of gross estate. The composition of estates does not vary markedly between taxable and nontaxable estates (not shown).

Table 1-4 provides information on estate tax deductions. Deductions account for 41 percent of gross estate on average, but this ratio varies dramatically with estate size. For estates with gross assets below $1 million, deductions accounted for 25 percent of gross estate. For estates above $20 million, deductions were 56 percent of gross estate.

The composition of deductions also changes with estate size. Bequests to surviving spouses account for between 60 and 75 percent of all deductions in each estate size category. In contrast, charitable contributions represent 11 percent of deductions for estates below $1 million but rise to 27 percent of deductions for estates above $20 million.

Because differences in deductions relative to gross assets are the main reason why some estates are taxable and some are not, it is not surprising that deduction patterns vary by taxable status. Among taxable returns, overall deductions, spousal deductions, and charitable contributions all rise as a share

14. Hoyert, Kochanek and Murphy (1999).
15. Federal Reserve Board (2000).
16. We thank Barry Johnson for providing this information.

Table 1-3. *Composition of Gross Estates, 1998*[a]

Percent

Asset category	All	Size of gross estate (millions of dollars)					
		0.6 under 1.0	1.0 under 2.5	2.5 under 5.0	5.0 under 10.0	10.0 under 20.0	20.0 and over
Personal residence	7.2	11.7	8.7	6.4	5.0	3.4	1.7
Real estate and real estate partnerships	11.4	13.0	12.0	10.7	11.5	9.8	9.0
Closely held stock	5.9	1.6	2.8	5.2	7.1	9.3	17.8
Limited partnerships	1.3	0.3	0.7	1.6	1.9	2.7	2.4
Other noncorporate businesses	0.7	0.3	0.5	1.0	0.8	1.2	1.2
Other stock	30.9	20.8	27.8	32.2	35.5	42.0	42.7
State and local bonds	10.6	8.4	10.5	12.6	14.6	11.8	8.3
Other bonds, bond funds, mortgages, and notes	7.4	8.9	7.6	6.8	6.1	6.6	6.5
Unclassifiable mutual funds	0.8	1.4	1.1	0.7	0.6	0.3	0.2
Cash and cash management accounts	11.0	18.6	11.9	8.7	7.0	6.5	4.7
Insurance	3.3	4.2	4.7	3.3	2.4	1.1	0.5
Farm assets	0.5	0.6	0.6	0.4	0.4	0.3	0.2
Annuities	6.9	8.5	9.5	8.1	5.1	2.9	1.2
Art	0.4	0.0	0.1	0.3	0.4	0.5	1.7
Other assets	2.0	1.9	1.9	2.2	1.9	1.7	2.0

Source: Internal Revenue Service (2000a).

a. Columns do not total 100, due to rounding.

Table 1-4. *Estate Tax Deductions as Percentage of Gross Estate, 1998*
Percent

Type of return and deduction	All	Gross estate size (millions of dollars)					
		0.6 under 1.0	1.0 under 2.5	2.5 under 5.0	5.0 under 10.0	10.0 under 20.0	20.0 and over
All							
Bequests for surviving							
spouses	28.4	16.4	27.9	34.1	34.4	35.3	34.2
Charity	6.2	2.8	3.8	5.3	7.4	9.9	15.2
Other	6.1	5.6	6.3	6.1	6.1	6.7	6.3
Total deductions	40.8	24.8	38.0	45.5	48.0	51.8	55.5
Taxable							
Bequests for surviving							
spouses	10.4	0.5	3.2	9.4	14.5	19.8	23.1
Charity	5.4	0.5	1.8	3.0	7.3	9.0	14.1
Other	6.2	5.0	6.5	6.5	6.2	6.4	6.5
Total deductions	22.0	6.0	11.5	18.9	28.1	35.2	43.7
Nontaxable							
Bequests for surviving							
spouses	54.7	28.2	57.6	72.5	79.7	77.8	75.7
Charity	7.4	4.6	6.2	8.9	7.6	12.3	19.1
Other	5.9	6.0	5.9	5.4	5.9	7.5	5.4
Total deductions	68.0	38.8	69.7	86.9	93.3	97.3	99.5

Source: Internal Revenue Service (2000a).

of estate as estate size rises. For nontaxable returns, deductions are much higher as a proportion of estate size, and in particular bequests to a surviving spouse are substantial. Barry W. Johnson, Jacob M. Mikow, and Martha Britton Eller provide extensive additional data in chapter 2 in this volume on features of decedents and asset and deduction patterns in estate tax returns.

Projections

Under current law, the unified credit is scheduled to rise in stages to $345,800 in 2006, raising the effective exemption to $1 million per person (table 1-5). Despite the increase in the effective exemption, the Joint Committee on Taxation (JCT) forecasts that the proportion of adult deaths resulting in taxable estates will be about the same in 2008 as in 1999.[17]

Table 1-5 also provides information on transfer tax revenues. In 1999 federal transfer taxes collected about $28 billion in revenue. Both the JCT and the Congressional Budget Office (CBO) project that estate and gift tax revenues will rise over the next decade. The increase is because of a number of factors. The aging of the population will raise the number of deaths; the stock market boom has increased wealth; the expansion of the spousal deduction in 1981 deferred estate tax revenues; and the tightening of the generation-skipping transfer tax in the Tax Reform Act of 1986 may cause additional increases. According to the CBO, during the next ten years estate and gift taxes are projected to raise nearly $400 billion, with annual revenue of nearly $50 billion by 2010.[18] Notably, neither the JCT nor the CBO forecasts that revenues will rise relative to gross domestic product (GDP).

History

Taxes on the transfer of wealth were levied in Egypt as far back as the seventh century B.C.[19] In the year 6 A.D., the emperor Augustus introduced to Rome the *vicesima hereditatum*, which taxed away one-twentieth of inheritances but exempted heirs in the direct line of descent. During the Middle Ages in Europe there were various levies owed at death to the feudal lord and to the Church, and by the end of the seventeenth century the established national monarchies in England, France, Spain, and Portugal all had inheritance taxes of one form or another.

17. Joint Economic Committee (1999); Congressional Budget Office (2000b).
18. CBO (2001).
19. This paragraph is based on West (1893) and Shultz (1926).

Table 1-5. *JCT and CBO Projections of Taxable Estates and Receipts from Estate, Gift, and Generation-Skipping Transfer Taxes, 1999–2010*

Year	Unified credit (dollars)	Exemption value of unified credit (dollars)	Joint Committee on Taxation				Congressional Budget Office	
			Number of taxable estates	Percent of deaths	Receipts (billions of dollars)	Receipts as percent of GDP	Receipts (billions of dollars)	Receipts as percent of GDP
1999	211,300	650,000	49,200	1.96	27.7	0.30	28	0.31
2000	220,550	675,000	51,700	2.03	28.8	0.29	30	0.31
2001	220,550	675,000	54,200	2.10	29.8	0.29	32	0.31
2002	229,800	700,000	57,000	2.17	30.8	0.28	33	0.31
2003	229,800	700,000	59,800	2.25	32.7	0.29	35	0.31
2004	287,300	850,000	62,800	2.33	33.8	0.28	36	0.30
2005	326,300	950,000	54,600	1.99	34.4	0.28	37	0.30
2006	345,800	1,000,000	50,400	1.82	35.7	0.27	38	0.29
2007	345,800	1,000,000	52,600	1.87	37.7	0.28	40	0.30
2008	345,800	1,000,000	56,200	1.97	39.7	0.28	42	0.30
2009	345,800	1,000,000	n.a.	n.a.	n.a.	n.a.	45	0.30
2010	345,800	1,000,000	n.a.	n.a.	n.a.	n.a.	48	0.31
2001–05	n.a.	n.a.	n.a.	n.a.	161.5	0.28	173	0.30
2001–10	n.a.	n.a.	n.a.	n.a.	n.a.	n.a.	386	0.30

Source: Joint Committee on Taxation (1999), Congressional Budget Office (2000a and 2000b), and authors' calculations.
n.a. = Not available.

In the United States, the first federal tax on wealth transfers dates back to 1797 when, faced with the expenses of dealing with French attacks on American shipping, Congress imposed a stamp duty on receipts for legacies and probates for wills. The tax was eliminated in 1802. An inheritance tax was instituted in 1862, during the Civil War, and was repealed in 1870. In 1894 Congress passed and the president signed into law an income tax that included all property acquired by gift or inheritance. This tax, however, was declared unconstitutional by the Supreme Court on the grounds that it inappropriately discriminated among residents of different states. In 1898 to help finance the Spanish-American War, the federal government imposed its first estate tax, which was subsequently repealed in 1902.

The Sixteenth Amendment to the Constitution was ratified by the states in 1913 and eliminated the constitutional barriers noted above. The precursor to the modern U.S. income tax became law in 1913, and the estate tax followed soon thereafter, in 1916. Like its precursors, the modern estate tax originated in a time of war preparation, if not war itself. Unlike its predecessors, the tax survived the war's aftermath. At least in part, its introduction and survival were because of the movement of the late nineteenth century and early twentieth century to reduce the reliance of federal revenue on customs and excise taxes, viewed by many to be regressive, with more progressive tax methods.

In 1916 the new estate tax exempted the first $50,000 of wealth transfers and featured rates ranging from 1 percent on the first $50,000 of taxable transfers to 10 percent of transferred assets over $5 million. Rates, brackets, and the tax base have changed many times since then.

In an effort to stem tax avoidance, the first gift tax was imposed in 1924 but was then repealed in 1926. In 1932 the gift tax was reintroduced at rates equal to three-quarters of the estate tax rate. Cumulative lifetime gifts below $5,000 were exempt from transfer taxes. In 1942 the exemption for lifetime gifts was raised to $30,000, and an annual gift exclusion of $3,000 was added.

In 1942 Congress attempted to equalize the treatment of spousal bequests across community property and noncommunity property states. This proved very complex. In 1948 the law was revised to provide the donor spouse with a 50 percent deduction for property transferred to the other spouse. Life insurance paid to the estate was added to the tax base in 1954, and a ten-year payment period for small businesses was introduced in 1958. There was then little legislative action on transfer taxes until 1976.

The Tax Reform Act of 1976 was a watershed event for transfer taxes and significantly altered the structure of the tax by reducing rates, raising exemptions, closing loopholes, and allowing adjustments for some special circumstances. The act provided a single, "unified" rate structure for lifetime gifts and transfers at death; raised the effective exemption, in the form of a unified credit, to $175,625 of otherwise taxable transfers; reduced the top rate to 70 percent; created a 100 percent deduction for the first $250,000 of assets given to a surviving spouse; made all gifts given in the three years before death includable in gross estate; allowed closely held business to be valued at "use value" provided certain conditions were met; extended the payment period for estate taxes on closely held businesses to fourteen years, with only interest payments for the first four years; and imposed a tax on generation-skipping transfers.[20]

The Economic Recovery and Tax Act of 1981 significantly cut the rates and the base of the estate tax. It also greatly expanded the effective exemption provided by the unified credit to $600,000 and introduced an unlimited deduction for spousal transfers, including cases in which the recipient spouse did not have control of the disposition of the asset after his or her death but did have an income interest in the property while alive. The annual gift tax exemption was raised to $10,000.

The Tax Reform Act of 1986 made further changes, including tightening the generation-skipping transfer tax. The top transfer tax rate fell to 50 percent at the end of 1992, but the Omnibus Budget Reconciliation Act of 1993 restored the 55 percent top rate retroactively to January 1, 1993. The Taxpayer Relief Act of 1997 enacted a series of increases in the effective exemption provided by the applicable credit amount from $625,000 in 1998 to $1 million in 2006 (table 1-5). The 1997 act also instituted new exclusions for qualified family businesses and for land subject to conservation easements.

Even this short history shows that many of the issues prevalent today have existed for decades. Concerns about high rates, avoidance through gifts, liquidity problems of small businesses, and so on have played a central role in the evolution of the nation's transfer tax system.

---

20. Interestingly, the act also changed the income tax treatment of capital gains at death. Before 1976 (and currently), unrealized capital gains on assets that were bequeathed at death were never taxed under the income tax; the tax basis faced by the heirs was "stepped up" to equal the asset value as of the date of valuation for estate tax purposes. The 1976 act changed this provision to incorporate "carry-over" basis for capital assets. Under this provision, heirs who receive an asset with unrealized capital gains would retain the decedent's tax basis. Thus, if and when the asset was subsequently sold, the heir would have to pay taxes on all capital gains the asset had accrued. The carry-over basis rule never went into effect, however. Implementation of the provision was first delayed and then, in 1980, was retroactively repealed, and the step-up basis rule was reinstated.

Figure 1-1. *Marginal Federal Estate Tax Rates at Various Wealth Levels*

Marginal tax rate (percent)

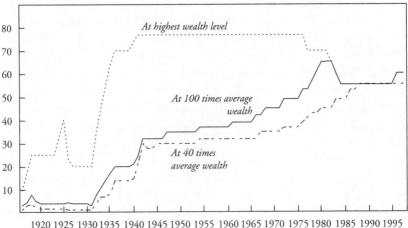

Source: Authors' calculations.

The broad impacts of previous legislation can be summarized in a few figures. Figure 1-1 shows the marginal estate tax rates that have applied to the top wealth level, and to 40 and 100 times per capita net worth. Rates were relatively low by current standards through the 1920s. In 1931 the top rate stood at 20 percent, while the marginal rate at 100 times average wealth was just 3 percent. The rate schedule started to increase sharply in 1932, reaching a top rate of 70 percent in 1936 and 77 percent in 1941. The rate at 100 times average wealth rose as well, reaching 20 percent in 1936 and 32 percent by 1941. From 1941 to 1976 the rate schedule remained fixed, which meant that inflation and real wealth increases raised the effective marginal tax rates at given relative wealth levels. In 1977 the top tax rate began a gradual decline to today's 55 percent rate, but the rate that applies to 40 or 100 times average wealth is considerably higher now than in the past.

The real value of the effective exemption has also changed dramatically over time (figure 1-2). The real exemption fell sharply in the early 1930s, at the same time that the rates rose. After an increase in the nominal exemption from $40,000 to $60,000 in 1942, the real value steadily eroded as the exemption remained at $60,000 until 1976. The real exemption rose fivefold between 1976 and 1987 and then steadily eroded until 1997.

Figure 1-2 also shows the ratio of taxable estate tax returns to adult deaths. Not surprisingly, this ratio rose from the early 1940s to 1976, as the real exemption declined. At its apparent peak in 1976, taxable estates accounted

Figure 1-2. *Estate Tax Exemption Level and Taxable Estate Tax Returns as a Percentage of Adult-Deaths*

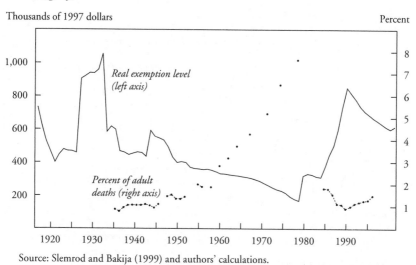

Source: Slemrod and Bakija (1999) and authors' calculations.

for 7.65 percent of adult deaths.[21] By 1998, only one-fourth as many deaths resulted in estate tax payments.

The rate structure, exemption level, and tax base affect the revenue yield of the tax, shown in figure 1-3. Estate and gift taxes raised nearly 10 percent of federal revenue in 1936 and more than 5 percent of revenues in certain other years in the 1930s. Since World War II, however, the tax has constituted less than 4 percent of revenues in any year and has generally raised between 1 and 2 percent of federal revenues. Of course, it was during World War II that the individual income tax changed from a "class" tax to a "mass" tax, and federal revenues vastly expanded, never to return to their pre-war levels. Transfer tax revenues have stayed well below 0.5 percent of GDP since World War II.

The reduction in estate tax revenues in the late 1970s and early 1980s reflects the lowered rates and the expanded unified credit enacted in the tax acts of 1976 and 1981. The introduction of the unlimited marital deduction, which took effect in 1982, probably reduced collections at that point but also likely raised future estate tax collections upon the death of surviving

---

21. Because data on the number of taxable estate tax returns are not available for many years in the 1970s, it is conceivable but unlikely that the ratio was higher in another year.

Figure 1-3. *Federal Estate and Gift Tax Revenue as a Percentage of Total Tax Revenue and GDP, 1917–97*

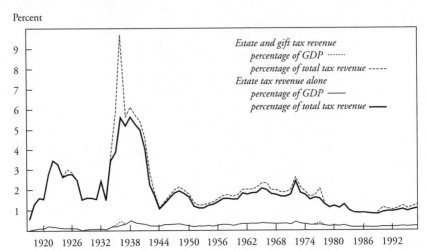

Source: Joulfaian (1998), Slemrod and Bakija (1999), and authors' calculations.

spouses. This may be part of the explanation for the increased revenues beginning in the late 1980s.

Figure 1-3 also shows gift tax collections, in the era when it was a separate tax and in the post-1976 era when gift and estate taxes have been "unified." As David Joulfaian notes, the history of gift tax revenues reveals the importance of anticipated changes in taxes. The huge increase in fiscal 1977 gift tax receipts undoubtedly reflects gifts made in anticipation of higher future gift tax rates brought about by the Tax Reform Act of 1976. Joulfaian argues that the strong growth in gift tax receipts in the late 1980s may reflect the deferral of gifts in the early 1980s, as estate tax rates declined gradually from 70 percent to 50 percent.[22]

Other Countries

The United States is not alone in taxing wealth transfers. Almost all of the Organization for Economic Cooperation and Development (OECD) member countries impose some type of wealth transfer tax. Australia phased out its estate tax starting in 1977. The Canadian federal capital transfer tax was abolished in 1972 as part of a federal tax reform that included the introduc-

---

22. Joulfaian (1998). Anticipated increases in gift tax rates are also plausibly part of the explanation for the relatively high collections in fiscal years 1935, 1936, and 1942.

tion of a capital gains tax that applied to bequests and gifts (except to spouses).[23] New Zealand abolished estate taxes for people who died after 1992. Of the twenty-one industrialized countries that levy a wealth transfer tax, seventeen levy an inheritance tax, and two (Switzerland and Italy) levy taxes that have some features of both an inheritance tax and estate tax. Only the United Kingdom and the United States levy "pure" estate taxes.[24]

It is difficult to compare such taxes across countries because of different exemptions, rate structures, valuation techniques, and other factors. Nevertheless, one common measure focuses on the share of revenues raised by transfer taxes. In 1997 the United States raised about 1.12 percent of revenues from transfer taxes (table 1-6). This figure is well above the OECD average of 0.44 percent and exceeds the transfer tax share of revenues in all OECD countries other than Korea and Japan. Transfer taxes were 0.33 percent of gross domestic product (GDP) in the United States. Only France and Japan exceeded that figure.

However, one-time taxes on wealth transfers may be closely related to recurrent taxes on net wealth. Wealth taxes exist in fourteen of the countries listed in table 1-6. Notably, Korea, Japan and the United States—the three countries with the highest share of revenues owing to transfer taxes—do not have wealth taxes. The average OECD country raises 1.05 percent of revenues from wealth and transfer taxes combined, slightly less than the United States (1.12 percent).

Motives for Intergenerational Transfers

Because estate and gift taxes place burdens on wealth transfers, their effects should depend on why people give transfers.[25] Previous research has considered several different motives but does not reach a consensus about the relative importance of each.

In the accidental bequest model, people face uncertain life spans and accumulate assets to save for retirement. They do not plan or desire to give

23. At the time of abolition of the federal death taxes, almost all the provinces (in Canada) and the states (in Australia) had estate and gift taxes. In both countries, the abolition of federal wealth transfer taxes was followed by abolition of the subfederal taxes.

24. In Switzerland, transfer taxes are imposed at subfederal levels. The seventeen industrialized countries with inheritance taxes are Austria, Belgium, Denmark, Finland, France, Germany, Greece, Iceland, Ireland, Japan, Luxembourg, Netherlands, Norway, Portugal, Spain, Sweden, and Turkey. Many U.S. states also levy inheritance taxes.

25. To be precise, the behavioral and efficiency effects of transfer taxes will vary across transfer motives to the extent that alternative motives correspond to different utility functions for donors and recipients.

Table 1-6. *Transfer and Recurrent Wealth Taxes in OECD Countries, 1997*

Country	Revenue from transfer taxes		Revenue from transfer and recurrent wealth taxes	
	Percent of GDP	Percent of revenue	Percent of GDP	Percent of revenue
All OECD[a]	0.16	0.44	0.40	1.05
Australia	0.00	0.00	0.00	0.00
Austria	0.05	0.11	0.06	0.14
Belgium	0.34	0.75	0.37	0.80
Canada	0.00	0.00	0.40	1.09
Czech Republic	0.03	0.07	0.03	0.07
Denmark	0.19	0.39	0.19	0.39
Finland	0.23	0.50	0.28	0.60
France	0.49	1.08	0.74	1.64
Germany	0.11	0.30	0.34	0.91
Greece	0.27	0.79	0.27	0.79
Hungary	0.04	0.11	0.04	0.11
Iceland	0.09	0.28	0.79	2.46
Ireland	0.17	0.52	0.17	0.52
Italy	0.07	0.16	0.41	0.93
Japan	0.48	1.66	0.48	1.66
Korea	0.26	1.20	0.26	1.20
Luxembourg	0.16	0.33	2.60	5.60
Mexico	0.00	0.00	0.00	0.00
Netherlands	0.28	0.67	0.51	1.22
New Zealand	0.00	0.01	0.00	0.01
Norway	0.10	0.22	0.70	1.63
Poland	0.02	0.05	0.02	0.05
Portugal	0.08	0.23	0.08	0.23
Spain	0.19	0.57	0.35	1.03
Sweden	0.10	0.19	0.40	0.77
Switzerland	0.30	0.88	1.67	4.93
Turkey	0.01	0.04	0.01	0.04
United Kingdom	0.20	0.56	0.20	0.56
United States	0.33	1.12	0.33	1.12

Source: OECD (1999).
a. Arithmetic mean of percentages for countries in OECD.

bequests, but they do not annuitize their wealth either, as would occur in a simple life-cycle model, because of imperfect or missing annuity markets or because they are also saving for precautionary reasons against, say, uncertain future health expenses. Under these assumptions, people will generally have positive asset holdings when they die, even though they do not derive positive utility from bequests.

Accidental bequests may account for a large fraction of aggregate wealth (and can help to explain puzzling wealth accumulation patterns of the elderly). But substantial evidence from patterns of inter vivos giving, life insurance purchases, and annuity choices indicates that some portion of transfers are intended. The existence of estate planning and tax avoidance techniques further suggests that not all bequests are accidental.[26]

In the pure altruism model, parents care about their own consumption and the utility of their children. Parents make transfers and leave bequests until the marginal cost in terms of their own forgone consumption is equal to the marginal benefit to the parents of the increase in their children's consumption. Bequests are given differentially across children to compensate for differences in endowments or outcomes. Variations of altruism with and without a mechanism that allows a parent to commit to a given transfer level are examined extensively in the literature.[27]

Nigel Tomes and Gary Becker and Tomes provide support for the altruistic model. But other research has rejected three sharp empirical implications of altruism. First, Joseph G. Altonji, Fumio Hayashi, and Laurence J. Kotlikoff show that the division of consumption within the family is not independent of the division of income, contrary to the predictions of an altruism model with operative transfers. Second, several studies find that, among families where parents make transfers to children, a one-dollar increase in parents' resources coupled with a one-dollar reduction in children's resources does not raise transfers by a dollar, although it should under altruism.[28] Third, under altruism, siblings with lower incomes should receive larger inheritances than siblings with higher incomes, but empirically they typically do not. The last rejection is striking because equal division of estates among children

26. Abel (1985); Davies (1981); Hurd (1987); Bernheim (1991); Gale and Scholz (1994); Kotlikoff (1989); Laitner and Juster (1996); McGarry (1997); Page (1997).

27. Barro (1974); Becker (1974); Bruce and Waldman (1990, 1991); Lindbeck and Weibull (1988); Perozek (1996).

28. Tomes (1981); Becker and Tomes (1979, 1986); Altonji, Hayashi, and Kotlikoff (1992); Altonji, Hayashi, and Kotlikoff (1997); Cox (1987); McGarry and Schoeni (1995). Although, see McGarry (2000), who considers a model of altruism where parents and children interact for several time periods and concludes that this test is mis-specified.

appears to be the norm. B. Douglas Bernheim and Sergei Severinov show that this norm can arise if parental altruism is combined with the assumptions that bequests are observable, that a child derives utility from her perception of parental affection toward her relative to her siblings, and that bequests are viewed as signals of parental affection.[29]

A variety of "exchange" models posit that bequests or transfers are the payment for some good or service provided by children. In the strategic bequest model parents care about their own consumption, their children's utility, and services obtained from children. These services may represent standard market goods or services (lawn mowing, for example) or more personal items, such as visits, attention, or children's choices regarding marriage, childbearing, education, career, and location of residence. Parents pay for services with bequests, rather than inter vivos transfers. By delaying payment, parents can control children's actions for a longer period and extract the entire consumer surplus out of the exchange relationship. In Donald Cox parents buy services from their children via inter vivos gifts, and the exchange may be mutually beneficial. Empirical tests of exchange models have generated mixed results.[30]

James Andreoni argues that people obtain utility from the act of giving itself. Another specification simply adds the after-tax bequest to the donor's utility function.[31] Each of these approaches may be considered structural, where the household derives utility directly from the after-tax bequest, or reduced-form, consistent with different structural motivations for transfers. No formal tests have been implemented.

Each motive listed above is plausible and draws support from at least some research, but each motive that has been tested has also been rejected. This suggests that households may be influenced by several motives or that the importance of each may vary across households.[32]

It is worth emphasizing that analysis of the estate tax requires evidence on the motives of the very wealthiest households. But there is even less known about the very wealthy than about the moderately wealthy or middle-class households that are the mainstay of most empirical work on transfers, and the richest households may well have different motives for, and patterns of, giv-

---

29. Menchik (1980, 1988); Wilhelm (1996); Bernheim and Severinov (2000).

30. For the strategic bequest model see Bernheim, Shleifer, and Summers (1985); Cox (1987); Perozek (1998).

31. Andreoni (1989); Blinder (1976); Carroll (2000).

32. Differences in empirical outcomes may also be due in part to data limitations and the difficulty of distinguishing rejection of the underlying behavioral model from rejection of the maintained assumptions needed to generate testable hypotheses.

ing and wealth accumulation. Recent work has only begun to examine the behavior of the very wealthy in detail.[33]

Incidence and Equity

Transfer taxes raise several controversial issues relating to incidence and equity. In this section, we examine the incidence of the tax, a variety of horizontal equity issues, and issues raised by taxation at the time of death.

Incidence

The estate itself bears the statutory burden of paying estate taxes. The economic incidence—which must be traced to individuals—depends on the base, the rate structure, the enforcement regime, and any behavioral responses the tax induces. These responses, in turn, will depend on the motivation for transfers and other factors. Because it is unclear what proportion of transfer taxes are borne by donors, recipients or others, we consider each possibility.

Examining the incidence of a tax also requires addressing the prior question of how to classify individuals or families in order to construct a distributional table. For the estate tax, a natural ordering unit is estate size. Other taxes, however, are typically distributed by annual income. We pursue both approaches below, though neither approach is without problems.[34]

Assigning the Burden to Donors. If it is borne by decedents, the estate tax is extraordinarily progressive. Because of the effective exemption, about 96 percent of decedents do not even file an estate tax return in a typical year. Among those that file, the deductions noted above remove half from any estate tax liability. Thus, only about 2 percent of decedents have taxable estates.[35]

---

33. See, for example, Slemrod (2000).

34. Ideally, data would match estate tax returns to lifetime income measures. No such income measure currently exists, although Joulfaian (this volume) uses a data set that matches decedents' estate tax returns with the previous ten years' worth of income tax returns. Joulfaian (1994) uses data from a Treasury collation study that links estate tax returns to the income tax return in the last full year the decedent was alive. But income in the last year of life, when people are typically elderly and retired, and often are ill, may not be a very meaningful indication of the taxpayer's lifetime affluence.

35. For example, Hoyert, Kochanek, and Murphy (1999) report 2,258,366 deaths of persons 20 years old and older in 1997. The number of taxable returns in 1998 was 47,843 (table 1-2), equal to 2.1 percent of 1997 adult deaths.

Among returns with positive tax liabilities in 1998, 84 percent had wealth between $600,000 and $2.5 million; these accounted for just 27.5 percent of transfer tax revenues (table 1-7). About 10 percent of taxable returns had estates between $2.5 million and $5 million and accounted for 19 percent of tax payments. The 6 percent of taxable returns with wealth above $5 million paid 53 percent of all transfer taxes.

Table 1-8 shows that the average estate tax return in 1998 had gross estate worth $1,776,000, paid federal estate taxes of about $208,000 and total transfer taxes, including gift taxes and state taxes, of about $274,000. This corresponds to an average federal estate tax rate of 12 percent and an average overall transfer tax rate of 15 percent.

Average transfer tax rates rise with estate size. Among all returns below $1 million, the average rate is just 4 percent. This figure rises to 26 percent for estates above $10 million. Among taxable estates, the average transfer tax rate is 8 percent for estates below $1 million, rising to between 33 and 35 percent for estates above $5 million.[36]

Assuming it is borne by decedents, the estate tax is much more progressive than the income tax. The Office of Tax Analysis (OTA) of the Department of the Treasury has undertaken a distributional analysis based on annual income and assuming that estate and gift taxes are borne by decedents. Expected estate tax payments for each family are calculated by imputing family wealth, calculating estate tax liabilities as a function of wealth and marital status, and applying a mortality probability based on age.[37] The resulting distribution of estate taxes is shown in table 1-9, along with Treasury estimates of individual income tax burdens. Estate tax burdens are highly skewed toward high-income individuals. More than 99 percent of the burden falls on the top quintile, 96 percent on the top decile, 91 percent on the top 5 percent, and 64 percent on the top 1 percent of the income distribution. The estate tax is clearly more progressive than the income tax, under the OTA assumptions. To the extent that income in the last year of life understates true lifetime

---

36. The slight decline in average tax rate to 33 percent for estates above $20 million compared with 35 percent for estates between $5 million and $20 million is because of higher deductions relative to estate size for spousal and charitable bequests among estates in the largest estate size category.

37. For the OTA analysis see Cronin (1999). To impute wealth, OTA capitalizes a measure of capital income using a 7 percent rate of return. Capital income includes interest, imputed accrued capital gains, real earnings on IRAs, Keoghs, pensions and life insurance, rental income including imputed rental income from owner-occupied housing, and the capital component of sole proprietor, partnership, and subchapter S corporation income. To calculate estate tax liability, OTA assumes that when the first spouse in a couple dies, no estate tax is incurred. OTA also assigns average charitable deductions by estate size.

Table 1-7. *Allocation of Returns, Gross Estate, and Tax Payments by Estate Size among Taxable Returns, 1998*

Item	Total	Percent of total, by size of gross estate (millions of dollars)					
		0.6 under 1.0	1.0 under 2.5	2.5 under 5.0	5.0 under 10.0	10.0 under 20.0	20.0 and over
Number of taxable returns	47,483,000	42.3	41.8	9.8	3.9	1.4	0.8
Total gross estate among taxable returns[a]	103,020,298	15.9	28.3	15.6	12.2	9.2	18.9
Total estate taxes paid[a]	20,349,840	4.5	23.8	20.6	17.0	12.4	21.7
Total transfer taxes paid[a]	26,695,286	5.0	22.5	19.3	16.4	12.6	24.3

Source: Internal Revenue Service (2000a).
a. Thousands of dollars.

Table 1-8. *Average Estate Size, Tax Payments, and Tax Rates by Estate Size, 1998*

		Size of gross estate (millions of dollars)					
	All	0.6 under 1.0	1.0 under 2.5	2.5 under 5.0	5.0 under 10.0	10.0 under 20.0	20.0 and over
All returns							
Average estate size[a]	1,776	771	1,467	3,426	6,806	13,762	55,139
Average estate tax paid[a]	208	19	133	545	1,300	2,665	9,896
Average total transfer taxes paid[a]	274	28	165	670	1,645	3,563	14,565
Average estate tax rate	0.12	0.02	0.09	0.16	0.19	0.19	0.17
Average transfer tax rate	0.15	0.04	0.11	0.20	0.24	0.26	0.26
Taxable returns							
Average estate size[a]	2,170	813	1,469	3,458	6,863	13,831	51,863
Average estate tax paid[a]	429	46	244	904	1,887	3,656	11,801
Average total transfer taxes paid[a]	562	66	302	1,109	2,383	4,885	17,347
Average estate tax rate	0.20	0.06	0.17	0.26	0.27	0.26	0.23
Average transfer tax rate	0.26	0.08	0.21	0.32	0.35	0.35	0.33

Source: Internal Revenue Service (2000a).
a. Thousands of dollars.

Table 1-9. *Estimated Distribution of Income and Estate Taxes, 1999*
Percent

Income quintile or percentile	Share of income		Allocation of total tax burden	
	Estate and gift taxes	Individual income tax	Estate and gift taxes	Individual income tax
Lowest quintile	0.0	−2.4	0.0	−0.6
Second quintile	0.0	0.8	0.0	0.5
Third quintile	0.0	5.6	0.0	6.9
Fourth quintile	0.0	7.8	0.8	16.3
Highest quintile	0.5	13.7	99.2	76.6
Top 10 percent	0.7	15.4	96.2	61.3
Top 5 percent	0.9	16.9	91.0	49.1
Top 1 percent	1.3	20.2	64.2	29.5
All	0.3	10.1	100.0	100.0

Source: Cronin (1999).

income, the Treasury methodology will understate the true progressivity of estate taxes.[38]

Daniel R. Feenberg, Andrew W. Mitrusi, and Poterba provide an alternative estimate, based on public-use income tax return files supplemented with data on nonfilers. They allocate the burden of estate and gift taxes to units with someone over the age of 65 in proportion to each unit's share of capital income in excess of $30,000.[39] Thus, they assume that the tax is borne by decedents and provide no special adjustments for a surviving spouse. Table 1-10 shows the resulting distribution of imputed estate and income tax liability by income class for 1991. Because taxpayers with annual incomes of more than $200,000 constitute about 1 percent of the total population, it is straightforward to compare the results with those of OTA. Feenberg, Mitrusi, and Poterba calculate that this group bears 58 percent of estate taxes, slightly below the 64 percent estimate provided by OTA.

38. Although the JCT does not currently estimate estate and gift tax burdens, JCT (1993) describes a methodology used in the past, in which the burden of (changes in) the estate tax was assigned to the decedent based on the decedent's income in the year preceding the year of death. The gift tax was not distributed. JCT does not report a distribution of the current existing estate tax that is comparable to table 1-4.

39. Feenberg, Mitrusi, and Poterba (1997). Capital income is defined as the sum of dividends, taxable and tax-exempt interest, (realized) capital gains, trust income from trusts, partnerships, subchapter S corporations, rents and royalties.

Table 1-10. *Estimated Distribution of Estate and Gift,*
and Income Taxes, 1991

Percent

Income level (thousands of dollars)	Share of income		Allocation of tax burden	
	Estate and gift taxes	Individual income tax	Estate and gift taxes	Individual income tax
0–10	0.0	−1.3	0.0	−0.3
10–20	0.0	2.4	0.0	2.0
20–30	0.0	5.9	0.0	6.0
30–40	0.0	7.9	0.9	8.1
40–50	0.0	8.7	0.9	8.9
50–75	0.1	9.9	7.3	19.6
75–100	0.2	12.1	8.2	12.6
100–200	0.5	15.1	21.8	16.4
200 or more	1.2	22.2	58.2	26.8
200–500	...	...	19.1	...
500–1,000	...	...	10.0	...
1,000 or more	...	...	29.1	...
All	0.3	10.7	100.0	100.0

Source: Feenberg, Mitrusi, and Poterba (1997), tables 8 and 10, and authors' calculations.

Assigning the Burden to Recipients. Assigning the burden to recipients of inheritances (or those that would have been recipients had taxes been lower) may seem to be a polar alternative to the assumption that donors bear the burden. In practice, however, the implications for progressivity appear similar, because the recipients of large inheritances tend to have very high income and (noninheritance) wealth themselves.

Joulfaian examines data on households that received inheritances from estates of 1982 decedents that were subject to estate tax. Among these recipient households, the average adjusted gross income (AGI) was $47,433 in 1981. Recipients of inheritances from estates valued between $2.5 million and $10 million had average AGI of $123,000. For estates in excess of $10 million, recipients' AGI averaged $271,000. These results suggest that recipients are quite well off. By comparison, mean family income was $25,838 in 1981, and average money income in the top 5 percent of the distribution was $74,482.[40] Thus, while there may be significant contro-

40. Joulfaian (1998); Bureau of the Census (2000a, 2000b).

versy over whether donors or recipients bear the burden of estate taxes, the controversy does not matter very much for purposes of understanding the progressivity of the tax with respect to current income (and, we conjecture, lifetime income). Both donors and recipients are quite well off.

General Equilibrium Considerations. None of the estimates discussed above allow for general equilibrium effects. These effects will in turn depend on how people who give and receive bequests adjust their labor supply and saving. For example, if the tax reduces personal saving and that reduces (domestic) capital accumulation, the resulting long-term reduction in wages could reduce to some degree the progressivity of the tax.

Along these lines, Joseph Stiglitz shows that, if the estate tax reduces saving, it can have perverse effects on the distribution of income.[41] Specifically, the reduction in saving reduces the capital stock, which raises the return on capital and reduces wages. In the long run, an increase in the estate tax could raise the share of income accruing to capital.

John Laitner in chapter 6 in this volume develops an intergenerational simulation model that incorporates altruistic transfer motives and shows that removing the estate tax in his framework would raise saving, as Stiglitz assumes. But Laitner also finds that removing the estate tax would increase the concentration of wealth, especially among the top 1 percent of wealth holders. These results imply that the tax is progressive, even taking into account general equilibrium considerations.

Progressivity: Further Discussion

Progressivity has long been a principal justification for the estate tax. The large increase in the concentration of before-tax income and wealth during the past two decades arguably makes the case for progressive taxes even more compelling.[42] Our analysis certainly suggests that transfer taxes in the United States are highly progressive but raises some additional issues.

First, one might reasonably ask why the desired progressivity could not be achieved solely through the income tax. The answer usually given is that the capacity of the income tax to impose progressive burdens is limited by several factors, most notably the preferential treatment of capital gains. Capital gains are taxed at a lower rate than other capital income and are taxed only when

41. Stiglitz (1978).
42. Graetz (1983); Slemrod and Bakija (1999).

the underlying assets are sold as opposed to when the gains accrue. Most important, gains are excused from income taxation at death.

Capital gains generally are concentrated among high-income and high-wealth households. Poterba and Scott Weisbenner in chapter 10 in this volume find that 37 percent of all estate value among estates above $500,000 is due to unrealized capital gains. Thus, the return to a substantial proportion of wealth is never taxed under the income tax. Unrealized gains are particularly heavily concentrated in the largest estates. Poterba and Weisbenner estimate that, among estates valued at more than $10 million, 56 percent of estate value was in the form of unrealized capital gains. Thus, the role of the estate tax as a "backstop" to the income tax is closely related to the progressivity of the estate tax.

To the extent that the estate tax is meant to capture tax on previously accrued but unrealized capital gains, the tax should apply only to unrealized capital gains and should be capped at the highest capital gains tax rate. Needless to say, that is not how the estate tax is designed. But if there are other reasons not to impose all of the desired progressivity through the income tax, the estate tax may well exceed the capital gains tax rate and apply to a broader measure of wealth than unrealized gains.[43]

Second, it is often claimed by both opponents and supporters of the tax that the estate tax has failed to reduce the concentration of wealth. It is true that the concentration of wealth is not obviously lower in the era of high estate taxes than it was before. But many factors affect the concentration of wealth. Furthermore, a tax that in a typical year raises revenue equal to just 0.3 percent of GDP and 0.1 percent of household net worth is unlikely to make a serious dent in overall wealth inequality, even if the tax is progressive.[44]

Horizontal Equity

While progressivity issues focus on the treatment of those with higher income or wealth relative to those with less, horizontal equity focuses on how "equals"—different households with the same income or wealth—are treated relative to each other. The estate tax raises many controversial issues along these lines.

43. To the extent that a taxpayer has evaded income tax obligations, the estate tax can serve a second backstop role by collecting taxes at the time of death.

44. McCaffery (1994); Graetz (1983). A related argument is that policy should be concerned not with the concentration of wealth but rather the concentration of consumption or well-being. If the estate tax encourages people to spend money while they are alive, it exacerbates inequality in living standards (McCaffery 1994) but not necessarily in utility (Kaplow, chap. 4, in this volume).

For example, among families of the same (considerable) means, the estate tax will not burden those that spend every penny on themselves or give their wealth to charity. But the tax will burden families that pass their good fortune to their children. From the perspective of the donor, this violates principles of horizontal equity.[45] However, from the perspective of the next generation, inheritance provides an advantage to some rather than others. Supporters of estate taxes claim the advantages created by unequal inheritance are unearned and unfair. These two perspectives appear to create an irreconcilable difference in views on whether taxes on transfers are horizontally equitable.

A second line of debate concerns parental versus societal rights regarding inheritance. Opponents of the tax argue that parents should have unlimited rights to pass along wealth to their children. They note that other forms of transfers—investing in human capital, providing social contacts and networks, bringing children into a family business, giving gifts of up to $10,000 per year, and so one are tax free and question why transfers at death should be treated differently. Supporters of the tax agree that large transfers can already be made tax free and conclude that the ability to provide adequately—indeed, generously—for one's offspring is not hampered by transfer taxes. But they see a need to level the playing field—or at least to limit the tilt—among the recipients of inheritances, for equity reasons. Irwin M. Stelzer also notes that placing limits on the use of personal property is a natural, continuing, and appropriate role for society to play. Others have argued that inheritance is a civic right, not a natural right, so government has not only the discretion but the duty to regulate such activity.[46]

A third set of horizontal equity issues relates to the treatment of married versus single taxpayers. Bequests to surviving spouses are not only deductible from taxable estate, they also enjoy the benefits of "basis step-up" for assets with capital gains. Moreover, married couples can reduce the effective tax rate on a given total bequest by dividing the bequest between the two estates, thus taking advantage of the unified credit and progressive rate structure two separate times. These two features provide added benefits to a married couple relative to either a single person with the same wealth as the couple or to two single people with the same combined wealth as the couple. This marriage bonus has to our knowledge never been measured but could potentially run in the millions of dollars for some wealthy families.

---

45. McCaffery (1994).
46. Stelzer (1997); see Erreygers and Vandevelde (1997).

All of these fairness issues hinge to a significant extent on value judgments, fairness being always and everywhere "in the eye of the beholder." As a result, it is difficult to resolve these issues analytically and even more difficult to do so in a political arena.

Taxing at Death

Compounding the grief of the family of the deceased with a *tax*, of all things, seems a bit heartless, to be sure. It is this queasiness that opponents play on by labeling the estate and gift tax system the *"death tax."* As evocative as it is, this label is misleading.

Death is neither necessary nor sufficient to trigger transfer taxes. It is unnecessary because transfers between living persons can trigger gift taxes. It is insufficient because 98 percent of people who die pay no estate tax. In addition, although death may trigger a tax liability, payment can be made at different times. Estate tax liabilities can be effectively pre-paid, via life insurance purchases tied to the expected tax liability. And in the case of qualified family businesses, the tax can be paid over a fourteen-year period.

But while contemplation of death is not pleasurable, that does not make taxing at death inappropriate or ineffective. Indeed, death may prove a convenient time to impose taxes in several ways. First, the probate process may reveal information about lifetime economic well-being that is difficult to obtain in the course of enforcement of the income tax but is nevertheless relevant to societal notions of who should pay taxes. Second, taxes imposed at death may have smaller disincentive effects on lifetime labor supply and saving than taxes that raise the same revenue (in present value terms) but are imposed during life.[47] Third, if society does wish to tax lifetime transfers among adult households, it is difficult to see any time other than death at which to assess the total transfers made.

Much of the public griping about taxation at death, however, is simply a smokescreen designed to hide opposition to a progressive tax. If taxation at death were really a problem, the logical solution would be to design equally progressive taxes imposed during life that would substitute for the estate tax.

Efficiency

A tax has an efficiency cost to the extent that it causes people and firms to make choices different than those they would have made in the absence of

---

47. This view has been expressed by McCulloch (1848); Mill (1994); Musgrave (1959); Pechman (1983); A. C. Pigou (1960) and others.

the tax, holding real income constant and ignoring externalities. From this perspective, a uniform tax on (or at) death is a highly efficient lump-sum tax, given the inevitability of death.[48] The estate and gift tax, however, is not a tax on death but on wealth transferred (other than to spouses or charities) during life and at death. Thus, the relevant behavioral responses concern the accumulation of wealth, to whom that wealth is transferred, and the avoidance measures taken.

Optimal Taxation

Optimal tax theory indicates that, on pure efficiency grounds, taxes should distinguish among the different uses of labor income only to the extent that the uses are more or less complementary to leisure, which is not taxable. Taxing complements to leisure at a higher rate than other goods reduces the inefficiency created by the inability to tax leisure.

A labor income tax, or a consumption tax, distorts the choice between leisure and all consumption but not among the uses of income, including bequests. In contrast, an estate tax distorts the choice between lifetime consumption and bequests and between leisure and bequests. If lifetime consumption and bequests are equally complementary with respect to leisure, then both of these uses of labor income should be taxed equally in an efficient system, and there should be no special tax on bequests.[49] If bequests were more (less) complementary to leisure than consumption is, there would be a case on pure efficiency grounds to tax transfers more (less) heavily than consumption. To our knowledge, no evidence exists on this issue. This strong theoretical conclusion, however, may be tempered by several factors.

Trade-offs between Equity and Efficiency

An optimal tax system balances efficiency and equity. The inclusion of equity considerations alone would not necessarily change the conclusions above. That is, if bequests and consumption were equally complementary to leisure, the most efficient way to impose progressivity would be to make the labor income (or consumption) tax progressive, rather than to create a separate tax on bequests, according to Louis Kaplow in chapter 4 in this volume.

---

48. The timing of death may be somewhat sensitive to financial considerations. Kopczuk and Slemrod (2000) investigate the timing of deaths around major changes in the estate tax and find some evidence that the date of (reported) death is prolonged into the period after a tax reduction.

49. Kaplow, chap. 4, in this volume.

However, if for structural reasons the income tax cannot generate as progressive a tax burden distribution, relative to its efficiency cost, as society would prefer, then there is a potential role for the estate tax. As Joel Slemrod and Shlomo Yitzhaki address, the optimality conditions that balance equity and efficiency require equating each tax's marginal efficiency cost adjusted for its contribution to progressivity. In this context, the marginal efficiency cost is simply measured as the ratio of the marginal revenue collected in the absence of behavioral responses to the marginal revenue collected in the presence of whatever behavioral responses occur, plus a correction for administrative and compliance costs. This implies that, because the estate tax can be more progressive than other taxes, it could still be part of an optimal tax system even if its marginal efficiency cost were somewhat higher than other taxes. The efficiency cost cannot, however, be ignored. For example, if even low estate tax rates raised no net revenue—perhaps because they induced avoidance activity that reduced the revenue from the estate tax and the income tax, as suggested by Bernheim—the marginal efficiency cost would be infinite and, even allowing for its progressivity, the estate tax would not be a part of the optimal tax system.[50]

Imperfect Annuity Markets

In general, the efficiency effects of taxation depend on the pre-existing structure of markets. In particular, a common assumption in analyses of Social Security and other fiscal policies is that markets for private annuities are incomplete, owing in part to adverse selection or moral hazard. Wojciech Kopczuk shows that an estate tax that finances income tax reductions provides a sort of annuity for taxpayers. With imperfect markets, this coupling of policies can raise utility. He estimates that the insurance effect reduces the marginal cost of funds for the estate tax by as much as 30 percent and that the resulting marginal cost of funds is within the range of estimates found for the income tax.[51]

The Role of Transfer Motives

Standard optimal tax theory does not in general incorporate transfer motives. The efficiency implications of taxes on intergenerational transfers depend in crucial and surprising ways on why people give transfers and bequeath wealth.

50. Slemrod and Yitzhaki (2001); Bernheim (1987).
51. See Brown and Warshawsky (2001); Kopczuk (2000).

As noted above, one explanation for bequests is that they are unintended, in the sense that people die before they expect to and thus do not manage to consume all of their wealth. If this were the only reason for bequests, an estate tax would have no effect on the donor's behavior because it changes the relative price of something—the bequest—to which the donor attributes no value. Thus, the tax creates no excess burden, as would be true under a lump-sum tax. But, unlike a lump-sum tax, the estate tax in this case does not make the donor worse off. This makes such a tax look like a "utility machine," as it produces revenue for the government without hurting the donor. Of course, the potential inheritors would be worse off because of the tax.

Alternatively, bequests may be payment for services provided by potential heirs. In this case, the estate tax is simply an excise tax on purchases of services by the donor from the recipient. If bequests are simply payments for services provided, the standard commodity tax argument applies, so that a relevant consideration is the price elasticity of the parents' demand for such services. If the elasticity is very low—as could be the case if there are no good substitutes for the child's love and attention—then the optimal tax rate would be higher than otherwise. If bequests are strategically manipulated by donors to alter children's behavior, the efficiency effects may be more complex but have not been thoroughly worked out.[52]

In pure altruism models, transfers create a sort of externality. Suppose a parent cares about her own utility and her child's utility but not about the size of the transfer, while the child cares only about his own utility. In equilibrium, the parent chooses transfers by trading off the reduction in her own utility from reduced consumption and the increase in her utility from the child's increased consumption. In contrast, a planner maximizing a social welfare function that summed the utilities of all individuals would consider the same two effects *plus* the effect of the transfer on the child's utility. In general, the child's marginal utility from the transfer will be positive. As a result, in equilibrium too few transfers will be provided, leading to an efficiency argument for a *subsidy*, rather than a tax, on transfers to children.[53]

These findings, however, are sensitive to alternative modeling assumptions. Combining parental altruism with opportunistic behavior on the part of children gives rise to a "Samaritan's Dilemma": if the parent is altruistic toward the child, and the child knows that, the child has incentives to

---

52. As payments for services see Cox (1987); as strategic see Bernheim, Shleifer, and Summers (1985).

53. Barro (1974); Becker (1974). This analysis assumes that there are no labor supply effects of giving or receiving transfers. If larger transfers cause recipients to reduce their labor supply, then the case for a subsidy is weakened (Kaplow, chap. 4, in this volume). See also Bernheim (1989).

behave in ways that are counter to the parent's overall interest.[54] For example, the child would have incentives to overconsume when young in order to elicit a larger bequest from the parent. In this case, by making it more difficult for the parent to transfer resources to the child, the estate tax reduces the extent of overconsumption by the child and thus may have welfare-*improving* properties, according to William Gale and Maria Perozek in chapter 5 in this volume.

Another motive for bequests may be that people enjoy the act of giving, independent of the utility level achieved by the child.[55] Suppose now that the parent cares about her own utility and the amount she bequeaths, whereas the child cares only about his own consumption. Again, in equilibrium, the parent will make transfers until the loss in her utility from the reduction in her consumption equals the gain in her utility from the higher bequest. But a social planner would include those two effects plus the effects of the increased bequest on the child's utility. As before, given the utility functions, this leads to an underprovision of the transfer and an optimal subsidy.

The analysis above shows that the efficiency effects of transfer taxes depend crucially on the operative transfer motive. But caution is warranted in interpreting some of the results. For example, the joy-of-giving model has a particularly unappealing feature from a welfare perspective. Because the donor's utility depends on consumption as well as gifts given, a social welfare function that sums up the value of the donor's and recipient's utility functions would under some circumstances favor a policy that lowers the consumption of both generations, if a greater amount of the lower level of consumption is financed by wealth transfers. The positive utility the donor derives from the increased transfers could offset reductions in each person's utility caused by reductions in their own consumption.

This problem does not arise in the pure altruism or Samaritan's Dilemma models because each person's utility in those models is a function only of the parent's and child's consumption. Thus, in those models a reduction in everyone's consumption would never be favored by a social welfare function that added up each person's utility (as long as each person's utility entered the other person's utility function in a non-negative manner).

These considerations suggest that simple descriptions of optimal policy toward transfers are difficult to establish. If it could be determined that motives varied systematically across different types of donors or across different types of gifts, this information would be useful in designing optimal

---

54. Bruce and Waldman (1990).
55. See Andreoni (1989) and Kaplow, chap. 4, in this volume.

transfer tax policy.[56] In the absence of such data, however, the multiplicity of possible transfer motives, the inability of the empirical literature to distinguish very clearly among motives, and the significant differences in optimal taxation under different motives imply that conclusions about the optimal taxation of transfers must be reached very cautiously.

Administrative Issues

Administrative issues are central to the analysis of estate taxes. Critics argue that the tax spawns a host of avoidance schemes that waste resources, create horizontal inequities, and erode the potential revenue yield. In that vein, George Cooper labeled the estate tax a "voluntary" tax. Bernheim argued that the revenue yield of the estate tax, net of the avoidance schemes it induced, was approximately zero. Although many of the avoidance schemes that Cooper and Bernheim discussed have been closed off or otherwise mitigated by subsequent legislation, others remain.[57]

Compliance and Administrative Costs

The cost of collecting the estate tax has two components. Compliance costs are borne directly by taxpayers as time or money spent on tax advice and implementation of tax planning devices, and by claimants to the estate in complying with the estate tax itself. Administrative costs are borne directly by the IRS, in operating, monitoring, and enforcing the system.

Estimates of the compliance cost of the estate tax vary enormously, partly because the methodologies are suspect. Alicia H. Munnell is cited as claiming that "the costs of complying with the estate tax laws are roughly the same magnitude as the revenue raised."[58] But Munnell actually wrote that compliance costs "may well approach the revenue yield." Even this more modest conclusion, however, is based on a number of rough calculations and more or less informed guesses, rather than hard evidence.

Munnell noted that, at the time, the American Bar Association reported that 16,000 lawyers cited trust, probate, and estate law as their area of concentration. Valuing their time at $150,000 a year on average and assuming they spend half of their time on estate taxes yields $1.2 billion in avoidance

56. See Kaplow, chap. 4, in this volume.
57. See Cooper (1979); Bernheim (1987); Schmalbeck, chap. 3, in this volume.
58. Munnell (1988); Joint Economic Committee (1998).

costs, compared with estate tax revenues of $7.7 billion in 1987. To get from $1.2 billion to close to $7.7 billion, Munnell refers to "accountants eager to gain an increasing share of the estate planning market," financial planners, and insurance agents who devote considerable energy to minimizing estate taxes, and the efforts of the individuals themselves, and concludes that the avoidance costs "must amount to billions of dollars annually." It is also worth noting that Munnell's estimates are now out of date and that estate tax revenues have risen dramatically during the intervening period. Thus, even if compliance costs at that point were almost equal to revenues, they may not be today.

Charles Davenport and Jay A. Soled estimate tax planning costs by surveying tax professionals about average charges for typical estate planning in six different estate size classes and applying these estimates to the number of returns filed in 1996.[59] This yields estimated costs for planning of $290 million. Using fairly ad hoc but not implausible adjustments for such factors as the number of nontaxable decedents that do tax planning and tax planning that has to be repeated when tax laws change, they estimate planning costs of $1.047 billion in 1999. They add $628 million for estate administration costs, based on taking one-half of the total lawyers' fees and other costs reported on estate tax returns, and reducing that number by 45 percent to reflect the tax deductibility of the costs. (The last reduction is inappropriate for measuring the social, rather than private, costs of the activity.) The sum of their estimates for planning and estate administration comes to $1.675 billion in 1999, or about 6.4 percent of expected receipts. They allocate another 0.6 percent of revenues for the administrative costs of IRS estate tax activities for an estimated total cost of collection of 7.0 percent of revenues.

The Davenport-Soled (DS) estimate is more recent and more detailed than Munnell's. Although both estimates require some arbitrary assumptions, it is difficult to see how the basic DS methodology could be redone with an alternative set of reasonable assumptions to yield an estimate that avoidance costs are close to 100 percent of revenues.

The estimates above are based on suppliers of estate tax avoidance techniques. Another approach would be to survey the demanders of the service, the wealth owners. This approach has been employed with some success for the U.S. individual income tax and the corporation income tax. As a point

---

59. Charles Davenport and Jay A. Soled. 1999. "Enlivening the Death-Tax Death-Talk," *Tax Notes*, July 26, 1999, special report, pp. 591–630.

of comparison, based on such studies, Slemrod concludes that collection costs for the U.S. individual and corporate income tax are about 10 percent of the revenue collected.[60]

Unfortunately, no reliable and comprehensive survey research has been carried out for the estate tax. What does exist applies only to businesses and may be considered suspect. Astrachan and Aronoff surveyed businesses in the distribution, sale, and service of construction, mining, and forestry equipment industry, and separately surveyed businesses owned by African Americans.[61] Each of these are very special and small subsamples of the estate tax population, and the methodology employed is worrisome on several dimensions. For example, the authors include as a cost of avoidance the amount spent on insurance premiums to provide liquidity for paying the estate tax. This expense is properly thought of as prepaying the tax liability, and to consider it as a cost in addition to the tax liability itself is surely inappropriate double counting.

Joseph H. Astrachan and Roger Tutterow survey 983 family businesses in a variety of industries and find that family business owners have average expenditures of more than $33,000 on accountants, attorneys, and financial planners working on estate planning issues; family members averaged about 167 hours spent on estate planning issues during the previous six years (the time frame for the dollar expenditures is not made clear).[62] However, these estimates include life insurance fees that represent prepayment of estate tax liabilities. In addition, an unknown fraction of the costs is due to estate planning, among other things about intergenerational succession of the business, that is unrelated to taxation. James R. Repetti, while corroborating in surveys of estate tax attorneys the broad magnitude of the Astrachan and Tutterow results, argues that a significant portion of these costs would be incurred even in the absence of estate taxes.[63]

In sum, there is some evidence on the costs of estate planning for small businesses, but the estimates are marked by conceptual problems and disagreement about the fraction of costs owing to the estate and gift tax as opposed to nontax factors or other taxes. For the broader population, there is no informative evidence from surveys of wealth owners.

60. Slemrod and Sorum (1984); Blumenthal and Slemrod (1992); Blumenthal and Slemrod (1996); Slemrod (1996).

61. Astrachan and Aronoff (1995).

62. Astrachan and Tutterow (1996).

63. James R. Repetti, "The Case for the Estate and Gift Tax," *Tax Notes*, March 13, 2000, pp. 1493–1510.

Extent of Avoidance and Evasion

Estimating the extent of (legal) avoidance and (illegal) evasion is difficult. Edward N. Wolff and Poterba attempt to do so by comparing tax revenues and the distribution of estates reported on tax forms and similar statistics calculated from a procedure that estimates these items using data on individuals' mortality probability and wealth measured in the Survey of Consumer Finances.[64] Because of a number of methodological differences, they reach vastly different conclusions, with Wolff arguing that the estate tax captures only about 25 percent of the potential tax base, and Poterba concluding that it catches nearly all of it. Martha Britton Eller, Brian Erard, and Chih-Chin Ho in chapter 9 in this volume point out that any such exercise is highly sensitive to a few essentially arbitrary assumptions about the allocation of deductions and credits, the differential mortality of married and unmarried individuals, and the first spouse in a couple to die.

Audit coverage of estate tax returns is relatively high. According to Eller and Johnson, in 1992, 19 percent of estate tax returns filed (not all of which were taxable) were audited.[65] The audit rate rose with the size of the gross estate, with 11 percent of estates below $1 million being audited, rising to over 48 percent for estates over $5 million. By concentrating on the largest estates, the audits covered returns with 63 percent of the reported tax liability.

Eller, Erard, and Ho show that 60 percent of audited estates in 1992 resulted in an additional positive assessment, 20 percent resulted in no change in tax liability, and 20 percent resulted in a reduced tax bill. Extrapolating from the results of a sample of those estate tax returns that were audited, Erard estimated overall evasion to be 13 percent of the potential tax base, which is slightly lower than the estimated tax gap for the income tax.[66]

Implications of Avoidance and Evasion

Conclusions about avoidance and evasion have important implications for the equity, efficiency, revenue yield, and reform of transfer taxes.

Equity. Some opponents of the estate tax assert that avoidance and evasion renders the tax regressive, at least among the highly wealthy that are subject

---

64. Wolff (1994); Poterba (2000).
65. Eller and Johnson (1999).
66. Erard (1998).

to the tax. For example, in commenting on 1997 estate tax returns, the Joint Economic Committee writes:

> One way to measure vertical equity is to compare the average tax rates for different income or asset levels. Based on this criterion, the estate tax does not exhibit vertical equity. According to IRS data, the average estate tax rate for the largest estates (gross estate over $20 million) is actually *lower* than the average tax rate for estates in the $2.5 million to $5 million range."[67]

It is true that in 1997, the ratio of net estate tax to gross estate was lower for estates above $20 million (11.8 percent) than for estates between $2.5 million and $5 million (15.0 percent). But this apparent anomaly in the face of graduated tax rates occurs for simple reasons that are certainly not related to evasion or to any sophisticated tax planning schemes. The wealthier group had higher charitable deductions, 28.4 percent of gross estate versus 5.7 percent, and higher credits for gift taxes and for state death taxes, 5.6 percent of gross estate versus 3.3 percent.[68] Moreover, the pattern that arose in the 1997 returns did not arise in 1998. Estate taxes in 1998 were 16 percent of gross estate for estates between $2.5 million and $5 million, and 17 percent for estates above $20 million. For all transfer taxes, the average tax rates are 20 percent and 26 percent, respectively (table 1-8). These figures thus provide no evidence that evasion or sophisticated avoidance strategies undermine the progressivity of the estate tax.

Efficiency. Administrative and compliance costs have two effects on efficiency. First, they should be added to the standard costs of distorted behavior in determining the overall welfare effects. A second issue is the extent to which avoidance and evasion opportunities reduce the effective marginal tax rate imposed by the estate tax and thus mitigate any disincentive effects the tax would otherwise cause. For example, it is sometimes claimed that transfer taxes are easy to avoid and—at the same time—a serious deterrent to wealth accumulation. At first glance, these arguments sound inconsistent: if they were so easy to avoid, why would the taxes hurt wealth accumulation? As Slemrod shows, however, these two claims need not be logically inconsistent. Whether they are depends on the pricing structure of the avoidance technology.[69]

Richard Schmalbeck in chapter 3 in this volume suggests that, for all but the largest estates, the avoidance technology often features a fixed fee for an avoidance device (for example, a trust) that reduces the effective tax rate on

67. Joint Economic Committee (1998, p. 31). Emphasis in original.
68. Johnson and Mikow (1999).
69. Slemrod (2001).

an unlimited amount of wealth that is passed through the device. This reduces the effective marginal tax rate (on wealth above the level that makes the fixed cost of using this device worthwhile), and therefore reduces the effective progressivity of the estate tax. For the largest estates, Schmalbeck notes that there is often an hourly fee for advice and planning. If the fee is not related to the size of the tax saving, the same conclusion applies.

Schmalbeck's findings imply that avoidance opportunities typically do reduce the effective marginal tax rate at high wealth levels and therefore do reduce the deterrence to wealth accumulation below what the statutory rate structure suggests.

Just as there is heterogeneity in bequest motives, there are also differences in the extent to which people pursue tax avoidance opportunities. There are undoubtedly people who maximize the after-tax bequest. But many others do not pursue even the most basic tax planning strategies. Poterba documents that most wealthy people do not take advantage of the annual $10,000 per donor, per recipient exemption for inter vivos gifts.[70]

Moreover, just as alternative transfer motives have different implications for the efficiency of transfer taxes, the different reasons why people may choose not to avoid transfer taxes may have important efficiency implications. There are several plausible explanations for at least part of the lack of giving, including precautionary motives among donors. To the extent that infrequent giving is because people find it uncomfortable to contemplate their own demise, the efficiency costs are not as large as they might otherwise be.

Revenue. Avoidance of any tax, by definition, reduces revenue. But the effect of estate tax avoidance on revenue is of particular interest because many of the easiest and most popular methods of reducing estate tax liability—inter vivos gifts, charitable contributions during life, and so on also end up reducing overall income tax liabilities of the donor and recipient. Thus, the net effect of estate tax avoidance on revenues is the net revenue earned by the estate tax less any avoidance of income taxes induced by the existence of the transfer tax system. Bernheim's calculations suggest that the loss in income tax revenue from estate tax avoidance in the 1980s was plausibly of the same order of magnitude as estate tax revenues. There are, to our knowledge, no reliable, recent estimates of the extent of income tax avoidance engendered by the existence of the estate tax.[71]

---

70. Poterba (2001).
71. Bernheim (1987); see McCaffery (1994) for a critique.

Reform. Even if avoidance and evasion of the estate tax are prevalent, the appropriate direction for reform may still be in question. For example, tightening loopholes could reduce avoidance and evasion, while at the same time raising the revenue yield. Thus, the extent of avoidance and evasion, and the accompanying compliance costs, are important inputs into reform decisions but do not dictate the nature of reform by themselves.

Effects on Saving, Labor Supply, and Entrepreneurship

Critics argue that the estate tax significantly reduces the saving, labor supply, and entrepreneurship that are essential to economic prosperity.

Saving

There is a strong presumption that estate taxes should influence saving. The implied marginal tax rates on the return to saving from the estate and income tax can be very high. Nevertheless, there are few formal models of estate taxes and saving. Laurence J. Kotlikoff and Lawrence H. Summers estimate that a one-dollar decline in gross transfers reduces the capital stock by about seventy cents, but they do not estimate how transfer taxes affect gross transfer levels. Jordi Caballe develops an altruistic model with endogenous growth, human capital, and bequests and finds that estate taxes reduce the capital stock. This model, however, focuses only on the special case where taxes on estates and on capital income have identical effects.[72]

Laitner in this volume provides the most sophisticated model of estate taxes to date, embedding them in an overlapping generations simulation model with altruistic bequest motives. He finds that removing estate taxes would have a small positive effect on the long-term ratio of capital to labor. It is sometimes claimed that the growth effects of removing the estate tax would raise revenue more than sufficiently to offset the revenue loss from abolishing the estate tax. Laitner, however, finds that other tax rates have to increase to maintain revenue neutrality.

Gale and Perozek in this volume show that the impact of transfer taxes on saving, like the efficiency effects, will depend critically on why people give transfers. If bequests are unintentional, estate taxes will not affect saving by the donor, but they will reduce the net-of-tax inheritance received by the

---

72. Poterba (2000); Gale (2000); Kotlikoff and Summers (1981).

recipient and thereby raise the recipient's saving. If bequests are payment for services provided by children, the impact of taxes depends on the elasticity of parents' demand for services. If demand is inelastic, higher taxes will raise total parental expenditure on services and thereby raise their saving. If bequests are motivated by altruism, the effects are ambiguous, but simulations suggest that the effect will be positive or non-negative under many circumstances.

Like previous theoretical work, empirical studies of the impact of estate taxes on saving are also limited in number. Kopczuk and Joel Slemrod in chapter 7 in this volume use estate tax return data from 1916 to 1996 to explore links between changes in the estate tax rate structure and reported estates. These links reflect the impact of the tax on both wealth accumulation and avoidance behavior. They find that an aggregate measure of reported estates is generally negatively associated with summary measures of the level of estate taxation, holding constant other influences. In pooled cross-sectional analyses that make use of individual decedent information, however, the relationship between the concurrent tax rate and the reported estate is fragile and sensitive to the set of variables used to capture exogenous tax rate variation. The negative effect of taxes seems stronger for those who die at a more advanced age and with a will, both of which are consistent with the theory of how estate taxes affect altruistic individuals. Perhaps of most interest, the tax rate that prevailed at age 45, or ten years before death, is more clearly (negatively) associated with reported estates than the tax rate prevailing in the year of death. This suggests that future research should concentrate on developing lifetime measures of the effective tax rates.[73]

Other empirical work has focused on saving by the recipient of the inheritance. Weil shows that the past or anticipated receipt of an inheritance raises a household's consumption by between 4 and 10 percent, after controlling for income, age, education, and other factors.[74] Given the magnitude of typical household saving rates, Weil's results suggest that reduced inheritances owing to estate taxes would substantially raise the donee's saving out of earned income.

Douglas Holtz-Eakin, Joulfaian, and Harvey S. Rosen show that receipt of a large inheritance raises the likelihood that a household starts a business and raises the probability of the recipient's existing business surviving and expanding.[75] Thus, to the extent that inheritances relieve liquidity constraints

73. Fiekowsky (1966) and Chapman, Hariharan, and Southwick (1996) also examine issues relating to the estate tax and saving.
74. Weil (1994).
75. Holtz-Eakin, Joulfaian, and Rosen (1994a, 1994b).

associated with investment, reduced inheritances because of estate taxes could reduce investment among recipients.

Labor Supply

As noted, the estate tax can be considered a tax on one use of labor income and so reduces the real wage. The numerous studies of how taxes affect labor supply, which generally find that the aggregate substitution effect is rather small, are therefore relevant.[76] However, with one exception no one has attempted to directly measure the impact of estate taxes on the labor supply of potential donors. Holtz-Eakin, using data from two national surveys, shows that, in raw cross-tabulations, individuals 50 years and older who face higher estate tax rates work less. This could be a reflection of the estate tax reducing labor supply, or—in our view more likely—may simply reflect the fact that leisure is a normal good and households that face higher estate tax rates have higher wealth.[77]

There has been more fruitful work on the impact of inheritances, and by implication the effect of any change in inheritances caused by the estate tax, on aspects of labor supply. Holtz-Eakin, Joulfaian, and Rosen show that receipt of an inheritance of $350,000 reduces labor force participation rates by 12 percentage points for singles and reduces the likelihood of married couples having two workers by 14 percentage points. Holtz-Eakin, Joulfaian, and Rosen and Joulfaian and Mark O. Wilhelm find small reductions in the labor supply of inheritors who remain in the labor force.[78]

Closely Held Businesses and Farms

The impact of the estate tax on family-held businesses and farms has taken on a hugely disproportionate role in public policy debates. This role has been fueled by anecdotal evidence on the adverse effect of the tax on particular families or businesses.

Holtz-Eakin provides supporting evidence.[79] Using a survey of about 400 business owners in New York state, he concludes from regression analysis that businesses in which the owner would be subject to the estate tax if

76. This literature is surveyed in MaCurdy (1992).
77. Douglas Holtz-Eakin, "The Death Tax: Investments, Employment, and Entrepreneurs," *Tax Notes* 84, August 2, 1999, pp. 782–92.
78. Holtz-Eakin, Joulfaian, and Rosen (1993); Joulfaian and Wilhelm (1994).
79. Holtz-Eakin, "The Death Tax."

he or she died immediately had significantly less employment growth during the previous five years than other firms. However, the regressions do not control for the age of the owner. One might suspect that older owners were more likely to be wealthy, and thus more likely to be subject to estate taxes upon death, but less likely to push for aggressive growth than younger owners. Moreover, the data are based on responses to a mail survey and so may not be very representative.

Other survey evidence should be viewed as highly suspect, in part because it is based on people's stated intentions rather than their actions. Astrachan and Tutterow report that in a survey of 983 family-owned businesses, more than 60 percent reported that paying estate taxes will limit business growth, 13 percent said it would make growth impossible, more than 60 percent said paying would threaten business survival, 8 percent said it would make survival impossible, and 33 percent said that paying estate taxes will require selling all or part of the business. Estate taxes were also thought to affect current business behavior: 36 percent said the tax shortens the time that owners wait for an investment to pay off, and 68 percent said it reduces the acceptable risk associated with investment. Finally, 60 percent of respondents said that if estate taxes were eliminated, they would immediately hire more workers and revenues would grow at least 5 percent faster than otherwise anticipated.[80]

Several important caveats apply to these figures. First, somewhat contradictorily, 45 percent of respondents said they had no knowledge of their likely estate tax liability. Second, the effects seem hugely out of proportion with the actual impact of estate taxes. The vast majority of family businesses undoubtedly do not ever face estate tax because they fail well before the death of the owner or because their value is well below the estate tax exemption. Neil E. Harl, for example, reports that 95 percent of farms could have passed to heirs with no estate tax liability under the rules in place in 1995.[81]

Third, insuring the life of a business owner is good business practice, even without an estate tax but is especially good practice for owners of closely held business who want the business to remain in family hands after their own death. Thus, if business owners were especially concerned about their ability to pass on the business to their descendants, they might be expected to be heavily insured. This does not appear to be the case, though. Holtz-Eakin, Phillips and Rosen show that small business owners do hold somewhat more

80. Astrachan and Tutterow (1996).

81. Neil E. Harl, "Does Farm and Ranch Property Need a Federal Estate and Gift Tax Break?" *Tax Notes*, August 14, 1995, pp. 875–77.

life insurance than others with the same wealth.[82] But they also find that the insurance purchases of business owners are less responsive to estate tax considerations than are the purchases of other households. This suggests either that business owners do not anticipate problems—given their current life insurance holdings and other assets—in passing the business along to their descendants, do not consider giving the business to their descendants a high priority, or are planning poorly.

Nor does it appear that many business owners would have difficulties paying estate taxes without liquidating the business. Holtz-Eakin, Phillips, and Rosen find that 58 percent of business owners could pay estate tax liabilities out of insurance, liquid assets, stocks and bonds alone, without having to use any nonliquid assets or the business itself to pay estate taxes.[83] On average, business owners can cover more than 80 percent of their projected estate tax liability without affecting the business. These estimates surely understate the true percentage of businesses that can pass to recipients without fear of being broken up by the estate tax, because the authors do not allow for any reduced valuation of businesses, or any other estate tax planning or avoidance, which would reduce estimated estate taxes, and they omit life insurance held in trusts, nonfinancial assets, and balances in 401(k)s or other pension accounts, each of which would raise available resources with which to pay estate taxes. Thus, the vast majority of closely held businesses do not appear to face imminent demise because of estate tax considerations.

Beyond the heartrending anecdotes and questionable surveys, however, there is little logic or evidence that suggests that the impact of estate taxes on family farms and businesses is a major concern. We offer several reasons for this conclusion.

First, family farms and businesses already receive special treatment under the estate tax. Taxpayers are entitled to calculate the taxable value of the real estate used in a farm or closely held business on the basis of their current-use value, rather than market value. As already noted, this can reduce the value of the taxable gross estate by up to $770,000 for decedents who died in 2000.[84] And because such assets do not trade in liquid markets, there is often substantial discretion (and hence substantial discounts) used in determining value. Furthermore, legislation enacted in 1997 permits a special deduction for family-owned farms and businesses when they constitute at least 50 percent of an estate and in which heirs materially participate.

82. Holtz-Eakin, Phillips, and Rosen (1999).

83. Holtz-Eakin, Phillips, and Rosen (1999).

84. The special use value of real estate is obtained by capitalizing the income expected from the property in its current use.

Taken together, these effects can be sizable. Consider a couple with a business worth $3.9 million. Suppose the value for estate tax purposes can be reduced by one-third using the valuation techniques noted above; Schmalbeck in this volume suggests that this would not be an unexpected outcome. The remaining value, $2.6 million, would not be taxable, given the business deduction and the unified credit. The entire business could pass to heirs in a tax-free manner. Thus, the various deductions, exemptions, and valuation procedures already in place provide a very high effective floor under which family businesses can pass tax free.

Empirical evidence also suggests that valuation discounts, or other avoidance measures, are substantial. Poterba and Weisbenner, in this volume, table 10-8 apply mortality probabilities to household wealth data in the 1998 Survey of Consumer Finances (SCF) and project that about 49 percent of the wealth in estates above $10 million was due to active businesses and farms. In contrast, the corresponding figure in actual estate tax returns, reported in table 1-3, is between 13 percent and 22 percent. This suggests that businesses are able to evade or avoid the estate tax quite successfully.

Any estate tax liability that is due to family farms and businesses can be paid in installments over a fourteen-year period, with only interest charged for the first four years. The applicable interest rate is 2 percent on estate tax liability stemming from the first $1 million of taxable assets with higher, but still below-market, rates on larger amounts. This not only reduces the cash flow needs for the business, it significantly reduces the present value of estate tax liabilities.

Second, a significant portion of the value of the family-owned businesses consists of unrealized capital gains. Arthur Kennickell and David Wilcox peg the figure at two-thirds using the 1989 SCF. Evidence in Poterba and Scott Weisbenner in chapter 10 in this volume suggests that the figure was 80 percent in 1998.[85] This income has never been taxed under the income tax and would never be taxed at all if exempted from the estate tax.

Third, small businesses already receive numerous income tax subsidies—for investment, for example. Fourth, there is an issue of horizontal equity: why, between two families with the same size estate, should the one whose assets are in business form have a smaller tax liability? The answer is presumably that in some sense the family owning the business is less well off or has

---

85. Kennickell and Wilcox (1992). Poterba and Weisbenner (chap. 10, in this volume, table 10-8) show that total estate value in their sample was $118 billion, of which 7.2 percent ($8.5 billion) consisted of active businesses and farms. At the same time, total unrealized capital gains in estates were $42.8 billion, of which 15.9 percent ($6.8 billion) was due to active businesses and farms. Thus, unrealized gains in active businesses and farms were 80 percent of the total value of active businesses and farms.

assets that are less diversified or less liquid than those of the other family. If so, the same tax represents a larger burden to the business-owning family. Nevertheless, the current adjustments in the estate tax for small businesses already address if not eliminate these concerns.

The analysis above suggests that claims for additional special treatment on behalf of family businesses and farms should be treated with great skepticism. In practice, the claims made by opponents of the tax go well beyond special treatment; many argue that the problems of family businesses and farms are sufficient to merit the abolition of the estate tax. This seems extreme, though.

Farms and other small businesses represent a small fraction of estate tax liabilities. Farm assets were reported on 6 percent of taxable returns filed in 1998; farm real estate was reported on 12 percent. Together, these items constituted just 1.7 percent of taxable estate value. About 8.7 percent of taxable returns in 1998 listed closely held stock, which accounted for 6.6 percent of taxable estate value. Limited partnerships and "other noncorporate business assets" accounted for an additional 2.6 percent of taxable estate. Thus, using a very expansive definition, farms and small businesses account for at most 11 percent of assets in taxable estates.[86] Clearly, the vast majority of estate taxes are paid by people who own neither farms nor small businesses, and the effects on farms and small businesses do not justify abolishing the estate tax.[87]

Serious empirical analysis of the role of the estate tax in the demise of family-run businesses would be enlightening. With that information in hand, one could estimate the efficiency cost of "breaking up" small businesses. This should start with the presumption that the tax system should be neutral with respect to whether a family member continues to run the business but could also incorporate the role of life insurance, business and estate planning in the absence of estate taxes, market imperfections because of credit constraints,

---

86. IRS (2000a). Holdings of farms and businesses are particularly low among the smallest taxable estates. Among taxable estates worth less than $1 million, only 1.0 percent of taxable estate value was due to small businesses. For those between $1 million and $2.5 million, small businesses account for only 2.6 percent of taxable estate value. But among the largest estates—those in excess of $20 million—closely held businesses account for 32 percent of taxable estate.

87. To put these figures in perspective, consider the following exercise. First, note that any estate with less than half of its wealth in farm or business assets could pay estate tax liability out of the rest of the estate without hurting the business. Second, in 1998, about 3 percent of taxable estates had more than half of gross assets in farm and small businesses. See Committee on Ways and Means (2000). Suppose the federal government had given each such estate $1 million in cash—surely a sufficient amount, given all of the other inducements for businesses, to allow any well-run, profitable small business to pay the 2 percent interest costs for 5 years and probably for longer than that. The total cost, $1.4 billion, would have composed only 6 percent of transfer tax revenue in 1998. *Budget of the U.S. Government, Fiscal Year 2000.*

and the incentives that other aspects of the tax system (for example, basis step-up on appreciated assets) have on the outcome.

Effects on Gift-Giving, Charity, and Capital Gains Realizations

Besides their alleged impact on the factors that generate economic growth, transfer taxes can influence many other forms of behavior, including inter vivos gifts during life, charitable gifts during life and at death, and the timing of capital gains realizations.

Inter Vivos Giving

Although federal estate and gift taxes are said to be "unified," gifts and bequests are taxed differently, as noted above. The estate tax is based on the gross-of-tax estate, while the gift tax is imposed on the net-of-tax gift. An appreciated asset given as a bequest benefits from "basis step-up;" the same asset, given as an inter vivos gift, does not.[88]

Although these two features work in opposite directions in favoring gifts versus bequests, several other features of the transfer tax system favor gifts. First, the annual gift exemption of $10,000 per donor per recipient has a "use-it-or-lose-it" feature. Gifts that fall under the exemption level add to the total lifetime giving that can be done tax free. Second, making transfers earlier rather than later exempts not only the transfer itself from tax but also all future growth of the asset. Thus, for example, people who wish to maximize the value of gifts should use up their entire effective exemption in inter vivos gifts rather than waiting until they die to transfer resources. Third, the two factors directly above would favor gifts over bequests even if the estate tax rate structure were flat. The fact that estate tax rates are graduated accentuates these incentives, by providing extra incentives to minimize the size of taxable lifetime transfers.[89]

Level of Giving. Despite these incentives, large (reported) gifts are small relative to bequests. Gifts in excess of the annual exemption must be re-

---

88. McGarry (2000) provides a thorough and thoughtful review of the literature on the determinants of inter vivos giving. Note that this implies that, for a given amount of total transfers, households should give high-basis assets as inter vivos gifts and low-basis assets as bequests.

89. For further discussion, see McCaffery (1994) and Poterba (1998).

ported on estate tax returns. Among 1998 returns, taxable gifts constitute only about 4 percent of total taxable estates and less than 6 percent in each estate size category. Only about 18 percent of taxable estates report taxable gifts, including a majority of taxable estates above $5 million. Interestingly, 7 percent of all nontaxable returns, and 33 percent of such returns above $5 million, report (previously) taxable gifts.[90]

Tax data showing small gifts may simply reflect evasion. Gale and John Karl Scholz use data from the 1983 and 1986 Surveys of Consumer Finances and find that large transfers are relatively rare—less than 10 percent of households gave $3,000 or more to other households in the three-year period. Nevertheless, they find that overall inter vivos transfers are substantial, amounting to between 67 percent and 75 percent of annual bequest flows. Kathleen McGarry, using data from the Health and Retirement Study, and Poterba, using data from the 1995 SCF, confirm that large inter vivos transfers are relatively rare, even among households whose wealth exceeds the estate tax filing threshold but do not estimate aggregate transfer flows.[91]

Timing of Transfers. The choice of inter vivos gifts versus bequests is one example of the timing of gifts, and there is significant evidence that the timing of gifts is sensitive to estate tax rates. McGarry shows that, in a regression that controls for wealth and other factors, whether a family would be subject to the estate tax has a large positive impact on its inter vivos giving. A simulation based on these results indicates that elimination of estate taxes would reduce inter vivos transfers by about 30 percent. Poterba finds, in a cross-sectional regression, that transfers are positively associated with wealth, consistent with the view that higher estate tax rates encourage transfers. Bernheim, Robert Lemke, and Scholz use several cross-sections from the Surveys of Consumer Finances and find that households in wealth groups whose estate tax rates fell after the 1997 tax changes provided fewer inter vivos transfers in 1998 than in earlier years.[92]

Jonathan S. Feinstein and Chih-Chin Ho in chapter 11 in this volume provide new evidence on estate tax avoidance by examining how health status interacts with wealth to affect inter vivos giving. They show that wealthy households in poor health—that is, with a higher probability of dying soon—are more likely to make transfers than wealthy households in good health.

Another example of the timing of transfers is whether the bequests of a married couple are made upon the first death or upon the death of the surviving

---

90. IRS (2000a).
91. Gale and Scholz (1994); McGarry (1999); Poterba (1998).
92. McGarry (1999); Poterba (1998); Bernheim, Lemke, and Scholz (2000).

spouse. Two aspects of the tax system affect this choice. First, there is an unlimited deduction for spousal bequests. Second, the graduated estate tax gives rise to an incentive to split the total nonspousal bequest between the two estates. If it were known with certainty that the two spouses would die at the same time, the tax-minimizing strategy would split nondeductible bequests exactly in two. Otherwise there is an offsetting incentive, owing to the time value of money, to have the estate of the first spouse that dies be somewhat smaller.[93]

Bernheim tests the sensitivity to estate tax provisions of the timing of transfers to one's ultimate heirs by comparing estate tax return data from 1977 and 1983.[94] Most of the former data are for estates treated under 1976 law, before the changes in the Tax Reform Act of 1976, and most of the latter data concern returns taxed under the Economic Recovery Tax Act of 1981, which removed the limitations on marital deductions. He finds that, among estates with approximately similar minimum value, in 1977 married decedents left forty-eight cents out of every dollar to their spouses, but by 1983 this figure had increased to fifty-nine cents. This change could be due to the introduction of the unlimited marital deduction. He also finds that the fraction of married decedents who claimed deductions for spousal bequests rose from 90 percent to 95 percent. This increase is not likely to be due to the increase in tax-free spousal bequests but is consistent with the lower estate tax rates in 1983 reducing the penalties associated with transferring wealth first to one's spouse, and then, upon the spouse's death, to one's children.

The Intra-Family Division of Wealth. To the extent that transfer taxes alter the relative magnitudes of inter vivos gifts and bequests, they may also affect the intrafamily division of wealth. Studies of probate records, existing wills, and estate tax returns show that estates are divided approximately equally among children most of the time. Whether inter vivos gifts are also usually equal is more controversial. Cox and Cox and Rank found evidence that parents give *more* to better-off children, the reverse of what the basic altruistic model would suggest. However, subsequent research suggests the opposite: that less well-off children benefit disproportionately from inter vivos transfers.[95]

McGarry notes that making full use of the $10,000 per donor per donee gift exemption may require people to give unequal amounts to the families of

93. See Schmalbeck, chap. 3, in this volume.

94. Bernheim (1987).

95. Menchik (1980, 1988); Dunn and Phillips (1997); Wilhelm (1996); Cox (1987); Cox and Rank (1992); Altonji, Hayashi, and Kotlikoff (1997); McGarry and Schoeni (1995, 1997); McGarry (1997).

their children, depending on the size of the children's family. In cross-section regressions, she finds that transfers are given differentially across children, but that there is little evidence that the deviations from equal division are motivated by tax planning.[96]

Charitable Contributions

Econometric analysis of the impact of the estate tax on charitable giving faces a difficult problem in distinguishing the impact of the marginal estate tax rate—which varies as a function of estate size—from the impact of variations in wealth. This problem also arises in examining the impact of income taxes on charitable contributions, of course. One solution is to assume that other components of income or wealth are fixed and calculate the marginal tax rate that applies at zero contributions. This "first-dollar" tax rate is sometimes used as an instrumental variable for the "last-dollar" tax rate that is presumed to determine the relative prices on the margin.

Although the complicated nature of the decision problem is often recognized, empirical work on charitable bequests has generally specified giving simply as a function of estate size, the price of charitable bequests relative to bequests to children, and other standard socioeconomic determinants of giving. Most studies calculate the marginal estate tax rate as a "first-dollar" rate.[97]

Another important econometric issue is the treatment of spousal bequests, which are currently fully deductible. Almost all previous work assumes that spousal deductions are unchanged when charitable contributions change. This does not appear to us a credible assumption, but it is difficult to know what the appropriate assumption ought to be.

Gerald Auten and Joulfaian use a data set that matches the estate tax returns of 1982 decedents to both their 1981 federal income tax return and the 1981 returns of their heirs.[98] They find that charitable contributions at death are sensitive to tax rates during life and at death. Joulfaian, in this volume, matches estate tax returns filed between 1996 and 1998 with the decedents' income tax returns for 1987 through 1996. He finds that the relative composition of giving during life and at death changes markedly with wealth, with the extremely wealthy giving a much greater share of their contributions at

96. McGarry (1997); Page (1997) makes use of the variation in effective state estate and inheritance taxes to investigate the impact of taxes on inter vivos gifts. But of the 384 households in his sample, only 14 had wealth over $600,000, so this study likely may not reveal much about the behavior of people who are subject to the federal estate tax.

97. For example, Clotfelter (1985); McNees (1973); Boskin (1976); Joulfaian (1991); Auten and Joulfaian (1996); Joulfaian (2000); Joulfaian, chap. 8, in this volume.

98. Auten and Joulfaian (1996).

death. These estimates also document that giving at death is sensitive to the marginal tax rates applied in the estate tax.

Thus, most studies find that the deduction in the estate tax for charitable contributions generates a significant increase in contributions at death. The estate tax may well encourage giving during life as well. Indeed, this is precisely one of the avoidance techniques that Bernheim emphasizes could reduce estate and income tax revenues.[99]

These effects may be especially large among the wealthiest households, who also face the highest estate tax rates and typically face the highest income tax rates too. For example, in 1998, among taxable estates with gross estate valued at more than $20 million that made charitable contributions, the average contribution was $13.2 million.[100]

Opponents of the estate tax counter with two claims. First, they note that the effects of the estate tax deduction for charitable giving are small relative to the overall funds raised by the nonprofit sector. Estate tax returns filed in 1998 provided charitable bequests of $11 billion. In contrast, total revenue of the nonprofit sector in 1996 was $704 billion, of which $137 billion came from contributions, gifts, and grants. Note, however, that a sizable portion of the income of the nonprofit sector may reflect the earnings of endowments, which may represent prior charitable contributions.[101]

Second, opponents argue that eliminating the estate tax would raise wealth among the wealthiest families, which would in itself increase charitable bequests. This claim, of course, is inconsistent with the view that the estate tax does not effectively reduce the concentration of wealth. In addition, if wealth did rise among the wealthiest families, but the price of charitable bequests rose by 122 percent, it is not obvious that charitable bequests would rise.[102]

Capital Gains Realizations

Because assets whose value consists in part of unrealized capital gains receive basis step-up at death, the estate tax may interact with incentives to give inter vivos gifts and to realize capital gains. Auten and Joulfaian examine the impact of the Economic Recovery Tax Act of 1981, which reduced capital gains tax rates and reduced estate tax rates. Using a sample of matched income and

99. Bernheim (1987).
100. IRS (2000a).
101. IRS (2000a, 2000b).
102. The 122 percent increase is calculated from the ratio of (a) the price of a one-dollar charitable bequest with no estate tax ($1) and (b) the price of a one-dollar charitable bequest with a 55 percent estate tax rate ($0.45).

estate records, their results suggest that lower estate tax rates reduce lifetime capital gains realizations, thus increasing the lock-in effect associated with basis step-up. Poterba shows that, controlling for net worth, households with larger unrealized capital gains are less likely to make inter vivos gifts. This suggests that the gain from basis step-up is an important consideration in choosing the level of gifts and which assets to give away.[103]

Proposals for Change

The policy debate on transfer taxes is remarkable not only for the variety of proposals that have been made in recent years but also for the extent to which proposals often cut across the lines that traditionally demarcate such discussions.[104] Naturally, some liberals applaud the tax, and some conservatives detest it, all for the usual reasons. But certain liberals acknowledge that the transfer tax system is flawed. Some propose strengthening the system to increase progressivity, while others claim that abolition would reduce inequality in consumption. On the other side, the case in favor of near-confiscatory taxes on bequests is made most forcefully by Stelzer, who describes himself as a libertarian, and who sees large inheritances as affirmative action for the children of the wealthy.[105]

The most radical reform would be to abolish the tax. This removes the existing problems but may create serious additional issues. It would eliminate what is by far the most progressive tax instrument in the federal tax arsenal, just after an extended period over which the distributions of income and wealth have become far more skewed. It could hurt nonprofit organizations. It may not even raise saving, labor supply, or growth, as its advocates hope, and would probably reduce state revenues as well.[106] Finally, abolition would expose a gaping loophole with regard to capital gains in the income tax and would open up other possibilities for tax avoidance, and resulting revenue loss, under the income tax.[107]

103. Auten and Joulfaian (1998); Poterba (1998).

104. Jane G. Gravelle and Steven Maguire, "Estate and Gift Taxes: Economic Issues," *Tax Notes*, July 24, 2000, pp. 551–69, provide a comprehensive and informative discussion of policy options.

105. Aaron and Munnell (11992); McCaffery (1994); Stelzer (1997).

106. In fiscal year 1997, state governments raised $5.91 billion from inheritance and estate taxes Rafool (1999). By comparison, federal estate tax returns filed in 1997 reported state tax credits of $4.33 billion.

107. See Jonathan G. Blattmacher and Mitchell M. Gans, "Wealth Transfer Tax Repeal: Some Thoughts on Policy and Planning," *Tax Notes*, January, 15, 2001, pp. 393–99; John Buckley, "Transfer Tax Repeal Proposals: Implications for the Income Tax," *Tax Notes*, January 22, 2001, pp. 539–41, for preliminary discussions.

Elimination, or scaling back, of the estate tax could be coupled with the extension of the capital gains tax to the gains accrued but unrealized at death. This proposal, however, according to Poterba and Weisbenner in this volume, would raise only about a quarter of the revenue of the estate tax, and would be much less progressive. CBO reports that this option would raise $78 billion between 2001 and 2010, compared with $386 billion from the estate tax (table 1-5). In addition, this alternative would have many of the complexities of the estate tax, so it is neither an attractive nor likely option by itself.[108]

The bill passed in Congress in 2000 tied elimination of the estate tax to another significant change in the taxation of capital gains, under which heirs would assume the decedent's basis for capital gains purposes—"carryover basis." Exemptions would apply to transfers below $1.3 million and to interspousal transfers of $3 million. Linking the two changes is designed to address the concern that the appreciated value of some assets might escape all taxes if the income tax featured basis step-up and there were no estate tax. However, this proposal would raise even less revenue than taxing gains at death. According to the CBO, instituting carryover basis with no exemption level would raise about $48 billion over the next ten years, or about 12 percent as much revenue as the existing estate tax (table 1-5).[109] However, at the generous exemption levels stipulated in the bills described above, the actual revenue would be significantly smaller. Another problem is that allowing basis to be carried over would be more complicated, in part because records would have to be kept for an even longer period (and across generations). A similar item was passed in the late 1970s but was repealed before it ever came into effect partly because of anticipated implementation problems.

Leonard Burman and Soled propose other ways to alter the current treatment of capital gains and estates.[110] Burman would allow deductions in the estate tax for the tax basis of capital assets. This would reduce the lock-in effect associated with the current tax treatment of capital gains. Soled proposes that the decedent (while alive) be given the option of electing carryover basis at death for any asset. If the decedent elects that an asset be taxed on a carryover basis, the estate would receive a credit equal to the value of the capital gains tax rate times the unrealized gain on the asset at the time the asset is valued for estate tax purposes.

---

108. CBO (2000b).
109. CBO (2000b).
110. Leonard E. Burman, "Estate Taxes and the Angel of Death Loophole," *Tax Notes*, August 4, 1997, pp. 675–78; Jay A. Soled, "Carryover Basis Election at Death," *Tax Notes*, January 1, 2001, pp. 99–105. James R. Repetti, "The Case for the Estate and Gift Tax," *Tax Notes*, March 13, 2000, pp. 1493–1510.

All of the proposals above that modify the treatment of capital gains could make some aspects of estate and portfolio planning even more difficult and cumbersome than current law. Even the proposal to abolish the estate tax with no other changes may not prove as simple as it first appears, since prudent investors would be well advised under those circumstances to plan for the possibility that the estate tax might be reinstated.

Another direction for reform would be to replace taxes on estates and gifts given with taxes on gifts and inheritances received, as is the practice in several U.S. states and many foreign countries. Under a progressive inheritance tax (but not under an estate tax), spreading a given bequest among more legatees reduces the total tax burden and thus encourages the splitting of estates. A unified tax system would also tax all sources or all uses of income. Currently, the income tax burdens sources, and the estate tax falls on a particular use of resources. In contrast, the income tax combined with a tax on inheritances and gifts received would cover all major sources of income over the lifetime. And placing the statutory burden of the tax on recipients rather than the donor may reduce some of the moral outrage generated by estate taxes.

Perhaps the most plausible reform would be to follow the strategy invoked for income taxes in the Tax Reform Act of 1986: raise the exemption level, close loopholes, and cut rates. Raising the exemption would reduce the number of people paying the tax while still taxing the "truly wealthy" and chipping away at the concentration of wealth. It would also help smaller family-owned businesses but without the horizontal equity problems that are involved in giving preferential treatment to business assets. Closing loopholes by treating different assets in a more similar fashion would reduce sheltering opportunities and thus make the tax simpler and fairer; Jane G. Gravelle and Steven Maguire and Schmalbeck discuss numerous options to achieve this objective, including ways to crack down on aggressive valuations. Modestly reducing rates would reduce the incentive to shelter or change behavior in the first place. Besides these changes, indexing the effective exemption and the tax brackets for inflation would automatically keep the tax burden at any particular real wealth level constant over time.[111]

Conclusion

The appropriate role and effects of transfer taxes are still open questions. Any conclusion about the appropriate taxation of intergenerational transfers must

---

111. Gravelle and Maguire (2000); Schmalbeck, chap. 3, in this volume.

take into account transfer motives, the political and technical limitations on other tax instruments, the limited knowledge about such taxes that is currently available, and other factors.

In a real world filled with practical difficulties, political compromises, and economic uncertainties, it may take a variety of taxes to meet social goals, and the estate tax may well play a small but important role in the government's portfolio of tax instruments. It adds to progressivity in a way that the income tax cannot easily do, because of capital gains issues, and that society may choose not to do through income taxes, because taxing at death may have smaller costs than taxing during life. The supposed negatives of the estate tax—its effects on saving, compliance costs, and small businesses—lack definitive supporting evidence and in some cases seem grossly overstated. And there are some presumed benefits from increased charitable contributions and improved equality of opportunity.

Nevertheless, it is equally clear that there is a problem. A tax with high rates and numerous avoidance opportunities is ripe for change. Even given the goals and constraints noted above, many people feel that transfer taxes could be better structured. Many others feel that having no transfer taxes would be preferred to the existing situation.

Economic analysis cannot fully resolve these issues. What it can do is clarify the various trade-offs involved in tax policy decisions, illuminate which value judgments—about which economics has no say—are involved, and identify the crucial conceptual and empirical issues. Compared with many tax questions, the trade-offs that affect estate taxes are more difficult to analyze because they involve more than one generation. The value judgments are more difficult because they involve life-and-death issues about which people feel strongly. And empirical analysis is more difficult because the data are more elusive and the relevant behaviors span at least a lifetime.

The chapters in this volume address all of these issues—they rethink the estate and gift tax in a rigorous way. It is our hope and expectation that the chapters will provide a solid base of knowledge to inform future policy discussions and a springboard to encourage continuing analysis of transfer tax issues.

References

Aaron, Henry J., and Alicia H. Munnell. 1992. "Reassessing the Role for Wealth Transfer Taxes." *National Tax Journal* 45 (June): 119–43.

Abel, Andrew B. 1985. "Precautionary Saving and Accidental Bequests." *American Economic Review* 75 (September): 777–91.

Altonji, Joseph G., Fumio Hayashi, and Laurence J. Kotlikoff. 1992. "Is the Extended Family Altruistically Linked? Direct Tests Using Micro Data." *American Economic Review* 82 (December): 1177–98.

———. 1997. "Parental Altruism and Inter Vivos Transfers: Theory and Evidence." *Journal of Political Economy* 105 (December): 1121–66.

Andreoni, James. 1989. "Giving with Impure Altruism: Applications to Charity and Ricardian Equivalence." *Journal of Political Economy* 97 (December): 1447–58.

Astrachan, Joseph H., and Craig E. Aronoff. 1995. "A Report on the Impact of the Federal Estate Tax: A Study of Two Industry Groups." Unpublished paper. Kennesaw State College, Family Enterprise Center.

Astrachan, Joseph H., and Roger Tutterow. 1996. "The Effect of Estate Taxes on Family Business: Survey Results." *Family Business Review* 9 (Fall): 303–14.

Auten, Gerald, and David Joulfaian. 1996. "Charitable Contributions and Intergenerational Transfers." *Journal of Public Economics* 59 (January): 55–68.

Auten, Gerald, and David Joulfaian. 1998. "Bequest Taxes and Capital Gains Realizations." U.S. Department of the Treasury. Mimeo.

Barro, Robert. 1974. "Are Government Bonds Net Wealth?" *Journal of Political Economy* 82 (November–December): 1095–117.

Becker, Gary S. 1974. "A Theory of Social Interactions." *Journal of Political Economy* 82 (November–December): 1063–93.

Becker, Gary S., and Nigel Tomes. 1979. "An Equilibrium Theory of the Distribution of Income and Intergenerational Mobility." *Journal of Political Economy* 87 (December): 1153–89.

———. 1986. "Human Capital and the Rise and Fall of Families." *Journal of Labor Economics* 4 (July, part 2): S1-S39.

Bernheim, B. Douglas. 1987. "Does the Estate Tax Raise Revenue?" In *Tax Policy and the Economy*, edited by Lawrence H. Summers, vol. 1, 113–38. NBER and MIT Press Journals.

Bernheim, B. Douglas. 1989. "A Neoclassical Perspective on Budget Deficits." *Journal of Economic Perspectives* 3 (Spring): 55–72.

———. 1991. "How Strong Are Bequest Motives: Evidence Based on Estimates of the Demand for Life Insurance." *Journal of Political Economy* 99 (October): 899–927.

Bernheim, B. Douglas, Robert Lemke, and John Karl Scholz. 2000. "Estate Tax Changes and Inter Vivos Transfers." October 8 (Mimeo).

Bernheim, B. Douglas, Andrei Shleifer, and Lawrence H. Summers. 1985. "The Strategic Bequest Motive." *Journal of Political Economy* 93 (December): 1045–76.

Bernheim, B. Douglas, and Sergei Severinov. 2000. "Bequests as Signals: An Explanation for the Equal Division Puzzle, Unigeniture, and Ricardian Non-Equivalence." Working Paper 7791. Cambridge, Mass.: National Bureau of Economic Research (July).

Blinder, Alan S. 1976. "Intergenerational Transfers and Life Cycle Consumption." *American Economic Review* 66 (May): 87–93.

Blumenthal, Marsha, and Joel Slemrod. 1992. "The Compliance Cost of the U.S. Individual Income Tax: A Second Look after Tax Reform." *National Tax Journal* 45 (June): 185–202.

———. 1996. "The Income Tax Compliance Cost of Big Business." *Public Finance Quarterly* 24 (October): 411–38.

Boskin, Michael. 1976. "Estate Taxation and Charitable Bequests." *Journal of Public Economics* 5 (January–February): 27–56.

Brown, Jeffrey R., and Mark J. Warshawsky. 2001. "Longevity-Insured Retirement Distributions from Pension Plans: Market and Regulatory Issues." Working Paper 8064. Cambridge, Mass.: National Bureau of Economic Research.

Bruce, Neil, and Michael Waldman. 1990. "The Rotten-Kid Theorem Meets the Samaritan's Dilemma." *Quarterly Journal of Economics* 105 (February):155–65.

———. 1991. "Transfers in Kind: Why They Can Be Efficient and Non-Paternalistic." *American Economic Review* 81(December): 1345–51.

Bureau of the Census. 2000a. March Current Population Survey. "Table F-3: Mean Income Received by Each Fifth and Top 5 Percent of Families (All Races): 1966 to 1999" (October 30).

———. 2000b. March Current Population Survey. "Table F-6: Regions—Families (All Races) by Median and Mean Income: 1953 to 1999" (October 30).

Caballe, Jordi. 1995. "Endogenous Growth, Human Capital, and Bequests in a Life-Cycle Model." *Oxford Economic Papers* 47 (January): 156–81.

Carroll, Christopher D. 2000. "Why Do the Rich Save So Much?" In Joel B. Slemrod, ed., *Does Atlas Shrug? The Economic Consequences of Taxing the Rich*, 465–84. Russell Sage Foundation and Harvard University Press.

Chapman, Kenneth, Govind Hariharan, and Lawrence Southwick Jr. 1996. "Estate Taxes and Asset Accumulation." *Family Business Review* 9 (Fall): 253–68.

Churchill, Winston S. 1906. *Lord Randolph Churchill*. London: Macmillan.

Clotfelter, Charles T. 1985. *Federal Tax Policy and Charitable Giving*. University of Chicago Press.

Committee on Ways and Means. 2000. "Background on the Estate and Gift Tax." Washington.

Congressional Budget Office. 2000a. "The Budget and Economic Outlook: An Update." Washington (July).

———. 2000b. "Budget Options." Washington (March).

———. 2001. "The Budget and Economic Outlook: Fiscal Years 2002–2011." Washington (January).

Cooper, George. 1979. *A Voluntary Tax? New Perspectives on Sophisticated Estate Tax Avoidance*. Brookings.

Cox, Donald. 1987. "Motives for Private Income Transfers." *Journal of Political Economy* 95 (June): 508–46.

Cox, Donald, and Mark R. Rank. 1992. "Inter-Vivos Transfers and Intergenerational Exchange." *Review of Economics and Statistics* 74 (May): 305–14.

Cronin, Julie-Ann. 1999. "U.S. Treasury Distributional Analysis Methodology." Office of Tax Analysis. Working Paper 85. Department of Treasury.

Davies, James B. 1981. "Uncertain Lifetime, Consumption, and Dissaving in Retirement," *Journal of Political Economy* 89 (June): 561–77.

Dunn, Thomas A., and John W. Phillips. 1997. "The Timing and Division of Parental Transfers to Children." *Economics Letters* 54 (February): 135–37.

Eller, Martha Britton, and Barry W. Johnson. 1999. "Using a Sample of Federal Estate Tax Returns to Examine the Effects of Audit Revaluation on Pre-Audit Estimates." Washington: Internal Revenue Service.

Erard, Brian. 1998. "Estate Tax Underreporting Gap Study: A Report Prepared for the Internal Revenue Service Economic Analysis and Modeling Group." Order TIRNO-98-P-00406. Washington: Internal Revenue Service.

Erreygers, Guido, and Toon Vandevelde, eds. 1997. *Is Inheritance Legitimate? Ethical and Economic Aspects of Wealth Transfers*. Berlin: Springer-Verlag.

Federal Reserve Board of Governors. 2000. "Flow of Funds Accounts of the United States: Annual Flows and Outstandings: 1991–1999." Washington.

Feenberg, Daniel R., Andrew W. Mitrusi, and James M. Poterba. 1997. "Distributional Effects of Adopting a National Retail Sales Tax." In James M. Poterba, ed., *Tax Policy and the Economy*, edited by James M. Poterba, 49–89. MIT Press.

Fiekowsky, Seymour. 1966. "The Effect on Saving of the United States Estate and Gift Tax." In *Federal Estate and Gift Taxes*, edited by Carl S. Shoup, 228–36. Brookings.

Gale, William G. 2000. "Commentary on Chapter 10: The Estate Tax and After-Tax Investment Returns, James Poterba." In *Does Atlas Shrug? The Economic Consequences of Taxing the Rich*, edited by Joel B. Slemrod, 350–54. Russell Sage Foundation and Harvard University Press.

Gale, William G., and John Karl Scholz. 1994. "Intergenerational Transfers and the Accumulation of Wealth." *Journal of Economic Perspectives* 8 (Fall): 145–60.

Graetz, Michael J. 1983. "To Praise the Estate Tax, Not to Bury It." *Yale Law Journal* 93 (December): 259–86.

Holtz-Eakin, Douglas, David Joulfaian, and Harvey S. Rosen.1993. "The Carnegie Conjecture: Some Empirical Evidence." *Quarterly Journal of Economics* 108 (May): 413–35.

———. 1994a. "Sticking It Out: Entrepreneurial Survival and Liquidity Constraints." *Journal of Political Economy* 102 (February): 53–75.

———. 1994b. "Entrepreneurial Decisions and Liquidity Constraints." *Rand Journal of Economics* 25 (Summer): 334–47.

Holtz-Eakin, Douglas, John W. Phillips, and Harvey S. Rosen. 1999. "Estate Taxes, Life Insurance, and Small Business." Working Paper 7360. Cambridge, Mass.: National Bureau of Economic Research.

Hoyert, Donna L., Kenneth D. Kochanek, and Sherry L. Murphy. 1999. "Deaths: Final Data for 1997." *National Vital Statistics Report* 47(19): 1–105.

Hurd, Michael D. 1987. "Savings of the Elderly and Desired Bequests." *American Economic Review* 77 (June): 298–312.

Internal Revenue Service. 1999. "Instructions for Form 706 (Revised July 31 1999) United States Estate (and Generation-Skipping Transfer) Tax Return." Washington.

———. 2000a. "Estate Tax Returns Filed in 1998: Gross Estate by Type of Property, Deductions, Taxable Estate, Estate Tax and Tax Credits, by Size of Gross Estate. Statistics of Income." Washington.

———. 2000b. "Nonprofit Charitable Organizations, 1996." *Statistics of Income Bulletin* (Winter 1999-2000): 107–14.

Johnson, Barry W., and Jacob M. Mikow. 1999. "Federal Estate Tax Returns, 1995-1997." *SOI Bulletin* 19 (Summer): 69–129.

Joint Committee on Taxation. 1993. *Methodology and Issues in Measuring Changes in the Distribution of Tax Burdens*. June 14. Washington.

———. 1998. "Present Law and Background Relating to Estate and Gift Taxes." Testimony before the House Committee on Ways and Means, January 28. 105 Cong. 2 sess. Government Printing Office.

———. 1999. "Present Law and Background on Federal Tax Provisions Relating to Retirement Savings Incentives, Health and Long-Term Care, and Estate and Gift Taxes," prepared for public hearing, June 16. 106 Cong. 1 sess. GPO.

Joint Economic Committee. 1998. *The Economics of the Estate Tax*. Washington (December).

Joulfaian, David. 1991. "Charitable Bequests and Estate Taxes." *National Tax Journal* 44 (June): 169–80.

———. 1994. "The Distribution and Division of Bequests in the U.S.: Evidence from the Collation Study." Office of Tax Analysis Paper 71. Department of the Treasury.

———. 1998. "The Federal Estate and Gift Tax: Description, Profile of Taxpayers, and Economic Consequences." Office of Tax Analysis Paper 80 (December).

Joulfaian, David, and Mark O. Wilhelm. 1994. "Inheritance and Labor Supply." *Journal of Human Resources* 29 (Fall): 1205–34.

Kennickell, Arthur, and David Wilcox. 1992. "The Value and Distribution of Unrealized Capital Gains: Evidence from the 1989 Survey of Consumer Finances." Washington: Federal Reserve Board (Mimeo).

Kopczuk, Wojciech. 2000. "The Trick Is to Live: Estate Taxes as Annuities for the Rich." University of Michigan. Mimeo.

Kopczuk, Wojciech, and Joel Slemrod. 2000. "Dying to Save Taxes: Evidence from Estate Tax Returns on the Death Elasticity." University of Michigan. Mimeo.

Kotlikoff, Laurence J. 1989. "Estimating the Wealth Elasticity of Bequests from a Sample of Potential Decedents." In *What Determines Savings?* edited by Laurence J. Kotlikoff, 404–28. MIT Press.

Kotlikoff, Laurence J., and Lawrence H. Summers. 1981. "The Role of Intergenerational Transfers in Capital Accumulation." *Journal of Political Economy* 89 (August): 706–32.

Laitner, John, and F. Thomas Juster.1996. "New Evidence on Altruism: A Study of TIAA-CREF Retirees." *American Economic Review* 86 (September): 893–908.

Lindbeck, Assar, and Jorgen W. Weibull. 1988. "Altruism and Time Consistency: The Economics of Fait Accompli." *Journal of Political Economy* 96 (December): 1165–83.

MaCurdy, Thomas. 1992. "Work Disincentive Effects of Taxes: A Reexamination of Some Evidence." *American Economic Review* 82 (May): 243–49.

McCaffery, Edward J. 1994. "The Uneasy Case for Wealth Transfer Taxation." *Yale Law Journal* 104 (November): 283–365.

McCaffery, Edward J. 1999. "Grave Robbers: The Moral Case against the Death Tax." *Tax Notes*, December 13, 1999, special report, 1429–43.

McCulloch, John Ramsay. 1848. *A Treatise on the Succession to Property Vacant by Death: Including Inquiries into the Influence of Primogeniture, Entails, Compulsory Partition, Foundations, etc. over the Public Interests.* London: Longman, Brown, Green, and Longmans.

McGarry, Kathleen. 1997. "Inter Vivos Transfers and Intended Bequests." Working Paper 6345. Cambridge, Mass.: National Bureau of Economic Research (December).

———.1999. "Inter Vivos Transfers or Bequests? Estate Taxes and the Timing of Parental Giving." September (Mimeo).

———. 2000. "Behavioral Responses to the Estate and Gift Tax: *Inter Vivos* Giving." *National Tax Journal* 53 (December): 913–31.

———. 2000. "Testing Parental Altruism: Implications of a Dynamic Model." Working Paper 7593. Cambridge, Mass.: National Bureau of Economic Research. (March).

McGarry, Kathleen, and Robert F. Schoeni. 1995. "Transfer Behavior: Measurement, and the Redistribution of Resources within the Family." *Journal of Human Resources* 30//supp: s184–s226.

———. 1997. "Transfer Behavior within the Family: Results from the Asset and Health Dynamics Survey." *Journal of Gerontology* 52B (May, special edition): 82–92.

McNees, Stephen. 1973. "Deductibility of Charitable Bequests." *National Tax Journal* 26 (March): 79–98.

Menchik, Paul L. 1980. "Primogeniture, Equal Sharing, and the U.S. Distribution of Wealth." *Quarterly Journal of Economics* 94 (May): 299–316.

———. 1988. "Unequal Estate Division: Is It Altruism, Reverse Bequests, or Simply Noise?" In *Modeling the Accumulation and Distribution of Wealth*, edited by Denis Kessler and Andre Masson, 105–16. Oxford: Clarendon Press.

Mill, John Stuart. 1994. *Principles of Political Economy and Chapters on Socialism*, edited by Jonathan Riley. Oxford: Oxford University Press.

Munnell, Alicia H. 1988. "Wealth Transfer Taxation: The Relative Role for Estate and Income Taxes." *New England Economic Review* (November): 3–28.

Musgrave, Richard A. 1959. *The Theory of Public Finance: A Study in Public Economy.* McGraw-Hill.

Organization for Economic Cooperation and Development. 1999. *Revenue Statistics 1965–1998.* Paris.

Page, Benjamin R. 1997. "Bequest Taxes, Inter Vivos Gifts, and the Bequest Motive." Congressional Budget Office. September (Mimeo).

Pechman, Joseph A. 1983. *Federal Tax Policy.* Brookings.

Perozek, Maria G. 1996. "The Implications of a Dynamic Model of Altruistic Intergenerational Transfers." Federal Reserve Board.

———. 1998. "A Re-examination of the Strategic Bequest Motive." *Journal of Political Economy.* 106 (April): 423–45.

Pigou, A.C. 1960. *A Study in Public Finance.* Third rev. ed. London: Macmillan and Co.

Poterba, James. 2000. "The Estate Tax and After-Tax Investment Returns." In *Does Atlas Shrug? The Economic Consequences of Taxing the Rich*, edited by Joel B. Slemrod, 329–49. Russell Sage Foundation and Harvard University Press.

———. 2001. "Estate and Gift Taxes and Incentives for Inter Vivos Giving in the U.S." *Journal of Public Economics* 79 (January): 237–64.

Rafool, Mandy. 1999. "State Death Taxes." National Conference of State Legislatures.

Shultz, William J. 1926. *The Taxation of Inheritance.* Houghton Mifflin.

Slemrod, Joel. 1996. "Which Is the Simplest Tax System of Them All?" In *The Economics of Fundamental Tax Reform*, edited by Henry Aaron and William Gale, 355–92. Brookings.

———, ed. 2000. *Does Atlas Shrug? The Economic Consequences of Taxing the Rich.* Russell Sage Foundation and Harvard University Press.

———. 2001. "A General Model of the Behavioral Response to Taxation." *International Tax and Public Finance* 8 (March): 119–28.

Slemrod, Joel, and Jon Bakija. 1999. "Does Growing Inequality Reduce Tax Progressivity? Should It?" Working Paper 99-3. Office of Tax Policy Research.

Slemrod, Joel, and Nikki Sorum. 1984. "The Compliance Cost of the U.S. Individual Income Tax System." *National Tax Journal* 37 (December): 461–74.

Slemrod, Joel, and Shlomo Yitzhaki. Forthcoming. "Integrating Expenditure and Tax Decisions: The Marginal Cost of Funds and the Marginal Benefit of Projects." *National Tax Journal.*

Stelzer, Irwin M. 1997. "Inherit Only the Wind." *Weekly Standard*, March 26, 1997, 27–29.

Stiglitz, Joseph. 1978. "Notes on Estate Taxes, Redistribution, and the Concept of Balanced Growth Path Incidence." *Journal of Political Economy* 86 (April): S137–50.

Tomes, Nigel. 1981. "The Family, Inheritance, and the Intergenerational Transmission of Inequality." *Journal of Political Economy* 89 (October): 928–58.

———. 1988. "Inheritance and Inequality within the Family: Equal Division among Unequals, or Do the Poor Get More?" In *Modeling the Accumulation and Distribution of Wealth*, edited by Denis Kessler and Andre Masson, 79–104. Oxford: Oxford University Press.

Weil, David N. 1994. "The Saving of the Elderly in Micro and Macro Data." *Quarterly Journal of Economics* 109 (February): 55–81.

West, Max. 1893. *The Inheritance Tax.* New York: Columbia University Studies in History, Economics, and Public Law.

Wilhelm, Mark O. 1996. "Bequest Behavior and the Effect of Heirs' Earnings: Testing the Altruistic Model of Bequests." *American Economic Review* 86 (September): 874–92.

Wolff, Edward N. 1994. "Trends in Household Wealth in the United States: 1962-1983 and 1983–1989." *Review of Income and Wealth* 40 (June): 143–74.

BARRY W. JOHNSON
JACOB M. MIKOW
MARTHA BRITTON ELLER

2 | *Elements of Federal Estate Taxation*

FOR MOST OF the twentieth century, and throughout American history, the federal government has relied on estate or inheritance taxes as sources of funding. The modern transfer tax system, introduced in 1916, provides revenue to the federal government through a tax on transfers of property between living individuals—inter vivos transfers—as well as a tax on transfers of property at death. The tax on transfers of property at death, the federal estate tax, historically has affected only the wealthiest 1 or 2 percent of the U.S. decedent population. Revenue from the estate tax has contributed less than 2 percent to annual federal budget receipts.

Proponents of transfer taxation embrace it as a "fair" source of revenue and as an effective tool for preventing the concentration of wealth in the hands of a few powerful families. Opponents claim that transfer taxation creates a disincentive to accumulate capital and thus is detrimental to the growth of national productivity. Controversy over the role of inheritance in democratic society and the propriety of taxing property at death is not new but is rooted firmly in arguments that have existed since Western society emerged from its feudal foundations.

Early Estate Taxation

The modern transfer tax system follows a long history of taxation that began as early as 700 B.C. in ancient Egypt.[1] Some seven centuries later, at the turn of the first century A.D., Roman Emperor Caesar Augustus imposed a transfer tax on successions and legacies to all but close relatives.[2] During the Middle Ages in feudal England, the crown owned all real property and granted its use to certain individuals during their lifetimes. At the death of a grantee, the grantee's estate retained the property only if an estate tax was paid. If no tax was paid, the granted property returned to the crown.[3]

In America, the first tax imposed at death was a death stamp tax in 1797, which provided for revenue to finance the undeclared naval war with France in 1794. Federal stamps were required on wills offered for probate, on inventories, on letters of administration, receipts, and discharges for legacies and on intestate distributions of property. A federal inheritance tax, as enacted by the Tax Act of 1862, helped fund the Civil War. The 1862 act included a document tax on the probate of wills and letters of administration and a legacy tax on transfers of personal property. Congress reenacted the provisions of the 1862 Act with the Internal Revenue Law of 1864. A tax on bequests of real property, a succession tax, was added, as well as increased legacy tax rates and a tax on transfers of real property made during a decedent's life for less than adequate consideration, the nation's first gift tax. The 1864 law introduced several features that later formed the foundation of the modern transfer tax system: the exemption of small estates, the taxation of certain lifetime transfers that were testamentary in nature, the special treatment of bequests to the surviving spouse, and tax deductions for bequests to charitable organizations. The 1864 law was repealed in 1870. The War Revenue Act of 1898 reintroduced a transfer tax to provide revenue for the Spanish American War. This time, the estate itself, not its beneficiaries, was taxed, making the 1898 tax a precursor to the modern federal estate tax. Tax rates varied based on the size of the estate and a beneficiary's relationship to the decedent. The tax was repealed in 1902 at the end of the war.

While the inheritance tax of 1862 had enjoyed relatively broad support, the 1898 tax provoked heated debate, largely because of changes in the U.S. social structure that were the result of industrialization and widespread immigration. Populist reformers called for curbs on unrestrained capitalism

1. Paul (1954, p. 3).
2. Smith (1776/1913, p. 311).
3. Wong (1996).

and limits on the dynastic accumulation of wealth. While congressional debate surrounding the role of transfer taxation swelled, no further legislative action was taken until 1916, when the federal government realized a mounting deficit, the result of World War I. To address its financial needs, Congress passed the Revenue Act of 1916, which introduced the modern federal estate tax. While the new estate tax was appealed to the Supreme Court in *New York Trust Company* v. *Eisner*, Justice Oliver Wendell Holmes, who wrote for the majority, upheld its legality. Thus the federal estate tax became a lasting component of the federal tax system.

The 1916 estate tax was applied to the net value of estates, defined as the value of all property owned by a decedent, the gross estate, less deductions. A $50,000 filing threshold was adopted in deference to the right of states to tax small estates. Gross estate included all property, personal and real, owned by a decedent; life insurance payable to the estate; property transfers made for inadequate consideration and those made within two years of death; and transfers that took effect on or after death. Also included in gross estate was all joint property, except that fraction attributable to the surviving cotenants' contribution. A deduction was allowed for administrative expenses and losses, debts, claims, and funeral costs, as well as for expenses incurred in the support of a decedent's dependents during the administration of the estate. The tax rates were graduated from 1 percent on the first $50,000 of net estate to 10 percent on the portion exceeding $5 million. Taxes were due one year after the decedent's death, and a discount equal to 5 percent of the liability was allowed for payments made within one year of death. A late payment penalty of 6 percent was assessed unless the delay was deemed "unavoidable."[4]

Significant Tax Law Changes: 1916 to the Present

Since its inception in 1916, the basic structure of the modern federal estate tax, as well as the law from which it is derived, has remained largely unchanged. However, in the eight decades that followed the Revenue Act of 1916, Congress has enacted several important additions to, and revisions of, the modern estate tax structure (table 2-1). There have also been occasional adjustments to the filing thresholds, tax brackets, and marginal tax rates (table 2-2).

---

4. For a more complete history of U.S. taxation of estates and inheritances, see Johnson and Eller (1998, pp. 61–90).

Table 2-1. *Highlights of Tax Law Changes, 1916–1997*

Year	Revision
1916	Federal estate tax introduced
1918	Spouse's dower rights, exercised general powers of appointment, and insurance payable to estate and insurance over $40,000 payable to beneficiaries included; charitable deduction added
1924	Gift tax enacted (two-year duration); credit for state death tax; revocable transfers included
1932	Gift tax reintroduced (allowed up to $50,000 in lifetime gifts, tax free)
1935	Optional alternate valuation date introduced
1942	Insurance purchased by decedent, all unlimited powers of appointment, and full value of community property (less spouse's contribution) included
1948	Marital deduction added (replaced 1942 community property rules); couples allowed to share gifts
1951	Powers of appointment rule relaxed
1954	Most life insurance included
1976	Unified estate and gift tax structure created; generation-skipping tax (GST) added; orphan deduction, carryover basis rule, and special valuation and payment rules for small business and farms added; marital deduction increased
1980	Carryover rule repealed
1981	Unlimited estate and gift tax marital deduction introduced; unified credit to be increased over 6 years; marital deduction allowed for qualified terminable interest property (QTIP); inclusion of pension benefits (full value); only half of joint property included; orphan deduction repealed; top tax rate lowered
1986	Employee stock ownership plan (ESOP) deduction introduced (dropped in 1989); GST modified (again in 1988)
1987	Phase-out of graduated rates and unified credit for estates over $10 million; "estate freeze" eliminated (modified in 1988, 1990, and 1996)
1988	Qualified domestic trust (QDT) allowed for marital deduction
1993	Top tax rate schedule revised
1997	Increase of the "applicable exclusion amount" (filing threshold) over 9 years; a deduction for family-owned businesses and an exclusion for qualified conservation easements established

Table 2-2. *Estate Tax Filing Requirements and Tax Rates, 1916–2006*

Year	Filing threshold amount (dollars)	Initial marginal rate (percent)	Maximum marginal rate (percent)	Top bracket amount (dollars)
1916	50,000	1	10	5,000,000
1917	50,000	2	25	10,000,000
1918–23	50,000	1	25	10,000,000
1924–25	50,000	1	40	10,000,000
1926–31	100,000	1	20	10,000,000
1932–33[a]	100,000	1	20	10,000,000
1934	100,000	1	20	10,000,000
1935–39	100,000	1	20	10,000,000
1940[b]	100,000	1	20	10,000,000
1941	100,000	1	20	10,000,000
1942–53	100,000	1	20	10,000,000
1954–76	60,000	3	77	10,000,000
1977	120,000	18	70	5,000,000
1978	134,000	18	70	5,000,000
1979	147,000	18	70	5,000,000
1980	161,000	18	70	5,000,000
1981	175,000	18	70	5,000,000
1982	225,000	18	65	4,000,000
1983	275,000	18	60	3,500,000
1984	325,000	18	55	3,000,000
1985	400,000	18	55	3,000,000
1986	500,000	18	55	3,000,000
1987–97[c, d]	600,000	18	55	3,000,000
1998[e]	625,000	18	55	3,000,000
1999[e]	650,000	18	55	3,000,000
2000–01[e]	675,000	18	55	3,000,000
2002–03[e]	700,000	18	55	3,000,000
2004[e]	850,000	18	55	3,000,000
2005[e]	950,000	18	55	3,000,000
2006[e]	1,000,000	18	55	3,000,000

Note: Estate tax figures are estimates based on samples.

a. A supplement tax was in effect from 1932 to 1953.

b. 10 percent war surtax added.

c. Tax rate was to be reduced to 50 percent on amounts beginning in 1988, but reduction was postponed until 1992, then repealed retroactively in 1993 and set permanently to the 1987 levels.

d. Graduated rates and unified credits phased out for estates between $10,000,000 and $21,040,000.

e. Graduated rates phased out for estates between $10,000,000 and $17,184,000.

The first important addition to the law of 1916 was a tax on inter vivos, or lifetime, gifts, as introduced by the Revenue Act of 1924. Congress realized that, without a gift tax, wealthy individuals could effectively circumvent the estate tax, imposed at death, by transferring property, tax free, during their lifetimes. However, this federal gift tax was short lived. Because of strong opposition to estate and gift taxes during the 1920s, the gift tax was repealed by the Revenue Act of 1926.[5] Then, just six years later, when the need to finance federal spending during the Great Depression outweighed opposition to the gift tax, the federal gift tax was reintroduced by the Revenue Act of 1932. A donor could transfer $50,000 free of tax during his or her lifetime, with a $5,000 per donee annual exclusion from the gift tax.

The Revenue Act of 1935 introduced the optional valuation date election. Although the value of the gross estate on the date of death determined whether an estate tax return had to be filed, the act allowed an estate to be valued, for tax purposes, one year after the decedent's death. With this revision, if the value of a decedent's gross estate dropped significantly after the date of death—a situation common during the Great Depression—the executor could choose to value the estate at its reduced value. The optional valuation date, today referred to as the *alternate valuation date*, later was changed to six months after the decedent's date of death.

Most outstanding among the pre-1976 changes to federal estate tax law were the estate and gift tax marital deductions, as well as the rule on "split gifts," introduced by the Revenue Act of 1948. The estate tax marital deduction, as enacted by the 1948 act, permitted a decedent's estate to deduct the value of property passing to a surviving spouse, whether passing under the will or otherwise. However, the deduction was limited to one-half of the decedent's adjusted gross estate—the gross estate less debts and administrative expenses. In a similar manner, the gift tax marital deduction allowed a donor spouse to deduct one-half of an interspousal gift of noncommunity property assets. Furthermore, the 1948 act introduced the rule on split gifts, which permitted a nondonor spouse to act as donor of half the value of the donor spouse's gift. The rule on split gifts effectively permitted a married couple to transfer twice as much wealth tax free in a given year.

With a few exceptions, the Congressional Record remained free of reference to the estate tax and the entire transfer tax system until the enactment of the Tax Reform Act (TRA) of 1976. By creating a unified estate and gift tax framework that consisted of a single, graduated rate of tax imposed on both lifetime gift and testamentary dispositions, the act eliminated the cost

5. Zaritsky and Ripy (1984, pp. 12–13).

differential that had existed between the two types of giving. Before the act, it cost substantially less to transfer property during life than to leave it at death due to the lower marginal tax rates applied to inter vivos gifts. The TRA of 1976 also merged the estate tax exclusion and the lifetime gift tax exclusion into a single, unified estate and gift tax credit. This credit could be used either to offset gift tax liability during the donor's lifetime or, if unused at death, to offset the deceased donor's estate tax liability. An annual gift exclusion of $3,000 per donee was retained.

The 1976 tax reform package also introduced a tax on generation-skipping transfers (GSTs). Before passage of the act, a transferor, for example, could create a testamentary trust and direct that the income from the trust be paid to his or her children during their lives and then, upon the children's deaths, that the principal be paid to the transferor's grandchildren. The trust assets included in the transferor's estate would be taxed upon the transferor's death. Then, any trust assets included in the grandchildren's estates would be taxed at their deaths. However, the intervening beneficiaries, the transferor's children in this example, would pay no estate tax on the trust assets, even though they had enjoyed the interest income derived from those assets. Congress responded to this tax leakage in the TRA of 1976. The act added a series of rules that applied to GSTs valued at more than $250,000 and were designed to treat the termination of the intervening beneficiaries' interests as a taxable event. In 1986 Congress simplified the GST tax rates and increased the amount a grantor could transfer, tax free, into a GST trust, from $250,000 to $1 million. As with the gift tax exclusion, married persons could combine their GST tax exemptions, thus allowing a $2 million exemption per couple.

The Economic Recovery Tax Act (ERTA) of 1981 brought several notable changes to estate tax law. Before 1982, the marital deduction was permitted only for transfers of property in which the decedent's surviving spouse had a terminable interest—an interest that grants the surviving spouse power to appoint beneficiaries of the property at his or her own death. Ultimately, such property is included in the surviving spouse's estate. However, the ERTA of 1981 changed tax law and allowed a marital deduction for life interests that were not terminable, as long as the property was "qualified terminable interest property"(QTIP). To qualify, the surviving spouse needed to have sole right to all income during his or her life, payable at least annually. To utilize the deduction, however, the QTIP must be included in the surviving spouse's gross estate. The 1981 act also introduced unlimited estate and gift tax marital deductions, thereby eliminating quantitative limits on the amount of estate and gift tax deductions available for interspousal transfers.

In addition, the ERTA of 1981 increased the unified transfer tax credit, the credit available against both gift and estate taxes. The increase, from $47,000 to $192,800, was to be phased in over six years, and the increase would effectively raise the tax exemption, or filing threshold, from $175,000 to $600,000 over the same period. The ERTA of 1981 also raised the annual gift tax exclusion to $10,000 per donee, and an unlimited annual exclusion from gift tax was allowed for the payment of a donee's tuition or medical expenses. Finally, through the ERTA of 1981, Congress enacted a reduction in the top estate, gift, and GST tax rates from 70 percent to 50 percent, applicable to transfers greater than $2.5 million. The reduction was to be phased in over four years. However, later legislation, both the Deficit Reduction Act of 1984 and the Revenue Act of 1987, delayed the decrease in the tax rate from 55 percent to 50 percent until after December 31, 1992. The Revenue Act of 1987 also provided for the gradual phase-out of the tax savings due to the structure of the marginal tax rates and the unified credit for taxable estates larger than $10 million. This was achieved by applying a 5 percent surtax to the amount of taxable estate in excess of $10 million but not over $21,040,000 (at $21,040,000, the effects of the graduated rates and the unified credit were completely recaptured so that the entire estate was taxed at the maximum rate of 55 percent). Later, with the passage of the 1993 Revenue Reconciliation Act, Congress again revised the top tax rate schedule, imposing a marginal rate of 53 percent on taxable transfers between $2.5 million and $3.0 million, and a maximum marginal tax rate of 55 percent on taxable transfers exceeding $3.0 million, applied retroactively to January 1, 1993.

The next significant change to estate and gift tax law, and most current, was the Taxpayer Relief Act of 1997. The most dramatic change introduced by the TRA of 1997 was the increase in the unified credit, now called the "applicable exclusion amount." This change effectively raised the filing requirement over a nine-year period to $1 million by the year 2006. Another key provision of the 1997 Act, targeted at family-owned businesses that were more than 50 percent of an estate, allowed the deduction of up to $675,000 of a qualified business. The total value of this credit, combined with the value of the applicable exclusion amount, is limited to $1.3 million. Thus the allowable business credit will gradually decrease to $300,000 by the year 2006. Besides having been predominately family owned, a qualified business must also have had the decedent or a member of the decedent's family as a material participant in the business for five of the eight years before the decedent's death. The last notable modification of this act, the qualified conservation easement, permitted executors to exclude up to 40 percent of the value of land that meets certain conservation, preservation, or education criteria.

Current Estate Taxation

In the course of its Estate Tax Study, the Statistics of Income Division (SOI) of the Internal Revenue Service (IRS) collects data from federal estate tax returns filed for wealthy decedents before an IRS audit. A stratified random sample of estate tax returns is selected across a three-year cycle in which each cycle year corresponds to a filing year. Since almost 99 percent of returns for decedents who die in a given year are filed by the end of the second calendar year following the year of death, the three-year selection cycle permits the collection and analysis of estate tax data by both filing year and year of death. Year-of-death estimates are preferred for analyzing the demographic and financial characteristics of a cohort of decedents within a consistent tax law and economic environment while filing-year data are useful for federal revenue estimates. This section provides an overview of current estate law, along with estimates of estate tax revenue and the scope of the tax, as measured by the size of the decedent population for whom estate tax returns are filed.

A federal estate tax return, Form 706, must be filed for every U.S. citizen or resident whose gross estate, valued on his or her date of death, combined with adjusted taxable gifts made by the decedent after December 31, 1976, and total specific exemptions allowed for gifts made between September 8, 1976, and the end of the year, equals or exceeds the filing threshold applicable for the decedent's year of death (table 2-2). In 1998, the most recent filing-year data available from SOI, 97,868 estate tax returns were filed for decedents who were citizens or residents of the United States.

The estate of a nonresident alien of the United States must also file a federal estate tax return, Form 706NA, if the nonresident alien's U.S. property, at death, exceeds $60,000. In filing year 1998, 346 federal estate tax returns were filed for nonresident aliens.[6] The U.S. total gross estate for nonresident aliens reached $110.3 million in 1998.

For decedents who were U.S. citizens or residents, the gross estate comprises all property, whether real or personal, tangible or intangible, including all property in which the decedent had an interest at the time of death, the decedent's share of jointly owned and community property assets, as well as the dower or curtesy of a surviving spouse. Also considered are most life insurance proceeds, certain annuities, property over which the decedent possessed a general power of appointment, and transfers made during life

---

6. Berkowitz (2000).

that were revocable or made for less than full consideration.[7] Finally, qualified terminable interest property—property in which the surviving spouse had only an income interest, but for which a decedent's estate previously received an estate tax deduction under Internal Revenue Code (IRC) §§2056(b)7—must be included in the estate of the surviving spouse. Assets are valued on the day of the decedent's death, although an estate is allowed to value assets on a date up to six months after a decedent's death, if the value of assets, as well as the estate tax, declines during this period. Special rules for determining real estate values and a tax deferral plan are available to an estate that is primarily composed of a small business or farm. In addition, special valuation rules were recently enacted for real estate subject to a qualified conservation easement. Combined total gross estate in 1998 exceeded $173.8 billion, an amount that reflects a reduction of more than $214.9 million due to the use of alternate valuation, and a reduction of nearly $190.7 million due to special valuation of farm or business real estate.

Expenses and losses incurred in the administration of the estate, funeral costs, and the decedent's debts are allowed as deductions against the estate for the purpose of calculating the tax liability. A deduction is also allowed for the full value of bequests to the surviving spouse, including bequests in which the spouse is given only a life interest, subject to certain restrictions. Bequests to qualified charities are also fully deductible. Finally, a limited deduction for the value of a qualified family-owned business was recently enacted. Estate tax returns filed in 1998 reported total allowable deductions of $70.9 billion, including $49.4 billion for bequests to the surviving spouse, $10.9 billion for bequests to qualified charities, and $10.6 billion for estate administration expenses and other debts.

The taxable estate is calculated by subtracting allowable deductions from the gross estate. Taxable estate and post-1976 taxable lifetime transfers (taxable gifts) are then added together to yield the tentative tax base, or adjusted taxable estate, to which unified estate and gift tax rates are applied, yielding the tentative, or gross, estate tax. An initial rate of 18 percent is applied to the first $10,000 of adjusted taxable estate, while the maximum tax rate, 55 percent, is applied to that portion of adjusted taxable estate that exceeds $3 million. And for returns with adjusted taxable estate between $10,000,000 and $17,184,000, the tax savings due to the structure of the marginal tax

7. Payment from pure annuities and benefits paid to the decedent from defined-benefit pension plans that terminate at death are not included in gross estate. Survivor benefits from joint annuities and survivor annuities are included in gross estate under sec. 2039. Survivor benefits associated with defined-benefit pension plans must be included in gross estate if the decedent contributed to the cost of the plan.

rates is phased out by applying a 5 percent surtax, which effectively creates a 60 percent tax bracket.[8] In 1998 more than 92,500 estates, or 94.5 percent of all estate tax returns filed in that year, reported combined tentative estate tax of more than $43.3 billion assessed on total adjusted taxable estate of $107.8 billion, including combined taxable gifts of $4.7 billion reported for 11,917 decedents.

Gift taxes paid on post-1976 transfers, as well as allowable credits against the estate tax, are subtracted from the tentative estate tax. An applicable exclusion amount, equal to the estate tax liability on the filing requirement in effect for the decedent's year of death, is allowed for every decedent who dies after December 31, 1976. Other credits are also allowed for death taxes paid to states and other countries, as well as for a portion of gift tax paid on pre-1977 transfers included in gross estate. The credit for death taxes paid to states is limited to a graduated percentage of adjusted taxable estate, which is the federal taxable estate less $60,000. Most states limit their estate tax assessments to the allowable credit amount rather than administering a separate estate or inheritance tax system.

Estates that filed in 1998 reported gift taxes paid on post-1976 transfers of more than $933.4 million. These estates also claimed $24.3 billion in tax credits. The applicable exclusion (allowable unified credit), the largest single credit claimed by 1998 estates, totaled $18.8 billion. The state death tax credit was claimed on 58.7 percent of all returns reporting gross estate tax, and the credit totaled more than $5.3 billion. Other credits, combined, totaled $134.1 million in filing-year 1998.

The residual of the total estate tax before credits, less post-1976 gift taxes already paid and other allowable credits, is the net federal estate tax payable. For filing-year 1998, 47,483 estates reported estate tax liability that totaled $20.3 billion, nearly 19.8 percent of the gross estate reported for these decedents. The reported tax liability in 1998 represented only about 1.2 percent of total federal budget receipts in that year (table 2-3). In general, as the number of estate tax filers and reported liability have increased in recent years, the share of federal budget contributed by the estate tax, while still quite small, has also increased. Table 2-3 also shows that estate taxes are assessed on fewer than 2 percent of all U.S. decedents annually.

---

8. Before the Taxpayer Relief Act of 1997, the surtax was intended to recapture the tax savings due to both the structure of the marginal tax rates and the applicable credit and was applied to estates with adjusted taxable estates between $10,000,000 and $21,040,000. The change was the result of a clerical error introduced during preparation of the final text of the 1997 legislation. P.L. 105-34, sec. 501 (a) (1) (D). Congress subsequently elected to retain the change.

Table 2-3. *Estate Tax Filings, Total Federal Revenue, and Estate Tax Filers as a Percentage of All Decedents, 1987–1998*[a]

Filing year	Number of filers	Number of taxable returns	Reported tax liability (millions of dollars)	Total federal receipts (millions of dollars)	Estate tax as a percentage of total federal receipts[b]
1987	45,113	21,335	6,358	854,353	0.88
1988	43,683	18,948	6,299	909,303	0.99
1989	45,695	20,695	7,467	991,190	1.11
1990	50,367	23,104	8,999	1,031,969	1.18
1991	53,576	24,781	9,100	1,055,041	1.25
1992	59,176	27,397	10,109	1,091,279	1.29
1993	60,207	27,506	10,335	1,154,401	1.45
1994	68,595	31,918	12,391	1,258,627	1.46
1995	69,755	31,563	11,841	1,351,830	1.62
1996	79,321	37,711	14,456	1,453,062	0.99[c]
1997	90,006	42,901	16,637	1,579,292	1.05[c]
1998	97,868	47,482	20,350	1,721,798	1.18[c]

a. In general in this table, figures are based on returns filed in a particular calendar year, which represent decedents who died in a number of different years (see note b for exceptions). Estate tax figures are estimates based on samples.

b. Percentages are calculated as the number of estate tax decedents who died in each year divided by the total decedents in that year.

c. Preliminary estimates.

Table 2-4 shows that more than half of all 1998 estates that reported a tax liability were assessed tax at a maximum marginal tax rate of 39 percent or less.[9] The liability reported by these estates, less than $1.2 billion, represented only about 5.7 percent of total revenue reported on all estate tax returns filed that year. The estate tax liability reported by these estates represented 5.0 percent of their combined total gross estate. In contrast, just 4,468 estates, or just 9.4 percent of all estates filing returns in 1998, were assessed tax at the maximum 55 percent marginal tax rate. These estates accounted for 63.6 percent of the total revenue reported in that year, more than $12.9 billion. These largest estates reported a tax liability that was 30.2 percent of their combined gross estate. The 5 percent surtax was assessed on just 676 estates and raised $201.1 million, or 1.0 percent of the total estate tax revenue reported in 1998.

9. The applicable exclusion amount effectively offsets the tax liability assessed at marginal rates less than 37 percent for decedents who died after 1986.

Table 2-4. *Estate Tax Returns Filed in 1998 Reporting a Tax Liability,*
by Highest Applicable Marginal Tax Rate

Top marginal tax rate (percent)	Number of returns	Total gross estate^a (thousands of dollars)	Allowable deductions (thousands of dollars)	Net estate tax (thousands of dollars)
37	10,153	8,896,797	1,959,492	156,670
39	13,739	14,337,983	2,690,354	1,001,160
41	6,929	9,468,034	1,877,580	1,094,924
43	4,083	6,982,319	1,620,779	1,010,126
45	4,350	9,035,667	1,885,909	1,667,010
49	2,348	6,409,352	1,439,106	1,363,028
53	1,413	5,073,560	1,453,750	1,120,162
55	4,468	42,816,587	9,786,831	12,936,761
Total	47,483	103,020,299	22,713,801	20,349,841

Note: Estate tax figures are estimates based on samples.

a. Gross estate is shown at the value used to determine estate tax liability.

The federal estate tax return (Form 706) must be filed within nine months of the decedent's death unless a six-month extension is requested and granted. Taxes owed for generation-skipping transfers in excess of the decedent's $1 million exemption are due concurrently with any estate tax liability. Interest accumulated on Treasury bonds redeemed to pay transfer taxes is exempt from federal income taxation.

Under IRC §6166, the executor can elect to defer paying the estate tax liability for five years and then pay the deferred taxes in ten installments when paying the tax on the due date would force liquidation of a business or farm. The first installment and the last year of the deferral period coincide, meaning that the maximum extension is fourteen years. During the five-year deferral period, interest payments, calculated at an annual interest rate as low as 2.0 percent, are due annually. To qualify, the decedent's interest in a closely held business must be at least 35 percent of the adjusted gross estate (total gross estate minus expenses, losses, taxes, and indebtedness allowed as deductions under IRC §2053 and §2054). An amount of tax that bears the same ratio as the closely held business bears to the amount of adjusted gross estate may be deferred. The percentage of estates electing to defer taxes under §6166 declined from 1.7 percent of taxable estates in 1995 to 1.2 percent in 1998 (table 2-5). The amount of deferred tax rose modestly from $420.4 million to $470.1 million over this same period. On average, these estates deferred 63.4 percent of their total reported tax liability. One reason that this

Table 2-5. *Election of Tax Deferral under Section 6166 of the IR Code for Estates, by Sex of Decedent, 1995–1998*

Thousands of dollars, except as indicated

Estate tax returns	Gross estate for tax purposes		Adjusted gross estate[a]	Closely held business	Net tax	Tax deferred
	Number	Amount				
Filed in 1995						
Female	206	909,323	818,868	565,671	268,289	162,365
Male	332	2,832,285	2,485,482	1,857,516	415,143	258,049
Total	538	3,741,608	3,304,350	2,423,187	683,432	420,414
Filed in 1996						
Female	212	920,259	842,029	567,270	286,896	183,775
Male	350	2,475,079	2,090,349	1,565,458	464,661	283,915
Total	562	3,395,338	2,932,378	2,132,728	751,557	467,690
Filed in 1997						
Female	173	1,099,717	1,012,741	743,205	330,896	224,692
Male	289	1,867,018	1,598,140	1,161,515	369,073	230,812
Total	462	2,966,735	2,610,881	1,904,720	699,969	455,504
Filed in 1998						
Female	251	828,828	754,456	488,978	244,520	146,049
Male	314	1,991,395	1,695,477	1,214,688	480,670	324,031
Total	565	2,820,223	2,449,933	1,703,666	725,190	470,080

Note: Estate tax figures are estimates based on samples.

a. Adjusted gross estate is total gross estate less deductions allowed under IRC sections 2053 and 2054 (expenses, indebtedness, taxes, and losses).

provision is elected so infrequently is that only a few estates are composed of businesses that constitute a sufficient share of the adjusted gross estate to qualify. A second reason this provision is not more popular is that, under IRC §6324, a lien, in the amount of the deferred tax, is required to secure the debt. Such a lien may make future borrowing difficult for farmers who, because of the cyclical nature of their income, often use short-term loans to purchase seeds and other supplies at the start of a growing season.

Profile of Taxpayers

Decedents for whom estate tax returns are filed represent a small fraction of the entire U.S. decedent population in any given year. The demographic characteristics of these relatively wealthy decedents vary distinctly from those of the overall decedent population in a number of significant ways. An understanding of these differences is essential to evaluating arguments for and against taxation of estates, since many of these discussions focus on the economic inefficiencies that arise from behavioral responses to the tax. For example, it is often argued that estate taxes decrease incentives to accumulate wealth, thereby retarding the growth of capital stock, and that the costs attributable to estate tax avoidance schemes outweigh revenue gained from the tax. Demographic data present on federal estate tax returns provide useful information for evaluating the influence of the estate tax on the acquisitive and financial planning behavior of the elite segment of the population who are affected by the tax.

Sex and Age Composition, Geographic Location

In 1995 there were an estimated 78,023 U.S. decedents with gross estates above the $600,000 filing threshold in effect for that year. Male decedents outnumbered female decedents in the estate tax population, 54.9 percent to 45.1 percent (table 2-6). Males also outnumbered females in the overall U.S. decedent population in 1995, but by a smaller percentage, 50.7 percent to 49.3 percent.[10] Estate tax decedents, on average, not only lived longer than their counterparts in the general decedent population but also showed a less pronounced difference in age at death between genders. Female estate tax decedents, on average, lived 2.0 years longer than women in the general decedent population, while the difference in the age at death for males was larger, 2.8 years. Female decedents in the general population had an average age at death that was 6.4 years higher than average age at death for males. This difference was only 5.6 years for estate tax decedents. Factors such as access to better health care, better nutrition, and safer work environments contribute to the relative longevity of estate tax decedents.

The geographic distribution of estate tax decedents, by region, differed somewhat from that of the overall U.S. decedent population. In general, estate tax decedents were more highly concentrated in the West and in the Northeast compared with the overall decedent population. The Northeast accounted for 22.6 percent of all estate tax decedents but only 21.2 percent of all U.S. decedents (table 2-7).[11] Similarly, 23.6 percent of estate tax decedents

10. National Center for Health Statistics (1997, pp. 5, 15).
11. National Center for Health Statistics (1997, p. 64).

Table 2-6. *All U.S. Decedents and Estate Tax Decedents, by Sex and Age, 1995*

	Decedent group	
Item	Estate tax	All United States
Male		
Number	42,864	1,172,959
Percent	54.9	50.7
Female		
Number	35,159	1,139,173
Percent	45.1	49.3
Total	78,023	2,312,132
Average age at death		
Male	75.3	72.5
Female	80.9	78.9
Difference	5.6	6.4

Source: Data for all U.S. decedents are from National Center for Health Statistics (1997, pp. 5 and 15).
Note: Estate tax figures are estimates based on samples.

lived in the West, compared with 18.2 percent of the general decedent population. Conversely, estate tax decedents were less highly concentrated than decedents in the general population in both the South and Midwest, where the differences were −4.8 percent and −2.0 percent, respectively. These regional differences are attributable to many factors, including economic conditions, weather, and recreational opportunities.

Table 2-7. *All U.S. Decedents and Estate Tax Decedents, by Region, 1995*

	Estate tax decedents[a]		All U.S. decedents	
Region	Number	Percent	Number	Percent
West	18,391	23.6	422,000	18.2
Midwest	17,631	22.6	568,000	24.6
South	24,288	31.2	833,000	36.0
Northeast	17,601	22.6	490,000	21.2

Source: Data for all U.S. decedents are from National Center for Health Statistics (1997, p. 64).
Note: Estate tax figures are estimates based on samples.
a. Excludes 112 estate tax decedents who were nonresident U.S. citizens at death.

Marital Status

A comparison of the distribution of sex and marital status in the estate tax decedent population with the distribution in the entire U.S. decedent population revealed some notable differences. Of the 42,864 male decedents in the estate tax decedent population, 27,720, or 64.7 percent, were married, significantly higher than the 57.1 percent of the total 1995 U.S. decedent male population that was married (table 2-8).[12] Only 8,684, or 24.7 percent, of female estate tax decedents were married, almost the same as the 25.6 percent of the U.S. female decedent population who were married at death. While only 23.1 percent of male estate tax decedents were widowed at death, most of the female estate tax decedents, 62.3 percent, were widowed. In the overall U.S. decedent population, 18.2 percent of males and 57.4 percent of females were widowed. The percentages of estate tax decedents who were classified as single or as separated or divorced were similar for both sexes. Only 8.0 percent of males and 8.8 percent of females were single, while 4.2 percent of both males and females were separated or divorced. In the U.S. decedent population, 13.6 percent of males and 8.2 percent of females were reported as single, while 11.2 percent of males and 8.7 percent of females were divorced.

Male decedents were, on average, wealthier at death than their female counterparts. The overall average gross estate of male decedents was $1.9 million compared with $1.6 million for females. However, the sex-based differences in wealth varied significantly by marital status. The largest sex-based difference in average gross estate size was observed for divorced decedents. Divorced males had an average gross estate of $2.2 million, while the average for divorced females was only $1.5 million. Married males, the largest group of male decedents, had an average gross estate of $2.0 million while married females had an average gross estate of $1.6 million. The smallest sex-based difference in average estate size was observed for widowed decedents, $1.7 million for males and $1.6 million for females. The smaller average estate size for females may be due, in part, to age at death. Since female estate tax decedents outlived males by an average of 5.6 years, females may use more of their lifetime savings for living expenses.

Occupation

Marked differences exist in the distribution of decedent occupations, as reported on the death certificate, between 1995 estate tax decedents and the

12. National Center for Health Statistics (1997, p. 60).

Table 2-8. All U.S. Decedents and Estate Tax Decedents, by Sex and Marital Status, 1995

Sex and marital status	U.S. decedents[a]		Estate tax decedents		Total gross estate, for tax purposes[b] (thousands of dollars)	Average gross estate (thousands of dollars)	Total estate tax liability (thousands of dollars)
	Number	Percent	Number	Percent			
Female							
Married	287,106	25.6	8,684	24.7	13,911,063	1,602	5,499,970
Widowed	643,383	57.4	21,920	62.3	34,576,545	1,577	6,451,966
Single	91,939	8.2	3,082	8.8	4,077,106	1,323	471,241
Separated or divorced[c]	97,491	8.7	1,472	4.2	2,166,319	1,471	319,346
Total	1,119,919	100.0	35,158	100.0	54,731,033	5,973	12,742,524
Male							
Married	654,472	57.1	27,720	64.7	54,894,675	1,980	1,946,566
Widowed	208,633	18.2	9,920	23.1	16,954,664	1,709	3,117,336
Single	155,487	13.6	3,429	8.0	5,548,178	1,618	643,131
Separated or divorced[c]	128,586	11.2	1,795	4.2	4,010,128	2,234	794,250
Total	1,147,178	100.0	42,864	100.0	81,407,645	7,541	6,501,283
Total	2,267,097	...	78,022	...	136,138,678	13,515	19,243,806

Source: Data for U.S. decedents are from National Center for Health Statistics (1997), p. 60.

Note: Estate tax figures are estimates based on samples.

a. Includes all decedents age 15 years and older.

b. Gross estate is shown at the value used to determine estate tax liability. It could be reported as of the date of death or six months thereafter (that is, the alternate valuation method).

c. "Separated or divorced" includes decedents who were legally separated or divorced at the time of their death, as well as decedents whose marital status at death was unknown.

overall 1995 U.S. decedent population.[13] The executive and managerial occupation category accounted for the largest percentage of male estate tax decedents, 27.7 percent, almost three times greater than the percentage of all U.S. male decedents in this category (table 2-9). Decedents working in educational and sales occupations made up the second and third largest groups of male estate tax decedents, accounting for 12.3 percent and 10.6 percent, respectively, of these wealthy decedents, while these occupations together accounted for fewer than one-tenth of all males in the U.S. decedent population. Likewise, although 8.9 percent of male estate tax decedents had occupations in health care, less than 1 percent of males in the overall decedent population had occupations in this category. Conversely, while just over half of all U.S. male decedents had worked in construction, production, labor, transportation, or service occupations, only 9.2 percent of male estate tax decedents had worked in one of these occupations. Nearly the same proportion of decedents in both groups had worked in agricultural or military occupations.

The distribution of occupations for female estate tax decedents was also quite different from that of females in the overall 1995 decedent population. Educational occupations were the largest occupation category for female estate tax decedents, accounting for 14.8 percent of all wealthy female decedents, more than three times the percentage of U.S. female decedents in this category. Executives made up 8.0 percent of female estate tax decedents, almost double the percentage of U.S. decedent businesswomen. In contrast, decedents who had worked in service, production, or laborer occupations accounted for more than one-fifth of all U.S. female decedents but only 2.5 percent of female estate tax decedents. Administrative support occupations were the second largest category for women in both groups, accounting for almost 10 percent of all occupations for female decedents. Occupation was reported as "none" or "homemaker" for nearly half of all female decedents in both groups.

13. The seventeen occupation categories chosen were based on the Standard Occupational Classification (SOC) manual developed by the Department of Commerce. The percentages for 1995 U.S. decedents were based on unpublished figures obtained from the National Center for Health Statistics (NCHS) as reported by the following states: CO, GA, ID, IN, KS, KY, ME, NH, NJ, NV, NM NC, OH, RI, SC, UT, VT, WV, and WI. The distribution of occupations for estate tax decedents from all fifty states was nearly identical to that of estate tax decedents who were residents of the states for which NCHS data were available. Occupation for all U.S. decedents was coded as "unknown" or "none" for 10.2 percent of males and 49.8 percent of females. For estate tax decedents, occupation was coded as "unknown" or "none" for 2.8 percent of males and 51.3 percent of females. For both groups, a significant portion of these cases were reported as either "retired," or, for female decedents, "homemaker."

Table 2-9. *All U.S. Decedents and Estate Tax Decedents, by Occupation and Sex, 1995*[a]

Sex and occupation category	Percentage of all U.S. decedents	Percentage of all estate tax decedents	Average gross estate[b] (thousands of dollars)
Male			
Executive and managerial	9.6	27.7	2,601
Engineer and architect	2.2	7.3	1,291
Scientist, social scientist	1.5	2.7	1,299
Lawyer and judge	0.4	4.7	1,948
Teacher and counselor	1.4	12.3	1,864
Healthcare	0.9	8.9	2,109
Entertainer and athlete	0.9	1.8	2,338
Technologist	1.4	0.6	1,171
Sales	8.0	10.6	1,609
Administrative support	3.9	1.3	1,263
Service	11.7	1.7	1,092
Agricultural	7.7	8.9	1,414
Construction and extractive	9.2	3.2	1,472
Production	13.9	2.5	1,276
Transportation	7.1	1.4	1,354
Laborer	8.3	0.4	1,639
Military	1.7	1.3	1,004
Female			
Executive and managerial	4.2	8.0	1,606
Engineer and architect	0.0	0.2	1,117
Scientist, social scientist	0.6	1.6	1,095
Lawyer and judge	0.0	0.5	1,652
Teacher and counselor	4.6	14.8	1,180
Healthcare	2.4	4.2	1,801
Entertainer and athlete	0.6	2.1	2,167
Technologist	1.2	0.3	897
Sales	5.2	3.2	1,389
Administrative support	9.7	9.6	1,215
Service	11.1	1.5	1,106
Agricultural	0.6	1.4	1,258
Construction and extractive	0.1	0.1	2,165
Production	7.4	0.9	886

(continued)

Table 2-9. (*continued*)

Sex and occupation category	Percentage of all U.S. decedents	Percentage of all estate tax decedents	Average gross estate[b] (thousands of dollars)
Transportation	0.2	0.0	761
Laborer	2.0	0.1	874
Military	0.1	0.0	684

Source: U.S. decedents were based on unpublished figures obtained from the National Center for Health Statistics (NCHS) as reported by the following states: Colorado, Georgia, Idaho, Indiana, Kansas, Kentucky, Maine, Nevada, New Hampshire, New Jersey, New Mexico, North Carolina, Ohio, Rhode Island, South Carolina, Utah, Vermont, West Virginia, and Wisconsin.

Note: Estate tax figures are estimates based on samples.

a. The seventeen occupation categories chosen were based on the Standard Occupational Classification system. The distribution of occupations for estate tax decedents from all fifty states was nearly identical to that of estate tax decedents who were residents of the states for which NCHS data were available. Occupation for all U.S. decedents was coded as "unknown" or "non" for 10.2 percent of males and 49.8 percent of females. For estate tax decedents, occupation was coded as "unknown" or "non" for 2.8 percent of males and 51.3 percent of females. For both groups, a significant portion of these cases was reported as either "retired" or, for female decedents, "homemaker."

b. For estate tax decedents.

Significant differences in wealth, as measured by average gross estate, existed between male and female estate tax decedents who had worked in similar occupations. Male estate tax decedents had larger average gross estates than females in all but one occupation category. The largest difference in average gross estate, $1.0 million, was for decedents with executive and managerial occupations. Male executives had an average gross estate of $2.6 million compared with female executives who had an average gross estate of just $1.6 million. Interestingly, the service occupation category was the only category in which the average gross estate for females was larger than that of males. However, the difference in average estate size was only $14,000, the smallest for all occupation categories examined. Decedents with military occupations had the lowest average gross estate, $1.0 million for males and $0.7 million for females.

Asset Portfolio

Much has been written about the possible effects of estate taxation on national savings and investment rates. Of particular concern are the possible effects of estate taxation on small businesses and farms. It is frequently suggested that these types of enterprises are often liquidated to satisfy estate tax obligations. Data from federal estate tax returns provide a rich source of portfolio data for decedents. From these data, it is possible to examine differences in portfolio composition for decedents of different age groups and different gross estate sizes.

Estate tax returns filed for 1995 decedents reported $136.3 billion in combined gross estate. For young men, those under age 50, the face value of life insurance made up the largest single component of total gross estate, accounting for 30.5 percent of the total (table 2-10). Real estate investments constituted the second largest share, 21.2 percent, with the personal residence accounting for $245.7 million, or 45.0 percent of total real estate holdings. Equity investments were the third largest component of gross estate, totaling $495.4 million, or 19.2 percent of the total. Stock in closely held corporations accounted for 63.4 percent of all equity holdings for these young males.

Male decedents, 50 to 65 years old, invested the largest portion of their portfolio, $3.8 billion or 30.3 percent of their gross estate, in stock, including $2.5 billion, or 65.9 percent of all equity investments, in closely held corporations. Real estate constituted 23.0 percent of gross estate, the second largest component, and totaled almost $2.9 billion, 30.7 percent of which was the value of the personal residence. For male decedents 65 and older, the portfolio shifted to publicly traded stock and tax-preferred securities. Stock was the largest component of gross estate, amounting to 22.4 billion, but with only 24.3 percent of these equity holdings made up of shares in closely held corporations. Bond holdings were the second largest component of gross estate, accounting for 19.0 percent of the total, or $12.6 billion, of which 68.2 percent was invested in tax-exempt bonds issued by state or municipal governments. Real estate constituted 18.0 percent of gross estate, with the value of the personal residence accounting for a third of total real estate holdings.

Overall, publicly traded stock and real estate dominated the portfolio held by female decedents, while bond holdings, particularly tax exempt issues, were featured much more prominently in their portfolio than in that of male decedents. However, female decedents held a smaller portion of their gross estate in retirement assets, and their estates included less life insurance than male decedents in the same age groups. For female decedents under 50, real estate made up 27.0 percent of the gross estate, with the personal residence accounting for 43.8 percent of total real property. Equity investments accounted for 22.8 percent of the gross estate. Stock in closely held corporations accounted for 45.7 percent of total equity holdings, a much smaller percentage than that held by male decedents of comparable age.

Table 2-10. *Composition of Gross Estate at Date of Death,*
by Age, Sex, and Size of Gross Estate, 1995 Estate Tax Decedents
Thousands of dollars, except as indicated

Sex and gross estate component	Age at death			Total	Percentage of total gross estate
	Under 50	50 up to 65	65 and older		
Female					
Total	886,046	4,740,712	49,185,700	54,812,458	100.0
Publicly traded stock	109,967	891,672	14,504,767	15,506,406	28.3
Closely held stock	92,474	246,788	992,753	1,332,015	2.4
Bonds	76,608	482,034	11,096,807	11,655,449	21.3
Cash	61,700	374,757	6,790,501	7,226,958	13.2
Real estate	134,386	1,165,475	5,196,106	6,495,966	11.9
Personal residence	104,915	483,597	3,587,795	4,176,307	7.6
Life insurance	106,391	133,940	294,840	535,170	1.0
Annuities	61,469	340,908	1,365,859	1,768,236	3.2
All other assets	138,138	621,542	5,356,277	6,115,957	11.2
Male					
Total	2,580,153	12,595,871	66,307,522	81,483,546	100.0
Publicly traded stock	181,160	1,301,055	16,992,021	18,474,236	22.7
Closely held stock	314,209	2,510,291	5,446,706	8,271,207	10.2
Bonds	87,854	592,719	12,579,765	13,260,337	16.3
Cash	143,884	687,206	6,847,340	7,678,430	9.4
Real estate	300,284	2,006,095	7,931,733	10,238,112	12.6
Personal residence	245,728	886,672	3,976,745	5,109,145	6.3
Life insurance	786,100	1,560,199	1,630,086	3,976,384	4.9
Annuities	228,962	1,698,536	4,436,052	6,363,550	7.8
All other assets	291,973	1,353,104	6,467,089	8,112,165	10.0
Total	3,466,198	17,336,583	115,493,222	136,296,004	...

Note: Estate tax figures are estimates based on samples. Detail may not add to totals because of rounding.

Middle-age female decedents, those 50 to 65, held the largest share of their portfolio as real estate, 34.8 percent, with 29.3 percent of all real estate consisting of the value of the personal residence. Stock accounted for 24.0 percent of gross estate, with less than a quarter of that made up of stock in closely held corporations. For women 65 and older, stock accounted for the largest share of gross estate, 31.5 percent, with only 6.4 percent of all stock invested in closely held corporations. Bonds made up the second largest share of their portfolio, 22.6 percent of gross estate, with 66.6 percent of bond holdings invested in tax exempt issues. Real estate accounted for 17.9 percent of gross estate, with the personal residence accounting for 40.8 percent of total real estate.

Using data from returns filed in calendar year 1998, the Treasury Department estimates that just over 6,400 estates included farm assets, defined as farm equipment, crops, livestock, or real estate used in farming activities, including grazing, orchards, or crop production.[14] Only 642 estates, or 1.4 percent of all taxable estates, had farm assets that constituted at least 50 percent of the total gross estate. For these estates, combined gross estate exceeded $939.1 million, an average of nearly $1.5 million per estate. The total tax liability was almost $151.0 million, an average of about $235,000 per estate, or about 16.1 percent of gross estate. Another 6,198 estates included either closely held stock or noncorporate business assets. These business assets constituted 50 percent or more of total gross estate for only 521 estates, or 1.1 percent of all taxable estates. For these 521 estates, the average value of gross estate was $7.9 million, while the average tax liability was $1.5 million, or about 19.1 percent of reported gross estate.

Jointly Owned Property

Several recent studies have attempted to estimate the degree to which estates with gross assets above the filing requirement actually file a return. The nonfiler tax gap is difficult to estimate because there are no administrative records that give a full picture of an individual's wealth. One approach to studying this problem is to use household survey data, in combination with U.S. Vital Statistics data, to generate an estimate of the number of decedents for whom estate tax returns should have been filed. One problem with this approach

---

14. Office of Tax Policy Analysis (2000, unpublished estimates). The value of farm real estate, often the most valuable farm asset, was not available for 1995 decedents. This information was first collected by SOI for returns filed during calendar year 1998.

is apportioning assets in married households to the husband and wife in order to determine whether or not either or both individuals' wealth would exceed the applicable estate tax filing threshold. The following data on the magnitude of jointly owned assets and community property reported in the estates of wealthy decedents provide some insight about asset ownership in married households.

Under IRC §2040, all of a decedent's property held either as "joint tenants with right of survivorship" or as "tenants by the entirety" must be included in the gross estate. These assets are reported on a separate schedule of Form 706.[15] Under both forms of ownership, the distinguishing feature of such property is the right of survivorship. In the case of joint property held solely with a spouse, only one-half the full value is included in the decedent's estate. In the case of property held with someone other than a spouse, the full value of joint property is considered part of the estate, excluding any portion for which the surviving tenant(s) contributed adequate consideration toward the acquisition of the property.

The estates of 21,226 married male 1995 decedents reported assets that were owned jointly with the surviving spouse, 76.6 percent of all married males for whom an estate tax return was filed. For males who held some joint spousal assets, only $4.7 billion, or 11.7 percent of total gross estate, was jointly owned (table 2-11). The majority, 86.8 percent, held a joint bank account, but the value of jointly held cash accounted for only 28.5 percent of total cash holdings for these males. The personal residence was owned jointly by 61.3 percent of males for whom some joint property was reported. Federal savings bonds and other real estate were owned jointly by more than half of the males who owned such assets. Only 7.0 percent of males who held stock in a closely held business held the stock jointly. The percentage of males who owned some publicly traded stock jointly was somewhat higher, 36.4 percent, but the value of jointly held stock accounted for only 6.3 percent of the value of all publicly traded stock for men reporting joint assets. Noncorporate business assets and farms were held jointly by a relatively small percentage of males whose estates included these assets.

Of the 8,684 married 1995 female estate tax decedents, 71.5 percent, or 6,210, owned some assets jointly with their husbands. Like married male decedents, the bulk of their gross estate, $7.4 billion or 83.0 percent, was separate property with only $1.5 billion owned jointly. Joint bank accounts were owned by 80.5 percent of married women, a slightly lower percentage than

---

15. Property held as tenants in common and community property are also included in a decedent's gross estate but are reported along with separate property on the appropriate schedules.

Table 2-11. Joint Assets and All Assets for 1995 Estate Tax Decedents Who Owned Some Joint Property with a Spouse, by Sex

| | Female decedents | | | | | Male decedents | | | | |
| | All assets | | Joint assets | | | All assets | | Joint assets | | |
Asset type	Number	Amount (thousands of dollars)	Number	Amount (thousands of dollars)	Joint as percentage of all assets	Number	Amount (thousands of dollars)	Number	Amount (thousands of dollars)	Joint as percentage of all assets
Personal residences	4,741	950,134	2,679	433,849	45.7	14,697	2,565,479	9,006	1,161,354	45.3
Real estate	3,673	1,291,807	1,665	288,282	22.3	12,929	5,407,306	6,539	1,040,684	19.2
Closely held stock	756	338,668	72	13,704	4.0	4,305	4,987,359	302	103,710	2.1
Publicly traded stock	4,870	2,286,730	1,715	198,900	8.7	16,342	8,135,807	5,942	508,920	6.3
Tax-exempt bonds	3,881	1,302,816	1,133	160,698	12.3	11,274	4,259,026	3,897	497,338	11.7
Other federal bonds	1,967	335,308	461	66,115	19.7	6,152	1,030,231	1,708	116,597	11.3
Federal savings bonds	863	45,894	529	30,289	66.0	3,293	147,500	1,699	33,004	22.4
Corporate bonds	1,184	69,394	294	8,948	12.9	3,637	215,545	1,096	24,123	11.2
Mixed bond funds	676	24,352	165	1,906	7.8	2,351	114,161	653	9,148	8.0
Mixed portfolio mutual funds	1,604	93,644	478	17,913	19.1	6,268	438,018	2,421	98,262	22.4
Cash	6,015	961,393	4,841	222,232	23.1	20,724	2,967,808	17,994	847,138	28.5
Life insurance	2,726	175,849	3	177	0.1	16,509	2,736,039	68	3,486	0.1
Farm assets	255	44,409	58	2,479	5.6	1,800	200,602	209	15,147	7.6
Limited partnerships	1,045	179,171	223	5,083	2.8	3,805	798,452	1,153	23,296	2.9
Noncorporate business assets	492	159,181	122	8,404	5.3	3,022	596,364	492	22,940	3.8
Annuities	3,056	345,968	72	2,417	0.7	13,930	4,279,892	475	24,134	0.6
Art	134	14,765	45	5,112	34.6	460	157,997	122	5,745	3.6
Depletables/intangibles	251	49,024	38	15,617	31.9	1,177	123,735	142	4,118	3.3
Other	5,498	252,264	2,278	34,800	13.8	18,946	833,972	8,525	124,268	14.9
Total	6,210	8,920,771	6,210	1,516,925	17.0	21,226	39,995,292	21,226	4,663,412	11.7

Note: Estate tax figures are estimates based on samples.

for married males who died in that same year, with 23.1 percent of the value of all cash holdings held jointly. Federal savings bonds were owned jointly by 61.3 percent of married women. Like their male counterparts, the personal residence was owned jointly by more than half of these married females. Notably, the percentage of females who owned joint assets is lower that that of married males in the majority of asset categories presented in table 2-11. In particular, this is true for real estate and financial assets other than federal savings bonds.

Community Property

Community property is all property acquired by a husband and wife while domiciled in a community property state. Although the specific laws vary by jurisdiction, most state laws exempt property acquired separately by gift, devise, bequest, or descent. Income generated by property usually follows the character of the property from which it is derived, so that separate property generates separate income. States currently governed by community property laws are Arizona, California, Idaho, Louisiana, Nevada, New Mexico, Texas, Washington, and Wisconsin. For federal estate tax purposes, only one-half the value of an asset owned as community property is included in a decedent's estate. Further, when a surviving spouse inherits a decedent's community property interest, the basis of both the decedent and surviving spouse's interests in that property, for capital gains tax purposes, becomes the value of the asset used for estate tax purposes.

Of the 7,438 married male decedents who were residents of community property states at the time of their deaths, 6,112, or 82.2 percent, owned some assets as community property (table 2-12). This property totaled almost $6.8 billion, or 69.8 percent of their total gross estate. More than 80 percent of the value of real estate (including the personal residence), farm assets, and federal savings bonds was reported as community property. Smaller shares of most other financial assets were held as community property. Notable among this group was equity interests in closely held corporations. For these, only 35.6 percent of the value of all such stock was reported as community property for these married males.

A higher percentage of estate tax returns filed for married female decedents who were residents of community property states reported community property, 88.2 percent. A greater percentage of their total gross estate, 84.2 percent, or almost $3.5 billion, was also community property. Nearly all the value of stock in closely held corporations, as well as farm assets, was community

Table 2-12. *Community Property and All Property for 1995 Estate Tax Decedents Who Owned Some Community Property, by Sex*

	Female decedents					Male decedents				
	All property		Community property		Community as a percentage of all property	All property		Community property		Community as a percentage of all property
Asset type	Number	Amount (thousands of dollars)	Number	Amount (thousands of dollars)		Number	Amount (thousands of dollars)	Number	Amount (thousands of dollars)	
Personal residences	2,024	406,204	1,848	380,435	93.7	4,926	1,026,185	4,416	908,304	88.5
Real estate	635	684,923	554	634,608	92.7	1,503	513,379	1,282	429,940	83.7
Closely held stock	499	304,664	467	295,648	97.0	1,074	1,435,820	874	511,096	35.6
Publicly traded stock	2,078	863,719	1,845	629,368	72.9	4,806	1,892,785	4,340	1,196,323	63.2
Tax-exempt bonds	1,716	531,122	1,508	393,972	74.2	3,689	1,303,678	3,183	1,110,430	85.2
Other federal bonds	880	115,580	763	94,402	81.7	2,148	332,828	1,918	232,989	70.0
Federal savings bonds	381	4,134	247	2,235	54.1	656	17,130	516	15,378	89.8
Corporate bonds	585	34,028	526	16,902	49.7	1,051	54,985	826	38,292	69.6
Mixed bond funds	292	7,432	273	6,411	86.3	873	33,846	751	30,386	89.8
Mixed portfolio mutual funds	779	40,216	700	34,393	85.5	1,772	93,046	1,573	77,962	83.8
Cash	2,541	410,317	2,380	338,634	82.5	6,081	930,898	5,521	715,537	76.9
Life insurance	1,176	55,143	928	41,633	75.5	4,343	479,796	3,355	330,595	68.9
Farm assets	152	34,975	145	34,665	99.1	591	67,168	564	58,278	86.8
Limited partnerships	711	95,984	640	89,732	93.5	1,339	171,823	1,161	130,764	76.1
Noncorporate business assets	462	112,161	410	102,310	91.2	1,192	190,848	1,020	149,927	78.6
Annuities	1,473	248,713	1,368	237,288	95.4	3,978	777,879	3,327	570,430	73.3
Art	103	6,637	98	6,598	99.4	271	23,007	222	11,974	52.0
Depletables/intangibles	246	16,585	192	9,793	59.0	901	85,336	682	54,843	64.3
Other	2,432	173,580	2,253	141,348	81.4	5,926	262,343	5,413	189,505	72.2
Total	2,583	4,146,117	2,583	3,490,374	84.2	6,112	9,692,781	6,112	6,762,953	69.8

Note: Estate tax figures are estimates based on samples.

property. However, a somewhat larger percentage of the value of certain financial assets was held as separate property in the portfolios of married women compared with the portfolios of married males. These assets included investments in publicly traded stock, tax exempt bonds, federal bonds, corporate bonds, and diversified mutual funds.

Valuation of Assets

Estate and gift tax regulations specify that assets should be valued at fair market value for the purpose of determining estate tax liability. Fair market value is defined as "that price at which the property would change hands between a willing buyer and a willing seller neither being under any compulsion to buy or sell and both having reasonable knowledge of the relevant facts," according to the Code of Federal Regulations 26CFR20. 2031-1 (b). In practice, however, determining the fair market value is complex, and most practitioners recognize the importance of using professionals to determine the value of assets for estate tax purposes.

IRS regulations provide some guidance for valuing the assets in a decedent's portfolio. For example, marketable securities—those that are traded either on an exchange or over the counter—are valued, for tax purposes, using the mean value of the highest and lowest bid on the valuation date or nearest trading day. Real estate is valued either by looking at comparative sales, or, in the case of rental properties, such as apartment houses or office buildings, by using a capitalization of income method.[16] Tangible assets, such as art or antiques, are valued by experts who focus on historical cost, condition, and recent sales. Partial interests, such as income interests, remainder interests, and annuities are valued using valuation tables produced by the IRS. These valuation tables take into account life expectancies and market rates of return on investments. Present value factors are calculated using Treasury obligations on instruments with maturities ranging from three months to nine years. Closely held businesses pose some of the most difficult valuation issues. Valuations must reflect earning potential, net worth, dividend paying potential, past performance, and overall financial soundness.

Valuation, then, is more art than science. Indeed, there is much potential for legitimate disagreement among qualified professionals. For example, a single case produced the following per share values for a closely held

16. Bittker, Clark, and McCouch (1996, p. 577).

publishing company: $516 (estate tax return), $1,000 (revenue agent), $4,000 (ninety-day letter), $980 (first expert), $822 (second expert), $1,320 (third expert), $4,000 (government first expert), $3,400 (government second expert), $2,200 (court).[17] In a recent SOI study of audited estate tax returns that included closely held businesses, 37.0 percent were revalued.[18]

Special Use Valuation

In some regions, urban sprawl has, over the years, increased the value of farm and ranch land, as well as real estate used for business purposes, relative to farm or business income. In determining the tax liability under section 2032A, an executor may elect to value property used as a farm or used in a trade or business at its current use rather than at its "highest and best use." This provision was enacted because Congress believed that it was inappropriate to value land on the basis of potential use, especially since it wanted to encourage the continued use of property for farming and other small business purposes. Valuing such property at its highest use, rather than actual use, could result in higher estate taxes that would make continuation of farming, or the closely held business activities, infeasible.[19]

To qualify for the special use valuation election, the real property must satisfy several statutory tests designed to ensure that the property was being used for farming or other business purposes prior to and at the time of the decedent's death. The business must also constitute at least 50 percent of the value of adjusted gross estate (the fair market value of property net of mortgages and debts associated with that property), and at least 25 percent of the adjusted gross estate must consist of qualifying real estate. Finally, the decedent's heirs must agree to continue to use the property for farming or business purposes for ten years following the decedent's death. The value of a farm is determined, in most cases, using a cash flow basis, calculated by dividing the excess annual gross cash rental for comparable land in the same general region as the subject property, by the prevailing interest rate on Federal Land Bank loans. For business interests, a variety of generally acceptable valuation methods may be used to determine the value of business assets in

---

17. See *Estate of Kelly* v. *Commissioner* 14 T.C.M. (CCH) 476 (1955).

18. Eller and Johnson (1999, pp. 3–10).

19. General Explanation of the Tax Reform Act of 1976, 94 Cong. 2 sess. 537 (1976), reprinted in 1976-3 C.B. (vol. 2), p. 549. P.L. 94-455.

their current use. The reduction in value as a result of special use valuation is limited to $750,000, although Congress amended §§2032A(a)(3(B) as a part of the Taxpayer Relief Act of 1997, adding an inflation adjustment to this limit, calculated in increments of $10,000, for decedents dying in calendar year 1997 and thereafter. If the decedent's heirs dispose of specially valued real property within ten years of the decedent's death, additional tax, equal to the original estate tax savings, is assessed.

Despite the seemingly generous provisions of this section of the code, it is rarely used. For returns filed during 1995–98, only about 1 percent of all returns reporting estate tax liability elected to specially value real property (table 2-13). Most of the elections were for farm property in each of these years. The reduction in gross estate resulting from the election grew from $115.9 million in 1995 to $190.7 million in 1998, an increase of 64.5 percent during the four-year period. The average reduction in value ranged from $359,963 in 1995 to $411,782 in 1998, far less than the statutory limit of $750,000 in effect for all returns filed during this period. In 1995, 47.2 percent of estates that elected special use valuation had total gross estates of less than $1 million. The percentage under that threshold increased to 51.2 percent in 1996 and 57.5 percent by 1998.

Among the chief reasons for the low number of estates that elect special use valuation is the difficulty of satisfying all of the restrictions. Few estates meet the eligibility requirements for the size of the business and the value of real property in relation to the adjusted gross estate. It is also often difficult to gain agreement from all the heirs to operate the farm or business for at least ten years after the decedent's death. The increasing demand for housing, particularly near urban areas, often means that the heirs would be financially better off selling the land rather than continuing to use it for a family farm or business.

Minority and Marketability Discounts

An important valuation issue, primarily affecting the valuation of business assets, but increasingly infiltrating the valuation of a host of other asset types, is the practice of claiming discounts to reflect the purported difficulty of finding a willing buyer for fractional or minority ownership interests. This practice takes full advantage of current tax laws by coupling minority discounts and lack of marketability discounts, two ideas that courts have held as conceptually distinct, but which, in practice, are often used jointly.[20] Minority

20. *Estate of Newhouse* v. *Commissioner,* 94 *Tax Court,* pp.193–249 (1990).

Table 2-13. *Estate Tax Returns Filed 1995–98*
for Estates Electing Special Use Valuation
Thousands of dollars, except as indicated

Estate tax returns	Number	Fair market value	Adjusted value	Reduction in value
Filed in 1995				
$600,000 up to $1 million	152	86,398	41,193	45,205
$1 million or more	170	161,556	90,853	70,703
Total	322	247,954	132,046	115,908
Farm property	282	221,413	115,885	105,527
Nonfarm property	40	26,541	16,161	10,380
Filed in 1996				
$600,000 up to $1 million	209	121,427	62,870	58,557
$1 million or more	199	200,735	122,703	78,031
Total	408	322,162	185,573	136,588
Farm property	387	298,110	170,723	127,387
Nonfarm property	21	24,052	14,851	9,201
Filed in 1997				
$600,000 up to $1 million	261	171,331	70,004	101,327
$1 million or more	158	175,524	89,131	86,394
Total	419	346,855	159,135	187,721
Farm property	373	300,370	143,254	157,116
Nonfarm property	46	46,485	15,881	30,604
Filed in 1998				
$600,000 up to $1 million	266	181,888	91,032	90,856
$1 million or more	197	215,276	115,478	99,799
Total	463	397,164	206,510	190,655
Farm property	448	385,156	199,852	185,304
Nonfarm property	16	12,009	6,657	5,352

Note: Estate tax figures are estimates based on samples.

discounts recognize that the owner of a noncontrolling interest in a business is, to some extent, at the mercy of the controlling owners, making such interests less desirable and thus less valuable.[21] Lack of marketability discounts, however, are appropriate when no ready market exists for a particular asset, requiring the seller to incur extraordinary expenses to locate a willing buyer.

21. Laura E. Cunningham, "Remember the Alamo: The IRS Needs Ammunition in Its Fight against the FLP," *Tax Notes*, March 13, 2000, p.1462.

There are also a few other discounts that recognize extraordinary circumstances that might depress asset values. Blockage discounts are appropriate when marketing large blocks of securities or property temporarily lowers the overall market for those assets by creating a sudden excess supply. Key man discounts are claimed when the loss of the manager of a one-man or small business has a depressing effect on the value of the business and are most acceptable when no suitable personnel are available to take over operations.[22]

A number of court rulings in recent years have provided increased opportunities for asset values to be diluted through the creative use of discounting. Key to this has been the courts' rejection of the practice of aggregating family-owned assets to value a decedent's estate, known as the doctrine of "no family attribution." The idea is that a decedent's assets must be valued independently of all other owners, regardless of their relation to the decedent. In practice, this means that a minority interest can be claimed when one spouse owns less than 50 percent of a business, even if the other spouse is the owner of a large percentage of the remaining share. This concept has been extended so that even assets in a QTIP trust cannot be merged with the second spouse's separate assets for estate tax valuation purposes at the time of the surviving spouse's death.[23] The repeated affirmation of this practice by the courts and its subsequent acceptance by the IRS in Revenue Ruling 93-12 have created what practitioners call "discount opportunities" for astute estate planners, with the family limited partnership (FLP) as the most common mechanism for exploiting these opportunities.

Family limited partnerships, or family limited liability companies, are created primarily to hold investment and personal assets rather than closely held businesses.[24] Parents transfer assets to a general partnership and create limited partner shares. The parents then make annual gifts of the limited partner shares to children, while retaining the controlling, general partnership interest. When the parents die, the remaining interests pass through the estate. When executed effectively, minority and lack of marketability discounts are available for estate and gift tax purposes.

Minority and lack of marketability discounts were claimed on more than 6,200 of the 97,868 returns filed during calendar year 1998, about 6.3 percent of all returns filed.[25] The value of discounts claimed was almost

---

22. Revenue rulings 59-60 §§ 4.02 (b) 1959-1 C. B. 237, 239–240.

23. *Estate of Bonner* v. *Commissioner* U.S. 84 F 3rd 196 5th Circuit Court 1996.

24. Cunningham (2000, p. 1464).

25. Discount data were captured by SOI for the first time on returns filed during calendar year 1998. These returns were primarily filed for 1997 decedents but include decedents who died in other years as well.

$2.8 billion, or 10.4 percent of total assets reported for these decedents. The size of these discounts ranged from about 10 percent to almost 40 percent of the full value of the asset (table 2-14). The largest discounts reported on returns reporting a tax liability, 36.3 percent on average, were claimed for limited partnerships. While assets in a family limited partnership were disaggregated by SOI during data collection whenever possible, it is likely that some of the limited partnership interests reported in table 2-14 are actually FLPs.[26] Closely held stock was also discounted steeply, an average of 29.8 percent for estates reporting a tax liability and 28.3 percent for nontaxable estates. Relatively large deductions were also claimed for interests in noncorporate business assets and farms. Overall, the discounts reported in table 2-14 are consistent with those reported in interviews SOI has conducted with attorneys and estate tax examiners, as well as with those discounts reported in estate planning literature.

Allowable Deductions

In the computation of tax liability, deductions are allowed for debts and mortgages owed by the decedent, losses and expenses incurred during administration of the estate, bequests to the surviving spouse, and bequests to qualified charities. For 1995 decedents, deductions totaled $60.1 billion, or 44.1 percent of gross estate (table 2-15). Of this amount, estates of male decedents deducted $44.7 billion, or 74.4 percent of the total deductions, while estates of female decedents deducted $15.4 billion.

Overall, the marital deduction was the largest deduction from gross estate for 1995 decedents, amounting to $40.9 billion. Bequests to qualified charities accounted for another $10.1 billion, the second largest deduction, while the third largest deduction was for decedents' debts, which totaled $6.3 billion. Expenses and losses related to the administration and settlement of the estate accounted for almost $3.2 billion of allowable deductions.

Marital Deduction

Because an estate can deduct an unlimited amount for bequests to the surviving spouse, the tax status of returns filed for married decedents is

26. The discounts shown for each asset type were prorated by SOI when the discount was reported as a percentage of a body of assets, such as assets held in a limited partnership or trust. For example, the discounts shown for tax exempt bonds reflect discounts taken on a trust or FLP containing these bonds.

Table 2-14. *Composition of Gross Estate for Estate Tax Returns Filed in 1998 Claiming Minority Discounts*

Asset type	Nontaxable returns[a]				Taxable returns[a]			
	Number	*Discount amount (thousands of dollars)*	*Taxable amount (thousands of dollars)*	*Percent discount*	*Number*	*Discount amount (thousands of dollars)*	*Taxable amount (thousands of dollars)*	*Percent discount*
Real estate	921	126,049	733,721	14.7	2,025	273,929	1,740,414	13.6
Closely held stock	1,273	399,095	1,010,710	28.3	1,251	1,289,332	3,043,264	29.8
Publicly traded stock	72	28,570	281,922	9.2	100	109,133	977,773	10.0
Bonds	28	82	13,216	0.6	16	8,239	63,082	11.6
Farm assets	51	6,320	20,977	23.2	153	14,008	37,818	27.0
Limited partnerships	330	62,200	131,326	32.1	673	336,548	590,572	36.3
Other noncorporate	145	17,368	35,945	32.6	281	70,107	228,232	23.5
Mortgages and notes	23	1,446	8,698	14.3	95	7,768	48,306	13.9
All other	112	15,345	69,309	18.1	91	12,597	250,914	4.8
Total	2,454	656,475	2,305,823	22.2	3,755	2,121,662	6,980,376	23.3

Note: Estate tax figures are estimates based on samples.

a. Nontaxable returns are returns filed for decedents with gross estate greater than or equal to the filing threshold but for which deductions and tax credits completely offset any tax liability. Taxable returns are those reporting a net tax liability after deductions and tax credits.

Table 2-15. *Deductions for 1995 Estate Tax Decedents,*
by Sex and Tax Status

Sex and type of deduction	Nontaxable returns[a]		Taxable returns[a]	
	Number	Amount (thousands of dollars)	Number	Amount (thousands of dollars)
Female				
Funeral expenses	11,552	72,477	20,794	128,874
Executors' commissions	2,805	73,879	11,858	455,579
Attorneys' fees	6,037	83,874	18,781	385,186
Other expenses and losses	7,786	49,472	20,455	308,615
Debts and mortgages	9,407	717,649	19,195	894,704
Bequests to surviving spouse	6,984	5,636,018	1,345	1,802,503
Charitable deduction	3,198	2,401,236	5,352	2,421,881
Total deductions	13,427	9,034,606	21,719	6,397,342
Allowable deductions	13,427	9,010,417	21,719	6,397,208
Male				
Funeral expenses	24,155	168,620	14,390	95,567
Executors' commissions	3,054	82,664	8,400	423,841
Attorneys' fees	10,570	129,791	12,961	348,930
Other expenses and losses	13,477	80,215	13,776	330,062
Debts and mortgages	17,853	2,869,475	12,971	1,801,436
Bequests to surviving spouse	23,731	25,222,950	3,335	8,258,237
Charitable deduction	2,864	2,181,029	2,869	2,699,230
Total deductions	28,009	30,734,742	14,841	13,957,302
Allowable deductions	28,009	30,715,665	14,841	13,952,903
Total allowable deductions	41,436	39,726,082	36,560	2,350,111

Note: Estate tax figures are estimates based on samples.

a. Nontaxable returns are returns filed for decedents with gross estate greater than or equal to the filing threshold but for which deductions and tax credits completely offset any tax liability. Taxable returns are those reporting a net tax liability after deductions and tax credits.

b. The total of allowable deductions is less than the sum of all reported deductions (total deductions) because, under certain circumstances, some amounts claimed as deduction are disallowed under the tax code.

determined, in large part, by the marital deduction. Overall, the marital deduction was the largest deduction from gross estate for 1995 decedents, accounting for 68.1 percent of all deductions and 30.1 percent of total gross estate. Bequests to the surviving spouse accounted for 49.4 percent of total deductions for taxable estates and 77.6 percent for nontaxable estates.[27] In terms of the amount deducted, bequests to the spouse totaled $10.1 billion, or 12.8 percent of total gross estate, for taxable estates and $30.9 billion, or 53.7 percent of total gross estate, for nontaxable estates. Of the 42,864 returns filed for male decedents, 27,066, or 63.1 percent, included spousal bequests, totaling $33.5 billion. By comparison, only 8,328, or 23.7 percent, of the 35,159 returns filed for female decedents included a deduction for spousal bequests, totaling $7.4 billion. Since male estate tax decedents, on average, died before female estate tax decedents, and since the estates of male decedents used the marital deduction at almost 3 times the rate of estates held by female decedents, it is not surprising to find that estates of female decedents who died in 1995 incurred proportionately more of the total estate tax liability.

Qualified Terminable Interest Property

Trusts can be useful estate planning tools for protecting the interests of both a surviving spouse and a decedent's children. Generally, the decedent creates a trust that provides income to the surviving spouse for life, along with limited powers to invade the corpus of the trust under certain circumstances. The remainder of the trust passes to the decedent's children upon the death of the survivor spouse. Thus, while providing for the surviving spouse, the trust can protect a decedent's children in the event that the surviving spouse remarries. However, while the unlimited marital deduction is allowed for most direct bequests to a surviving spouse, IRC §§2056(b)(1) specifies that a bequest consisting of a life estate or other terminable interest does not qualify for the deduction. This is because allowing the deduction for terminable interest property would essentially exempt it from ever being subject to the estate tax, since this type of property is not included in the surviving spouse's estate for estate tax purposes. In 1981 Congress provided an exception to the terminable interest rule by enacting IRC §§2056(b)(7), which provided a

27. In some cases, paying some tax at the time of the first spouse's death is a sound strategy for minimizing estate taxes. By carefully dividing the taxable estate between both spouses and by taking advantage of the structure of the marginal tax rates, a lower overall tax liability can often be achieved.

marital deduction for "qualified terminable interest property," or QTIP.[28] For property to qualify as QTIP, the trust must provide a "qualifying income interest for life" to the surviving spouse, meaning that all trust income must be paid to the surviving spouse. Most important, by electing to treat terminable interest property as a QTIP, the property must be included in the value of the surviving spouse's estate.

QTIP trusts were reported on 11,321 returns, or 31.1 percent of all returns filed for married 1995 decedents, and had a total value of over $16.4 billion, 78.3 percent of the $21.0 billion marital deduction claimed by these estates (table 2-16). The percentage of estates reporting QTIP trusts as part of the marital deduction increased with the size of gross estate, rising from 21.9 percent of married decedents with gross estates under $1 million to 74.1 percent of those with gross estates over $20 million. For male decedents whose marital bequest included a QTIP trust, the size of the trust, as a percentage of the total marital deduction, increased with the size of gross estate as well. Those with gross estates less than $1 million reported QTIP trusts that were 66.2 percent of the total marital deduction, while those whose estates were greater than $20 million reported QTIP trusts that were 88.6 percent of the marital deduction. Overall, female decedents elected to place more of the marital deduction property in trust than males with comparable gross estate sizes. For female decedents whose marital bequest included a QTIP trust, the size of the trust increased from 69.1 percent of the marital deduction for women with gross estates less than $1 million to 98.0 percent for those with estates greater than $20 million.

Charitable Contributions

Charitable contributions are allowed as a deduction from gross estate under IRC §2055. The decision to include charities among the beneficiaries of an estate depends on many factors. The estate tax deduction for gifts to charity, in theory, provides an incentive for making such bequests by lowering the price of giving to charitable donees relative to noncharitable donees. Some researchers have found that, in fact, the estate tax deduction does stimulate charitable bequests and that higher estate tax rates increase the amount bequeathed to charities.[29] Such a finding suggests that eliminating the estate tax might have a serious impact on the finances of nonprofit organizations.

28. Bittker, Clark, and McCouch (1996, pp. 524–29).
29. Joulfaian (1991, pp. 169–80).

Table 2-16. *Gross Estate and Selected Deductions for 1995 Estate Tax Decedents Reporting QTIP Trusts, by Sex and Size of Estate*[a]

Thousands of dollars, except as indicated

Sex and size of estate	Number	Total gross estate	Allowable deductions	Marital bequests	QTIP[a]
Female					
$600,000 up to $1 million	939	747,007	245,298	209,555	144,790
$1 million up to $5 million	1,699	3,061,756	1,986,399	1,789,556	1,369,503
$5 million up to $10 million	97	668,322	518,198	469,508	350,586
$10 million up to $20 million	33	463,818	358,251	302,711	254,923
$20 million or more	14	1,195,958	1,132,997	1,053,656	1,032,300
Total	2,784	6,136,861	4,241,143	3,824,986	3,152,102
Male					
$600,000 up to $1 million	2,907	2,353,094	924,033	838,529	555,219
$1 million up to $5 million	4,816	9,709,932	6,631,222	6,129,174	4,148,893
$5 million up to $10 million	490	3,341,920	2,769,589	2,527,139	1,982,432
$10 million up to $20 million	193	2,652,780	2,163,774	1,960,855	1,526,334
$20 million or more	132	8,385,245	7,235,384	5,702,830	5,055,268
Total	8,537	26,442,971	19,724,002	17,158,527	13,268,145
Total	11,322	32,579,832	23,965,145	20,983,513	16,420,248

Note: Estate tax figures are estimates based on samples.
a. QTIP is qualified terminable interest property.

Of course, other factors, such as the satisfaction gained from helping others and the desire to create a permanent legacy, play a role as well. Living dependents, such as a spouse or children, compete directly with charities for a decedent's distributable assets. Interestingly, estates reporting a tax liability claimed only 6.5 percent of gross estate as a charitable deduction, less than the 8.0 percent claimed by estates reporting no tax liability. For estates reporting a tax liability, clearly, factors other than tax reduction had an important influence on the disposition of the assets. A look at the characteristics of decedents who made charitable bequests in 1995 is useful for assessing the possible impact of changes in the estate tax on charitable giving and, to those in the nonprofit sector, for targeting fundraising efforts.

Of the estimated 78,023 estate tax decedents in 1995, 14,283, or 18.3 percent, made charitable bequests. For those decedents who gave, the deduction for gifts to charities totaled $9.7 billion, or 26.9 percent of net worth, defined as total gross estate less mortgages and other debts. Taxable estates deducted $5.1 billion for charitable bequests, 25.2 percent of total deductions, while nontaxable estates deducted $4.6 billion, only 11.5 percent of total deductions. Compared to smaller estates, larger estates bequeathed a higher percentage of their net worth to charities. Of estates that contributed to charities, those with net worth under $1 million gave, on average, about 18.1 percent of their net worth, while those with net worth in excess of $10 million gave, on average, about 43.4 percent of their net worth.

Besides varying by size of net worth, the propensity to give and the amount bequeathed to charities also varied considerably by sex and marital status. Overall, single decedents were more likely to give to charitable organizations than decedents who were married, widowed, separated, or divorced. An estimated 38.3 percent of single male decedents and 48.9 percent of single female decedents made charitable bequests (table 2-17). While the 5,793 widowed female decedents who made charitable bequests constituted the largest group of female decedent donors, accounting for 67.8 percent of all female benefactors, only 26.4 percent of all widowed female decedents made charitable bequests. The 2,296 widowed male decedents who gave to charity constituted the largest group of male benefactors, accounting for 40.0 percent of male charitable donors. However, only 23.1 percent of all widowed males made charitable bequests. Married decedents of both sexes were least likely to make charitable bequests. Only 6.9 percent of married males and 9.1 percent of married females included charities among their beneficiaries. This finding supports other research that found that marriage has a negative effect on charitable bequests, since married decedents tend to substitute bequests to dependents, spouses, and children for charitable gifts.[30]

Single decedents of both sexes gave a larger share of their net worth to charities than decedents who were married, widowed, separated, or divorced. Single males gave a total of 52.1 percent of net worth to charitable institutions, while single females gave 36.5 percent of their net worth to charities. Widowed females, as a group, bequeathed the most property to charities,

---

30. Boskin (1976, p. 46).

Table 2-17. *Charitable Deductions for 1995 Estate Tax Decedents Who Made Charitable Bequests, by Sex and Marital Status*
Thousands of dollars, except as indicated

Sex and marital status	Number	Net worth[a]	Charitable deduction
Female			
Married	788	1,494,053	165,299
Single	1,508	2,360,708	826,618
Widowed	5,793	12,496,909	3,547,319
Separated or divorced[b]	461	777,696	283,880
Total	8,550	17,129,366	4,823,116
Male			
Married	1,917	10,047,304	1,845,973
Single	1,312	2,644,493	1,348,699
Widowed	2,296	5,785,195	1,567,859
Separated or divorced[b]	208	506,885	117,727
Total	5,733	18,983,877	4,880,258
Total	14,283	36,113,243	9,703,374

Note: Estate tax figures are estimates based on samples.

a. Net worth is calculated as total gross estate less debts and mortgages. Negative values of net worth are constrained to zero.

b. "Separated or divorced" includes decedents who were legally separated or divorced at the time of their death, as well as decedents whose marital status at death was unknown.

$3.5 billion or 28.4 percent of their net worth. Widowed males bequeathed $1.6 billion to charities, 27.1 percent of their net worth. Married decedents contributed the smallest percentage of net worth to charitable organizations, 18.4 percent for males and 11.1 percent for females. Married 1995 male decedents, as a group, gave $1.8 billion to charities, a bequest greater than that of widowed males. This is due, primarily, to four decedents who made charitable gifts of well over $100 million each. The median bequest for married males, $30,000, was almost 31 percent lower than the median bequest for widowed males, $43,155.

Charitable institutions receiving bequests from 1995 estate tax decedents were classified into one of the following six categories: institutions that benefit society as a whole; arts and humanities organizations; religious institutions; educational, medical, or scientific institutions; private foundations; and other, a category for contributions to organizations not includable elsewhere. Of these, religious organizations had the largest number of contributors, 8,401, or 58.8 percent of all contributing estates. Educational, medical, or scientific institutions had the second largest number of contributors (7,309) followed by institutions in the "other" category (6,355), private foundations (981), arts and humanities organizations (932), and institutions that benefit society (611). Decedents gave, on average, to 1.7 types of organizations and contributed 87.0 percent of all charitable bequests to the following three groups: educational, medical, and scientific institutions (31.6 percent); private foundations (30.9 percent); and other (24.5 percent). Private foundations received the largest share of total charitable bequests from male decedents, 38.5 percent, while organizations classified as educational, medical, or scientific in nature received the largest share of total charitable bequests from female decedents, 31.9 percent. Organizations that work to improve society as a whole, including those involved in promoting civil rights, community development, social science research, or government effectiveness, received the smallest percentage of total bequests from both male and female decedents, accounting for only 0.4 percent and 1.0 percent, respectively.

Summary

Many of the arguments for abolishing the federal estate tax rest on assumptions about inefficiency costs that arise in response to its high marginal tax rates. Estimates of these costs are problematic, because of the uncertainty surrounding behavioral responses to any tax and compounded by a paucity of demographic and financial information on the very wealthy. This chapter offers a range of basic estate tax data essential to any systematic evaluation of the merits, as well as the shortcomings, of the estate tax. The chapter also demonstrates that the characteristics of the estate tax decedent population, only a small portion of the general U.S. decedent population, are different from the rest of the decedent population in rather significant ways. For example, the life spans of estate tax decedents exceed those of decedents in the general population, and, compared with the general decedent population, estate tax decedents more often were married at death, worked in professional occupations, and lived in western or northeastern states.

The federal estate tax is often asserted as a "backstop" for the federal income tax. Under current federal income tax regulations, capital gains are taxed as they are realized, that is, after an asset is sold. When property is transferred at death, the basis of that property, for capital gains purposes, becomes the value as determined on the transferor's date of death. Thus financial gains on property held until death escape the income tax but are taxed under the estate tax. Estate tax data show that a significant share of assets owned by estate tax decedents is invested in real estate and stocks, both of which are likely to have accrued substantial unrealized gains. Therefore, by capturing tax revenues lost by the federal income tax system, this feature of the estate tax code offsets some of the tax costs often associated with the estate tax. Data also show that small business assets, including farms, closely held stock, and noncorporate businesses, are owned as part of a widely diversified portfolio for all but a few estate tax decedents. Only 1,163 estates reported business or farm assets that constituted more than 50 percent of their total gross estate. For these estates, recent changes in the tax code, such as allowing a deduction for qualified family owned businesses and raising the estate tax filing threshold, coupled with existing provisions, should prevent families from having to liquidate business assets to satisfy any estate tax liability.

Finally, when first adopted, the federal transfer tax system had goals beyond simply raising tax revenue. These objectives included breaking up large concentrations of wealth, limiting the extent to which wealthy parents could confer unearned advantages on their children, and adding greater progressivity to the overall tax system.[31] At this writing, the future of the estate tax is unknown. Both houses of the 106 Congress voted to phase out the tax over ten years, but that bill was vetoed by former president Bill Clinton. Still, popular sentiment seems to support major revision to, or complete abolition of, the transfer tax system, ensuring it prominence in the budget negotiations between the 107 Congress and the administration of George W. Bush.

31. Cooper (1979, p. 9).

COMMENT BY

C. Eugene Steuerle

Taxation in practice differs remarkably from taxation in theory. A standard method of assessment in the tax policy arena is to see how well practice or law conforms to theory, for example, how well an income tax represents a pure tax on all income or differs from a pure tax on consumption. In the case of estate taxation this type of approach is limited by the lack of any uniform agreement over any one or even two theories that should guide the design of the tax. This compels us to at least consider an alternative—not superior, just different—method of assessment: to let the data themselves reveal the preferences of the public and their elected officials for just what this tax is supposed to be. Such an approach, of course, does not preclude us from seeing whether the tax appears to meet these revealed goals well or to determine whether the goals themselves are worthwhile ones. To use a revealed preference approach, we start with the type of basic research and data gathering performed by Barry W. Johnson, Jacob M. Mikow, and Martha Britton Eller.

The Revealed Purpose of the Tax: To Limit the Dynastic Accumulation of Wealth

One theory of estate taxation is that it is a rough method of taxing ability to pay on a lifetime rather than annual basis.[32] Under this theory, the basic equation is that lifetime endowment is approximated by the present value of all consumption plus the present value of all gifts given or the present value of all wages plus the present value of all inheritances received. The present estate tax, however, makes an inexact fit into this equation for a variety of reasons. In the presence of a tax on all bequests or inheritances, for instance, there would be no need to tax capital income. Still, this type of theory does fit well with what I believe to be most economists' perception of the role of an estate tax. But Johnson, Mikow, and Eller reveal that only a tiny portion of all bequests are actually taxed. Using some rough estimates of total private wealth, it appears that much less than .5 of 1 percent of all bequests in the economy fall into the measure of taxable estates and gifts. And this measure, moreover, ignores all the additional transfers that take place in the form

---

32. These various goals and the equity issues surrounding trying to tax on the basis of lifetime ability or endowment are examined in Steuerle (1980).

of educational subsidies and other transfers of human capital from one generation to the next.

A second theory is that the estate tax is a once-a-generation tax on property as a measure of ability to pay. Historically, property was often a base of taxation, especially in societies that were largely rural and ruled over by a propertied class. William the Conqueror's recording of valuation of landed "estates" in England after his conquest—in no small part to set up a system of taxation—was perhaps appropriately known as the *Domesday Book*. But the theory of taxing property rather than income or property income is not without merit. One can spend out of capital as well as income, so one could argue that wealth also provides some additional ability to pay. Moreover, property income—as opposed to wage income—is measured quite poorly, and, therefore, some tax on property value might be considered an appropriate alternative to a tax on capital income.[33] One important reason for the inexactness of taxes on property income measures is that it is difficult to measure and tax capital gains as they accrue. Many wealthy accumulators, therefore, are taxed at very low rates on their income throughout their lives. Johnson, Mikow, and Eller show how this issue arises in recent debates over the estate tax—through the argument that the estate tax should be retained in lieu of capital gains at death. Note, by the way, that in many tax proposals in the United States and in some tax reforms in other countries, some form of capital gains taxation is substituted for an estate tax. Unfortunately, here again the data call the theory into question. So little property is subject to taxation under the estate tax that it can hardly be seen as a tax on property, even once a generation.

Indeed, viewed as a tax on property, the estate tax has never been a primary revenue source, and its relative role has been declining for a long time. During the twentieth century industrial economies expanded their taxes first by applying progressive income taxes to income and then, especially in the post–World War II period, bumping up flatter rate taxes on wages and consumption. Property taxes of all sorts, whether federal estate taxes or state taxes on equipment, inventory, and personal property, have waned in importance during this process.

If revealed not to be a tax on ability to pay, whether in terms of property or lifetime endowment, then just what do we learn from the Statistics of Income data? We mainly learn that the tax represents an attempt to reduce the intrafamily transfer of *large* amounts of wealth between generations. In effect, the concentration of the tax on very large estates reveals its basic purpose to be antidynastic.

33. See Steuerle (1985).

Another feature of the estate tax distinguishes it from all other taxes—the allowance of a complete deduction for charitable contributions. Unlike the income tax, this means that anyone, no matter how rich, can avoid paying the tax. It is a totally discretionary tax. Individuals only pay it if their bequests are made to later generations of their family or some other selected group of individuals. Thus, it is not a tax on transfers or bequests but on *some* transfers. If individuals wish to transfer to society, there are easy ways to do this through the charitable deduction. Government will not claim any of the resources.

The estate tax also allows a complete marital deduction; alternatively, it attempts to apply some limit on the benefits of passing transfers on to much later generations through "generation-skipping" taxes. These reveal attempts—not always successful—to assess the tax once and only once a generation on large wealth transfers.

Other special deductions or deferrals detailed by Johnson, Mikow, and Eller are sometimes harder to interpret other than as attempts to favor particular groups or to meet their special needs and circumstances. Nonetheless, these preferences, such as for farmers and closely held businesses, tend to be limited in size and scope. Very large estates benefit little, if at all, from these exceptions. What this reveals, once again, is that the tax is mainly aimed at large transfers of wealth within families, and, therefore, limiting the creation of dynastic types of wealthholding.

Other Issues

We are indebted to Johnson, Mikow, and Eller for developing and presenting the data in a way that greatly enhances our understanding of this particular tax. In a couple of cases, however, there is some danger of over-interpreting their data. To give two examples, the authors note that those who pay estate tax tend to live longer than the average person in the population. However, the selection of individuals into the estate population automatically means that they have above-average wealth. We also know that among accumulators those who accumulate for longer periods are more likely to end up with more wealth because they have more years for their wealth to compound. Since older people have more years to accumulate, we might expect top wealth holders to have lived longer than those who accumulated less. To take an extreme case, assume there are three people in society, one of whom lives to 30 and two of whom live to 90, and that one of those living longer falls into the estate population. That the average age of the non-estate population is 60 and that of the estate population is 90 may tell us

nothing about whether wealth adds to life expectancy. In fact, given this selection factor, I am surprised that age of the average estate decedent is not
even older relative to other decedents in the population.

Second, for jointly owned property, we know that exactly half of its value
is owned by men and half by women. The data that indicate that there are not
similar percentages in the estate filing population do not tell us very much.

But these are quibbles. Johnson, Mikow, and Eller provide the basic research on which so many economists, lawyers, and other policy analysts perform their applied research. They make clear what type of tax is revealed by
the data and the design of the law. And like so many basic researchers, their
reward is seldom commensurate with their contribution.

Finally, I would like to suggest the need for additional research and recording of data in two important areas. First, in their population for one year the
total gross estate reported on 227 estates with $20 million or more of estate
size was just a little more than $14 billion. Yet we know that there are a
number of individuals in our society who by themselves have a net worth
of billions. This reality warns us that we are dealing with a unique population from which a few observations can very much affect the aggregate data.
To understand estate taxation better, we need better samples of truly top
wealth holders over long periods and of those to whom they pass this wealth.
This can only be done within the Internal Revenue Service since the data are
confidential.

Second, there has been a vast increase in the percent of assets held in
defined-contribution pension plans. We need a better way of tracking how
these assets will be affected by estate taxation. Returns from these assets can
be subject to a high rate of tax without adequate estate planning. That is because the estate tax at the margin does not get a complete deduction against
income subject to income tax when withdrawals are later made by inheritors
from these types of pension plans.[34]

References

Berkowitz, Daren. 2000. "Nonresident Alien Estates, 1997–98." *Statistics of Income Bulletin*
(Summer). Internal Revenue Service.
Bittker, Boris, Elias Clark, and Grayson McCouch. 1996. *Federal Estate and Gift Taxation.*
Little, Brown, and Co.

34. The estate tax is "averaged" across all assets, so that at the margin an extra dollar in pension
assets might add one dollar to taxable estate at some rate, say, 55 percent, but the estate tax will be
prorated across all assets, including those for which no additional income tax is still owed.

Boskin, Michael J. 1976. "Estate Taxation and Charitable Bequests." *Journal of Public Economics* 5: (January–February): 27–56.

Cooper, George. 1979. *A Voluntary Tax? New Perspectives on Sophisticated Estate Tax Avoidance.* Brookings.

Eller, Martha B., and Barry W. Johnson. 1999. "Using a Sample of Federal Estate Tax Returns to Examine the Effects of Audit Revaluation on Pre-Audit Estimates." In *1999 Proceedings of the Section on Government Statistics and Section on Social Statistics.* Alexandria, Va.: American Statistical Association.

Johnson, Barry W., and Martha B. Eller. 1998. "Federal Taxation of Inheritance and Wealth Transfers." In *Inheritance and Wealth in America*, edited by Robert Miller and Stephen McNamee. Plenum Press.

Joulfaian, David. 1999. "Charitable Bequests and Estates Taxes." *National Tax Journal* 44 (June): 169–80.

National Center for Health Statistics. 1997. "Report of Final Mortality Statistics, 1995." *Monthly Vital Statistics Report* 45 (11): supplement 2.

Paul, Randolph E. 1954. *Taxation in the United States.* Little, Brown and Co.

Smith, Adam. 1776/1913. *An Inquiry into the Nature and Causes of the Wealth of Nations.* Dutton.

Steurle, Eugene. 1980. "Equity and the Taxation of Wealth Transfers." *Tax Notes* (September 8): 459–64.

———. 1985. "Wealth, Realized Income, and the Measure of Well-Being." In *Horizontal Equity, Uncertainty, and Economic Well-Being*, 2d ed., edited by Timothy Smeeding and Martin David. University of Chicago Press.

Wong, Jacqueline J. 1996. "Treasury Defends Imposition of Estate and Gift Taxes." *Tax Notes Today*, 96 TNT 47-61 (online reference service).

Zaritsky, Howard, and Thomas Ripy. 1994. "Federal Estate, Gift, and Generation Skipping Taxes: A Legislative History and Description of Current Law." Report 84-156A. Washington: Congressional Research Service (August).

RICHARD SCHMALBECK

3 | *Avoiding Federal Wealth Transfer Taxes*

T HE CURRENT debate about the future of federal wealth
transfer taxes is influenced by two widely held assump-
tions. The first is that people can easily avoid these taxes. The second is
that the public and private costs associated with the transfer tax system are
too large.

The first assumption is to some degree belied by the sizable annual revenue generated by the transfer taxes, much of which is paid by the estates
of very wealthy and presumably well-advised decedents. Although it is un-
deniable that avoidance devices exist and are to a considerable degree effective in reducing the size of a taxable estate, popular and professional accounts
have frequently exaggerated the efficacy of these devices.

The second assumption is somewhat at odds with the first: if avoidance
strategies were easy, then private avoidance costs would be minimal. And if
those strategies were certain and comprehensively effective, then public enforcement efforts would be unproductive and hence unnecessary. In truth,
whether the public and private costs of the transfer tax system are un-
acceptably large is not a question subject to definitive resolution, both because
the costs are difficult to assess precisely and because there can be no consensus on what constitutes acceptable costs. However, this chapter argues that,
just as the ease of avoidance has been exaggerated, so too have the costs, and
that there is little reason to believe that the transfer tax system is significantly

113

less efficient, in terms of the relationship between costs and revenues, than other taxes.

This chapter explores the major avoidance options currently in use, highlighting devices meant to be representative of the strategies in most common contemporary use, based on interviews with estate planners currently practicing in New York, Washington, Charlotte, Raleigh, and Winston-Salem, as well as officials of the Treasury Department and the Internal Revenue Service.[1] The chapter also analyzes the costs of tax avoidance from several different perspectives and offers suggestions for reform of federal wealth transfer taxes.

Federal Wealth Transfer Tax System

The following brief sketch of the federal wealth transfer tax system provides a background for the discussion of the avoidance devices.

The Federal Estate Tax

The centerpiece of the transfer tax system is of course the federal estate tax, which has in various forms applied to decedents' estates since 1916. In its current form, it imposes a transfer tax on the passage of assets from an estate to the decedent's heirs and beneficiaries when the value of the taxable estate so transferred exceeds $675,000. The $675,000 exemption—which is technically achieved through the use of a "unified credit" equal to the tax on a taxable estate of precisely that size—is scheduled under current law to increase in unequal increments over the next several years until it reaches $1,000,000, effective for estates of decedents dying in 2006 or later years.[2] Although the statutory rate structure runs from 18 percent to 55 percent, the actual marginal rate faced by estates subject to the tax begins at 37 percent for estates just over the $675,000 exemption level, reaches its highest mar-

---

1. I am grateful to the several estate planners who were kind enough to grant interviews during the preparation of this draft, all of whom preferred to remain anonymous. I am also indebted to Charles Clotfelter, Deborah Geier, Jay Soled, Larry Zelenak, and the participants in the Brookings conference on the future of the transfer tax system for their helpful comments on earlier drafts of this chapter.

2. The Taxpayer Relief Act of 1997, which will phase in a higher unified credit over the coming years, also changed the estate planning jargon. Although the caption of Internal Revenue Code (IRC) sec. 2010 still refers to the "unified credit," the actual words of the code now describe the concept as "the applicable credit amount," and this latter term has come into common parlance among estate planners. However, because "applicable credit amount" is descriptively empty, this chapter will continue to use the term "unified credit" (which does at least convey the linkage between the gift and estate taxes) to refer to the IRC sec. 2010 credit.

ginal rate of 60 percent on estates between $10,000,000 and $17,184,000, and reverts thereafter to the statutory maximum rate of 55 percent.[3] Congress has tried to give the estate tax a fairly broad reach, so that assets may be included in an estate even if the decedent enjoys less than full ownership of those assets at the time of death. For example, if a testator gives away a remainder interest in property but retains a life estate, the value of the entire property will generally be included in the testator's estate.[4] Similar rules apply to property over which a testator has retained a power of appointment; life insurance owned by the decedent (which ordinarily does not pass through the decedent's probate estate but is rather paid directly to the beneficiaries); annuities; certain transfers three years or less prior to the decedent's death; and so on.[5]

However, the reach of the tax is circumscribed by several deductions, among which two are particularly important: an unlimited marital deduction, so that any part of the estate left to a surviving spouse may be deducted in full;[6] and an unlimited charitable deduction, allowing deduction in full of any testamentary gifts to charitable organizations or governmental units.[7] The impact of these deductions can hardly be overstated. For estates filing returns in 1997 the aggregate total of reported *gross* estates was

3. IRC, sec. 2001(c)(1). The rates below 37 percent are irrelevant because they are fully offset by the unified credit. Actual tax liabilities begin at the point that the credit is exhausted, and the rate schedule by that point is at 37 percent. The 60 percent bracket is intended to phase out the benefit of the rate brackets below the 55 percent bracket. Until 1997 the 60 percent bracket was also intended to phase out the benefits of the unified credit, but a technical defect in the Taxpayer Relief Act of 1997 omitted that effect. If this is corrected by a subsequent technical corrections bill, the 60 percent rate would fall back to the 55 percent rate on an estate of $24,100,000 by the time the $1,000,000 exemption is effective in 2006.

4. A testator is simply a person who makes a legally valid will. (Readers unfamiliar with some of the other terms in this paragraph, such as "life estate" or "remainder interest," may wish to skip ahead to the section explaining some rudimentary trust concepts and terminology.) See IRC, sec. 2036. There is, however, a credit for any gift tax paid on the original transfer of the remainder interest during the testator's life.

5. IRC, sec. 2041; IRC, sec. 2042; IRC, sec. 2039. Only annuities having a death benefit or refund feature, or those covering multiple lives, are includable under these provisions. A single-life annuity does not ordinarily pass anything to anyone at the death of the annuitant and would not be included in a decedent's estate. IRC, sec. 2035.

6. IRC, sec. 2056. The marital deduction, like a number of other rules in the estate and gift tax area, only applies in this way if the heir is a U.S. citizen. To avoid undue complications, it will be assumed throughout this chapter that all transactions described are between U.S. citizens. Those who are interested in the treatment of gifts to non-U.S. spouses can look forward to the eventual publication of a work-in-progress by the author of this chapter, who, for nontax reasons, married a Canadian citizen. The forthcoming article is titled "I Married an Alien" (with an eye toward sale of the movie rights) and explains in horrific detail the unfortunate tax treatment of couples of mixed citizenship.

7. IRC, sec. 2055. This section covers more or less the same ground as IRC sec. 170, which provides the rules for income tax deductibility of charitable gifts.

over $162 billion.[8] The $73 billion difference between that number and the aggregate total of *taxable* estates reported in the same year (about $89 billion) is largely explained by the marital deductions claimed of $49 billion and the charitable deductions of $14 billion.[9] Thus, it may be said that the federal estate tax is intended to apply to a broad sense of the decedent's wealth transferred at or because of death, but only to the extent that wealth is transferred to someone other than a surviving spouse or a charitable entity.[10]

The Federal Gift Tax

If the tax rules are intended to impose significant tax burdens on transfers of wealth at death, the possibility that wealth transfers can—and in the absence of comparable burdens, probably will—take place in advance of death must be addressed. The salience of this point was apparently not obvious to the Congress that first enacted the federal estate tax, for that tax had no counterpart gift tax. However, the avoidance opportunity had become clear enough by 1924, when Congress finally enacted the first gift tax.[11] For roughly the next half-century, the estate and gift taxes proceeded in parallel but along separate courses, with each having its own exemptions and rate structures. The absence of coordination between the two taxes encouraged wealthy individuals to make sizable gifts during life to use up the gift-tax exemption and the lower ranges of the gift tax rates because the advantages of those features would be lost once the individual died.

Congress unified the estate and gift taxes in the Tax Reform Act of 1976, creating more or less the structure that prevails to this date. Under the unified structure, lifetime gifts are accumulated and only become taxable when

8. Johnson and Mikow (1999, p.104). These were the most recent estate tax return data available at the time this book went to press.

9. Johnson and Mikow (1999, p.105, table 1c, col. 60 [marital deduction] and 62 [charitable deduction]). The balance of the deductions was composed largely of the deduction for estate debts ($6 billion, col. 58) and attorneys' and executors' fees ($2 billion, col. 54 and 52, respectively). The total of all other deductions was about $1 billion.

10. While the estate tax returns presumably provide reasonably accurate data on marital deductions and charitable gifts, they are highly unreliable on the question of the total wealth transferred. As will be seen, virtually all avoidance devices take value out of the estate altogether (such as insurance trusts), or reduce the valuation of the property, in many cases below what would appear to be an appropriate market valuation (such as family partnerships). What is reported as the gross estate on the estate tax return, unfortunately, is a net number that is reached after estate planners have implemented their avoidance strategies.

11. That gift tax was repealed a year later; however, in 1932 Congress enacted another gift tax that has, with important modifications from time to time, been continuously in force in subsequent years.

total gifts exceed the $675,000 level that is protected by the unified credit. Once exhausted through lifetime gifts, the unified credit is no longer available to shelter subsequent transfers during life, nor transfers at the decedent's death. If partially exhausted due to lifetime gifts, the credit is reduced to that extent. Under this structure, a transfer of a given amount from one generation to the next will generally produce the same dollar value of transfer tax liability regardless of whether some or all of that value was transferred during the decedent's life, or exclusively at death.[12]

Like the estate tax, the gift tax was intended to reach broadly all gratuitous property transfers, whether direct or indirect. For example, if a corporation sells property for less than its value to a relative of a major shareholder, the arrangement is subject to recharacterization as a dividend to the shareholder, followed by a potentially taxable gift from the shareholder to the relative.[13] Similarly, arrangements such as interest-free loans may create taxable gifts.[14]

Also like the estate tax, the gift tax permits unlimited deductions for gifts to spouses and charitable entities.[15] The gift tax rules also permit an "annual exclusion" of gifts of up to $10,000 in value to any donee during any year.[16] Married taxpayers can, with the consent of both spouses, claim exclusions for gifts of up to $20,000 a year, per donee, regardless of which spouse is the source of the gifted property.[17] This exclusion is subject to one important caveat, however: gifts will not qualify for the annual exclusion if they are gifts of "future interests."[18] And, though the point is an obvious one, it is so important that it should be emphasized: while the exclusion is part of the gift tax provisions, it is effectively an exclusion for estate-tax purposes as well,

12. This is not to say that all incentives for lifetime giving have been eliminated; as will be discussed below, substantial advantages continue to be available to wealthy people who are willing to part with their property in advance of their deaths. In particular, because the gift tax is the legal liability of the donor, payment of the tax depletes the estate to that degree; effectively, then, there is an estate tax deduction for gift taxes paid, as well as a credit in the computation of the unified estate and gift tax.

13. Such recharacterization would depend on a number of circumstances and would never be automatic. A case in which precisely these facts were presented is *Epstein* v. *Comm'r*, 53 T.C. 459 (1969). (Note that a gift is only potentially taxable, because it may be within the donor's lifetime exemption or eligible for the annual exclusion from the gift tax explained below.)

14. This rule was first determined by the Supreme Court, in *Dickman* v. *Comm'r*, 465 U.S. 330 (1984). The rule was subsequently codified by Congress in IRC, sec. 7872, added to the code later the same year.

15. IRC, sec. 2523 and 2522, respectively.

16. IRC, sec. 2503(b). The $10,000 exclusion is to be adjusted, pursuant to sec. 2503(b)(2), in $1,000 increments, to reflect inflation after 1998; no such adjustment has been required to date.

17. IRC, sec. 2513.

18. IRC, sec. 2503(b)(1). An explanation of this concept, and a discussion of its implications in estate planning, are offered in the section on use of the annual exclusion.

since any funds transferred irrevocably during life will not be present in the gross estate when the estate tax liability is computed. Similarly, subsequent earnings generated by property given away during the testator's life will also fall wholly outside the gross estate.

Trusts

Because many of the estate planning devices to be described involve trusts, a few words about trust terminology may be helpful. A trust is a legal entity created by one or more *grantors* (sometimes called *settlors*) to hold and manage property for the benefit of one or more *beneficiaries* (which can include the grantor). The property transferred to a trust may be referred to as its *principal*, or *corpus*, which is to be distinguished from the *income* generated by the corpus while it is held in trust. Trust documents typically instruct the *trustees* (who are responsible for managing the trust property and protecting the rights of the beneficiaries) to distribute income periodically to particular beneficiaries (who are said to have *income interests* in the trust) and to preserve the corpus for distribution at the conclusion of the trust term to other beneficiaries (who are said to have *remainder interests* in the trust). However, trusts can be designed to accumulate some or all income or to permit *invasion of corpus*, generally or for specific purposes. Trusts can be created for a specific duration or for the lifetime of one or more individuals (usually the grantor or a beneficiary). Trusts are usually *irrevocable*, in which case transfers of assets to the trust are treated as complete for most tax purposes; but trusts can be *revocable* if the trust agreement so provides, meaning that the grantor can cause the return of the assets to himself by simply choosing to cancel the trust agreement. The assets in a revocable trust are generally treated for tax purposes as belonging to the grantor. The income tax treatment of trusts is governed by subchapter J of the Internal Revenue Code (IRC) (sections 641 through 692, inclusive), and can be complex. Depending on the provisions of the trust and the actions of the trustees, the income generated by the corpus in the trust may be taxable to the grantor, the beneficiaries, or the trust itself.

The Federal Generation-Skipping Transfer Tax

Before 1976, there were transfer-tax advantages associated with trusts that would leave an income interest in the trust to one (or more) of the decedent's children, for the duration of that beneficiary's life, with a remainder interest to be paid to one or more of the decedent's grandchildren. The transfer of property into the trust from the grandparent's estate would be a taxable transfer by the deceased grandparent, but the enjoyment of the remainder interest by the grandchildren at the death of the member(s) of the intermediate generation was not generally subject to a transfer tax. This was typically true even if the trustees had some powers to invade the corpus of the trust for the benefit of the member(s) of the intermediate generation. If the testator so chose, more than one generation could be skipped; that is, a trust could create a series of lifetime income interests cascading down through subsequent generations, each one beginning tax free at the death of a member of the previous generation, with a remainder interest vesting in a member of the fourth or fifth generation following the testator whose will created the trust.[19] A majority of Congress in 1976 believed that the enjoyment of the value of the property by the intermediate generation(s) was sufficient that the passage of value from each generation to the next should be subject to a federal transfer tax. Accordingly, Congress created the aptly named "generation-skipping transfer tax" (GST tax) in that year.[20]

The GST tax can be complex, but essentially it treats the termination of the life interests of any intermediate generation in a situation of the sort described (or certain others deemed equivalent by Congress) as a taxable event, effectively imputing the value of the interest passing to the next generation as a part of the estate of the member of the intermediate generation. The GST tax also taxes certain "direct skips" that do not pass through the intermediate generation. The saving grace of the GST tax is that it only applies to transfers within its ambit to the extent that they exceed $1,030,000 per transferor.[21] Largely because of the generous exemption, the GST tax collects very little revenue—about $86 million in 1997, or about half of 1 percent of the total federal transfer tax collections.[22] However, it is one of those taxes—rather like the alternative minimum tax—whose impact is to discourage taxpayer

19. Historically, trusts could not endure indefinitely as a matter of law. Most states limited the duration of trusts by some variant of the "rule against perpetuities," which generally requires that the interests created by the trust must vest within a period measured by the duration of any life existing at the time the trust is created, plus twenty-one years. See generally the William Hurt/Kathleen Turner film *Body Heat*, which is thought to be the cinematic debut of this wonderful common law concept. Some form of this rule, which effectively limits trusts to four or five generations, in most cases, continues to apply in most states. However, a handful of states have recently abolished their versions of the rule against perpetuities, and institutions in some of those states (Delaware and Alaska seem particularly prominent) have begun actively marketing so-called dynasty trusts that exploit the absence of such limitations. See the discussion under "Other Devices."

20. IRC, sec. 2601, and following; see also Tax Reform Act of 1976, P.L. 9 4-455, sec. 2006 (c).

21. IRC, sec. 2631(a). The figure in the text is for the year 2000. The exemption level is now indexed and may be adjusted in subsequent years.

22. Johnson and Mikow (1999, p.107, table 1c, col. 86.)

behavior by imposing strong disincentives. To the extent that the tax succeeds in this effort, its effects would not be reflected in the revenue collected but rather in the generation-skipping bequests that it discourages. While the effects of the tax are not easily measured, the point is that the GST tax should not be regarded as unimportant simply because of its negligible revenue impact.

The Avoidance Options

Several of the more important avoidance options result in the removal of transfers from the transfer tax base altogether. Others operate primarily to diminish the tax value of the assets included, by exposing the transfer to tax when the value of the transferred interest is low or by achieving in some other way a valuation that understates somewhat the likely true value of the property transferred. For the most part, each of these options is self-sufficient.[23] Accordingly, they can be discussed seriatim, beginning with the three options that are based on the major deductions or exclusions from the estate and gift tax, namely, the annual exclusion, the charitable deduction, and the marital deduction.

Use of the Annual Exclusion

By far the simplest strategy available to wealthy individuals who wish to make tax-free transfers to subsequent generations involves the committed, regular use of the annual exclusion. A typical married couple in their fifties, for example, may have two children, each of whom may have a spouse, as well as two children of their own. Each of these eight potential beneficiaries could be given, free of any transfer tax, $20,000 a year. Over a period of twenty years (well within the life expectancies of the couple), this practice would distribute more than $3 million to subsequent generations without giving rise to any transfer taxes at any time. If one also considers the income produced by the funds given away in this manner (which will enrich the donees, rather than augmenting the estate), the potential reduction in the estate would be around $6 million altogether from the strategy outlined, assuming a 6 percent rate of return. If the family is larger, or

---

23. Many of the devices can be combined in one way or another with other devices. For example, many of the devices involve creation of trusts; and a trust can contain a wide range of assets, some of which could consist of such things as units in a family limited partnership.

if the donors live longer or are willing to spread their largesse more widely (for example, to nieces, nephews, cousins, and so on), then this sum could of course be much larger. One recent study suggested that roughly one-quarter of the wealth transfers between succeeding generations could be sheltered from transfer taxes by the use of this simple device.[24] This device is also nearly free of the transactions costs that commonly accompany more complicated estate-reduction devices. The donors need only open their checkbook once a year and make the transfers. If all gifts during the year are within the annual exclusions for each donee, then it is not even necessary to file a gift tax return.[25]

Despite the obvious tax-avoidance efficacy of a strategy making maximum use of the annual exclusion, few people pursue the strategy to the fullest degree possible. In the aggregate, it is estimated that, at most, only about 15 percent of the value of the annual exclusion gifts that could be made tax free from potentially taxable estates are in fact made.[26] Several explanations have been offered. For estates that are in the low seven-figure range, a plausible claim can be made that the potential donors feel a need to retain all or most of their assets as protection against catastrophic medical expenses, rampant inflation, and other potential uncertainties. Other prominent explanations include the possible damage done to young donees who may in some cases receive as much (or more) by gift as they are able to earn on their own in the labor force,[27] and the possibility that testators prefer to retain their assets until death as a way of retaining some control over the behavior of their children and others who imagine themselves to be, eventually, targets of bequests.[28] But some observers have forcefully argued that the

24. Poterba (1998a, p. 24). The paper presents a variety of estimates, ranging from 22 to 33 percent, depending on the underlying assumptions.

25. IRC, sec. 6019(1).

26. Poterba (1998, p. 25). Poterba estimates that annual giving levels within the annual exclusion could be approximately $443 billion; estimates of actual gifts qualifying for the annual exclusion vary, but no estimate is higher than about $62 billion.

27. If both parents and as many as four grandparents make the maximum tax-free gifts, a child or grandchild could receive up to $60,000 a year from this source. As will be explained, however, the present interest requirement of the annual exclusion operates somewhat differently in the case of gifts to minor children; so concerns about the ability of a child to exercise wise stewardship over gifts of this magnitude do not present any genuine obstacles. Such gifts may, however, because of the fiduciary relationships involved, have somewhat higher transactions costs.

28. Bernheim, Shleifer, and Summers (1985, p. 1046). Still other explanations, having to do with the possibilities that the older generation may have more attractive investment opportunities; that they may lack sufficient liquidity to make lifetime gifts; or that they are reluctant to forgo the stepped-up basis opportunities provided by IRC, sec. 1014, for assets held at death, are considered in Poterba (1998, pp. 1, 7–8).

real barrier to full use of the annual exclusion is the strong preference of potential donors for the retention of economic power.[29]

Gifts to a minor can generally qualify for the annual exclusion even if the value of the gifts is not made immediately available to the child. Under the provisions of the Uniform Transfers to Minors Act (UTMA), which has been enacted in some form in most states, the transfer is made to a custodian who holds the assets for the child until the child reaches the age of 21.[30] The donor can be the custodian of a gift to a minor, but if the donor dies during the custodianship period, the assets will typically be included in the donor-custodian's estate as a revocable transfer.[31] Thus, the regular use of the annual exclusion in making gifts to minors as an estate planning device is advanced more reliably by designating as custodian someone other than the donor. By means of regular use of the annual exclusion, a married couple could thus transfer up to $420,000 to each child free of any transfer taxes (21 years times $20,000 a year), as could each pair of grandparents, if they survive to the age of majority of their grandchildren.

Of course, the possibility that a child or grandchild might enjoy a birthday gift of $1,260,000 or more upon attaining the age of 21 is not something that every family regards as desirable.[32] To avoid this possibility, while retaining as much as possible of the benefits of regular use of the annual exclusion, many donors resort to so-called Crummey trusts,[33] a name that sounds pejorative but is so perhaps only to the IRS. Under a Crummey trust, the beneficiary is given a power (a Crummey power) to demand distribution of each year's contribution by the donor to the trust; but if the power is not exercised within a reasonable time, then the power lapses. The limited power to demand distribution transforms what would otherwise be a future interest into a present interest, which in turn qualifies the annual contribution to

29. See, for example, Thurow (1975, pp. 139–42). Thurow was speaking principally of the then greater tax advantages associated with lifetime giving under the pre-1976, preunified, estate and gift tax system. However, his observations would seem to have equal relevance to the use of the annual exclusion.

30. The relevant age of majority is one of the several ways in which each state's version of this model legislation may vary. In several states, the age of majority for UTMA purposes is eighteen, rather than twenty-one.

31. IRC, sec. 2038. Even though the gifts in such cases are not in fact revocable, this provision has been interpreted broadly to authorize inclusion in the estate because of the retained power of the grantor to affect the timing of the benefit to the minor child. See, for example, *Lober* v. *U.S.*, 346 U.S. 335 (1953) (interpreting predecessor provision under the 1939 code); Rev. Rul 57-366, 1957-2 C.B. 618.

32. This assumes that each parent, and each of four grandparents, made the maximum excludable gift during each year of the child's minority. If no distributions had been made from the trust, the accumulated earnings would of course make the hypothetical gift much larger.

33. These trusts take their name from the case in which their use was first fully endorsed by the courts, *Crummey* v. *Comm'r*, 397 F.2d 82 (9th Cir., 1968).

the trust for the annual exclusion. The period during which the power to demand distribution may be exercised can apparently be quite short; in one case litigated on other issues, the IRS did not challenge the validity of Crummey powers that could only be exercised within fifteen days.[34] Though Crummey trusts thus do involve the possibility of limited invasion of the trust corpus by the beneficiary, presumably those beneficiaries understand that to exercise their rights to demand immediate distributions contrary to the donor's wishes would jeopardize future contributions to the trust. For that reason beneficiaries are willing to accede to the donor's wish to allow the trust to accumulate with the help of the regular use of the annual exclusion.[35]

Other devices involve the use of the annual exclusion to pass partial interests in property each year to the next generation, but they will be explained subsequently as each of those devices is outlined.

Charitable Gifts

At the most basic level, a simple cash bequest to a charitable organization will eliminate the tax that would have been paid on that amount had it been left to noncharitable beneficiaries. The cost of such gifts may accordingly be formulated as the gift itself times one minus the marginal tax rate, which—in view of marginal rates ranging from 37 to 60 percent—yields a cost ranging from sixty-three cents on the dollar to as little as forty cents on the dollar.

An even lower after-tax cost of giving can be achieved if gifts are made during the donor's life, however, because of the income tax deductions available for such gifts.[36] A donor who is in the highest rate bracket as to both the in-

---

' 34. *Cristofani Est.* v. *Comm'r*, 97 T.C. 74 (1991). The estate planners interviewed for this chapter recommended periods of at least thirty days, and some preferred exercise periods of up to one year. Reasonable notice of their rights to distributions from the trust should be provided to the beneficiaries if the annual exclusion is to protect the transfer from gift tax liability, though there is some precedent to the effect that actual notice is not legally necessary. (See *Estate of Holland* v. *U.S.*, T.C. Mem. 1997-302.)

35. Only two of the estate-planner interviewees had ever witnessed an actual exercise of a *Crummey* power, and one of these knew of only a single instance.

36. Some very high-wealth taxpayers get little or no income tax benefit from charitable giving because of the limits of IRC sec. 170(b), which allows deductions only up to an amount equal to 50 percent (or less in some cases) of the taxpayer's "contribution base," which is essentially the taxpayer's adjusted gross income. An individual whose wealth is largely in the form of highly appreciated (but as yet untaxed) assets, such as the stock of company created by the taxpayer, may have the willingness and capacity to make gifts that greatly exceed this level, but he will have to do so without benefit of an income tax deduction. (Unused deductions may be carried over for up to five years; even so, some high-wealth individuals find themselves in a persistent situation of having contributions that exceed the annual limits and thus never have years in which carried-over deductions from prior years can be claimed.)

come and estate taxes can achieve an after-tax cost of giving as low as twenty-four cents on the dollar; that is to say that a dollar given during the donor's life to charity may cost the heirs as little as twenty-four cents in lost net inheritance.[37] This tax arithmetic makes clear that lifetime charitable giving has nearly as much to do with estate tax avoidance as it does with income tax considerations, particularly for elderly donors or others of limited life expectancy.

Of course, simple cash bequests do not exhaust the estate planner's repertory in the charitable giving area. Several interesting options involve split-interest gifts, in which an income interest is given to one party and a remainder interest to another. If either party is a charitable entity, there will be either income tax or transfer tax advantages (or both) associated with the gift.

A family of similar transactions, under which the charitable entity receives a remainder interest, are typically known by their acronyms: CRATs, and CRUTs—charitable remainder annuity trusts, and unitrusts, respectively. These involve a gift from a donor (usually during the donor's life) to a trust, which distributes income from the trust to the donor or another noncharitable party for a period of years or for a period measured by the life of a natural person (typically the donor), following which the corpus of the trust is distributed to a charitable entity. The actuarial value of the remainder given to charity is deductible from income taxes by the donor in the year the assets are irrevocably transferred into the trust; the estate tax benefit comes simply from the removal of the entire corpus of the trust from the taxable estate. Although quite popular estate planning tools, these vehicles will not be further detailed in this chapter because their benefits are thought to involve primarily avoidance of income taxes.[38] From an estate tax perspective,

---

37. Had the dollar of income not been sheltered from income tax by the charitable deduction, only a bit more than 60 cents would have remained after that tax had been paid. The 60 cents remaining in the estate would have incurred—albeit at some indefinite future date—a further estate tax liability as high as 60 x .6, or 36 cents. Thus, the 40 cents of income tax savings, plus the 36 cents of estate tax savings, leave a net cost as low as 24 cents lost by the heirs for every dollar given to charity during the donor-testator's life. (Note, however, that the usual reduction in the cost of giving associated with gifts of appreciated property ordinarily does not apply in the context of estate planning. That reduction involves the implicit assumption that, besides ordinary income sheltering, there is a sheltering of the income tax on the capital gain that would have been incurred had the appreciated asset been sold. However, because heirs who receive property take that property with a basis equal to the fair market value of the property as of the date of death (or the alternate valuation date) pursuant to IRC, sec.1014, there is no capital gains tax to be avoided as to the unrealized gain on appreciated property. Thus, a charitable gift of appreciated property that would otherwise be retained until death neither adds to nor subtracts from the tax advantages of charitable giving.)

38. In particular, these devices can provide an attractive means of diversifying a concentrated portfolio of appreciated assets. Because the trust is itself tax exempt, it can liquidate appreciated assets without immediate tax consequences, the proceeds of which can then be invested in a diversified portfolio to provide, for example, a secure stream of retirement income to the donor.

they typically do not accomplish much more than a straightforward, non-charitable annuity contract might.

Estate tax considerations are more important in the other sort of split-interest charitable gift, the charitable lead trust. In this vehicle, the donor transfers assets to a trust with instructions to pay an income interest to a charitable entity, with the remainder interest being distributed at the end of the trust term to a noncharitable beneficiary. The income interest can be given in the form of a guaranteed annuity (a charitable lead annuity trust) or in the form of a fixed percentage of the annually appraised fair market value of the assets in the trust (a charitable lead unitrust). Although the donor may usually deduct for income tax purposes the actuarial value of the income interest given to charity, the tax benefit of this deduction is offset by the requirement that the donor include the trust income going to charity in later years in the donor's own adjusted gross income.[39] This is an appropriate income tax result, in that the charitable lead trust effectively replicates what would happen if a donor had simply received investment income and then transferred that income each year to a charitable entity; the charitable deduction would offset the investment income but would not shelter any other income.[40]

The transfer tax benefit of the charitable lead trust is that it transfers assets into the hands of the ultimate beneficiaries at reduced values. The charitable lead trust is considered a taxable transfer to the beneficiary at the time the assets are transferred into trust, in an amount equal to the difference between the value of the assets and the value of the charitable income interest. Thus, a gift of trust assets consisting in substantial part of growth stocks[41] might be valued for transfer tax purposes at a fraction of its present value as of the date of the gift (because of the reduction for the charitable interest), but the entire value of the corpus (which would be expected to have grown because of the corporate earnings reinvestment strategy) can be passed without additional transfer tax consequences to the ultimate donee at the end of the trust term or the end of the measuring life (typically the donor's).

---

39. Both clauses of this sentence presume that the trust will be structured as a grantor trust. If the trust is structured instead as a nongrantor trust, then the initial deduction is unavailable but so also is the subsequent trust income excludable.

40. Charitable lead trusts can have favorable income tax consequences in some cases, however. In particular, if the donor's tax bracket is expected to decline in future years, the benefit of the immediate deduction of the discounted present value of the future income going to charity will not be fully offset by the subsequent inclusion of that income in the taxpayer's taxable income in future years.

41. The donor will typically wish to include some income-producing assets to enable the trust to discharge the obligations to the charitable donee without liquidation of significant trust assets.

By itself, this is not very different from the results that could be obtained by simply dividing the trust corpus into a share that would go directly and immediately to charity (generating a charitable deduction of that amount), and another share that would go directly and immediately to the noncharitable beneficiary (generating a taxable gift of that amount); if invested in the same way that the trustees would have, the latter share would grow to the same amount that would constitute the expected remainder interest at the termination of the lead trust, with similar tax consequences.[42] Again, however, estate planners frequently encounter a preference by donors to defer the full enjoyment of their gifts, both charitable and familial. On the charitable side, an income interest ensures that the gift will have the endowment-like quality that many charitable donors seem to prefer; on the familial side, the enjoyment of the gift can be deferred until the donee has acquired the maturity to handle responsibly the receipt of the wealth in question.[43]

While charitable split-interest gifts can accomplish significant transfers of value to charities, they have also been subject to a good deal of abuse in recent years. Schemes involving charitable remainder trusts using very high payout rates produce mostly income-tax avoidance; descriptions appearing elsewhere will not be repeated here.[44] But a very recently developed form of aggressive transfer tax avoidance involves the use of charitable lead trusts. This device—like many in this area—exploits the fact that the valuation of remainder interests is usually based on tabular life expectancies applied to the "measuring life" of the income interest. Under a so-called vulture trust, the grantor would employ as a measuring life the life of a person—typically a stranger recruited for this purpose by the vulture—who was suffering from AIDS or some similar condition having radically depressing effects on life expectancy. Thus, a thirty-five-year-old person with a tabular remaining life expectancy of perhaps forty years, but an actual remaining life expectancy of perhaps two to five years, would be used as the measuring life. This would establish a very low value for the remainder interest, because the actuarial expectation would be that the death

---

42. In the direct gift alternative described here, much or all of the corpus would presumably be invested in growth stocks, so that the donee could benefit from the favorable effects of the deferral of income taxation on unrealized appreciation.

43. Because the death of a parent frequently occurs when the children are in middle age, the intention of the donor-testator is frequently to provide a store of wealth adequate to ensure the children's comfortable retirement.

44. Congress addressed some of the more serious abuses in this area by amending IRC, sec. 664, in the Taxpayer Relief Act of 1997. For a brief explanation of these devices, see IRS Notice 94-78, 1994-2 CB 555, and Auten, Clotfelter, and Schmalbeck (1998).

of the person whose life was the measuring stick would not occur for many years.[45] In fact, that measuring life is chosen precisely because the individual's death is close at hand; and when it does occur a few years later, very large values could pass—free of any additional transfer tax—to the noncharitable remainderman. The IRS has (probably) shut down this abusive use of charitable lead trusts by proposing regulations that would limit the selection of measuring lives to close relatives.[46] But this egregious device remains an instructive illustration of a pattern that runs through a number of the devices to be described here: the use of tabular assumptions as to life expectancy and rates of return that allow individuals to engage in various adverse selection games that employ the tabular rates when they are helpful, while avoiding them when they are not.

Several estate planners—especially those with the most experience with very large estates—mentioned the continuing high interest in setting up private foundations. Again, nothing particularly fancy in the way of tax avoidance is involved in establishing a private foundation; such gifts are simply another form of charitable contribution and thus qualify for deductions from the income, gift, and estate tax bases. Their desirability comes from the opportunity they provide to wealthy donors (or their designates) to retain a good deal of control over the assets of the foundation (which may, for example, be stock of a family corporation, though this is subject to several restrictions)[47] and control over the direction of the income from those assets to the ultimate charitable beneficiaries funded by the foundation's grants. Foundations have some drawbacks, which include the exposure to the elaborate array of excise taxes applying to such organizations, and the fact that, for income tax purposes, a limitation exists on the percentage of gross income that can be deducted for gifts to foundations (generally 30 percent rather than 50 percent for public charities). Limitations also exist on the ability to deduct the fair market value of appreciated property (generally, only certain publicly traded stock can be deducted at full value when given to a private foundation) rather than being limited to the property's tax basis. However, neither of these latter drawbacks comes into play in the area of estate and gift taxes; all gifts to charitable entities—whether public charities or private foundations—are fully deductible.

45. For example, at a 6 percent discount rate, a remainder interest that would not ripen for forty years would have a value equal to about 9.7 percent of the value of the corpus.

46. See *Tax Notes*, vol. 87, April 10, 2000, p. 207, which describes proposed amendments to the Treasury Regs., sec. 25.2522(c)-3, that would restrict the choice of measuring lives.

47. See generally the rules on excess business holdings, IRC, sec. 4943, which impose the major restrictions in this area.

Marital Deductions

Federal transfer taxes apply separately to each natural person and allow each decedent a substantial exemption and the benefit of lower marginal tax rates on the first $3,000,000 transferred. When an unlimited marital deduction is added to these structural features, a basic tax-minimization strategy is immediately evident: estate plans for married couples should at a minimum be structured to ensure that the full value of both exemptions can be claimed. By doing so, the estate plan ensures that the married couple enjoys an effective exemption of $1,350,000. Under some circumstances, they may wish to ensure as well that the couple's wealth makes two trips through the lower rate brackets, thus insulating their estates from the highest rates on the first $6,000,000 transferred, regardless of the division of wealth between them.[48]

For smaller to medium-sized taxable estates (in perhaps the two- to ten-million-dollar range) ensuring effective use of both unified credits is the estate planner's first step. Because it is again true that even the simplest strategies in this area can be highly effective, a few minutes of skilled draftsmanship can often produce transfer tax savings of hundreds of thousands of dollars. Ideally, any transfers necessary to ensure that each spouse makes full use of the unified credit would be done during life, since a partner with little or no wealth may die first, leaving the surviving spouse with all or most of the wealth, but no one qualified to receive a marital deduction gift.[49] But, though exceptions abound, the husband is generally the wealthier and older member of the couple and possessed of a shorter overall life expectancy as well. Under those circumstances, it may suffice simply to ensure that a hus-

---

48. The benefits of taking two credits, and two trips through the rate brackets, can be considerable. As an illustration, a $6,000,000 taxable estate would generate an estate tax liability, after allowance of the unified credit, of $2,720,250. Two $3,000,000 estates, in contrast, would generate a total tax liability of only $2,140,500, thus saving $579,750, or 21.3 percent of the liability that would be incurred on a single estate of $6,000,000. Of this savings, $220,550 is generated by the availability of the second credit, and the balance by the lower rates on the first $3,000,000 transferred. However, intentionally exposing half of the total value of the couple's wealth to an estate tax at the death of the first to die may not always be the best strategy. If the surviving spouse is in good health, any estate tax potentially owed at the first death can be deferred indefinitely by making sure that the marital deduction shields all but the amount that can be absorbed by the unified credit. In fact, the surviving spouse may not only be able to defer the tax by continuing to live but may also be able to use the annual exclusion, for example, in subsequent years to transfer much of the potential estate to the next generation free of any transfer tax. The couple will not know, of course, when their wills are drafted, the ages at which each will die. But it is probably sensible when the testators are relatively young to pursue a strategy that makes maximum use of the marital deduction, thus deferring any tax that might fall due if one of them dies prematurely.

49. Although widowhood is a correctable condition, couples engaged in estate planning do not typically wish to explore the ramifications of that notion in any great detail.

band in such a situation has a will that passes substantial assets to his wife, so that she may take full advantage of the unified credit.

Problems can arise, however, in trying to make the best use of the two credits when the tax-minimization strategy is not completely harmonious with the dispositive preferences of the couple. For example, in small to medium estates, and especially where the marriage is a stable first marriage for both parties, the couple's first instinct is often to leave all of the estate to the surviving spouse. If they do so, the estate of the first to die will receive no benefit from the unified credit because the marital deduction will reduce the taxable estate to zero. At the other end of the spectrum of preferences, someone who remarries late in life may wish to leave all or most of the estate to children of a prior marriage and may not want to leave enough to a surviving spouse to enable him or her to use the full measure of the unified credit (or the lower rate brackets) at the death of the second to die.

To a limited degree, either preference can be accommodated at only modest loss in the value of the double-credit strategy. If the preference is to leave as much to the spouse as possible, but still to create enough of a taxable estate at the first death to absorb the credit (and the lower rates, if desired), property can be left to a "credit shelter trust" that may pay the surviving spouse an income interest for life (or, less expansively, merely permit invasion of corpus if needed for support of the surviving spouse), with a remainder interest to one or more children, with the specific intention that the income interest passing to the spouse would nevertheless *not* be marital deduction property. The trust corpus will then be included in the estate of the first spouse to die and will pass to the next generation without inclusion in the estate of the surviving spouse.

If the situation is the reverse—that is, if the desire is to leave less to the surviving spouse than the amount that would be necessary to allow the spouse fully to absorb the credit and the lower rates at his or her death— then the standard approach would be to set up a "qualified terminable interest property trust," known in the trade as a QTIP trust.[50] This is a trust over which the surviving spouse has just enough rights to the income from the trust to qualify the transfer of property to the trust for the marital deduction (taking it out of the first estate for tax purposes), with the ancillary consequence of being includable in the estate of the surviving spouse at the time of that later death. The income rights necessary to qualify a

---

50. The desire to leave less to a surviving spouse than the amount necessary to absorb the credit may be frustrated by state laws requiring "forced shares" of estates to go to surviving spouses. This will depend on the size of the estate, the particulars of state law, the presence and content of an antenuptial agreement, and other circumstances.

QTIP trust are fairly detailed,[51] but they include such things as a requirement of at least annual payments of the trust income, a bar on investment
of the corpus in unproductive property without the surviving spouse's con-
sent, and other similar measures designed to ensure that the right to the income from the trust cannot be easily defeated by a testator whose real preference is to leave as much as possible to the children or other beneficiaries
than the surviving spouse. Arrangements other than QTIP trusts are also
available to accomplish the purposes of making sure that an appropriate
share of the couple's total wealth is taxed at the death of the second to die,
such as the marital deduction power of appointment trust, and certain types
of legal life estates outside of a trust situation.

Credit-shelter and QTIP trusts, and other, similar devices are widely used
and certainly can reduce transfer taxes, compared with some alternative disposition patterns that could be reasonably imagined. Whether this makes
them "tax-avoidance devices" depends on what is meant by that phrase. This
seems particularly worth noting in this context because Congress was well
aware of what actions it was sanctioning when it added the QTIP provisions
to the code in 1981, as part of the expansion of the marital deduction. Creation of an unlimited marital deduction without things like a QTIP trust
would have imposed unduly harsh choices, in congressional eyes, between
tax avoidance and dispositive preferences.[52] In light of their fairly explicit invitation to manipulate the marital deduction in this way, QTIP trusts and
similar vehicles might be better viewed as simply features of the transfer tax
system, rather than the creation of fertile minds bent on subverting congressional intent.

Insurance Trusts

Life insurance proceeds on a decedent's life that are payable to the estate or
to beneficiaries named by the decedent are ordinarily included in the decedent's gross estate.[53] However, this result can be reversed if the decedent had

---

51. See IRC, sec. 2056(b)(7), and the regulations promulgated thereunder, for fuller details.

52. As the Ways and Means Committee report put it: "Unless certain interests which do not
grant the spouse total control are eligible for the unlimited marital deduction, a decedent would be
forced to choose between surrendering control of the entire estate to avoid imposition of estate tax
at his death, or reducing his tax benefits at his death to insure inheritance by the children. The committee believes that . . . tax consequences should not control an individual's disposition of property."
H.R. Rept. 201, 97 Cong. 1 sess. (Government Printing Office, 1982), reprinted in 1981-2 C.B.
352, 377–78. There is no evidence of any conscious irony in this last sentence.

53. IRC, sec. 2042.

no "incidents of ownership" of the policies at the time of his death.[54] This rule has led to the widespread use of insurance trusts, to which the insured has either transferred ownership of the policies, or funds with which to purchase the policies. If certain formalities are observed, it is not difficult to make the trust the owner of the policies rather than the person whose life is insured, thereby accomplishing the wonderful result of entirely removing the proceeds of the policies from the gross estate. Insurance trusts are especially useful in providing indirect liquidity to an estate, since the relatively small investment values in the policy become much larger when the insured's death triggers payment of the (nontaxable) proceeds.[55]

The transfer to the trust of the policies themselves or funds to pay premiums to purchase or maintain the insurance can create gift tax liabilities if the value of the policy is large. However, it is frequently possible to use the annual exclusion to avoid all or most of those liabilities, especially if the trust has multiple beneficiaries among whom the gift would be spread. The use of Crummey powers[56] is common to ensure that the gifts qualify as present interests for purposes of the gift tax annual exclusion. Under such an approach, cash for each year's premium may be transferred to the trust, with notice to the beneficiaries of their rights to withdraw all or part of the newly transferred amount. If and when the withdrawal right lapses (which can be within a few weeks), the funds are transferred to the insurance company to pay the premiums on the policy. Although this device is simple, powerful, and relatively foolproof, it does not appear to be well known by the general public. For that reason, it is one of the more impressive tools that an estate planner can reveal—one imagines with some flourish—to new clients. One of the unfortunate consequences, one further imagines, is to incline laymen toward a belief that virtually any kind of estate planning magic is possible, given the gross violation to common sense that tax treatment of insurance trusts exemplifies.

54. Before 1981, transfers within three years of death were routinely brought back into the estate for estate tax purposes under IRC, sec. 2035. Since that year, those rules apply to a much more limited range of property; however, property that would have been included in an estate as proceeds of life insurance remains subject to the three-year rule. Therefore, if the decedent dies lacking incidents of ownership because he has transferred them within the three-year period preceding his death, the proceeds will be included in his estate under IRC, sec. 2035. Conversely, if the incidents of ownership lapse without action on the part of the decedent within the three years immediately before his death, then the insurance will not be brought back into the estate.

55. The liquidity is indirect because the insurance proceeds are not payable to the estate but to a beneficiary. The beneficiary can then use the proceeds to buy property from the estate, thus providing the estate with funds with which to pay the estate tax.

56. See description under "Use of the Annual Exclusion."

Family Limited Partnerships

A powerful tool for reducing the value subject to transfer tax liabilities that has become more popular in recent years is the family limited partnership.[57] Under this device, assets are transferred to a limited partnership whose limited partners are typically the family members of the person who creates the partnership and transfers assets to it; the general partner is often a corporation set up specifically to hold the general partnership interest. The gratuitous transfer of interests in a limited partnership—or, alternatively, the gratuitous transfer of assets to a partnership in which others already hold interests—is likely to be a gift for gift tax purposes. However, by making small transfers seriatim over a period of years, the donor may be able to use the annual exclusion to insulate much or all of the transfers from actual gift tax incidence. And, of course, at the donor's death, there is reason to hope that only the donor's share of the partnership assets would remain to be included in the estate.

From this bare-bones description, it may be difficult to infer any advantages over a simple transfer of the assets directly to the beneficiaries, without the frequently clumsy interposition of the limited partnership. There are several, however. First, there may be nontax advantages to the partnership vehicle. The control of the assets by the general partner may permit better, and in any event more centralized, management of the assets than if they had been distributed among a number of beneficiaries who would all become coowners of the assets. Second, there may be enhanced protection of the assets from creditors of the donor and the donees. This depends on the various state laws governing partnerships and access to debtors' assets, but in general creditors can attach a limited partner's interest in the partnership, but not the partnership assets themselves; thus creditors may be entitled to distributions as assignees of the debtor partner but cannot require dissolution of the partnership or cessation of a partnership business.

The tax advantages—besides providing a convenient way of using the annual exclusion—consist mostly in the systematic undervaluation of the assets transferred by gift. Because all that the donee receives in a typical family limited partnership is a minority interest in that partnership, the value attached to that transfer is generally conceded to be much less than the pro-

---

57. In many states, it is preferable to use a limited liability company ("LLC") rather than a limited partnership. The differences among limited partnerships, LLCs, and other so-called pass-through entities are not generally critical to the issues described in this chapter, so the term "limited partnership" will be used to described this type of entity generically.

portionate interest in the value of the assets transferred to the partnership by the donor. This is nicely illustrated by a recent district court case from Texas, *Church* v.*U.S.*[58] In that case, a decedent had transferred, just before her death, an interest in ranch land worth about $400,000, and about $1.1 million in marketable securities, to a limited partnership. In exchange, she received an interest in a new limited partnership that was valued by the estate at just over $600,000. (The decedent's children made smaller transfers to the same partnership and received smaller partnership interests.) The IRS argued in District Court that either the decedent's interest in the limited partnership had a true value of about $1.5 million, or, alternatively, she had made a gift to her children in the amount of the difference between the value of the assets she contributed to the partnership and the value of the partnership interest she received in exchange. The court rebuffed both of these claims, essentially countenancing a situation in which more than half the value of Mrs. Church's assets disappeared when those assets went into partnership solution.

Most cases do not go quite as far, and this one may be reversed on appeal. But there is a sense among practitioners that deep discounts in valuation are appropriate, because the assets have been moved from a direct ownership situation to a mediated ownership situation that outside buyers would find much less attractive. A ranch, this reasoning goes, may be worth $1,000,000 if it could be purchased outright. But if that ranch is contributed to a limited partnership, and a 10 percent interest in that limited partnership is given to the child of the erstwhile individual owner of the ranch, appropriate valuation of that interest should recognize that the partnership share of the underlying assets could not be readily marketed for anything approaching the $100,000 proportionate value of the underlying assets.

What is the appropriate discount in such a situation? There is no firm guidance on this question. Practitioners in the interviews I conducted indicated that it was well known in the trade that appraisers at one large national bank routinely give appraisals that reflect 40 percent discounts from the value of the assets in the limited partnerships (as long as the interest was a minority interest), while appraisers working for another major bank are known to appraise at even larger discounts. It was asserted that even the IRS would allow discounts in the 10 to 20 percent range without any dispute. And, generally, the East Coast practitioners interviewed for this chapter believe that the approach in this region is fairly conservative, and that appraisals

58. 85 A.F.T.R. 2d 804 (W.D. Tex., 2000).

in Texas (obviously viewed as a renegade state for these purposes) are often as high as 80 percent.[59] Although practitioners vary in their discount comfort levels, all but one interviewee seemed to feel that sizable discounts are appropriate.[60] An observer outside the system is likely to find them rather troubling, however. The discounts put the donor-testator in the position of arguing, in effect, that a lower value should be attached to his property because he has vandalized it. He has taken assets worth $2X and intentionally placed them into a solution that has a value of only $X. The awkwardness of this argument is exacerbated by the fact that the original assets are all still owned, however indirectly, by the same family, and that that family could, at least if they act in concert, restore the status quo ante arrangement, and its $2X value, at any time. Still, estate planners and their clients seek low appraisals, appraisers oblige them, and many courts seem willing to endorse the idea of deep discounting. This is arguably the greatest single force diminishing valuations for transfer tax purposes currently in use.[61]

Another tax advantage sometimes claimed for family limited partnerships is that if the partnership interests are distributed to family members well in advance of the donor's (expected) death, and if the assets are ones that are likely to enjoy significant appreciation during the balance of the donor's life,[62] then a sizable tax advantage can occur in having the transfer valued at a date well in advance of the testator's death. Whatever truth there is in this expectation would also be true of direct transfers of those assets at similarly early dates; so one could say that the use of the partnership vehicle adds lit-

59. The discount found by the appraiser (and approved by the court) in the *Church* case was just under 58 percent; but this is apparently not the maximum to be found in Texas or elsewhere. One well-known Texas estate planner has published articles that appear, by example, to endorse the idea that discounts of 65 percent or more might be justified in particular circumstances. Eastland (1993, pp. 59, 61–62).

60. The estate planners interviewed for this article seemed to regard discounts in the range of 20 to 40 or 45 percent as reasonable (though "defensible" was a more commonly used term), depending on the circumstances, especially the type of property in the limited partnership. All of these planners, probably accurately, described themselves as conservative.

61. For an excellent analysis of minority discounts and their impact on the transfer tax system, see Repetti (1995). Family partnership discounts are discussed on pp. 452–57.

62. Economists will point out that, generally, an asset's value at any time reflects the reasonable market expectations about possible appreciation scenarios. But to the extent that the expected improvement in value will result from reinvested company profits, the appreciation will not necessarily be reflected in price until those profits are earned. And, of course, the availability of inside information to the executives of a corporation may give them reason to believe that significant appreciation in the market value is highly likely; if the market lacks that information, the fair market value of the stock will not reflect it.

tle to the tax-avoidance efficacy. However, the mediated form of ownership may sometimes make it easier for the donor to part with the assets in question, since the donor can continue to exercise control over the affairs of the partnership even after some significant share of the economic value of the enterprise has been passed to other members of the family, while direct transfer of the assets may make that much more difficult. This is likely to be especially important for a family partnership that actually operates an active business. The partnership approach also has nontax advantages for real estate interests, as it is much easier and less costly to transfer fractional shares of a real estate partnership than it is to record new deeds showing fractional ownership of the underlying real estate assets.

And, as noted, the annual exclusion can usefully leverage the advantages of the systematic undervaluation of family limited partnerships. The donor creates the partnership and transfers substantial assets to it; then she distributes fractional interests in the partnership over several years to each of several beneficiaries, so that each such transfer is taxable, if at all, only to the extent that its (highly discounted) value exceeds $10,000. Because audits of gift tax returns are infrequent,[63] and, since 1997, more difficult to review after the passage of three years,[64] many of these steep discounts will never be effectively questioned by the IRS.

Because of the complexity of the limited partnership vehicle, and the year-to-year costs of maintaining that structure, the family limited partnership is not generally promoted for estates with less than $5 million or so of wealth.[65] For estates above this figure, however, a good deal of activity of this sort occurs. The most significant legal risk appears to be that the IRS will propose (and may ultimately persuade a court) that the creation of the partnership

63. David Cay Johnston, "IRS Sees Increase in the Evasion of Taxes on Gifts to Heirs," *New York Times*, April 2, 2000, p. A1. The article relates IRS statistics that show an overall gift-tax-return audit rate of less than 1 percent; however, about three-quarters of the 2,194 gift-tax returns filed in 1999 showing gifts in excess of $1,000,000 were audited.

64. IRC, sec. 2504(c). Before 1997, it was common to audit gift tax returns at the time of the donor's death. Since then, a three-year statute of limitations has applied to gift tax returns, as long as they fully disclose the basis for valuation of the gifts. The IRS will often be able to avoid the statute of limitations by successfully claiming defects in the disclosure. But, obviously, in at least some cases, the disclosure of even a daring undervaluation will be found by a court to have been sufficiently complete to interpose the statute of limitations as a bar to further collection of transfer taxes.

65. This was true among the group of estate planners interviewed for this article. Some of them, however, said that more aggressive planners were pushing the family partnership model even for estates that would be at the lowest end of taxability. Possibly, this inappropriately ignores the costs of maintaining the partnership vehicle; alternatively, perhaps some planners believe that they have found ways of minimizing the costs of establishing and maintaining partnerships. Note that the *Church* case involved a family partnership containing no more that about $1.5 million of assets.

lacked business purpose and so should be disregarded.[66] Because the achievement of centralized management is the obvious business purpose that can be asserted by estates, it is thought that assets that consist largely of small business interests or real estate—where centralized management is a logical desideratum—are reasonably resistant to such an attack. In contrast, partnerships whose assets are largely passive portfolio investments may be in some jeopardy on these grounds. Nevertheless, many family limited partnerships do apparently consist mostly or even exclusively of portfolio investments.[67] Although some practitioners eschew portfolio partnerships flatly, others believe that creation of such partnerships is well within ethical bounds and that the response to their greater riskiness lies simply in full disclosure and explanation of the risks to the client.

Grantor Retained Trusts

Another family of avoidance devices are the various grantor retained trusts, which, like their charitable relatives, are known by their acronyms: GRITs, GRATs, and GRUTs, for grantor retained income trusts, annuity trusts, and unitrusts. The basic form of these trusts involves establishment by a donor of an irrevocable trust, under which the donor retains an income interest for a stated period of years, while assigning the remainder interest to some named beneficiary. The present value of the remainder interest would be a taxable transfer, though the gift-tax value would of course only be a fraction of the value that will ultimately pass to the remainderman because of time-value discounting.

As in the case of the family partnership, the transfer tax advantages associated with this vehicle may not be immediately evident. The gift-tax valuation is lower, but if the lifetime exemption is exhausted, it will be currently taxable; and there is no advantage in lowering the absolute amount of a tax if the current tax is simply the present value of the larger tax that could be deferred into the future. Until 1990, however, there were significant op-

66. See generally Toth (1997, p. 346). Several practitioners noted a practical obstacle as well: the device depends on execution of documents actually transferring property to the limited partnership. Failure of testators reliably to follow through on such transactions, or otherwise to observe the niceties of the limited partnership form, have led to inclusion of some transferred assets in the estates of the transferors. See, for example, *Est. of Schauerhamer* v. *Comm'r*, 73 T.C.M. 2855 (1997), and *Estate of Reichardt* v. *Comm'r*, 114 T.C. No. 9 (2000).

67. In the *Church* case about 75 percent of the assets consisted of portfolio investments that were held in street name by Paine Webber; at least as to those assets, the occasional "thank you, Paine Webber" would seem to have provided all the management necessary.

portunities to fund the trust with appreciating property, which diminished the actual, but not necessarily the assumed, value of the income interest. Donors also had some opportunities to engage in adverse selection if the actual facts of particular cases varied from the standard assumptions used by the IRS to value the income and remainder interests.[68]

Since 1990, however, Congress has imposed a valuation rule on grantor retained trusts that effectively values the income interest at zero (unnaturally inflating the remainder interest that is subject to the gift tax) unless the remainderman is not closely related to the donor or the income interest retained by the grantor is a "qualified interest."[69] The nonfamily grantor retained trust therefore remains a viable vehicle but only for the relatively uncommon situation involving a large gift outside of a family context.[70]

Within families, there are three important types of qualified interests now in common use. The first is a "qualified personal residence trust" (a QPRT), under which the grantor transfers title to a personal residence to a trust, retaining a possessory interest in the residence, but assigning the remainder to one or more donees. The second and third types of qualified transactions are simply the GRATs and GRUTs, which require that the trust fix the income interest in terms of mandatory annual payments of either a specific dollar amount (the GRAT) or a specific percentage of the trust corpus, as annually appraised (the GRUT).

A nettlesome tax feature of grantor retained trusts is that they typically do not accomplish their purposes if the donor dies during the term of the trust. In that case, the corpus of the trust is pulled back into the estate as a "retained life estate,"[71] and credit is given for any gift tax that had been paid on the remainder interest when the trust was created. This is not a disastrous consequence, but it does mean that some amount of planning and trust administration will have produced no tax benefit. To minimize this risk, some planners set up the trusts with relatively short terms (three years or so seems common) and use relatively high annuity payouts to reduce the value of the remainder interest (and thus reduce the size of the current gift). If the assets

68. In particular, it was thought that the IRS discount rates during the 1980s may have been too high. This had the effect of reducing the value assigned to the remainder interest, which was, of course, what went into the gift tax base.

69. The rules are contained in IRC, sec. 2702, and the regulations promulgated thereunder. These provisions were added by the *Omnibus Budget Reconciliation Act of 1990*, P.L. 101-508, 104 Stat. 1388.

70. The family is defined for this purpose to include spouses, ancestors and lineal descendants, brothers and sisters, and anyone who is the spouse of any people in the foregoing categories. IRC, sec. 2704(c)(2).

71. IRC, sec. 2036.

in the trust appreciate quickly, these trusts can remove considerable value from the estate at a modest gift tax cost. They may be especially useful, then, for an individual who thinks that his company may make an initial public offering of its stock within the trust's term, or the like.

Although all of the permissible forms of retained interest trusts are used to some degree, especially among the very wealthiest families, one of the most common uses appears to be the QPRT, especially for vacation or other nonprimary homes. Real estate is thought reliably to appreciate, so the advantages of fixing a relatively low current value at the creation of the trust seem especially appealing in those cases.

Other Devices

Several other devices appear to be used somewhat less frequently and so will be described cursorily in this section. The first device is the *intentionally defective grantor trust*, or IDGT. In some cases, creators of trusts seek to avoid grantor trust status, since the income of such trusts continues to be taxable to the grantor. For an IDGT, the grantor trust prohibitions are intentionally breached, so that the grantor continues to diminish her own estate by the amount of the income tax obligations accruing to the trust, and so that the trust can undertake transactions with the donor that would be income-tax recognition events were it not for the grantor trust rules. Frequently, these trusts are used to purchase property from the grantor of the trust, the advantage being that the grantor trust rules make the purchase and sale a nontaxable event, since they are viewed for tax purposes as being bought and sold by the same person. IDGTs are, however, subject at the moment to some legal uncertainties, and some practitioners do not appear to regard the advantages as worth the risks and complexities.[72]

Some practitioners recommend the use of private annuities, by which title to a valuable asset is transferred, typically to a relative who might otherwise have received the property by bequest in exchange for a promise to pay annuity benefits for the remainder of the transferor's life. The idea is that the property will be removed from the estate, but without any gift tax consequences. However, if the annuity is properly valued, and the grantor lives to a normal life expectancy, the annuity benefits will roughly replace the value

---

72. For a description of some of these uncertainties, though in a context of some approbation nevertheless, see Schlesinger and Mark (2000, pp. 742–44). This was a point of some divergence among the group of interviewees for this chapter, with some believing that any risks could be adequately contained, and that the IDGT could be a very useful device.

transferred out of the estate, leaving little net benefit. And if the annuity benefits are less than the expected value transferred, there should be a taxable gift in the amount of the difference. In some cases, however, there may be some tax advantages to transferring out of the estate property that is expected to appreciate, in exchange for a stream of payments that will equal the property's present value, but would be less than the expected value of the property at the time of the transferor's death.

Asset protection trusts, under which assets are transferred to a trust in a jurisdiction that has adopted rules that make it more difficult for creditors of the grantor to reach assets held in such trusts,[73] are by all accounts increasingly popular, though the estate planners who were the sources of background information for this chapter reported very little interest by their clients in such trusts. By itself, such a trust accomplishes little estate tax avoidance, though it may be that one of the other trust vehicles discussed would be used in combination with the sort of creditor protection opportunities now available. Some Treasury officials believe that many of these trusts, at least when they are created in foreign jurisdictions that do not freely share tax information with the United States, are devices not of avoidance, but of evasion, of both income and transfer taxes. Because of the possibly illicit motivations behind such trusts, it is obviously difficult to develop any significant information on the extent of such activity.

An avoidance device that is intended to allow wealthy families to avoid transfer taxes after the first death is the so-called *dynasty trust*. These trusts are intended to be perpetual and so are set up in one of the jurisdictions that has repealed any sort of rule against perpetuities. They create vehicles that the GST tax was intended to reach, but, because their initial capitalization is set at (or below) the $1,030,000 GST tax exemption level, they slip under the reach of that tax. Some estate planners reported that their clients are not sufficiently interested in benefiting remote heirs to bother with creating such trusts. Others, however, said that very wealthy families often find these quite attractive, especially when structured in trusts that give the trustees broad powers to distribute benefits only to the needy members of the grantor's descendants, such as those with disabilities.

One final option to be considered is the possibility that wealthy testators might avoid the gift and estate taxes by *greater consumption*. This option does not require the wise counsel of tax advisers and perhaps for that reason was

---

73. The Cayman Islands have been a popular destination for such trust funds; however, in recent years Delaware and Alaska, among other U.S. jurisdictions, have begun competing for these funds by adopting trust law provisions that apparently provide similar insulation from creditors.

not mentioned by the panel of estate planners consulted in preparation of this chapter. But it may be worth mentioning, if only because the possibility is thought to present one of the major moral hazards associated with the estate and gift taxes.[74] One obstacle to reducing transfer taxes through greater consumption for the very wealthy, of course, is that they can hardly spend their wealth quickly enough to prevent it from further accumulating. An individual who owns $1 billion of assets, conservatively invested, say, in tax exempt bonds paying a 5 percent annual return, would be saddled with about $137,000 of (tax free) income to dispose of each day of the year. Such individuals may find that even their attempts at consumption involve incidental investment qualities that result in further, unintended accumulation. They may, for example, strenuously consume the fair rental value of that charming apartment in the Fifth Arrondissement, or a nicely outfitted yacht, year after year, only to find that these assets keep appreciating anyway, enriching their heirs against their will, as it were. It has been noted that the very wealthy do indeed save a great deal—more than can be explained by the usual life-cycle explanations of savings.[75] But at the same time there is some evidence that wealth accumulation is adversely affected by transfer taxes,[76] suggesting at least a possible role for consumption. Suffice it to say at this point that one encounters very little anecdotal evidence suggesting that the very wealthy embark on spending sprees as a means of reducing their estates; at the same time, it cannot be denied that transfer taxes, by taxing wealth transfers, clearly provide incentives for additional consumption, compared with a tax system in which all consumption taxes remained in place but from which wealth transfer taxes had been removed.

Post Mortem Estate Planning and Valuation Issues

Although "post mortem estate planning" seems a contradiction in terms,[77] executors can do a number of things to reduce the tax burdens of their deceased clients. One major area of attention is ensuring that the marital deduction has been appropriately balanced to minimize total transfer taxes

---

74. See, for example, McCaffrey (1994, pp. 318–24).

75. See Carroll (2000, p. 366). This article focuses in large part on the possibility that having great wealth is itself a major source of utility and so continues to be pursued even by those who already have achieved such great wealth that the buying power afforded by that wealth would seem at the margin to have lost its meaning.

76. See chapter 7 by Kopczuk and Slemrod in this volume.

77. Estate planners seem to have a taste for this sort of thing, since they also refer sometimes to "pre-mortem probate" issues.

on the two estates that a husband and wife will leave. For example, if circumstances make it desirable, the executor can elect not to include certain property that would qualify for the marital deduction in the schedule of property for which a marital deduction is claimed. Similarly, in some cases heirs may wish to disclaim gifts, which can generally be done without incurring transfer tax liabilities. Again, counseling by the executor or legal adviser to the estate about the consequences of such disclaimers can frequently achieve a better result than would obtain without explicit consideration of this option.

Probably the most important role in this area is not usually considered "planning" but rather simply intelligent completion of the estate tax return. One of the executor's duties is to value the assets of the decedent, an area in which a good deal of judgment is often involved. Unsurprisingly, that judgment is usually exercised in a way that resolves all doubts in favor of lower values.[78]

Several valuation-discount doctrines have emerged from cases in which estates have successfully argued for lower values than the IRS believed appropriate. One of the major discount situations is presented when the estate has a large quantity of a particular kind of property, most typically, the stock of a corporation. In such cases, a "blockage" discount may be claimed on grounds that disposition of a large number of shares within a short time would inevitably push down the price; the demand over any period, it is argued, is relatively fixed, so sudden expansions of the supply of tradable stock must have a negative effect on fair market value. This theory is applied to provide modest discounts from the trading price on the valuation date of 5 percent or so even on publicly traded stock.[79] With respect to the stock of corporations that is not publicly traded, there is of course no clear benchmark from which the discount can even be measured. But, as an illustration, in one tax court case last year, the court found a block of stock to be worth only $276 a share, even though the estate itself had sold some of the stock not long after the valuation date for a price of $355 a share.[80]

---

78. This is of course only true as to taxable estates; in ones that are below the threshold of taxability, incentives exist to shade the valuations on the high side, if anything, because the reported valuation also sets the tax basis under IRC, sec. 1014, for the heirs who receive the property.

79. See, for example, *Foote* v. *Comm'r*, 77 T.C.M. 1356 (1999) (3.3 percent discount); *Gillespie* v. *U.S.* 23 F.3d 36 (2d Cir., 1994) (4.85 percent discount).

80. *Branson* v. *Comm'r*, 78 T.C.M. 78 (1999). The block of stock sold represented a bit less than 10 percent of the total shares held by the estate. The discount allowed from this sale price was about 22 percent. The estate had initially claimed a discount of nearly 50 percent, computed on the basis of the actual sale price.

Discounts have also been allowed for real estate[81] and even works of art. Georgia O'Keeffe's estate, for example, consisted primarily of some 400 works of art that had been appraised at more than $72 million. The court divided the works into two equally valuable groups: those that could be sold within a reasonably short period, and those that might have required more deliberate marketing; it then applied a 25 percent discount to the former, and a 75 percent discount to the latter, reaching an ultimate valuation for the estate of about $36 million.[82]

The theory behind these discounts is troubling, at least insofar as it seems to lead to liquidation or "fire-sale" valuations. In fact, the estate is typically under no compulsion to liquidate the assets; except for the payment of the estate tax itself,[83] there is no need generally for the estate to liquidate the assets at all, much less to do so quickly. Rather, the assets can and usually are passed on in kind to the heirs. The regulations do call for a fair market valuation as of a particular date, and courts have over time come to view that as meaning the value that could be produced by an immediate sale. But the effect of this seems to be to undervalue substantially the assets in large estates, precisely because they are either very large overall or concentrated in one asset.

Discounts are also routinely sought and allowed, in varying amounts, in various other situations, involving such things as restrictions on transferability of the shares; the fact that the shares held by the estate represent a minority interest in the corporation; the possibility that the shares may be worth less precisely because of the death of the testator, who may have been a key executive of the company; and so on.

Effectiveness of Avoidance Measures

How effective overall are the avoidance devices described? Clearly, many of the examples provided, some of which are drawn from actual decided cases, indicate that discounts of 50 percent or more are not beyond the range of

81. See, for example, *Auker* v. *Comm'r*, 75 T.C.M. 2321 (1998). This case allowed a 6 percent discount from the appraised value of three apartment complexes that were in the estate, to allow for market absorption of the buildings. The estate had sought a 15 percent discount.

82. *O'Keeffe* v. *Comm'r*, 63 T.C.M. 2699 (1992). Remarkably, the estate initially appealed this outcome, but the appeal was later withdrawn. See also "Georgia O'Keeffe's Estate," *Wall Street Journal*, April 15, 1992.

83. The estate tax return is due nine months after death, and payment of the tax is ordinarily made with the return. If the estate consists largely of closely held business interests, however, payment of the tax can be deferred for five years and paid in installments over the following ten years. See IRC, sec. 6166.

possibility. Indeed, in smaller estates, good planning could certainly reduce a potentially taxable estate to one that would be below the threshold for taxability. Mrs. Church's estate provides a concrete example.[84] A more representative, though hypothetical, case might involve a couple in their sixties, in which one spouse holds $3,000,000 of wealth, while the other owns only trivial assets. The potential estate of the spouse holding the wealth would be right on the edge of the top estate tax marginal rate bracket of 55 percent, and would face a potential estate tax liability of $1,070,250.[85] But suppose that the couple spends any income and appreciation in value of the estate over their remaining, retirement years; gives gifts to each of two children and four grandchildren of $20,000 a year for ten years, depleting their estates by $1,200,000; achieves, through a family partnership or otherwise, a 30 percent discount in value of the remaining $1,800,000 of assets, thus producing an estate valuation of $1,260,000; and uses any of several mechanisms to divide the potential estate of the wealthy spouse more or less evenly between the two. They, or rather their heirs, will then find that no federal transfer taxes will have been paid during the couple's lives, nor owed at death, on the transfer of the total of $3,000,000 to the next generation.

Larger estates are likely to find it more difficult to avoid transfer taxes altogether. However, the experienced estate planners interviewed for this chapter believed that discounts of about one-third of the value of even very large estates could be achieved through good planning, perhaps a bit more or less depending on the circumstances of the testator, including such things as his or her age, marital status, the number of intended beneficiaries (which affects the ability to use annual gift tax exclusions effectively), and the nature of the assets in the estate. This is an extremely rough and unscientific guess at the percentage that escapes from the estate tax. Besides data collection problems, estimating this percentage involves at least one troubling conceptual question as well: if A transfers $X of value to her child early in life, and the value of the property comes to be, say, $4X by the time of A's death, is the amount of wealth transferred to the next generation equal to $X, or $4X, or perhaps at some intermediate figure that represents the value as of the first date that the child had unfettered access to the assets? If one wishes to exaggerate transfer-tax avoidance, date of death valuations would be chosen. Most unbiased observers would probably choose the intermediate value,

---

84. See note 58.

85. This is a slight overstatement, since the estate would almost certainly have some deductions, if only for probate fees, and likely some credits for state death taxes as well. Still, it would be quite possible to reach a total transfer tax liability of $1,000,000, if the spouse who owns the assets is the second to die and undertakes no steps to reduce exposure to those taxes.

at the point where the child actually gains control of the value. But certainly a reasonable argument can be made that, once the parent has irrevocably transferred value out of her own portfolio, any subsequent gains cannot be said to be wealth that she has transferred, but rather are earnings that at all times belonged to the child. No guidance on this question was given to the interviewees who estimated that at least one-third of all wealth transferred from planned estates escapes taxation. So, together with data questions, it must be conceded that doubts about this major issue in transfer tax cannot be put aside.

Nevertheless, assuming for the moment that their best guess is about right, and that one-third or a bit more of the potential base of the transfer taxes eludes the reach of that tax, what should be made of that? On the one hand, it represents a sizable leakage from the potential tax base. But on the other, it certainly falls far short of confirming the popular belief that the very wealthy can completely avoid transfer taxes through clever planning.

It appears that the popular view exaggerates the ease of wholesale avoidance of the transfer taxes for several distinct reasons. First, this view tends to ignore that many of the avoidance devices require earlier disposition of assets than most testators feel comfortable with, or, alternatively, they require asset transfers—from outright, direct ownership into an indirect ownership form, such as through a partnership—that testators regard as inconvenient. Many avoidance devices, in many circumstances, carry private costs that exceed their value in terms of transfer-tax reduction.

Second, many devices—especially those that are designed to "freeze" the value of an estate at something approximating its level at some particular starting point—benefit from what might be called a hindsight fallacy. Because both corporate stock and real estate investments have, as a whole, performed spectacularly well over the past decade, devices that positioned the moment of transfer taxability at some date in the early 1990s now appear to have been very wise. The property, or more typically some kind of remainder interest in property, was transferred for tax purposes when the value was relatively low, and now, years later, the actual transfer of the remainder interest occurs when the value is much higher. In a period of relatively stable or falling asset valuations, however, many avoidance devices offer little prospect of lowering transfer taxes; at most, they lower somewhat the absolute amount of the transfer tax but accelerate the incidence of the tax, so that the present value of the tax paid is about as much or more than it would have been absent any special planning. A simple example will illustrate this point: if a donor were to put $1,000 into a trust at the beginning of year 1, with a qualified remainder interest in the trust going to a beneficiary after ten years, any gift tax liability would be based on the discounted present value of a ten-year deferred gift, as of year one. At an 8 percent discount rate, the remainder interest in those assets would be valued at about $463, and the transfer tax based on that sum would be no more than 60 percent of that, or $278. If the assets in the trust rise over the decade to, say, $5,000, this will have been a good deal: $5,000 of assets will have been transferred at a cost of only $278 of tax. However, if the value of the assets instead remains in the vicinity of $1,000, no real tax avoidance will have been accomplished. At an 8 percent discount rate, $278 at the beginning of a ten-year period has precisely the same present value as $600 does at the end of that period.[86] And if the value falls, the donor will in effect have suffered a transfer-tax penalty.

A third source of exaggeration of the potency of avoidance measures is related to the second. It stems from a more general tendency to ignore time-value considerations in assessing tax avoidance. If a wealthy person has $X of wealth at some point in time, and devices can be created to transfer the same amount to the heirs some years later, without explicit payment of a wealth transfer tax, it may be thought by some that no transfer tax burdens have been absorbed, even though the income from the assets during the period in question is unavailable to anyone in the family. Charitable lead trusts have this quality and are featured prominently in many discussions of avoidance. For example, George Cooper, in his book on sophisticated estate planning, offered a hypothetical plan by which the then current generation of the duPont family might avoid transfer taxes completely.[87] But one of the major devices required transfer of about half of the family's assets into a charitable lead trust of twenty-four years' duration. At the time Cooper was writing, interest rates were in the double-digit range; at those rates, the value of a twenty-four-year income interest in a fund would constitute more than 90 percent of the total value of the fund. Because that fund constituted about half of their potential estates, Cooper would have the duPonts avoiding transfer taxes by giving away about 45 percent of the value of their property to charity. Of course, transfer taxes should be completely avoidable only if *all* the property is given to charity, so Cooper's strategies—which also involved some shuffling of assets to generate a plausible basis for claiming substantial discounts—certainly would have accomplished a considerable reduction in the transfer-tax burdens borne by the family. But to say that the

86. An 8 percent rate, compounded over ten years, yields a multiplier of 2.159, which, when multiplied times the $278 of tax, equals $600. Six hundred dollars, of course, is the maximum transfer tax that would be paid on the transfer of $1,000.

87. Cooper (1979). The book was an expanded and updated version of an article that Cooper published in 1977 in the *Columbia Law Review*.

family would be completely free of transfer tax burdens ignores the substantial cost of losing a twenty-four-year income stream from a large portion of the family assets.

Some popular accounts of the transfer tax avoidance dynamic contain elements of all three of these sources of exaggeration. For example, a famous *New York Times* article of a few years ago begins with the story of a New Jersey tax lawyer, who, at age 40, reportedly transferred title to the family residence (which he owned outright, without any mortgage) to his three children, the oldest of whom was then 11, in exchange for the right to live in the house rent free for the next twenty-five years.[88] The house was then worth $539,000, but the donor projected that the value of the house would rise by about 4 percent a year, and would, by the end of the twenty-five-year period, be worth about $1.4 million. Even though that value would then pass to the children, the valuation of the gift for tax purposes was only about $84,000—the then current value of the house, less the $455,000 value assigned to the right retained by the donor to continue living in the house for twenty-five years. And, because the donor had not used up his unified credit, no immediate gift tax was owed, even though the gift was not one of a present interest.[89]

This is a clever idea. But it accomplishes somewhat less tax avoidance than might at first be supposed. To begin with, although the assumption that the house will appreciate by 4 percent a year sounds conservative at first blush, it is not quite so conservative if one accounts for the fact that the house is also producing a return in the form of its rental value, which should be around $4,000 a month, or something in the range of an 8 percent (or higher) rate of return. The 4 percent appreciation assumption, stacked on top of that, means that the donor expects at least a 12 percent return on the capital invested in this house. That may happen to some houses, in some neighborhoods, at some times, but developing a model based on an assumption of a 12 percent compound return over twenty-five years is, as a general matter, rather speculative. It is, in a sense, the inverse of the hindsight fallacy: instead of looking backward, and deciding that a tax-avoidance strategy was good, when all that happened was that the market was good,

---

88. Christopher Drew and David Cay Johnston, "Rushing Away from Taxes: Preserving the Legacy—A Special Report," *New York Times*, December 22, 1996, p. A1. Though the article describes the transaction as though it were a direct gift of a remainder interest to the children, it was presumably a transfer instead to a qualified personal residence trust, of the sort described under "Grantor Retained Trusts," since the latter type of transfer would have produced much better tax results.

89. As explained under "The Federal Gift Tax," the effect of this will be to make $84,000 more of Shenkman's estate taxable at death, because of the partial exhaustion of the lifetime unified credit.

this strategy looks forward and assumes an exceptionally good market performance into the future.

But suppose the good-market assumption is borne out by subsequent events. Will this turn out to be a good idea? Perhaps so, but mostly because this arrangement will benefit from a form of leverage. Instead of getting a net return of 4 percent on an investment of $84,000, the 4 percent return compounds on an investment of $539,000, the full value of the house. The cleverness of the idea is in using the offsetting obligation (to provide housing to the donor's family rent free) to reduce the size of the current net transfer and hence the transfer tax. It is rather as if the donor had given his children $84,000 for a down payment on the house and loaned them the remaining $455,000 of the amount needed to buy the house, with their "virtual mortgage" being paid back in the form of the twenty-five-year rental value of the house.

In fact, it might have been better if the donor had done that somewhat simpler transaction; that is, if he had simply given the children enough for a down payment on some house other than the family residence. If the rent received in the market covered the mortgage payment, property tax, insurance, and maintenance, they would still be in a position to enjoy the leveraged benefits of the appreciation on the full value of the house, even though their investment only represented a small slice of it. Or simply putting $84,000 into a NASDAQ index fund, leveraged with as much margin as they could manage, would also have done very well. Why might those have been preferable? Because there are some major inconveniences to using a family's own residence to fuel this device. If the donor decides that he wants to move within the twenty-five-year period, he will need to undertake some fairly complicated corrective actions to comply with the terms of the agreement. And what about improvements to the house? What if the donor decides in 2010 to do a major kitchen remodeling? This sort of periodic infusion of home improvement capital is the sort of thing that is usually necessary to offset the natural depreciation of buildings over time (and to maintain any hope of achieving that 4 percent annual appreciation). But in this case, it seems likely that each such capital infusion would also constitute a new gift at that time to the children.[90] Finally, when the property is ultimately transferred to the children, it is likely that they would not be eligible for the forgiveness of up

90. Of course, the IRS is not nearly vigilant enough to pick up on this sort of thing as a routine matter; indeed, gifts in kind are thought to be routinely unreported, even when they exceed the annual exclusion or are not present interests. See Johnston, "IRS Sees Rise." Still, the possibility that subsequent, potentially taxable gifts might be involved in this device is the sort of thing that should give a tax lawyer some pause, especially if this "product" is to be marketed to clients as part of an overall tax avoidance strategy.

to $500,000 of capital gain that is now available to homeowners on the sale of their personal residences, since they would presumably no longer reside in the house by the time their remainder interest ripens.[91]

In summary, it seems that what magic there may appear to be in this arrangement depends mostly on making a heavily leveraged investment in a (presumably) rising market, for a twenty-five-year period. That scenario will always produce happy results, as long as subsequent events bear out the assumptions. And the remaining magic inheres in the idea of making transfers to children earlier in life rather than later, so that the asset appreciation never shows up in the parents' own base of wealth to be transferred. But that is an easy move; the personal residence strategy does not really improve on that move very much, except insofar as it provides a convenient means of leveraging the gift.[92]

One is reminded a little of the days before the Tax Reform Act of 1986, when it was nearly impossible to attend a cocktail party or barbecue without hearing some discussion of the latest income tax shelter.[93] Even the devices that probably worked were never as attractive overall as they seemed to

---

91. This provision is contained in the 1997 amendments to IRC, sec. 121, which was enacted after the trust in this case was created. This illustrates, among other things, one of the perils of clever tax planning on a twenty-five-year time horizon: Congress changes the tax laws each legislative session, and the strategy that appears best at one point may not be as attractive in subsequent years, under new rules.

92. The other items mentioned in the *New York Times* article mostly consist of devices described elsewhere in this article, such as the use of family partnerships and insurance trusts. They also mention the use of transferred stock options, which is again an opportunity to transfer a leveraged investment to a younger generation, which will seem very attractive as long as the investment does well. Also mentioned is the dubious technique of having a surviving spouse buy the children's right to inherit, as a means of stripping the parent's estate; but it is not clear, even from the favorable description in the article, that this technique works from a legal or an economic point of view. The parties in the case on which this was based paid substantial taxes in the first instance and settled the estate tax question with the IRS for an undisclosed additional sum—hardly a result that seems likely to spawn legions of imitators. Finally, the article mentions enforcement difficulties that can result when a decedent held assets in secret foreign bank accounts. These may be significant, but the problem in this area is largely one of evasion of tax, about which reliable information is inherently difficult to find. The estate planners consulted for this article reported, naturally, that they would never encourage or cooperate in any scheme of tax evasion. Somewhat more surprising, they reported that their clients themselves showed little interest in such options. It does seem likely that very wealthy persons would be quite risk averse as to criminal sanctions: if one has great wealth already, one would think that illegal means of preserving more of that wealth for their heirs would not be worth even a remote chance of a stay in Leavenworth. While it must be conceded that the sample of estate planners drawn for the preparation of this chapter was neither a random nor a cross-sectional slice of the profession, but rather distinctly tilted toward the upper end, it should also be noted that most high-wealth individuals seek out precisely the sort of practitioner who was interviewed for this chapter.

93. Possibly, this was only true if one happened to be a tax lawyer, as one does indeed happen to be. But tax shelters appeared to be of general interest among upper-middle and upper-bracket taxpayers at the time.

be when described by the promoters, or their true believers, and many had serious tax or economic shortcomings that only became apparent when the details of the plan were carefully examined.

The Costs of Transfer Tax Avoidance

There are several different sorts of costs associated with transfer-tax avoidance. Some of the strategies affect the actions of testators, and in that sense distort those actions from what they would presumably be in a system that imposed no transfer taxes. There are also direct costs of effecting the transfer-tax-avoidance strategies, consisting of fees paid to lawyers, accountants, trustees, and appraisers. And there are public costs associated with the need to police the tax-avoidance efforts and ensure that the law is reasonably enforced. Each of these will be considered separately.

Distortion

Much of the cost of transfer-tax avoidance results from engaging in tax-favored dispositive arrangements that are, from a nontax viewpoint, less desirable than one or more of the alternatives available. Thus, wealthy individuals may leave more (or less) to a spouse than they would in the absence of transfer-tax considerations. Wealthy individuals may make significant transfers of wealth during their lives because of the tax features associated with some such transfers, when their preferences otherwise would be to retain all (or in any event more) of their property until death. Testators may make charitable gifts that they would not make, or in forms that would not be used, but for transfer-tax considerations. The distortion of choice implicit in these devices often becomes too great, which substantially explains why testators generally do not adopt the most aggressive estate plans imaginable under their particular circumstances and why many will always "volunteer" to pay more transfer tax than some hypothetical minimum.

Those who do adopt tax avoidance strategies surely suffer welfare losses of some magnitude as a result of distorted choices. However, in most cases, the distortions involve making transfers earlier than the testators desire or to a different beneficiary.[94] Under these circumstances, there would be little or no systematic effect on resource allocation and hence little or no welfare loss

---

94. The status of the beneficiary has salience primarily in the marital context. As explained under "Charitable Gifts," there are circumstances in which the tax-wise disposition will require a larger transfer to a spouse, and other circumstances in which it will require a smaller transfer. In either case, the transferor will lose utility if she makes a tax-induced second-best transfer.

overall. Consumption opportunities are simply transferred to spouses or to subsequent generations differently than they might have been but in ways that merely shuffle utility rather than destroying it.[95]

Besides affecting the timing of transfers and the choice of individual beneficiaries, transfer-tax avoidance no doubt motivates some charitable gifts. But the analysis just described seems equally applicable in the charitable context: the utility of the individual testator is reduced, compared with a tax-free state in which the charitable gift would not have been made, but in a way that presumptively preserves aggregate utility, which is simply transferred to the indirect beneficiaries of the charitable enterprise supported by the gift in question.

There are some exceptions, however, to the general notion that transfers among natural persons and from natural persons to charitable entities preserve welfare. It seems likely that wealthy Americans buy more life insurance than they otherwise might because of transfer tax avoidance efforts. Estimating the welfare loss created by this distortion is beyond the scope of this chapter. But a few points do mitigate this distortion. First, many testators seek insurance to provide estate liquidity for reasons that have more to do with orderly conduct of an ongoing business that they do with wealth transfer taxes. For example, if two unrelated individuals conduct a partnership business together, they are likely to seek some sort of buy-sell arrangement, under which the estate of the first to die must sell the estate's share of the business to the survivor. Insurance would often be used to provide the resources to effect such a purchase and sale and would be desirable in such cases without regard to any wealth transfer tax considerations.

Second, insurance has a substantial financial value that is independent of the motive for its purchase. Even if an individual would not have purchased a particular policy but for tax-avoidance motives, it does not follow that the premiums paid for that insurance are a net loss to the individual (much less to society overall). Even in the case of term insurance, in which investment values are intentionally minimized, the value of the pure life expectancy gamble—roughly, the death benefit times the probability of death within the period covered by the premium—remains an asset of the testator. So the social cost of

95. The archetypal tax-avoidance-induced transfer is from an elderly person of wealth, who will likely hold the assets until death if he does not give them away earlier, to a person in youth or middle age, who is much likelier to spend them. It might seem that the younger person would get more utility from using the resources than the elderly person gets from merely holding them, but such a judgment involves the sort of interpersonal utility comparison that most economists find extremely problematic. The archetypal transfer may also have implications for savings rates: if very wealthy elderly people save more than less wealthy younger people, and if transfer taxes induce earlier wealth transfers from older people to younger ones, then the overall savings rate will decline. Again, however, there is no clear welfare loss in this; the new savings rate is presumably the optimal one for whatever the new wealth distribution is.

this distortion seems quite limited and could be thought of casually as the cost of having a somewhat larger than optimal number of people employed in sales, clerical, and actuarial functions in the insurance industry, rather than in similar functions elsewhere in the broader financial services sector.

Distortion possibilities may also inhere in the rearrangement of assets that is sometimes undertaken to lower valuations. Testators certainly claim that the market value of such things as interests in family limited partnerships is well below the net asset valuation of the property owned by the partnership, which suggests, as noted, that testators have to some degree vandalized their property in their frantic search for transfer-tax avoidance. However, on closer analysis, it appears that what testators typically do in these cases is to lower the marketability of the property, making investments less attractive to outsiders, it is hoped, without doing serious damage to the income-producing power of the property itself. There is a loss of liquidity in that process and that is surely a genuine welfare loss; but its magnitude would be of a much lower order than the amount of the discounts sought by testators engaging in valuation-lowering strategies of this sort. In fact, even while they are arguing the case for discounting the value of partnership interests, testators (or their representatives) typically argue that the partnerships were set up to advance the interests of the businesses and investments contained within the partnership vehicle, by consolidating management of disparate bits of an enterprise, for example.[96] If there is truth to that claim, then there would be in those cases no loss from transfers of property into partnership solution.[97]

Direct Costs

The direct costs of estate planning consist of the fees of the professionals—typically lawyers and accountants—who put together the plan, trustees who administer funds transferred into trust, and in some cases the appraisers who help wealthy individuals set the values claimed on gift and estate tax returns.

96. Such an argument anticipates an IRS argument that the partnership can be disregarded as a mere device to reduce taxes, with no other purpose. See discussion under "Family-Limited Partnerships." The IRS has raised this argument in cases such as *Estate of Schauerhamer* v. *Comm'r*, 73 TCM 2855 (1997), but has not achieved definitive resolution of whether some sort of business purpose need be shown to sustain recognition of the limited partnership as the true holder for tax purposes of the assets to which it had legal title.

97. It should not be argued that such asset transfers represent a positive welfare change, however, since the argument noted in the text is that these moves are made, for nontax business reasons, to achieve the most efficient deployment of assets. In this view, if these moves happen, somewhat paradoxically, to lower transfer tax valuations, then that is merely a happy by-product of a transaction that would have taken place anyway; to attribute any efficiency improvements to the transfer tax rules would thus contradict the basic premise of the argument.

Although these fees may seem large in some absolute sense, they are typically quite modest as a percentage of the transfer tax saved and almost negligible as a percentage of the assets transferred. About half of the estate planners consulted in the preparation of this paper reported that they had rather standard packages that they would make available to individuals who would leave estates in the $3 to $10 million range that might be provided for as little as $3,000 to $5,000. Larger estates, or any estate requiring substantial variations from the standard plans, would typically pay the planner an hourly fee that is likely to be in the range of $250 to $550, depending on the experience of the planner, the cost factors of the relevant legal market, and the like.[98] But even quite wealthy individuals, who might save millions of dollars of transfer tax by a sound estate plan (compared with the tax that might be imposed by a transfer at death pursuant to a state's laws of intestate succession), might pay an estate planner less than $20,000 for their plans. If a plan involves difficult valuation issues, appraisal fees are likely to be involved and may be significant.

The estate planners interviewed for this chapter were also asked to estimate what percentage of their work was not directly related to the transfer tax rules but rather to the need simply to transfer substantial assets to beneficiaries in an orderly way. Specifically, they were asked to engage in the thought experiment of imagining that the transfer taxes had been repealed.[99] Putting aside transitional effects, and looking forward to a steady-state situation in which repeal was believed to be permanent, those planners who were willing to guess on this point generally thought that about half of the current level of services would continue to be required.[100]

Thus, while the interviews on which this chapter was prepared do not provide a firm basis for empirical findings on the aggregate cost of estate

98. This was the range of fees among estate planners consulted for this article, all of whom were practicing for large, urban law firms. In many cases, estate planning services are offered by lawyers in smaller towns, accountants, and financial planners, many of whom would presumably charge lower fees. It thus seems likely that the overall average rate for estate planning services is toward the lower end of the range mentioned in the text.

99. One estate planner noted astutely that for at least the five years following repeal, estate planners would enjoy great demand for their services, because their clients would not regard the repeal as permanent and would be scrambling to take advantage of a window of opportunity to get assets out of their estates free of transfer tax, while at the same time striving to retain as much control over the use of those assets as possible. Even if the repeal were taken as permanent, there would be a considerable one-time need for review of estate plans for provisions that involved some compromise between tax considerations and dispositive preferences, which could then be amended to more perfectly effect the latter.

100. Even this number may turn out to be pessimistic, from the estate planners' viewpoint. See Jonathan Clements, "Estate Planning Outlives 'Death' Tax," *Wall Street Journal*, July 25, 2000, p. C1, which suggests that the bulk of estate planning currently undertaken would still be required even in a post-transfer-tax situation.

planning, they do permit a rough guess. If there are about 5,000,000 American families (about 5 percent of the total), who have sufficient wealth that they should be at least a little concerned about wealth transfer taxes,[101] and if those families engage in a thorough review of their estate plans every ten years, on average, at an average cost of $5,000 a review, and if 50 percent of the cost of that review is attributable to tax minimization concerns, then the planning costs attributable to transfer tax considerations would amount to about $1.25 billion a year.

Others who have analyzed estate planning costs have come to widely varying conclusions. Henry Aaron and Alicia Munnell offered an informed guess that overall transfer tax compliance costs were "a sizable fraction" of the total revenue generated by the tax, which at the time was about $6 billion.[102] However, it seems likely that in the years since their article, revenue has grown much more quickly than estate planning costs. Revenue has increased approximately fourfold; comparably precise estimates of compliance costs are not available, but there have been no reports of the sort of widespread increase in either individual fees or the number of professionals engaged in estate planning that would support a guess that those costs had increased by anything approaching the same proportion.

In their excellent and comprehensive survey of current transfer tax issues, Charles Davenport and Jay Soled estimated the aggregate costs of estate planning and reviewed a number of estimates made by others.[103] Their estimates for both the costs of estate planning and of administering the estates were based on their own interviews with estate planners and on analysis of costs reported on estate tax returns. They estimated planning costs for 1999 at a bit in excess of $1.047 billion and administration costs at $856 million gross, with a net cost to the estates (because administration costs are deductible against the estate tax) of $471 million.[104]

Joseph Astrachan and Roger Tutterow analyzed the results of polling data conducted among small business owners, which produced much higher estimates of estate planning costs.[105] Their pool of more than 1,000 owners of "family businesses" reported spending an average of $33,137 for estate plan-

101. In 1995 only about 3.4 percent of all deaths resulted in the filing of an estate tax return, suggesting that the 5 percent parameter is generous. Johnson and Mikow (1999, p. 71).

102. Aaron and Munnell (1992, pp. 119, 138). They did not indicate what a "sizable fraction" might be, but they did conclude that high avoidance costs suggested that the "ratio of excess burden to revenue of wealth transfer taxes is among the highest of all taxes," which they appeared to find deeply troublesome (p. 139).

103. Charles Davenport and Jay A. Soled, "Enlivening the Death-Tax Death-Talk," *Tax Notes,* vol. 84, July 26, 1999, pp. 619–25.

104. Davenport and Soled, "Enlivening the Death-Tax Death-Talk," pp. 621, 622, respectively.

105. Astrachan and Tutterow (1996).

ning services from lawyers, accountants, and financial planners.[106] There is some basis for skepticism about the results of this survey, for a few reasons. First, the questions about the cost of estate planning come in the context of an overall survey that surely invited hostility to transfer taxes.[107] And some of the results seem at least mildly internally inconsistent.[108] Furthermore, the consumers of financial and estate planning services may not be in a position to know in any detail what part of the professional time for which they were billed might have been necessary for nontax reasons. Mostly, however, the results of the survey simply strain credulity, in the light of what is known about what estate planners can and do produce for their clients: a handful of relatively simple documents, most of which have been only lightly customized for the particular client. At billing rates of $300 an hour, which seems a reasonably generous estimate of the average billing rate for professionals in this field, $33,137 would buy more than 100 hours of professional time. While this much time might not be unusual for planning the estate of an individual of great wealth, it seems well above the amount of time reasonably necessary to produce an estate plan of the sort needed by the average owner of a small- to medium-sized business.[109]

Public Costs

The public costs of administering and policing the transfer tax system seem modest. In fact, they may well be too modest: it is likely that substantial ad-

---

106. Astrachan and Tutterow (1996, p. 306). Family businesses in the pool had revenues of at least $1,000,000 annually and had at least two officers or directors with the same last name.

107. The survey invited respondents to report on how the estate tax limited business growth, threatened survival of the business, affected investment horizons, affected employment decisions, and other similar questions. (Of course, it must be admitted that the estate planners who were the primary sources for this chapter, and for Davenport and Soled's article, are not disinterested either, and may have bias in the opposite direction from that observed among family business owners.)

108. For example, the survey indicated that 45 percent of the respondents had "no knowledge of amount of [their own] estate tax liability." But it also indicated that 60 percent of respondents "would immediately hire [more] workers" if the estate tax were repealed. Astrachan and Tutterow (1996, p. 306). This means that at least 15 percent of the respondents know nothing about their potential liabilities, but are nonetheless sure that repeal would lead to expansion of their businesses. Sixty percent of respondents also reported that their revenues would grow by 5 percent or more if transfer taxes were eliminated. One wonders how even those who know what their transfer tax liabilities are would have any reasonable basis for believing that.

109. Two other recent works explore the costs of estate planning but do not develop their own estimates. Miller (1999) draws on the work cited above of Astrachan and Tutterow and on the earlier analysis of Aaron and Munell (1992). James R. Repetti, "The Case for the Estate and Gift Tax." *Tax Notes*, vol. 86, March 13, 2000, p.1507, relies primarily on Davenport and Soled, "Enlivening the Death-Tax Death-Talk," p. 619.

ditional revenue could be collected with relatively small increments to the enforcement budget, but these increments have nevertheless not been forthcoming. Davenport and Soled estimated the share of the IRS budget that could be properly attributed to transfer taxes in 1996 at $152 million.[110] Their discussion of this estimate makes clear that it is somewhat conjectural, but the estimate seems reasonable in light of the fact that the overall IRS budget is only around $8 billion, and only a small fraction of that budget is devoted to estate and gift tax questions.[111] For example, the most recently available projected statistics indicate that estate and gift taxes will amount to about 1.6 percent (fiscal 2001) of federal revenues, .16 percent of all returns filed, and .8 percent of returns audited.[112] Earlier IRS reports have indicated that about 2 percent of ruling requests had estate and gift taxes as their subject.[113] Thus, the Davenport and Soled estimate, which comes under 2 percent of the IRS budget, appears to be rather generous, toward the higher end of the range of possibilities.

If Davenport and Soled, and the views expressed in this article, which are generally consistent with their findings, are correct, then the estate and gift taxes are reasonably efficient. Under this view, the total costs of administering and complying with those taxes would appear to be around 6 to 7 percent of the revenue generated by those taxes.[114] This would put those taxes somewhere between the 10 percent of revenue estimated by Slemrod as the administrative and compliance costs of the individual and corporate income taxes, and the 3 to 5 percent estimated by Slemrod for the value-added taxes and 2 to 5 percent for the sales tax.[115]

Conclusions

The transfer tax system depicted in this chapter has two faces. On the one hand, a number of devices are available that significantly reduce the base of the transfer tax. At the threshold of the taxable range—those estates that

110. Davenport and Soled, "Enlivening the Death-Tax Death-Talk."

111. *Budget of the United States Government, Fiscal Year 2001*, table 32-2, presents an estimate for all tax administration costs, presumably including those of the Office of Tax Policy of the Treasury Department, of $8.054 billion, for the fiscal year that will end on September 30, 2000.

112. The first of these numbers is derived from the *Budget of the United States Government, Fiscal Year 2001*, table S-11. The second and third are, respectively, from IRS (1997, table 2, table 11).

113. The IRS does not appear to publish this information anymore. The number in the text is taken from the *1976 IRS Annual Report*, p. 48.

114. Davenport and Soled, "Enlivening the Death-Tax Death-Talk," pp. 622–23.

115. Slemrod (1996, pp. 368–74).

might be potentially in the $1-3 million range—a reasonably attentive approach to the marital deduction, the annual gift tax exclusion, and the lifetime transfer-tax exclusion can eliminate much or all of the tax liability. In the higher ranges—above about $20 million, those deductions and exclusions become relatively insignificant, but other devices, such as family partnerships and grantor-retained trusts, are available to reduce the size of the estate by at least one-third its potential size, and more in some circumstances. In the range between those two extremes, some parts of both approaches may be useful in significantly cutting transfer tax liabilities.

On the other hand, the devices have limits; the stories of complete avoidance of transfer taxes by the very wealthy are mostly hyperbolic. Massive transfers to charity or a surviving spouse can transfer wealth without wealth transfer taxes, but most other large wealth transfers will be subject to significant effective rates of tax. Further, the hypothetical strategies that could minimize the transfer tax liabilities of an individual will frequently be eschewed because of nontax considerations. In particular, the estate planners consulted in preparation of this chapter consistently noted that their clients do not like paying gift taxes; yet a willingness to pay some gift tax is a virtual necessity for large estates if they wish to minimize their total transfer tax liabilities.[116] More fundamentally, as one estate planner put it: people simply do not like to give away their property while they are alive. And, as the foregoing explanations should make clear, most of the more effective strategies require a considerable willingness to make truly irrevocable transfers during the donor's life. To be sure, wealthy individuals are not all alike; some have less trouble than others in making transfers (and paying gift taxes, if necessary). And even those who find lifetime transfers and gift tax liabilities problematic usually manage to surmount their reluctance. But they do so only to a degree, and that degree falls well short of minimizing their transfer taxes.

The best proof of that is in the revenue itself: it is projected that about $30.5 billion in transfer tax will be paid this year,[117] about a third of it by the thousand or so estates with more than $10 million in assets.[118] It is virtually impossible to imagine that estates of this size did not have access to good advice and even more unimaginable that any significant number of them "volunteered" in any meaningful sense to pay as much tax as they did.

---

116. One source said she thought that this was related in part to the possibility of imminent repeal of transfer taxes; most sources, however, seemed to think that this reluctance was very deep-seated and long-standing.

117. *Budget of the United States Government, Fiscal Year 2001*, table S-11.

118. Johnson and Mikow (1999, p. 102).

Nor does it appear that the devices used are particularly expensive. The basic strategies are not difficult to understand. Their implementation may be somewhat more complicated than the simple descriptions in this chapter have captured, but not greatly so. And while the IRS probably should spend more to enforce the transfer tax rules, it will never be in a position to spend so much that those costs will be significant as a portion of the revenue raised by these taxes.

So we have overall a highly imperfect transfer tax system, but one that is sounder at the core than it is generally assumed to be. Reform is clearly indicated and clearly possible. A full description of the reforms needed is beyond the scope of this chapter, but I note that most of the major problems have to do in one way or another with valuation issues. Congress made a start on these in 1990, when it added a new subchapter to the code providing special valuation rules for certain transferred business interests and transfers in trust. But it can go much further than it did. And Congress can be draconian in its approach, if it really desires comprehensive reform. For example, Congress in IRC, sec. 2702, has said, essentially, that the grantor retained interest in nonqualifying grantor retained trusts is to be valued at zero.[119] That does not mean that those interests have a true market value of zero; it only means that Congress has decided that they should be so treated, so as to avoid undervaluation of the interest passing to the donee. A similar "deemed value" approach could be imagined in the valuation of family partnerships: Congress could say that limited partnership interests should be deemed to have a value equal to the proportionate net asset valuation of the partnership assets, regardless of the amount of any discount an appraiser might think should apply for the lack of marketability of such partnership shares. Similarly, Congress could say that any remainder interest in a grantor-retained trust lasting for less than ten years should be revalued as of the time that such remainder interest is finally distributed, with additional gift tax being payable at that time, if the value has risen.

To say that Congress could do these things is not the same as saying that there is any reasonable likelihood that Congress will. And because some of the key conceptual guides to valuation have become deeply embedded in the case law, most meaningful reform will probably have to come from Congress, which, unlike the Treasury (and the IRS), has the power to overrule the courts. Because the last expression of the views of the current Congress on the transfer tax system was that the system should be repealed altogether, such reform does not seem likely in the short run. But, just possibly, those

---

119. See explanation under "Grantor Retained Trusts."

reforms could be bargained for, perhaps in the company of significant rate relief, as a realistic alternative to transfer-tax repeal.

Again, the analogy to the Tax Reform Act of 1986 seems apt: if Congress were to lower rates and do the sometimes difficult work of closing loopholes, we would end up with what would surely be a better tax, with a broader base, but lower rates, yielding about the same revenue. If Congress were willing to spend some of that revenue, it could do so by increasing the exemption level applying to transfer taxes. Undertaking that reform would do a great deal to relieve the stress felt by owners of small- and medium-sized businesses, who have served as the stalking horses for the current effort to repeal the tax. If that is really the group that Congress is concerned about, a combination of rate reduction, loophole closing, and exemption raising will achieve the best result.

COMMENT BY
Jane Gravelle

Richard Schmalbeck's chapter suggests that the important efficiency costs of estate tax avoidance are the distortion in timing and allocation of bequests rather than the direct cost of estate planning. He presents some evidence for this view. These efficiency costs generally mean making a transfer earlier than preferred or transferring assets to a less preferred beneficiary.

My comments are directed to policy options that might reduce these distortions (while retaining an estate and gift tax). Essentially, this discussion focuses on various elements of estate tax reform. One can imagine a revenue neutral plan, where rate changes offset base broadening or narrowing. Alternatively, since some sentiment exists for reducing the estate tax, one could also use a potential revenue loss to reform as well as reduce. The following policy options mostly include base broadening but also consider proposals that would lose revenues.

Schmalbeck's chapter suggests that a handful of provisions seem to be most involved in constructing avoidance mechanisms. Clearly, one approach to estate tax reform is to consider reform of the underlying structures. Four basic areas relate to these underlying mechanisms: the marital deduction, the annual gift exclusion, the charitable deduction, and valuation issues.

First, let us look at the unlimited marital deduction. Although an unlimited marital deduction probably reduces the need for estate planning, it has ironically also created problems. For example, a spouse who wishes to leave assets mostly to the surviving spouse can pay a tax price: he or she effectively loses the flat exemption and the lower rate brackets that would apply to transfers to children. However, if the first spouse leaves part of the estate to children, he or she uses his exemption, and perhaps lower rate brackets, and the second spouse's estate will also benefit from these provisions. This problem arises from the unlimited marital deduction; without the deduction the flat exemption and lower rates would be used both times. This is an example of how a benefit introduces an implicit cost.

Another, and related, problem also occurs: a spouse who wishes to leave assets to children rather than the surviving spouse can lose out because again the children benefit from only one exemption and one walk through the lower rate brackets.

These provisions distort choices unless children and parents arrange some sort of implicit contract between themselves (which cannot be easily enforced). A spouse might prefer to leave assets to the surviving spouse to deal with freely. Thus the credit shelter trust, which provides an income stream and allows a way to use assets for ordinary support while disqualifying the corpus from the unlimited marital deduction, may be an imperfect device for satisfying preferences.

Or a spouse may have children from a previous marriage that the surviving spouse might be unlikely or unwilling to leave money to. This one is a bit more easily fixed with a QTIP (which qualifies the property for the marital deduction), which can direct the disposition of the corpus of the trust. However, that approach is also imperfect, particularly if the spouse has a long prospective life and the receipt by children will be long delayed.

These problems arising from the unlimited marital deduction also have a peculiar effect as one moves through the wealth distribution. Estates with the smallest amount of wealth will never exceed the single first exemption. The superwealthy can probably use up exemptions and lower rate brackets by leaving only a small share of the estate to either party (surviving spouse or children). This treatment has the effect of allowing larger exemptions for larger estates when there is a wish to leave the bulk of the estate either to the surviving spouse or to the children, and limiting these exemptions for intermediate-sized estates.

This problem has several possible solutions. One solution is to let the second spouse inherit the unused exemptions and lower rates of the first. Another is to let spouses voluntarily agree to apportion all exemptions and lower rates between them to the spouse who dies first or the spouse who dies second.

Others have made proposals of this nature. The inheritance of the exemption has been proposed in a recent law review article by Jay Soled.[120] He points out that most married couples with a long-term stable relationship may well prefer simply to leave all of the assets to the surviving spouse, and inheriting the exemption would permit this simplification. Such an inheritance of exemptions has also been proposed in the Democratic substitute to H.R. 8 in the House of Representatives, that is, for expanded exemptions for farms and small businesses.[121]

The annual gift exclusion also affects estate planning and the development of distortions. This provision looms large in several estate planning mechanisms (Crummey trusts, insurance trusts). Ideally a tax system would make inter vivos gifts and gifts at death subject to the same tax burdens. This ideal system would require several changes, which have been discussed in other chapters, but among them would be eliminating, or at least reducing,

120. Soled (1997).
121. Bureau of National Affairs (2000).

the annual gift exemption. One approach would be disallowing all or part of the annual gift exclusion. Of course, some de minimis exclusion would be desirable (to deal with gifts such as birthday and wedding gifts). An alternative would be a single limit for all donees.

A more specialized approach might be to require all insurance on the life of the decedent to be included in the estate regardless of who owns the policy, which would eliminate the use of Crummey trusts to shift insurance out of the estate.

A third applicable provision, sometimes combined with the gift tax, is the charitable deduction. Approaches to reducing estate taxes with charitable contributions, as in the charitable lead trust, involve a benefit from asymmetric information (as in the vulture trust, with respect to life, or with respect to expected appreciation). When the value at the end of the trust period is significantly larger than the value for gift tax purposes for these reasons, the taxpayers saves money. One approach to these games is to delay the gift tax and only allow it to be completed when actually transferred. That is, disallow recognition of gifts until the recipient gets the gift, then pay gift tax; if delayed until death, simply add to the estate the value at that time (or pay the estate tax when the money is actually received).

The use of private foundations is also linked to the charitable deduction. Private foundations are subject to the same problems as exchange value of charitable contributions in general, that the donor gets some private benefit; here the private benefits are potentially quite high. While funds cannot be used for private benefits, the heirs maintain power and influence over the disposition of the charitable gifts. There is a long history of debate on the merits and potential abuses of the private foundation.

Finally, an important tool for reducing the estate and gift tax is the valuation discount. Some valuation problems are, by their nature, very difficult, such as the value of a business, which is not a readily marketable asset. But other valuation issues can be addressed directly by legislative changes.

First, prohibit fire-sale valuations. With the availability of loans, and with other assets in the estate, it is not necessary in most cases to sell the entire estate quickly. This approach would be supplemented with a look-back option. If the sale actually occurred (quickly) and the value was reduced, taxes could be refunded.

Second, prevent minority discounts. One could simply make the valuation of assets in a limited partnership proportionate to the minority interest. Or one could disallow discounts for property, such as bonds and publicly traded stock, that has a market value regardless of the form the asset is held in. Some of these provisions have been included in recent proposals. For example, the administration tax proposals called for disallowing discounts for marketable assets. The Democratic alternative to recent tax legislation also included such a proposal, and it included provisions to disallow minority discounts if related individuals have voting control.

Besides these revisions that relate to the major tax planning devices, some other provisions have been addressed in the administration's 2001 tax proposals that may help to reduce the distortions induced by estate planning techniques.[122] One such provision is the allocation of basis for a transaction that is part sale and part gift. Under current law, a transaction that is part gift and part sale assigns a basis to the asset for the donee that is the larger of the fair market value or the amount actually paid. The donor pays a tax on the difference between amount paid and his basis and may frequently recognize no gain. The administration proposal would allocate basis proportionally to the gift and sale portions. For example, suppose an asset with a basis of $50,000 but a market value of $100,000 is sold to the donee for $50,000. The donor would realize no gain and the gift amount would be $50,000, with the donee having a basis of $50,000. Eventually, the gain would be taxed when the donee sold the property, but that tax would be delayed. However, if the asset were divided into a gift of $50,000 with a basis of $25,000 and a sale of $50,000 with a basis of $50,000, the donor would realize a gain of $25,000; the donee would now have a basis of $75,000. Half of the gain would be subject to tax immediately. (These split rules would not apply when the fair market value is less than basis, that is, where a loss rather than a gain occurs, and it is advantageous to realize the loss earlier.)

Another proposal made by the administration is to ensure that assets in a QTIP trust are included in at least one of the spouse's estates. In some cases, the second spouse's estate has argued that there is a defect in the trust arrangement and excluded the trust; the administration proposes to include the trust in the second estate if it is excluded from the first.

In closing I look at a future potential avoidance technique, namely, the expanded exemptions for farms and small businesses, proposals that are currently popular as a less dramatic way to deal with potential liquidity problems of family businesses (despite considerable evidence that very few family businesses even pay an estate tax, much less are driven to liquidate because of it). Proposals have been made to expand, and even to provide, a complete exemption for these types of assets. Certainly, such provisions are an invitation for wealthy individuals to shift assets into these forms. Just as the unlimited marital deduction was a benefit that ultimately created new

122. Department of the Treasury (2000).

planning complications and new distortions, so could these expanded exemptions for family businesses.

References

Aaron, Henry J., and Alicia H. Munnell. 1992. "Reassessing the Role for Wealth Transfer Taxes." *National Tax Journal* 45 (June): 119–43.

Astrachan, Joseph, and Roger Tutterow. 1996. "The Effects of Estate Taxes on Family Business: Survey Results."*Family Business Review* IX (1996): 309, 303–14.

Auten, G., C. Clotfelter, and R. Schmalbeck. 1998. "Charitable Giving among the Wealthy." Working Paper 98-15. University of Michigan, Office of Tax Policy Research.

Bernheim, Douglas, Andrei Shleifer, and Lawrence H. Summers. 1985. "The Strategic Bequest Motive." *Journal of Political Economy* 93 (December): 1045–76.

Bureau of National Affairs. 2000. *Daily Tax Report* (June 8): G-7.

Carroll, Christopher. 2000. "Why Do the Rich Save So Much?" in *Does Atlas Shrug? The Economic Consequences of Taxing the Rich*, edited by Joel Slemrod, 465–84. Russell Sage Foundation and Harvard University Press.

Cooper, George. 1979. *A Voluntary Tax? New Perspectives on Sophisticated Estate Tax Avoidance*. Brookings.

Eastland, Stacy. 1993. "Family Limited Partnerships: Transfer Tax Benefits." *Probate and Property* (July): 50–63.

Gale, William. 2000. "Do Estate Taxes Reduce Saving?" Working Paper. University of Michigan, Office of Tax Policy Research.

IRS. 1997. *Data Book*.

Johnson, B., and J. Mikow. 1999. "Federal Estate Tax Returns, 1995–1997." *Statistics of Income Bulletin* (Summer): 69–129.

McCaffrey, Edward. 1994. "The Uneasy Case for Wealth Transfer Taxation." *Yale Law Journal* 104 (November): 318–24.

Miller, Daniel. 1999. "The Economics of the Estate Tax," report for the Joint Economic Committee. S. Rept. 105-89. Government Printing Office.

Poterba, J. 1998a. "The Estate Tax and After-Tax Investment Returns." Working Paper Series 98-11. University of Michigan, Office of Tax Policy Research.

———. 1998b. "Estate Tax Avoidance by High Net Worth Households: Why Are There So Few Tax-Free Gifts?" *Journal of Private Portfolio Management* 1 (Summer): 1–9.

Repetti, James R. 1995. "Minority Discounts: The Alchemy in Estate and Gift Taxation." *Tax Law Review* 50 (Spring): 415–86.

Schlesinger, Sandford J., and D. Mark. 2000. *Valuation, Taxation, and Planning Techniques for Sophisticated Estates*, vol. 35. Practising Law Institute.

Slemrod, Joel. 1996. "Which Is the Simplest Tax System of Them All?" In *Economic Effects of Fundamental Tax Reform*, edited by Henry Aaron and William Gale, 355–91. Brookings.

Soled, Jay. 1997. "A Proposal to Make Credit Shelter Trusts Obsolete." *Tax Lawyer* 51 (Fall 1997): 83–107.

Thurow, L. 1975. *Generating Inequality*. Basic Books.

U.S. Department of the Treasury. 2000. *Greenbook 2000*.

LOUIS KAPLOW

4 A Framework for Assessing Estate and Gift Taxation

E STATE AND GIFT taxation is a controversial subject. Some commentators propose extending transfer taxation to a larger segment of the population, increasing tax rates, and eliminating various means of tax avoidance. Others favor substantial reductions or outright abolition. Moreover, the approach to estate and gift taxation varies among developed countries; most use an inheritance tax instead of estate and gift taxes, and some have abolished transfer taxation.[1]

Two elements are necessary to develop a coherent assessment of estate and gift taxation. First, we need a sound conceptual framework that is explicit

I am grateful to Gerard Brannon, Pierre Pestieau, Richard Schmalbeck, and Alvin Warren for comments, Yoram Keinan for research assistance, and the John M. Olin Center for Law, Economics, and Business at Harvard Law School for financial support. Many of the points developed here are drawn from a draft book chapter that received limited circulation in 1996 and 1997, and some were sketched in Kaplow (1998).

1. For prior discussions of these issues, see, for example, Aaron and Munnell (1992); Graetz (1983); Joint Economic Committee (1999); McCaffery (1994); Repetti (2000); essays in Erreygers and Vandevelde (1997); and *Tax Law Review* (1996). For background information on the system in the United States, see the chapter by Johnson, Mikow, and Eller in this volume. For arguments concerning the distinct subject of wealth taxation (that is, taxing individuals' holdings of wealth rather than their transfer of wealth to others), see *Tax Law Review* (2000).

about the objectives to be served and that organizes thinking about a range of complex and conflicting effects of tax regimes. Second, we need empirical evidence, particularly concerning donors' motives for giving and donees' behavior in response to the receipt of gifts. Much prior work and some of the chapters in this volume address the latter need.[2] This chapter, by contrast, concentrates on the former, because without a framework, it is difficult to determine the policy implications of empirical findings and to establish research priorities for future investigation.

The thesis advanced here is that a framework for assessing estate and gift taxation should be developed systematically, beginning with first principles of welfare economics and standard results in optimal taxation. From that starting point, one should then ask what it is that makes bequests and inter vivos gifts distinctive. Thus, if voluntary transfers were no different from expenditures on some ordinary good or service, the correct conceptual approach would be straightforward in the light of prior work on the economics of taxation, which has already addressed the factors bearing on differential taxation of various types of consumer expenditures. If the proper method of analysis for giving differs, therefore, it must be because of the manner in which making gifts is unlike using resources for one's own consumption. Accordingly, thinking about the optimal tax treatment of transfers should start from benchmark understandings of how we should tax ordinary consumption and then consider modifications (perhaps substantial ones) that reflect the unique features of transfer behavior.

The foregoing approach is pursued in the next section. The discussion begins with a nontechnical review of the optimal taxation of different forms of expenditure in the standard optimal income tax framework. (It should be noted that most of the insights gleaned from optimal income tax analysis will be relevant even in a world in which the prevailing income tax is not set optimally.) Use of this framework is appropriate not only because it is the most systematic method that economists have developed for analyzing tax policy but also because, in fact, countries that make use of estate and gift taxes also have income taxes (and/or consumption taxes) in place. Hence, to analyze behavior and to assess welfare, we must take into account the combined impact of transfer taxes and income taxes. Relatedly, there is the question of how income (or consumption) taxes should treat gifts, and, one presumes, a tax

2. See, for example, the sources cited in note 24 and the chapter by Kopczuk and Slemrod in this volume.

on transfers administered through an income tax will have the same effect as an equivalent one imposed under the auspices of a transfer tax regime.

When such a framework is employed, the question of transfer taxation can be stated as follows: How much more or less (if at all) should we tax, at the margin, a dollar that a donor transfers to a donee *compared to the situation in which the donor instead spends the dollar on own-consumption?*[3] Putting the question this way reinforces the need to examine the particular characteristics of gifts. The main feature to note is that the donor's act of giving—which can be viewed as a species of consumption by the donor—is simultaneously a source of income—and thus, prospectively, consumption—to the donee. (This is the case for "true gifts," those not involving some form of exchange between the donor and donee.) One consequence is that, in assessing social welfare, there will be a positive effect—a positive externality of sorts—on an individual (the donee) other than the one whose behavior is initially the subject of examination (the donor). Another important consequence is that the receipt of gifts may be expected to affect the behavior of donees in a manner that will be relevant to social welfare. Notably, the receipt of gifts will have an income effect, tending to reduce labor effort, which has a negative effect on income tax revenues—a negative externality on the public fisc.

After this preliminary analysis, the inquiry is broadened by considering the range of transfer motives that underlie giving behavior. Although motives are not important in themselves in assessing social welfare, different motives suggest different forms of utility functions. And, when utility functions differ, policies will have different effects on behavior. In addition, assessments of welfare depend on the form of individuals' utility functions. Hence, transfer motives are important in assessing transfer tax policy.

Using the framework developed in the first sections of this chapter, a number of the familiar policy considerations in the debate over estate and gift taxation are revisited. These topics include redistribution (viewed both within and between generations), raising revenue, savings, administrative and compliance costs, and concentration of wealth and power. A recurring theme in this section is that many of the common ways of discussing these issues are incomplete and, sometimes, misleading, because they are not rooted in first principles of policy assessment (welfare economics) and of optimal tax theory.

At the conclusion of the foregoing analysis, a number of additional subjects are examined briefly: the relevance of human capital, which, on one view, is by far the largest component of intergenerational transfers, yet is largely

---

3. It is also instructive to restate the question for the case of in-kind transfers. If, say, an individual buys a set of golf clubs, should the person's overall tax burden be higher or lower (and by how much) if the golf clubs are given to one's child rather than used for oneself?

ignored in most analyses of estate and gift taxation; possible differences between inter vivos gifts and bequests; taxation of the family, recognizing that a substantial portion of all transfers are between spouses; charitable giving; and the possibility that gifts are not always the result of maximizing behavior by donors.[4]

The Taxation of Transfers in an Optimal Income Tax Framework

In this section, the individuals' utility maximization problem, with a budget constraint that reflects both income taxation and possible transfer taxation, will first be presented, followed by a statement of the social welfare maximization problem. Then, the optimality of differential taxation will be analyzed, first, in the case in which expenditures on transfers are not qualitatively different from expenditures on other forms of consumption and, second, in the case in which transfers are distinctive.

Throughout most of the discussion in this section and the rest of this chapter, it will ease exposition to make a number of simplifications.[5] Thus, the analysis considers the aggregate net taxation of transfers, not distinguishing whether the tax is part of an income or consumption tax system or a separate transfer tax regime. Inter vivos gifts and bequests are simply referred to collectively as gifts or transfers. The analysis often focuses on a single donor and donee (although the interpretation, of course, is that these are representative individuals).[6] Although the donor and donee may have any relationship, the usual interpretation offered is that of intergenerational transfers, from par-

---

4. Another important subject, beyond the scope of the present inquiry, concerns the question of transfer tax *reform* per se—that is, how one should make the transition to another transfer tax regime and whether the fact that a given tax system is currently in place bears on what sort of reform would be optimal. For example, in the present analysis it is assumed that inheritances must come from somewhere—from donors—who in turn must have earned the funds at some point (or received them from another donor who once earned the funds, and so forth); this is relevant because such prior behavior is presumed to be subject to the same overall tax system, taken to be in place throughout time. By contrast, when new taxes are suddenly implemented (that is, are unanticipated), it is always possible to tax some (indeed, all) existing capital without distortion; likewise, unexpected repeals will generate windfalls.

5. The list in the text is hardly exhaustive. Also ignored are many other matters, including strategic behavior by donors (for example, gifts intended to shape donees' utility functions to induce possible return gifts of care or of funds in the future) and by donees (for example, the Samaritan's dilemma and rent-seeking behavior).

6. The possibility that the donee might in turn save a gift and later give it to others, such as members of a subsequent generation, is implicitly captured by the analysis, for the subsequent gift can be treated as simply another instance of a gift involving a different donor-donee pair.

ent(s) to child(ren).[7] Transfers are usually taken to involve true gifts, rather than transfers that are one component of an exchange relationship. And individuals are assumed to behave as informed, rational maximizers of their utility. Each of these assumptions, however, is addressed to some extent in subsequent sections.

Donors' Utility Maximization Problem

Consider the following simple utility maximization problem. There are two periods. In the first period, an individual chooses a level of labor effort, ℓ, yielding before-tax income of $w\ell$. Taxes on labor income are $T(w\ell)$; that is, there is an income tax that may be nonlinear. (It also may provide for negative taxes, that is, welfare support payments.) After-tax income may be spent on consumption in period 1, c_1, or deferred, earning interest at the rate r, until period 2. Then, remaining resources may be spent on ordinary (own) consumption, c_2, or on another good, c_g. Ultimately, c_g will be interpreted as expenditures on gifts, but the model will also be interpreted where c_g refers to expenditure on some other good or activity, such as playing golf. There are taxes t_r on the return to savings and t_g on consumption of c_g (each of which may be negative, that is, subsidies).

Thus, the individual chooses a level of labor effort and levels of each type of consumption to maximize

$$U(c_1, c_2, c_g, \ell),$$

subject to the budget constraint[8]

$$w\ell - T(w\ell) = c_1 + \frac{c_2 + (1 + t_g)c_g}{1 + r(1 - t_r)}.$$

---

7. The donor might be a representative parent and the donee a representative child. Likewise, only net transfers, in a single direction, will be considered.

8. Such a budget constraint is sometimes written as

$$w\ell - T(w\ell) = (1 + t_1)c_1 + \frac{(1 + t_2)c_2 + (1 + t_g)c_g}{1 + r},$$

where the taxes t_1, t_2, and t_g are levied on each type of consumption, c_1, c_2, and c_g, respectively. This expression is equivalent to that in the text: t_1 is redundant: one can divide both sides by $1 + t_1$ and restate $T(w\ell)$, t_2, and t_g ; then, one can restate the taxes on the two forms of period 2 consumption as a tax on interest earnings, t_r, and an additional tax (or subsidy, if negative) on c_g (relative to c_2), further restating the other tax terms. Then, the budget constraint would be the same as that in the text.

Setting $t_g = 0$ for the moment, consider two standard interpretations of this expression. First, when $t_r = 0$, this formulation is a standard labor income (wage) tax, which is also equivalent to a tax on lifetime consumption. Second, when $t_r = t$, where t is the uniform marginal tax rate on labor income, this corresponds to a standard proportional income tax (which here includes investment income).[9]

Social Welfare Maximization Problem

Consider the following simplified formulation of the social welfare maximization problem. As in the standard optimal income tax problem, assume that there is a continuum of individuals, where their type, w, distributed according to the density function, $f(w)$, indicates individuals' earnings ability, which is not observed by the government. (Hence, redistributive taxation must use income as a signal, and redistribution will involve distortion of the labor/leisure choice.)

Society is assumed to choose tax schedules and rates in order to maximize a utilitarian social welfare function

$$\int U(w) f(w) dw$$

subject to a revenue constraint (that tax revenues equal transfer payments plus expenditures on public goods) and individuals' maximizing behavior, where individuals are assumed to take the government's policy as given and maximize their utility functions, as described in the preceding subsection.

Two simplifications, which do not fundamentally affect the analysis to follow, should be noted. First, this formulation of the social welfare function is utilitarian, though one could allow, say, for a welfare function that is strictly concave in individuals' utilities—indicating additional aversion to inequality. Second, public goods are suppressed, so the problem is stated as if taxes are purely redistributive. One could instead include public goods in individuals' utility functions, in which case the government's welfare maximization problem would involve choosing the level of public goods as well as tax schedules and rates.

---

9. To allow for a nonlinear tax that combines labor and investment income, one would have to rewrite the budget constraint; the present, simpler formulation clarifies analysis of the taxation of savings and its relationship to transfer taxation.

Analysis Where c_g Refers to Expenditures on Another Form of Ordinary Consumption

It is useful as a benchmark to begin the analysis not with gifts, but with the case in which c_g refers simply to expenditures on some ordinary form of period 2 consumption, such as playing golf during one's retirement years. In this case, the problem can be restated as whether expenditures in the second period on golf should be taxed more or less heavily (and to what extent) than expenditures in the second period on other goods and services (for example, dining in restaurants). The solution to this problem is familiar; see, for example, the work of Atkinson and Stiglitz.[10]

Case of Weak Separability. First, assume that individuals' utility functions are weakly separable in labor (leisure), in which case they can be written as

$$U\big(x\big(c_1, c_2, c_g\big), \ell\big),$$

where x is a subutility function. The interpretation of weak separability is that the marginal disutility of labor effort does not depend on how one allocates disposable income among different types of consumption. Another interpretation of this condition is that individuals' allocations among different types of consumption depend only on the effective prices (including taxes) of different types of consumption and on their disposable income, not on the level of labor effort required to produce their income.

Now, in this case, it is familiar that the optimum involves no differential taxes on different types of consumption.[11] That is, one should set equal to zero both t_r^* and t_g^*, the optimal tax (subsidy) rates on investment earnings (that is, the deferral of consumption from period 1 to period 2) and on playing golf. The reason for this result is that differential taxes on different types of consumption expenditures cause distortions among types of consumption but do not alleviate the labor/leisure distortion. Hence, they involve a cost but produce no benefit.

Before proceeding, it is worth pausing to emphasize some of the factors that this result does *not* depend on. First, it does not depend on individuals' "motives" for engaging in the different types of consumption. Thus, whether

---

10. Atkinson and Stiglitz (1976); Stiglitz (1987).

11. There are other assumptions implicit in this framework that are explored in the optimal taxation literature and will not be pursued here. Conceivably, some would have particular relevance to transfer taxation.

individuals play golf because they like fresh air, swinging clubs, or viewing the color green (or tan or blue, as the case may be) is irrelevant. (This point is mentioned because, when interpreting c_g as expenditures on gifts, the question of motivation is often raised; motives for giving will prove to be relevant, but only indirectly.)

Second, these results disfavoring differential taxation do not depend on the magnitude of the pertinent elasticities—of savings, in the case of t_r, and of playing golf, in the case of t_g. (And in the much discussed case of savings, the result does not depend on whether the uncompensated savings elasticity is positive, negative, or zero, either with respect to the price of period 2 consumption in general or with respect to the price of c_g in particular.) Of course, the *extent* of any distortion will depend on the relevant (compensated) elasticities.

A further important observation is that it is not optimal in the present setting to impose differential taxes on different forms of consumption in order to redistribute income. For example, suppose that c_g is a form of consumption (playing golf) that is undertaken disproportionately by the rich. Furthermore, assume that more redistribution would in principle be desirable. Does it follow that $t_g^* > 0$? No. The reason is that one can tax the rich more heavily through the income tax itself. If that tax is set optimally, attempting further redistribution indirectly necessarily lowers welfare; further indirect redistribution is less efficient than further direct redistribution because the former involves an additional consumption distortion (with no offsetting benefit) and further direct redistribution was already determined not to be optimal. Note, moreover, that even if there were too little redistribution at the outset—the income tax was not set in a sufficiently redistributive manner—it still will be true that further indirect redistribution would not be optimal. As just explained, further direct redistribution, through the income tax itself, would be a dominant strategy.[12]

---

12. This general idea (including the fact that it does not depend on the preexisting income tax regime being optimal) has been developed in a long line of literature. See, for example, Hylland and Zeckhauser (1979); Shavell (1981); Ng (1984); Kaplow (1996c). For some qualifications, see Slemrod and Yitzhaki (2000).

For political reasons, it is possible that a suboptimal strategy would be sensible when an optimal strategy is politically infeasible. Thus, perhaps, certain special interests successfully lobby for inefficient regulations that favor them when they believe that direct transfers, which would be more efficient, would be more visible and thus politically infeasible. With regard to the estate and gift tax, however, it seems unlikely that the rich are unaware that such taxes (as currently formulated) fall disproportionately on them, and thus that they would fail to oppose such a tax when they would have opposed income tax increases with a similar effect on themselves.

Cases in Which Savings Should Be Taxed or Subsidized; Relevance for t_g. Suppose that for some reason it is not optimal to set the tax rate on investment earnings (savings), t_r, equal to zero, but instead that it should be positive. (The reason may be due to violation of the separability assumption, the existence of externalities involving savings, or some other factor outside the present model.) The main point for present purposes is that this would not, in itself, provide any reason for imposing a positive tax, that is, $t_g > 0$, on c_g, playing golf in the second period. The reasoning is similar to that offered previously: a tax specifically on c_g would distort the choice between it and c_2, without offering any benefit in return. If the motive for taxing c_g were really that a higher tax on all consumption in period 2 would be optimal, it obviously would be best to raise that tax rate, t_r, directly.

This analysis also applies in reverse. Suppose one believed that the tax rate on second-period consumption (savings), t_r, was too high. It would not follow that it would be optimal to reduce an otherwise optimal tax on c_g, t_g—whether from a zero level to a negative level (a subsidy) or from a positive level to a lower (or zero, or negative) level.

Reasons for Setting $t_g \neq 0$. Let us now consider what *are* the good reasons in the present setting to employ differential taxation among expenditures in period 2, that is, to choose $t_g \neq 0$. Initially, we should think of relaxing the assumption that c_g and (period 1) leisure are weakly separable. Perhaps whether one's period 2 expenditures are on playing golf rather than on other goods and services affects the marginal utility of leisure after all. One view would be that golf is relatively time-intensive and thus is a leisure complement. But if we are considering playing golf during retirement (a useful interpretation of period 2 for present purposes), such a result is hardly obvious. In any event, when weak separability is violated, a differential tax—or subsidy, depending on the direction of the effect—may be optimal.

There are other, familiar reasons for imposing a differential tax (or subsidy) on a particular activity. The main one involves correcting for an externality. Some activities cause pollution or congestion, negative externalities, or provide direct pleasure to others or indirectly benefit them such as through network effects, positive externalities. Then a differential tax or subsidy, as the case may be, would be optimal.

Analysis Where c_g Refers to Gifts

We are now in a position to consider expenditures on gifts. We do not, however, begin in a vacuum. Rather, we begin from where we left off in the preceding discussion. That is, the benchmark in our minds at the outset should be the optimal treatment of an ordinary expenditure, and the baseline for that case is one of no differential tax or subsidy. If the optimal tax (or subsidy) on gifts should be different from this, it must be because of distinctive features of expenditures on gifts.

Following the analysis above, we can first inquire whether expenditures on giving are leisure complements or substitutes, favoring a tax or subsidy, respectively, in order to mitigate the labor/leisure distortion caused by the income tax. To my knowledge, there has been no empirical study of this matter. As a matter of speculation, the answer is hardly obvious. On one hand, it might appear that gifts are a leisure substitute because, when one gives away income rather than spending it on oneself, say, for a vacation, one no longer needs as much leisure time to engage in consumption. On the other hand, an important use of leisure time may involve vicarious consumption through observing the direct consumption of donees—for example, spending time with one's grandchildren, whom one helps to support. (For bequests, however, this factor would be inoperative.) Suffice it to say that too little is presently known to decide whether this consideration involving the interaction between giving and the demand for leisure is significant and, if so, which way it cuts.[13]

Next, we can inquire into the existence of externalities. In this respect, it seems that gifts typically are distinctive from ordinary consumption. Consider the case of true gifts, those that are not really part of an exchange (a possibility considered below). Here, it seems that, ordinarily, the giving of a gift benefits not only the donor (who, one presumes, would not otherwise have made the gift) but also the donee.[14] To introduce formally this into the preceding model, one could rewrite individuals' budget constraints as follows:

$$wl + g - T(wl) = c_1 + \frac{c_2 + (1 + t_g)c_g}{1 + r(1 - t_r)},$$

where g refers to the total value of gifts *received*. (The present notation implies that one receives gifts in the first period of one's life and also that the receipt

13. To illuminate this question, one could imagine studying, say, whether individuals who make larger gifts to their children are more likely to retire sooner or to work longer.

14. This is another way of describing the familiar point that true gifts do not exhaustively consume resources but rather transfer command over the resources to another individual. The formulation presented in the text has the advantage of focusing attention on possible externalities, which, if present, have direct implications for policy design.

of gifts is not independently subject to tax. Both simplifications are for convenience.)[15] This modification would seem to have two fairly direct effects.[16]

First, because donees are now better off, other things being equal, their utility is higher, and hence social welfare is higher. This involves a positive externality.[17] If this were the only consideration, it would appear that a gift subsidy, $t_g < 0$, would be optimal.

Second, the receipt of gifts will have an income effect. Because donees are better off, as just described, their marginal utility of consumption will fall and, accordingly, we would expect their labor effort to fall.[18] In the presence of an income tax, this involves a negative externality.[19] The reason is that, when individuals are induced to work less, they do not take into account that they are contributing less to the government fisc. (This is simply another way of describing an aspect of the familiar labor/leisure distortion.) Interestingly, this factor raises the possibility that an individual's receipt of manna could reduce social welfare in a second-best world.

Several observations are in order. Initially, something can be said about the optimal level of tax on transfers that is implied by consideration of the second factor alone. Receipt of a gift of magnitude g should depress labor earnings, in the standard case, by an amount less than g. (The reason is that, when earnings fall by g, the marginal utility of income will be restored to its pre-gift level but, due to the fall in labor effort, the marginal disutility of labor will be somewhat lower, so the individual will wish to increase labor effort relative to that point.) It follows, therefore, that taxing g at the donee's marginal income

15. The latter simplification is interesting because of the interaction between taxes on giving levied on donors and those levied on donees. Under most plausible formulations for individuals' utility functions, all that should matter is the aggregate net tax on the gift. To simplify notation, one can assume that any net tax or subsidy is levied on the donor. If one introduces further complications, such as nonlinear taxes, which may depend on the aggregate of gifts given or gifts received (the latter corresponding to an inheritance or accessions tax), then the present simplification would not suffice.

16. There is a third effect that should be considered in a complete analysis: giving affects donors' and donees' marginal utility of income. See Kaplow (1998). One might suppose that this effect would be positive in the former case, because those who give spend less on their own consumption, and negative in the latter case. Differences in utility functions are usually ignored in welfare economic analysis because differences are assumed to be unobservable; implicitly, individuals are taken to have identical utility functions. But when giving patterns differ among otherwise similar individuals, the assumption of identical utility functions is no longer as plausible, and the observed differences in giving may be taken as indicators of differences in utility functions.

17. See, for example, Atkinson (1971, p. 222, n.1); Kaplow (1995); Stiglitz (1987, p. 1035).

18. See, for example, Holtz-Eakin, Joulfaian, and Rosen (1993); Imbens, Rubin, and Sacerdote (1999); Joulfaian and Wilhelm (1994).

19. See Kaplow (1998).

tax rate would be more than sufficient to make up for this externality.[20] Interestingly, taxing g at the donee's marginal income tax rate has been proposed by those who favor taxing gifts as income and forgoing a separate estate and gift tax system (these views are discussed further below).[21] It should be recalled, however, that such a tax not only is more than what is required to account for the negative tax revenue externality, but also that such an analysis ignores the positive externality from giving.

In addition, it should be noted that, although the income effect usually involves a reduction in work effort and thus a negative tax revenue externality, this is not necessarily the case in the present context. For example, some gifts relax liquidity constraints and thereby facilitate investment by donees, whether in human capital or in entrepreneurship.[22] Indeed, this prospect may motivate some gifts, or at a minimum affect their timing. In such cases, it would be possible to have a positive tax revenue effect because donees would ultimately earn more income on account of receiving gifts and thus pay more taxes.[23]

The remarks in the present subsection are suggestive. Obviously, it would be useful to work out explicitly the optimal income taxation problem with transfer behavior fully incorporated. In doing so, one would need to make explicit the form of donors' utility functions that leads them to make transfers in the first place, which is the subject of the next section.

Transfer Motives and Tax Policy

Until the recent past, there was little interaction between the literatures on transfer motives and on tax policy. Recently, however, the importance of transfer motives to tax policy has been increasingly recognized. Nevertheless, it is worth asking at the outset exactly why it is that motives matter. After all, motives did not play any direct role in the preceding analysis.

20. The reason is that, as just explained, earnings would not fall by the full amount g, so a tax on the full amount would not be necessary to internalize the externality. (It should also be noted that imposing a positive tax on g will lead to a reduction in g, which will reduce the income effect; nevertheless, the tax would be imposed on the resulting level of g in any event.)

21. See, for example, Simons (1938).

22. See, for example, Blanchflower and Oswald (1998); Cox (1990); Holtz-Eakin, Joulfaian, and Rosen (1994a, 1994b).

23. Donees' labor supply could be affected in other ways as well. There may, for example, be a further negative influence on account of the Samaritan's dilemma; that is, donees may work less hard, anticipating that altruistic donors (for example, their parents) will bail them out. Or there may be the opposite effect: it may be understood that future gifts are contingent on productive behavior, leading donees to work harder or to invest more in their human capital in order to please prospective donors.

The first, and most obvious, reason that motives matter is that they bear on donors' behavior. In order to know whether and how much various tax regimes would influence gifts and bequests, it is necessary to understand why transfers are made in the first place.

A second reason—more direct even if less attended to—is that motives typically indicate the form of donors' utility functions which, in turn, indicate what utility donors receive from their giving. Moreover, motives may bear on donees' utility. These factors can have an important influence on optimal transfer tax policy. Consider two examples.

First, assume that we are uncertain whether donors leave bequests "accidentally" (that is, due to the incompleteness of annuity markets) or intentionally (say, on account of altruism). Suppose, now, that a confiscatory estate tax is under consideration. Even ignoring the effects of such a tax on behavior, the welfare assessment would be different depending on the motive. If bequests were purely accidental, the tax would reduce donees' (but not donors') utility with a corresponding gain to the fisc. If the bequests were altruistically motivated, then, in addition to these two effects, there would *also* be a reduction in donors' utility. Hence, it is conceivable that what would be a desirable policy given one motive would be a detrimental one given another. (To be sure, there would also be differences in behavioral effects, which would make the analysis more complicated.)

Second, consider an example in which it is unclear whether what appear to be gifts are "true gifts" or really involve some sort of exchange (perhaps the donee provides services to the donor). Assume, moreover, that in either case a proposed tax would reduce giving to the same extent. Furthermore, we could suppose that the donor's utility loss from imposing the tax was the same, independent of the motive. It would remain true, nevertheless, that the welfare effects would differ. When the gift really involves an exchange, a lower gift implies a lower level of exchange; hence, the reduction in the donee's receipt is offset (at least in part) by the donee's providing fewer services. Thus, the donee's utility loss will be less than in the case of the pure gift, where the reduction in the donee's receipt will not be offset by anything.

These illustrations suggest that understanding donors' motives is extremely important in formulating estate and gift tax policy. The remainder of this section examines briefly a number of the motivations that have been offered in the literature and sketches some of their implications.[24] To simplify the exposition, it will be useful to consider a one-period model, where c will denote the

24. For discussions of transfer motives, see, for example, Davies (1996); Masson and Pestieau (1997); Stark (1995). A more complete analysis of some of the issues discussed in this section appears in Kaplow (1998).

donor's expenditures on own-consumption.[25] It will also be imagined in each subsection that gifts are explained by a single motive, whereas in fact donors' motives may be mixed and different donors may have different motives.[26]

Altruism

Consider the following standard formulation of the altruistic donor's utility function:

$$U(c, c_g, \ell) = \alpha u(c, \ell) + \beta v(c_v + c_g, \ell_v),$$

where u is the donor's "self-regarding" utility function, v is the donee's utility function, c_v refers to donee's expenditures on consumption from disposable income, ℓ_v refers to donee's labor effort, and α and β are weights (a relatively larger value of β indicating a greater degree of altruism). For clarity, the gift, c_g, is entered explicitly in the donee's utility function rather than appearing through the donee's budget constraint.

The analysis in this case follows that already presented in the initial, general analysis of gifts. Ignoring for the moment any effects on tax revenue due to the donee's choice of labor effort, a gift subsidy (that is, $t_g < 0$) would be optimal because of the positive externality on the donee. Even though the donor is altruistic, the weight placed on the donee's utility is only β. By contrast, a utilitarian social welfare function would, with regard to a given donor/donee pair, place a weight of $1 + \beta$ on the donee's utility, v, the 1 representing that the donee counts in his or her own right, and the additional β reflecting the benefit to the donor from increases in the donee's utility.[27]

---

25. The donor's budget constraint for this version of the model is

$$w\ell - T(w\ell) = c + (1 + t_g)c_g.$$

26. Such heterogeneity, combined with the government's presumed inability to observe motives directly, complicates the problem of policy formulation if indeed different motives imply that different policies are optimal. In practice, the government will have to base policies on averages, although sometimes it may be able to have policies depend on observable features of gifts (such as whether the gift is financial or involves human capital, whether it is given during life or as a bequest, and how the donor and donee are related—issues addressed below) that are correlated with transfer motives.

27. To illustrate, in a two-person society, the utilitarian social welfare function would be $\alpha u + (1 + \beta)v$, the sum of the donor's utility function and the donee's. Some have questioned whether altruistic preferences should "count" in assessments of social welfare, but the reasons for ignoring tastes about others (such as those one loves) when counting all sorts of tastes (including preferences regarding the behavior of individuals one does not love, such as performers that one pays to see) are obscure. Moreover, using a social welfare function that omits altruistic utility would have troubling policy implications (for examples, bans on supporting children and on highly skilled individuals engaging in various low-paying helping professions may be welfare-improving under such a view).

Hence, the donor's gift will be below the welfare-maximizing level in the absence of a subsidy.

But it should also be apparent that a positive subsidy, which induces the donor to make a larger gift, will in the standard case reduce the donee's labor effort and thus the level of income tax collections, producing a negative externality as well. In all, the case of altruistically motivated gifts fits well the analysis presented previously.

Utility from Giving Per Se

Some donors may be motivated, not by altruism, but by the direct utility they receive from the act of giving, whether due to some internal feeling of virtue arising from sacrifice in the aid of others, a desire for prestige, or some other source of benefit. (James Andreoni refers to this phenomenon as "warm glow" giving.)[28] For comparison with the case of altruism, the donor's utility function may be stated as

$$U(c, c_g, \ell) = \alpha u(c, \ell) + \beta v(c_g),$$

where v is no longer interpreted as the donee's utility function but rather as a direct indicator of pleasure that the donor receives from the act of giving. The main difference, as is well known in the literature on transfer motives, is that v does not depend on other sources of consumption for the donee.

Despite the difference in motives, the analysis of the welfare effects of a tax or subsidy on giving is qualitatively similar. A subsidy will still increase the level of giving, the increase will involve a positive externality in that the greater gift benefits both the donor and the donee, and the gain to the donee will tend to affect tax revenue, negatively in the standard case.

It should be observed, however, that the preceding formulation (which is analogous to that used, for example, by Andreoni),[29] may not be the best representation of the stated motive. It is supposed that the donor is really motivated in a manner that depends on his or her own sacrifice, and not on the benefit to the donee from all sources (including the public fisc), as in the case of altruism. Accordingly, it would appear that the donor's benefit should not depend on the gross gift, c_g—as in the above expression—but rather on the net amount that the donor actually gives up, which here is $(1 + t_g)c_g$, an

28. Andreoni (1990).
29. Andreoni (1990).

amount that is less than c_g when there is a subsidy (when $t_g < 0$).[30] In this case, the donor's utility function would be

$$U(c, c_g, \ell) = \alpha u(c, \ell) + \beta v((1 + t_g)c_g).$$

The effect of a gift subsidy on social welfare is quite different under this formulation. A higher subsidy (a lower, or more negative, level of t_g) now has the direct effect of reducing the donor's utility from giving because a lesser sacrifice is involved for a given level of gift. A higher subsidy (lower tax) may produce a larger gross gift, but the utility benefit to the donee is matched by a utility loss to the donor. The situation can be characterized as one involving induced redistribution rather than a double benefit. Hence, the optimal tax (subsidy) on giving would be higher (lower) if—taking as given that donors are motivated by the act of giving per se—it is the net sacrifice rather than the gross gift that determines the donor's level of utility. To my knowledge, the existing empirical work on this transfer motive does not attempt to determine which of these two versions more accurately describes such donors' behavior.

Exchange-Related Motives

The most straightforward instance of exchange-motivated giving occurs when the donor gives the donee resources in exchange for services.[31] Here, the interpretation of the donor's utility function, $U(c, c_g, \ell)$, is simply that c and c_g are two different forms of ordinary consumption of goods and services. In this case, the previous analysis of gifts as another form of ordinary consumption is directly applicable: gifts are not distinctive and there is no a priori argument for applying any differential tax or subsidy. It also follows in this setting that

30. To test this intuition, suppose that the subsidy on giving was not given to donors at all, but instead was given directly to donees, in the form of a matching grant. Should one assume that donors who do not care directly about the donee's utility or about other sources of financial support the donee might receive view such a government grant as part of their own sacrifice? Another consideration is that, if donors cared only about their own sacrifice and not at all about what donees received, then a confiscatory tax on donees' gift receipts would not reduce donors' utility from giving, which seems implausible. Obviously, the factors determining donors' utility from giving—even assuming that the present motivation correctly describes an important fraction of giving—raises empirical questions that, as noted in the text to follow, do not seem to have been explored.

31. See Cox (1987). More subtle versions, such as the strategic motivation explored by Bernheim, Shleifer, and Summers (1985), are no different for present purposes. The argument in Buchanan (1983) that potential heirs will engage in rent-seeking behavior to induce donors to make transfers also seems similar if one supposes that such behavior involves providing something of value to donors.

"gift" receipts of donees should be included in their taxable income, for in the typical case the receipts are wages, although received in an informal market.[32] In fact, this case supplied one of the motivations for Henry Simons's argument that gifts should be taxed as income to donees.[33]

Other forms of exchange are also possible. Notably, what may appear to be unidirectional transfers may really be loans that are expected to be repaid or elements of various types of insurance and annuity schemes.[34] These sorts of exchanges likewise do not call for any special tax or subsidy. Under an income tax, the proper treatment of many such arrangements is to ignore transfers, except when they involve (explicit or implicit) payments of interest; under a consumption tax (of a personal, cash-flow type), all receipts would be included in the tax base and all payments would be deductible.

Accidental Bequests

Purely accidental bequests involve the transfer of remaining assets at death to one's heirs when the only reason any assets are in one's estate is on account of the inability to annuitize completely (and otherwise obtain insurance). To model this phenomenon obviously requires the introduction of uncertainty. The main ideas for present purposes, however, can be understood intuitively. First, there is the familiar point that, if bequests are purely accidental, they can be confiscated completely, with no effect on donors' behavior or utility. Yet this point does not, by itself, imply that such taxation would be optimal, for such a tax obviously reduces the utility of donees.[35]

---

32. Interestingly, if the donee provided the same services as a gift—that is, with no payment expected in return—there would be no tax under the standard income tax system. The donee may be regarded as providing nonmarket labor services, but such imputed income generally is not taxed. Under current law, if the donor—without any formal obligation—reciprocates with a return gift, both halves of the transaction are exempt from the income tax, whereas if one transfer is the quid pro quo for the other, the exchange is subject to tax (although, as a practical matter, evasion on such transactions is undoubtedly high).

33. Simons (1938).

34. See, for example, Kotlikoff and Spivak (1981); Lucas and Stark (1985). Data on inter vivos transfers often do not distinguish among pure gifts, loans, loan repayments, insurance payments, and other forms of transfers, which makes the interpretation of empirical work difficult.

35. It is also important to distinguish purely accidental bequests—from individuals who would prefer to annuitize completely—from bequests by individuals who cannot bring themselves to write a will or engage in other forms of planning. Even if the latter group were to exhibit little behavioral response to estate taxation, it still may not be optimal to impose such a tax because it is possible that such donors do derive utility from contemplation of their descendants' prospective inheritances, which would be reduced by the prospect that their bequest would be taxed.

This leads to the second point, which concerns income distribution—or, from an ex ante perspective, allocation of risk. To make matters simple, assume that the revenue from estate taxation would be distributed pro rata among otherwise identical members of the generation of prospective donees.[36] Such an estate tax would operate as a pure insurance arrangement among donees: some would otherwise receive large bequests, others little or no bequest, but with the tax, all will receive an equal amount.[37] If individuals are risk averse, as most probably are, such a scheme would tend to raise welfare.[38]

Rethinking Standard Criteria for Assessing Estate and Gift Taxation

As suggested in the introduction, the standard criteria for assessing estate and gift tax policy concern such matters as redistribution, raising revenue, effects on savings, and other considerations. Unfortunately, discussion of these desiderata often is not tied directly to an explicit statement of ultimate objectives or to a formal analysis of the tax system as a whole. As a result, analysis is often incomplete or misleading. Some suggestion of the shortcomings appears above. The present section offers a more complete examination of how optimal income tax analysis illuminates the standard criteria and sketches some further extensions of that analysis.

Redistribution, Conventionally Understood

Perhaps the most commonly suggested link between concerns about redistributing income from the rich to the poor and the instrument of estate and gift taxation is that transfers are made disproportionately by the wealthy, so

36. As is familiar, if one were examining an optimal tax regime, then it would not matter at the margin how the revenues were used, in which case the scenario considered in the text would suffice to demonstrate the conclusion. In any event, the proposed thought experiment should serve to illustrate why steep taxation of bequests would tend to be optimal in the case of purely accidental bequests.

37. One can usefully compare to confiscatory estate taxation the alternative scheme of taking individuals' assets—say, at age 65—and giving back an annuity with a present value equal to the assets taken. If the reason for the failure to annuitize was adverse selection, such a solution might enhance welfare even more.

38. It should be noted, however, that those receiving the largest bequests in the absence of taxation would be those whose parents died earliest. Such individuals might be supposed ordinarily to have lower utility than others on this account, and their larger bequests might be viewed as compensatory. The argument in the text implicitly assumes that such utility differences due to nonpecuniary factors do not affect individuals' marginal utility of income. In such a case, optimal insurance equalizes income, and thus marginal utility—not utility levels—across states of nature.

that an estate and gift tax system can aid in the redistributive enterprise. It was explained earlier, however, that this intuition is in error, for it is generally better to increase the extent of redistribution—if that would be optimal—directly, through adjusting the income tax system.

One way to understand this basic point is to reformulate the question of optimal transfer tax policy as follows: *As between two donors with identical income (etc.), should we tax (or subsidize) more heavily—and how much more— the one who spends an additional $1 on a gift rather than on own-consumption?* As explored previously, there may well be reasons to tax more or less heavily expenditures that are made on gifts. But none of these considerations has any direct connection with increasing the extent of redistribution. That is, there is no particular reason (on purely redistributive grounds) that a rich person who spends a marginal dollar on a gift should have to make a greater contribution to supporting the poor than an equally rich person who instead spends the marginal dollar on him- or herself.

The preceding discussion is, however, incomplete in an important respect. One should expand the analysis to take into account that multiple generations are involved and that gifts affect income distribution through effects on donees. Formally, the situation defined in the initial presentation of the problem could be extended in several ways. One would be to incorporate two generations that overlap (so that period 2 for the first generation was period 1 for the second, with gifts potentially being made during the period of overlap, from the older to the younger generation). Another way, which has been explored in some of the literature, involves incorporating an infinite series of overlapping generations into the model.[39] To keep matters simple, most of the discussion to follow speaks in terms of the first version. Also, to make the exposition concrete and to focus on the most pertinent case, suppose that rich members of the first generation give disproportionately more than do others, that most of the giving is by individuals of above-average income taking the two generations as a whole, and that the average recipient is not as rich as the corresponding donor but is as rich or richer than average for members of the second generation.[40]

What, then, are we to make of a transfer from a member of the first generation to a member of the second? One perspective would be to examine the effect of transfers on the distribution of *living standards* within each of the two

39. See, for example, Bevan and Stiglitz (1979) and the chapter by Laitner in this volume.

40. There are, of course, settings in which this description would be inaccurate. For example, if there were substantial regression toward the mean in income and if transfers were highly equalizing, it is possible that average recipients would (pre-gift) be of below-average income. See, for example, Bevan and Stiglitz (1979).

generations and for the two generations viewed as a whole. For the first generation, giving reduces inequality in living standards (because, by assumption, the rich give disproportionately more). For the second generation, giving increases inequality in living standards (because the average recipient is of at least the average living standard before receiving the gift). Finally, and perhaps most importantly, if the two generations are viewed as a single society for purposes of analysis, gifts reduce inequality; indeed, the typical gift can be seen as a sort of voluntary redistribution.[41] To be sure, the reduction in inequality does not primarily involve transfers to the poorest members of society, most of whom do not have wealthy parents; nevertheless, the average gift involves moving resources to a donee whose standard of living is relatively lower than that of the corresponding donor.

A problem with the preceding analysis is that living standards are not the ultimate matter of concern; rather, it is supposed that social welfare consists in some aggregate of individuals' utilities, their levels of well-being. On this account, the analysis is more complicated, for gifts cannot be understood to reduce the *utility* (as opposed to the living standard) of donors, for otherwise they would not have made their gifts. Taking this into account, it seems entirely possible that gifts would increase inequality in utilities, combining the two generations together.

That said, there is a further and more important difficulty with all of the analysis of intra- and intergenerational inequality that has just been presented (and much of that in the literature): it considers inequality in a vacuum, rather than examining social welfare as a whole and taking into account the income tax system. Indeed, the preceding analysis suggests that, even if gifts are made disproportionately by the rich, it does not follow that gifts should be taxed to further redistributional objectives. Rather, it tends to be optimal to make adjustments in the income tax and transfer system. Whether gifts should be taxed (or subsidized) *relative to expenditures by equally rich individuals on own-consumption* depends not on the income level of donors, but rather on other factors identified in the preliminary analysis, notably, the positive and negative externalities associated with gifts.

41. The discussion in the text sheds light on analyses that examine the effects of voluntary transfers—and of transfer taxation—on the *steady-state* extent of inequality in an infinite, overlapping generations model. This measure of inequality is akin to focusing, in the present, simpler setting, on inequality in the second generation alone. As the point in the text suggests, and as Bevan and Stiglitz (1979) and others have previously noted, such a focus can be misleading.

Another issue raised by considering multiple generations is the problem of aggregation, sometimes addressed under the rubric of generational discounting. Exploring this issue, which obviously involves questions going well beyond estate and gift taxation, is outside the scope of the present inquiry. The basic points made in the text do not seem to depend on precisely how the matter is resolved.

Moreover, even in a world with no income tax, confining attention to the effects of giving on inequality, rather than social welfare, can be problematic. Suppose, for example, that one is contemplating a simple policy of abolishing giving (which may well be the consequence of a confiscatory tax on giving, which some have proposed). Under the stated assumptions of the present example, such a policy would reduce inequality in utilities. (Abolishing giving would reduce the utility of donors who no longer have the utility-enhancing option of making gifts—they, by assumption, are richer than average—and it would reduce the utility of donees who no longer receive gifts—donees, by assumption, were of at least average income and of above-average income including their gifts.) Nevertheless, this inequality-reducing policy would be Pareto inferior, for it reduces the well-being of donors and donees and helps no one else. Even if one were to employ a social welfare function that was highly egalitarian, such a policy would reduce welfare as long as the welfare function respected the Pareto principle. Thus, knowing how a policy affects inequality—even combined with knowledge about how the policy affects total wealth—is insufficient in the present setting to determine even the *direction* of the effect of the policy on social welfare.

Other Distributive Objectives

The preceding subsection considered issues of inequality and redistribution using the framework that has become familiar in economic policy analysis. Not all distributive objectives that have been advanced, however, seem on their face to be reducible to such terms, and this is certainly true of public policy toward transfers, notably, involving the intergenerational transmission of wealth.

Perhaps the most common alternative criterion is some notion of "equal starting points." Focusing on the generation of recipients of gifts, the concern is that inheritance (combined with inter vivos transfers) gives some individuals an unfair advantage over others. Sometimes the point is cast in terms of providing equality of opportunity (which could refer to the opportunity to enjoy life or to take advantage of various opportunities that are more accessible to those with greater initial wealth). Consider, now, two variations of this notion, which differ with respect to whether financial gifts are distinguished from other sources of unequal opportunity.

Under one view, the problem is with unequal opportunity, whatever its source. As will be discussed below, the greatest cause of unequal starting points involves human capital—differences in genetic endowments, living environments, and other sources of parental support that affect future earnings and other life opportunities.[42] Explicit transfers of the sort that are or may be subject to estate and gift taxation might in some instances mitigate such inequality but more often probably augment it (due to the positive correlation between parental financial resources and these other sources of inequality).

The problem of basic inequality, however, is familiar, and it is the problem that the standard welfare economic framework and optimal redistributive taxation analysis are designed to handle. From this perspective, there is nothing special about financial transfers. An extended optimal income tax framework, with overlapping generations and gifts, would already take the effect of transfers into account. And, whatever is the weight of the social concern for inequality, it will be reflected in the social welfare function. As already discussed, there is no simple, direct connection between the desire to redistribute income and the optimality of imposing taxes on gifts.

Under another view, financial gifts are seen as a particularly undesirable source of inequality in starting points. Some have suggested a distinction between individuals' rights to the proceeds from their own labor and to the receipt of financial transfers from others. Although the grounds for this distinction are unclear, arguments of this sort have been offered in favor of taxation of gifts.[43] Such an approach, however, fundamentally conflicts with the welfare economic approach of assessing policies based upon their effects on individuals' well-being and in a manner that suggests that the former approach should not be followed.

It is useful to elaborate upon the latter point because the basic tension, although often acknowledged at some level, does not seem to be fully appreciated. Suppose, for example, that we would (that society should) be willing to sacrifice up to R in resources to reduce inequality in the next generation by the amount I when the inequality was caused, say, by differences in talent, physical disabilities, or market luck. The posited distributive objective supposes that we should be willing to spend *something more than R in resources* to reduce inequality in the next generation by *the same amount I* when the cause is financial inheritance. In principle, this would be true even when those

---

42. See Davies (1982). For example, Bradford (1986) indicates that if a 90th percentile male received, at age 40, the 90th percentile inheritance, his lifetime wealth would increase by a mere 4.2 percent.

43. Some suggest that earned income should be treated preferentially to unearned income from inheritances. This view, however, ignores that earned income itself is largely determined by sorts of inheritance, as already noted in the text. Moreover, one should ask whether the view makes problematic the taxation of earned income under the income tax or under a consumption tax. (Indeed, if what appear to be gifts are really payments for services, it is generally uncontroversial that a tax should be levied on the transfer. As discussed below, earned income is fully taxed whereas gift receipts are generally exempt under the United States income tax; this approach seems to be the opposite of that suggested by this notion about how different sources of receipts should be treated.)

suffering from the inequality were the same people in both instances, since the notion depends on the *source* of reduced well-being and not purely on the extent to which well-being is reduced.

The foregoing analysis implies that, in a world in which ordinary constraints are present, following the prescription of this view will result in *less* reduction in overall inequality than if this special notion received no weight. At whatever constrained optimum we could achieve under the proposed view, we could shift some resources from reducing inequality caused by financial inheritance to reducing inequality caused by other factors; by assumption, the marginal cost being incurred for inequality reduction is greater for the former than for the latter source of inequality. Hence, the shift would, at given cost, reduce inequality more.[44] And because, as noted, this analysis holds true even when it is the same individuals who suffer from both sources of inequality, it follows that a change in policy that gives less weight to the posited principle could make everyone—in particular, the poorest members of society— better off.

Indeed, it is possible to show formally that any such principle that is not grounded exclusively in a concern for individuals' well-being (that is, a principle of assessment not based solely on utilities but that instead looks, for example, to the sources of utility) will in some cases conflict with the Pareto principle.[45] Thus, other distributive objectives—whether based on a notion of equal starting points or otherwise—are troubling, to the extent that individuals' well-being is deemed to be important in assessing social policy.

Revenue

It is sometimes suggested that estate and gift taxes are useful supplements to other taxes in raising revenue to finance public expenditures. In the present

44. Suppose, for example, that at the posited optimum under the distributive view that gives special weight to inequality caused by financial inheritance, the marginal tradeoff between deadweight loss and given reductions in inequality is 12 for inequality due to financial inheritance but 10 for all other sources of inequality. One could then raise inequality with the former cause by 1.0 unit, freeing up 12 in resources, which could be used to reduce inequality due to other causes by 1.2 units.

45. See Kaplow and Shavell (2001). Seemingly nonwelfarist distributive principles such as the equal starting points notion may, however, be understood differently, as focusing on a proxy indicator that is related to individuals' well-being rather than as constituting an independent evaluative principle, to be pursued at the expense of individuals' well-being. One interpretation would be that the notion refers simply to general concerns for inequality, urging us not to lose sight of the distributive impact of transfers on the donee generation. Another interpretation might be that the notion reflects concern about a particular sort of envy among members of the donee generation, suggesting that there is a negative externality produced by intergenerational transfers. Under that view, the relevant question would be the magnitude of such an externality (that is, the strength of such individual tastes) and how it compares to other such externalities, which are noted briefly below.

setting, this suggestion is misleading. As suggested briefly above, the standard formulation of the optimal income taxation problem takes into consideration any social benefits from raising revenue, whether for financing redistributive transfers or for funding public goods. The subsequent analysis then explored when taxes (or subsidies) on giving—relative to other forms of expenditures by individuals—were optimal. Although the need to raise revenue is present in the background, it does not bear directly on whether transfer taxation increases social welfare.

The most important exception to the conclusion that revenue-raising considerations should not guide estate and gift tax policy involves problems of tax enforcement.[46] Tax avoidance can be a serious problem, even in developed economies with sophisticated enforcement machinery. As a consequence, it may be optimal to employ certain taxes that otherwise would be inefficient in order to address income tax noncompliance. The easiest example in which to see this point is to consider that excise taxes on luxury goods might be optimal because some individuals may earn high incomes in the underground economy that otherwise would go untaxed. If there are income groups for whom income tax evasion is substantial and difficult to eliminate, but enforcement of estate and gift taxation is feasible, there would be grounds for favoring such taxation.

In practice, the appropriate role of transfer taxes in addressing enforcement gaps in the income tax (or in consumption taxes) is unclear. On one hand, if illegal sources of income are kept as cash or sent to untraceable offshore accounts, it seems unlikely that one could readily collect transfer taxes on such funds. On the other hand, some such income may be laundered and then used to purchase assets in the regular economy. These assets may be observable as part of individuals' estates. In such cases, however, the optimally set consumption tax, applicable to the initial purchase of such assets, may suffice as a second-best instrument. Estate taxes might nevertheless be a useful supplement when assets are purchased secretly—or in other jurisdictions—but can be identified as part of an estate. In any event, this potential role of transfer taxation deserves further exploration, and it seems likely that a transfer tax system designed with such enforcement problems in mind would look rather different from that currently employed. (Notably, it might tax only certain types of assets, or provide for exemptions if assets were purchased

---

46. It is sometimes suggested that political constraints may favor the use of transfer taxes rather than, say, greater progression of income taxes, although, as note 12 indicates, the basis for such a view is unclear.

through qualified accounts in which all deposits had been subject to income taxation.)[47]

Savings

The relationship between transfer taxation and savings was explored (implicitly) above.[48] The main connection between transfer taxation and savings that has been identified is that donors often fund transfers out of their savings. This is not inevitably so; for example, transfers in support of minor children are often funded out of current earnings or even from borrowing. But many transfers, including bequests, come out of savings derived from previous receipts.[49]

As explained previously, one can, in the simple two-period model presented, view gifts as one type of expenditure in period 2, the other type being on own-consumption. A tax on giving is an example of a tax on a subset of consumption in period 2. (In the earlier discussion, recall, the problem was discussed with the differential tax being applied to expenditures on playing golf.) A tax on a subset of period 2 consumption can be viewed in part as a tax on period 2 consumption and hence as a tax on savings.

It is helpful, however, to decompose such a tax so that we can view separately its two components: an average tax rate on period 2 expenditures (whether gifts or own-consumption) and a differential tax/subsidy on particular components. Thus, a tax on gifts is equivalent to (a) raising the average tax rate on period 2 expenditures (taxing savings), by an amount equal to the tax rate on gifts times the fraction of period 2 expenditures on gifts, combined with (b) a tax on gifts and a subsidy on own-consumption, which sum (in absolute values) to the originally posited tax on gifts.

Viewed in this manner, the analysis is straightforward. The first component is simply an ordinary tax on savings, which has been subject to extensive prior analysis. (The optimal income tax analysis of such a tax, in certain basic settings, was explored earlier.) Obviously, one can in principle adopt such a tax without taxing transfers differentially. Likewise, if the effect of taxing

---

47. See also the discussion below on whether estate and gift taxes do raise significant revenue and on their own compliance costs.

48. Literature on transfer taxation and savings includes Johnson, Diamond, and Zodrow (1997) and also the chapter by Gale and Perozek in this volume.

49. It is familiar that this tendency poses an empirical puzzle, for giving earlier is tax-favored in the present United States estate and gift tax system, yet most gifts are delayed, often until the time of death. See, for example, Poterba (2001).

transfers were thought to be detrimental because of how such a tax affects savings, one could offset such effects by directly adjusting the tax rate on savings. Furthermore, other policy instruments may be used to influence savings more directly.[50] This suggests that estate and gift tax policy should probably be based on other considerations. (The reason for supposing that transfer taxes tend to be an inferior means to influence savings is that adjusting them from what would otherwise be optimal will involve a further distortion, of transfer behavior, whereas interventions that act directly on savings will not have this effect.)

The second component, a tax on gifts *relative to* own-consumption, has nothing to do with savings per se. It is this aspect of the tax on gifts (or subsidy, as the case may be) that has been the subject of analysis in the rest of this chapter. This is not to deny that a differential tax on different components of period 2 expenditure may have an effect on savings. It can—just as the case with any differential tax on different forms of expenditures. Such effects, however, will be more indirect than that attributable to the previously described first component of a tax on transfers. It is important in analyzing the effects of transfer taxes on savings to distinguish these two components. Moreover, one should distinguish gross effects—which may not have welfare consequences— from distortions, which ordinarily do adversely affect individuals' well-being.

Administrative and Compliance Costs

All actual tax systems, including systems of estate and gift taxation, involve administrative and compliance costs. Indeed, it is often suggested that these costs are particularly high for transfer taxes because large expenditures are made on expert advice and rearranging financial affairs and that these expenditures significantly reduce the tax owed, although it is not clear the extent to which this is actually the case.[51] This point does not, however, have obvious implications for tax reform, because such costs may be reduced either by eliminating transfer taxation or, perhaps, by making it more comprehensive (such as by eliminating tax benefits from inter vivos transfers, which are often made in complex ways in order for donors to retain control of resources during their lifetimes).

Other complications involve interactions between the income tax and transfer taxes. To some degree, one may serve as a backstop to the other. Such

50. See Stiglitz (1978).
51. See, for example, Cooper (1979); Munnell (1988); and the chapter by Schmalbeck in this volume.

an argument is sometimes made about the United States income tax provision that steps up the basis of appreciated assets at death, estate taxes on the transfer of such assets substituting for capital gains taxation of the unrealized appreciation.[52] When a real problem exists, however, it is often better to deal with it directly, here, by changing the income tax treatment of capital gains, if that is indeed deficient.[53] In addition, as discussed above, it may be that one tax (the estate tax) is able to collect revenue on funds not previously taxed (under the income tax) due to evasion. Yet another possibility that has been explored is that attempts to avoid one tax may affect receipts under the other, such as when estate tax planning reduces income tax receipts.[54]

Administrative and compliance costs as well as the complex interactions among different tax systems are all relevant to a welfare economic assessment of estate and gift tax policy. Further analysis of the empirical and, in some cases, analytical issues that underlie these matters are beyond the scope of this chapter.

Are Gifts and Bequests "Income"?

It has long been suggested that gifts and bequests are "income" to the donee and hence should be included in the donee's taxable income.[55] This argument was made by Simons and has been subsequently advanced, sometimes to support income taxation of gift receipts as an alternative to estate and gift taxation.[56]

If gifts and bequests were included as taxable income (they are excluded in the United States under section 102 of the Internal Revenue Code), this would result in a major tax increase on transfers for the vast majority of the

---

52. For empirical evidence on the relative magnitudes of savings in capital gains taxes from step-up and estate taxes paid, as a function of the size of estates, see the chapter by Poterba and Weisbenner in this volume.

53. There are other possible shortcomings of the income tax that a transfer tax might play a role in remedying. For example, aggregate gifts and bequests may be correlated to lifetime income whereas the income tax is assessed on annual income. It would seem, however, that the correlation is significantly confounded by other factors (notably, saving and giving behavior, which vary even taking lifetime income as given) and that more direct solutions, such as restoring some degree of explicit lifetime averaging, would be a superior means of achieving such an end.

54. For example, Bernheim (1987) indicates that this effect may result in an income tax revenue loss sufficient to offset the revenue raised through the United States estate and gift tax system. For a contrasting view, see Repetti (2000).

55. Analogous reasoning can be offered with regard to a consumption tax: a gift would be viewed as consumption by the donor, and the donee's expenditure of the gift receipts would be viewed as another act of consumption.

56. See Simons (1938).

population, whose transfers are too low to be subject to estate taxation but who pay income taxes at nontrivial marginal tax rates. For the most wealthy, top income tax rates are currently below estate tax rates, so net transfer taxes would fall, although if income taxation were in addition to the estate and gift tax system, transfer taxes would rise substantially for this group.

The main point to be made regarding this argument about income taxation of gifts is that it is a semantic one that does not really bear in any manner on social welfare.[57] Whether a definition of "income" that includes transfer receipts is better in some sense as a matter of language usage does not inform us about the effects of taxation on individuals' behavior or on their well-being. Thus, a number of commentators have suggested abandoning such appeals to definitions when assessing tax policy, in favor of direct application of the welfare economic framework. That is the approach employed in this chapter.

Note, furthermore, that it should not matter—either for determining individuals' behavior or for assessing effects on individuals' well-being—whether taxes on transfers are nominally levied as part of the income tax, through a separate estate and gift tax regime, or some combination of the two. Of course, certain differences may arise from using one or another approach—such as whether the marginal tax rate on gifts varies with one's annual earnings, one's total level of giving, or both—but such considerations are secondary and, if important, could be altered. There may also be differences in administrative and compliance costs between the regimes. (For example, if gifts were deemed to be income to donees, it may be more difficult for alleged tax evaders to claim that their unexplained cash holdings were gifts from a now-deceased relative and thus were properly not reported.)

Concentration of Wealth and Power

Estate and gift taxes are sometimes favored on the ground that they tend to diminish undesirable concentrations of wealth and power. To consider this objective, it is useful to distinguish two questions, whether and why society should seek to reduce concentrations of wealth or power, and, if such a goal is an important one, whether use of transfer taxation is a sensible means of pursuing it.

---

57. Another interesting point, advanced by Brennan (1978), is that the existing single tax levied on the donor, who earns the income, already serves to reduce the level of gifts. For example, if individuals give a fixed fraction of their disposable income, a tax that reduces disposable income by t also reduces net gifts by t. One could argue that this point does not really suffice to establish that gifts are already "taxed" as "income," but this would merely extend the semantic debate without illuminating the welfare implications of transfer taxation.

With regard to the first question, two opposing views are often expressed. On one hand, it is suggested that undue concentrations of wealth are undesirable. Among the more common reasons for this view is that wealthy individuals are able to obtain disproportionate influence, on the political system or otherwise, as a result. Perhaps they or those whom they favor would have an advantage in seeking elective office or in inducing government officials to do their bidding.

On the other hand, it is argued that concentrations of wealth enhance democracy by providing important sources of countervailing power. It may be that incumbent individuals or political parties are sometimes able to insulate themselves from opposition forces, yet the existence of outsiders with significant wealth makes it possible to unseat incumbents if they become too unresponsive. In this regard, it may be important whether a few families have large accumulations of wealth or there are many wealthy people, with differing interests and points of view. Clearly, further study is required to ascertain which, if either, of these views is compelling, and to assess other possible effects, positive or negative, of concentrations of wealth.[58]

Suppose, for the sake of argument, that those individuals with large amounts of wealth do exercise a disproportionate and undesirable influence on the political system. Is transfer taxation a sensible means of addressing such a problem? The first point to note is that the problem, as usually described, really involves wealth, not its transfer, suggesting that a wealth tax—or a steeper income tax that would regulate the accumulation process—is more suitable to the task.[59] Relatedly, it is not clear that transferring wealth to the

---

58. Separately, it is sometimes suggested that wealth should be taxed because holding wealth is itself a source of utility. There are two problems with this argument. First, as explained above, a proper approach to social welfare maximization is not concerned with taxing utility per se. Second, that wealth may produce two sources of utility (one while it is held and another when it is consumed) has no implication regarding the marginal utility of holding wealth. Many activities produce utility in multiple ways (for example, health club membership may provide entertainment, offer an opportunity to meet people, contribute to health, and improve one's appearance). Regardless, maximizing individuals will equate the marginal utility of different activities (spending on food, health clubs, savings, and so forth) so that, regardless of the number of sources of marginal utility of an activity, the aggregate marginal utility from each activity will be equal (unless there are distortions, such as those caused by taxation).

59. A transfer tax might be thought of as a wealth tax that is imposed once a generation rather than, say, once a year or once and for all. (The existence in the United States of a spousal exemption and a generation-skipping transfer tax is consistent with this conception.) But generations vary greatly in length and, in any event, the amount of wealth transferred may not be that closely related to the amount held or used (whether to obtain influence or otherwise) during the donor's lifetime. It should also be clear that wealth taxes and transfer taxes have different effects on incentives, the former applying directly to the savings (wealth accumulation) margin and the latter applying to the choice between own-consumption and giving, independent of whether one is expending current income, drawing on savings, or borrowing against future income.

next generation is more problematic than using it to buy influence in the present generation. For example, Edward McCaffery notes the case of wealthy individuals who make large expenditures in attempts to become elected to high public office.[60] (Indeed, to the extent that transfers spread the wealth more evenly, they may reduce concentration in the relevant sense.) Second, more focused regulation—such as limits on campaign contributions—seem more directly related to the problem. Nevertheless, if direct means are inadequate, there may be second-best grounds for resort to transfer taxation.[61]

Symbolic Effects of Giving and of Transfer Taxation

Another factor relevant to the social desirability of some policies concerns their symbolic effects. One reason symbolic effects may be relevant to social welfare is that individuals may have tastes for certain rules or regimes. (For example, they may derive satisfaction from knowing that the legal system will punish individuals who commit heinous crimes, independent of the tendency of such punishment to reduce crime.) Another possibility is that certain laws or policies may reinforce or undermine various social norms that regulate society. (For example, laws requiring people to clean up after their dogs may send or reinforce messages about proper behavior that tend to be influential independent of formal enforcement, such as by inducing guilt feelings and the fear of social disapprobation.)

Some of the controversy surrounding transfer taxation may involve these factors. Individuals may be envious of the rich (particularly those who live off inheritances) or may disapprove of their behavior (in general, or the particular act of spoiling their children), in which case heavy transfer taxation may seem appealing. On the other hand, transfer taxation may be viewed as a penalty on success—or, worse, on success combined with generosity toward one's children—in which case transfer taxation may be seen as undesirable because it is corrosive of social norms favoring hard work and caring for one's family.[62]

Regardless of the actual importance of these factors to social welfare, a good deal of the political rhetoric about estate and gift taxation does seem

60. McCaffery (1994).

61. One might suppose that direct means are politically infeasible, in part perhaps due to the political power of the wealthy. If this is the case, however, one might expect, as suggested in note 12, that they would similarly oppose aggressive transfer taxation designed to address the same problem indirectly.

62. With regard to the former, opposition to applying estate taxes to successful small businesses may be viewed in this light (and, of course, also in the light of special interest pleading).

to echo these themes. Relatedly, such factors may help to explain why estate and gift taxation is unpopular among individuals who are unlikely ever to have to pay the tax.

Additional Topics

A number of further considerations seem important in assessing estate and gift tax policy, some of which have received only limited attention in prior work. In this section, a brief sketch will be presented. More questions will be raised than answers offered, suggesting a number of avenues for further research.

Human Capital

Begin with two factual observations. First, human capital is undoubtedly a substantial majority of all wealth.[63] It constitutes virtually all of wealth for a large segment of the population and, especially at younger ages, the bulk of wealth for all but a small fraction of society.

Second, contributions to human capital represent a sizable fraction of all intergenerational transfers, broadly construed.[64] Much of human capital is obviously attributable to innate abilities, which may be described (not just metaphorically) as genetic inheritance. Many of the other leading contributors to human capital can also be traced to parents. Our environment—the atmosphere in our homes, the neighborhood in which we grow up, the public schools we attend—are all determined significantly by parental choices, which are often made with effects on children in mind. The time parents spend with children (imputed income, which is untaxed under income and consumption taxes) also is an important factor. In addition, there are direct expenditures on education (private elementary and secondary schools, college, postgraduate education) and contacts, business opportunities, and other benefits that flow from parents to their children. Even the efforts individuals exert to develop and make use of their human capital are shaped by genetic inheritance of various predispositions and by socialization that is determined largely by the aforementioned factors.

Interestingly, essentially none of this huge component of social wealth, much produced by various sorts of intergenerational transfers, is subject to estate and gift taxes, either existing or proposed. Most of these sources of

---

63. See, for example, Davies and Whalley (1991); Jorgenson and Fraumeni (1989).
64. On the contribution of families to children's human capital, see Taubman (1996).

human capital would be viewed as analogous to tax-free imputed income under an income tax or (in the case of genetic inheritance) simply ignored. Of course, the benefits of exemption from both income and transfer taxes (where applicable) is great. Even the most explicit of such transfers—tuition payments for postsecondary education—are exempt from transfer taxation in the United States. (It should be noted, however, that all such transfers are implicitly taxed under income and consumption taxes, to the extent that the human capital is productive and ultimately gives rise to income and consumption.)[65]

If it is optimal to eliminate estate and gift taxation (and not to tax bequests and gifts under income and consumption taxes), this state of affairs is unproblematic. If, however, significant transfer taxes (or subsidies) are optimal, it should be asked whether there is good reason for heavily taxing (or subsidizing) some types of transfers while exempting others.[66] Is the omission of human capital just an oversight by the tax system, among scholars, and in popular beliefs? Or is there some fundamental difference that justifies exemption for one set of transfers but not for the other?

As a benchmark, there would be seem to be a prima facie basis for assuming that transfers should be treated uniformly, for otherwise behavior would be distorted. Differential treatment would have to be justified by reference to the sorts of arguments developed in previous sections concerning the optimal tax treatment of transfers. To suggest one possible ground for a distinction, transfers of human capital may tend to create positive tax revenue externalities (because they result in greater earnings by the beneficiaries, to the benefit of the fisc on account of higher income and consumption tax revenues), whereas other transfers tend to produce a more typical income effect that depresses labor supply and thus generates a negative tax revenue externality.[67] From other perspectives, such as that favoring equal starting

65. If such income or consumption taxation is deemed sufficient, one must ask why analogous taxation of transfers of cash (or other financial or physical wealth) is deemed insufficient. That is, if earnings have already been taxed under an income tax, why is that not sufficient taxation if the subsequent income taxation of human capital transfers is deemed adequate? Likewise, under a consumption tax, if the ultimate taxation of consumption by donees of their earnings from transferred human capital is sufficient, why would the same level of taxation of other transfers not be enough?

66. Analogous points regarding income versus consumption taxation of human capital versus physical and financial capital are developed in Kaplow (1994, 1996a).

67. Other externalities might depend on whether gifts involve human capital. For example, envy of those who live lives of leisure may be greater than envy of individuals whose education or businesses are subsidized but who must work hard in order to reap the benefit. Gifts of human capital may also reduce socially undesirable behavior (notably, crime) more than in the case of financial transfers.

points, discussed previously, transfers of human capital may be the most problematic, whereas large receipts of financial wealth later in life may be less of a concern.

Other differences between the two types of transfers should be studied as well. Perhaps motives that typically underlie the creation or transferring of resources that contribute to human capital differ from those behind other transfers. This would suggest that taxation of the two different categories of transfers would have different behavioral and welfare effects. Whether the difference would favor more generous treatment of human capital transfers, as now exists, is an open question. In sum, human capital is simply too large a fraction of wealth and of intergenerational transfers to be ignored in serious study and analysis of estate and gift tax policy.

Inter Vivos Gifts versus Bequests

This chapter, like much work on estate and gift tax policy, has for the most part not carefully distinguished inter vivos gifts from bequests. To the extent that the issue is addressed in the literature, the most common view seems to be that the two types of giving, which are often close substitutes for both donors and donees, should be treated in a unified manner. The 1976 tax reform in the United States was designed to move in this direction, although significant gaps remain and are the subject of many reform proposals.[68]

Although the assumption that inter vivos gifts and bequests should be viewed symmetrically in tax policy analysis seems to be the right starting point, a number of differences between them exist. Inter vivos gifts, especially those given when donees are younger, may have different effects on donees. Early gifts may contribute to human capital; they may relax liquidity constraints, allowing donees to engage more freely in entrepreneurial activity; and so forth. Later gifts and bequests are less likely to have such effects. Those received mid-career may primarily have an income effect, depressing work effort. Those received during retirement may have no labor supply effect. On

---

68. Not all of the gaps and loopholes, however, favor inter vivos giving; transferring appreciated assets at death can have the advantage of saving capital gains taxes, due to the step-up of basis. Also, it should be noted that one of the more significant gaps, involving charitable transfers (addressed below), is not usually mentioned. There, even ignoring the estate and gift tax system, there is a large income tax benefit from inter vivos giving, namely, one gets a full income tax deduction for such gifts (up to certain limits that most individuals do not reach) but no such deduction for pure bequests.

the other hand, anticipation of such gifts and bequests may affect labor supply negatively and also should be expected to reduce savings.[69]

One should also consider donors. Perhaps earlier gifts (as noted above) may, on average, be given based on different motives than later gifts or bequests.[70] If so, this will bear on donors' behavior and their welfare. Because motives cannot be observed directly by the government, it might make sense to treat differently various types of behavior (such as inter vivos giving versus bequests) that may signal different underlying motives. It also seems relevant in this regard (as explored below) that donors' inter vivos gifts are substantially lower than optimizing behavior—taking into account the tax benefits of inter vivos giving—would seem to imply, which raises questions about whether their motivations are well explained by existing theories of transfer behavior.[71]

Of course, whatever conclusions one reaches in principle about the appropriate difference between optimal taxation of inter vivos gifts versus taxation of bequests, maintaining asymmetric rules will create planning opportunities. These will tend to reduce the effect of any difference in stated tax rates and also lead to additional expenditures of resources on tax planning.

Distinguishing among Different Donor-Donee Pairings; Taxation of the Family

Under estate and gift tax regimes, different donor-donee pairings are often taxed quite differently. In the present system in the United States, for example, transfers between spouses are completely exempt, certain forms of transfers to children (notably, support and education, as well as many in-kind transfers) are exempt, other transfers to children and most transfers to others

---

69. In considering effects on savings, even if they are relevant to policy (see the above discussion), one should be careful to keep track of donors and donees together. See the chapter by Gale and Perozek in this volume. The donee who is saving less may be matched by a donor who is saving more, later to make a gift from such savings. By contrast, suppose that the donee receives the gift earlier in life. Then the donor is not saving as much. On the other hand, the donee—assuming that the gift will be spent in the same periods as it would have been spent if it was received late in life—will be saving correspondingly more. Thus, it is not clear that the timing of gifts will directly affect net savings. When the timing and extent of transfers are uncertain, however, one would expect there to be an effect; most likely, early giving would reduce saving by donees more than would later giving with the same expected value. Also, if recipients are liquidity constrained, earlier gifts would tend to reduce net savings.

70. For example, purely accidental transfers (accidental bequests) would not emerge as inter vivos gifts. Also, some evidence suggests that the pattern of inter vivos giving (which favors poorer children) is more consistent with altruism than that of bequests (which tend to be divided equally). See, for example, Dunn and Phillips (1997).

71. See, for example, Poterba (2001).

(that is, other people, not charitable organizations) are taxed, and transfers to more distant generations are subject to an additional, generation-skipping transfer tax.

A natural presumption would seem to be that, whatever is the optimal differential taxation of transfers (versus expenditures on own-consumption), all donor-donee pairings should be treated in the same manner. Yet, there are reasons that may justify differences.[72] Notably, as discussed above, it may be that different levels of taxation (or subsidy) are optimal, depending on donors' motives. But, as noted in the preceding subsection, if different motives cannot be observed directly and, moreover, certain observable characteristics (such as the relationship between the donor and donee or the type of gift) are signals of different motivations, then different tax treatment may be appropriate. Further work must be undertaken, however, to determine the relationships, if any, between possible categories of donees and various transfer motives in order to determine which distinctions, if any, are welfare promoting.[73]

Finally, it is worth connecting the present discussion to the problem of the optimal tax treatment of different family configurations. The proper income tax (or consumption tax, or welfare program) treatment of different types of family units has proved contentious, and practices vary significantly among countries. The important point for present purposes is that a major defining feature of a family, from the perspective of the use of resources, is that there is substantial (even if incomplete) sharing of income. That is, there are significant transfers among household members, usually from earners to others (whether to spouses who earn less or do not provide market labor or to children). Related to the foregoing discussion, there arises the question of how, if at all, such transfers should be taxed, in principle.[74] The further suggestion here is that this question is intimately related to family unit issues under other tax systems, for what matters to particular families, with particular patterns of earnings, sharing, and expenditures, is the aggregate tax burden they bear, not how much of their tax obligation is denominated as arising under the in-

---

72. For reasons relating to the distribution of wealth, see Cremer and Pestieau (1988).

73. Another question concerns whether any tax or subsidy should be applied to donors, as is done under an estate and gift tax system, or to donees, as is done under inheritance or accessions taxes. This question becomes relevant when the tax or subsidy is not applied at a uniform rate but may depend on the totality of gifts given or gifts received (particularly when a single donor gives to multiple donees or a single donee receives gifts from multiple donors) or on donors' or donees' marginal income tax rates in a graduated income tax system.

74. Administrative considerations, such as the difficulties of untangling the sources and uses of funds within a household, may favor certain regimes, such as exemption of intra-household transfers.

come tax or under transfer taxes. Indeed, the method of taxing different family units can be interpreted as corresponding to different forms of presumptive taxation of transfers within the family.[75]

Charitable Gifts and Bequests

A significant (although minority) fraction of giving, inter vivos and at death, is to donees that are charitable institutions. Moreover, the United States estate and gift tax system, through an exemption for charitable gifts, provides a large implicit subsidy to such transfers in the case of wealthy individuals who would pay significant estate and gift taxes if they instead transferred such funds to individual donees.[76] (By contrast, there is no estate and gift tax preference for charitable transfers versus own-consumption, although there is an income tax preference for such transfers.)[77]

To analyze tax policy toward such transfers, it is useful to apply the analysis developed throughout this chapter, supplemented by consideration of the distinctive features of charities as recipients. Thus, in the model initially presented, one could decompose second-period expenditures on gifts, c_g, into two components, c_{gc} and c_{gi}, corresponding to gifts to charities and gifts to individuals, respectively; similarly, one could tax (or subsidize) each type of gift at its own rate, t_{gc} or t_{gi}. The analysis could then proceed in three steps.

First, as before, one would consider gifts as if they were simply another form of ordinary consumption and determine what, if any, differential taxation (versus expenditures on own-consumption in the second period) was optimal. Second, one would again examine the distinctive features of gifts, now as a whole (considering both gifts to charities and gifts to individuals). Observe, importantly, that most of the considerations examined in this chapter in the context of what were presumed to be gifts to individuals are applicable to gifts to charities as well. Thus, gifts to charities similarly involve a transfer of resources, which provides utility both to donors and to donees. In addition, the range of motives for giving explored earlier all seem potentially applicable to gifts to charities (with the possible exception of purely accidental bequests). Hence, arguments about the optimal taxation of trans-

75. For exploration of some aspects of the problem of income taxation of families, which takes account of the nature of intra-family transfers, see Kaplow (1996b).

76. See, for example, Auten, Clotfelter, and Schmalbeck (2000) and the chapter by Joulfaian in this volume.

77. As indicated in note 68, in examining the incentives under the current United States estate and gift tax regime to make inter vivos gifts rather than bequests, the charitable contribution deduction under the income tax—a significant preference favoring gifts rather than bequests—must be kept in mind.

fers that depend on different types of transfer motives seem presumptively applicable to charitable gifts (although the frequency of different types of motives may well differ between the two types of gifts).

These points are emphasized because it seems that, in tax policy analysis and debate, charitable giving is often treated as if it were an entirely separate subject from ordinary giving.[78] Yet, in many respects, charities can be viewed as representatives or conduits that serve as intermediaries between donors and ultimate recipients. For example, giving to an organization that provides shelter for homeless people is analogous to making many small gifts to homeless people; the organization may realize economies of scale, represent donors' paternalistic wishes, and so forth, but the ultimate beneficiaries are still the individuals whom the organization serves.[79]

There should, however, be a third step in the analysis, which asks what (if anything) is distinctive about gifts to charities, compared with gifts to individuals. (This is, of course, analogous to the second question, emphasized earlier, concerning what is distinctive about gifts in general, compared with expenditures on own-consumption.) The preceding point suggests that little may in fact be distinctive, but important differences still exist, at least on average, that may warrant differential treatment. In particular, gifts to charities often involve public goods. For example, it may be that only parents or close relatives care especially about a particular child, who even without the gift would get along well in life, whereas a large number of people may have a sympathetic interest in the plight of the poor.[80] Likewise, funding for the arts, medical research, or religious institutions may benefit many

78. This point is applicable not only to estate and gift taxation per se but also to income (or consumption) tax treatment of various types of gifts.

79. The argument is more indirect, although conceptually similar, for other types of charities. Thus, gifts to support medical research can be seen as gifts to individuals who might ultimately benefit from such research.

80. See Hochman and Rodgers (1969). Preferential tax treatment of charitable giving is often advocated on the ground that it is redistributive. In addition to the public goods argument made in the text, further redistribution generally is beneficial from the perspective of overall social welfare, assuming that one's social welfare function is sufficiently egalitarian. The problem of the optimal mix of redistributive taxation and subsidy to voluntary redistribution merits further study. There is the separate question of the extent to which gifts are indeed redistributive. As already noted, there is a sense in which most gifts to individuals are redistributive, and the same is probably true of gifts to charities. For example, among those who regularly attend the opera, it is probably true, on average, that the largest donations come from the richer patrons, to the benefit of all opera-goers. However, redistribution from rich opera supporters to average opera afficionados is not the sort of redistribution that most advocates of the present argument probably have in mind. And, one supposes, a significant fraction of charitable giving—to the arts, to educational institutions, to one's own religious institutions (such as a local church or synagogue)—involves the support of organizations that benefit individuals who have levels of income not that different from those of many donors.

others, beyond the donor's immediate family. Hence, there may well be reasons for preferring charitable giving over other giving or other forms of expenditure.

Nevertheless, it is not obvious that the existing scheme of tax preferences is optimally designed to serve this purpose. In particular, the level of subsidy under the estate and gift tax depends primarily on the level of one's giving to individuals (for that determines one's marginal tax rate). It does not depend on the nature of the organization and hence on the extent to which one's gift funds valued public goods that benefit a large number of individuals. Moreover, it should be clear that if it is optimal to subsidize charitable giving, it is hardly necessary to do it through the transfer tax system. If, for example, it turned out that transfer taxation of ordinary gifts was not optimal but subsidization of charitable gifts was, one could simply operate a direct subsidy to charitable giving, such as through matching grants.

The Possibility That Transfers Are Not the Result of Maximizing Behavior by Donors

Not all economic behavior is accurately described as the product of the pure maximizing behavior that is stipulated in standard economic models. In many settings, departures from rationality may be insignificant or may have little effect in the aggregate. It is hardly obvious, however, that the same can be said in the present context. First, it is well known that a substantial portion of donors who will be subject to transfer taxation fail—by a wide margin—to take full advantage of inter vivos giving opportunities that would reduce their tax burden.[81] Moreover, although some of this behavior can be explained on rational grounds, the evidence seems to suggest that a good deal of it cannot (or at least not in a straightforward manner that would be consistent with the standard models of transfer behavior). Second, it is often suggested that many donors are uneasy about contemplating their own death and that this unease may affect their transfer behavior. This sort of consideration may help to explain the difficulty of reconciling the empirical evidence on transfer behavior with any of the transfer motives that have seemed most plausible to researchers. Hence, this aspect of donors' behavior deserves further study.

Pending the outcome of such work, it is worth contemplating briefly the possible implications of nonmaximizing behavior—in particular, of the sort often postulated in the present setting—for transfer tax policy. Some have suggested that the presence of such behavior strengthens the case for high estate

81. See, for example, Poterba (2001).

taxation, for if individuals do not think about what happens after death, there will be no incentive effects (on labor supply, savings, and giving) of such a tax. Of course, the extent to which this is true is an empirical question, and the simple version of the argument is unlikely to be substantially true, as evidenced by the large expenditures on estate tax planning and avoidance. Moreover, it does not follow from individuals' resistance to planning—or to making early transfers—that their behavior will be unaffected. If their bequests are not truly accidental (in the sense discussed above), it is still possible that they adjust their labor supply, savings, and giving in the light of the anticipated tax burden. And, in any event, if they do receive utility from the contemplation of their children's enjoyment of funds that are transferred and they are aware of any tax, it will have the effect of reducing the well-being of donors and donees even if donors' giving behavior does not react much to the tax.

A separate behavioral issue is that individuals may behave myopically, greatly discounting the future. This topic has received attention recently in many contexts, including the analysis of savings behavior.[82] From this perspective, it might seem that taxes in the future, including estate taxes (and gift taxes, which may be incurred long after income is earned and has been saved) would have less of an effect on behavior.[83] (A more dramatic implication might be that repeal of the income tax and payroll tax, substituting consumption taxes, would greatly reduce labor supply distortions because much consumption—notably, retirement spending—is delayed until long after the time that the money is earned.) It should also be noted that a given behavioral response to taxation will be more distortionary if, for example, due to individuals' failure to behave rationally, their decisions concerning earning, saving, and giving are already distorted in the same direction.

Whatever the precise nature of any departures from maximizing activity in the present context, it should be clear that they may upset a wide range of the arguments presented in this chapter. And, in particular, presumptions such as one that inter vivos giving and bequests should be taxed neutrally may be weakened significantly. For example, taking the simple and extreme case in which some individuals are rational maximizers and some do not think about their bequests or estate taxes at all, it may be optimal to employ high (even confiscatory) estate taxes, allowing for easy avoidance through

82. See, for example, Laibson, Repetto, and Tobacman (1998).

83. Whether this is true will depend on the particular model. (To illustrate a different possibility, suppose that individuals in their high-earnings and savings years are well aware that there is a steep estate tax, but do not engage in tax planning until their later years, at which time they learn that they can avoid much of the tax; then, their behavior in earlier years may implicitly be affected as if the effective estate tax rate were higher than it actually is.)

inter vivos gifts.[84] The only taxes collected would be on individuals whose behavior and utility is unaffected, whereas for the group on whom it might be inefficient to impose the tax, the tax would be fully avoided, and at little cost. One of the main purposes of considering such an example and exploring the topic more generally is to highlight the potential benefit of further investigation of this dimension of transfer behavior.

Political Economy of Estate and Gift Taxation

The present inquiry is concerned with offering a normative and analytical framework to assess estate and gift tax policy, in particular, to determine what sort of policy best advances social welfare, understood as some aggregate of the well-being of individuals in a society. A rather different question concerns what sort of estate and gift tax regime would be adopted under the assumption that the legislative process is largely controlled by self-interested political actors. The political economy of estate and gift taxation, however, is a subject outside the scope of this chapter.

Nevertheless, some of the analysis presented here may bear on transfer tax politics. First, the analysis clarifies what the effects of transfer taxation are likely to be under various assumptions. Second, it has been suggested that transfer taxes, in the context of a larger tax system, may have a different role to play regarding redistribution, raising revenue, influencing savings, and other matters from what is commonly understood. It is possible that an improvement in the understanding of these interactions would influence which groups favor which reforms. Finally, the foregoing may shed some light on popular views about estate and gift taxation, which are sometimes seen as a bit of a mystery since many who are probably beneficiaries of such taxation seem to favor its reduction or repeal. (See, for example, the discussion of the symbolic effects of transfer tax policy.)

Conclusion

The two main purposes of this chapter have been to relate the many criteria that have been used to assess estate and gift taxes explicitly to the standard

---

84. Or, to consider another example, if donors' irrationality consisted in thinking only about the taxes that they themselves paid and not about the net gift received by donees, then switching from an estate and gift tax system to an inheritance or accessions tax regime, wherein the tax is instead imposed on the donee, would avoid distortions of donors' behavior.

welfare economic framework and to integrate analysis of transfer taxation with that of the income tax. When transfers are viewed simply as one of many forms of expenditures that donors may make, many insights into the optimal taxation of giving can be obtained. This analysis, however, had to be modified in important ways to take into account the distinctive nature of gifts and bequests, namely, that expenditures on transfers tend to raise donors' utility by transferring resources rather than by using them up, as in the case of ordinary consumption. On one hand, this suggests that gifts often involve positive externalities, because donees benefit along with donors when the latter choose to spend on gifts rather than on own-consumption. On the other hand, the receipt of gifts may well have an effect on donees' labor supply, reducing it in the standard case, resulting in a negative tax revenue externality. It was seen, however, that this analysis is directly applicable only to pure gifts of certain types; other transfer motives are associated with different welfare consequences.

Several of the traditional criteria for assessing transfer taxation, as well as standard arguments that appeal to them, were seen to be incomplete or even misleading once the explicit welfare economic analysis, taking into account the income tax, was performed. Other familiar concerns are indeed valid but can be better illuminated if one makes use of the framework that has been developed by economists to analyze other aspects of the tax system.

The present investigation is incomplete: it offers a preliminary sketch of issues rather than a thorough, rigorous analysis, it does not provide the empirical evidence necessary to resolve important questions, and it only suggests how one might incorporate additional dimensions, such as the treatment of human capital, different giving patterns and family configurations, and transfers to charitable organizations. Much research remains to be done, and it is hoped that this chapter is helpful in organizing part of the necessary agenda.

COMMENT BY
Pierre Pestieau

It should not be too difficult to get a majority of economists to agree on the desirability of death taxation.[85] If one were able to convince them that all existing bequests were accidental, their size increasing with the lifetime income of heirs, they would be in favor of a very high rate of taxation. If all bequests were voluntary and compensatory (with unlucky kids inheriting more than lucky ones), however, and if the actual level of saving were too low, relative to some socially optimal one, they would be in favor of a very low rate of taxation.

But we do not find that kind of evidence in reality, In other words, the existing empirical studies indicate that no one type of bequest prevails, and furthermore that quite often bequeathing is influenced by a mix of motives.

In this comment on Louis Kaplow's chapter, which I agree with in the main, I would like to raise several questions and grapple with a few puzzling phenomena on the topic of death taxation. I realize that, like many others who have worked on this subject, I raise more questions than I answer and only partially clear up some of the enigmas. My viewpoint throughout is a Continental European one.

Two main differences between Continental Europe and the United States are worth emphasizing. First, in Europe, compliance is a serious issue. Capital mobility makes it easy to hide a number of assets, mostly financial, from the tax authorities. Second, in many European countries death taxation is not imposed on the estate of the deceased but on the share received by the heirs, this share being equal for all.

Especially puzzling is that in countries in which equal division is not imposed, it turns out to be a general practice. Similarly, in spite of a wide heterogeneity in tax systems, most countries in the OECD draw less than 1 percent of total tax revenue from their death taxes. Finally, one observes the overwhelming importance of bequests relative to inter vivos gifts, even when inheritance seems to be motivated by unrestricted altruism.

85. CREPP, Université de Liège, CORE, Delta, and CEPR. This comment is a spin-off of recent surveys: Arrondel and others (1997); Masson and Pestieau (1997); Pestieau (2000). I will use the term *death taxation* to cover either inheritance or estate taxation and not inter vivos gifts.

Table 4-1. *Share of Gift and Estate Taxation in Total Revenue, 1997*
Percent

Germany	0.30	Italy	0.17
Spain	0.52	Japan	1.70
United States	1.10	Netherlands	0.67
France	.89	United Kingdom	0.62

Source: OECD (1998).

The Best and the Worst Tax

For Aesop, the writer of fables, tongue was at the same time the best and the worst dish, depending on the way it was cooked. The same can be said of death taxation. For many political scientists, social philosophers, and economists, estate taxation is to be viewed as an ideal tax, the best way to ensure some equality of opportunity. Yet reality is deceptive. The fact is that the yield from estate and gift taxation is uniformly low, as shown in table 4-1 for a sample of OECD countries.

This poor result seems to be independent of the type of death taxation, inheritance, or estate duty, as well as of the progressivity of the rates and of the techniques used to skip it through evasion or avoidance. It seems that in the balance between avoidance and evasion, Americans would favor the first and Europeans the second. This contrast raises an interesting question. Given that the death tax yield is about the same in the United States and France, is it better to elude its burden by giving away money to foundations, or to invest it in tax havens such as Luxembourg or Switzerland?

Just as an illustration, Denis Kessler and Pierre Pestieau estimated that the effective inheritance and gift tax rate were equal to 6.25 percent in France, whereas standard statutory tax rates are around 40 percent.[86]

Mixed Political Support

Poor compliance with the death tax is not uniform across households. Sometimes families bear the full burden of death taxation for a number of reasons, including (why not?) citizenship. Two of the most cited reasons for full compliance are sudden death and conflict within the family. In the first case there is no time for avoidance; in the second, it is too risky to do anything illegal

---

86. Kessler and Pestieau (1991).

or even questionable, as this could be exploited by one family member against the others. As a result, the burden of death taxation is unevenly distributed across families of similar wealth. In other words, it is fundamentally unfair as it violates basic horizontal equity. These two arguments: poor yield and horizontal inequity, explain why some people (even on the left) advocate abandoning death taxation.

A further argument makes death taxation unpopular among low-income households: the hope or rather the fantasy that anyone can become a millionaire. Note in that respect that the threshold below which there is no taxation is quite a bit lower in most European countries than in the United States, and thus that the death tax in Europe concerns a rather wide share of the population. As a consequence, it is increasingly difficult, even for social democratic governments, to make death taxation more effective. In fact, if there is to be a reform in that direction, it is more likely to come from conservative governments along the lines of the "Nixon goes to China" principle.

Meade's Report

I totally agree with Kaplow's idea that the death tax cannot be separated from a general discussion of the whole tax system. In that respect, one might note that estate taxation is much less flexible than inheritance taxation (the tax burdens varying with the number of heirs and their relationship to the deceased) or the accession tax (the tax burden varying with the lifetime income of heirs). I will come back to this point.

The spirit of Meade's report and also of the Blueprints was that the best form of taxation was a progressive expenditure tax coupled with an effective death taxation.[87] This would dominate the then-prevailing income tax, combined with an already deceptive estate tax. More than two decades later, this approach is still theoretically correct. Following Anthony B. Atkinson and Joseph S. Stiglitz, we know that with weak separability between consumption and labor, and with observability of bequests, one should have a progressive tax on earnings (which is equivalent to an expenditure tax) and a high and progressive tax on bequests.[88]

In reality, however, if the amount of an inheritance cannot be ascertained and thus effectively taxed, this recommendation is no longer valid. Indeed, one can show that, besides a progressive tax on earnings, a flat rate capital income tax can be desirable as an indirect way of taxing inherited wealth.[89]

87. Meade (1978); Bradford (1977).
88. Atkinson and Stiglitz (1980).
89. Cremer, Pestieau, and Rochet (2000); Boadway, Marchand, and Pestieau (2000).

Mixed Bequest Motives

The design of death taxation is closely related to the bequest motive. We now have a good understanding of what the optimal structure should be given the bequest motive. Furthermore, the relative importance of each type of bequest is an empirical question for which new evidence continuously occurs. There is, however, a serious problem; the same evidence seems to point to the co-existence of different motives. Typically, a number of bequests can be at the same time accidental and altruistic. Parents may have very little motive for altruism, but faced with inefficient and costly annuity markets, they may opt for traditional saving that in case of premature death results in bequests that are both altruistic and accidental.[90] Designing death taxation with mixed motives is theoretically difficult.

Furthermore, consider a society of individuals with different bequest motives, some altruistic and some others nonaltruistic. In such a society, if altruists leave positive bequests, one can show that the traditional Ricardian equivalence holds and also that a death tax can be Pareto worsening. This result holds even if there is only a small minority of altruists.[91]

Washing Out Utilities

When one deals with altruism in an intertemporal framework, one cannot avoid the philosophical issues about the welfare criterion used to assess the desirable death tax. If each parent derives utility from his own consumption and also from altruism, how do we treat altruism when utilities are aggregated over time? There are two views: one paternalistic, the other individualistic. According to the latter, the social planner does not intervene in the way that individuals evaluate their own behavior. Then, if individuals derive some utility from the level of welfare of their children, or from the mere act of giving, adding up individual utilities over time, even with a discount factor, yields a strong bias toward the future. For example, children of the first generation are counted twice: directly in the planner's welfare function and indirectly through their parents' utility. Basically, this outcome may lead to the encouragement of capital accumulation even beyond the golden rule benchmark.

An alternative assumption consists of *washing out* individuals' utilities from their altruistic component. In so doing, one avoids the double counting that might generate an overaccumulation. However, such overaccumu-

90. Friedman and Warshawsky (1990)
91. Michel and Pestieau (1998); Laitner (forthcoming).

lation of capital results from the fact that people like to give and is not because of missing markets. Admittedly, the case for washing out utilities is stronger with pure altruism than with what I call "warm glow" giving. With pure altruism, the social planner chooses a Pareto optimal solution, which is not the case when he treats the joy of giving as a negative externality. In that case, the optimal solution that can be achieved with a death tax is definitively Pareto inefficient.

My intention in raising this point is not to argue in favor of one viewpoint or the other but to illustrate the complexity of an appropriate policy objective when bequests are motivated by altruism. To illustrate this point, take the utility function used in Kaplow's chapter for warm glow gifts:

$$U_t = u(c_t, \ell_t) + \beta v(c_{gt+1}),$$

where t denotes the period and the generation. Using Kaplow's notation, $u(\cdot)$, $v(\cdot)$ are utility functions; c, own consumption; ℓ, labor supply; and c_g, the amount of bequest.

If one takes as social objective the discounted sum of U_t

$$\sum_t \gamma^t U_t$$

where $\gamma \leq 1$ is a discount factor, the social optimum is likely to result in overaccumulation (relative to the golden rule). In a second-best setting with death taxation, one should then have a subsidy on bequests. On the contrary, this would not occur with an objective function:

$$\sum_t \gamma^t u(c_t, \ell_t),$$

from which the altruistic component $v(c_{gt+1})$ has been removed.[92]

Two Contrasting Views

One way to contrast the two alternative approaches, the Anglo-Saxon and the Continental one, toward taxation and regulation of bequests is to focus on their respective view of family and state.[93] In the Continental (Napoleonic) view, the government makes good decisions, particularly regarding families

---

92. Michel and Pestieau (2000).
93. This is a summary of Pestieau (2000).

of different incomes; families are suspected of biases in the way they allocate resources among their children. As a consequence, equal sharing among children is mandatory; the tax base is the amount received by each heir, and the tax rate is related to consanguinity (for example, higher for a nephew than for a son).

According to the Anglo-Saxon view, parents make unbiased bequests and adjust them to the needs of each heir. Death taxation is therefore an estate tax, with its rate independent of the number of heirs and degree of consanguinity. With an estate tax, parents can disinherit their children or at least devote an important share of it to a charity, which is not possible in many European countries for households with children.

The issue of death taxation cannot be reduced to just designing a tax schedule; it also includes nontax regulations as shown by the following views:

	Anglo-Saxon	Continental
Freedom to bequeath	Free will	Equal sharing among children
Tax base	Aggregate estate	Share of estate
Tax rate	Neutral	Consanguinity-related

These views are part of a nation's culture but can also be explained by its history. For example, in England equal division of estate was made mandatory at time when there were a lot of remarriages together with mistreatment of stepchildren by stepparents.[94]

There is an interesting amount of evidence indicating that in a country with the freedom to divide one's estate, a large majority of parents choose equal sharing. Compensatory bequests seem to be rather rare even when there is evidence of income difference among children, whereas compensatory inter vivos gifts are rather frequent. One explanation seems to be that parents can control differences in gifts while they are alive and wish to avoid the risk of family disputes after their death.

Inter Vivos Gifts versus Bequests

One of the enigmas of inheritance is that even though a large fraction of transmitted wealth appears to be motivated by some kind of altruism, wealth

---

94. This has been labeled the *Cinderella effect*. See Brenner (1985); Bremo (1985); Pestieau (2000).

is usually bequeathed at death, namely, when the donees are around fifty, and not earlier in their lifetime when the gifts would be inter vivos. Donees who receive gifts while young tend to treat the gifts differently. Either they use them to relax their liquidity constraints, thus contributing to more consumption and sustaining aggregate demand. Or they invest them in a more aggressive way than they would if they receive the gifts at a later age.

For these reasons a number of governments have been trying to encourage gifts instead of bequests. Often gifts are tax exempt below a certain level or at least subject to lower tax rates than bequests. Undisclosed gifts are also used as a key instrument of death tax evasion. Yet, as already said, most altruistic transfers seem to occur at death.

A standard line of explanation for such a phenomenon is the wish of parents to keep control of their money or their children or both. Even though altruistic, they want to make sure that their children will be caring of them. Another reason might be that parents want to wait for more information about the real needs of their children. Whatever the reasons, it is an awkward situation for aging heirs who would have welcomed financial help from their parents at an earlier stage of their life.

Conclusion

What can one conclude? In all European Union countries, death taxation offers a poor yield and is widely unfair. Yet a majority of voters favor keeping it for symbolic reasons that pertain to an ideal of equal opportunity for all and a desire to make sure the wealthy pay their due.

If what we want is to tax wealth as effectively as possible in order to get some revenue and achieve some redistribution, conceivably, an annual wealth tax or a withholding capital income tax will prevail over a tax at death. In any case what is needed in the EU, and possibly in the OECD area, is some capital tax harmonization and information exchange on capital flow. As long as this objective is not achieved, the tax system in general and death taxation in particular will appear to a large number of taxpayers as unfair, which indicates the lack of a real political will among European governments to change things.

References

Aaron, Henry J., and Alicia H. Munnell. 1992. "Reassessing the Role for Wealth Transfer Taxes." *National Tax Journal* 45 (June): 119–43.

Andreoni, James. 1990. "Impure Altruism and Donations to Public Goods: A Theory of Warm-Glow Giving?" *Economic Journal* 100 (June): 464–77.

Arrondel, Luc, Andre Masson, and Pierre Pestieau. 1997. "Bequests and Inheritance: Empirical Issues and French-U.S. Comparison." In *Is Inheritance Legitimate? Ethical and Economic Aspects of Wealth Transfers*, edited by G. Erreygers and T. Vandevelde, 89–125. Berlin: Springer-Verlag.

Atkinson, A. B. 1971. "Capital Taxes, the Redistribution of Wealth and Individual Savings." *Review of Economic Studies* 38 (April): 209–27.

Atkinson, A. B., and Joseph E. Stiglitz. 1976. "The Design of Tax Structure: Direct versus Indirect Taxation." *Journal of Public Economics* 6 (July–August): 55–75.

———. 1980. *Lectures on Public Economics.* London: McGraw-Hill.

Auten, Gerald E., Charles T. Clotfelter, and Richard L. Schmalbeck. 2000. "Taxes and Philanthropy among the Wealthy." In *Does Atlas Shrug? The Economic Consequences of Taxing the Rich*, edited by Joel Slemrod, 392–426. Russell Sage Foundation and Harvard University Press.

Bernheim, B. Douglas. 1987. "Does the Estate Tax Raise Revenue?" In *Tax Policy and the Economy*, edited by Lawrence H. Summers, 113–38. MIT Press.

Bernheim, B. Douglas, Andrei Shleifer, and Lawrence H. Summers. 1985. "The Strategic Bequest Motive." *Journal of Political Economy* 93 (December): 1045–76.

Bevan, D. L., and Joseph E. Stiglitz. 1979. "Intergenerational Transfers and Inequality." *Greek Economic Review* 1 (August): 8–26.

Blanchflower, David G., and Andrew J. Oswald. 1998. "What Makes an Entrepreneur?" *Journal of Labor Economics* 16 (January): 26–60.

Bradford, David F. 1977. *Blueprint for Basic Tax Reform.* Department of the Treasury.

———. 1986. *Untangling the Income Tax.* Harvard University Press.

Bremo, Gabrielle. 1985. "Why Did Inheritance Laws Change?" *International Review of Law and Economics* 5 (June): 91–106.

Brennan, Geoffrey. 1978. "Death and Taxes: An Attack on the Orthodoxy." *Public Finance* 33 (July): 201–24.

Brenner, Reuven. 1985. *Betting on Ideas.* University of Chicago Press.

Buchanan, James M. 1983. "Rent Seeking, Noncompensated Transfers, and Laws of Succession." *Journal of Law and Economics* 26 (April): 71–85.

Cooper, George. 1979. *A Voluntary Tax? New Perspectives on Sophisticated Tax Avoidance.* Brookings.

Cox, Donald. 1987. "Motives for Private Income Transfers." *Journal of Political Economy* 95 (June): 508–46.

———. 1990. "Intergenerational Transfers and Liquidity Constraints." *Quarterly Journal of Economics* 105 (February): 187–217.

Cremer, Helmuth, and Pierre Pestieau. 1988. "A Case for Differential Inheritance Taxation." *Annales d'Économie et de Statistique* 9, special issue (January–March): 167–82.

Cremer, Helmuth, Pierre Pestieau, and Jean-Charles Rochet. Forthcoming. "Capital Income Taxation When Inherited Wealth Is Not Observable." *International Economic Review.*

Davies, James B. 1982. "The Relative Impact of Inheritance and Other Factors on Economic Inequality." *Quarterly Journal of Economics* 97 (August): 471–98.

———. 1996. "Explaining Intergenerational Transfers." In *Household and Family Economics*, edited by Paul L. Menchik, 47–82. Boston: Kluwer Academic Publishers.

Davies, James B., and John Whalley. 1991. "Taxes and Capital Formation: How Important Is Human Capital?" In *National Saving and Economic Performance*, edited by B. Douglas Bernheim and John B. Shoven, 163–200. University of Chicago Press.

Dunn, Thomas A., and John W. Phillips. 1997. "The Timing and Division of Parental Transfers to Children." *Economics Letters* 54 (February): 135–37.

Erreygers, Guido, and Toon Vandevelde, eds. 1997. *Is Inheritance Legitimate? Ethical and Economic Aspects of Wealth Transfers.* Berlin: Springer-Verlag.

Friedman, Benjamin M., and M. J. Warshawsky. 1990. "The Cost of Annuities: Implications for Saving Behavior and Bequests." *Quarterly Journal of Economics* 105 (February):135–54.

Graetz, Michael J. 1983. "To Praise the Estate Tax, Not to Bury It." *Yale Law Journal* 93 (December): 259–86.

Hochman, Harold M., and James D. Rodgers. 1969. "Pareto Optimal Redistribution." *American Economic Review* 59 (September): 542–57.

Holtz-Eakin, Douglas, David Joulfaian, and Harvey S. Rosen. 1993. "The Carnegie Conjecture: Some Empirical Evidence." *Quarterly Journal of Economics* 108 (May): 413–35.

———. 1994a. "Entrepreneurial Decisions and Liquidity Constraints." *Rand Journal of Economics* 25 (Summer): 334–47.

———. 1994b. "Sticking It Out: Entrepreneurial Survival and Liquidity Constraints." *Journal of Political Economy* 102 (February): 53–75.

Hylland, Aanund, and Richard Zeckhauser. 1979. "Distributional Objectives Should Affect Taxes but Not Program Choice or Design." *Scandinavian Journal of Economics* 81: 264–84.

Imbens, Guido W., Donald B. Rubin, and Bruce Sacerdote. 1999. "Estimating the Effect of Unearned Income on Labor Supply, Earnings, Savings, and Consumption: Evidence from a Survey of Lottery Players." Working Paper 7001. Cambridge, Mass.: National Bureau of Economic Research (March).

Johnson, Craig E., John Diamond, and George R. Zodrow. 1997. "Bequests, Saving, and Taxation." In *1996 Proceedings of the National Tax Association* 37–45. Washington: National Tax Association–Tax Institute of America.

Joint Economic Committee. 1999. *The Economics of the Estate Tax.* Government Printing Office.

Jorgenson, Dale W., and Barbara M. Fraumeni. 1989. "The Accumulation of Human and Nonhuman Capital, 1948–84." In *The Measurement of Saving, Investment, and Wealth*, edited by Robert E. Lipsey and Helen Stone Tice, 227-82. University of Chicago Press.

Joulfaian, David, and Mark O. Wilhelm. 1994. "Inheritance and Labor Supply." *Journal of Human Resources* 29 (Fall): 1205–34.

Kaplow, Louis. 1994. "Human Capital under an Ideal Income Tax." *Virginia Law Review* 80 (October): 1477–514.

———. 1995. "A Note on Subsidizing Gifts." *Journal of Public Economics* 58 (November): 469–77.

———. 1996a. "On the Divergence between 'Ideal' and Conventional Income-Tax Treatment of Human Capital." *American Economic Association Papers and Proceedings* 86 (May): 347–52.

———. 1996b. "Optimal Distribution and the Family." *Scandinavian Journal of Economics* 98 (March): 75–92.

———. 1996c. "The Optimal Supply of Public Goods and the Distortionary Cost of Taxation." *National Tax Journal* 49 (December): 513–33.

———. 1998. "Tax Policy and Gifts." *American Economic Association, Papers and Proceedings* 88 (May): 283–88.

Kaplow, Louis, and Steven Shavell. 2001. "Any Non-Individualistic Social Welfare Function Violates the Pareto Principle." *Journal of Political Economy* 109 (April): 281–86.

Kessler, Denis, and Pierre Pestieau. 1991. "The Taxation of Wealth in the EEC." *Canadian Public Policy* 17 (September): 309–21.

Kotlikoff, Laurence J., and Avia Spivak. 1981. "The Family as an Incomplete Annuities Market." *Journal of Political Economy* 89 (April): 372–91.

Laibson, David I., Andrea Repetto, and Jeremy Tobacman. 1998. "Self-Control and Saving for Retirement." *Brookings Papers on Economic Activity 1:1998:* 91–172.

Laitner, J. Forthcoming. "Secular Changes in Wealth Inequality and Inheritance." *Economic Journal.*

Lucas, Robert E., Jr., and Oded Stark. 1985. "Motivations to Remit: Evidence from Botswana." *Journal of Political Economy* 93 (October): 901–18.

Masson, André, and Pierre Pestieau. 1997. "Bequest Motives and Models of Inheritance: A Survey of the Literature." In *Is Inheritance Legitimate? Ethical and Economic Aspects of Wealth Transfers,* edited by Guido Erreygers and Toon Vandevelde, 54–88. Berlin: Springer-Verlag.

McCaffery, Edward J. 1994. "The Uneasy Case for Wealth Transfer Taxation." *Yale Law Journal* 104 (November): 283–365.

Meade, J. E. 1978. *The Structure and Reform of Direct Taxation.* Report of a Committee Chaired by J. E. Meade. London: Allen and Unwin.

Michel, Philippe, and Pierre Pestieau. 1998. "Fiscal Policy in a Growth Model with Both Altruistic and Nonaltruistic Agents." *Southern Economic Journal* 64 (January): 682–97.

———. 2000. "Fiscal Policy in a Growth Model with Bequest-as-Consumption." University of Liège.

Munnell, Alicia H. 1988. "Wealth Transfer Taxation: The Relative Role for Estate and Income Taxes." *New England Economic Review* (November): 3–28.

Ng, Yew-Kwang. 1984. "Quasi-Pareto Social Improvements." *American Economic Review* 74 (December): 1033–50.

Organization for Economic Cooperation and Development. 1998. *Revenue Statistics of OECD Member Countries.* Paris.

Pestieau, Pierre. 2000. "Gifts, Wills, and Inheritance Law." In *Encyclopedia of Law and Economics,* edited by B. Buckaert and G. De Geest, 888–906, vol. 3. Aldershot, UK: Edward Elgar.

Poterba, James. 2001. "Estate and Gift Taxes and Incentives for *Inter Vivos* Giving in the United States." *Journal of Public Economics* 79, special issue (January): 237–64.

Repetti, James. 2000. "The Case for the Estate and Gift Tax." *Tax Notes* (March 13): 1493–510.

Shavell, Steven. 1981. "A Note on Efficiency vs. Distributional Equity in Legal Rulemaking: Should Distributional Equity Matter Given Optimal Income Taxation?" *American Economic Review, Papers and Proceedings* 71 (May): 414–18.

Simons, Henry C. 1938. *Personal Income Taxation.* University of Chicago Press.

Slemrod, Joel, and Shlomo Yitzhaki. 2000. "Integrating Expenditure and Tax Decisions: The Marginal Cost of Funds and the Marginal Benefit of Projects." Unpublished.

Stark, Oded. 1995. *Altruism and Beyond: An Economic Analysis of Transfers and Exchanges within Families and Groups.* Cambridge University Press.

Stiglitz, Joseph E. 1978. "Notes on Estate Taxes, Redistribution, and the Concept of Balanced Growth Path Incidence." *Journal of Political Economy* 86 (April, pt. 2): S137–50.

———. 1987. "Pareto Efficient and Optimal Taxation in the New New Welfare Economics." In *Handbook of Public Economics*, vol. 2, edited by Alan J. Auerbach and Martin Feldstein. Amsterdam: North-Holland.

Tax Law Review. 1996. "Colloquium on Wealth Transfer Taxation." 51 (Spring): 357–637.

———. 2000. "Symposium on Wealth Taxes." 53 (Spring and Summer): 257–498, 499–695.

Taubman, Paul. 1996. "The Role of the Family in the Formation of Offsprings' Earnings and Income Capacity." In *Household and Family Economics*, edited by Paul L. Menchik. Boston: Kluwer Academic Publishers.

WILLIAM G. GALE
MARIA G. PEROZEK

5) Do Estate Taxes Reduce Saving?

T HE ESTATE TAX is one of the most controversial components of tax policy, but its economic effects are not yet well
understood. For example, there appears to be a general presumption that
higher estate taxes will reduce saving and aggregate capital accumulation.[1] If
correct, this presumption implies that estate taxation reduces the long-run
growth prospects for the economy. Reductions in saving could also affect the
distribution of income by reducing the capital-labor ratio, thereby raising the
return to capital and reducing wages. There are a number of reasons to suspect that estate taxes have an important effect on saving. Most important, the
estate tax places a one-time levy on wealth that is not bequeathed to a spouse
or given to charity. There is at least a *prima facie* case that a wealth tax reduces
saving. Because it is a tax on capital value and because of interactions with
other taxes, the estate tax can impose very high effective tax rates on capital

We have received helpful comments from Leonard Burman, Donald Cox, Eric Engen, Roger
Gordon, Douglas Holtz-Eakin, Michael Kremer, Gilbert Metcalf, Lise Vesterlund, and participants
at the AEA meetings, Brookings, Northwestern, the University of Michigan, the University of North
Carolina. Gale gratefully acknowledges financial support from the National Institute on Aging
through grant number AG11836. The opinions expressed are our own and should not be ascribed
to Brookings or to the Board of Governors of the Federal Reserve System.
    1. Kotlikoff and Summers (1981); McCaffery (1994); Stiglitz (1978).

income. In addition, bequests and inter vivos transfers plausibly account for half or more of all wealth accumulation in the United States and other countries. Finally, although the estate tax only directly affects the very wealthiest households, large inter vivos transfers, bequests, and wealth are also concentrated among wealthy households.[2] However, despite these concerns, despite a massive literature on the magnitude, patterns, and motives for intergenerational transfers, and despite an even larger literature on the effects of capital income taxation on saving and capital formation, there has been little formal analysis of how the estate tax affects saving and capital accumulation.

To investigate these issues, this chapter develops a simple model of a parent and child making life-cycle consumption and saving choices. We use the model to examine how alternative motives for giving transfers influence the effect of the estate tax on the parent's and child's saving. We also consider how different uses of the estate tax revenues affect the results.

Several key findings emerge. First, the effects of estate taxes on saving depend on the donor's motives for bequests and for wealth accumulation. This suggests important links between transfer motives and the impact of estate taxes that might be exploited in future theoretical and empirical work. Second, the response of the potential transfer recipient can materially affect the overall impact of estate taxes on saving. Thus, analysis of the estate tax should consider the saving behavior of both the donor and the recipient. Third, under every transfer motive examined, estate taxes can actually raise net saving by the donor and recipient. This raises doubts about the robustness of what appears to be conventional wisdom that estate taxes always reduce wealth. Fourth, recycling estate tax revenues generally reduces the effect of the tax on saving but does not necessarily make the effect negative.

We begin by describing the estate tax, reviewing evidence on transfer motives, and examining previous work on estate taxes, inheritances, and saving. The next section presents a general model of intergenerational transfers and estate taxes, featuring a parent and child that overlap for two periods. The subsequent sections examine estate taxes and saving in a variety of special cases of the general model that generate different transfer motives and incorporate different uses of the revenues. The last section discusses some interpretations and extensions of the research.

2. Shoven and Wise (1996); Poterba (2000); (Gale 2000); Gale and Scholz (1994); Kotlikoff and Summers (1981); Masson and Pestieau (1997); Modigliani (1988); Aaron and Munnell (1992); Carroll (2000); Gale and Scholz (1994); Menchik and David (1983).

Background

The tax base for the unified estate and gift tax is the sum of the value of net wealth held at the time of the taxpayer's death and the value of gifts made (above a $10,000 per recipient per year exemption) while the decedent was alive.[3] Deductions are provided for bequests to a surviving spouse, contributions to charitable organizations, and expenses relating to administration of the estate and the decedent's funeral.

Before 1997, a lifetime tax credit against estate and gift taxes effectively eliminated taxes on the first $600,000 of the estate. The Taxpayer Relief Act of 1997 raised the credit so that the effective exemption will rise to $1 million by 2006 (and also introduced special adjustments for owners of family farms and small businesses). The tax-inclusive tax rate that applies to the first dollar of taxable estate is 37 percent.[4] This statutory rate rises to 55 percent for taxable estates in excess of $3 million, and the effective rate rises to 60 percent for taxable estates between $10 million and $17.18 million, owing to a phase-out of the "preference" received from less-than-55 percent tax rates on lower estate amounts.[5]

Taxes on estates and gifts directly affect only the wealthiest households. In recent years only about 2 percent of decedents have had taxable estates. In 1998 the average taxable estate paid $562,000 in taxes. Among taxable estates, payments are highly concentrated among very large estates. In 1998 estates above $20 million accounted for 0.8 percent of taxable returns but 24 percent of tax payments. According to William Gale and Joel Slemrod in chapter 1 in this volume, taxable estates in excess of $5 million accounted for 6.1 percent of taxable returns but more than 53 percent of revenues.

Motives for Intergenerational Transfers

Previous research has considered several classes of models of intergenerational transfers. In the accidental bequest model, bequests are "accidental" because people face uncertain life spans and die before they can consume all of their wealth. These accidental bequests arise in a life-cycle framework

---

3. Information on the estate tax may be found in Joint Committee on Taxation (1998); see chap. 1 by William Gale and Joel Slemrod in this volume; and chap. 2 by Barry W. Johnson, Jacob M. Mikow, and Martha Britton Eller in this volume.

4. Although the federal gift and estate taxes are said to be unified, the gift tax is imposed on the net-of-tax gift, while the estate tax is imposed on the gross estate.

5. Internal Revenue Service, *Instructions for Tax Form 706* (revised July 3, 1999, U.S. Estate and Generation Skipping Tax Return).

because people are unwilling or unable to annuitize all of their wealth—perhaps because of annuity market imperfections or uninsurable risks, such as the risk of catastrophic nursing home expenses. Under these assumptions, people will generally have positive asset holdings when they die, even though they do not have a bequest motive.

Accidental bequests may account for a large fraction of aggregate wealth and may help to explain puzzling wealth accumulation patterns of the elderly.[6] But substantial evidence from patterns of inter vivos giving, life insurance, and annuity choices suggests that some portion of transfers are intended.[7] The existence of estate planning and tax avoidance techniques further suggests that not all bequests are accidental.

In the pure altruism model, parents care about their own consumption and the utility of their children.[8] Parents make transfers and leave bequests until the marginal cost in terms of their own forgone consumption is equal to the marginal benefit to the parents of the increase in their children's consumption. In general, bequests are given differentially across children to compensate for differences in endowments or outcomes.[9]

Gary S. Becker and Nigel Tomes provide support for the altruism model. But other research has rejected three sharp empirical implications of altruism. First, Joseph G. Altonji, Fumio Hayashi, and Laurence J. Kotlikoff show that the division of consumption within the family is not independent of the division of income, contrary to the predictions of an altruism model with operative transfers. Second, several studies find that, among families where parents make transfers to children, a one-dollar increase in parents' resources coupled with a one-dollar reduction in children's resources does not raise transfers by a dollar, although it should under altruism.[10] Third, there does not appear to be empirical support for the implication that siblings with lower incomes should receive larger inheritances than siblings with higher incomes. The last rejection is striking because equal division of estates among children appears to be the norm. However, B. Douglas Bernheim and Sergei Severinov show

6. Abel (1985); Davies (1981); Hurd (1987).

7. Bernheim (1991); Gale and Scholz (1994); Kotlikoff (1989); Laitner and Juster (1996); McGarry (1997); Page (1997). Brown (2000), however, shows that the evidence and conclusion in Bernheim (1991) fail to hold up when using data from the Health and Retirement Study.

8. Barro (1984); Becker (1974).

9. Variations of the altruism model with and without a mechanism that allows a parent to commit to a given transfer level are examined in Bruce and Waldman (1990, 1991), Lindbeck and Weibull (1988), and Perozek (1996).

10. Tomes (1981, 1988); Becker and Tomes (1979, 1986); Altonji, Hayashi, and Kotlikoff (1992); Cox (1987); McGarry and Schoeni (1995). McGarry (2000) considers a dynamic model of altruism and concludes that this test is mis-specified.

that this norm can arise when parents are altruistic, parental preferences are unobservable, and each child derives utility from his perception of his parents' affection for him relative to his siblings.[11]

A variety of "exchange" models posit that bequests or transfers are the payment for some good or service provided by children. In the strategic bequest model, parents care about their own consumption, their children's utility, and services obtained from children.[12] These services may represent standard market goods (lawn mowing, for example) or more personal items, such as visits, attention, or children's choices regarding marriage, childbearing, education, career, and location of residence. Parents pay for services with bequests rather than inter vivos transfers because by delaying payment, parents can control children's actions for a longer period and extract all of the consumer surplus out of the exchange relationship. In Cox, parents buy services from their children via inter vivos gifts, and the exchange may be mutually beneficial. Empirical tests of exchange models have generated mixed results.[13]

Laurence Kotlikoff and Avia Spivak offer an alternative exchange model, where parents face uncertain lifetimes and imperfect annuity markets. To insure against outliving their resources, parents essentially buy annuities from their children and pay for the annuities with bequests. The model suffers from the empirical problem that large, ongoing flows of wealth from children to living parents are rarely observed, but that may be due to the sizable annuities that the government already provides in the form of Medicare and Social Security.[14]

Other specifications simply assume that households acquire utility directly from wealth or from the after-tax bequest they leave. This specification is sometimes offered as a structural model. Henry J. Aaron and Alicia H. Munnell, Gurdip S. Bakshi and Zhiwu Chen, and Christopher D. Carroll, for example, argue that (pre-estate-tax) wealth may enter the utility function as a separate argument, above and beyond the conventional consumption goods it can finance, because wealth may also provide social status, power, social connections, and so on. A related case occurs if households care directly about the size of the after-tax bequest they provide. Alternatively, the specifications using pre- or post-tax wealth may be thought of as reduced forms

---

11. Joulfaian (1992); Menchik (1980, 1988); Wilhelm (1996); Bernheim and Severinov (2000).

12. Bernheim, Shleifer and Summers (1985).

13. Cox (1987); Bernheim, Shleifer, and Summers (1985); Cox (1987); and Perozek (1998). The equal division puzzle is a problem for the strategic bequest motive, although Bernheim, Shleifer, and Summers (1985) offer a reconciliation.

14. Kotlikoff and Spivak (1981); Gale and Scholz (1994).

consistent with different structural motivations for transfers. Carroll presents casual evidence consistent with the utility-of-wealth model, but no formal tests of either model exist.[15]

Each motive above plausibly describes some portion of transfers and draws support from some research, but each motive that has been tested has also been rejected. This suggests that households may be influenced by several motives or that the importance of each may vary across households.[16] It is worth emphasizing that analysis of the estate tax requires evidence on the motives of the very wealthiest households. But there is even less known about the very wealthy than about the moderately wealthy or middle-class households that are the mainstay of most empirical work on transfers, and relative to other households, the wealthiest households may have different motives, at the margin, for wealth accumulation.[17]

Previous Analysis of Estate Taxes, Inheritances, and Saving

The debate about the impact of transfer taxation on saving dates back to Adam Smith and David Ricardo, who thought such taxes reduced capital formation, and Jeremy Bentham and John Stuart Mill, who believed any negative impact was minimal. More recently, Richard A. Musgrave, Seymour Fiekowsky, Gerard M. Brannon, and Joseph A. Pechman have suggested that substitution of an estate tax for a lifetime income tax could generate positive effects on capital formation.[18]

Joseph Stiglitz notes that estate taxes induce income and substitution effects for donors, negative wealth effects for recipients, and revenue for governments. He surmises that effects on capital accumulation are likely to be negative but does not model these effects.[19]

Laurence J. Kotlikoff and Lawrence H. Summers examine the steady-state, partial-equilibrium effects of transfer taxes in an altruism model. Owing to separability assumptions, transfer taxes have income effects on lifetime consumption and earnings but not substitution effects. Income effects

---

15. Aaron and Munnell (1992); Bakshi and Chen (1996); Carroll (2000); Blinder (1976).

16. Differences in empirical outcomes may also be due in part to data limitations and the difficulty of distinguishing rejection of the underlying behavioral model from rejection of the maintained assumptions needed to generate testable hypotheses.

17. Recent work has only begun to examine the behavior of the very wealthy in detail. See, for example, the papers in Slemrod (2000).

18. See the discussion in Graetz (1983) and McCaffery (1994). See Musgrave (1959); Fiekowsky (1966); Brannon (1973); and Pechman (1983).

19. Stiglitz (1978).

are based on the difference between growth rates and interest rates. Using historical averages for these values, they estimate that a one-dollar decline in gross transfers reduces the capital stock by about 70 cents, but they do not estimate how transfer taxes affect gross transfer levels.[20]

Excellent surveys by Michael J. Graetz, Holtz-Eakin, and Andre Masson and Pierre Pestieau discuss how different bequest motives could have differential impacts on the donor's saving but typically do not examine the effect on the recipient. Edward J. McCaffery provides the reasoning behind the view that estate taxes reduce saving.[21]

Despite these previous discussions, there are few formal models of the impact of estate taxation on saving. Jordi Caballe develops an altruism model with endogenous growth, human capital, and bequests and finds that estate taxes reduce the capital stock. A feature of his model, however, is that estate taxes and capital income taxes have identical effects, which appears to be a special case. Shigeki Kunieda develops a much simpler model that focuses on donor behavior and obtains similar results.[22]

Carroll simulates a particular parameterization of the utility-of-bequests model and finds that higher estate taxes reduce donor's saving but does not examine saving by potential recipients.[23] Robert B. Rebelein examines Ricardian equivalence in a dynamic model with and without strategic interaction among household members. He introduces estate taxes and shows via simulation that, relative to lump sum taxes, estate taxes have higher crowding out effects and higher welfare losses.[24] John Laitner in chapter 6 in this volume examines the role of estate taxation in a sophisticated overlapping generations simulation model. He finds that the estate tax reduces the steady state concentration of wealth and capital stock.

There are few empirical studies of the estate tax and saving. Wojciech Kopczuk and Joel Slemrod in chapter 7 in this volume use estate tax return data from 1916 to 1996 and find that increases in estate tax rates tend to reduce the amount of wealth held in the largest estates. As they note, this evidence is consistent with higher estate taxes increasing tax avoidance or reducing saving by the donor, but the evidence is somewhat fragile. They

---

20. Kotlikoff and Summers (1981).
21. Graetz (1983); Holtz-Eakin (1996); Masson and Pestieau (1997); McCaffery (1994).
22. Caballe (1995); Kuneida (1989, chap. 3).
23. Carroll (2000). In related work, Ihori (1998) examines wealth taxation in intergenerational models with endogenous growth and finds that increased taxes on financial bequests (as opposed to transfers of human capital) alter intragenerational equality, while increased taxes on transfers of human capital have ambiguous effects. Mulligan (1997, chapter 5) shows that progressive estate taxes increase intergenerational mobility of households.
24. Rebelein (1998).

also show estate tax rates that prevailed at age 45 (or ten years before death) are more clearly negatively associated with reported estate size than is the rate prevailing in the year of death.[25]

Several articles examine the behavior of recipients. Recipients of inheritances from estates subject to federal estate taxation tend to be middle-aged, high-income households, and the typical inheritance for these recipients is several times the recipients' income. Holtz-Eakin, Joulfaian, and Harvey S. Rosen show that receipt of an inheritance of $350,000 reduces labor force participation rates by 12 percentage points for singles and reduces the likelihood of having two workers by 14 percentage points for married couples. Holtz-Eakin, Joulfaian, and Rosen and Joulfaian and Mark O. Wilhelm find small reductions in the labor supply of inheritors who remain in the labor force. David N. Weil shows that the past or anticipated receipt of an inheritance raises a household's consumption by 4 to 10 percent, after controlling for income, age, education, and other factors. Given the magnitude of typical household saving rates, Weil's results suggest that inheritances substantially reduce a household's saving out of earned income. All of these empirical results suggest that if transfer taxes reduce inheritances, they should raise saving by recipients. However, Holtz-Eakin, Joulfaian, and Rosen show that receipt of a large inheritance raises the likelihood that a household starts a business and raises the probability of the business surviving and expanding. Thus, to the extent that inheritances relieve liquidity constraints associated with investment, reduced inheritances could reduce saving.[26]

A Framework for Analyzing the Effects of Estate Taxes on Saving

This section discusses a simple but general framework for examining estate taxes. The formal model equations and solutions are derived in the Appendix to this chapter. The model consists of a parent and child, each of whom is alive in the first period. The child survives to the second period with certainty, while the parent survives with probability less than or equal to 1.

25. Earlier studies by Fiekowski (1966), Southwick (1996), and Chapman, Hariharan, and Southwick (1996) examine the effects of estate taxes on saving.
26. Joulfaian (1998); Wilhelm (1996); Holtz-Eakin, Joulfaian, and Rosen (1993, pp. 426–27, 1994a, 1994b); Joulfaian and Rosen (1993); Joulfaian and Wilhelm (1994); Weil (1994, pp. 73–74); Imbens, Rubin, and Sacerdote (1999) show that winning a lottery prize of about $15,000 per year for 20 years has little if any effect on the recipient's labor supply, but winning a prize of $80,000 per year for 20 years significantly reduces labor force participation, hours worked, and labor earnings.

The parent derives utility from her own lifetime consumption and may also care about the well-being of the child or services the child provides to her. The different sources of utility correspond to different transfer motives, as discussed below. The parent receives exogenously determined income in the first period and, if alive, the second period.[27] If the parent is alive in the second period and estate tax revenues are rebated in lump sum manner, she also receives a transfer from the government. The parent's lifetime budget constraint is that the discounted value of her own consumption plus her pretax bequest must be no larger than the sum of the discounted value of her exogenous income and any tax rebate. The estate tax is assumed to be proportional with no exempt amount. Given these constraints, the parent maximizes lifetime utility by choosing first-period saving and a planned net-of-tax inheritance to the child in the second period. If the parent dies at the end of the first period, the bequest will in general differ from the planned bequest that would have occurred at the end of the second period.

The child cares about his own consumption and may also care about services provided to the parent but does not care directly about the parent. He receives exogenous income in each period and may receive an inheritance in the second period. He maximizes his lifetime utility by choosing consumption in each period subject to a lifetime budget constraint that requires that the discounted value of his consumption not exceed the discounted value of his wages plus the after-tax inheritance received. The determination of services provided to the parent is described in the discussion of the exchange motive below.

Before turning to the analysis of estate taxes, a few comments on the model are warranted. First, our analysis focuses on how estate taxes that are imposed in the second period affect saving in the first period. Second, although we focus on estate taxes, nothing of substance would change if the transfer were labeled a gift and the tax called a gift tax. Third, in the general framework noted, the timing of moves by the parent and child has not been specified carefully. The timing will vary across transfer motives, and is described in subsequent sections.

Accidental Bequests

To model accidental bequests, we assume that the parent cares only about her own consumption, and that the parent lives to the second period with prob-

27. The second period income is assumed not to be bequeathable if the parent dies at the end of the first period.

ability less than 1. To ensure that the parent does not die with negative wealth, we impose the constraint that parental saving in the first period is non-negative. In this framework, the parent does not intentionally provide a bequest. Thus, if the parent lives to the end of the second period, she bequeaths nothing. However, if she dies at the end of the first period with positive wealth, she will accidentally leave a bequest. Thus, with no estate tax, the expected value of the inheritance received by the child is positive.

Now consider estate taxes. If estate tax revenues are not recycled, an increase in the estate tax rate would have no effect on the parent's saving but would reduce the expected inheritance received by the child and thereby raise the child's saving. Thus, raising the estate tax would raise the sum of parent's and child's saving.

If the revenue is recycled to the parent in the second period, the analysis changes somewhat.[28] Relative to the no-tax case, the parent now has higher expected value of second-period income, and therefore of lifetime income, if she lives to the second period. Even though the parent does not know in period 1 whether she will live the full two periods, the increase in second period income contingent on survival causes her to raise consumption in the first period— that is, to reduce saving. The rise in the estate tax reduces the child's expected inheritance for two reasons: first, the higher tax directly reduces the after-tax inheritance flowing from a pretax bequest of a given size; second, the reduction in the parent's saving reduces the pre-tax bequest should the parent die at the end of the first period. Thus, the child's first-period saving rises. As a result, the net effect on first period saving by the parent and child is ambiguous.

Bequests as Exchange

In the exchange framework, the parent values a service (or good or action) that the child provides, and the parent purchases the service by promising to bequeath additional funds. For simplicity, we assume the parent survives to the second period with certainty and the parent cares about her own consumption and the services provided by the child but not the child's well-being.

To simplify further, we assume the child does not care directly about the service provided and that the child must work a fixed number of hours but

---

28. Obviously, if a particular parent dies at the end of period 1, she cannot receive the recycled revenue in period 2. This problem can be easily accommodated by adjusting the model to allow for many families, where some of the parents die at the end of period 1 and the rest live until the end of period 2.

can allocate those hours between working at the market wage and providing attention to the parent. Since the child is indifferent between working in the labor market and providing services for the parent, in equilibrium the child will have to receive the same payment from an hour of work and an hour of providing services.

Thus, with exchange-motivated bequests, the parent saves in period 1 to finance second period consumption and to purchase services from the child. The estate tax is simply a tax on those purchases. The effect of the estate tax on the parent's first-period saving depends on the parent's price elasticity of demand for services. If the demand for services is inelastic, then a higher estate tax raises total parental expenditure on services, and the parent's saving rises. If demand is elastic, a higher estate tax rate will reduce the gross estate and reduce parental saving in the first period.

If the revenue is not recycled, the relevant price elasticity above is based on an uncompensated demand curve. If the revenue is recycled, the same intuition applies, but the relevant price elasticity is now derived from a situation in which the parent is compensated in lump sum for the tax payments made. Revenue recycling will raise the parent's lifetime income compared to when revenue is not recycled. This will raise the parent's consumption of all normal goods. Thus, if first period consumption is normal, the parent's first-period saving will fall by more (rise by less) under revenue recycling than when revenue is not recycled.

Empirically, the demand for attention is more likely to be inelastic if the attention provided is child-specific and few suitable market substitutes are available. Demand is likely to be more elastic when there are market substitutes for the service provided by the child.[29]

We have focused on the parent's saving in response to changes in the estate tax rate. As in Bernheim, Shleifer, and Summers, the discussion above assumes that the parent is able to extract all of the surplus from the transaction with the child, and therefore, in equilibrium, the child is indifferent on the margin between providing the service and working in the labor market.[30] These assumptions also imply that the child's total resources and therefore the child's saving, do not change as the estate tax or the transfer from the parent changes.

29. This point is related to a result derived by Cox (1987), who focuses on the role of the parent's income elasticity of demand for services provided by children in attempting to distinguish between altruism and exchange motives.
30. Bernheim, Shleifer, and Summers (1985).

In an earlier version of this chapter, we examine models where parents obtain utility from after-tax bequests or from the act of giving itself.[31] The effects of estate taxes on saving in these models are very similar to those obtained when bequests are a means of exchange. In all three cases, the parent derives utility from the after-tax bequest—without regard to the child's utility—and the effects of estate taxes depend on the elasticity of the parent's total (pre-tax) bequest with respect to the tax rate.

Altruism Models

To model purely altruistic preferences we assume the parent cares about her own consumption and the well-being of the child, but not the size of the transfer per se. For simplicity, we assume that neither the parent nor the child cares about services provided by the child, and that the parent lives to the second period with certainty.

In a dynamic setting, altruistic parents may face a Samaritan's Dilemma. Specifically, if the parent does not have a credible mechanism for committing to transfer levels independent of the child's outcome, and if the child's outcome depends on the child's behavior, then a selfish child will consume more in the first period than he would if the parent could commit to a transfer scheme. The child knows that the resulting reduction in his own wealth will be at least partially compensated by an increased transfer from the parent.

We first examine the altruism model when parents possess the power to commit to the level of future transfers. This simpler model establishes the benchmark for the efficient solution. Then we compare those results with the solution to the model when parents cannot commit to a future transfer level.

Altruism with Commitment Power

When the parent can credibly commit to future transfer levels, the analysis is straightforward. First, because the child cannot manipulate the parent's transfer, the child maximizes his own lifetime utility, taking the transfer as given. Then, knowing the child's saving as a function of the transfer, the parent chooses first-period saving and the second-period transfer to maximize her lifetime utility. In effect, if a transfer is given, the parent chooses the distribution of family resources that maximizes her lifetime utility.

---

31. Gale and Perozek (2000); Blinder (1976); Carroll (2000); Andreoni (1989).

Figure 5-1. *Inheritance under Altruism with Commitment Power*

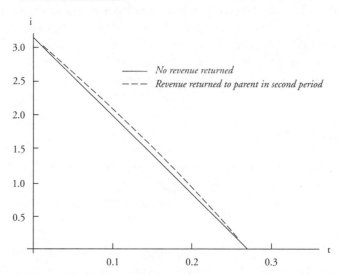

In this theoretical framework, the effect of the estate tax is ambiguous; the tax reduces the parent's saving and raises the child's saving (see the appendix at the end of the chapter). To gain further insights, we specify a numerical model. For each person i (i = parent, child), we assume the within-period utility function is isoelastic, that is, $u_i(c) = c^{1-\gamma}/(1-\gamma)$, and lifetime utility is additively separable. We also assume the time preference rate is zero, and parents value their child's utility at half the level of their own utility. We parameterize income by assuming that $W_{p1} = 50$, $W_{p2} = 20$, $W_{k1} = 10$, and $W_{k2} = 40$, where W_{ij} gives the exogenous income of person i in period j (= 1 or 2). These income values imply that family resources in the two periods are equal, which implies the efficient level of family saving is zero.[32] The coefficient of relative risk aversion, γ, is set to 3.

With these assumptions, the effects of higher estate tax rates, with and without revenue recycling, are shown in figures 5-1 to 5-4. We first exam-

32. The income values can be thought of as representing the second and third of three periods of the parent's life—i.e., the parent's middle-age and retirement period—and the first and second of three periods of the child's life—young adulthood, and then middle age. This would justify the downward sloping profile for the parent and the upward sloping profile for the child, although those slopes are not necessary to establish the results in the paper. It may seem counterfactual that the child has fewer lifetime resources than the parent, but this condition, or a high degree of altruism, is necessary, under the assumptions of the model, to generate positive transfers from the parent to the child.

Figure 5-2. *Child's Saving under Altruism with Commitment Power*

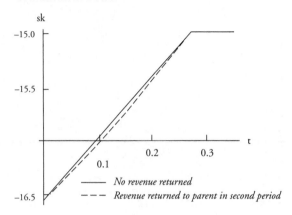

Figure 5-3. *Parent's Saving under Altruism with Commitment Power*

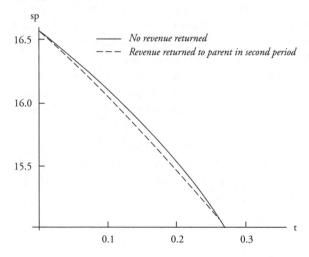

Figure 5-4. *Total Family Saving under Altruism with Commitment Power*

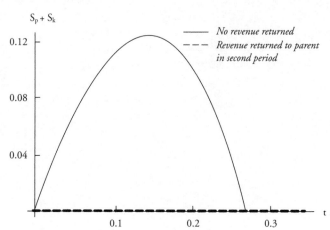

ine the effects with no revenue recycling (shown by the solid lines in figures 5-1 through 5-4.) As the estate tax rate rises, the net-of-tax inheritance falls, and vanishes at a tax-inclusive rate of about 27 percent (figure 5-1). Raising the estate tax rate also raises the child's saving (figure 5-2) and reduces the parent's saving (figure 5-3).

Figure 5-4 shows the main result of this section, the impact of the estate tax on family saving. When the tax rate is zero, total family saving is zero. As the tax rate rises, family saving first increases and then decreases until the transfer is no longer operative, at which point family saving returns to zero. Hence, for a range of tax rates between 0 and t^*, where t^* is the rate at which saving peaks, increases in the tax raise family saving. Moreover, with this parameterization, every positive tax rate produces a level of saving at least as high as a zero tax rate does.

Although the quantitative effects shown in figure 5-4 are quite small, the intuition behind the qualitative patterns is worth pursuing. Calculations in the appendix show that, under the assumptions above, as the estate tax rate changes, family saving changes according to:

(1) $$ds/dt = (B/2)(\epsilon_{Bt} + 1),$$

where the s is the sum of the parent's and child's saving, B is the pre-tax bequest, $\epsilon_{Bt} = (dB/dt) * (t/B)$ and represents the elasticity of the gross bequest with respect to the estate tax rate, and t is estate tax rate. Equation (1) shows that the sign of the effect on saving of increasing the estate tax rate depends on the elasticity of gross (pre-tax) bequests with respect to the tax rate. When the elasticity is greater than negative one, the derivative is positive—that is, raising the estate tax rate *raises* saving. Evaluated at $t = 0$, the elasticity has to be greater than negative one, since t enters the numerator of the elasticity. As a result, equation (1) implies that starting from a zero estate tax rate, raising the tax rate by a small amount will raise family saving. This finding explains the initial increase in saving shown in figure 5-4. Simulations confirm that as t rises, ϵ_{Bt} falls in value, reaching a value of -1 at $t = t^*$, where t^* is defined above.

The results with revenue recycling are shown by the dashed lines in figures 5-1 through 5-4. Whether the revenue is returned to the parent in the second period or not has very little quantitative influence on the results in figures 5-1 through 5-3. Relative to the no-recycling case, recycling raises the inheritance (figure 5-1), reduces first-period saving by the child (figure 5-2), and reduces first-period saving by the parent (figure 5-3).

In contrast, revenue recycling has a major effect on the qualitative results for overall family saving (figure 5-4). With recycling, the estate tax is completely neutral with respect to family saving. Because the parent can effectively choose family saving, she will choose the level of saving that is efficient given the distribution of resources over time. But when tax revenues are recycled to the parent, total resources available to the family in each period are the same as in the no-tax case. Thus, family saving is the same as in the no-tax case.

Altruism without Commitment Power

When the parent cannot commit to future transfer levels, parental altruism provides an incentive for the child to undersave in the first period, where "undersave" is defined relative to the case with commitment described above. As described in the appendix, the absence of commitment changes the ordering of moves and the nature of the maximization problem. The key difference is that when the parent has no commitment power, the child can manipulate the size of the transfer by consuming more in the first period than is optimal from the parent's perspective. In particular, as the child's second period wealth rises, the parent's preferred transfer falls. This decline acts like a tax on the child's wealth, so that the child chooses to save less than he would in the commitment case, where the transfer is fixed given the exogenous distribution of family income.

Theoretical analysis (see the appendix) shows that when parents lack commitment power, higher estate taxes lead to higher saving by the parent and lower saving by the child; the net effect of the tax increase on total saving is

Figure 5-5. *Inheritance under Altruism without Commitment Power*

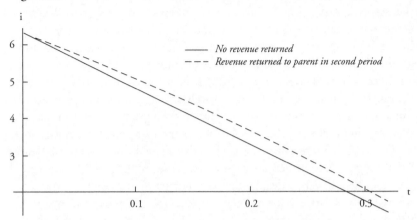

indeterminate. Thus, we turn again to numerical solutions, using the same parameterization as in the commitment case described above.

We focus first on the results with no revenue recycling (the solid lines in figures 5-5 through 5-8). Figure 5-5 shows that the net-of-tax inheritance falls as the tax rate rises when there is no commitment power. Comparison of figures 5-1 and 5-5 shows that the net-of-tax inheritance is much larger when there is no commitment power. At a tax rate of zero, the inheritance is about twice as large when there is no commitment, and it remains operative until the tax rate rises to about 36 percent, compared with 27 percent in the commitment case, using the same parameter values.

Figure 5-6 shows that when there is no commitment power, the child's saving rises as the estate tax rate rises. Comparison of figures 5-2 and 5-6 shows that the child saves much less when there is no commitment power, demonstrating the disincentive effects on saving of the parent's policy to reduce her transfer as the child's saving rises.

Figure 5-7 shows that the parent's saving unambiguously declines as the tax rate rises when there is no commitment power. However, relative to the case with commitment shown in figure 5-3, parents save slightly more in the no-commitment case for low tax rates and slightly less for higher tax rates. The intuition for this result stems from Neil Bruce and Michael Waldman.[33] In the absence of commitment mechanisms, parents are either forced by the opportunistic behavior of their children to give more than they would with

---

33. Bruce and Waldman (1990).

Figure 5-6. *Child's Saving under Altruism without Commitment Power*

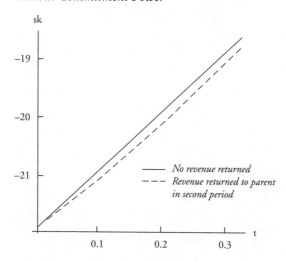

Figure 5-7. *Parent's Saving under Altruism without Commitment Power*

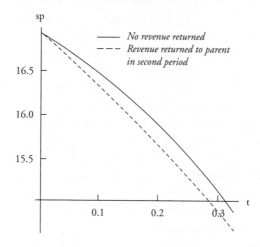

Figure 5-8. *Total Family Saving under Altruism without Commitment Power*

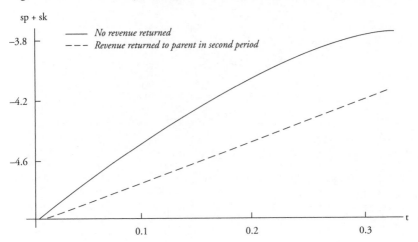

full commitment, or they must find some way to make credible the threat not to give more. One way to make the threat credible is simply to consume the resources themselves. As the estate tax rate rises, the relative costs of using this threat mechanism decline, so that parental consumption rises relative to the full-commitment case as the estate tax rises.

Figure 5-8 shows that, when there is no commitment power, total saving rises as the estate tax rises. Comparison of figures 5-4 and 5-8 shows that the level of family saving is lower when the parent does not have commitment power. However, the marginal effect on saving of raising the estate tax rate is larger in absolute value when there is no commitment power. This result can be illustrated by examining extreme cases. When $t = 1$ (actually, when t is as low as .37 using the parameters specified), there is no operative bequest in either model, so saving will be the same in both. However, when $t = 0$, there is less saving in the no-commitment model because of the Samaritan's Dilemma. Thus, the effect on saving of raising t (from 0 to 1) must be larger in the no-commitment model. The intuition is that, in the absence of credible parental commitment, the estate tax provides a way of credibly making it more difficult for the parent to give transfers. This forces the child to raise saving by more, for a given increase in the estate tax, in the no-commitment case than in the commitment case.

Given the absence of commitment power, whether the revenue is recycled does not have a very large effect on any of the results. Because the tax revenue is refunded to the parent in the second period, the parent's second period income is higher than in the case in which the revenue is not recycled. As a result, the parent saves less in the first period (figure 5-7). In addition, the parent gives a larger transfer (figure 5-5), which reduces the child's saving (figure 5-6). This implies that total saving by the parent and the child is lower with revenue recycling (figure 5-8) than without. Nevertheless, the main qualitative result is the same: over a range of tax rates, increases in the estate tax raise total saving by the parent and child.

Discussion

Our analysis generates three central conclusions: the effects of estate taxes on saving depend crucially on transfer motives; the overall effects require analysis of both the donor and the potential recipient; and in a surprising number of cases, higher estate taxes appear to raise saving.

The central role of transfer motives should not be surprising. Motives for intergenerational transfers play an important role in several other topics in public finance, including the effects of government debt, the effects of subsidies for charitable giving, the appropriate treatment of gifts and bequests under a consumption tax, and the effects of consumption taxes.[34]

The effects of estate taxes vary across transfer motives because different motives make the effects hinge on completely different behavioral responses. Under the exchange motive, for example, the price elasticity of demand for children's services is the key variable. Under altruism, the effects will vary depending on the level of commitment power that the parent possesses. An implication of this finding is that all behavioral and efficiency aspects of the estate tax should depend in some degree on transfer motives. Louis Kaplow in chapter 4 in this volume shows that the efficiency effects of transfer taxes vary with motives for giving.[35] Our models confirm and extend those results. For example, when parents lack commitment power, it can be shown that the parent can achieve a higher level of lifetime utility at certain values of $t > 0$ than when $t = 0$. To understand why, recall that with altruism and no commitment power, the child saves too little. The estate tax raises the cost of giving a second period transfer. It provides, if not a commitment device, at least an increase in the marginal cost of giving the transfer, which reduces the size of the transfer, causes the child to raise saving, and thus helps to offset the inefficient behavior induced by the lack of commitment power.

34. Barro (1989); Bernheim (1980); Andreoni (1989); Fried (1999); Metcalf (1995); Johnson, Diamond, and Zodrow (1997).
35. See also Kaplow (1995, 1997).

Transfer motives will also affect the impact of the estate tax on the cost of capital. Poterba models the impact of the estate tax on the donor's cost of capital by adding to the standard cost of capital formula the product of the statutory estate tax rate times the donor's one-period mortality risk.[36] It is not clear, however, which if any transfer motives would generate that formula. Under accidental bequests, the estate tax has no impact on how the donor perceives the cost of capital. Under the exchange motive, the estate tax acts as an excise tax on parental purchases of children's services. This imposes a constant cost per service requested, and the cost is independent of when the parent dies. And under altruism, the parent is concerned about the child's lifetime well-being. Since the parent knows she will die at some point, it is not clear how or why the parent's mortality risk should enter the cost of capital formula. In any case, the relation among the estate tax, bequest motives, and the donor's cost of capital merits further investigation, especially given the extraordinary attention in policy debates to the effects of the estate tax on small businesses and entrepreneurship. Transfer motives will also affect the economic incidence of the estate tax and the impact on labor supply and the distribution of wealth.

Our second central finding is that the overall effects of estate taxes depend critically on the recipient's response as well as the donor's. As described above, many previous analyses examine the impact on the donor or the recipient. A large portion of the policy debate focuses only on the effect on donor's saving. Our results, however, suggest that the overall impact may be different in magnitude and direction than the effect just on donors.

Our third and perhaps most striking finding is that under several different circumstances, higher tax rates on estates can raise saving. The results are strongest when tax revenues are not recycled. Under these circumstances, higher estate tax rates generate higher net family saving among the affected families if bequests are accidental. If bequests are motivated by exchange, the effect is ambiguous but plausibly positive, since there are often few good substitutes for a child's attention. When bequests are altruistic and parents have commitment power, our simulations and parameter values generate positive effects of higher estate taxes for a range of tax rates, and family saving with a positive tax rate is never below saving with no tax. When bequests are altruistic and parents lack commitment power, family saving rises with increases in the estate tax rates.

---

36. Poterba (2000).

Partly, the effects noted occur because of the assumption that revenue is not recycled to the donor or recipient.[37] When the revenue is not recycled, higher estate taxes impose substitution and income effects. The income effects reduce family consumption in both periods and therefore raise saving in the first period. But the results without recycling are still of interest, especially for policy purposes. Virtually all proposed revisions or abolitions of the estate tax do not involve compensating adjustments for the families involved; rather, they involve significant shifts in the distribution of tax burdens across income classes.[38] Thus, the policy debate about the effects of estate taxes focuses on the effects of uncompensated estate tax changes. This chapter shows that such changes can lead to net increases in saving by the affected donors and recipients under all of the transfer motives considered above.

We also show that, in the presence of revenue recycling, the effects on saving are less likely to be positive. This should not be surprising, since recycling the revenue removes the negative income effect and the reduction in first-period consumption it causes. Nevertheless, even with revenue recycling the results are far from the conventional wisdom that estate taxes always reduce saving. With accidental and exchange-motivated bequests, the effects are ambiguous. With altruistic bequests and commitment power, the estate tax is neutral with respect to family saving. And when parents face a Samaritan's Dilemma, the effects of higher estate taxes remain positive.

Our modeling strategy has followed earlier work, in examining the effects of transfers among one generation of parents and one generation of children.[39] This allowed us to examine estate taxes in models that have been commonly used to examine transfer motives. Examining models with a series of overlapping generations is an important next step. In addition, the model might usefully be extended to consider general equilibrium effects, tax avoidance possibilities, interactions among inter vivos gifts, bequests, and estate and gift taxes, and other motives for transfers and wealth accumulation.[40]

37. The implicit assumption is that the revenue is spent by the government on a public good that enters the parent's and child's utility function in a separable manner.

38. See Gale and Slemrod, chapter 4, in this volume.

39. Altonji, Hayashi, and Kotlikoff (1997); Bernheim, Shleifer, and Summers (1985); Bernheim and Severinov (1998); Bruce and Waldman (1990, 1991); Cox (1987, 1990).

40. Stiglitz (1978); Laitner, chap. 6 in this volume; McGarry (2000); Bernheim and Severinov (2000); Curry and Davies (1998); Pollak (1988); Frank (1997); and Michael Kinsley, "The Super-rich Are Different," Time, May 23, 1988.

Appendix

This appendix provides the formal modeling that generates the results discussed in the text of the chapter. We model the behavior of a parent and child, each of whom is alive in the first period. The child survives to period 2 with certainty, while the parent survives with probability $q < = 1$. The parent derives utility from her own consumption, and may also care about the well-being of the child (U_k), or about an action (a) taken by the child—this action may be thought of as services provided by the child to the parent. The parent's degree of altruism is θ and the discount factor is β. The parent receives exogenously determined income in the first period and, if alive, the second period, denoted W_{p1} and W_{p2}, respectively. The parent may also receive a transfer from the government (T) in the second period if the estate tax revenue is rebated. Given a flat, tax-inclusive tax rate t on bequests to children (with no exempt amount), the parent chooses saving (s_p) in the first period and a planned net-of-tax inheritance (I) to the child in the second period to maximize lifetime utility U_p:

$$Max_{s_p, I} \quad U_p = u_p(c_{p1}) + \beta q u_p(c_{p2}, a) + \theta U_k(c_{k1}, c_{k2}, a)$$

$$\text{subject to:}$$

(A1)
$$c_{p1} = W_{p1} - s_p$$

$$c_{p2} = W_{p2} + T + (1 + r)s_p - \frac{I}{1 - t}.$$

The constraints imply that first-period consumption (c_{p1}) equals first period resources (W_{p1}) less saving, and second period consumption (c_{p2}) equals second period resources ($W_{p2} + T + (1 + r)s_p$) less the total cost of the transfer $I/(1 - t)$, where I is the after-tax inheritance received by the child.

The child receives endowments of W_{k1} and W_{k2} and chooses first-period saving (s_k) and a second-period action (a) to maximize lifetime utility U_k:

$$Max_{s_k, a} \quad U_k = (c_{k1}, c_{k2}, a) = u_k(c_{k1}) + \beta E[u_k(c_{k2}, a)]$$

$$\text{subject to:}$$

(A2)
$$c_{k1} = W_{k1} - s_k$$

$$c_{k2} = W_{k2} + (1 + r)s_k + (1 - Q)I + Q(1 + r)(1 - t)s_p$$

$$Q = \begin{cases} 0 \text{ with probability } q \\ 1 \text{ with probability } 1 - q. \end{cases}$$

The constraints imply that first period consumption (c_{k1}) equals income (W_{k1}) less saving (s_k), and second period consumption (c_{k2}) equals the sum of income (W_{k2}), accumulated first-period saving $(1 + r)s_k$, the intended after-tax inheritance (I), and—if the parent does not survive to the second period—the parent's accumulated saving intended for her own second period consumption, net of the estate tax: $(1 + r)(1 - t)s_p$.

In equilibrium, the parent chooses s_p^* and I^*, while the child chooses s_k^* and a^*. Each maximizes lifetime utility subject to the resource constraints above and the constraints of the game, which will change as motivations for transfers change. For simplicity, and without loss of generality, we assume the return on saving and the rate of time preference equal 0 ($r = 0$ and $\beta = 1$), and the second period transfer is operative ($I > 0$).

Accidental Bequests

To model accidental bequests, we assume the parent cares only about her own consumption and lives to the second period with probability $q < 1$. To ensure that the parent dies with non-negative wealth, we require parental saving to be non-negative. In the absence of formal or family annuity markets, the parent chooses saving to maximize lifetime utility:

$$Max_{s_p} \quad U_p = u_p(c_{p1}) + qu_p(c_{p2})$$

$$subject \ to:$$

(A3)

$$c_{p1} = W_{p1} - s_p$$

$$c_{p2} = W_{p2} + T + s_p$$

and the parent will choose saving to satisfy

(A4)
$$\frac{\dfrac{\delta u_p}{\delta c_{p1}}}{\dfrac{\delta u_p}{\delta c_{p2}}} \geq q; \quad s_p \geq 0.$$

When there is no revenue recycling ($T = 0$), the estate tax has no effect on the parent's saving. Although the parent has no intended transfer, she will leave a positive bequest if she dies at the end of the first period. Hence, with probability $1 - q$ the parent will leave an estate of size s_p at the end of the first period, of which the child will inherit $(1 - t)s_p$. The child's saving thus depends on the parent's saving and the estate tax rate, and he will choose s_k to maximize lifetime utility:

$$Max_{s_k} \quad U_k = u_k(c_{k1}) + E[u_k(c_{k2})]$$

$$subject\ to:$$

(A5)
$$c_{k1} = W_{k1} - s_k$$

$$c_{k2} = W_{k2} + s_k + Q(1 - t)s_p$$

$$Q = \begin{cases} 0\ with\ probability\ q \\ 1\ with\ probability\ 1 - q. \end{cases}$$

Intuitively, if the parent saves nothing, the child's saving is unaffected by estate taxes. If the parent's saving is positive, expected inheritances will be positive, but will be reduced by estate taxes. Thus, higher estate tax rates reduce the expected inheritance.

Formally, the child chooses saving (s_k) to satisfy

(A6) $\quad F(s_k, t) = -\dfrac{\delta u_k}{\delta c_{k1}} + (1 - q)\dfrac{\delta u_k}{\delta(c_{k2}|Q = 1)} + q\dfrac{\delta u_k}{\delta(c_{k2}|Q = 0)} = 0$

and, by the implicit function theorem, the child's saving increases as the estate tax increases:

(A7)
$$\frac{\delta s_k}{\delta t} = \frac{(1 - q)\,u''(c_{k2}|Q = 1)s_p}{u''(c_{k1}) + E[u''(c_{k2})]} > 0.$$

The outcome is ambiguous when estate tax revenue from deceased parents is recycled to parents who survive for two periods. The transfer raises second-period and lifetime resources of surviving parents. Consequently, all parents will consume more and thus save less in the first period, relative to the case with no recycling. Substituting the condition $T = t(1 - q)s_p$ into (A4) and totally differentiating shows that higher estate taxes reduce the parent's saving:

(A8)
$$\frac{\delta s_p}{\delta t} = \frac{-qu''(c_{p2})s_p(1 - q)}{u''(c_{p1}) + qu''(c_{p2})(1 + t(1 - q))} \leq 0.$$

As before, the child maximizes expected utility conditional on the expected inheritance, with the optimal choices satisfying (A6). With $T > 0$, however, the child recognizes that an increase in the tax not only reduces the after-tax inheritance, but also reduces the gross estate s_p. Formally,

$$(A9) \quad \frac{\delta s_k}{\delta t} = \frac{-(1 - q)\, u''(c_{k2}|Q = 1)\left(-s_p + (1 - t)\dfrac{\delta s_p}{\delta t}\right)}{u''(c_{k1}) + E[u''(c_{k2})]} > 0.$$

Equation (A9) is identical to (A7) except for the added term $(1 - t)\partial s_p/\partial t$, which is equal to zero when there is no revenue recycling.

Bequests as Exchange

In the exchange framework, the parent values the child's attention (a) and purchases attention by promising to bequeath additional funds. For simplicity, we assume the parent survives to the second period with certainty ($q = 1$) and the parent is not altruistic ($\theta = 0$).

To simplify further, we assume the child does not care directly about the action a. Also, the child must work H hours, but can allocate those hours between working at the market wage, ω ($= W_{k2}/H$) per hour, and providing attention to the parent at a net wage of ω_a per hour. Since the child is indifferent between working in the labor market and working for the parent, the equilibrium price of attention ω_a will equal the market wage ω. Thus, for each hour of attention the parent requests and the child provides, the child will receive an additional ω_a in after-tax inheritances. However, due to the estate tax, the parent pays—that is, has to accumulate in wealth—an amount equal to $p_a = \omega_a/(1 - t)$ to obtain an hour of attention.

The model is solved as follows. The parent solves the second-period problem by choosing a to maximize second period utility given s_p and the second-period budget constraint:

$$(A10) \quad \begin{aligned} Max_a \; &u(c_{p2}, a) \\ &subject\ to\text{:} \\ c_{p2} = \; &W_{p2} + T + s_p - p_a a. \end{aligned}$$

The parent's demand for attention, a^*, must satisfy the first-order condition:

$$(A11) \quad \frac{\delta u}{\delta c_{p2}} \frac{\delta c_{p2}}{\delta a} + \frac{\delta u}{\delta a} \leq 0; \; a \geq 0.$$

If $a > 0$, then in the first period the parent chooses s_p to maximize:

$$Max_{s_p} \ u\left(c_{p1}\right) + u\left(c_{p2}, a\left(s_p\right)\right)$$

$$subject \ to$$

(A12)
$$c_{p1} = W_{p1} - s_p$$

$$c_{p2} = W_{p2} + T + s_p - p_a a\left(s_p\right)$$

$$a\left(s_p\right) = a^*\left(s_p, T\right)$$

and therefore, with no revenue recycling satisfies

(A13) $$F\left(s_p, a\right) = -\frac{\delta u}{\delta c_{p1}} + \frac{\delta u}{\delta c_{p2}}\left[1 - p_a \frac{\delta a^*}{\delta s_p}\right] + \frac{\delta u}{\delta a^*}\frac{\delta a^*}{\delta s_p} = 0,$$

which reduces to the following expression if $a > 0$:

(A14) $$F\left(s_p, t\right) = -\frac{\delta u}{\delta c_{p1}} + \frac{\delta u}{\delta c_{p2}} = 0.$$

To solve for the effect of the estate tax on parental saving, note that:

$$\frac{\delta s_p}{\delta t} = \frac{\delta s_p}{\delta p_a}\frac{\delta p_a}{\delta t}$$

(A15) $$where$$

$$\frac{\delta p_a}{\delta t} = \frac{\omega_a}{\left(1 - t\right)^2} > 0.$$

Since the second term in (A15) is positive, we only need to solve for $\partial s_p / \partial p_a$, which is given by:

(A16) $$\frac{\delta s_p}{\delta p_a} = -\frac{\dfrac{\delta F}{\delta p_a}}{\dfrac{\delta F}{\delta s_p}} = \frac{u''\left(c_{p2}\right)a^*\left[\dfrac{p_a}{a^*}\dfrac{\delta a^*}{\delta p_a} + 1\right]}{u''\left(c_{p1}\right) + u''\left(c_{p2}\right)\left[1 - p_a \dfrac{\delta a^*}{\delta s_p}\right]} \begin{matrix} > \\ < \\ = \end{matrix} 0.$$

The denominator is the second-order condition and is therefore negative. Thus, the sign of $\partial s_p / \partial p_a$ depends only on the sign of

$$\left[\frac{p_a}{a^*} \frac{\delta a^*}{\delta p_a} + 1 \right].$$

That is, the price elasticity of demand for attention determines the effect of the tax on saving.

When revenues are recycled, the problem is only slightly different. The parent's total resources do not change as the tax rate changes. This leaves only the substitution effect, implying that the parent purchases less attention as the tax rate and the price of attention rise. Whether total expenditure on attention falls, though, depends on the compensated elasticity of demand for attention. The formal analysis is sufficiently similar to that described above that we omit the details.

Altruism with Commitment Power

To model altruism, we assume the child's utility enters the parent's utility function with weight $\theta > 0$, neither the parent nor the child cares about the action the child takes, and the parent lives to the second period with certainty. With commitment power, the model is solved in the following order. First, because the child cannot manipulate the parent's transfer, the child takes the transfer as given and chooses saving to maximize his lifetime utility,

(A17)
$$\underset{s_k}{Max} \; u_k\left(c_{k1}\right) + u_k\left(c_{k2}\right)$$

subject to:

(A18)
$$c_{k1} = W_{k1} - s_k$$

(A19)
$$c_{k2} = W_{k2} + s_k + I.$$

The child's optimal saving, $s_k^*(I)$, given the after-tax transfer I, satisfies the first-order condition:

(A20)
$$-\frac{\delta u_k}{\delta c_{k1}} + \frac{\delta u_k}{\delta c_{k2}} = 0.$$

That is, the child chooses saving to smooth consumption over the two periods.

Knowing the child's saving function, $s_k^*(I)$, the parent chooses first-period saving (s_p) and the second-period transfer (I) to maximize lifetime utility:

$$\underset{I, s_p}{Max} \; u_p(c_{p1}) + u_p(c_{p2}) + \theta\{u_k(c_{k1}) + u_k(c_{k2})\}$$

subject to:

(A21) $\qquad c_{p1} = W_{p1} - s_p$

(A22) $\qquad c_{p2} = W_{p2} + T + s_p - I/(1-t)$

$\qquad\qquad c_{k1} = W_{k1} - s_k^*(I)$

$\qquad\qquad c_{k2} = W_{k2} + s_k^*(I) + I.$

The parent's choice of the transfer (I) and saving (s_p) must satisfy the first-order conditions:

(A23)
$$\frac{\delta}{\delta s_p} = -\frac{\delta u_p}{\delta c_{p1}} + \frac{\delta u_p}{\delta c_{p2}} = 0$$

$$\frac{\delta}{\delta I} = -\frac{1}{1-t}\frac{\delta u_p}{\delta c_{p2}} + \theta\frac{\delta u_k}{\delta c_{k2}} \leq 0; \quad I \geq 0.$$

In this framework, the effect of the tax on total saving is ambiguous. To gain further insights, we assume that the utility function is isoelastic, that is, $u_i(c) = c^{1-\gamma}/(1-\gamma)$, $i = p, k$. Under these assumptions, if $I > 0$, optimal transfers and saving are given by:

(A24) $s_p^* = \dfrac{1}{2(1+\alpha)}\left[(2+\alpha)W_{p1} - \alpha(W_{p2} + T) - \dfrac{\alpha}{(1-t)}(W_{k1} + W_{k2})\right]$

(A25) $\quad I^* = \dfrac{1}{(1+\alpha)}[(1-t)(W_{p1} + W_{p2} + T) - \alpha(W_{k1} + W_{k2})]$

$s_k^* = \dfrac{1}{2(1+\alpha)}[(1+2\alpha)W_{k1} - W_{k2} - (1-t)(W_{p1} + W_{p2} + T)],$

(A26)
$$where \; \alpha = \theta^{-\frac{1}{\gamma}}(1-t)^{\frac{\gamma-1}{\gamma}}.$$

Given these expressions, with no revenue recycling ($T = 0$), it is straightforward, if tedious, to show that increases in the estate tax rate reduce inheritances and the parent's saving and raise the child's saving, and have a generally ambiguous effect on family saving. However, with revenue recycling, the estate tax is neutral with respect to family saving.

To understand these results, note that with isoelastic utility and a zero time preference rate, (A20) implies that $c_{k1} = c_{k2}$. Substituting these values into (A18) and (A19) and rearranging yields

(A27) $$s_k^* = \tfrac{1}{2}\left(W_{k1} - W_{k2} - I^*\left(t\right)\right).$$

Similarly, for the parent, equations (A21) and (A22) imply that

(A28) $$s_p^* = \tfrac{1}{2}\left(W_{p1} - W_{p2} - T^*\left(t\right) + I^*\left(t\right)/\left(1 - t\right)\right).$$

Setting $T = 0$ and taking the derivatives of (A27) and (A28) with respect to t, noting that $B^* = I^*(t)/(1 - t)$, adding the results, and rearranging yields:

(A29) $$d\left(s_p + s_k\right)/dt = \left(B/2\right)\left(\epsilon_{Bt} + 1\right),$$

where $\epsilon_{Bt} = (dB/dt) * (t/B)$ and represents the elasticity of the gross bequest with respect to the estate tax rate.

However, with revenue recycling,

(A30) $$T^* = t\left(I^*/\left(1 - t\right)\right).$$

Differentiating (A27), (A28), and (A30) with respect to t, and substituting the third derivative into the formula for the second yields the result that $d(s_p + s_k)/dt = 0$.

Altruism without Commitment Power

When the parent cannot commit to future transfer levels, the model is solved by backward induction. The parent takes the government transfer T as exogenous. In the second period, the parent observes the financial status of the child, $W_{k2} + s_k$, and chooses I:

(A31)
$$\underset{I}{Max} \quad u_p\left(c_{p2}\right) + \theta u_k\left(c_{k2}\right)$$
$$subject\ to:$$
$$c_{p2} = W_{p2} + T + s_p - I/\left(1 - t\right)$$
$$c_{k2} = W_{k2} + s_k + I.$$

The optimal I^* satisfies the first-order condition:

$$(A32) \qquad -\frac{1}{1-t}\frac{\delta u_p}{\delta c_{p2}} + \theta\frac{\delta u_k}{\delta c_{k2}} \leq 0; \qquad I \geq 0$$

given the child's saving and the parent's saving. If $I > 0$, then:

$$(A33) \qquad \frac{\delta I^*}{\delta s_k} = \frac{-\theta u_k''(c_{k2})}{\dfrac{u_p''(c_{p2})}{(1-t)^2} + \theta u_k''(c_{k2})} < 0$$

and

$$(A34) \qquad \left|\frac{\delta I^*}{\delta s_k}\right| < 1.$$

Equations (A33) and (A34) illustrate the disincentive effects of the altruistic transfer policy on the child's saving. If the child saves an additional dollar, the transfer is reduced by $|\delta I^*/\delta s_k|$. This implicit tax leads the child to overconsume in the first period relative to the efficient solution described above.

Next, the child takes the parent's transfer policy $I^*(s_k)$ as given and chooses saving, s_k, to maximize lifetime utility:

$$(A35) \qquad \begin{array}{c} \underset{s_k}{Max} \quad u_k(c_{k1}) + u_k(c_{k2}) \\[4pt] subject\ to: \\[4pt] c_{k1} = W_{k1} - s_k \\[4pt] c_{k2} = W_{k2} + s_k + I^*(s_k). \end{array}$$

The child's optimal saving, s_k^*, satisfies the first-order condition:

$$(A36) \qquad -\frac{\delta u_k}{\delta c_{k1}} + \frac{\delta u_k}{\delta c_{k2}}\left(1 + \frac{\delta I^*}{\delta s_k}\right) = 0.$$

After the child chooses saving, the parent chooses s_p, given $s_k(s_p)$ and $I^*(s_p, s_k^*(s_p))$, to maximize lifetime utility,

$$(A37) \qquad \underset{s_p}{Max} \quad u_p(c_{p1}) + u_p(c_{p2}) + \theta\{u_k(c_{k1}) + u_k(c_{k2})\}$$

subject to:

$$c_{p1} = W_{p1} - s_p$$

$$c_{p2} = W_{p2} + T + s_p - I^*\left(s_p, s_k^*(s_p)\right)\Big/(1 - t)$$

$$c_{k1} = W_{k1} - s_k(s_p)$$

$$c_{k2} = W_{k2} + s_k^*(s_p) + I^*\left(s_p, s_k(s_p)\right),$$

which implies

$$(A38) \quad -\frac{\delta u_p}{\delta c_{p1}} + \frac{\delta u_p}{\delta c_{p2}}\left[1 - \frac{1}{(1 - t)}\left(\frac{\delta I^*}{\delta s_p} + \frac{\delta I^*}{\delta s_k^*}\frac{\delta s_k^*}{\delta s_p}\right)\right] + \theta\frac{\delta u_k}{\delta c_{k2}}\frac{\delta I^*}{\delta s_p} = 0.$$

When revenue is recycled, the condition that $T^* = t\,I^*/(1 - t)$ is imposed at this point. No analytic solutions are available. Simulations are discussed in the text.

COMMENT BY

Roger H. Gordon

What is the effect of the estate tax on aggregate savings? The conventional wisdom has certainly been that savings are reduced by the estate tax. The source of this "wisdom" rests on several presumptions. To begin with, the desire to leave a bequest is presumed to be an important if not a key motivation for savings, as seen in the evidence in Laurence J. Kotlikoff and Lawrence H. Summers. Second, the presumption has been that a drop in the rate of return on savings results in a fall in savings.[41] Given the results in Kotlikoff and Summers, it has been natural to extend this presumption about the effects of a tax on the return to savings more broadly to the effects on savings of a tax on an important use for savings–bequests.

The underlying reason for focusing on the effects of the estate tax on savings is that any induced changes in savings are presumed to have important efficiency consequences. In particular, owing to the existing taxes on the return to savings and investment, the presumption has been that the level of the capital stock is far below the efficient level. Externalities provided by new investment, as suggested by J. Bradford De Long and Lawrence H. Summers and by the endogenous growth literature more broadly, strengthen this view that increases in savings and investment are valuable on efficiency grounds.[42] Together, these arguments imply that cutting the estate tax rate should raise savings and thereby raise efficiency.

In contrast, William Gale and Maria Perozek find in general that the forecasts from the theory are ambiguous regarding the effects of the estate tax on savings, once effects on the children as well as effects on the parent are taken into account. Many of their results in fact suggest that savings rise in response to the estate tax. Their results therefore undermine one important argument for a reduction or elimination of the estate tax.

Their argument has two parts. First, they argue that the presumption that savings fall because of a tax on bequests has not been adequately examined closely. Gale and Perozek explore more formally the effects of the estate tax

---

41. Kotlikoff and Summers (1981). Of course, the theory is ambiguous regarding the effects on savings of a change in the rate of return to savings. While the price effect is positive, the income effect is negative. In particular, if the rate of return earned on savings rises, then the individual would need to save less in order to leave the same bequest, suggesting that savings fall unless the desired bequest rises significantly. Specifically, savings rise only if the price elasticity of bequests exceeds one, which is normally assumed. See, for example, Boskin (1978) and Summers (1981).

42. De Long and Summers (1991).

on savings in a variety of models that have been proposed in the literature to explain why parents leave bequests. While past intuition seems to rely on parents obtaining utility directly from bequests, Gale and Perozek show that several of the other models lead to somewhat different results. However, the presumption remains that the effects of the tax on the savings of the parents are small or negative.

Second, and more important, they explore the effects of the estate tax on the savings rate of the children. While the theory is ambiguous whether savings rise or fall in response to the estate tax, the theory is clear that the size of the bequest (net of the estate tax) falls. If kids expect to receive a smaller bequest because of the tax, then Gale and Perozek argue that they will save more themselves in order to offset this reduced transfer. Therefore, the estate tax, by reducing bequests, increases the kids' savings. Since the tax increases kids' savings and has ambiguous effects on the parents' savings, the combined effect on savings remains ambiguous, though numerical examples suggest that the tax *increases* savings, contrary to the conventional wisdom.

In my comments, I raise a few questions about their forecasts on the behavior of both parents and children.

Estate Taxes and Savings of Parents

Gale and Perozek analyze the effects of taxes on parents' savings using several different models of bequests. In two of these models, the tax simply has no effect. These models are not at all implausible, so that this forecast must carry some weight. In one model, parents do not care about how much they leave as a bequest. However, they are unable to buy annuities, or more generally to buy reverse mortgages on their house and consumer durables, implying that any remaining wealth when they die is left as a bequest. In the other model, they get utility from wealth per se, so hold some wealth that they never plan to consume. In both cases, they simply do not care what happens to their estate after they die.

The other models they explore have implications more consistent with the conventional wisdom. In one, parents buy services from their kids, paying for these services with a promised estate. In the other, parents care about their kids' utility directly or at least about the size of their net-of-tax bequest. In all three cases, bequests are used to buy a particular good that provides utility. If the price elasticity of this good exceeds one, then expenditures on the good fall when the price goes up.

The past literature has presumed that these price elasticities do exceed one. However, the empirical support for this presumption is surprisingly weak. In a recent survey of past studies of the interest-rate elasticity of savings, Timothy Besley and Costas Meghir find at least as many studies estimating an elasticity below one as estimating an elasticity above one.[43] I know of no studies looking at the price elasticity of demand for kids' services or of desired transfers to one's kids.

In addition, however, having a price elasticity above one for (net bequests, transfers, services from kids) only implies that expenditures on bequests fall when the price goes up. While expenditures on other goods in total therefore must go up, expenditures on any particular good can still fall. For example, if the price of help from one's kids goes up, then parents will likely shift to hiring nurses, maids, or other such services from the market instead. These alternatives are presumably more expensive, suggesting that expenditures on services for the elderly can easily go up even if expenditures on help from one's kids go down due to the estate tax, that is, the price elasticity of kids' services may be above one even while the price elasticity of services for the elderly generally is below one. If so, then savings will rise in response to the tax in order to finance these more expensive alternatives. Similarly, if the estate tax makes transferring money to one's children more expensive, then parents will likely consider giving charitable donations instead, as an alternative way to generate "fond memories." Donations presumably are a less effective way to generate "fond memories," so that donations can easily go up by more than the fall in bequests to one's kids. Formally, the claim is that C_2 should be a close substitute for B, to the point that C_1 may well fall when B falls. Any effects on savings depend on what happens to C_1.

For these reasons, I think that they understate their challenge to the conventional wisdom that parents' savings fall owing to the estate tax.

Taxes and Savings of the Kids

The key omission from the previous literature that they point out, however, is the effects of the estate tax on the savings of the kids. In their model, this effect is necessarily positive, since the kids will need to increase their own savings to offset the fall in the transfer they can expect to receive from their parents.

Their model, however, assumes that kids receive a bequest during their last period of life—any savings occurred in earlier periods so savings drop in response to higher expected income in the last period. Results can quickly change if the bequest is received at a younger age.

43. Besley and Meghir (1998).

To provide a simple illustration of the issues, assume that the kids live for T years and know they will receive a bequest of size B at some point in their life.[44] Then consumption at each age goes up by B/T, regardless of the kids' age when they receive the bequest. By age t, their wealth changes by $-tB/T$ if they have not yet received the bequest, and by $B - tB/T$ if they have already received it.

To calculate the long-run effect of a change in B on kids' wealth, we need to aggregate over different cohorts. If each cohort will receive a bequest of B at age n, but the cohorts are otherwise identical, then the long-run effect of a change in B on the wealth of the heirs equals $(T - n)B - \int_t tB/Tdt = B[T/2 - n]$. If $n > T/2$, as implicitly assumed by Gale and Perozek, then savings does fall on net in response to B, and the estate tax will increase kids' savings. However, this forecast reverses if $n < T/2$, since the fact that bequests are added to savings in order to finance future consumption becomes a dominant effect. When $n < T/2$, a cut in B because of the estate tax lowers kids' savings.

What can we say about the age when kids normally receive a bequest, compared with the range of ages at which their consumption is changed in response to the (anticipated) bequest? Assume, for example, that kids reach maturity at age 20 and live to age 80, so that $T = 60$ and $T/2 = 30$. In that case, wealth falls on net due to bequests if $n > 30$, or if bequests are received after age 50. Probably, the representative age of kids when they receive a bequest is more like 55 or 60. If so, bequests do reduce savings on net.

More plausibly, however, a better approximation is that savings (like life!) begins at 40: before then, many kids will be credit constrained, or at least too young to be focusing on retirement savings. In that case, $T/2 = 20$ and bequests reduce savings only if $n > 20$ or if bequests are received after age 60. This seems less assured, particularly once one takes into account the fact that the size of the bequest should vary with the age of death of the parents. In particular, the size of the bequest should be smaller the older the age at which the parents die (so the older the age of the kids when they receive it), as long as parents have not fully annuitized the wealth they are using to finance their own consumption. If kids receiving bequests at a younger age receive a larger bequest, then they should get more weight when calculating effects on aggregate savings. Therefore, the weighted average age of receipt will be below the average age of receipt.[45]

---

44. Formally, I assume in addition that utility equals $\int_0^T u(C_t)dt$, so ignore the interest rate and the utility discount rate, or at least assume they are equal and offsetting.

45. However, wealthier parents may live longer, pushing in the opposite direction.

This example ignores so far the possibility that the kids will increase their bequest to the grandkids in response to receiving a larger bequest from their parents. Assume they increase the size of their own bequest by a for each dollar they receive in bequests from their parents. Then the change in their wealth at age t equals $-(1 - a)tB/T$ if they have not yet received a bequest, and $B - (1 - a)tB/T$ if they have. Aggregating across cohorts, the long-run change in savings equals $B[T(1 + a)/2 - n]$. Savings therefore fall in response to bequests only if $n > T(1 + a)/2$. The larger is a, the less likely this condition is to be satisfied.

A theory for effects on savings in the long run may not be the most interesting measure, however, given that the long run can be forty or even sixty years from now according to the theory. What will be the immediate effects on kids' savings during the years immediately following an unanticipated drop in the estate tax? Assume that, as of some date (Dec., 2000?), kids unexpectedly increase the size of bequest they anticipate receiving by b.[46] Past bequests remain unchanged, so that the wealth of kids who have already received a bequest will not be affected (except in their role as parents of the grandkids). Note, however, that the past consumption of younger kids also cannot go up in response to the now larger anticipated bequest. If they were age t when the policy change was announced, then consumption each year thereafter goes up by $b/(T - t)$. After c years, the individual's wealth changes by $-cb/(T - t)$ if (s)he has not yet received a bequest, and by $b - cb/(T - t)$ if (s)he has. After c years, aggregate wealth of the kids changes by

$$cb - \int_c^{n+c} \frac{cb}{T - t}\, dt - \int_0^c \frac{tb}{T}dt = cb\left[1 - \frac{c}{2T} - \ln\left(\frac{T - c}{T - n - c}\right)\right].$$

This expression is obviously much more complicated than before. If $T = 60$ and $n = 35$, however, numerical calculations show that aggregate wealth of the kids goes up during the first four years following the reform, even though wealth declines in the long run.

Summary and Implications

Gale and Perozek have effectively shown that the conventional wisdom that the estate tax reduces savings rests on a very weak foundation. They provide

---

46. For simplicity, I assume that b does not vary by future cohort, even though the tax change is unanticipated. This would be true, for example, if parents view donations and bequests as very close substitutes, so they can immediately respond to a change in incentives.

a rich exploration of the implications of the formal models of bequest behavior for the effects of the estate tax on aggregate savings and find that the effects are ambiguous or even positive. While their results are largely consistent with the conventional wisdom that the estate tax reduces (or perhaps leaves unchanged) the savings of the parents, they point out that the conventional wisdom has ignored effects of the estate tax on savings of the kids: they argue that kids' savings should rise in response to the tax.

Compared with the authors, I find it a bit more plausible that parents' savings rise owing to the estate tax, strengthening their challenge to the conventional wisdom. However, contrary to their arguments, I find it very plausible that kids' savings fall because of the estate tax. The net effect is still ambiguous, however.

The main point of the chapter is only reinforced, however: assessing the effects of the estate tax on savings is much more complicated than has been recognized in the past literature, and results can easily be very different than have been presumed in the past. This is a careful and important contribution to the discussion of the effects of the estate tax.

References

Aaron, Henry J., and Alicia H. Munnell. 1992. "Reassessing the Role for Wealth Transfer Taxes." *National Tax Journal* 45 (June): 119–43.

Abel, Andrew B. 1985. "Precautionary Saving and Accidental Bequests." *American Economic Review* 75 (September): 777–91.

Altonji, Joseph G., Fumio Hayashi, and Laurence J. Kotlikoff. 1992. "Is the Extended Family Altruistically Linked? Direct Tests Using Micro Data." *American Economic Review* 82 (December): 1177–98.

———. 1997. "Parental Altruism and Inter Vivos Transfers: Theory and Evidence." *Journal of Political Economy* 105 (December): 1121–66.

Andreoni, James. 1989. "Giving with Impure Altruism: Applications to Charity and Ricardian Equivalence." *Journal of Political Economy* 97 (December): 1447–58.

Bakshi, Gurdip S., and Zhiwu Chen. 1996. "The Spirit of Capitalism and Stock-Market Prices." *American Economic Review* 86 (March): 133–57.

Barro, Robert. 1974. "Are Government Bonds Net Wealth?" *Journal of Political Economy* 82 (November–December): 1095–117.

Barro, Robert. 1989. "The Ricardian Approach to Budget Deficits." *Journal of Economic Perspectives* 3 (Spring): 37–54.

Becker, Gary S. 1974. "A Theory of Social Interactions." *Journal of Political Economy* 82 (November–December): 1063–93.

Becker, Gary S., and Nigel Tomes. 1979. "An Equilibrium Theory of the Distribution of Income and Intergenerational Mobility." *Journal of Political Economy* 87 (December): 1153–89.

Becker, Gary S., and Nigel Tomes. 1986. "Human Capital and the Rise and Fall of Families." *Journal of Labor Economics* 4 (July): S1–39.

Bernheim, B. Douglas. 1989. "A Neoclassical Perspective on Budget Deficits." *Journal of Economic Perspectives* 3 (Spring): 55–72.

Bernheim, B. Douglas. 1991. "How Strong Are Bequest Motives: Evidence Based on Estimates of the Demand for Life Insurance." *Journal of Political Economy* 99 (October): 899–927.

Bernheim, B. Douglas, Andrei Shleifer, and Lawrence H. Summers. 1985. "The Strategic Bequest Motive." *Journal of Political Economy* 93 (December): 1045–76.

Bernheim, B. Douglas, and Sergei Severinov. 2000. "Bequests as Signals: An Explanation for the Equal Division Puzzle." Working Paper 7791. Cambridge, Mass.: National Bureau of Economic Research. July.

Bernheim, B. Douglas, and Oded Stark. 1988. "Altruism within the Family Reconsidered: Do Nice Guys Finish Last?" *American Economic Review* 78 (December): 1034–45.

Besley, Timothy, and Costas Meghir. 1998. "Tax Based Savings Incentives." Mimeo.

Blinder, Alan. 1976. "Intergenerational Transfers and Life Cycle Consumption." *American Economic Review* 66 (May): 87–93.

Boskin, Michael J. "Taxation, Savings, and the Rate of Interest." *Journal of Political Economy* 86 (April 1978): S3–27.

Brannon, Gerard M. 1973. "Death Taxes in a Structure of Progressive Taxes." *National Tax Journal* 26 (September): 451–57.

Brown, Jeffrey R. 2000. "Differential Mortality and the Value of Individual Account Retirement Annuities." Working Paper 7560. Cambridge, Mass.: National Bureau of Economic Research. February.

Bruce, Neil, and Michael Waldman. 1990. "The Rotten-Kid Theorem Meets the Samaritan's Dilemma." *Quarterly Journal of Economics* 105 (February): 155–65.

———. 1991. "Transfers in Kind: Why They Can Be Efficient and Non-Paternalistic." *American Economic Review* 81 (December): 1345–51.

Caballe, Jordi. 1995. "Endogenous Growth, Human Capital, and Bequests in a Life-Cycle Model." *Oxford Economic Papers* 47 (January): 156–81.

Carroll, Christopher D. 2000. "Why Do the Rich Save So Much?" In *Does Atlas Shrug? The Economic Consequences of Taxing the Rich*, edited by Joel B. Slemrod, 465–84. Russell Sage and Harvard University Press.

Chapman, Kenneth, Govind Hariharan, and Lawrence Southwick, Jr. 1996. "Estate Taxes and Asset Accumulation." *Family Business Review* 9 (Fall): 253–68.

Coate, Stephen. 1995. "Altruism, the Samaritan's Dilemma, and Government Transfer Policy." *American Economic Review* 85 (March): 46–57.

Cox, Donald. 1987. "Motives for Private Income Transfers." *Journal of Political Economy* 95 (June): 508–46.

———. 1990. "Intergenerational Transfers and Liquidity Constraints." *Quarterly Journal of Economics* 105 (February): 197–217.

Curry, Philip A., and James B. Davies. 1998. "Evolution and Intergenerational Transfers." University of Western Ontario. December. Mimeo.

Davies, James B. 1981. "Uncertain Lifetime, Consumption, and Dissaving in Retirement." *Journal of Political Economy* 89 (June): 561–77.

De Long, J. Bradford, and Lawrence H. Summers. 1991. "Equipment Investment and Economic Growth." *Quarterly Journal of Economics* 106 (May): 445–502.

Fiekowsky, Seymour. 1966. "The Effect on Saving of the United States Estate and Gift Tax." In *Federal Estate and Gift Taxes*, edited by Carl S. Shoup, 228–37. Brookings.

Frank, Robert H. 2000. "Progressive Taxation and the Incentive Problem." In *Does Atlas Shrug? The Economic Consequences of Taxing the Rich*, edited by Joel B. Slemrod, 490–507. Cambridge University Press.

Fried, Barbara. 1999. "Who Gets Utility from Bequests? The Distributive and Welfare Implications for a Consumption Tax." Colloquium on Tax Policy and Public Finance, Spring.

Gale, William G. 2000. Comment on "The Estate Tax and After-Tax Investment." *Does Atlas Shrug? The Economic Consequences of Taxing the Rich*, edited by Joel B. Slemrod, 350–54. Russell Sage and Harvard University Press.

Gale, William G., and Maria G. Perozek. 2000. "Do Estate Taxes Reduce Saving?" Brookings Institution and Federal Reserve Board of Governors. April. Mimeo.

Gale, William G., and John Karl Scholz. 1994. "Intergenerational Transfers and Accumulation of Wealth." *Journal of Public Economics* 8(4): 145–60.

Graetz, Michael J. 1983. "To Praise the Estate Tax, Not to Bury It." *Yale Law Journal* 93: 259–86.

Holtz-Eakin, Douglas. 1996. "The Uneasy Empirical Case for Abolishing the Estate Tax." *Tax Law Review* 51: 496–515.

Holtz-Eakin, Douglas, David Joulfaian, and Harvey S. Rosen. 1993. "The Carnegie Conjecture: Some Empirical Evidence." *Quarterly Journal of Economics* 108 (May): 413–35.

———. 1994a. "Sticking It Out: Entrepreneurial Survival and Liquidity Constraints." *Journal of Political Economy* 102 (February): 53–75.

———. 1994b. "Entrepreneurial Decisions and Liquidity Constraint." *Rand Journal of Economics* 25 (Summer): 334–47.

Hurd, Michael D. 1987. "Savings of the Elderly and Desired Bequests." *American Economic Review* 77 (June): 298–312.

Ihori, Toshihiro. 1998. "Wealth Taxation and Economic Growth." University of Tokyo. Mimeo.

Imbens, Guido W., Donald B. Rubin, and Bruce Sacerdote. 1999. "Estimating the Effects of Unearned Income on Labor Supply, Earnings, Savings, and Consumption: Evidence from a Survey of Lottery Players." Working Paper 7001. Cambridge, Mass.: National Bureau of Economic Research (March).

Johnson, Craig E., John Diamond, and George R. Zodrow. 1997. "Bequests, Saving, and Taxation." *1996 Conference Proceedings*, 37–45. National Tax Association, Tax Institute of America.

Joint Committee on Taxation. 1998. *Present Law and Background Relating to Estate and Gift Taxes*. Testimony before the House Committee on Ways and Means, January 28.

Joulfaian, David. 1992. "The Distribution and Division of Bequests in the U.S.: Evidence from the Collation Study" (December).

———. 1998. "The Federal Estate and Gift Tax: Description, Profile of Taxpayers, and Economic Consequences." Office of Tax Analysis Paper 80 (December).

Joulfaian, David, and Mark O. Wilhelm. 1994. "Inheritance and Labor Supply." *Journal of Human Resources* 29 (Fall): 1205–34.

Kaplow, Louis. 1995. "A Note on Subsidizing Gifts." *Journal of Public Economics* 58 (November): 469–77.

———. 1997. "Transfer Motives and Tax Policy." Working Paper 6340. Cambridge, Mass.: National Bureau of Economic Research (December).

Kotlikoff, Laurence J. 1989. "Estimating the Wealth Elasticity of Bequests from a Sample of Potential Decedents." In *What Determines Savings?* MIT Press.

Kotlikoff, Laurence J., and Avia Spivak. 1981. "The Family as an Incomplete Annuities Market." *Journal of Political Economy* 89 (April): 372–91.

Kotlikoff, Laurence J., and Lawrence H. Summers. 1981. "The Role of Intergenerational Transfers in Capital Accumulation." *Journal of Political Economy* 89 (August): 706–32.

Kunieda, Shigeki. 1989. "Does the Estate Tax Matter?" Harvard University (Mimeo).

Laitner, John, and F. Thomas Juster. 1996. "New Evidence on Altruism: A Study of TIAA-CREF Retirees." *American Economic Review* 86 (September): 893–908.

Lindbeck, Assar, and Jorgen W. Weibull. 1988. "Altruism and Time Consistency: The Economics of Fait Accompli." *Journal of Political Economy* 96 (December): 1165–83.

Masson, Andre, and Pierre Pestieau. 1997. "Bequest Motives and Models of Inheritance: A Survey of the Literature." In *Is Inheritance Legitimate?* edited by G. Erreygers and T. Vandevelde, 54–88. Berlin: Springer.

McCaffrey, Edward J. 1994. "The Uneasy Case for Wealth Transfer Taxation." *Yale Law Journal* 104 (November): 283–365.

———. 1997. "Inter Vivos Transfers and Intended Bequests." Working Paper 6345. Cambridge, Mass.: National Bureau of Economic Research (December).

McGarry, Kathleen. 2000. "Testing Parental Altruism: Implications of a Dynamic Model." Working Paper 7593. Cambridge, Mass.: National Bureau of Economic Research (March).

McGarry, Kathleen, and Robert F. Schoeni. 1995. "Transfer Behavior within the Family: Results from the Asset and Health Dynamics Survey." Working Paper 5099. Cambridge, Mass.: National Bureau of Economic Research (April).

Menchik, Paul. 1980. "Primogeniture, Equal Sharing, and the U.S. Distribution of Wealth." *Quarterly Journal of Economics* 94 (May): 299–316.

Menchik, Paul, and Martin David. 1983. "Income Distribution, Lifetime Savings, and Bequests." *American Economic Review* 73 (September): 672–89.

Menchik, Paul L. 1988. "Unequal Estate Division: Is It Altruism, Reverse Bequests, or Simply Noise?" In *Modelling the Accumulation and Distribution of Wealth,* edited by Denis Kessler and Andre Masson, 105–16. Oxford: Oxford University Press.

Metcalf, Gilbert E. 1995. "The Lifetime Incidence of a Consumption Tax." In *Distributional Analysis of Tax Policy,* edited by David F. Bradford, 295–303. Washington: American Enterprise Institute Press.

Modigliani, Franco. 1988. "The Role of Intergenerational Transfers and Life-Cycle Saving in the Accumulation of Wealth." *Journal of Economic Perspectives* 2 (September): 15–40.

Mulligan, Casey B. 1997. *Parental Priorities and Economic Inequality.* University of Chicago Press.

Musgrave, Richard A. 1959. *The Theory of Public Finance: A Study in Public Economy.* McGraw-Hill.

Page, Benjamin R. 1997. "Bequest Taxes, Inter Vivos Gifts, and the Bequest Motive." Congressional Budget Office (September).

Pechman, Joseph A. 1983. *Federal Tax Policy.* Brookings.

Perozek, Maria G. 1996. "The Implications of a Dynamic Model of Altruistic Intergenerational Transfers." Federal Reserve Board.

———. 1998. "A Re-examination of the Strategic Bequest Motive." *Journal of Political Economy.* 106 (April): 423–45.

Pollak, Robert A. 1988. "Tied Transfers and Paternalistic Preferences." *American Economic Review* 78 (May): 240.

Poterba, James. 2000. "The Estate Tax and After-Tax Investment." In *Does Atlas Shrug? The Economic Consequences of Taxing the Rich*, edited by Joel B. Slemrod, 329–49. Russell Sage and Harvard University Press.

Rebelein, Robert B. 1998. "Strategic Behavior and Ricardian Equivalence in a Dynamic Environment." Department of the Treasury.

Shoven, John B., and David A. Wise. 1996. "The Taxation of Pensions: A Shelter Can Become a Trap." Working Paper 5815. Cambridge, Mass.: National Bureau of Economic Research (November).

Slemrod, Joel B., ed. 2000. *Does Atlas Shrug? The Economic Consequences of Taxing the Rich*. Cambridge University Press.

Stiglitz, Joseph. 1978. "Notes on Estate Taxes, Redistribution, and the Concept of Balanced Growth Path Incidence." *Journal of Political Economy* 86 (April): S137–150.

Summers, Lawrence. 1981. "Capital Taxation and Accumulation in a Life Cycle Growth Model." *American Economic Review* 71 (September): 533–44.

Tomes, Nigel. 1981. "The Family, Inheritance, and the Intergenerational Transmission of Inequality." *Journal of Political Economy* 89 (October): 928–58.

Tomes, Nigel. 1988. "Inheritance and Inequality within the Family: Equal Division among Unequals, or Do the Poor Get More?" In *Modeling the Accumulation and Distribution of Wealth*, edited by Denis Kessler and Andre Masson, 79–104. Oxford: Oxford University Press.

Weil, David N. 1994. "The Saving of the Elderly in Micro and Macro Data." *Quarterly Journal of Economics* 109 (February): 55–81.

Wilhelm, Mark O. 1996. "Bequest Behavior and the Effect of Heirs' Earnings: Testing the Altruistic Model of Bequests." *American Economic Review* 86 (September): 874–92.

JOHN LAITNER

6 Inequality and Wealth Accumulation: Eliminating the Federal Gift and Estate Tax

R ECENT POLITICAL debates include proposals to reduce or eliminate the federal unified gift and estate tax. This chapter analyzes the possible long-run consequences of such changes, focusing on national wealth accumulation and the degree of inequality in the cross-sectional distribution of net worth among households.

This chapter works with a structural model. Economists have proposed many theories of intergenerational transfer behavior, including ones in which transfers arise inadvertently from incomplete annuitization, others in which they constitute repayment for services (such as care for an elderly donor), and theories in which transfers occur intentionally as donors seek to augment their descendants' resources.[1] Since an array of exemptions and credits imply that the federal tax only affects large gifts and estates, I concentrate on intentional transfers. Among theories for intentional transfers, some stress a donor's joy of giving, and others a donor's concern for his heirs' well-being. The former do not necessarily have clear tax implications—as a donor might derive joy in proportion to his gross or net-of-tax estate. The latter, so-called altruistic models, avoid this potential problem. Altruism is consistent with the "representa-

I owe thanks to conference participants, especially Douglas Holtz-Eakin, for helpful comments and suggestions on an earlier version of this chapter.

1. See, for example, Laitner (1997).

tive agent" paradigm, which macroeconomic theorists employ widely, and with the casual empirical observation that very prosperous families are the ones most likely to leave estates.[2] Our analysis adopts the altruistic framework.

This chapter constructs an intertemporal general equilibrium model with heterogeneous households, a simple government sector, and an aggregate production function. Households have differing earning abilities, and they may care about their grown children to different degrees. A household lives for a number of periods, and life-cycle saving is important. Since households may care about the utility of their descendants, intergenerational transfers may also occur in the form of inter vivos gifts or bequests. Altruistic households with high earning abilities relative to their children are, for example, likely to make intergenerational transfers. Expectations are fully rational. The complexity of the framework limits our analysis to long-run, steady-state equilibria. The model generates a stationary distribution of wealth. I compare it with the actual distribution and study the consequences for it of changes in the gift and estate tax. I also consider the long-run effects of the tax on aggregative national wealth.

Overview

This chapter constructs an intertemporal general equilibrium model. The model's parameters characterize household preference orderings and aspects of the production technology; they are invariant with respect to tax changes. If we alter gift and estate taxes, the model enables us to follow the consequences for the aggregate capital stock in a context in which other taxes adjust to preserve the government's budget constraint, and in which the interest rate moves to a new equilibrium level. Since the model, after trend corrections, determines a stationary equilibrium distribution of wealth, we can also study how wealth inequality changes subsequent to modification of the tax system. Although later the chapter references propositions about existence and provides a diagram that summarizes several aspects of the analysis, quantitative results stem from numerical solutions of the model.

The model has life-cycle saving for all families. This part of the framework includes children, retirement, income taxes, and Social Security taxes and benefits. Labor supply is inelastic. Annuity and life insurance markets exist and function. There is an exogenous distribution of family earning abilities.

2. See Modigliani (1986).

Each household learns its lifetime earning ability early in adulthood, and earning abilities are heritable to a degree within family lines. A fraction λ of family lines are dynastic; the remaining fraction, $1 - \lambda$, are not. Nondynastic families care only about their own lifetime consumption, including the consumption of minor children living with them. They do not make inter vivos gifts or bequests to their grown children.

Dynastic, or "altruistic," families care as well about the consumption of their adult children, grandchildren, and so on. Dynastic families have earning ability draws from the same distribution as households in general, and their life cycles are analogous to those of other families. The descendants of dynastic families are also dynastic. Dynastic families may choose to make intergenerational transfers, although the latter must be nonnegative. Parents with high earnings or a large inheritance are likely candidates to make transfers, especially if their children have lower earning abilities than they do. Life-cycle saving, private intergenerational transfers, and the overall distribution of earnings determine wealth holdings. The analysis in this chapter considers only long-run, steady-state equilibria.

Later the model is calibrated. There are four key parameters. One determines the slope with respect to age of life-cycle consumption profiles. I set this parameter from survey data on consumer expenditures. A second parameter determines the weight altruistic parents assign to descendants' well-being relative to their own. I calibrate the second parameter so that numerical solutions replicate the empirical aggregate stock of wealth. The third key parameter, γ, jointly sets risk aversion and willingness to substitute consumption over different ages. The fourth parameter is λ, the fraction of dynastic households in the economy. This chapter jointly calibrates γ and λ to match the empirical degree of wealth inequality and federal gift and estate tax revenues.

A surprising result is that when $\lambda = 1$, so that all families are dynastic, private intergenerational transfers contribute rather modestly to overall wealth inequality. In fact, when $\lambda = 1$, the model falls short of explaining the degree of inequality of the empirical distribution of wealth. For consistency with the empirical distribution of bequests and estate tax collections, however, the model seems reasonably satisfactory.

When only a fraction of households are altruistic, the model can match the actual distribution of wealth more closely. A value of λ of about .05 seems to yield good results. In other words, bequests and inheritances can explain a high degree of wealth inequality when only a small minority of households are altruistic. With a low λ, however, the simulated distribution of bequests deviates from the empirical distribution: in the simulations nearly all altruistic households leave multimillion dollar estates, whereas data from tax returns imply that estates of this magnitude are very rare.

At this point, the model then offers either a plausible distribution of bequests but an overly equal distribution of wealth or a reasonably good match with the empirical distribution of wealth but a less than entirely satisfactory distribution of bequests.

The chapter studies the long-run consequences of eliminating the federal gift and estate tax. After eliminating the tax, I calculate a new steady-state equilibrium interest rate, adjusting income taxes to maintain the former ratio of government spending to output. For the best calibration with $\lambda = 1$, eliminating the estate tax has almost no effect on the economy's long-run capital intensivity. The steady-state distribution of wealth becomes moderately less equal: its Gini coefficient rises slightly, although the fraction of wealth held by the top 1 percent increases by 16 percent. For the best calibration with $\lambda = .05$, however, eliminating the estate tax causes the aggregative capital to output ratio to increase about 2.5 percent in the long run, with the gross of tax interest rate falling as much as sixty basis points. In view of the relatively small revenues of the gift and estate tax, these effects are impressive. Wealth inequality rises more sharply than before, however, with the fraction of wealth of the top 1 percent expanding by 32 percent.

With either choice of calibration, the analysis suggests that reducing the federal gift and estate tax is likely to raise the concentration of the cross-sectional distribution of wealth. If one's primary goal is to increase the aggregative capital-to-output ratio, perhaps policies such as paying down the national debt deserve careful consideration as alternative options.

The Model

The model is neoclassical. Parts are conventional. Technological change is exogenous, and there is an aggregate production function. As in standard overlapping generations frameworks, households have finite lives. However, the model has three distinctive features. First, households may be "altruistic" in the sense of caring about the utility of their grown-up descendants.[3] Second, within each birth cohort there is an exogenous distribution of earning abilities. Third, households face borrowing constraints: because of bankruptcy

---

3. In this chapter, parents may care about their grown children, but children, by assumption, do not reciprocally care about their aged parents.

laws, creditors will not extend loans without collateral; hence, households cannot have negative net worth. The first two features lead to a distribution of intergenerational transfers: a high-earning-ability, altruistic parent with a low-earning-ability child will want to make an inter vivos gift or a bequest, but a low-earning-ability parent with a high-earning-ability child, or a non-altruistic parent, will not. The third feature creates another reason for inter-generational transfers, in particular, inter vivos gifts: even parents who do not intend to make bequests at death may want to make lifetime transfers to their grown children if the children are liquidity constrained, say, when they are in their twenties.

There is a long-standing controversy within the economics profession over the relative importance for national wealth accumulation of life-cycle saving and estate building.[4] Following the lead of Alan Blinder and James Davies, this paper incorporates both motives for wealth accumulation.[5] The calibrations later in the chapter determine their relative roles. If only bequest-motivated saving was included, my analysis might overstate the significance of estate tax-ation for overall wealth accumulation. Furthermore, a model without life-cycle saving compels inheritance to explain wealth inequality entirely—again risk-ing exaggeration of the effects of estate-tax reform.

In contrast to Blinder, parents in this chapter's model determine their be-quests by balancing their own resources and needs against their adult children's earning abilities and needs. The model is more analogous to Davies, although this chapter's computations proceed all the way to a long-run equilibrium with a stationary distribution of inheritances and wealth. The basic framework is similar to John Laitner, although this chapter incorporates estate taxes, assumes that earning abilities are heritable within family lines, and allows lim-ited altruism in the sense that a parent caring about his grown children may, in his calculations, weight the children's lifetime utility less heavily than his own.[6] Further—and this turns out to be significant in the calibrations—this chapter allows a fraction of households to be altruistic, while the remainder are not.

Other comparisons to the existing literature are as follows. In contrast to Gary S. Becker and Nigel Tomes, Glenn C. Loury, and many others, this chapter omits special consideration of human capital.[7] In contrast to James B. Davies, Benjamin M. Friedman and Mark J. Warshawsky, Andrew Abel,

---

4. For example, Kotlikoff and Summers (1981); Modigliani (1988); Kotlikoff (1988).
5. Blinder (1974); Davies (1982).
6. See Laitner (1992).
7. Becker and Tomes (1979); Loury (1981).

Jagadeesh Gokhale, and others, this chapter assumes that households purchase actuarially fair annuities to offset fully mortality risk; consequently, all bequests are intentional.[8] In contrast to B. Douglas Bernheim and Kyle Bagwell, this chapter assumes perfectly assortative mating—adopting the interpretation of Laitner, who shows that a model of one-parent households, each having one child, can mimic the outcomes of a framework in which each set of parents has two children and mating is endogenous.[9]

In contrast to Blinder, Auerbach and Kotlikoff, and others, this chapter assumes that households supply labor inelastically.[10] Similarly, each surviving household retires at age 66. Presupposing an inelastic labor supply eliminates, of course, potentially interesting implications about the work incentives of heirs (see, for example, Holtz-Eakin).[11] This ultimately may lead to an understatement of the importance of intergenerational transfers: in practice, a parent having an exceptionally high earning ability may decide, on the basis of the principle of comparative advantage, to work long hours and to build a very large estate, letting his descendants enjoy higher consumption than they could otherwise afford and more leisure than the donor takes for himself.

Finally, this chapter's model does not explore possible strategic behavior on the part of heirs.[12] For example, the child of a high-earning-ability parent might intentionally save nothing in youth in order to extract a larger bequest.

Framework

In the analysis, time is discrete and the population is stationary. Think of each household as having a single parent and single offspring (see the reference to assortative mating above). The parent is 22 years old when a household begins. The parent is 26 when his child is born. When the parent is 48, the child is 22. At that point, the child leaves home to form his own household. The parent works from age 22 through 65 and then retires. No one lives beyond age 87. There is no child mortality. In fact, for simplicity we assume all parents live at least through age 48. Between 49 and 87, the age of death is uncertain.

Because of experiential human capital, each household's earnings rise naturally with age. There is also labor-augmenting technological progress at a

---

8. Davies (1981); Friedman and Warshawsky (1990); Abel (1985); Gokhale and others (1999).
9. Bernheim and Bagwell (1988); Laitner (1991).
10. Blinder (1974); Auerbach and Kotlikoff (1987).
11. Holtz-Eakin and others (1993).
12. See William Gale and Maria Perozek in this volume.

constant rate, affecting all households equally. Finally, each adult has an individual earning ability. There is an intergenerational stochastic process for abilities, such that each adult's ability is the geometric average of his father's ability and random sampling from an exogenous distribution. The intergenerational correlation of abilities follows estimates from Gary Solon.[13] The exogenous shock comes from a noncentral T—distribution—allowing thicker tails than the more traditional choice of a normal distribution. The stochastic process assigns an ability to each adult at age 22. The ability remains fixed throughout the adult's life, and it is public knowledge (visible, in particular, to the adult's parents). A household's earnings at a given age are the product of its human capital, ability, the state of overall technology, and the wage rate. My analysis is limited to steady-state equilibria in which the wage rate, interest rate, income tax rate, and Social Security tax rate are constant over time.

Preferences are homothetic. This allows a steady-state equilibrium despite technological progress. As explained, each household is thought of as having a single adult and raising a single child. An adult's life has two phases. The first begins at age 22 and closes after age 47. At 22, the adult learns his earning ability and the present value of all transfers that he will receive from his parent. He chooses a terminal net worth level (for age 47), and then he solves a life-cycle problem for ages 22–47. He must pay a proportional income tax and a proportional Social Security tax up to the latter's statutory earnings maximum. Other than paying taxes and saving to meet his terminal goal, the adult allocates consumption between his minor child and himself to maximize private utility. He does face, however, a nonnegativity constraint on net worth at every age. In choosing his net worth for the close of his first phase of life, an adult seeks to maximize his subsequent expected utility.

This chapter assumes that parents part with their transfers to their adult children as late as they can. This enables them to limit the potential strategic behavior of their children, and it seems consistent with donors' apparent reluctance to distribute their estates through gifts instead of bequests (see, for example, Joseph A. Pechman, as well as James Poterba).[14] Thus, in the first phase of life, until his parent dies an adult will actually receive in any given year only the portion of his inheritance needed to lift his current liquidity constraints. The remaining estate arrives, of course, at his parent's death. For simplicity, we assume that if the parent remains alive at age 74 (when the child is 48), the remaining transfer takes place then—and is called a "be-

---

13. Solon (1992).
14. Pechman (1987, table 8.2); Poterba (1998, table 4).

quest."[15] The model has no generation-skipping transfers from parents to grandchildren.

The second phase of life runs from age 48 to 88. At age 48 an adult's inheritance is complete, and his child has become an adult. He learns his child's earning ability and sets his transfer. As above, he implements the transfer through inter vivos gifts over years in which his child is liquidity constrained, and through a bequest at death or age 74. The parent annuitizes the remainder of his assets, and he uses the assets plus his remaining earnings and Social Security benefits for his own life-cycle consumption.

To determine a household's asset goal for the close of age 47 and its desired intergenerational transfer to its adult child, we must solve a pair of so-called Bellman equations. Appendix A to this chapter provides the details of these equations and of the life-cycle calculations outlined above.

The remainder of the economy is more straightforward. There is a Cobb-Douglas aggregate production function through which the economy's aggregate physical capital stock and total effective labor supply determine the current GDP. (The model omits government capital and consumer durables.) Setting the price of units of GDP to 1 and assuming perfect competition, the marginal products of effective labor and physical capital determine the wage and interest rate.

The model has government debt—the empirical government debt seems too large to overlook in the calibrations later in this chapter. We assume that the ratio of debt to total GDP is constant through time; that the ratio of Social Security retirement benefits to GDP is constant; that the Social Security system is unfunded, so that current Social Security tax revenues just equal current benefits; and that government spending on goods and services is an unchanging fraction of GDP. Later pages describe the gift and estate tax, which is the most elaborately specified tax in the model. Finally, there is a proportional tax on interest and wage income. Each simulation solves for the income tax rate necessary to preserve balance in the government's budget constraint.

The economy is closed. Thus, Walras law implies that equilibrium requires two conditions. First, the sum of the current effective labor from all households provides the aggregate supply of labor, and the production sector provides the aggregate demand. For (our neoclassical) equilibrium, we

---

15. The reason for the arbitrary age limit of 74 for transfers is as follows. After age 74, the grandchild's earning ability is revealed. While the additional information would affect the parent's planning in theory, in practice it seems unlikely that surviving 75-year-olds alter their consumption and wills appreciably in view of their grandchildren's early success in the labor market.

need the total labor supply to equal the labor input of the aggregate production function. Second, the sum of the current net worth of all households
provides the economy's supply of financing. The demand for financing is
the sum of next period's government debt and next period's physical capital stock. Again, equilibrium requires equality of supply and demand. Put
another way, to calculate an equilibrium for the model one must find an
income tax rate and an aggregative capital-to-labor ratio such that (a) the
implied net-of-tax wage and interest rates from the aggregate production
function induce household wealth accumulation just sufficient to finance the
given capital-to-labor ratio, and (b) implied tax collections are just sufficient
to finance current government spending and debt service net of steady-state
debt growth. In fact, this chapter focuses exclusively on steady-state equilibria in which factor payments and tax rates are indefinitely constant and capital, effective labor, and GDP grow at the rate of technological progress.
Appendix A to this chapter presents details of the framework.

Computation of Equilibrium

Figure 6-1 summarizes the sectoral components of our model.

Figure 6-1. *The Steady-State Equilibrium Demand and Supply of Financing*

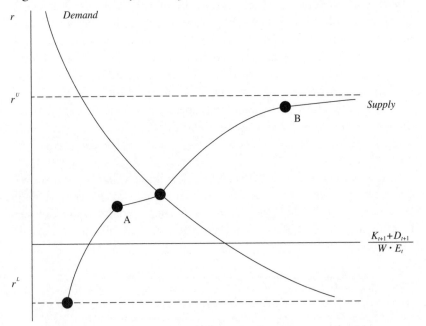

On the vertical axis we have potential steady-state gross-of-tax interest rates. Letting W be the steady-state gross-of-tax wage rate corresponding to a given r, E_t the aggregate effective labor supply, K_{t+1} the physical capital stock ready for use at the start of the next period, and D_{t+1} national debt which private-sector creditors must carry from t to $t + 1$, the horizontal axis gives the amount of credit at time t supplied by the household sector and used by government and business. Our Cobb-Douglas aggregate production function implies a constant ratio of factor shares, leading to a hyperbolic relation of r and $K_t/(W \cdot E_t)$—hence, given a steady state, of r and $K_{t+1}/(W \cdot E_t)$. Our assumptions about government debt make $D_{t+1}/(W \cdot E_t)$ constant. Thus, uses of credit determine the demand curve in figure 6-1. (Appendix A provides details.)

For any interest rate, household behavior and the government budget constraint determine a long-run supply of credit (relative to the wage bill). For given any r, we can jointly solve for the household sector's supply of credit and the income tax rate satisfying the government's budget constraint. This determines the supply curve in figure 6-1. Straight-forward amendments of Propositions 1–3 in Laitner establish that the supply curve has an asymptote at r^U specified in appendix A.[16] An inter-section in figure 6-1 determines a steady-state equilibrium for the model. There are no steady states above the asymptote (household net worth is infinite in that range). Although multiple intersections are theoretically possible in figure 6-1, they do not arise in the numerical computations below.

Appendix A lays out a series of numerical steps which generate points on the curves in figure 6-1, enabling one to compute their intersection.

Digressing for a moment, the shape of the supply curve in figure 6-1 has great potential interest. The supply of credit must become extremely interest elastic near its asymptote. If our steady-state equilibrium occurs in that range, for example, near point B, we have an implication reminis-cent of Robert Barro: a larger national debt, sliding the demand curve to the right, will barely change the equilibrium interest rate at all.[17] We might label this the "Ricardian region" of the supply curve. At a point such as A, in contrast, an increase in government debt affects the econ-omy as in the familiar overlapping generations model without bequests of Peter Diamond.[18]

16. Laitner (1992).
17. Barro (1974).
18. Diamond (1965).

Calibration

The model has fifteen parameters. Using 1995 as our base year, we set them to match data on the U.S. economy as closely as possible. With the parameters fixed, the next section, "Tax Changes," changes the federal gift and estate tax and computes new long-run equilibria.

We calibrate most of the parameters from familiar sources. Appendix B in this chapter provides details of the steps. Since the parameters setting the shape of life-cycle consumption profiles and the degree of altruism are more subtle, we discuss them separately. We also devote extra attention to the distribution of earnings, since the model proves sensitive to it. This section also reviews the model's treatment of the existing federal gift and estate tax. Finally, I turn to the two most difficult parameters to calibrate.

Lifetime Consumption and the Degree of Altruism

Our specification of lifetime utility has a subjective discount factor β. This parameter specifies how heavily a household weights next-year's lifetime marginal utility relative to this year's. Although economists often surmise that $0 < \beta < 1$ because people are impatient, recent work by Robert Barsky finds some support for $\beta > 1$ from survey evidence.[19] We estimate β indirectly. The time path of life-cycle consumption for a liquidity-constrained household must follow the household's flow of resources. For unconstrained households, however, the age profile of consumption per adult equivalent depends on the interest rate, the intertemporal rate of substitution, and the subjective discount factor. Given values for the first two, we set β so that lifetime consumption growth follows 1984–97 data from the U.S. Consumer Expenditure Survey. The survey enables us to track the consumption of different age cohorts over time. We pick 30- to 39-year-olds as the least likely to have family composition changes or binding liquidity constraints. We find consumption per adult growing at about 2.5 percent a year. Appendix B provides details.

In their calculations of total utility, altruistic adults in our model weight their children's lifetime utility relative to their own with parameter ξ. We certainly expect $0 \leq \xi \leq 1$. The closer ξ is to 1, the closer parents are to valuing their grown children's utility as highly as their own; the closer it is to 0, the weaker altruism is. Lacking direct evidence, we set ξ so that at the

---

19. Barsky and others (1997).

Table 6-1. *Simulated Distributions of Earnings*
Percent, except as indicated

| Share | Huggett | Simulation with random shock that is | |
		Normal	T distribution
Gini coefficient	0.42	0.39	0.41
Top 1 percent	6	6	8
Top 5 percent	19	19	21
Top 10 percent	31	30	32
Top 20 percent	47	46	47

Source: Huggett (1996) and author's calculations based on Solon (1992), using equation A1 in the appendix.

1995 empirical interest rate, our steady-state equilibrium intersection in figure 6-1 has a ratio of wealth to labor income matching aggregative U.S. data.

Early simulations showed that the steady-state distribution of wealth was quite sensitive to the underlying distribution of earnings—in other words, to the distribution of earning abilities. The first column of table 6-1 presents empirical characterizations of the U.S. earnings distribution from Mark Huggett.[20] Following Solon, this chapter assumes that earning abilities evolve according to a log-linear equation, with a child's earning ability related to his father's with an intergenerational correlation of .45.[21] The equation also has a random component. Choosing a distribution and variance for the random component, the equation determines a stationary distribution. We adjust the variance of the random component so that the stationary distribution roughly matches U.S. Census data (see appendix B). With a normal distribution for the random component (in an equation determining the evolution of the log of ability), table 6-1 shows we obtain a distribution of earnings similar to Huggett's. Column 3 shows that a T-distribution with 9 degrees of freedom matches Huggett almost as closely. The T-distribution does allow a slightly larger share of total earnings for the top 1 percent of earners, however, and that leads to a noticeable improvement relative to empirical evidence in the simulated wealth distributions below. All of the simulations in this chapter use the T-distribution.

20. Huggett (1996).
21. Solon (1992).

Table 6-2. *Federal Estate Tax Rates, 1995*

Tax bracket (thousands of dollars)	Marginal tax rate (percent)
0–10	18
10–20	20
20–40	22
40–60	24
60–80	26
80–100	28
100–150	30
150–250	32
250–500	34
500–750	37
750–1,000	39
1,000–1,250	41
1,250–1,500	43
1,500–2,000	45
2,000–2,500	49
2,500–3,000	53
3,000–10,000	55

Source: Poterba (1998).

Estate Taxes

This discussion of the taxation of intergenerational transfers is limited to the federal gift and estate tax.[22] Recall that when a parent is age 48, his child leaves home and both the parent and child learn the latter's earning ability. At that point, the parent determines the present value of his total intergenerational transfer. Data show that although most wealthy decedents made gifts during their lives, actual taxable estates are an order of magnitude larger than taxable gifts.[23] Thus, in terms of tax liability, this chapter assumes that all private transfers are taxed as estates. Table 6-2 presents 1995 marginal estate tax rates.[24] In 1995 donors had a lifetime credit of $192,800, bequests to spouses

22. However, many states now set their estate taxes merely to pick up the credit that the federal tax allows to states. Therefore, since for calibration purposes below we adjust our assessment of federal estate tax collections to incorporate this credit, our treatment does, in effect, include most state death taxes.

23. Pechman (1987, table 8.2); Poterba (1998, table 4).

24. In practice, there was an eighteenth bracket with marginal rate .60, and a nineteenth bracket with rate .55—emerging from the phase-out of lower inframarginal rates. The simulations ignore the .60 bracket.

were tax free, and each parent could make a tax-exempt annual transfer of $10,000 per child. Elementary steps that a couple with two children could take to reduce their tax liability included using $40,000 of exemptions each year (a gift of $10,000 from each parent to each child), and transferring half of the ultimate bequest to children at each spouse's death. To capture these steps, our tax algorithm exempts $40,000 for each year of a child's life up to the date of the estate, it splits the remaining estate in half and applies table 6-2's rate schedule and the $192,800 credit to each half, then it combines the tax liabilities for both halves as the parent household's full estate-tax liability.[25] For any prospective transfer amount, the algorithm computes the tax liability for each possible (parent) age of death (up to 74), then it derives the expected value of the liability with mortality-table weights. A parent's estate pays taxes equaling the expected value amount (and the parent fully anticipates this). The model assumes that a parent who anticipates the possibility of a taxable estate can begin making tax-exempt $40,000 gifts before learning his child's earning ability and that the parent has sufficient liquidity to do so. Think of gifts of this description to minor children as funding trust accounts—counted as part of parental net worth in our distributional analysis below. In fact, we have argued that parents act as though they want to control their net worth as long as possible; thus, in computing parental net worth, we deduct only such transfers as occur between parent ages 48–74, do not exceed the parent's eventual estate, and are necessary to lift a child's liquidity constraints. In practice, the latter may exceed or fall short of tax-exempt gifts needed for maximal tax avoidance.[26]

Fraction of Altruists and Intertemporal Elasticity of Substitution

In our model, the fraction of family lines that are altruistic is λ. For the flow of utility at any age, the elasticity of utility with respect to consumption is γ. Selecting values for λ and γ is the remaining calibration task. We want to pick values so that the simulated distribution of wealth resembles the empirical distribution and so that simulated estate tax revenues resemble actual tax collections.

25. As stated above, to capture the effect of assortative mating, our model has one adult and one child per household. Nevertheless, our tax assessments reflect empirical households with two adults and two children.

26. For example, for a very large estate, gifts to lift liquidity constraints will exceed cumulative $40,000 exemptions, the parent in question would pay a gift tax in practice, and estate tax payments that our model computes will be correspondingly overstated. For a moderately large estate, in contrast, cumulative $40,000 exemptions may exceed the lifetime transfers we compute. Then for some ages, our computations will understate inter vivos transfers, overstate the wealth of the parent, and understate the wealth of the child.

Table 6-3. *U.S. Distribution of Net Worth*

Percent, except as indicated

Share	Survey of Consumer Finances, 1983	Panel Study of Income Dynamics, 1989
Gini coefficient	0.78	...
Top 1 percent	33	25.6
Top 5 percent	55	47.3
Top 10 percent	...	61.2
Top 20 percent	80	...
Top 25 percent	...	82.9

Source: SCF data are from Wolff (1996, tab. 4); PSID data are from Hurst, Luoh, and Stafford (1998, tab. 5).

Table 6-3 presents empirical information on the cross-sectional distribution of net worth among U.S. households. The first column uses the 1983 Survey of Consumer Finances aligned to national (flow of funds) totals.[27] Net worth includes government bonds, real estate, corporate stock, cash, the surrender value of life insurance, and so on, less debts. The data exclude most consumer durables, although not vehicles. The figures include defined-contribution pension accounts, but they omit the value of defined-benefit pension rights. Likewise, future Social Security benefits are not part of net worth. The second column is based on the *1989 Panel Study of Income Dynamics* augmented with information on the highest wealth holders from *Forbes* magazine and other sources.[28] The definition of net worth is similar to column 1. In both cases it seems likely that omission of defined-benefit pensions and consumer durables biases the concentration of wealth upward.

The distribution of wealth clearly is much more concentrated than the distribution of earnings—recall table 6-1. Net worth concentration may arise in part from the life-cycle pattern of wealth accumulation: households near retirement tend to have higher net worth than very young or very old families. Table 6-4 simulates a purely life-cycle model at a steady-state interest rate of .069 and an income tax rate $\tau = .2402$ (the latter is consistent with our model's government budget without estate tax revenues). Life-cycle accumulation explains 63 percent of the empirical ratio $(K_{t+1} + B_{t+1})/(W \cdot E_t)$. Recall that Laurence J. Kotlikoff and Lawrence H. Summers suggest that life-cycle saving explains 20 percent or less of U.S. national net worth, while Franco Modigliani

27. The first column is based on Wolff (1996).
28. The second column comes from Hurst and others (1998).

Table 6-4. *Simulated Distribution of Wealth with Life Cycle Saving Alone*
Percent, except as indicated

Share	Life cycle net worth
Gini coefficient	0.69
Top 1 percent	15
Top 5 percent	36
Top 10 percent	51
Top 20 percent	70

Source: Author's calculations; see text for details.

argues that it accounts for 70–80 percent.[29] Our results are in between, although closer to Modigliani. The Gini coefficient for the steady-state cross-sectional distribution of net worth generated from the life-cycle model is .69, and the shares of net worth for the top 1, 5, 10, and 20 percent of households are, respectively, 15, 36, 51, and 70 percent. Evidently the life-cycle model can account for part of the difference between the empirical earnings and wealth distributions; nevertheless, it falls short of explaining the wealth distribution's upper tail.

The 1999 *Economic Report of the President* shows 1995 federal revenues from the gift and estate tax of $14.8 billion.[30] Surrounding years suggest 1995 revenues were atypically low: tax revenues were $15.2 billion in 1994, $17.2 billion in 1996, $19.8 billion in 1997, and $24.1 billion in 1998. Further, Martha B. Eller shows the federal credit for state death duties was $3.0 billion.[31] Since money transferred to state governments does not alleviate the tax burden of individuals, a revenue figure of $18 to $19 billion seems an appropriate calibration target.

Table 6-5 presents simulation results with different combinations of λ and γ. In every case, the government budget constraint holds (with the proportional income tax rate adjusting for different estate-tax revenues), β is set so that lifetime consumption grows at the empirical rate, and ξ is set so that private net worth matches the empirical combination of physical capital plus government debt. Because in the model many "bequests" occur at age 74—rather than at death—we calculate cross-sectional wealth statistics in the simulations for ages 22–73.

29. Kotlikoff and Summers (1981); Modigliani (1988).
30. See table B-81, p. 422.
31. Eller (1997, table 1d).

Table 6-5. *Calibrated Simulations of the Distribution of Wealth for Different Combinations of* λ *and* γ[a]

Item	Value of γ				
	0	−1	−2	−4	−8
λ = 1.00					
Gini coefficient	0.73	0.73	0.73	0.73	0.73
Top 1 percent	18	19	20	21	21
Top 5 percent	41	42	42	43	43
Top 10 percent	56	57	57	57	57
Top 20 percent	74	74	74	74	74
Fraction zero bequest	0.62	0.68	0.73	0.74	0.77
Estate tax revenue					
($ billions)	9.9	22.6	30.2	36.8	39.3
λ = 0.10					
Gini coefficient	0.78	0.78	0.78	0.78	0.78
Top 1 percent	21	21	22	22	23
Top 5 percent	52	52	52	52	52
Top 10 percent	66	66	66	66	66
Top 20 percent	81	81	81	81	81
Fraction zero bequest	0.91	0.91	0.91	0.91	0.91
Estate tax revenue					
($ billions)	3.5	9.9	16.0	25.4	33.9
λ = 0.05					
Gini coefficient	0.80	0.80	0.80	0.80	0.80
Top 1 percent	23	23	24	25	26
Top 5 percent	57	57	57	57	57
Top 10 percent	69	69	69	69	69
Top 20 percent	82	82	82	81	81
Fraction zero bequest	0.95	0.95	0.95	0.95	0.95
Estate tax revenue					
($ billions)	3.0	7.3	13.1	23.2	36.9

Source: Author's calculations; see text for details.

a. Table reports results for distribution over ages 22–73.

The parameter λ measures the fraction of family lines which are dynastic. To the extent that life-cycle saving fails to explain total national wealth, dynastic families must on average have higher net worth than nondynastic households. When λ is small, the equilibrium average amount of extra wealth that dynastic families carry must be larger, and the corresponding degree of inequality in the distribution of net worth will tend to be greater.

The role of γ is more complicated. Gamma determines risk aversion and the (lifetime) intertemporal elasticity of substitution. A low γ denotes rigid preferences with regard to risk and consumption variation over time. The second characteristic means that a parent who has a low γ, who is altruistic, and who has high resources relative to his child's earning ability, will want to make a very substantial bequest. Accordingly, to maintain equality with the empirical capital-to-wage bill ratio, the simulations tend to require a lower ξ for a more negative γ. When both parameters are low, we end up with few, very large estates. In other words, a low γ tends to lead to high wealth inequality. Because of the progressive marginal rates in the estate tax, a more concentrated wealth distribution tends, in turn, to generate higher estate-tax revenues.

From table 6-5 we select two combinations of λ and γ as plausible matches with 1995 U.S. data.

The first candidate occurs in the rows with $\lambda = 1$, where all households are altruistic. Then column 2 produces rough agreement with 1995 empirical estate-tax revenues. Intergenerational transfers make the distribution of wealth somewhat more unequal than table 6-4's purely life-cycle economy: the Gini coefficient for the wealth distribution rises from .69 for the purely life-cycle economy to .73 in column 2; the fraction of wealth held by the top 1 percent of wealth holders rises from .15 to .19; and the fraction held by the top 5 percent rises from .36 to .42. Nevertheless, comparison with table 6-3 shows that simulated inequality remains below its empirical counterpart.

In the simulation with $\lambda = 1$ and $\gamma = -1$, 32 percent of all households receive an inheritance. Laitner and Henry Ohlsson find that about 40 percent of households in the Panel Study of Income Dynamics eventually inherit.[32] Other simulation output shows that inter vivos gifts make up 54 to 55 percent of private transfers in present value terms, and the average bequest is $91,000. Although the latter exceeds the average inheritance of $23,000 (in present value at age 50) which Laitner and Henry Ohlsson report for the PSID, they measure the average inheritance per capita whereas this chapter's $91,000 figure measures what an average couple would receive, this chapter's

---

32. Laitner and Ohlsson (2000).

simulation corresponds to 1995 whereas the PSID data come from 1984 (when the nominal GDP was only 54 percent as large as in 1995), heirs seem to have a general tendency to understate their inheritances in surveys, and wealthy households are underrepresented in the PSID.[33] In the distribution of estates, figures on numbers of decedents and numbers of taxable estates, figures from, for example, Barry W. Johnson, Jacob M. Mikow, and Martha Britton Eller, show that about 1.4 percent of U.S. decedents in 1995 had taxable estates, and figures from Eller show that about .8 percent had taxable estates over $1 million.[34] In the simulation with $\lambda = 1$ and $\gamma = -1$, the stationary distribution of bequests for 1995 has roughly 3.5 percent of households leaving estates over $600,000 and about 1.5 percent leaving $1 million or more. Since estate tax data refer to individuals, for comparability we need to divide simulated household bequests in half. Then less than 1 percent of decedents have estates over $1 million, and 1 to 1.5 percent have estates over $600,000.

A second candidate for a match has $\lambda = .05$ and $\gamma = -4$. The character of the long-run equilibrium is quite different from the first candidate. As stated, life-cycle saving alone accounts for about 63 percent of the economy's stock of wealth. When $\lambda = 1$ and $\gamma = -1$, all households are altruistic, and about 32 percent leave an estate at death. When $\lambda = .05$ and $\gamma = -4$, only 5 percent of households are altruistic, and slightly over 4.5 percent leave an estate. To generate the 37 percent of national wealth owing to intergenerational transfers, the bequests of the tiny fraction of altruistic families must be huge in the second case. In the first case, households with exceptionally high earnings share their good luck through moderate transfers to their descendants, and traces of the original fortune will tend to die out rather quickly. In the second case, a small group of families have great inherited wealth, and they perpetuate their dynasties' fortunes with large estates—bequests only dip to 0 for altruistic dynasties suffering through a long sequence of generations with low earnings.

When $\lambda = .05$ and $\gamma = -4$, intergenerational transfers substantially contribute to overall wealth inequality. The Gini coefficient for the simulated dis-

---

33. See Cox (1987) for data on surveys of heirs and Hurst and others (1998) for representation of wealthy households in the PSID.

34. See Johnson, Mikow, and Eller, chap. 2 in this volume, and Eller (1997). Although in 1995 about 3.4 percent of decedents left estates over the $600,000 minimum for filing an estate tax form, spousal and charitable deductions rendered many of these estates nontaxable. Our model's bequests exclude transfers to spouses, and our model treats charitable bequests as part of the lifetime consumption of the decedent; hence, our simulated distribution of bequests seems most comparable to data on taxable estates. Of course, tax avoidance (for example, see Schmalbeck in this volume) presumably creates a downward bias in the data.

tribution of wealth is .80, the empirical level reported in table 6-3 being .78. The fractions of wealth for the top 1, 5, 10, and 20 percent of households are .25, .57, .69, and .81, respectively, compared with .25–.33, .47–.55, .61, and .80, respectively, in table 6-3. Estate-tax revenues roughly match their actual 1995 value.

The problem with a very low λ comes from the bequest numbers themselves. With $\lambda = .05$ and $\gamma = -4$, although the average bequest is \$119,000, the average bequest among altruistic households is \$2.4 million. Virtually all altruistic households leave bequests, with well over 80 percent, in other words, over 4 percent of the total population of households, leaving over \$1 million. Slightly more than 3 percent of individual decedents have estates this large. One might rationalize the small fraction of households leaving an estate at all—slightly under 5 percent—in the simulations relative to the PSID (see above) by arguing that many of the PSID estates are small, perhaps being accidental transfers stemming from incomplete annuitization. However, the simulated distribution of bequests does not seem to resemble Eller's tax-return frequencies (as reported above) at all.

In the end, if one believes that all households have the same preferences, the top section of table 6-5 implies that intergenerational transfers do not entirely explain the observable wealth concentration. One might then want to investigate other theoretical frameworks to feel fully confident about the consequences of tax reform for inequality. Alternatively, if one believes that private intergenerational transfers are a major source of wealth disparity, table 6-5's best calibrations have $\lambda = .05$ and $\gamma = -4$. A problem then is that the very high bequests of many dynastic households in the simulations seem difficult to square with empirical evidence.

Table 6-6 presents derived values of β and ξ. Recall that ξ is the weight a parent places on his marginal utility relative to his child's at the same date, and $\beta^{26} \cdot \xi$ is the weight a parent puts on his own marginal utility at age 22 relative to his child's marginal utility at age 22. For $\lambda = 1$ and $\gamma = -1$, $\xi = .168$ and the age-corrected weight is .166; for $\lambda = .05$ and $\gamma = -4$, $\xi = .119$ and the age-corrected weight is .847. Evidently, parents favor their own utility over their adult children's by a considerable degree in the simulations.

Finally, note that Alan J. Auerbach and Laurence J. Kotlikoff choose $\gamma = -3$ for their base case simulations. More recently, Robert B. Barsky and others estimate $\gamma = -4$ on the basis of survey questions about intertemporal substitution, and $\gamma = -3$ to -11 from questions about risk aversion.[35]

35. Auerbach and Kotlikoff (1987); Barsky and others (1997).

Table 6-6. *Calibrated Simulations of Intertemporal and Intergenerational Preference Weights*

Parameter	Value of γ				
	0	*–1*	*–2*	*–4*	*–8*
λ = 1.00					
β	0.975	1.000	1.025	1.078	1.193
ξ	0.422	0.168	0.064	0.009	0.000
β²⁶ · ξ	0.216	0.166	0.122	0.062	0.012
λ = 0.10					
β	0.975	1.000	1.025	1.078	1.194
ξ	0.641	0.402	0.246	0.087	0.009
β²⁶ · ξ	0.328	0.397	0.469	0.620	0.943
λ = 0.05					
β	0.975	1.000	1.025	1.078	1.194
ξ	0.673	0.447	0.290	0.119	0.017
β²⁶ · ξ	0.344	0.442	0.554	0.847	1.735

Source: Author's calculations; see text for details.

These estimates seem roughly consistent with calibrations in table 5 of $\gamma = -1$ to -4.

Tax Changes

This section performs the comparative static exercise of eliminating the federal gift and estate tax. The analysis fixes parameters (including β and ξ) as in table 6-5 and then simulates without estate taxes. We adjust the proportional income tax rate so that the government's budget constraint holds despite lost estate-tax revenues, assuming that ratios of government spending to GDP and government debt to GDP remain as before. We are especially interested in what happens to private net worth and what happens to the degree of equality in the cross-sectional distribution of wealth. Table 6-7 presents results.

Since increases in the income tax offset decreases in estate taxes, we cannot be sure whether the economy's capital intensity will rise or fall after our policy change. Because of general equilibrium changes in factor prices, we cannot even know ahead of time whether wealth equality will rise or fall. Indeed, the table shows changes in either direction are possible for capital intensity or wealth inequality.

When $\lambda = 1$, our most interesting simulation has $\lambda = -1$. Compare tables 6-5 and 6-7 in this case. Eliminating the estate tax leads to a very slight increase in the economy's steady-state capital intensivity: the aggregative wealth-to-wage bill ratio, and hence the wealth-to-GDP ratio, rises about .25 percent, and the gross interest rate essentially remains unchanged. The Gini coefficient of the distribution of wealth rises from .73 to .74. The fraction of wealth owned by the top 1 percent shows the biggest effect: it rises from .19 to .22, an increase of 16 percent.

When $\lambda = .05$ and $\gamma = -4$, the steady-state aggregative wealth to GDP ratio increases 2.6 percent after the elimination of the estate tax. The gross of tax interest rate falls from 6.9 to 6.3 percent a year. Again, the Gini coefficient of the wealth distribution does not change much—from .80 to .81. However, the share of the top 1 percent of wealth holders increases substantially—rising from .25 to .33, an increase of 32 percent.

In sum, according to the model eliminating the estate tax has small effects on the economy's overall capital intensivity in the preferred calibrations with $\lambda = 1$. While the effect on the Gini coefficient of the cross-sectional wealth distribution is also small, the top of the distribution becomes more concentrated: the fraction of wealth held by the top 1 percent rises 16 percent. In the case with $\lambda = .05$ and $\gamma = -4$, the steady-state wealth-to-GDP ratio increases over 2 percent, a fairly impressive change given the small revenues of the estate tax. Again, wealth inequality rises as well, especially at the very top of the distribution, with the share of the wealthiest 1 percent of asset holders increasing 32 percent.

Conclusion

This chapter develops a neoclassical, general equilibrium model of the steady-state distribution of wealth. Calibration outcomes seem to leave two choices: either one can assume all households are altruistic, or one can assume that a small fraction of households are altruistic, and the remainder is not.

In the first case, the model does not explain the high degree of concentration evident in the U.S. distribution of wealth, though average simulated bequest amounts seem plausible, as does their distribution. In this case, the model predicts that eliminating the U.S. gift and estate tax would have very modest consequences for overall wealth accumulation and would moderately increase inequality in the long-run wealth distribution.

Alternatively, if we assume that only about 5 percent of all households are altruistic, the simulations are more consistent with the existing U.S.

Table 6-7. *Steady States with New Equilibrium Interest Rates,*
after Elimination of the Estate Tax[a]

Percent, except as indicated

Item	Value of γ				
	0	*−1*	*−2*	*−4*	*−8*
λ = 1.00					
Gini coefficient	0.74	0.74	0.73	0.73	0.72
Top 1 percent	22	22	21	21	20
Top 5 percent	44	44	43	43	42
Top 10 percent	59	58	58	57	57
Top 20 percent	76	75	75	74	74
Gross interest rate	0.068	0.069	0.069	0.070	0.073
New $g \cdot \dfrac{K + B}{W \cdot E}$	4.19	4.19	4.18	4.15	4.08
Prereform $g \cdot \dfrac{K + B}{W \cdot E}$	4.18	4.18	4.18	4.18	4.18
New average bequest ($)	104,000	99,000	94,000	88,000	78,000
Prereform average bequest ($)	96,000	91,000	87,000	74,000	76,000
λ = 0.10					
Gini coefficient	0.81	0.81	0.80	0.79	0.79
Top 1 percent	30	29	28	26	24
Top 5 percent	57	56	56	54	53
Top 10 percent	70	69	68	68	67
Top 20 percent	83	82	82	81	81
Gross interest rate	0.068	0.067	0.067	0.066	0.067
New $g \cdot \dfrac{K + B}{W \cdot E}$	4.21	4.23	4.24	4.25	4.23
Prereform $g \cdot \dfrac{K + B}{W \cdot E}$	4.18	4.18	4.18	4.18	4.18
New average bequest ($)	135,000	134,000	132,000	128,000	123,000
Prereform average bequest ($)	120,000	119,000	118,000	115,000	113,000

(*continued*)

Table 6-7. (*continued*)

Percent, except as indicated

Item	Value of γ				
	0	*-1*	*-2*	*-4*	*-8*
$\lambda = 0.05$					
Gini coefficient	0.83	0.83	0.82	0.81	0.80
Top 1 percent	37	36	35	33	30
Top 5 percent	62	62	61	60	59
Top 10 percent	72	72	72	71	70
Top 20 percent	84	84	84	83	82
Gross interest rate	0.067	0.066	0.065	0.063	0.063
New $g \cdot \dfrac{K + B}{W \cdot E}$	4.22	4.27	4.29	4.33	4.34
Prereform $g \cdot \dfrac{K + B}{W \cdot E}$	4.18	4.18	4.18	4.18	4.18
New average bequest ($)	143,000	144,000	142,000	141,000	135,000
Prereform average bequest ($)	121,000	122,000	121,000	119,000	117,000

Source: Author's calculations; see text for details.

a. Shares and Gini coefficients refer to distribution over ages 22–73.

distribution of wealth. Unfortunately, the new simulations generate seemingly unrealistically large average bequests for altruistic households. In this case, eliminating the estate tax causes quite large increases in the steady-state capital intensity of the economy (especially relative to the small magnitude of gift and estate tax revenues). Increases in long-run wealth inequality are also substantial, however—with simulated increases in the share of wealth of the wealthiest 1 percent of families of 32 percent in the favored case. In view of the possible consequences for inequality, if the objective of estate tax reform is to increase national wealth accumulation, our results suggest that one might want carefully to consider other options, such as lowering the national debt or strengthening the Social Security trust fund.[36]

36. For example, Laitner (2000).

Appendix A

This appendix presents this chapter's model in mathematical detail.

An adult who was born at time t and who has earning ability z supplies $e_s \cdot z \cdot g^{t+s}$ "effective" labor units at each age $s \geq 22$. If z' is the earning ability of the adult's child, following Gary Solon,

(A1) $\ln(z') = \rho \cdot \ln(z) + \eta,$

where $\rho \in (0,1)$ is a parameter and η is a random variable.[37] Solon assumes η has a normal distribution. In order to allow thicker tails on the earnings distribution, this chapter assumes η has a noncentral T-distribution. The latter has density

(A2) $$\frac{\Gamma\left(\frac{n+1}{2}\right)}{\sigma_\eta \cdot \Gamma\left(\frac{n}{2}\right) \cdot \sqrt{\pi \cdot n}} \cdot \frac{1}{\left(1 + \left(\frac{\eta - \mu_\eta}{\sigma_\eta}\right)^2 \Big/ n\right)^{(n+1)/2}},$$

where n is number of degrees of freedom.

This chapter focuses on steady-state equilibria in which the wage per effective labor unit, W, the interest rate, r, the income tax rate, τ, and the Social Security tax rate, τ^{ss}, are constant. The fraction of adults remaining alive at age s are q_s. One plus the net-of-tax interest factor on annuities for an adult of age s is

(A3) $$R_s = \frac{1 + r \cdot (1 - \tau)}{q_{s+1}/q_s}.$$

If an adult has consumption c at age s, his household derives utility flow $u(c,s)$. If his minor child has consumption c^k, the adult's household derives, at age s, an additional utility flow $u^k(c^k,s)$. Our analysis sets

$$u(c, s) = \begin{cases} \frac{c^\gamma}{\gamma}, & \text{if } s \leq 65, \\ \upsilon^{1-\gamma} \cdot \frac{c^\gamma}{\gamma}, & \text{if } s > 65, \end{cases}$$

$$u^k(c, s) = \begin{cases} \omega^{1-\gamma} \cdot \frac{c^\gamma}{\gamma}, & \text{if } 26 \leq s < 48, \\ 0, & \text{if } s \geq 48, \end{cases}$$

37. Solon (1992).

with $\gamma < 1$. Appendix B discusses the relative weights for retirement consumption, υ, and minor children, ω.

Consider a parent at 48 years old. Let t be the year he was born. Let his utility from remaining lifetime consumption be $U^{old}(A', z, t)$, where his earning ability is z, and his assets for remaining lifetime consumption are A'. Then

(A4)
$$U^{old}\left(A', z, t\right) = \max_{c_s} \sum_{s=48}^{88} q_s \cdot \beta^{s-48} \cdot u(c_s, s),$$

subject to:

$$A_{s+1} = R_{s-1} \cdot A_s + e_s \cdot z \cdot g^{t+s} \cdot W \cdot \left(1 - \tau - \tau_{ss}\right) + ssb(s, z, t) \cdot \left(1 - \frac{\tau}{2}\right) - c_s,$$

$$A_{44} = A' \quad \text{and} \quad A_{89} \geq 0,$$

where $u(\cdot)$ and q_s and R_s are as above, $\beta \geq 0$ is the lifetime subjective discount factor, A_s stands for the net worth the parent carried to age s, and $ssb(s, z, t)$ specifies Social Security benefits at age s.

The utility over ages 22–47 for a parent born in year t is $U^{young}(A, A', z, t)$ if he carries assets A into age 22, carries assets A' out of age 47, and has earning ability z. We have

(A5)
$$U^{young}\left(A, A', z, t\right) = \max_{c_s} \sum_{s=22}^{47} q_s \cdot \beta^{s-22} \cdot \left[u(c_s, s) + u^k\left(c_s^k, s\right)\right]$$

subject to: $A_{s+1} = R_{s-1} \cdot A_s + e_s \cdot z \cdot g^{t+s} \cdot W \cdot \left(1 - \tau - \tau_{ss}\right) - c_s - c_s^k,$

$$A_{22} = A \quad \text{and} \quad A_{48} \geq A',$$

$$A_s \geq 0 \quad \text{all} \quad s = 22, \ldots, 48.$$

We assume bankruptcy laws prevent households from borrowing without collateral, giving us the last inequality constraint in equation A5—but, for the sake of simplicity, that such constraints do not bind for older households, making them superfluous in equation A4.

A nonaltruistic household solves

(A6)
$$\max_{A' \geq 0}\left\{U^{young}\left(0, A', z, t\right) + \beta^{26} \cdot U^{old}\left(A', z, t\right)\right\}.$$

To incorporate altruism, let $V^{young}(A, z, t)$ be the total utility—combining utility from lifetime consumption and from the lifetime utility of descendants—of a 22-year-old altruistic household carrying initial assets A to age 22, having earning ability z, and born at time t. Let $V^{old}(A', z, z', t)$ be the total utility of a 48-year-old altruistic household, which begins age 48 with assets A' and has just learned that its grown child has earning ability z'. Then letting $E[\cdot]$ be the expected value operator and $\xi > 0$ the intergenerational subjective discount factor, we have a pair of Bellman equations

$$V^{young}(A, z, t) = \max_{A' \geq 0} \left\{ U^{young}(A, A', z, t) + \beta^{26} \cdot E_{z'|z}\left[V^{old}(A', z, z', t)\right] \right\},$$

$$V^{old}(A', z, z', t) = \max_{B \geq 0} \left\{ U^{old}(A' - B, z, t) \right.$$

$$\left. + \xi \cdot V^{young}(T(B, t), z', t + 26) \right\},$$

where B is the parent's intergenerational transfer and $T(B,t)$ the net-of-tax inheritance of the child. We require $B \geq 0$, implying that parents cannot compel reverse transfers from their children.

Because utility is isoelastic,

$$U^{young}(A, A', z, t) = g^{\gamma \cdot t} \cdot U^{young}\left(A/g^t, A'/g^t, z, 0\right),$$

and, assuming Social Security benefits rise with growth factor g between cohorts,

$$U^{old}(A', z, t) = g^{\gamma \cdot t} \cdot U^{old}\left(A'/g^t, z, 0\right).$$

Similarly, provided estate tax exemptions, credits, and brackets grow over time with factor g, one can deduce

$$V^{young}(A, z, t) = g^{\gamma \cdot t} \cdot V^{young}\left(A/g^t, z, 0\right),$$

$$V^{old}(A', z, z', t) = g^{\gamma \cdot t} \cdot V^{old}\left(A'/g^t, z, z', 0\right).$$

Substituting a for A/g^t and b for B/g^t, one can, therefore, rewrite the Bellman equations as

(A7)
$$V^{young}(a, z, 0) = \max_{a' \geq 0} \left\{ U^{young}(a, a', z, 0) \right.$$
$$\left. + \beta^{26} \cdot E_{z'|z}\left[V^{old}(a', z, z', 0)\right] \right\},$$

(A8)
$$V^{old}(a', z, z', 0) = \max_{b \geq 0} \left\{ U^{old}(a' - b, z, 0) \right.$$
$$\left. + \xi \cdot g^{\gamma \cdot 26} \cdot V^{young}\left(T(b, 0)/g^{26}, z', 0\right) \right\}.$$

If $\phi(s, t, z)$ is the net worth of a family of age s, ability z, and birthdate t, homotheticity also implies

$$\phi(s,t,z) = g^t \cdot \phi(s,0,z).$$

This chapter assumes all families have identical υ, ω, and β. At first all households have a common ξ as well. Later, however, we allow two values of ξ: a fraction λ of family lines have $\xi > 0$, but a fraction $1 - \lambda$ have $\xi = 0$.

In the production and government sectors, the aggregate production function is

$$(A10) \qquad Q_t = [K_t]^\alpha \cdot [E_t]^{1-\alpha}, \quad \alpha \in (0,1),$$

where Q_t is GDP, K_t is the aggregate stock of physical capital, and E_t is the effective labor force. K_t depreciates at rate $\delta \in (0,1)$. The price of output is always 1. Perfect competition implies

$$(A11) \qquad W_t = (1 - \alpha) \cdot \frac{Q_t}{E_t} \quad \text{and} \quad r_t = \alpha \cdot \frac{Q_t}{K_t} - \delta.$$

The government issues D_t one-period bonds with price 1 at time t. We assume

$$(A12) \qquad D_t/Q_t = \text{constant}.$$

Letting SSB_t be aggregate Social Security benefits, we assume

$$(A13) \qquad SSB_t/Q_t = \text{constant}.$$

The Social Security system is unfunded, so

$$(A14) \qquad SSB_t = \tau^{ss} \cdot W_t \cdot E_t.$$

If G_t is government spending on goods and services, assume

$$(A15) \qquad G_t/Q_t = \text{constant}.$$

Leaving out the Social Security system, in which benefits and taxes contemporaneously balance, the government budget constraint is

$$(A16) \quad G_t + r_t \cdot D_t = \tau \cdot [W_t \cdot E_t + r_t \cdot K_t + r_t \cdot D_t] + D_{t+1} - D_t + ET_t,$$

where ET_t is estate-tax revenues. Assume public-good consumption does not affect marginal rates of substitution for private consumption.

Normalizing the size of the time-0 birth cohort to 1 and employing the law of large numbers,

$$(A17) \qquad E_t = \sum_{s=22}^{65} g^t \cdot q_s \cdot e_s.$$

Households finance all of the physical capital stock and government debt. Letting $f(\cdot)$ be the density for z, and NW_t be the aggregate net worth held which the household sector carries from time t to $t+1$, the economy's supply and demand for credit balance, using the law of large numbers again, if and only if

$$(A18) \qquad \frac{K_{t+1} + D_{t+1}}{E_t} = \frac{NW_t}{E_t} \equiv \frac{\sum_{s=22}^{87} q_s \cdot \int_{-\infty}^{\infty} \phi\left(s, t - s, z\right) \cdot f(z) dz}{E_t}.$$

Alternatively, suppose a fraction of households λ are altruistic, and the remainder are not. As stated in the text, dynasties permanently fall into one group or the other: descendants of altruistic households are themselves altruistic, whereas descendants of nonaltruistic households are nonaltruistic. Nonaltruistic households, or "purely life-cycle households," solve equation A6 alone. Let such a household's net worth be $\phi^{LC}(s, t, z)$. (Recall that nondynastic and dynastic family lines have the same ρ and distribution for η.) Then in place of A18, one needs

$$(A18') \qquad \begin{aligned} &\frac{K_{t+1} + D_{t+1}}{E_t} = \frac{NW_t}{E_t} \equiv \\ &\frac{\sum_{s=22}^{87} q_s \cdot \int_{-\infty}^{\infty} \left[\lambda \cdot \phi(s, t - s, z) + (1 - \lambda) \cdot \phi^{LC}\left(s, t - s, z\right)\right] \cdot f(z) dz}{E_t}. \end{aligned}$$

This chapter treats λ as a parameter.[38]

In "equilibrium" all households maximize their utility and A1-A18 hold. A "steady state equilibrium (SSE)" is an equilibrium in which r_t and W_t are constant all t and in which Q, K, and E grow geometrically with factor g.

Proceeding to figure 6-1 of the text, note that perfectly competitive behavior on the part of firms and the aggregate production function yield

---

38. See, however, Stark (1999).

$$\frac{(r + \delta) \cdot K_t}{W \cdot E_t} = \frac{\alpha}{1 - \alpha},$$

where K_t/E_t is stationary in a steady state. Equations A10–A12 show D_t divided by $W \cdot E_t$ is stationary. Combining the two uses of credit,

(A19) $$\frac{K_{t+1} + D_{t+1}}{W \cdot E_t} = g \cdot \left[\frac{\alpha}{1 - \alpha} \cdot \frac{1}{r + \delta} + \frac{D_t}{W \cdot E_t}\right].$$

This yields the demand curve of figure 6-1, where $r^L \equiv -\delta$.

Define $\bar{r}$ from

(A20) $$(1 + \bar{r})^{26} \cdot (1 - \tau^{beq}) \cdot \xi \cdot \beta^{26} \cdot g^{(\gamma-1) \cdot 26} = 1,$$

where τ^{beq} is the maximal marginal tax rate on bequests. For any r with $r \cdot (1 - \tau) < \bar{r}$, we can solve our Bellman equations using successive approximations: set $V^{old,1}(\cdot) = 0$; substitute this for $V^{old}(\cdot)$ on the right-hand side of equation A7, and solve for $V^{young,1}(\cdot)$; substitute the latter on the right-hand side of (8), and solve for $V^{old,2}(\cdot)$; and so on. This yields convergence at a geometric rate: as $j \to \infty$,

$$V^{young,j}(.) \to V^{young}(.) \quad \text{and} \quad V^{old,j}(.) \to V^{old}(.).$$

This chapter's grid size for numerical calculations along these lines is 250 for net worth and 25 for earnings. The grids are evenly spaced in logarithms—except for even division in natural numbers for the lowest wealth values.

Turning to the distribution of inheritances and wealth, let the policy functions from A7–A8 be

$$a_{48} = a(a_{22}, z) \quad \text{and} \quad b = b(a_{48}, z, z').$$

Composing them we have a mapping from initial assets in one generation, a_{22}, to initial assets in the next, a'_{22}:

(A21) $$a'_{22} = b(a(a_{22}, z), z, z').$$

Lines (A1)–(A2) imply

(A22) $$z' = [z]^{\rho} \cdot e^{\eta},$$

where η has a known distribution. Together A21–A22 determine a Markov process from Borel sets of points (d'_{22}, z') to sets of tuples (d'_{22}, z') a generation later. We truncate the distribution of η so that its support is compact. Then as in Laitner, there are bounded intervals A and Z with $A \times Z$ an invariant set for the Markov process, and there is a unique stationary distribution for the process in this set.[39] In terms of distribution functions $F: A \times Z \rightarrow [0,1]$, the Markov process induces a mapping Ψ with

(A23) $$F^{t+26} = \psi(F^t),$$

where F^t is the distribution of intergenerational transfers at time t. Iterating equation A23 from any starting distribution on $A \times Z$, we have convergence to the unique stationary distribution. Again, our numerical grid in practice is 250×25. The stationary distribution and lifetime behavior yield expected net worth per household normalized by average current earnings. Using the law of large numbers, we treat the latter ratio, $NW_t/(W \cdot E_t)$, as nonstochastic. This generates the supply curve in figure 6-1. Laitner's propositions show the ratio $NW_t/(W \cdot E_t)$ varies continuously with r and has an asymptote at $r^U \equiv \bar{r}/(1 - \tau)$.[40]

Appendix B

Our model has parameters α, δ, μ_η, σ_η, n, ρ, υ, ω, τ^{ss}, g, τ, β, ξ, λ, and γ. We calibrate the first thirteen from sources described in this appendix. The text discusses the last two.

Letting 1995 wages and salaries from the *Economic Report of the President, 1999* be c_1, proprietor's incomes be c_2, and national income be c_3, labor's share of output, $1 - \alpha$, solves

$$1 - \alpha = \frac{c_1 + (1 - \alpha) \cdot c_2}{c_3}.$$

This generates our estimate $\alpha = .3251$. Using the 1995 GDP and stock of business inventories from the *Economic Report of the President, 1999* and combining the latter with the 1995 fixed private capital stock from the *De-*

---

39. Laitner (1992).
40. Ibid.

partment of Commerce, we have $K_t/Q_t = 2.3386$.[41] This implies an interest rate $r = .069$, closely resembling Auerbach and Kotlikoff's $.067$ and Cooley and Prescott's $.072$, if we set $\delta = .07$.[42] The latter is our choice of depreciation rate.

There is no population growth in our simulations. We simply set our technological progress factor g to 1.01.

We set a proportional tax τ^{ss} on earnings up to the 1995 Social Security limit ($61,200) so that taxes exactly cover 1995 retirement benefits ($287.0 bil.). Within each birth cohort, Social Security benefits are progressive: for each cohort, we allocate benefits across our twenty-five earning groups according to the benefit formula and maximum in the statistical supplement of the Social Security Administration.[43]

Using 1995 federal, state, and local expenditures on goods and services, $G_t/(W \cdot E_t) = .2765$. Taking the 1995 ratio of federal debt to $1 - \alpha$ times GDP, $D_t/(W \cdot E_t) = .6716$. Similarly, using K_t/Q_t from above, the empirical ratio $(K_t + D_t)/(W \cdot E_t)$ is 4.1367 for 1995.

We assume no child mortality and no adult mortality until age 48. Table 6B-1 presents figures for q_s, which reflect average 1995 mortality rates for U.S. men and women. The implied average life span is 77 years. Markets offer actuarially fair annuities and life insurance, and households fully annuitize their life-cycle consumption streams and insure their earnings.

Labor supply, by assumption, is inelastic. Column 2 of table 6B-1 presents the age profile for experiential human capital, taken from median money incomes of 1995 households. In (1), we set $\rho = .45$ on the basis of Solon.[44] We set μ_η so that the unconditional average z is 1; we truncate our distribution of η so that the minimum z is .2 and the maximum is 10,000; and, we set σ_η so that the unconditional variance of log earnings matches Martin D. Dooley and Peter Gottschalk's U.S. Census figure of .4510. Finally, we set the degrees of freedom of our T-distribution (see (2)) to 9, so that our unconditional earnings distribution resembles Mark Huggett's figures—see table 6-1 and the text.[45]

First-order conditions for lifetime optimization imply that an adult will choose υ times as much consumption after retirement, other things being equal, as before, and that he will allocate ω times as much consumption to

41. U.S. Department of Commerce (1997, p. 38).
42. Auerbach and Kotlikoff (1987); Cooley and Prescott (1995).
43. Social Security Administration (1998).
44. Solon (1992).
45. Dooley and Gottschalk (1984); Hugget (1996).

Table 6B-1. *Survival Rates and Experiential Human Capital*

Age	Survival rate (q_s)	Experiential human capital (e_s)	Age	Survival rate (q_s)	Experiential human capital (e_s)
22	1.0000	33,006	55	0.9678	59,922
23	1.0000	34,910	56	0.9608	58,532
24	1.0000	36,815	57	0.9533	57,141
25	1.0000	38,720	58	0.9451	55,751
26	1.0000	40,625	59	0.9362	54,361
27	1.0000	42,529	60	0.9264	52,971
28	1.0000	44,434	61	0.9158	51,580
29	1.0000	46,339	62	0.9042	50,190
30	1.0000	48,243	63	0.8918	48,800
31	1.0000	49,467	64	0.8785	47,409
32	1.0000	50,690	65	0.8643	46,019
33	1.0000	51,914	66	0.8493	...
34	1.0000	53,137	67	0.8333	...
35	1.0000	54,361	68	0.8163	...
36	1.0000	55,584	69	0.7982	...
37	1.0000	56,808	70	0.7789	...
38	1.0000	58,031	71	0.7585	...
39	1.0000	59,255	72	0.7370	...
40	1.0000	60,478	73	0.7143	...
41	1.0000	61,118	74	0.6904	...
42	1.0000	61,757	75	0.6654	...
43	1.0000	62,397	76	0.6393	...
44	1.0000	63,036	77	0.6120	...
45	1.0000	63,676	78	0.5835	...
46	1.0000	64,315	79	0.5539	...
47	1.0000	64,955	80	0.5233	...
48	1.0000	65,594	81	0.4918	...
49	1.0000	66,234	82	0.4476	...
50	0.9957	66,874	83	0.3875	...
51	0.9909	65,483	84	0.3098	...
52	0.9858	64,093	85	0.2169	...
53	0.9803	62,703	86	0.1197	...
54	0.9743	61,312	87	0.0396	...

Source: Survival rates are calculated from average death rates for 1990, and experiential human capital is extrapolated from household money income for 1995, using data from Department of Commerce, *Statistical Abstract of the United States, 1997*, pp. 89 and 466, respectively.

his minor child as to himself. People tend to have lower consumption needs after retirement: a recent TIAA-CREF brochure suggests, for example, that "you'll need 60–90 percent of your current income in retirement, adjusted for inflation, to maintain your standard of living when you retire;" and, a recent *Reader's Digest* article on retirement planning writes, "Many financial planners say it will take 70 to 80 percent of your current income to maintain your standard of living when you retire." Using the midpoint of these limits, we set $\upsilon = .75$. Randall P. Mariger estimates that children consume 30 percent as much as adults. Similarly, Richard V. Burkhauser and others estimate that consumption needs of four-person relative to two-person families have a ratio of 1.34–1.42.[46] We set $\omega = .3$.

Lifetime first-order conditions for adult consumption at different ages imply

$$q_s \cdot [c_s]^{\gamma-1} \geq q_{s+1} \beta \cdot R_s \cdot [c_{s+1}]^{\gamma-1} \Leftrightarrow [\beta \cdot (1 + r \cdot (1 - \tau))]^{1/(1-\gamma)} \cdot c_s \leq c_{s+1},$$

with equality when the nonnegativity constraint on household net worth does not bind. Tables from the 1984–97 *U.S. Consumer Expenditure Survey* present consumption data for households of different ages.[47] We adjust the treatment of service flows from owner occupied houses.[48] Then we compute the average ratio of consumption at age $s + 1$ to that at age s for households aged 30–39—attempting to avoid ages at which liquidity constraints bind, at which children leave home, and at which retirement begins. The average ratio is 1.0257; hence, we require

(B1) $$[\beta \cdot (1 + r \cdot (1 - \tau))]^{1/(1-\gamma)} = 1.0257.$$

Table 6B–2 summarizes the data so far. We fix our first ten parameters to the values in the table. For a particular λ and γ, we then adjust τ, β, and ξ until in the simulation the government budget constraint holds, consumption growth condition B1 holds for unconstrained ages, and the empirical capital stock plus government debt to earnings ratio matches the right-hand side of equation A18 or A18'. In these calculations, a higher ξ will lead to higher intergenerational transfers, always shifting figure 6-1's supply curve to the right.

---

46. Mariger (1986); Burkhauser and others (1996).

47. See http://stats.bls.gov.csxhome.htm. (June 2000).

48. The adjustment is as follows: we subtract mortgage payments and repairs to owner-occupied houses and scale remaining consumption to NIPA levels for aggregate consumption less housing flows. Then we distribute NIPA housing service flows across ages using proportional housing values given in the survey. See Laitner (2000).

Table 6B-2. *Parameter Values and Empirical Ratios*

Item	Value
Parameter	
α	0.3251
δ	0.0700
g	1.0100
τ^{ss}	0.0607
μ_η	−0.1964
σ_η	0.5930
n	9
ρ	0.45
υ	0.7500
ω	0.3000
Ratio	
$G_t/(W \cdot E_t)$	0.2765
$(K_t + D_t)/(W \cdot E_t)$	4.1367
$\left[\beta \cdot \left(1 + r \cdot \left(1 - \tau \right) \right) \right]^{\frac{1}{1-\gamma}}$	1.0257

COMMENT BY
Douglas Holtz-Eakin

John Laitner's contribution to this volume is a tour de force of economic and computational modeling. He has crafted an intricate and impressive model of economic growth that incorporates dynastic and nondynastic families, life-cycle and bequest motives for saving, borrowing constraints, intergenerationally correlated heterogeneity in earnings ability, inter vivos gifts, progressive estate taxation, a social security system, government finance through debt and taxes, and much more. Indeed, before proceeding it is only proper to congratulate the author and to warn readers that discussing every interesting aspect of the model is beyond the scope of these comments.

The chapter contains myriad numerical results. However, to my eye there are a few key results. First, he shows that a life-cycle model with perfect annuity markets and empirically plausible heterogeneity in earnings ability can produce substantial wealth inequality. However, such a model does not produce the "super-rich" concentration of wealth in the upper tail of the distribution that is the focus of attention in the estate tax debate.

Second, to generate a substantial upper tail, the author must choose parameters so that a small number of people ("families") are different (in this case "dynastic" and "altruistic") and have a sufficient incentive to accumulate and transfer wealth resources.

Third, in these circumstances, replacing the estate and gift tax with greater reliance on income taxation leads to greater wealth inequality and (perhaps) substantial increases in aggregate capital accumulation.

Fourth, the model implies that fairly small individual-level responses are consistent with potentially large macroeconomic effects. For example, the elasticity of bequests with respect to the "tax price" (defined as 1 minus the estate tax rate) is only 0.3; similarly, the elasticity of the ratio of net worth to earnings is roughly 0.1. Still, both of these relatively small magnitudes are consistent with an increase in the steady-state capital per worker of roughly 2.5 percent.

Finally, *replacing* the estate tax with an equal-yield income tax can result in substantial aggregate capital accumulation, leading one to suspect that the former has especially unattractive efficiency properties. That is, it suggests that an important topic for further research is the deadweight loss of the estate tax system.

Given the highly charged political debate surrounding the estate tax, I suspect that the most intriguing finding is that the estate tax reduces wealth inequality (or, more precisely, eliminating it leads to greater wealth inequality). For various reasons, a bit of caution is in order before translating this finding from the model into policy conclusions.

To begin, the model is designed only to simulate the steady-state distribution of wealth. We will never live long enough to "see" the steady state, and the model is by necessity silent on the day-to-day wealth inequality one would observe in an economy as it grew toward the steady state.

Second, we do not know the degree to which real world wealth inequality derives from the mechanisms in the model. The author assumes that there are inherent differences in earnings ability. As families shift some of their earnings toward retirement years (life-cycle saving), these differences translate into a modest degree of wealth inequality. However, to generate significant wealth inequality, the author must assume that there are two types of families. The dynastic ones recognize the odds that subsequent generations will not have earnings ability equal to their own.[49] Accordingly, they save for a second reason: to transfer wealth to their "poor" future relations. The estate and gift taxes are simply a tax on these transfers. The estate tax raises the cost of this activity (compared with its benefits) and leads to smaller bequests and less wealth inequality.

But there are other modeling assumptions that generate the same types of wealth inequality but have very different implications for the estate tax. For example, Jagadeesh Gokhale and coauthors generate essentially the same implication—bequests are an important contributor to wealth inequality but only in the presence of Social Security; that is, without Social Security, bequests actually reduce wealth inequality, though to a minor degree.[50] But in their model, bequests are entirely accidental and would not respond at all to estate taxation. In short, this is only one possible model of wealth inequality, and others may have very different implications for the effects of the estate tax.

Alternatively, one could compare the model to some of our (admittedly scant) empirical understanding of the estate tax. For example, the model generates bequests that are too large, on average. (This insight is not terribly original. To his credit, the author makes this point.) Or, to make the point another way, all of the rich people in the model have substantial inherited

---

49. In future work, it would be interesting to address the endogeneity of human capital accumulation (for example, through parents' paying for college education). The estate and gift tax may modify the relative price of cash versus human capital transfers in an important way not captured by the current model.

50. Gokhale and others (1999).

wealth. There are no entrepreneurial giants or self-made billionaires of the type that cause the *Forbes 400* to change from year to year.

Lastly, the normative implications of the rise in wealth inequality are not clear. Notice that the source of the rise in inequality is a voluntary transfer that raises the well-being of both generations in the family. And, because the aggregate capital-labor ratio rises, the remainder of the population will benefit from higher real wages. In short, despite our instincts to shy away from concentration of wealth, it is hard to imagine that this is a welfare-worsening policy shift.

With these general comments aside, let me turn to a few specific suggestions on the model and chapter. As noted at the outset, the simulation model is impressive in detail and complexity. Nevertheless, I think it would be useful to include more information.

To begin, I think the reader would benefit from additional measures of outcomes. The author focuses on capital accumulation and wealth inequality. These are important aspects of the problem and should be part of the menu. However, it is also possible to make explicit welfare computations (that is, evaluate the utility function), which would allow us to make explicit comparisons about the desirability of alternative steady states. For example, in this model there will be an underlying level of utility inequality owing to the assumption of differences in earnings ability. By focusing explicitly on the utility of each household, one would be able to determine the degree to which the estate and gift taxes increase or decrease the average level of utility and its dispersion in the population.

I think there is room for one more variation of the basic tax experiment. The author eliminates the estate tax and gift tax and replaces the revenue using the income tax. Because earnings ability is exogenous, and labor supply is fixed, the portion of the income tax that falls on wages will be nondistortionary. However, the portion that falls on capital income will introduce an intertemporal distortion of the consumption path. As mentioned earlier, one of the tantalizing results is that it may be possible that replacing the estate and gift tax with the income tax is Pareto-improving, suggesting that the capital income tax has a smaller distortion cost than the estate and gift tax.[51] Since the estate tax is frequently defended as a "fix" to problems with capital income taxes, this would be useful to sort out. However, to do so, one would

---

51. One needs to be careful. The economy is short of the modified Golden Rule level of capital accumulation, so policies that increase saving (and decrease consumption) will benefit the steady-state population at the expense of generations alive during the transition. For sensible reasons, the author focuses on comparative steady states; the model cannot address trade-offs involving the transition path.

have to compare each to a truly nondistortionary tax; for example, cut the estate tax and replace it with a lump sum tax on each dynastic family equal in present value to the estate taxes. One might even get greedy and wonder if the progressivity of the estate tax, or merely its existence, is the culprit, but these sorts of additional experiments with the slope of the estate tax schedule are beyond the scope of this chapter.

In addition, the reader would greatly benefit from a better sense of the contribution of each feature of the model. Now, this may be asking the impossible. But, for example, one might be curious about the degree to which borrowing constraints are central to inter vivos transfers and the overall contribution of these considerations to the bottom line.

Similarly, it would be useful to understand better the effect of the social security program in the model. The author assumes that private annuities are available at fair prices, so there is no social insurance role for the program. Instead, it amounts to a forced saving program, with a rate of return equal to the population plus productivity growth rate. For high-earning, high-bequest families, this will be a lifetime tax that provides an additional incentive to save. When the income tax replaces the estate tax, real wages will change and interact with the social security program. How much does this contribute to the saving profiles we observe?

In summary, it is perhaps fairest to say that these comments are motivated by greed more than is the wealth accumulation modeled in the chapter. The model is so rich, the behavioral responses so suggestive, and the question so important that it is hard not to be unfairly curious about alternatives. This chapter is a valuable contribution to our understanding of the estate tax and is the foundation for much more insight in the future.

References

Abel, Andrew. 1985. "Precautionary Saving and Accidental Bequests." *American Economic Review* 75 (September): 777–91.

Auerbach, Alan J., and Laurence J. Kotlikoff. 1987. *Dynamic Fiscal Policy*. Cambridge: Cambridge University Press, 1987.

Barro, Robert J. "Are Government Bonds Net Worth?" *Journal of Political Economy* 82 (November-December 1974): 1095–1117.

Barsky, Robert B., and others. 1997. "Preference Parameters and Behavioral Heterogeneity: An Experimental Approach in the Health and Retirement Study," *Quarterly Journal of Economics* 112 (May): 537–79.

Becker, Gary S., and Nigel Tomes. 1979. "An Equilibrium Theory of the Distribution of Income and Intergenerational Mobility." *Journal of Political Economy* 87 (December): 1153–89.

Bernheim, B. Douglas, and K. Bagwell. 1988. "Is Everything Neutral?" *Journal of Political Economy* 96 (April): 308–38.

Blinder, Alan S. 1974. *Toward an Economic Theory of Income Distribution*. MIT Press.

Bureau of the Census. 1997. *Statistical Abstract of the United States: 1997*.

Burkhauser, Richard V., Timothy Smeeding, and J. Merz. 1996. "Relative Inequality and Poverty in Germany and the United States Using Alternative Equivalence Scales." *Review of Income and Wealth* 42 (December): 381–400.

Cooley, Thomas F., and Edward C. Prescott. 1995. "Economic Growth and Business Cycles." In *Frontiers of Business Cycle Research*, edited by T. F. Cooley, 1–38. Princeton University Press.

Cox, Donald. 1987. "Motives for Private Income Transfers." *Journal of Political Economy* 95 (June): 508–46.

Davies, James B. 1981. "Uncertain Lifetime, Consumption, and Dissaving in Retirement." *Journal of Political Economy* 89 (June): 561–77.

———. 1982. "The Relative Impact of Inheritance and Other Factors on Economic Inequality." *Quarterly Journal of Economics* 97 (August): 471–98.

Diamond, Peter A. 1965. "National Debt in a Neoclassical Growth Model." *American Economic Review* 55 (December): 1126–50.

Dooley, Martin D., and P. Gottschalk. 1984. "Earnings Inequality among Males in the United States: Trends and the Effects of Labor Force Growth." *Journal of Political Economy* 92 (February): 59–89.

Eller, Martha B. 1997. "Federal Taxation of Wealth Transfers, 1992–1995." *Statistics of Income Bulletin* 16 (Winter 1996–97): 8–63.

Friedman, B. M., and M. J. Warshawsky. 1990. "The Cost of Annuities: Implications for Saving Behavior and Bequests." *Quarterly Journal of Economics* 105 (February): 135–54.

Gale, William G., and J. Karl Scholz. 1994. "Intergenerational Transfers and the Accumulation of Wealth." *Journal of Economic Perspectives* 8 (Fall): 145–60.

Gokhale, Jagadeesh, and others. 1999. "Simulating the Transmission of Wealth Inequality via Bequests." Working Paper 7183.

Holtz-Eakin, Douglas, David Joulfaian, and Harvey Rosen 1993. "The Carnegie Conjecture: Some Empirical Evidence." *Quarterly Journal of Economics* 108 (May): 413–36.

Huggett, Mark. 1996. "Wealth Distribution in Life-Cycle Economies." *Journal of Monetary Economics* 38 (December): 469–94.

Hurst, Erik, Ming Ching Luoh, and Frank P. Stafford. 1998. "The Wealth Dynamics of American Families, 1984–94." *Brookings Papers on Economic Activity 1: 1998: 267–37.*

Kotlikoff, Laurence, J. 1988. "Intergenerational Transfers and Savings." *Journal of Economic Perspectives* 2 (Spring): 41–58.

Kotlikoff, Laurence J., and Lawrence H. Summers. 1981. "The Role of Intergenerational Transfers in Aggregate Capital Accumulation." *Journal of Political Economy* 89 (August): 706–32.

Laitner, John. 1991. "Modeling Marital Connections among Family Lines." *Journal of Political Economy* 99 (December): 1123–41.

———. 1992. "Random Earnings Differences, Lifetime Liquidity Constraints, and Altruistic Intergenerational Transfers." *Journal of Economic Theory* 58 (December): 135–70.

———. 1997. "Intergenerational and Interhousehold Economic Links." In *Handbook of Population and Family Economics*, vol. lA, edited by Mark Rosenzweig and Oded Stark, chap. 5. Amsterdam: Elsevier.

————. 2000. "Secular Changes in Wealth Inequality and Inheritance." University of Michigan. Mimeo.

Laitner, John, and Henry Ohlsson. 2001. "Bequest Motives: A Comparison of Sweden and the United States." *Journal of Public Economics* 79 (January): 2005–236.

Loury, Glenn C. 1981. "Intergenerational Transfers and the Distribution of Earnings." *Econometrica* 49 (July): 843–67.

Mariger, Randall P. 1986. *Consumption Behavior and the Effects of Government Fiscal Policy.* Harvard University Press.

Modigliani, Franco. 1986. "Life Cycle, Individual Thrift and the Wealth of Nations." *American Economic Review* 76 (June): 297–13.

————. 1988. "The Role of Intergenerational Transfers and Life Cycle Saving in the Accumulation of Wealth." *Journal of Economic Perspectives* 2 (Spring): 15–40.

Pechman, Joseph A. 1987. *Federal Tax Policy.* Brookings.

Poterba, James. 1998. "Inter Vivos Transfers and the Incentive Effects of Estate and Gift Taxes in the United States." Massachusetts Institute of Technology and National Bureau of Economic Research.

Social Security Administration. 1998. "Annual Statistical Supplement Updates for 1998." *Social Security Bulletin* 61(2): 29–92.

Solon, Gary. 1992. "Intergenerational Income Mobility in the United States." *American Economic Review* 82 (June): 393–408.

Stark, Oded. 1999. *Altruism and Beyond.* Cambridge: Cambridge University Press.

U.S. Department of Commerce. 1997. "Fixed Reproducible Tangible Wealth in the United States: Revised Estimates for 1993–95 and Summary Estimates for 1925–96." *Survey of Current Business* 77 (September): 37–47.

Wolff, Edward N. 1995. "International Comparisons of Wealth Inequality." *Review of Income and Wealth* 42 (December): 433–51.

WOJCIECH KOPCZUK
JOEL SLEMROD

7 The Impact of the Estate Tax on Wealth Accumulation and Avoidance Behavior

WHETHER AN ESTATE tax deserves a role in the U.S. tax system depends in part on its impact on the behavior of potential donors. Opponents argue that an estate tax reduces the incentive to accumulate wealth in two ways: by reducing the incentive to earn income and by increasing the incentive to consume. Supporters downplay the salience of these incentives and often ascribe wealth accumulation to motives that are immune to taxation. For example, Cedric Sandford writes, "Much saving is undertaken with no thought of bequests in mind; people accumulate property for a variety of reasons—future security and enjoyment; the power that wealth confers; inertia—the sheer inability to spend their wealth; the desire to manage a large business; the posthumous glory of dying rich; and many others which are unaffected by death duty considerations."[1] Opponents of the estate tax also refer to the substantial avoidance it engenders. For example, the U.S. Joint Economic Committee report asserts, "Virtually any individual

We are grateful to the Statistics of Income Division of the Internal Revenue Service for allowing access to confidential estate tax return data under a data disclosure agreement. We especially thank Barry Johnson of SOI for patiently explaining the data structure and facilitating our analysis. Robert Greebel and Kassie Stone provided assistance on the history of estate tax provisions. Alan Auerbach, Julie Cullen, David Joulfaian, and conference participants provided helpful comments on an earlier draft.

1. Sandford (1984, p. 226).

who invests sufficient time, energy and money in tax avoidance strategies is capable of avoiding the estate tax altogether."[2] Both the impact on wealth accumulation and the "time, energy, and money" devoted to avoidance should be counted as costs of levying the estate tax, to be weighed against the revenue it raises in a highly progressive manner.

Although assertions about the impact of the estate tax are made with great confidence, almost no empirical evidence supports claims of a large effect or of a negligible effect. In this chapter we begin an empirical analysis of this issue.

Models of How the Estate Tax Affects Potential Donors' Behavior

The impact of the estate tax on potential donors' behavior depends critically on the nature and motivation behind the bequest motive. This fact poses an immediate challenge, because the literature considers several different bequest motives. Bequests may be accidental, as a consequence of uncertain lifespan and an imperfect market for life annuities.[3] They may reflect altruism, in the sense that the expected well-being of a child affects the utility of a parent.[4] A parent may enjoy giving, or he may enjoy being wealthy, preventing him from running down resources at the end of life.[5] Bequests may also reflect some strategic interactions, for example, parents attempting to manipulate their children's behavior by holding out the chance of an inheritance.[6] They may also be a form of contract between subsequent generations.[7] In what follows, we focus on a model with altruism and without strategic interactions between the parents and children to highlight how taxes affect the key incentives of the donor.

A Model with No Uncertainty

To later highlight the role of uncertainty, we begin with a simple model with none at all. Consider an individual who values leisure and consumption dur-

---

2. U.S. Joint Economic Committee (1998, p. 30).

3. Davies (1981); Hurd (1989).

4. See Barro (1974). There is also literature on two-sided altruism; for a survey see Laitner (1997, sec. 3.1).

5. See Yaari (1965) and Andreoni (1990) on the joy of giving and Carroll (2000) on the utility from holding wealth.

6. Bernheim, Shleifer, and Summers (1985).

7. Kotlikoff and Spivak (1981).

ing his life and who also values the well-being of his heir.[8] We can represent the individual's decision problem as follows:

(1)
$$\max_{C,L,G,A} u\left(C, L, G, v\left(y, I\right)\right)$$

(2)
$$W = wL - T\left(wL\right) - C,$$

(3)
$$I = W - G - E\left(W - G - A\right) - D\left(W, A\right).$$

Here C and L represent lifetime consumption and labor supply, respectively, w is the wage rate, $T(\cdot)$ is the income tax function, and W is the total bequeathable estate. G represents charitable bequests (which are deducted from the estate tax base). The individual cares about the heir's utility, v, which depends on his own endowment y and on I, the after-tax inheritance received by the heir; $E(\cdot)$ is the estate tax function. Taxes may be avoided at the cost of $D(W, A)$, where A represents the amount of taxable income reduction. This specification allows, as in Joel Slemrod, for the marginal cost of avoidance to be lower for larger estates, reflecting scale economies in avoidance, so that $D_W < 0$, $D_A > 0$, and $D_{AW} < 0$.[9] Combining the first-order conditions leads to the following characterization of the optimal plan:

(4)
$$C: \quad \frac{u_C}{u_v v_I} = 1 - E'\left(W - G - A\right) - D_W\left(W, A\right),$$

(5)
$$L: \quad -\frac{u_L}{u_v v_I} = w\left(1 - E'\left(W - G - A\right) - D_W\left(W, A\right)\right)\left(1 - T'\left(wL\right)\right),$$

(6)
$$G: \quad \frac{u_G}{u_v v_I} = 1 - E'\left(W - G - A\right),$$

(7)
$$A: \quad D_A\left(A\right) = E'\left(W - G - A\right).$$

The first-order conditions for this problem reveal that the marginal estate tax rate increases the cost of leaving an inheritance relative to consumption, leisure, and charitable bequests. As with any tax, there will also be an income effect that, as long as all the goods are normal, will reduce C and I, and increase L (because leisure, not its complement labor, is the normal good). Of more interest (because it is unique to an estate tax) is the substitution effect, which will certainly reduce I and will also increase C when it is not complementary to I (or, more precisely, complementary to the utility of children),

8. For present purposes, we model an unmarried person with a single heir.
9. Slemrod (2001).

as well as reduce L when leisure is not complementary to I. Absent complementarity, the substitution effect implies that end-of-life wealth will be lower with an estate tax, both because labor supply will be lower than otherwise and consumption will be higher than otherwise. In general, it is not possible to sign the uncompensated response. Finally, estate taxes are avoided up to the point where the marginal tax saving is equal to the marginal cost. To the extent that greater wealth facilitates avoidance ($D_{AW} < 0$), this mitigates the disincentive effect of the estate tax on saving and labor supply. Thus, whether avoidance opportunities soften the impact of the estate tax on "real" behavior depends on the technology of avoidance. This continues to be true in the models that follow, although for the sake of simplicity we ignore avoidance from this point on.

This model generalizes in a straightforward way to deal with multiple periods of life. For tractability, we consider a special case in which the utility of N different periods is additively separable, so that

$$u\left(C_1, L_1, \ldots, C_N, L_N, G, v(y, I)\right) = \sum_{i=1}^{N} \rho^i u\left(C_i, L_i\right)$$
$$(8) \qquad\qquad\qquad + \rho^{N+1} h\left(v(y, I), G\right),$$

where ρ is the per period rate of utility discounting and h is the utility derived from bequests to heirs and charities.[10] The optimum is characterized by a series of relationships.[11] First, there is an instantaneous optimality condition that relates consumption and leisure at each period of time,

$$(9) \qquad \frac{u_C\left(C_i, L_i\right)}{u_L\left(C_i, L_i\right)} = w\left(1 - T'\left(wL_i\right)\right),$$

which states that the marginal rate of substitution between leisure and consumption should be equal to the wage rate net of the marginal income tax rate. Second, there are Euler equations that describe the evolution of consumption and leisure over time,

$$(10) \qquad \frac{u_C\left(C_i, L_i\right)}{u_L\left(C_{i+1}, L_{i+1}\right)} = \rho(1 + r), \qquad\qquad i = 1 \ldots N - 1,$$

---

10. Because there is no uncertainty, there will never be a need for the individual to diverge from the consumption, work, and bequest plan set out at the beginning of life.

11. In deriving these conditions, we assume that there are no borrowing constraints and that terminal wealth is constrained to be non-negative.

$$(11) \quad \frac{u_L(C_i, L_i)}{u_L(C_{i+1}, L_{i+1})} = \rho(1 + r)\frac{1 - T'(wL_i)}{1 - T'(wL_{i+1})}, \quad i = 1 \ldots N - 1.$$

Equation 10 states that the marginal rates of substitution between consumption in adjoining periods should depend on the pure discount rate and the rate of interest (pretax, because we have not introduced capital taxes into the model). Equation 11 is the equivalent for labor supply, which must be adjusted across time for any changes in the marginal income tax rate. Finally, there are terminal conditions that relate consumption in the last period of life to the inheritance and charitable bequest,

$$(12) \quad \frac{u_C(C_N, L_N)}{h_v v_I(y, I)} = \rho(1 + r)(1 - E'(W_N - G)),$$

$$(13) \quad \frac{h_G(v(y, I), G)}{h_v v_I(y, I)} = 1 - E'(W_N - G),$$

$$(14) \quad -\frac{u_C(C_N, L_N)}{h_v v_I(y, I)} = \rho(1 + r)u(1 - T'(wL_N))(1 - E'(W_N - G)).$$

Without a bequest motive, the terminal condition would guarantee that the individual just exhausts his resources at the end of life. In the presence of a bequest motive, the estate is set so that the individual is just indifferent between consuming or working and leaving an inheritance. (This is conceptually identical to the analysis of the one-period model.) Holding wealth at the beginning of the last period constant, the estate tax induces an unambiguous substitution response toward more consumption and leisure.[12] Owing to the presence of a counteracting income response, it is not possible to sign the total effect. The Euler equations, which characterize the optimal paths of consumption and leisure, require that consumption (and leisure) in *each* period move in the same direction. In other words, a change in the estate tax shifts the lifetime consumption/labor profile without affecting its shape. However, both upward and downward shifts are consistent with the theory, depending on whether the income or substitution response to the estate tax of *lifetime* consumption and leisure dominates.

---

12. Because of the assumed additively separable form of the utility function, an increase in the price of inheritance induces a substitution response toward the composite good consisting of C and L. It does not affect the relative prices of consumption and leisure so that when both these goods are normal, as we assume, they both increase.

A Model with Uncertain Lifetime

In spite of Benjamin Franklin's injunction that the only certain things in life are death and taxes, uncertainty plays an important role in understanding the impact of estate taxes on donors' behavior. There is uncertainty about future income realizations of potential donors. This consideration originally gave rise to the literature on the precautionary motive for saving.[13] Uncertainty may be present about future medical expenses and long-term care. Uncertainty about the endowment and therefore the well-being of the future generations is considered by Michel Strawczynski.[14] Finally, there may also be uncertainty about the future rules that govern the taxation of wealth transfers. For example, individuals might want to avoid inter vivos gifts if they think that estate taxes may be reduced in the future.

We focus on the uncertainty about the lifespan of the donor, which affects decisions of the donor through a precautionary motive—the desire to avoid "outliving" one's resources. This aspect, in the presence of an imperfect market for annuities, produces accidental bequests.[15] As is conventional in this literature, we assume that consumers are not allowed to freely purchase life annuities but that some are exogenously available through Social Security benefits.[16]

As in the previous model, we consider an individual who maximizes an intertemporal utility function that depends on consumption, leisure, and bequests left at death.[17] In the presence of uncertainty, it is assumed that the individual is an expected utility maximizer and so seeks to maximize

$$(15) \qquad \sum_{i=1}^{N+1} \rho^i \left(a_i u \left(C_i, L_i \right) + m_i v \left(y, I_i \right) \right),$$

13. If the uncertainty regarding income or wealth is resolved after most labor supply, human capital, and saving decisions are made, then taxation of estates may be very efficient, because it is a tax on luck.

14. See Hubbard, Skinner, and Zeldes (1994) concerning future medical expenses. See also Strawczynski (1994).

15. Several papers are concerned with consumer behavior in this context. See, for example, Yaari (1965); Richard (1975); Davies (1981); Abel (1985); Hurd (1989); Bernheim (1991). Some of these papers (Davies 1981, Abel 1985) consider accidental bequests in isolation; others (Hurd 1989, Bernheim 1991) allow also for other types of bequest motives.

16. Barro and Friedman (1972) noted that when insurance markets are perfect and actuarially fair, mortality and survival rates do not affect consumption and bequest decisions. An intuition for this result is simple. A decrease in the mortality rate increases the value of future consumption to an individual. At the same time, it increases its price because annuities become more expensive when people are expected to live longer. With actuarially fair insurance markets, these two effects cancel out.

17. For simplicity, we do not model charitable bequests.

where as before C_i and L_i are consumption and labor in period i, I_i is the (after-tax) inheritance left in case of death in period i, $u(\cdot)$ and $v(\cdot)$ are the instantaneous utilities from consumption and inheritances respectively, N is the maximum possible age, and ρ is the rate of time preference.[18] We introduce some new notation, so that a_i is the survival rate and m_i is the mortality rate. The mortality rate m_i is the probability of dying at the beginning of period i, and a_i is the probability of being alive at the end of period i. The individual lives in the first period, so it is natural to assume that $a_1 = 1$ and $m_1 = 0$; she may live at most N periods so that $a_{N+1} = 0$. Mortality and survival rates are linked by the relation $m_i = a_{i-1} - a_i$ or, equivalently, $a_i = a_{i-1} - m_i$.

Optimization is, as in the certainty case, subject to the budget constraints,

(16) $$W_{i+1} = (1 + r)(W_i + wL_i - T(wL_i) - C_i),$$

(17) $$I_i = W_i - E(W_i).$$

The Euler equation in this model can be written as follows:[19]

(18)
$$u_C(C_i, L_i) = \rho(1 + r)\left(\frac{a_{i+1}}{a_i}\left(u_C(C_{i+1}, L_{i+1})\right.\right.$$
$$\left.\left. + \frac{m_{i+1}}{a_i} v_I(y, I_{i+1})(1 - E'(W_{i+1}))\right)\right)$$

(19)
$$\text{or } u_L(C_i, L_i) = \rho(1 + r)\frac{1 - T'(wL_i)}{1 - T'(wL_{i+1})}\left(\frac{a_{i+1}}{a_i} u_L(C_{i+1}, L_{i+1})\right.$$
$$\left. + \frac{m_{i+1}}{a_i} w(1 - T'(wL_{i+1}))(1 - E'(W_{i+1}))v_I(y, I_{i+1})\right).$$

Compare equation 18 to the certainty version of equation 10. The marginal benefit of consumption is unchanged, but the marginal benefit of postponed consumption now must account for the fact that it allows for either increased own consumption or an increased bequest, with the two weighted by the probability of surviving until the next period. The estate tax reduces the payoff to saving because it reduces the inheritance that a unit of postponed consump-

18. With an appropriate interpretation of the function $v(\cdot)$, it may also be considered as a reduced form of the altruistic model. See Abel and Warshawsky (1988).

19. It is assumed that the wealth constraints are not binding. If they were, this first-order condition would become an inequality, with equality whenever the constraint is not binding.

tion creates. This effect is present in every period, but only next period's marginal tax appears directly in any single Euler equation, and its effect is proportional to the mortality rate. It would be a mistake, however, to conclude that this is the full effect. Consumption after period $t + 1$ is also affected by taxes, and from the Euler equation we may conclude that (expected) consumption in period $t + 1$ is a sufficient statistic for the influence of estate taxes after that period.

The estate tax also affects labor supply, as demonstrated by the presence of the tax term in equation 19. The wage rate relevant for the labor supply/inheritance margin is $w(1 - T')(1 - E')$; that is, the estate tax reduces the payoff to working. As in the certainty case, labor supply and consumption at a point in time are instantaneously related by equation 9, so that the relevant wage rate on this margin is still $w(1 - T')$.

As stressed by Michael D. Hurd, in the last possible period of life two possibilities may occur: either an individual is willing to leave a bequest, in which case terminal conditions (12-14) apply, or not, in which case there are no such conditions, and final consumption is pinned down based on the budget constraint and the Euler equation.[20] In general, the more wealthy an individual is, the more likely a bequest will be left. Leaving a bequest with certainty may be guaranteed by imposing the condition that $\lim_{I \to 0} v_I(y, I) = +\infty$, which implies that one wishes at all costs to avoid the possibility of leaving no bequests at all.[21]

The Euler equation may be iterated forward to yield the following formula:

$$
\begin{aligned}
u_C(C_i, L_i) = {} & a_N \rho^{N-1}(1 + r)^{N-1} u_C(C_N, L_N) \\
& + \sum_{i=2}^{N} m_i \rho^{i-1}(1 + r)^{i-1} v_I(y, I_i)(1 - E'(W_i)).
\end{aligned}
$$
(20)

When the individual plans a bequest, this equation further simplifies to

$$
(21) \quad u_C(C_t, L_t) = \sum_{i=t+1}^{N+1} m_i \rho^{i-1}(1 + r)^{i-1} v_I(y, I_i)(1 - E'(W_i)).
$$

20. Hurd (1989). Note that even though one may not wish to leave bequests upon reaching a certain age, the marginal utility from bequests is still in the Euler equation because accidental bequests also yield utility.

21. If this assumption is made, the wealth constraint would never be binding because, if it was, the marginal utility from bequests would be infinite, which may not be optimal.

Equation 21 implies that consumption in any period depends on the value of $m_i(1 - E'(W_i))$ for all subsequent periods.

A Simulation Exercise

To gain more insights into the nature of behavioral response and to the empirical challenges we will confront later, we can simulate individual behavior using a stylized utility function. To do so, we assume that an individual maximizes lifetime utility given by

$$(22) \qquad \sum_{i=25}^{115} \rho^{-i}\left(a_i \frac{C^{1-\gamma}}{1-\gamma} + m_i \alpha \frac{B_i^{1-\delta}}{1-\delta} \right),$$

where C_i is consumption in period i, B_i is the bequest in case of death at the end of period i, ρ is the discount factor, a_i is the probability of survival until period i and m_i is the probability of death in period i. Initial wealth W_{25} is assumed to be zero. The simulated lifetime begins when at age 25, and the maximum possible age is 115. Mortality and survival rates are taken from the population actuarial life tables for males. Neither annuities nor life insurance is available, and the optimization is subject to the following two constraints,

$$(23) \qquad W_{i+1} = (1 + r)(W_i + Y_i - C_i), \qquad i = 0\ldots N,$$

$$(24) \qquad B_i = W_i - E(W_i), \qquad i = 1\ldots N + 1,$$

where Y_i is (exogenously given) income in period i, and $E_i(\cdot)$ is the estate tax function.

It is assumed that $\gamma = 2$, $\rho = .97$, $r = .03$, $\alpha = .1$, and $\delta = .5\gamma$. This last parameter implies that, over the lifetime, bequests increase approximately twice as fast as consumption. The individual is assumed to have a constant stream of income of $200,000 a year until the age of 65 and no income thereafter.

Figures 7-1 and 7-2 consider the case in which the representative individual starts his economic life facing the current U.S. tax system and is convinced that it will be in effect for the rest of his life. After twenty years of living in this regime, however, the tax system changes unexpectedly, and the estate tax is abolished completely. What effect does this have on the lifetime pattern of consumption and bequests?

Figure 7-1 shows the effect on the path of wealth accumulation for two individuals who differ only in level of endowment. Eliminating the tax increases

Figure 7-1. *Simulated Wealth over a Lifetime under the Current Estate Tax and under a Zero-Tax Regime Imposed at Age 45*

Wealth (thousands of dollars)

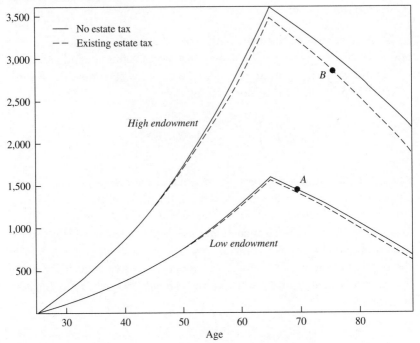

Source: This and all subsequent figures present author's models, as described in text.

wealth, and the effect gets larger with age. Figure 7-2 shows the effect on the path of consumption. Consumption falls immediately, but if one lives long enough, consumption may ultimately increase above what it would otherwise be. An intuition for this result is as follows: at the maximum possible age, an individual is planning to hold more wealth than he otherwise would. As a result, the marginal utility from leaving a bequest is lower, and thus there is an incentive to consume more (than one otherwise would) close to that date. Importantly, the response to the tax change is sensitive to the parameterization of the model.

This simple simulation offers several insights. First, the effect of the estate tax on wealth depends on the age of an individual. Second, the full effect is not visible until many years after the tax reform. Finally, compare points A and B in figure 7-1. Although point A is an observation from a zero estate tax regime and point B is an observation from a high estate tax regime, the estate at B ex-

Figure 7-2. *Simulated Consumption over a Lifetime under the Current Estate Tax and under a Zero-Tax Regime Imposed at Age 45*

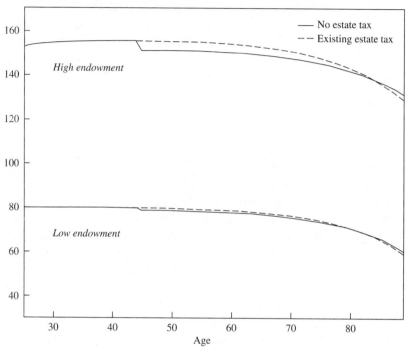

Consumption (thousands of dollars)

ceeds the wealth at A even though estate taxes reduce wealth accumulation in this simulation model. The behavioral response to taxation will be revealed in an empirical analysis only to the extent that the endowment can be held constant in some way. Because no information about lifetime income is available in the analysis below, other assumptions are required.

More generally, the response of wealth accumulation to a change in the estate tax will depend on the responsiveness of labor supply to a change in its net reward and on the responsiveness of lifetime consumption versus bequests to its relative price. This cannot be revealed by theoretical analysis but only by empirical analysis. Moreover, the income effect may partly or fully offset the relative price effects, so the sign of the net effect is not definite. Finally, as William Gale and Maria Perozek emphasize in this volume, the qualitative effect of the estate tax on private saving depends on why donors give bequests and how saving by the donee is affected. They argue that in plausible models the estate tax may increase the combined saving of the donor and donee.

The same point applies to the avoidance response: theoretical reasoning can determine neither the magnitude of the response nor the sensitivity of the response to the tax structure.

Both because the key parameters of the altruism model are unknown and because the "right" model of bequests, be it altruism or some other, is unknown, the response of potential donors to the estate tax is ultimately an empirical question. Before attempting to advance our understanding of this question later in this chapter, we briefly review some relevant literature.

Previous Empirical Literature on Effects of the Estate Tax

In his survey of the U.S. federal estate and gift tax, David Joulfaian notes that estate taxes may reduce the work effort and savings of parents motivated to leave large bequests to their children, but he states that "there is no empirical evidence" on either type of behavioral response.[22] Because the estate tax is a particular kind of tax on return to working and saving, the large empirical literature on how the income tax affects these two decisions is, however, certainly relevant. If taxes affect neither, it is unlikely that the estate tax could affect wealth accumulation. We cannot adequately survey the enormous literature on these topics here, although we refer the reader to the able surveys by Richard Blundell and Thomas E. MaCurdy on labor supply and by B. Douglas Bernheim on saving.[23] Although the consensus of these literatures—that neither is very responsive to taxes—suggests that the impact of the estate tax on wealth accumulation is not large, there is almost no direct analysis of this question.

In an earlier era, Seymour Fiekowsky argued that estate accumulators were not discouraged by the sharply increased death tax rates introduced in the 1930s and early 1940s. He asserts that if there had been such discouragement, one would have (but did not) observed three phenomena: "the distribution of estate taxpayer estates would have become more equal, as the larger estates failed to grow and the smaller estates (truly held for consumption) increased slightly; the proportion of widows among estate taxpayers would have risen, as active accumulators moved to thwart the IRS, since widows would report estates inherited from the prior generation of unthwarted accumulators; and a marked effort to minimize transfer tax liabilities by making gifts and creating generation-skipping transfers would have been manifested."[24]

---

22. Joulfaian (1998b, pp. 24–25).
23. Blundell and MaCurdy (1999); Bernheim (1997).
24. Fiekowsky (1966, p. 235).

Avoidance and Evasion

Alan A. Tait estimates the extent of avoidance of the estate tax in Great Britain by comparing the distribution of taxable estates in a low-tax year (1912) to the distribution in a high-tax year (1960). He first applies 1960 estate tax rates to the 1912 distribution and expresses the tax yield as a fraction of total wealth held in 1912. He then compares this figure to the actual 1960 revenue yield as a fraction of total wealth held in 1960 and finds that the 1912 figures exceed those of 1960 by 1.3 to 1.5 times. This leads Tait to conclude that avoidance amounts to 34 to 50 percent of the potential 1960 base.[25] Note, though, that the total wealth estimates in the denominator are themselves derived from estate tax returns and are thus skewed by any avoidance. Furthermore, the large time span between the two years suggests that much other than the tax structure changed and may confound the methodology.

Edward N. Wolff estimates U.S. estate tax avoidance by comparing the actual tax base to an estimate of what the base "should be" based on the comprehensive wealth survey in the 1992 Survey of Consumer Finances (SCF) conducted by the Federal Reserve Board. He first applies mortality rates by age, gender, and race to the population represented by the 1992 SCF file. He calculates the total net worth of decedents to be $241.5 billion in 1993, which compares to $99.4 billion reported on estate tax returns. He then adjusts the net worth of each "probabilistic" decedent by the average marital and charitable giving deduction in the estate class and applies the federal estate tax schedule. On this basis, Wolff's simulation indicates that estate tax collections should have been $44.5 billion in 1993, compared with $10.3 billion in actual collections. He concludes that more effective enforcement of the estate tax might have yielded another $30 billion in revenue in 1993.[26]

However, James M. Poterba performs a similar exercise and concludes that the estimated tax liability corresponds closely to actual estate tax liability.[27] The stark difference in conclusion is partly because Poterba uses a mortality table that describes the mortality experience of individuals who purchase single-premium annuities from life insurance companies, who are generally from the upper tail of the wealth distribution and are arguably representative of the population paying estate tax. In contrast, Wolff uses the population mortality table and may therefore be overestimating the fraction of wealthy

25. Tait (1967).
26. Wolff (1996).
27. Poterba (2000).

people who are subject to estate tax in a given year.[28] Martha Britton Eller, Brian Erard and Chih-Chin Ho, in this volume, revisit the Wolff-Poterba methodology and find that the conclusions are highly sensitive to assumptions about differential mortality rates of married and unmarried individuals and the distribution of charitable contributions across estates in a given gross estate category. Because of this sensitivity, they caution against taking too seriously estimates of avoidance or evasion based on this type of approach. Moreover, these studies are attempts to estimate the size of avoidance (and evasion), but none addresses the sensitivity of this magnitude to changes in the estate tax structure.

Not only avoidance, but also (illegal) evasion, may be sensitive to the tax structure. However, little is known about this effect. Certainly, the audit coverage of estate tax returns is relatively high. Martha Britton Eller and Barry W. Johnson report that in 1992, 11,338 estate tax returns were audited, which constitutes 19.2 percent of the total number of filed returns.[29] The audit rate increases with the size of the gross estates, with an 11.1 percent audit rate of estate under $1 million, 26.5 percent of estates between $1 million and $5 million, and 48.5 percent of estates larger than $5 million. Because of the concentration of audits on the largest estates, although 19.2 percent were audited, returns with 63.2 percent of the reported tax liability were subject to audit.

Eller and Johnson do not estimate an estate tax "gap," but report that as a result of audit, net estate tax liability increased by $559.8 million, which is 8.7 percent of the total reported tax liability of the returns that were audited. Of audited cases, 60.0 percent were closed with additional net estate tax owed, 19.0 percent were closed with no change in assessment, and 21.0 percent were closed with a reduction in the original net estate tax liability. Erard estimates the tax gap to be 13 percent (using 1992 data) of potential revenues.[30] Neither Eller and Johnson nor anyone else has tried to estimate the responsiveness of estate tax evasion to changes in either the tax structure or the level of enforcement resources and their application.

The closest antecedent to what we attempt in this chapter is Kenneth Chapman, Govind Hariharan, and Lawrence Southwick, who regress the logarithm of real revenues from the estate tax in 1958 through 1994 against the logarithm of real GNP and the logarithm of the marginal estate tax on an estate of real value equal to $1.4 million in 1989.[31] The response of revenues

28. Another difference is that Wolff uses a reweighted version of the SCF data set that generates larger wealth holdings than the public-use weights used by Poterba.
29. Eller and Johnson (2000, p. 3).
30. Erard (1999).
31. Chapman, Hariharan, and Southwick (1996).

should reflect avoidance and, with a lag, wealth accumulation. They estimate a significant negative coefficient on the tax rate variable, with an elasticity of revenues with respect to the marginal tax rate of about −2. They note, however, that three other definitions of the marginal tax rate "did not give as strong an effect," made no attempt to control for other influences on revenues other than the level of GNP, and included no time trend, which might be especially important given that the measure of marginal tax rate increases monotonically over this period. In the following empirical analysis, we examine a longer period over which the estate tax structure rises and falls and allow for nontax influences on reported estates as well as a time trend. Furthermore, we examine reported estates rather than revenues to separate out the behavioral effects of changes in the tax structure from the direct revenue impact of such changes.

In summary, although the literature has addressed aspects of the behavioral response to the estate tax, not much solid empirical research informs policy. To be sure, there are substantial methodological challenges to overcome in obtaining such evidence.

Analysis of Aggregate Time-Series Evidence

Although the technology of life and death means that panel data are (and will in the foreseeable future be) unavailable, investigating the impact on behavior of the changes over time in the rates and rules regarding the estate tax is still possible. Since its introduction in the Revenue Act of 1916, many changes have occurred in the rate structure, base, deductions, treatment of gifts, creditability of state estate and inheritance taxes, and other aspects of the tax.[32] We make use of some aspects of that variation to examine the impact of the estate tax on aggregate wealth accumulation and avoidance.

The ultimate goal of the empirical analysis is to provide evidence of how the estate tax structure has affected wealth accumulation and avoidance. Of course, the counterfactual—what estates would have been under a different tax structure—is not known. We are forced to rely on inference based on the relationship between what is observed—reported estates of the very wealthy—and some other variables. For example, one might examine the ratio of estates subject to the estate tax to the total of all estates, under the assumption that, were it not for the estate tax, this ratio would stay fairly constant. Alas, the amount of total estates is not known, because we do not observe

32. Luckey (1995).

the estates of the vast majority of the population that is not subject to estate taxation.

There is, however, information about the aggregate net worth of the whole population. If the relationship between aggregate net worth and total estates of decedents remains fairly constant over time, one can use net worth as a benchmark against which to examine the response of taxable estates to changes in the tax structure. We pursue this strategy in what follows. Studying this relationship qualitatively is in the spirit of the work of Daniel R. Feenberg and James M. Poterba, who in an influential article calculated the share of total taxable income received by the top 0.5 percent of income earners, and discussed the extent to which it could be explained by the variation in the income tax rates on this group relative to the population as a whole.[33]

The dependent variable we seek to explain is the ratio (to aggregate net worth) of total reported net estates (gross estate minus debts) of a fixed percentile of the largest estates. To avoid spurious results owing to changes over time in mortality experience (which would affect the total estates of a given fraction of the wealthiest taxpayers in a mechanical way), we normalize this variable by the mortality rate. The variable we construct is defined as

$$(25) \qquad\qquad estratio_t \equiv \frac{E_t}{0.005 m_t W_t},$$

where E_t is the value in year t of estates of the richest 0.5 percent of decedents, W_t is aggregate net worth, and m_t is the mortality rate. Noting that $0.005 m_t$ is just the ratio of the number of deaths in the top 0.5 percent to the total population, $estratio_t$ may alternatively be expressed as $\frac{\overline{E}_t}{\overline{W}_t}$, where $\overline{E}_t$ is the average estate of the wealthy decedent group, and $\overline{W}_t$ is the average wealth among the whole economy.

Note that we are examining the determinants of reported net worth on estates rather than reported taxable estates. Analyzing the latter raises a difficult empirical problem because the definition of taxable estate changed several times over the period we study, and we do not have sufficient data to construct a series according to a consistent definition. Not adjusting the data causes problems of interpretation, discussed in the context of taxable income in Joel Slemrod.[34] Over this period, the definition of gross estate and net worth was more stable, although there were certainly changes, regarding, for

33. Feenberg and Poterba (1993).
34. Slemrod (1998).

example, inclusion of the property owned jointly by a married couple, which we attempt to account for in our analysis. Thus, our analysis focuses on the association between the tax structure and gross estate or net worth, rather than taxable estate. This compromise because of data constraints almost certainly leads to an understatement of the true elasticity of the tax base. The data sources and estimation procedure are described in detail in the appendix to this chapter.

To investigate whether taxes had a significant impact on reported estates, we need a measure of the tax rate that is not in any way endogenously determined by the distribution of actual estates. We explore three such measures. The first is the statutory marginal tax rate that applies to the largest estates (TTOP). Clearly, no decisions of the taxpayers affect this value instantaneously. Although one could argue that over time the concentration of estates may, through the political process, influence the tax structure, we ignore this possibility. The other two measures of the tax rate we investigate are the marginal tax rate at 100 times (T100) and 40 times (T40) the level of aggregate wealth per capita. The tax rate at 40 times average wealth is of interest because it corresponds to a sequence of wealth that was subject to the estate tax throughout the whole period, and yet only very recently did the highest tax bracket apply to it.

Results

Figures 7-3 through 7-5 plot *estratio* against each of the three tax rate indicators. The tax rate measures are shown for each year, although *estratio* is only available (here and in the regression analysis that follows) for selected years. For both T100 and T40, there is an apparent and striking negative relationship between the tax variable and the estate/wealth ratio—the two series are practically mirror images of each other. Indeed, the simple correlations are −0.87 and −0.86 for T100 and T40, respectively. The sharp increase in the estate tax rates beginning in the early 1930s coincides with a sharp decrease in reported estates, and the halt and, in the case of T100, decline of the rates beginning in the early 1980s coincides with the timing of a turnaround in the estate ratio. For TTOP, the negative relationship is not quite as striking, but there is nevertheless a correlation of −0.49 between the two series.[35]

35. Not correcting for the mortality rate would make it even more striking, because the mortality rate was decreasing over time, and thus without this correction an additional downward-sloping time pattern would be present in the *estratio* series.

Figure 7-3. *Top Estate Tax Rate and the Estate-Wealth Ratio*

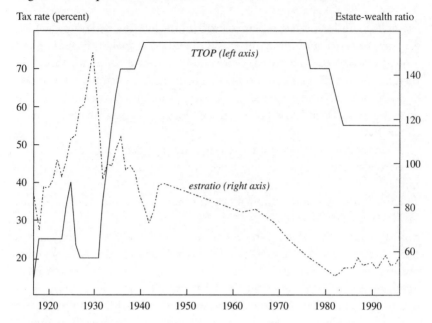

Tax rate (percent)

Estate-wealth ratio

TTOP (left axis)

estratio (right axis)

Figure 7-4. *Estate Tax Rate at 100 Times Average Wealth and the Estate-Wealth Ratio*

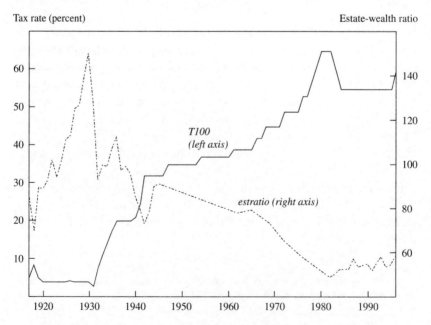

Tax rate (percent)

Estate-wealth ratio

T100 (left axis)

estratio (right axis)

Figure 7-5. *Estate Tax Rate at 40 Times Average Wealth and the Estate-Wealth Ratio*

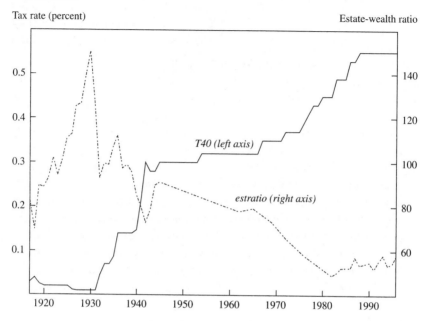

Tax rate (percent)   Estate-wealth ratio

A few features of the tax rate series are worth pointing out. Increases in T100 and T40 between 1942 and 1976 are solely due to "bracket creep"— the nominal tax brackets remained unchanged while the average wealth was increasing (in real terms and because of inflation). In the 1980s, the T100 series was equal to TTOP, and both series stabilized with the aggregate estates.[36] The T40 series, however, paints a different picture. Although the highest tax rates decreased in the early 1980s, this is not true for the tax rates that applied at this more moderate level of wealth. Instead, the marginal tax rate continued to increase owing to real and nominal changes in aggregate wealth. Legislated increases in the exemption level were just too small to matter.

The strong negative correlation between *estratio* and the tax rate measures does not establish that the changes in the estate tax *caused* the changes in reported estates. For one thing, other factors, coincidentally related to

36. The increase in T100 in 1996 is due to a phase-out of the exemption and lower tax rates at smaller estates that increases the marginal tax rate on estates between $10 and $21.4 million to 60 percent.

the evolution of the estate tax, may have influenced this variable. For instance, the correlation of *estratio* with the real S&P 500 index is −0.59. We can, of course, go beyond ocular econometrics and investigate formally the relationship between the estate/wealth ratio and the estate tax structure in a regression framework, in a way similar to Slemrod's investigation of the determinants of the Feenberg-Poterba high-income share of total income.[37] The multiple regression framework allows us to statistically hold constant nontax factors that changed over time that might be expected to influence this variable.

We investigate two nontax and two tax, but non-estate-tax, explanatory variables. The first nontax variable is the contemporaneous inflation-adjusted level of the S&P 500 stock market index. This is included because changes in asset values will affect the value of estates in a way that cannot be offset by changed behavior. On the reasonable assumption that the portfolio of high-wealth individuals is likely to be relatively more concentrated in stocks, we expect to find a positive relationship between the stock market index and *estratio*, a relationship that is unrelated to a behavioral response to taxation. We also include a ten-year lagged value of the inequality of income, measured as the share of income going to the richest 5 percent of the population (see the appendix for the source of this series). This variable is meant to proxy for the inequality of lifetime endowments which, other things equal, would later cause inequality in estates. Of course, income realizations depend not only on endowments but also on factors such as labor supply and effort, which may themselves have been affected by the estate tax structure, and therefore the income inequality measure may be endogenous. This problem is somewhat alleviated by use of the lagged value of the inequality measure.

To control for the possible effects of other tax variables, we also include as explanatory variables the individual income tax and, separately, the corporation income tax rates that applied to the highest bracket of individual and corporation income, respectively. Both of these variables were lagged ten years to account for the fact that they were more likely to be important during the individual's working years.

The regression results are presented in table 7-1. The dependent variable is the logarithm of *estratio*. In the basic specification, shown in the first three columns, the right-hand-side variables include a constant, the logarithm of one of the three measures of the net-of-tax rate $(1 - t)$, the inflation-adjusted stock market index, the income inequality measure, and the two lagged tax rate terms.

---

37. Slemrod (1996).

Table 7-1. *Aggregate Time-Series Results: The Effect of the Estate Tax Rate on the Reported Estate-Wealth Ratio*[a]

Independent variable	I	II	III	IV	V	VI
Log(1 – TTOP)	0.075 (0.069)	...	...	0.083 (0.027)	...	...
Log(1 – T100)	...	0.657 (0.130)	...	...	0.245 (0.115)	...
Log(1 – T40)	...	...	0.717 (0.104)	...	...	0.335 (0.171)
Log(1 – top income tax rate) (ten-year lag)	−0.263 (0.034)	−0.155 (0.035)	−0.132 (0.031)	−0.045 (0.019)	−0.046 (0.020)	−0.060 (0.022)
Log(1 – top corporate tax rate) (ten-year lag)	1.375 (0.385)	0.717 (0.268)	0.921 (0.195)	0.452 (0.163)	0.709 (0.133)	0.906 (0.140)
Log real S&P 500	0.234 (0.054)	0.227 (0.043)	0.307 (0.038)	0.443 (0.024)	0.414 (0.032)	0.418 (0.032)
Log inequality (ten-year lag)	0.512 (0.400)	0.252 (0.193)	0.182 (0.167)	−0.100 (0.152)	−0.408 (0.114)	−0.372 (0.119)
Log real aggregate wealth per capita	...	...	...	−0.805 (0.113)	−0.720 (0.115)	−0.616 (0.125)
Log death rate	...	...	...	−0.735 (0.118)	−0.715 (0.128)	−0.701 (0.132)
Time trend	...	...	...	−0.005 (0.002)	−0.003 (0.003)	−0.002 (0.003)
Constant	−2.913 (1.267)	−2.020 (0.648)	−1.990 (0.564)	7.038 (0.996)	7.326 (1.044)	6.307 (1.198)
$\bar{R}^2$	0.88	0.92	0.94	0.98	0.98	0.98
N	49	49	49	49	49	49
Modified DW[b]	0.72	0.96	1.04	2.18	2.07	1.93

Source: This and all subsequent tables report authors' calculations. See text.

a. The dependent variable is the logarithm of *estratio*, as defined in the text. Standard errors are in parentheses.

b. The Durbin-Watson statistic is calculated using only adjacent observations, that is, using 44 out of 49 observations.

The coefficients of the (net of) estate tax rate variables are in all cases positive and are in all but one case significant at the 1 percent level, suggesting that an increase in taxes is indeed associated with reduced reported estates relative to aggregate wealth. As expected, the stock market variable has a positive association with the estate variable, with an estimated coefficient between 0.23 and 0.31. The coefficient on lagged income inequality is also positive but not significantly different than zero.

Both the lagged individual and corporate income tax rates are significantly related to *estratio* but not necessarily in an expected way. Higher income tax rates are linked with an increase of the ratio of reported estates to aggregate wealth, while higher corporation income tax rates are associated with a decrease. The former result is not consistent with the idea that high income tax rates depress both labor and saving, causing lower wealth accumulation. The pair of results is, though, consistent with the idea, explored in Roger H. Gordon and Slemrod, that high individual income tax rates cause income to be retained by corporations rather than being paid out to business principals.[38] If, perhaps because of liquidity constraints, the shifting toward the corporate tax base reduces the propensity to consume, this could produce the pattern of associations with tax rates displayed in table 7-1.

Given that the key series appear to be trending, it is not surprising that the fit of these regressions is very good. The reported Durbin-Watson statistics are, however, low, reflecting significant positive autocorrelation. The presence of missing data makes it impossible to address the problem of autocorrelation using standard approaches, as it would require deleting all of the isolated observations. However, the observed autocorrelation may simply be caused by misspecification of the model, and when we control below for other relevant factors the problem is mitigated.

Our measure of the magnitude of the top estates is normalized by the aggregate wealth and the death rate. Implicitly, this procedure amounts to restricting the coefficients on wealth and the death rate in a regression explaining total estates to be equal to one. However, either of these variables may have an independent effect on the largest estates. For example, it may be that the inequality of wealth is systematically related to the level of development. Furthermore, during the twentieth century, there were significant trends in the mortality rate and the expected length of life.[39] These factors may affect the size distribution of estates by affecting the age structure of decedents and their lifetime behavior. The death rate may be used as a proxy for these considerations.

The next three columns of table 7-1 augment the original specification by adding as explanatory variables the level of aggregate wealth, the death rate, and a time trend. The coefficients on the tax rate variables remain significant in two out of three cases, although they are somewhat smaller. The coefficient on the S&P 500 index increases, while the coefficient on lagged income inequality becomes negative and significant in two out of three cases. We find

38. Gordon and Slemrod (2000).
39. Bureau of the Census (1975, series B181).

a negative time trend. Both aggregate wealth and the death rate enter significantly and negatively. The coefficients on the aggregate wealth are between −0.62 and −0.81, suggesting that a 1 percent increase in aggregate wealth is associated with only a 0.18 percent to 0.39 percent increase in the wealth of the rich. However, the relative wealth of the rich is also affected by changes in the stock market, which are undoubtedly causally related to aggregate wealth. This introduces a qualification to the interpretation of the estimated coefficient on wealth.[40]

The estimated coefficients on the measures of the net-of-tax rate are between 0.083 and 0.335. In the logarithmic specification, these coefficients can be interpreted as elasticities. However, one has to be careful in interpreting these coefficients as elasticities with respect to *the* tax rate, because one cannot adequately characterize the whole tax system by means of a single rate, and even if it were possible it is not clear how exactly our measures are related to it. Still, these estimates are suggestive in assigning to the estate tax a moderate but statistically significant role in the determination of aggregate reported estates of wealthy Americans.[41]

Caveats to Interpreting the Aggregate Analysis

Although the aggregate results are consistent with the notion that the estate tax causes lower reported estates, several caveats are in order. First of all, the rates themselves may respond to aspects of economic performance. Certainly the largest increase in rates occurred at the beginning of the Great Depression. Perhaps in a period of widespread destitution a highly progressive tax on wealth is more defensible. Notably, the drop in the estate/wealth ratio occurred before the estate tax increase began.

Our summary measures of the marginal estate tax rate also do not account for many relevant features of the estate and gift system. For example, the treatment of gifts changed dramatically over the period, leading to the present "unified" treatment of estates and gifts beginning in 1981. The treatment of state-level inheritance, estate, and gift taxes also changed dramatically, such that at first they were incremental taxes and by the end of the

---

40. Because wealth is in the denominator of the dependent variable, errors in measuring it will introduce a negative bias to the estimated coefficients.

41. We also investigated a number of other modifications of this specification, such as including lagged values of the S&P 500 index, adding dummies for years when the unlimited marital deduction was in effect, and for the World War II period. The qualitative results are robust to these changes. We also investigated adding a lagged value of the tax variable. Usually the estimated coefficient was insignificant, and the coefficient on the contemporaneous value was not qualitatively affected.

period they were largely creditable and therefore not incremental. These and certain other aspects of the U.S. tax system are not captured in this analysis. Undoubtedly, this imprecision adds measurement error to the tax variables that will tend to bias the estimated tax coefficients toward zero. Moreover, if the mismeasurement is systematically related to the included independent variables, it could lead to bias of any direction in the estimated coefficients. We leave refinement of these summary tax measures to future research.

A more technical issue concerns what has been labeled "rank reversals." This term refers to the possibility that in periods when taxes are high, the high estate group we are focusing on is no longer composed of the wealthiest individuals, but rather the relatively poor avoiders, or those who are unwilling to cut back on wealth accumulation. This phenomenon implies that the composition of this group changes systematically with tax changes. Note, though, that the direction of the bias is to find less response of reported estates to tax changes, because we would underestimate the true decrease in estates owing to an increase in taxes.

Because the decision to accumulate or spend wealth is usually made in the context of a family, conceivably people with differing marital status may react differently to the tax rates. For example, a couple may react differently to features of the estate tax that affect marital bequests (on the estate of the first spouse dying) than to taxes on estates of the second spouse. Such issues cannot be adequately analyzed with aggregate data, if the cross-sectional composition of families has changed over the sample period. Furthermore, as mentioned above, a varying amount of spousal bequests, changing in part because of the variation in the relevant tax incentives, may influence the extent to which wealth accumulation appears twice in the estate tax return data.

Finally, any analysis of annual aggregate data relies on a few tax changes and observations, so that definitive conclusions cannot be drawn. We stress that the results are consistent with a behavioral response to estate tax rates but do not decisively establish such a relationship.

Analysis of Pooled Estate Tax Return Data

Examining data from estate tax returns that are aggregated by years may obscure the relationship between the tax system on the one hand, and wealth accumulation and tax avoidance behavior on the other. To take a simple example, in a year when the tax law changed it does not allow us to differentiate the estates reported in the two different tax regimes.[42] More important, aggregate analysis precludes examining whether the impact of the tax system is moderated by individual-specific attributes, such as age at death or the presence of a surviving spouse.

In this section we examine the data from individual estate tax returns, with the goal of identifying the tax and nontax determinants of taxable estates. At first blush, one might expect that the greatest advantage of analyzing individual tax return data lies in the ability to calculate tax rates on a return-by-return basis, rather than having to use summary statistics that characterize the tax system in place but that do not vary by individual. However, the econometric analysis of taxation using microlevel estate tax return data is plagued by the ubiquitous problem that, in a graduated tax system like that of the United States, the marginal tax rate is a function (only) of the taxable estate. This raises the danger of detecting a positive correlation between the level of the estate and the marginal tax rate that is unrelated to any causal relationship between tax rates and behavior. This may obscure a causal negative relationship between the tax rate and reported estates. We return to this issue below.

As our foundation, we appeal to the model discussed under "A Model with Uncertain Lifetime," in which the only uncertainty is about longevity, and annuities are not available. In this case, wealth at death is a function of the present value of the endowment (including the ability to earn net-of-tax income and any inheritance received), the after-tax rate of return to saving, age at death, the individual's tastes regarding labor versus leisure, regarding bequests versus own consumption and present versus future consumption (the discount rate), and the estate tax structure. In what follows we first outline our empirical strategy for examining the impact of estate taxation on wealth accumulation and avoidance and then discuss the observable proxies for the marginal tax rate and other factors that influence the estate.

Our data come from estate tax returns collected by the IRS from 1916 until 1996. The data set, which was also the source of the aggregate analysis discussed earlier, is described in detail in the appendix. It contains information on almost 770,000 decedents. The filing threshold and, consequently, the coverage of the estate tax varied over the years, so that the composition of population subject to the tax in different years changed. Given that time series variation is an important source of identification, the varying coverage could

---

42. In the aggregate analysis we account for this problem by taking as a measure of the tax rate in a given year a weighted average of the relevant tax rates (with weights proportional to the time they were in effect).

lead to spurious conclusions. For that reason, we construct a more homogenous sample by analyzing, as in the aggregate analysis, the estates of the richest 0.5 percent of U.S. decedents in each year. This procedure ensures that every observation for every year of death represented in the data corresponds to an estate well above the filing threshold. This limits the sample to slightly more than 310,000 decedents.

Calculating the Individual-Specific Marginal Tax Rate

The key explanatory variable is the marginal estate tax rate applicable to an individual. It is a component of the "price" of leaving a bequest relative to lifetime consumption and relative to leisure, as well as being the reward to reducing through avoidance the taxable estate by one dollar. The marginal tax rate is not present explicitly on the tax return. We construct it by applying the actual tax schedule in effect at the time of death of the individual to a measure of the taxable estate. Details of this procedure may be found in the appendix.

We also investigate two measures of the marginal tax rate that might be expected during the lifetime of an individual: the tax rate at age 45 (RATE45) and the tax rate ten years before death (RATE10).[43] Both are evaluated at the actual taxable estate at death, denominated in dollars of the relevant year, but based on the tax rate schedule in effect in these earlier years. Investigating these tax rate measures may prove helpful in two other ways. First, if one believes that avoidance measures, as distinct from labor supply or consumption decisions, are decided late in life, then the response to the tax rates expected earlier in life may separately identify the wealth accumulation behavioral response. Second, these variables are much less susceptible to the possibility that they are, through a political reaction, endogenous to the economic situation.

The Marginal Tax Rate for Married Couples

In defining the marginal tax rate that affected wealth accumulation and avoidance decisions, an important issue is the treatment of spousal bequests. To see the issues involved, recall that the 1981 Economic Recovery Tax Act provided for an unlimited deduction for bequests to surviving spouses. Under previous law (going back to 1948) the deduction for spousal bequests was limited to one-half of the adjusted gross estate. (From 1977 to 1981 the deduction was the greater of $250,000 and one-half of the adjusted gross

---

43. For individuals who died before reaching age 45, we assume that RATE45 is equal to RATE.

estate).[44] Under these two regimes, what is the appropriate marginal tax rate on a given taxable estate for a decedent with a surviving spouse?

One possible approach to this question is to calculate the marginal tax rate for a constant spousal bequest. Comparing two returns with the same gross estate, this procedure assigns a marginal tax rate of zero to a return with a sufficiently large spousal bequest deduction, and assigns a positive tax rate to the one with no spousal bequest deduction. In the context of estimating the impact of the estate tax on charitable bequests, Joulfaian argues that the unlimited marital deduction helps to alleviate the problem of separating the wealth effect and the marginal tax rate effect; because estates vary greatly in the amount of spousal deduction, Joulfaian argues that this provides a source of variation in the effective tax rate for a given level of wealth.[45] But this procedure provides identification only under the assumption that the behavior under study, in this case charitable contributions, does not independently depend on whether there is a surviving spouse.

For estimating the tax disincentive effect on wealth accumulation, calculating the marginal tax rate ignoring the eventual taxation of the surviving spouse's estate is almost certainly inappropriate. In a model where the couple cares only about the total net-of-tax bequest, even if there is no tax levied upon the first decedent because all the estate is left to the surviving spouse, the effective tax rate is that of the last dying spouse. Because we cannot link estate tax returns from the same family, we are unable to measure that precisely. However, the size of the spousal bequest reveals some information about this matter, because this bequest becomes the inheritance of the surviving spouse, whose eventual estate equals that inheritance, plus any assets held separately at the time of the first spouse's death, plus subsequent earnings, minus consumption.

Furthermore, the household that cares only about the total net-of-tax bequest should equate the expected marginal tax rate levied on the two estates and will not do so only to the extent there are costs associated with it, such as, for example, liquidity constraints that may be faced by small business owners. If such nontax costs apply to the first spouse only, the relevant marginal cost of taxation is approximated by the rate faced by the second spouse, which is equal to the marginal tax rate of the first spouse plus the unobservable marginal cost.

This discussion suggests that the relevant marginal tax rate that would be expected to affect wealth accumulation decisions is not necessarily well

44. Luckey (1995, pp. 12, 14, 18).
45. Joulfaian (1998a).

measured by the observed marginal tax rate of one member of a married couple. Furthermore, the appropriate marginal tax rate depends on a number of unverifiable aspects of family decisionmaking. Faced with this indeterminacy, we investigate two different measures of the appropriate marginal tax rate. The basic one (denoted RATE) is simply the marginal tax rate that applies to the decedent's taxable estate at death assuming a fixed spousal bequest. Note that after 1981 this procedure assigns a tax rate of zero to a large estate that was entirely left to the surviving spouse. The other tax rate measure, RATEMAX, addresses the issues discussed concerning the treatment of married couples. It is the maximum of RATE and RATESP, where RATESP is equal for married decedents to the marginal tax rate calculated using the bequest to the spouse as the tax base, and is equal to RATE for unmarried individuals. This procedure attempts to implement the idea that the tax distortion faced by the household may be better measured by the tax paid by the second spouse.

Instrumenting for the Marginal Tax Rate

As already discussed, a critical methodological challenge is to identify an individual-specific marginal tax rate that is not a function of the estate itself. When studying behavior that is a component of or a deduction from the tax base, such as charitable contributions, this problem has been dealt with by assuming that the other components of the tax base are exogenous,[46] and using the marginal tax rate at zero (or, an average for similar returns) amount of contributions. This "first-dollar" marginal tax rate does not depend on the magnitude of the studied behavior and is thus exogenous. Because it is not the actual applicable "last-dollar" marginal tax rate, a common empirical strategy is to use the first-dollar marginal tax rate as an instrumental variable for the appropriate last-dollar marginal tax rate.

This approach is much more problematic when the behavior under study is a principal component or, as in this case, is *identical* to, the tax base. Thus, the literature on the elasticity of taxable income has focused on longitudinal data that bracket changes in the tax schedule.[47] In this way, comparing data over time allows one to look at the behavior at given levels of income but at different marginal tax rates.

Alas, the nature of the estate tax is such that one will never observe the same person paying estate tax under two (or more!) estate tax regimes. In

---

46. Although see, in the context of capital gains realizations, Burman and Randolph (1992).
47. Slemrod (1998).

cross-sectional or pooled cross-sectional data, simply regressing the estate value against the marginal estate tax rate will surely produce a bias toward finding a spurious positive relationship, owing to the graduated nature of the tax. Consequently, we seek instruments that are correlated with the tax rate but do not affect independently the estates of taxpayers. In what follows we will use the three tax system measures discussed earlier—TTOP, T100, and T40—as instruments for the actual marginal tax rate. These instruments vary only across years and not across individuals in a given year. Thus, using only these instruments would not make use of any cross-sectional variation in identifying the effect of marginal tax rates. This would still be an improvement over the aggregate analysis, however, because we can control for the potentially changing cross-sectional composition of the decedent population and for potential differential response to taxes.

We can, though, improve upon this approach. To make use of the cross-sectional variation, we note that decisions affecting the estate at death are made over the whole lifetime. Consequently, the marginal tax rate should be correlated with characteristics of the tax system in the years preceding death. This adds to our arsenal of potential instruments lagged values of the three measures of the tax (we use ten years' lagged values of these variables). More interestingly, it also allows us to construct a set of instruments that vary within a year: the three measures of the tax system in effect when the decedent was 45. The tax rate at age 45 is chosen to represent the tax rate when individuals begin to consider the ramifications of the estate tax. These instruments vary with age and the year of death of an individual, allowing for a richer source of identification. Furthermore, we include instruments accounting for changes in the taxation of spousal bequests: dummies for married and widowed individuals dying when a limited marital deduction was allowed (1948–81) and dummies for married and widowed individuals dying when an unlimited marital deduction was allowed (post-1981).

Nontax Independent Variables

The estate tax return data contain a number of other variables that might reasonably be expected to affect the estate.[48] By statistically controlling for these variables, we can presumably sharpen the estimate of the partial effect of taxation on the reported estate. Potentially more important, several variables would be expected to moderate the effect of taxation. For example, our theoretical model suggests that the effect of taxes on the estate would depend

---

48. Although, as discussed, we have no good indicator of the individual's lifetime income.

on age at death. Furthermore, the wealth accumulation of married individuals may differ from the patterns of wealth accumulation among single individuals for reasons unrelated to the tax rates. For example, the effect of uncertainty for a couple will usually be different than the sum of effects for two separate individuals.[49] Finally, reported estates may behave in a systematically different way in community property states, in which most family wealth is determined to be jointly owned by both spouses; we include a dummy variable for residence in a community property state.[50]

By including in the regression interaction terms between the tax rates and these other moderating variables, we can enrich our analysis in an important dimension. This is because now in high-tax periods we would expect not only an effect on the level of reported estates, but also an effect on the *relative* reported estates of decedents with different characteristics. For example, we would expect that in high-tax periods, the reported estates of young decedents would be relatively higher, because the estate tax had not had a chance to affect many years of wealth accumulation decisions.

To analyze differential effects by demographic groups, we interact the marginal tax rate with a dummy for being married, sex, age, and testate status. Of course, each of these variables interacted with the tax rate is endogenous to the size of the estate, for the same reasons discussed earlier.

Results of Micro Regression Analyses

We begin by estimating specifications that are similar to the aggregate ones whose results are reported in table 7-1. Table 7-2 contains the results of a regression of the logarithm of real net worth reported on the estate tax return on the log of the net-of-tax rate (denoted RATE), controlling only for the (economy-wide) variables used in the aggregate analysis. The first column presents the results when the three aggregate tax measures are used as instruments. The coefficient on the net-of-tax rate is equal to −0.05 and is not significantly different from zero.[51]

The next three columns of table 7-2 contain the results of using as the sole instrument one of the three summary measures of the tax rate struc-

---

49. Hurd (1994).

50. Eight states were community property states for the whole period considered: Arizona, California, Idaho, Louisiana, Nevada, New Mexico, Texas, and Washington. In 1986 the Uniform Marital Property Act, which approximates community property statutes, was introduced in Wisconsin.

51. We report standard IV errors. Potentially, they may be understated if there is significant within-year correlation in the error terms. This problem is somewhat alleviated because of the inclusion of the time trend and other time-dependent aggregate variables.

Table 7-2. *Pooled Cross-Section Regression Results with Alternative Instrument Sets: The Effect of the Estate Tax on Reported Net Worth*[a]

Independent variable	Instruments			
	All	TTAX	T100	T40
Log(1 – RATE)	−0.051	0.027	1.024	−0.277
	(0.038)	(0.042)	(0.114)	(0.050)
Log(1 – top income tax rate) (ten-year lag)	−0.071	−0.074	−0.111	−0.063
	(0.005)	(0.005)	(0.006)	(0.005)
Log(1 – top corporate tax rate) (ten-year lag)	0.456	0.440	0.236	0.502
	(0.028)	(0.028)	(0.038)	(0.028)
Log real S&P 500	0.341	0.337	0.282	0.354
	(0.006)	(0.006)	(0.009)	(0.006)
Log inequality (ten-year lag)	−0.304	−0.269	0.178	−0.405
	(0.030)	(0.031)	(0.058)	(0.033)
Log real aggregate wealth per capita	0.284	0.283	0.269	0.287
	(0.025)	(0.025)	(0.028)	(0.024)
Log death rate	−0.926	−0.906	−0.642	−0.986
	(0.027)	(0.028)	(0.041)	(0.028)
Time trend	−0.005	−0.004	0.007	−0.008
	(0.001)	(0.001)	(0.001)	(0.001)
Constant	12.398	12.250	10.339	12.831
	(0.238)	(0.242)	(0.334)	(0.242)
$\bar{R}^2$	0.1952	0.1931	0.1631	0.2007
N	309,136	309,136	309,136	309,136

a. The dependent variable is the logarithm of net worth in 1945 dollars. Standard errors are in parentheses. The set of instruments includes the top tax rate, the tax rates at 100 times average wealth, and at 40 times average wealth (all expressed as the logarithms of one minus the rate).

ture. This specification improves upon the aggregate analysis only by making use of the actual individual tax rates, which allows for an easier interpretation of the estimated coefficient. The estimated elasticities for two of the three instruments are positive, although quite different from the coefficients in the aggregate analysis. However, when T40 (the tax at forty times the average wealth) is used, the estimated elasticity is negative and significant. One possibility for this anomalous result is that, although asymptotically any instrument will do, the finite sample performance of different instruments may vary. In fact, although the sample contains more than 300,000 individuals, all of the instruments and the right-hand side variables are constant within a year, so that this procedure is equivalent to regressing the average logarithm of net worth within the year on the yearly average of the net-of-tax rate and the other explanatory variables.

Viewed in this way, there are only as many degrees of freedom as there are years in the sample (forty-nine, to be precise), and so finite sample bias may be significant.

A more intriguing explanation has to do with the composition of the sample. By construction, T40 should be most closely related to the marginal tax rates at relatively small estates, while the other two measures should be more correlated with the marginal tax rates at higher estates. If there are systematic differences in how high-wealth and very high-wealth individuals respond to the estate tax, different instruments may pick up the response of different groups (for example, if the marital status or gender composition of the two groups differs, and the response to the tax varies systematically with these demographic characteristics). Consequently, this result may simply reflect the heterogeneity of response within the sample.

Introducing Individual-Specific Nontax Controls

Next we introduce into the microregressions certain known characteristics of the decedents: marital status, sex, testate status, age and age squared, and dummy variables for residing in a community property state when married or widowed.[52] We also include the set of variables from table 7-2 and the values of the S&P 500 index lagged by five years, ten years, and at the time the decedent was 45.[53] This last variable is of particular interest, because it may help to control for any cohort effect and to disentangle cohort and age effects. A similar approach is taken in Arie Kapteyn, Rob Alessie, and Annamaria Lusardi in their study of the effect of Social Security programs on saving. They consider different indicators of economic conditions during the economic life of an individual: GNP per capita when the household entered the labor market (proxying for productivity changes), as well as changes in the Social Security system. Although these factors may be relevant for the general public, they are probably of less importance for the very rich group that we are studying. For this segment of population, the performance of financial markets is probably more relevant. In addition, the level of the stock market index helps to control for the endowment of different cohorts. It is also un-

---

52. Because most demographic information is unavailable before 1925, these results (and those of the later tables) are based on returns of decedents in 1925 and thereafter.

53. Although not reported in the tables, we also controlled separately for a dummy indicating the imputation of age (equal zero if not imputed), imputed age squared, and the S&P 500 at age of 45 multiplied by the age imputation dummy. The results are robust to limiting the sample to just individuals for whom the age at death is known.

doubtedly affected by productivity shocks, so that this aspect is not completely absent from our analysis.[54]

Table 7-3 shows the results of the regression specifications in which the only measure of the tax burden is the marginal tax rate at the time of death. For comparison with aggregate regressions, the first column presents the results when only the three tax measures are used as the instruments. The next two specifications extend the set of instruments, first by adding the lagged and age 45 tax measures, and then by additionally including the marital deduction dummies. The estimated elasticity with respect to the net-of-tax rate is between −0.11 and 0.09. It is negative and significant when smaller sets of instruments are used and becomes positive when the full set of instruments is used. We conclude that the estimated relationship between the reported estate and the marginal estate tax rate is quite fragile to the set of instruments used.

The estimated values on the other coefficients are of separate interest. The estimated coefficients on age and age squared correspond to an increasing wealth profile with people who are 70 years old having approximately 4.7 percent higher net worth than those who are 50. This pattern is consistent with some other empirical evidence.[55] Most of the other variables enter significantly as well. Estimated values of the marital status coefficients suggest that being divorced is associated with a relatively higher level of net worth on the estate, while being single is on average accompanied by lower net worth, when compared with other types of marital status.[56] Being a male is associated with slightly higher reported net worth. Testate status has the strongest effect in explaining net worth of all the dummy variables. People who die with a will have a net worth that is on average 27 percent higher than that of those who die intestate. This is consistent with the idea that the presence of a will is a good indicator of having a bequest motive. It is also plausible that having a will is more attractive when the estate tax is higher and so is an endogenous variable.

The S&P 500 index at the age of 45 enters significantly and with the expected positive sign. The estimated elasticity is, however, rather small. The elasticity with respect to the current level of the S&P 500 index is estimated to be about 0.25, not too far from the effect estimated earlier. Surprisingly, lagged values of the S&P 500 index enter negatively. It is possible that this reflects tax avoidance. The higher net worth is, the more important estate

---

54. See Kapteyn, Alessie, and Lusardi (1999). We do not include the level of GNP in our analysis, because there is no consistent annual series going back to the 19th century, when the economic life of many individuals in our sample began.

55. For example, Hurd (1987).

56. The dummy for being single is the omitted marital status category.

Table 7-3. *Pooled Cross-Section Regression Results with Decedent Characteristics and Alternative Sets of Instruments*[a]

Independent variable	I	II	III
Log(1 – RATE)	–0.084	–0.110	0.094
	(0.051)	(0.040)	(0.024)
Log(1 – top income tax rate)	–0.047	–0.045	–0.062
(ten-year lag)	(0.007)	(0.007)	(0.006)
Log(1 – top corporate tax rate)	0.199	0.197	0.212
(ten-year lag)	(0.039)	(0.039)	(0.039)
Log(1 – top income tax rate)	0.002	0.004	–0.008
(at age 45)	(0.005)	(0.005)	(0.004)
Log(1 – top corporate tax rate)	0.045	0.042	0.065
(at age 45)	(0.020)	(0.019)	(0.019)
Age	–0.001	–0.001	–0.001
	(0.001)	(0.001)	(0.001)
Age^2	0.00002	0.00002	0.00003
	(0.000007)	(0.000007)	(0.000007)
Divorced	0.084	0.081	0.106
	(0.012)	(0.011)	(0.011)
Married	0.050	0.051	0.043
	(0.006)	(0.006)	(0.006)
Separated	0.034	0.033	0.042
	(0.042)	(0.042)	(0.043)
Widow	0.008	0.006	0.017
	(0.006)	(0.006)	(0.006)
Male	0.020	0.020	0.020
	(0.003)	(0.003)	(0.003)
Testate	0.242	0.241	0.245
	(0.006)	(0.006)	(0.006)
Married, community	–0.026	–0.026	–0.029
property state	(0.005)	(0.005)	(0.005)
Widow, community property state	–0.029	–0.030	–0.025
	(0.006)	(0.006)	(0.006)
Log real S&P 500	0.258	0.259	0.248
	(0.009)	(0.009)	(0.009)
Log real S&P 500 (five-year lag)	–0.033	–0.033	–0.028
	(0.006)	(0.006)	(0.006)
Log real S&P 500 (ten-year lag)	–0.036	–0.037	–0.029
	(0.006)	(0.006)	(0.006)
Log real S&P 500 (at age 45)	0.014	0.014	0.015
	(0.005)	(0.005)	(0.005)
Log inequality (ten-year lag)	–0.219	–0.229	–0.148
	(0.035)	(0.033)	(0.031)

(continued)

Table 7-3. (*continued*)

Independent variable	I	II	III
Log real aggregate wealth per capita	0.531	0.538	0.485
	(0.036)	(0.035)	(0.034)
Log death rate	0.001	−0.021	0.147
	(0.089)	(0.085)	(0.082)
Time trend	−0.005	−0.006	−0.002
	(0.001)	(0.001)	(0.001)
Constant	7.889	7.926	7.638
	(0.347)	(0.343)	(0.347)
$\bar{R}^2$	0.1637	0.1644	0.1592
N	242,897	242,897	242,897

a. The dependent variable is the logarithm of net worth in 1945 dollars. In the regressions, we also controlled for age imputation dummy, imputed age, imputed age squared, and S&P 500 at age 45 interacted with the age imputation dummy. The three tax measures described in table 2 are used as instruments in specification I. The ten-year lagged values and the values at age 45 are added in specification II. In specification III, dummies for married and widowed individuals dying in years when the limited marital deduction was available (1948–81) and when the unlimited marital deduction was available (post-1981) are also included. Standard errors are in parentheses.

tax planning becomes, because higher estate tax rates may potentially apply to it. Shocks to net worth (for example, because of a booming stock market) may then induce an avoidance response and result in lower observed net worth a few years later.

The logarithm of the death rate is not significantly related to net worth reported on estate tax returns. Aggregate wealth may control for the unobservable endowment, in which case the positive coefficient is not surprising. The estimated negative effect of lagged income inequality is unexpected, although it is consistent with some of the aggregate results. The estimated effects of the lagged income tax rate variables are consistent with the aggregate results.

Allowing for Heterogeneity in the Response to Taxation

Table 7-4 presents the results of specifications that allow for differential response to the estate tax for different groups of taxpayers. The first specification reveals no differential response by sex. The next three specifications, which test for differential response by marital status, testate status, and age, are all of interest.

As mentioned earlier, the response of married couples may differ from the response of single individuals. This can occur because the expected longevity of a family (understood as the survival of one of the spouses) is higher than that

Table 7-4. *Pooled Cross-Section Regression Results:*
Interactions with the Tax Rate[a]

Independent variable	I	II	III	IV
Log(1 – RATE)	0.072	0.033	–0.048	–0.053
	(0.024)	(0.024)	(0.058)	(0.036)
Male*log(1 – RATE)	0.012			
	(0.015)	...	...	...
Married*log(1 – RATE)		–0.0788		
	...	(0.0193)	...	...
Age*log(1 – RATE)			0.0017	
	...	...	(0.0007)	...
Testate*log(1 – RATE)				0.162
	...	...	...	(0.031)
Log(1 – top income tax rate) (ten-year lag)	–0.061	–0.052	–0.059	–0.061
	(0.006)	(0.006)	(0.006)	(0.006)
Log(1 – top corporate tax rate) (ten-year lag)	0.211	0.210	0.217	0.211
	(0.039)	(0.039)	(0.039)	(0.039)
Log(1 – top income tax rate) (at age 45)	0.062	–0.005	–0.010	–0.008
	(0.019)	(0.004)	(0.005)	(0.004)
Log(1 – top corporate tax rate) (at age 45)	–0.007	0.066	0.076	0.064
	(0.004)	(0.019)	(0.020)	(0.019)
Age	–0.001	–0.001	–0.001	–0.001
	(0.001)	(0.001)	(0.001)	(0.001)
Age^2	0.00003	0.00003	0.00003	0.00003
	(0.000007)	(0.000007)	(0.000007)	(0.000007)
Divorced	0.104	0.104	0.103	0.108
	(0.011)	(0.011)	(0.011)	(0.011)
Married	0.043	0.024	0.045	0.044
	(0.006)	(0.007)	(0.006)	(0.006)
Separated	0.041	0.040	0.042	0.043
	(0.043)	(0.043)	(0.043)	(0.043)
Widow	0.016	0.016	0.017	0.019
	(0.006)	(0.006)	(0.006)	(0.006)
Male	0.024	0.020	0.019	0.019
	(0.006)	(0.003)	(0.003)	(0.003)
Testate	0.245	0.243	0.245	0.278
	(0.006)	(0.006)	(0.006)	(0.009)
Married, community property state	–0.029	–0.030	–0.029	–0.029
	(0.005)	(0.005)	(0.005)	(0.005)
Widow, community property state	–0.026	–0.025	–0.025	–0.025
	(0.006)	(0.006)	(0.006)	(0.006)
Log real S&P 500	0.249	0.254	0.251	0.247
	(0.009)	(0.009)	(0.009)	(0.009)

(continued)

Table 7-4. (*continued*)

Independent variable	I	II	III	IV
Log real S&P 500 (five-year lag)	−0.029 (0.006)	−0.032 (0.006)	−0.029 (0.006)	−0.028 (0.006)
Log real S&P 500 (ten-year lag)	−0.030 (0.006)	−0.035 (0.006)	−0.031 (0.006)	−0.029 (0.006)
Log real S&P 500 (at age 45)	0.015 (0.005)	0.014 (0.005)	0.014 (0.005)	0.015 (0.005)
Log inequality (ten-year lag)	−0.152 (0.031)	−0.195 (0.032)	−0.163 (0.031)	−0.153 (0.031)
Log real aggregate wealth per capita	0.488 (0.034)	0.518 (0.035)	0.496 (0.034)	0.490 (0.034)
Log death rate	0.136 (0.082)	0.060 (0.083)	0.125 (0.082)	0.148 (0.082)
Time trend	−0.002 (0.001)	−0.004 (0.001)	−0.002 (0.001)	−0.002 (0.001)
Constant	7.658 (0.346)	7.792 (0.344)	7.638 (0.346)	7.584 (0.347)
$\bar{R}^2$	0.1596	0.1619	0.1597	0.1591
N	242,897	242,897	242,897	242,897

a. The dependent variable is the logarithm of net worth in 1945 dollars. In the regressions, we also controlled for age imputation dummy, imputed age, imputed age squared, and S&P 500 at age 45 interacted with the age imputation dummy. The set of instruments includes all the ones listed in the notes to table 7-3 and, additionally, all these instruments interacted with the variable analyzed in a given specification. Standard errors are in parentheses.

of an individual. Consequently, the probability of a family paying the tax in any given period is smaller, and therefore the shape of its consumption profile is less affected. A family may also respond to the tax by modifying the timing of its taxable estates. Higher tax rates are usually associated with more progressive rate structures and thus introduce a stronger motive to equate the expected marginal tax rate (and therefore the estate) of both spouses. The second specification in table 7-4, which allows for a differential response by marital status, suggests that the married individuals (that is, those with a surviving spouse) respond to a lower net-of-tax rate by increasing their net worth (with an elasticity of −0.078), while the effect for single individuals is insignificant. This may be explained by the hypothesis of equalization of the marginal tax rates if, absent the tax, the report of the first spouse would be smaller than that of the second. Then, the tax rate of the first spouse, *other things being equal,* is negatively correlated with the tax rate of the second spouse. If so, the estimated negative coefficient for the married individuals may be consistent with reduction of the family's net worth in response to taxes.

Theory indicates clearly that the response of the estate to the tax rate is greater the larger the time one has to adjust to the tax rate. This may be crudely captured by interacting the marginal tax rate with age. Such a regression is presented in the third specification of table 7-4. As expected, the tax effect is increasing with age.

Finally, in the last column of table 7-4 we report the results of interacting testate status with the net-of-tax rate. If, as is highly plausible, having a will indicates a bequest motive, one would expect that wealth accumulation would be more sensitive to taxation for those who die with a will. The results strongly confirm this expectation, although as noted earlier, this conclusion must be tempered by the possible endogeneity of testate status.

Alternative Measures of the Effective Tax Rate

The marginal estate tax rate variable we have analyzed up to this point is evaluated at the time of death. However, the bulk of the behavioral response to estate taxation undoubtedly takes place in the years preceding death, perhaps throughout the whole economic life of an individual. Thus, arguably it is the tax structure in place during the life of an individual that affects the expectations about the actual tax at death and shapes the response. We investigate two measures of the tax rate expected earlier in life: the tax rate ten years before death (RATE10) and at the age of 45 (RATE45). Both are calculated by applying the relevant tax structure to the actual taxable estate at death denominated in dollars of the corresponding year. Table 7-5 shows the results. Each of these net-of-tax variables has a positive and significant impact on the reported estate. Furthermore, in results not reported here, in a "horse race" between either of these variables and the basic rate, the alternative measure robs the basic tax rate of its significance and has a significant positive coefficient. These results are consistent with the idea that most of the behavioral response takes place over a long horizon and suggests that future research should focus on such measures of the tax incentives.

The last variable we investigated is RATEMAX, equal to the maximum of the own and an estimated spousal tax rate for married individuals and equal to the decedent's own marginal tax rate for unmarried individuals.[57] The estimated coefficient is significantly negative. This finding may simply reflect the impact on the timing of spousal bequests discussed earlier or may indicate that RATEMAX does not successfully measure the expected effective tax rate of a married couple. For example, holding other things constant, the spousal be-

---

57. Because of the unavailability of spousal bequests before 1945, this specification is estimated for the post-World War II years only.

Table 7-5. *Pooled Cross-Section Regression Results:
Alternative Measures of the Tax Rate*[a]

Independent variable	I	II	III
Log(1 – RATE45)	0.160 (0.038)	...	...
Log(1 – RATE10)	...	0.100 (0.029)	...
Log(1 – RATEMAX)	...	...	–0.571 (0.163)
Log(1 – top income tax rate) (ten-year lag)	–0.052 (0.006)	–0.055 (0.006)	0.032 (0.016)
Log(1 – top corporate tax rate) (ten-year lag)	0.227 (0.040)	0.202 (0.039)	–0.245 (0.240)
Log(1 – top income tax rate) (at age 45)	–0.004 (0.004)	–0.007 (0.004)	–0.004 (0.005)
Log(1 – top corporate tax rate) (at age 45)	0.009 (0.022)	0.060 (0.019)	0.039 (0.024)
Age	–0.001 (0.001)	–0.001 (0.001)	–0.003 (0.001)
Age^2	0.00002 (0.000007)	0.00003 (0.000007)	0.00004 (0.000010)
Divorced	0.107 (0.011)	0.105 (0.011)	0.075 (0.022)
Married	0.041 (0.006)	0.043 (0.006)	0.041 (0.018)
Separated	0.041 (0.043)	0.041 (0.043)	0.004 (0.078)
Widow	0.016 (0.006)	0.017 (0.006)	–0.007 (0.020)
Male	0.020 (0.003)	0.019 (0.003)	0.015 (0.005)
Testate	0.245 (0.006)	0.245 (0.006)	0.182 (0.013)
Married, community property state	–0.029 (0.005)	–0.029 (0.005)	–0.003 (0.006)
Widow, community property state	–0.026 (0.006)	–0.025 (0.006)	–0.004 (0.008)

(continued)

Table 7-5. (*continued*)

Independent variable	I	II	III
Log real S&P 500	0.256	0.257	0.151
	(0.008)	(0.009)	(0.024)
Log real S&P 500 (five-year lag)	−0.027	−0.029	0.019
	(0.006)	(0.006)	(0.013)
Log real S&P 500 (ten-year lag)	−0.035	−0.038	−0.085
	(0.006)	(0.006)	(0.012)
Log real S&P 500 (at age 45)	0.009	0.015	0.008
	(0.006)	(0.005)	(0.007)
Log inequality (ten-year lag)	−0.192	−0.207	−0.083
	(0.029)	(0.030)	(0.094)
Log real aggregate wealth per capita	0.542	0.517	0.947
	(0.035)	(0.034)	(0.074)
Log death rate	0.088	0.083	0.641
	(0.080)	(0.080)	(0.203)
Time trend	−0.004	−0.003	−0.018
	(0.001)	(0.001)	(0.003)
Constant	7.514	7.749	3.183
	(0.350)	(0.345)	(0.776)
$\bar{R}^2$	0.1593	0.1593	0.0395
N	242,897	242,897	95,611

a. The dependent variable is the logarithm of net worth in 1945 dollars. In the regressions, we also controlled for age imputation dummy, imputed age, imputed age squared, and S&P 500 at age 45 interacted with the age imputation dummy. The set of instruments includes all the ones listed in the notes to table 7-3. Standard errors are in parentheses.

quest will be higher the *lower* is the marginal tax rate faced by the spouse. Consequently, the estimated negative value may be spurious. Understanding the effect of the estate tax on spousal bequests, and how empirical investigation might account for this, should be high on the agenda for future research.

Conclusions

This chapter represents a first attempt to learn from an extraordinary archive for estate tax return data. In the end we have, as first attempts usually do, raised as many questions as we have provided answers. We found that over time summary measures of the estate tax rate structure are generally negatively related to the reported aggregate net worth of the top estates as a fraction of national wealth. This conclusion is preserved when we control for other relevant influences in a multiple regression framework. This finding is consistent with estate taxation reducing either wealth accumulation or inducing avoidance, or both. We view this evidence as suggestive rather than definitive, because of the difficulty of controlling for other factors and of ascribing causality to an observed association.

We then turned to an analysis of the individual tax return data. We make use of both the time-series variation in the tax rate structure and the cross-sectional variation in observable individual characteristics. In particular, cross-sectional differences in age provide a potentially important source of identification because they correspond to differences in the tax structure effective during one's lifetime.

In our baseline specification the estimated elasticity of reported estates is positive (that is, negative with respect to the tax rate itself) and statistically significant. The response is also clearly positive for those who die testate and are older, which suggests that a behavioral response is present for older people who have a bequest motive.

When we investigate measures of the tax rate that prevailed during one's lifetime rather than at death, the estimated negative behavioral response to estate taxes is more pronounced. In particular, the marginal tax rate at the age of 45 dominates all other measures, and the estimated elasticity with respect to (one minus) the tax rate is 0.16, and is statistically significant. Such a number is also economically significant, because it implies that an estate tax rate of 50 percent would reduce the reported net worth of the richest half percent of the population by 10.5 percent when its effect is fully realized many years later.[58]

Our results do not tell us whether the estate tax deserves a role in the U.S. tax system. They are, though, a first step toward pinning down the magnitude of behavioral response to the tax, which is a crucial input for determining the optimal level of estate taxes.[59] A part of the measured effect on reported estates is due to reduced wealth accumulation, and another part is due to estate planning techniques. Only the former has implications for capital accumulation, although both are indicative of economic cost. Note, though, that to those who believe that a highly unequal distribution of wealth has negative consequences aside from its implications for individual levels of well-being, that the estate tax reduces the wealth accumulation of the most

58. The change in the log of net worth is $0.16\ln(1-.5) \approx -0.111$, which corresponds to a reduction in net worth of $1- \exp(-0.111) \approx 10.5$ percent.

59. See Kopczuk (2001) for a theoretical analysis of this question.

well-off families is an indication of policy success rather than policy failure. However, as discussed by Louis Kaplow in this volume, that is a controversial notion.

Appendix

In this appendix we describe in detail our data sources and procedures for constructing the variables used in the regression analyses.

Aggregate Data

To construct the aggregate estate-wealth ratio, *estratio*, we first calculate the number of total decedents in a given year using the mortality rates and the population from the Bureau of the Census and from the *Economic Report of the President*.[60] Using this information, we sum the net worth of the number of estates that is equal to 0.5 percent of total decedents with the highest net worth. After 1945, we use the population weights to calculate the size of the population represented by a given sample of estates. Between 1962 and 1976, the sample is representative of returns filed in the next year, so that calculated net worth corresponds to this population. This procedure gives us the total reported estates of the top 0.5 percent of decedents, all of whom are subject to the estate taxation over this period.

The denominator of *estratio*, aggregate economywide net worth, is based on a few sources. Up to and including 1945, it is taken from Raymond W. Goldsmith, Dorothy S. Brady, and Horst Menderhausen, with minor corrections for some years as in the Bureau of the Census.[61] After 1945 the data on net worth are taken from the Federal Reserve balance sheets of the U.S. economy. Both series are calculated at current cost. The series overlap between 1945 and 1958. They are very close for most of this period, although there is a discrepancy of approximately 10 percent for 1945. In calculating average wealth, we use the total U.S. population.

The series for the Consumer Price Index and the Standard and Poor's 500 Index are from the Bureau of the Census and the *Economic Report of the President*.[62]

---

60. Bureau of the Census (1975); *Economic Report of the President* (after 1968).
61. Goldsmith, Brady, and Menderhausen (1956, table W-1); Bureau of the Census (1975, series F422). The latter source does not contain the data for all years.
62. Bureau of the Census (1975, series E135) and the *Economic Report of the President* (1999).

The series on income inequality are based on two sources. Up to 1945, we use the share of income going to the top 5 percent of the richest *individuals*, constructed by Simon Kuznets and reprinted in the Bureau of the Census.[63] After 1945 we use the share of income going to the top 5 percent of *families*, constructed by the Bureau of Census.[64] The values of the two series are very close in the overlapping year of 1945. We are not aware of any consistent series for income inequality for the whole period that we consider.

The information on the estate tax structure is obtained from the Internal Revenue Code.[65] The series for the top tax rate and tax rates at the standardized levels of wealth are constructed based on the actual tax structures.[66] For the years when more than one tax law was in effect, we use a weighted average of the relevant tax rates under different regimes, with weights proportional to the time a given tax structure was in place. The Tax Reform Act of 1924 was repealed in 1926, so that estates of individuals who died between 1924 and 1926 were retroactively subject to the rates set before 1924. For these years the relevant tax structure is unclear, because repeal of the law was probably expected for part of this period. Nevertheless, we use the marginal tax rates that were effective during this period. In calculating the lagged tax rates, tax rate series are set to zero before 1916, although there were episodes when there was an estate tax, for example, in the years 1898–1902, when the death tax introduced by the War Revenue Act of 1898 was in effect. However, we assume that these taxes were expected to last for a short time only, so that they did not have an effect on the lifetime decisions of people who were young at the time.

Micro Data

The basic data are drawn from the estate tax returns collected by the IRS. The database contains data from the Statistics of Income studies for 1916 to 1945, 1962, 1965, 1969, 1972, 1976, and for each year from 1982 to 1996.[67] The prewar data contain a nearly 100 percent sample of estate tax returns for peo-

---

63. Bureau of the Census (1975).

64. Bureau of the Census (1996).

65. Luckey (1995) and McCubbin (1990) discuss the history of changes in the taxation of estates.

66. The top tax rate is defined as the marginal tax rate for the largest estate, not the maximum marginal tax rate. Because of the phase-out of the initial deduction after 1987 the latter is 60 percent, while the former is 55 percent.

67. The pre-1945 data are described in McCubbin (1990), and the later data are described in various studies in Johnson (1994).

ple who died between 1916 and 1945.[68] The postwar data are stratified samples of estate tax returns. Between 1962 and 1976 they are representative of the estates filed in one year following the nominal date of the study, resulting in a majority of the returns being for decedents who died in the year of the study. Starting in 1982, they are stratified to be representative of the population of decedents in a given year. We use the sampling weights in our regression.

The estate tax return data contain almost all the items on the tax return, but the tax form changed over the years so that only a subset of variables is present for all observations. With some exceptions, this subset includes the year of death, debts and mortgages, gross estate, charitable bequests, sex, marital status, testate status, and the presence of trust and gifts.[69] The pre-1945 data contain information on the number of children and the number of beneficiaries. The pre-1945 data and data for 1976 contain the length of the terminal illness. The postwar data additionally contain information on the size of the taxable estate, bequests to a surviving spouse, and any deduction for such bequests.

We define net worth to be the total gross estate minus debts reported on the tax returns. Notably, the before 1945 data set does not contain information on the estate subject to taxation, a natural subject of investigation. Although there is information about the total tax liability owed to the federal government, there is no information about the deductions for taxes already paid, such as the state estate, inheritance, and gift taxes, that were used to arrive at this number, making it impossible to calculate the taxable estate by inverting the tax liability using the actual tax structure.[70] Instead, we construct a measure of taxable income based on other information. As our measure of taxable estate before 1918, we simply take net worth. In 1918 the deduction for charitable bequests was introduced. It applies to estates of

---

68. There is a possibility that some of the returns were missing at the time the data were coded. However, McCubbin (1990) compared the number of returns present in the sample to the numbers reported by the IRS in its official publications from this period, and concluded that the coverage is extremely good. In fact, in some years the data set contains more returns than the IRS reported.

69. When the marital status is missing in the regression analyses, we treat it as a separate category. Age is missing in 1965 and for some observations in other years.

70. For example, under the Revenue Act of 1926 estates were allowed a tax credit not to exceed 80 percent of the total federal estate tax for estate, inheritance, legacy, or succession taxes paid to any of the several states, territories, or the District of Columbia. Before 1924 this credit was limited to 25 percent of the total liability, and when the tax was introduced in 1916 no credit was allowed. Furthermore, no credit was allowed against so-called additional taxes introduced by the Revenue Act of 1932, which constituted most of the tax liability. After 1926, estates were allowed a tax credit for gift taxes paid. This was a significant item, for example, for the returns filed in 1934, as it constituted 11 percent of the total tax liability.

decedents who died after December 31, 1917, and thus we define taxable estate to be equal to the difference between net worth and charitable contributions.[71] This measure ignores other deductions about which we have no information. The main missing components are deductions for the tax paid on property subject to the estate tax within the previous five years and administrative funeral expenses. After 1945, we use the actual adjusted taxable estate from the tax return. In the years 1962 to 1981 the marital deduction is present on the tax return, and after 1981 it is equal to the spousal bequest. Before 1948, there was no marital deduction.

The marginal tax rates are constructed by applying the actual tax structure at the time of death to the (constructed) taxable estate. Tax rates at the age of 45 and ten years before death are constructed by applying the tax structure in the relevant year (in effect on the same day of that year) to the actual taxable estate at the time of death denominated in the dollars for that year (deflated using the CPI). For decedents younger than 45, we use the actual tax rate at death as the tax rate at age 45.

Marital status is missing for 20 percent of the returns (and it is missing for all observations in 1965). The rest of decedents are classified as married (43 percent), widowed (27 percent), single (8 percent), separated (0.1 percent), or divorced (1.7 percent). We make use of separate dummies for each type of marital status and omit the dummy for being single.

Age is present for 88 percent of the sample. It is missing for all individuals who filed their returns in 1969 and for some subset of the remaining population. To avoid deleting these observations, we impute their age. This is done by regressing age on a constant and a time dummy for the rest of the population and using predicted values for the individuals with missing age.[72] In our regression we include as a separate variable a dummy for age being imputed, as well as a variable which is equal to the imputed age for individuals with missing age, and zero otherwise. We follow the same procedure for variables that were constructed using age (such as the tax rate at age of 45 and interactions of the tax rate with age). The coefficients on these variables are insignificant and are not reported. Most of our specifications were also run on the sample of individuals with a reported age. The results are not significantly different than the ones reported here.

Two other variables are present for the whole sample. The dummy variable for sex takes the value of one for men, who constitute 68 percent of the sample. Eighty-seven percent of the individuals are testate.

71. This change was retroactive, but we do not account for that aspect.
72. The predicted age in 1917 was 65.8, and the coefficient on the time dummy was .13.

COMMENT BY
Alan J. Auerbach

Perhaps because it relates to an event so unpleasant to contemplate, the estate tax generates more humorous comment than most other activities of the Internal Revenue Service. But attempting empirical work on the effects of the estate tax is no laughing matter. To begin with, one must deal with the problem of data confidentiality, which the authors have overcome through an agreement with the IRS. From there, the researcher must confront and model the many motives for leaving estates, the lifetime of decisions leading up to the final bequest, and, of course, the complex and changing estate tax rules themselves. Finally, one must finesse the many limitations of available data sources in attempting to tease meaningful results from them. Wojciech Kopczuk and Joel Slemrod are to be commended for their trailblazing efforts in tackling this problem. Their results are interesting and, although not robust enough to be fully convincing, are certainly suggestive of an impact of estate taxes on the size of estates. Future work on the subject surely will cite this chapter with appreciation, and appropriately so.

The authors begin their chapter with a discussion of the theory underlying their work. This is the right place to start, for it is important to justify the empirical approach they then implement. However, as the theoretical discussion is clear and not especially controversial, I will focus primarily on the empirical part of their work.

The empirical analysis is carried out in two parts: a time series analysis and a pooled cross-section analysis. However, unlike in other instances in which a researcher may analyze data organized in different formats, the underlying data here are the same. That is, the time series data are simply the aggregation of the cross sections from each corresponding year. All the information contained in the time series is also contained in the pooled cross sections.

As aggregation eliminates a lot of information, one might ask the purpose of carrying out the time series analysis first. One answer is that it is useful to begin with a graphical plot of the time series behavior of different series, to carry out the "ocular econometrics" referred to by the authors. This is likely to be more informative (and certainly less messy) than a scatter plot of 309,136 observations. But it is also possible that the time series relationship between tax rates and estates is governed by different factors than the cross-section variation at a given point in time. As is familiar from the empirical literature on the behavioral effects of taxation, identification of a model based on cross-section data requires variation in tax rates traceable to factors—

potential instruments—that can be excluded from the behavioral equation. Justifiable exclusion restrictions are sometimes scarce and, even if they can be found, the tax rate variation across individuals at a given point in time may have a different impact than the variation in tax rates over time. Thus we might wish to look at time series and cross section variation separately, in the language of econometrics, to examine the "between" and "within" estimators separately. But the authors do not do this; because they do not include time dummy variables in their pooled analysis, their estimates reflect the impact of both sources of tax rate variation. As a consequence of this approach, it is difficult to know how much additional information the pooled estimates provide, once we have considered the time series estimates.

The time series analysis, presented first, suggests a negative relationship between the estate tax rate and the share of wealth showing up in the top 0.5 percent of estates, a group subject to substantial estate taxes. This relationship is not surprising, given the relative movements of the dependent variable and tax variables shown in figures 7-1, 7-2, and 7-3. But these figures also raise some other issues. First, they show a strong downward trend in the dependent variable, one that is not predicted by theory. The authors deal with this by adding a time trend to their model, but doing so does not tell us where the trend comes from or whether the impacts of missing variables for which the time trend proxies are also being picked up to some extent by the tax variable.

These figures also suggests that the statistical properties of the dependent variable may have been different in the early years of the sample, before 1945, for which certain alternative data definitions are necessary. I wonder what the results look like for the postwar period. At the very least, it would be appropriate to control for the heteroskedasticity associated with the large fluctuations of this earlier period or, failing that, to report corrected standard errors that take this distributional property into account. This would likely make all the estate tax coefficients in the last three columns of table 7-1 insignificant at conventional levels. Finally, it is not clear what to make of the other coefficients. The lagged corporate income tax rate has the "correct" sign—higher taxes lead to lower estates—but the lagged personal income tax rate has the "wrong" sign. Perhaps most puzzling is the effect of lagged inequality. It is difficult to think of another variable that would be predicted to have as strong a positive impact on the share of wealth accounted for by the largest estates, but this variable has a negative sign. In summary, the coefficients on the estate tax variables themselves suggest a behavioral relationship between the estate tax and the size of estates, but there are many troubling elements of the estimates that should give us pause.

Turning next to the pooled estimates, we observe—without surprise, because the time series effects are incorporated in these estimates as well—that certain anomalies carry over from the time series analysis. Notable are the negative coefficients on the time trend (which should be positive, given that the dependent variable, the logarithm of real reported net worth on the top estate tax returns, should be growing with the economy) and the lagged inequality of income. Once again, it is likely that the standard errors are understated, in this case not only because of heteroskedasticity (the economy grows over time, and the size of the errors may as well) but also because the errors at any given date are likely to be strongly correlated.

As mentioned above, the challenge in cross section analysis is to find valid instruments for the individual's endogenous tax rate. The authors remind us that one can not look at prior estate tax rates for a given individual, given the biological reality that we mortals confront. Instead, they come up with a variety of instruments, including tax rates at different levels of wealth and lagged values of these tax rates. Some of these lagged values vary across individuals, as they are defined relative to the individual's age at death. Another thorny problem that arises in the analysis of microdata is how to account for intra-family estate planning. How should one treat the estate left by an individual with a surviving spouse? If the aim of the couple is to maximize their after-tax estate then they should organize their affairs in such a way as to shift enough from the deceased spouse to the surviving spouse so that the latter's expected estate tax rate equals that of the former. In this case, the observed estate tax rate is the right one to use in our analysis. But suppose, for reasons not apparent ("transaction costs"), that a husband dies and leaves everything in his large estate to his wife. Under current law, this estate faces a tax rate of zero, but it will face a much higher tax rate when the surviving wife eventually dies. Which tax rate should we attribute to the husband's estate? Kopczuk and Slemrod analyze two sensible candidates, the tax rate of the deceased (RATE) and the maximum of that rate and the rate of the surviving spouse, were that spouse to die with the estate just inherited (RATEMAX). Finally, in recognition of the fact that estate planning is, after all, estate *planning*, they consider the impact of tax rates from earlier periods, the tax rate that an individual's actual estate would have faced ten years earlier, or alternatively when the individual was forty-five years old.

Through the chapter's thorough analysis of different instrument sets, different treatment of family decisions, and different planning horizons, we learn, alas, that specification choices matter—a lot. For example, while a limited instrument set leaves the tax rate coefficient with the "wrong" sign (the quotes reflecting the fact that, in theory, the sign of the effect is ambiguous), this changes with the addition of more instruments (table 7-3). The individual's actual tax rate, the rate based on tax law ten years earlier, or on tax law when the decedent was forty-five, all have a small but significant effect in reducing estates (table 7-3, column 3 and table 7-5, columns 1 and 2). But the tax rate based on a comparison of the two spouses' tax rates (RATEMAX) causes the sign of the tax rate coefficient to change.

Where, then, are we, after this initial foray into the unknown? As already indicated, the results are suggestive, but their lack of robustness leaves us well short of being able to draw policy conclusions based on them. Still, we know more than we did before. In the short run, we could learn a little more through some straightforward econometric refinements. But substantial advances will not come as easily. For that, we need a combination of better data and more thought: data that might link estate tax returns to the income tax returns of the same individuals during their lives; and thought about further testable implications of the theoretical prediction that estates respond significantly to the estate tax. Some of us may be here to see these advances happen; others will provide additional observations for future research.

References

Abel, Andrew B. 1985. "Precautionary Saving and Accidental Bequests." *American Economic Review* 75 (September): 777–91.

Abel, Andrew B., and Mark Warshawsky. 1988. "Specification of the Joy of Giving: Insights from Altruism." *Review of Economics and Statistics* 70 (February): 145–49.

Andreoni, James. 1990. "Impure Altruism and Donations to Public Goods: Theory of Warm-Glow Giving." *Economic Journal* 100 (June): 464–77.

Barro, Robert J. 1974. "Are Government Bonds Net Wealth?" *Journal of Political Economy* 82 (November–December): 1095–1117.

Barro, Robert J., and James W. Friedman. 1977. "On Uncertain Lifetimes." *Journal of Political Economy* 85 (August): 843–49.

Bernheim, B. Douglas. 1991. "How Strong Are Bequest Motives? Evidence Based on Estimates of the Demand for Life Insurance and Annuities." *Journal of Political Economy* 99 (October): 899–927.

———. 1997. "Rethinking Savings Incentives." In *Fiscal Policy: Lessons from Economic Research*, edited by Alan J. Auerbach, 259–311. MIT Press.

Bernheim, B. Douglas, Andrei Shleifer, and Lawrence H. Summers. 1985. "The Strategic Bequest Motive." *Journal of Political Economy* 93 (December): 1045–76.

Blundell, Richard, and Thomas E. MaCurdy. 1999. "Labor Supply: A Review of Alternative Approaches." In *Handbook of Labor Economics*, vol. 3A, edited by Orley Ashenfelter and David Card, 1527–86. Elsevier/North Holland.

Bureau of the Census. 1975. *Historical Statistics of the United States, Colonial Times to 1970.*

———. 1999. "Historical Income Tables—Families, Table F.2 Share of Aggregate Income Received by Each Fifth and Top 5 Percent of Families (All Races)." October 4, 1996.

Burman, Leonard E., and William C. Randolph. 1992. "Measuring Permanent Responses to Capital-Gains Tax Changes in Panel Data." *American Economic Review* 84 (September): 794–809.

Carroll, Christopher D. 2000. "Why Do the Rich Save So Much?" In *Does Atlas Shrug? The Economic Consequences of Taxing the Rich*, edited by Joel Slemrod, 465–84. Harvard University Press and Russell Sage Foundation.

Chapman, Kenneth, Govind Hariharan, and Lawrence Southwick Jr. 1996. "Estate Taxes and Asset Accumulation." *Family Business Review* 9 (Fall): 253–68.

Davies, James B. 1981. "Uncertain Lifetime, Consumption, and Dissaving in Retirement." *Journal of Political Economy* 89 (June): 561–77.

Eller, Martha Britton, and Barry W. Johnson. 2000."Using a Sample of Federal Estate Returns to Examine the Effects of Audit Revaluation on Pre-Audit Estimates." *(http://www.irs.gov/prod/tax-stats/soi/est_etr.html* ESTAUDIT.PDF 47258 [December 2000]).

Erard, Brian. 1999. "Estate Tax Underreporting Gap Study: A Report Prepared for the Internal Revenue Service Economic Analysis and Modeling Group." TIRNO-98-P-00406. Internal Revenue Service.

Feenberg, Daniel R., and James M. Poterba. 1993. "Income Inequality and the Incomes of Very High-Income Taxpayers: Evidence from Tax Returns." In *Tax Policy and the Economy*, vol. 7, edited by James M. Poterba, 145–77. National Bureau of Economic Research, MIT Press.

Fiekowsky, Seymour. 1966. "The Effect on Saving of the United States of Estate and Gift Tax." In *Federal Estate and Gift Taxes*, edited by Carl S. Shoup, 228–36. Brookings.

Goldsmith, Raymond W., Dorothy S. Brady, and Horst Menderhausen. 1956. *A Study of Saving in the United States.* vol. 3. Princeton University Press.

Gordon, Roger H., and Joel Slemrod. 2000. "Are 'Real' Responses to Taxes Simply Income Shifting between Corporate and Personal Tax Bases?" In *Does Atlas Shrug? The Economic Consequences of Taxing the Rich*, edited by Joel Slemrod, 240–80. Harvard University Press and Russell Sage Foundation.

Hubbard, R. Glenn, Jonathan Skinner, and Stephen P. Zeldes. 1994. "The Importance of Precautionary Motives in Explaining Individual and Aggregate Saving." *Carnegie-Rochester Conference Series on Public Policy* 40 (June): 59–125.

Hurd, Michael D. 1987. "Savings of the Elderly and Desired Bequests." *American Economic Review* 77 (June): 298–312.

———. 1989. "Mortality Risk and Bequests." *Econometrica* 57 (July): 779–813.

———. 1994. "Measuring the Bequest Motive: The Effect of Children on Saving by the Elderly in the United States." In *Savings and Bequests*, edited by Toshiaki Tachibanaki, 111–36. University of Michigan Press.

Johnson, Barry W., ed. 1994. *Compendium of Federal Estate Tax and Personal Wealth Studies.* Department of Treasury, Internal Revenue Service 1773 (4–94).

Joulfaian, David. 1998. "Charitable Bequests and Estate Taxes: Another Look at the Evidence." November. U.S. Department of Treasury, Office of Tax Analysis (November).

———. 1998. "The Federal Estate and Gift Tax: Description, Profile of Taxpayers and Economic Consequences." Paper 80. U.S. Department of Treasury, Office of Tax Analysis

Kapteyn, Arie, Rob Alessie, and Annamaria Lusardi. 1999. "Explaining the Wealth Holdings of Different Cohorts: Productivity Growth and Social Security." Dartmouth College (August).

Kopczuk, Wojciech. 2001. "Optimal Estate Taxation in the Steady State." Ph.D. dissertation, University of Michigan.

Kotlikoff, Laurence J., and Avia Spivak. 1981. "The Family as an Incomplete Annuities Market." *Journal of Political Economy* 89 (April): 372–81.

Laitner, John. 1997. "Intergenerational and Interhousehold Economic Links." In *Handbook of Population and Family Economics*, vol. 1A, edited by Mark K. Rosenzweig and Oded Stark, 189–238. Elsevier/North Holland.

Luckey, John R. 1995. "A History of Federal Estate, Gift and Generation-Skipping Taxes." CRS Report for Congress 95-444A. Congressional Research Service (March).

McCubbin, Janet G. 1990. "The Intergenerational Wealth Study: Basic Estate Data 1916–1945." *Statistics of Income Bulletin* (Spring): 79–114.

Poterba, James M. 2000. "The Estate Tax and After-Tax Investment Returns." In *Does Atlas Shrug? The Economic Consequences of Taxing the Rich*, edited by Joel Slemrod, 329–49. Harvard University Press and Russell Sage

Richard, Scott F. 1975. "Optimal Consumption, Portfolio and Life Insurance Rules for an Uncertain Lived Individual in a Continuous Time Model." *Journal of Financial Economics* 2 (June): 187–203.

Sandford, Cedric. 1984. *Economics of Public Finance*. 3d ed. Oxford: Pergamon Press.

Slemrod, Joel. 1996. "High-Income Families and the Tax Changes of the 1980s: The Anatomy of Behavioral Response." In *Empirical Foundations of Household Taxation*, edited by Martin S. Feldstein and James M. Poterba, 169–89. University of Chicago Press.

———. 1998. "Methodological Issues in Measuring and Interpreting Taxable Income Elasticities." *National Tax Journal* 51 (December): 973–88

———, ed. 2000. *Does Atlas Shrug? The Economic Consequences of Taxing the Rich*. Harvard University Press and Russell Sage Foundation.

———. 2001. "A General Model of the Behavioral Response to Taxation." *International Tax and Public Finance* 8 (March): 119–28.

Strawczynski, Michel. 1994. "Government Intervention as a Bequest Substitute." *Journal of Public Economics* 53 (March): 477–95.

Tait, Alan A. 1967. *The Taxation of Personal Wealth*. University of Illinois Press.

U.S. Joint Economic Committee. 1998. *The Economics of the Estate Tax*. 98-J-842-48 (December).

Wolff, Edward N. 1996. "Discussant's Comments on Douglas Holtz-Eakin, 'The Uneasy Case for Abolishing the Estate Tax.'" *Tax Law Review* 51 (Spring): 517–22.

Yaari, Menahem E. 1965. "Uncertain Lifetime, Life Insurance, and the Theory of the Consumer." *Review of Economic Studies* 32 (April): 137–50.

DAVID JOULFAIAN

8 | *Charitable Giving in Life and at Death*

PEOPLE TRANSFER ABOUT $100 billion to charity a year.[1] An extensive body of literature examines the pattern of such giving during life. A smaller body addresses the determinants of charitable bequests. Few studies, however, examine the pattern of giving during life and at death, most important in the case of the wealthy, who transfer tens of billion of dollars to charity each year.[2]

Transfers to charity during life benefit from an income tax deduction. Transfers at death benefit from an estate tax deduction. Many studies find that income taxes greatly affect lifetime contributions. Other studies find that estate taxation influences charitable bequests. One study finds that estate taxation influences lifetime giving too.[3]

The scant evidence on the pattern of giving suggests that the wealthy make most of their transfers to charity at death. Using data from estate tax returns filed in 1977, Eugene Steuerle finds that contributions represent less than

This chapter greatly benefited from comments by Gerald Auten, David Ribar, and conference participants. I am particularly indebted to Jim Cilke for his expertise and guidance in manipulating panel data.

1. Giving USA (1999, p. 20).
2. Joulfaian (2000a).
3. Clotfelter (1985, chap. 2); Randolph (1995); Boskin (1976); Clotfelter (1985, chap. 6); Joulfaian (2000a); Auten and Joulfaian (1996).

5 percent of charitable bequests. Similarly, and using estate tax returns for decedents in 1982, David Joulfaian reports contributions as less than 6 percent of bequests, and much less for the very rich (less than 3 percent for those with assets of more than $10 million).[4] This reported pattern indicates an unwillingness by the wealthy to part with wealth during life and suggests that they may not pursue a tax minimization strategy in timing their giving.

Data availability has limited the scope of the few studies made on the timing of transfers. The evidence reported in Steuerle and Joulfaian, for instance, is based on data on contributions reported in the year before the date of death.[5] Although this one-year snapshot of giving is informative, a longer history of giving, well in advance of death, may shed more light on the mode of transfers that the rich prefer.

Many of the studies not only focus exclusively on one of the two modes of giving but also examine the effects of only one form of taxation. The literature on the determinants of lifetime charitable contributions, for instance, traditionally emphasizes income taxation, and, except for Auten and Joulfaian, ignores the effects of the estate tax.[6]

In this chapter, I examine the pattern of giving in life and at death. I investigate how the estate tax affects total giving and how total giving is allocated between transfers made during life and at death. I offer evidence on the pattern of giving by using estate tax returns and panel data reflecting the decedents' income history. The panel data consist of income tax returns for ten years spanning the period 1987 through 1996 and their associated estate tax returns for decedents during the years 1996 through 1998. The data contain rich information on the income sources and deductions claimed during life, as well as on the size of terminal wealth and its disposition at death. Such a long panel is a vast improvement over the one-year snapshot employed in past studies.

The evidence gleaned from this panel suggests that giving during life is far greater than that reported earlier. The very rich, however, continue to exhibit a greater preference for giving at death than those not very rich.

What Determines the Size and Timing of Giving?

A person may make transfers to charity during life as well as at death. Charitable contributions are deductible in computing the income tax liability but

4. Steuerle (1987); Joulfaian (1998, table 14).
5. Steuerle (1987); Auten and Joulfaian (1996); and Joulfaian (1998).
6. Auten and Joulfaian (1996).

only when deductions are itemized. The sum of charitable gifts, state and local taxes, mortgage interest, and a number of other items in excess of a certain threshold is deductible in computing taxable income. This threshold, or the standard deduction, ranged from \$3,760 to \$6,700 for joint filers over the 1987–96 period; \$2,540 to \$4,000 for single filers.[7]

For those who itemize deductions, the general rule is that charitable contributions are deductible as long as they do not exceed 50 percent of the adjusted gross income (AGI) or 30 percent for transfers other than cash. Special rules apply to lifetime transfers to private foundations; the limits become 30 and 20 percent, respectively. Unused amounts are carried over and used to reduce taxable income in subsequent years.

Beginning in 1987, and as provided for by the Tax Reform Act of 1986, donations that appreciated beyond the original donor basis were given preferential tax treatment by avoiding the alternative minimum tax (AMT), an extra 20–21 percent tax imposed on individuals and businesses that make excessive use of deductions. For those affected, the AMT treatment limited the deduction to the basis in the property transferred. This limitation was relaxed for appreciated tangible personal property in 1990, with museums being the primary beneficiaries, and done away with altogether in 1993.[8]

As provided by the Deficit Reduction Act of 1984, donors may deduct contributions of publicly traded stocks to private foundations at their full market value. This provision expired at the end of 1994, and the deduction became limited to the donor's basis. The full deduction was temporarily restored in the middle of 1996 and then of 1997, and permanently extended in 1998.[9]

For every dollar in contributions, the individual may save an amount t in income taxes, the marginal tax rate. If this is not consumed and saved until death, then the heirs receive $t(1 - e)$, where e is the estate tax rate.[10] Alternatively, the individual may postpone giving until death. Charitable bequests are deductible in computing the estate tax without any limits. For every dollar in bequests, the charity receives \$1 as in the case of giving during life, but nothing is left to the heirs. Table 8-1 summarizes the outcomes of the timing of charitable giving. A simple comparison of the consequences of the two modes of transfers to charity highlights the optimality of giving during life.

It follows from table 8-1 that when \$1 is transferred to a charity, the donor receives a tax reduction of t. Thus, the price of the gift, relative to con-

----

7. Commerce Clearinghouse (2000).

8. Commerce Clearinghouse (2000).

9. Commerce Clearinghouse (2000); U.S. Congress (1997, p. 86; 1998, p. 239).

10. Actually, the heirs receive $t(1 - e)(1 + \pi)^n/(1 + r)^n$, where π is the rate at which t appreciates, and r is the discount rate. These rates, here and below, are omitted to simplify exposition.

Table 8-1. *Outcome of the Timing of Charitable Giving*

Type of transfer	Charity receives	Consumption	Heirs receive
During life	1	t	$t(1-e)$
At death	1	0	0

Table 8-2. *Tax Price of Transfers*

	Tax price relative to	
Type of transfer	Consumption	Bequests to heirs
Charitable gifts during life	$1-t$	$(1-t)(1-e)$
Charitable bequests at death	1	$1-e$
Bequests to heirs	$1/(1-e)$	1

sumption, is $1 - t$, which is the traditional price measure employed in the literature on charitable contributions. If the gift is deferred and transferred at death, then the price is 1. If the gifts are to be bequeathed to heirs instead, the price of such bequests becomes $1/(1 - e)$. With a tax rate of 0.55, it will cost the donor $2.22 in forgone consumption for every dollar received by the heirs.

When measured relative to the price of bequests to heirs, the tax price of charitable contributions becomes $(1 - t)$ $(1 - e)$. This result is in stark contrast to the conventional measure of the tax price of $(1 - t)$ measured relative to the price of consumption. The price of charitable bequests is $1 - e$, consistent with the literature on charitable bequests. These prices are summarized in table 8-2 and suggest that giving to charity is less costly than giving to heirs. Along with the outcomes reported in table 8-1, they also suggest that a tax minimization strategy would require giving during life.

Many studies find that lifetime contributions are responsive to the income tax price, $1 - t$. These findings vary from study to study as well as between transitory and permanent effects.[11] A number of studies also find the estate tax an important influence on charitable bequests.[12]

While the above suggest that taxes may affect the size and timing of charitable transfers, many nontax factors may also influence such transfers.

11. Randolph (1995); Bakjia (1999); Auten, Clotfelter, and Sieg (1999).
12. McNees (1973); Boskin (1976); Clotfelter (1985); Joulfaian (1991, 1999, 2000a). A notable exception is Barthold and Plotnick (1984).

Andrew Carnegie, for instance, gave much of his fortune to charity at a time when estate and income taxes virtually did not exist. Indeed, Carnegie even strongly argued for the enactment of the estate tax in his "Gospel of Wealth" and other writings.[13]

The wealthy may give little to charity during life especially if much of their wealth is in the form of business assets or closely held corporate stocks. In part, this reluctance may reflect liquidity constraints. Such constraints, however, may be overcome by transfers of fractional interest. More to the point, the wealthy may not want to part with their wealth for fear of losing control of their businesses as they become minority owners. Thus, they may postpone giving until death.

Aside from business ownership, the wealthy may postpone giving simply because they enjoy wealth accumulation.[14] Charitable contributions reduce wealth held during life. If individuals derive utility from holding wealth, then giving during life reduces welfare; any gain in utility or "warm glow" resulting from giving is in part offset by utility reduction resulting from loss of wealth. Aside from the joy of wealth accumulation, the wealthy may hold on to wealth, and postpone giving, because of the benefits that wealth yields. Charitable organizations and others, for instance, are likely to be "nice" to them in anticipation of gifts.

Despite these two propositions, the wealthy may choose to make some transfers during life. One motivation for lifetime giving, perhaps a cynical one, is that these gifts provide the wealthy, invariably holders of large businesses interests, some goodwill, fame, or influence. Contributions may be viewed as a form of advertising or a public relations instrument. One extreme view is that donations may appease consumer groups or may influence government officials to take a softer stance in regulating business activities.

Empirical Evidence

To examine the pattern of giving and its determinants, I employ data on lifetime contributions obtained from a panel of income tax returns. In 1987 a stratified random sample of some 85,000 income tax returns were selected by the Statistics of Income (SOI) division of the Internal Revenue Service. These returns were followed over time through 1996. As people in the panel died, their estate tax returns, which provide information on bequests, were

13. Carnegie (1962).
14. Carroll (1997).

Table 8-3. *Ten-Year Panel Attributes*[a]

Thousands of dollars, except as indicated

Wealth	Number of observations	Mean wealth	Mean adjusted gross income	Mean age
Less than 1,000	126	876	79	74
1,000–2,500	205	1,771	375	75
2,500–5,000	148	3,779	680	74
5,000–10,000	131	7,955	1,234	76
10,000–20,000	111	14,798	2,036	78
20,000–50,000	80	32,360	3,079	79
50,000–100,000	45	70,424	5,656	78
100,000 and over	36	405,226	15,081	84
Total	882	27,286	1,836	76

Source: This and all subsequent tables present author's calculations using a sample of matched income and estate tax returns of decedents in 1996–98. In this and subsequent tables, all the income and wealth ranges are inclusive of the lower point.

a. Measured at 1997 levels, using a real discount rate of 4 percent. See text for details.

obtained. Given the estate tax filing threshold, only estate tax returns reporting assets of $600,000 and over are available. Thus, we are able to study only the behavior of the rich (table 8-3).

In this chapter, I focus on individuals in the panel who died in the years 1996–98, with income tax records filed in the years 1987–96. The resulting balanced panel consists of 882 individuals.[15] Table 8-3 describes these individuals classified by wealth. Wealth is defined as net worth at death, and all the variables are measured at 1997 levels using a real discount rate of 4 percent.

The average estate at death is $27 million and is well over $400 million for the top wealth category. One hundred and twenty-six individuals left estates valued under $1.0 million, and 36 left estates in excess of $100 million. The average income, defined as the adjusted gross income (AGI) is about $1.8 million, or $15 million for the wealthiest group. This represents about 7 percent of wealth but is less than 4 percent in the case of the wealthiest group; the wealthy realize little of their income.[16] The average age is 76, or 66 at the beginning of the panel, and generally rises with wealth. Overall,

15. About fifty-six died in 1998, and of the remaining observations about one-half died in each of 1996 and 1997. I exclude eighteen never-married individuals to allow for estimation and observations with negative wealth.

16. Steuerle (1985).

the sample is representative of the wealthiest and somewhat older segment of society (table 8-4).

Table 8-4 provides information on the income trend over the ten-year period again classified by size of estate. Mean AGI drops from about $3.1 million in 1987, to a low of $1 million in 1996, the last year in the panel. A similar pattern is observed for most wealth classes. Although this trend is interesting in its own right, given the constraints imposed by the tax code, it has implications for the deductibility of contributions as well.

Table 8-5 further documents wealth and income patterns and presents the frequency distribution of people in the sample by size of wealth and the ten-year mean AGI. The number of those with negative AGI reported in the first column is striking, which implies that these individuals will not be able to benefit from a deduction for lifetime contributions. Although generally the wealthy report high incomes, the underlying trend is uneven; some of the less wealthy report income much larger than that reported by the very wealthy.

Trends in Giving

The trend in charitable giving over the ten-year panel period is reported in table 8-6. The charitable deduction claimed on income tax returns is reported in the top panel. The average deduction peaks at a value of $223,000 in 1987, the first year of the panel, and declines to $108,000 in 1996. The average cumulated contributions deducted over the ten years is $1.6 million. The least wealthy deducted $138,000 on average, compared with about $20 million for those estates of more than $100 million.

Studies on lifetime contributions have traditionally focused on the reported deduction as the measure of charitable contributions, a practice dictated by available data. The top panel of table 8-6 follows such convention. Actual contributions, however, may not be adequately reflected in the claimed deduction, as the deductibility of gifts is subject to a number of limitations (20, 30, or 50 percent of AGI) depending on the type of underlying asset transferred. Unfortunately, and before 1991, SOI edited data did not provide such information.[17] For the remaining period, the actual contributions are reported in the bottom panel of table 8-6. The average contribution made in 1991 is $848,000, or about six times the deduction claimed in that year. In contrast to the smooth pattern of deductions reported in the top panel, contributions vary considerably over time.

17. For the years 1987 through 1990, the data provide information on contributions and carryovers. Such information, however, is adjusted to add up to the reported deduction.

Table 8-4. *Mean Adjusted Gross Income by Estate Size and Year* [a]

Thousands of dollars

Wealth	1987	1988	1989	1990	1991	1992	1993	1994	1995	1996	Mean
Less than 1,000	345	77	51	128	–47	15	64	20	12	124	79
1,000–2,500	1,043	521	432	406	306	275	200	183	167	221	375
2,500–5,000	2,264	885	778	605	519	491	346	304	330	281	680
5,000–10,000	3,056	2,117	1,472	1,075	731	1,165	765	599	664	692	1,234
10,000–20,000	3,127	3,134	2,493	2,482	1,545	2,357	1,736	1,333	1,236	917	2,036
20,000–50,000	5,155	5,851	4,213	3,696	2,352	2,636	2,184	1,701	1,538	1,467	3,079
50,000–100,000	7,908	9,971	7,966	5,904	4,829	4,704	4,070	3,996	3,969	3,246	5,656
100,000 and over	17,981	22,408	20,161	20,648	12,959	12,294	10,586	11,194	13,424	9,155	15,081
Total	3,124	2,944	2,382	2,165	1,443	1,599	1,284	1,168	1,240	1,007	1,836

a. See note to table 8-3.

Table 8-5. *Frequency Distribution of Individuals by Mean Adjusted Gross Income and Estate Size*[a]
Thousands of dollars

| | Adjusted gross income | | | | | | | | More than | |
Wealth	Negative	0–50	50–100	100–200	200–500	500–1,000	1,000–2,500	2,500–5,000	5,000	All
Less than 1,000	7	12	27	37	29	8	4	1	1	126
1,000–2,500	10	4	16	48	71	42	12	1	1	205
2,500–5,000	13	1	1	9	38	43	35	6	2	148
5,000–10,000	6	0	0	3	17	28	59	14	4	131
10,000–20,000	4	1	0	0	5	19	51	22	9	111
20,000–50,000	5	0	0	0	4	10	20	24	17	80
50,000 and over	4	0	0	0	0	0	8	24	45	81
Total	49	18	44	97	164	150	189	92	79	882

a. Ten-year mean adjusted gross income is measured at 1997 levels. See note to table 8-3.

Table 8-6. *Mean Contributions by Estate Size and Year*[a]

Thousands of dollars

Mean income tax deduction

Wealth	1987	1988	1989	1990	1991	1992	1993	1994	1995	1996	Cumulative
Less than 1,000	21	13	24	12	9	11	14	8	5	21	138
1,000–2,500	27	15	26	25	20	23	13	18	11	13	191
2,500–5,000	58	37	52	39	31	29	33	33	28	36	376
5,000–10,000	76	62	54	46	50	46	54	53	50	51	542
10,000–20,000	102	110	138	136	97	103	95	92	101	115	1,089
20,000–50,000	356	230	170	262	264	232	218	204	163	173	2,272
50,000–100,000	608	712	465	215	274	237	274	305	419	263	3,772
100,000 and over	2,857	2,569	2,315	1,847	1,857	1,872	2,121	1,787	1,612	1,096	19,933
Total	223	197	177	148	144	141	151	137	130	108	1,556

Mean actual contribution

Wealth	Carry-over to 1991	1991	1992	1993	1994	1995	1996	Cumulative
Less than 1,000	0	8	7	11	7	5	21	129
1,000–2,500	7	19	22	12	17	6	11	187
2,500–5,000	48	43	29	28	36	19	32	421
5,000–10,000	16	44	45	51	50	44	48	536
10,000–20,000	85	172	152	104	96	107	114	1,316
20,000–50,000	5	703	223	226	224	151	385	2,935
50,000–100,000		247	285	248	298	290	190	3,454
100,000 and over	111	17,906	3,295	12,875	1,539	1,263	1,026	54,866
Total	7,374	848	206	588	129	105	119	3,070

a. See note to table 8-3.

Table 8-7. *Mean Cumulative Contributions and Bequests, by Estate Size*[a]

Thousands of dollars, except as indicated

		Contributions		Bequests	
Wealth	*Total giving*	*Amount*	*Percent*	*Amount*	*Percent*
Under 1,000	129	129	100.00	0	0.00
1,000–2,500	213	187	87.79	26	12.21
2,500–5,000	452	421	93.14	31	6.86
5,000–10,000	728	536	73.63	192	26.37
10,000–20,000	1,851	1,316	71.10	535	28.90
20,000–50,000	6,059	2,935	48.44	3,124	51.56
50,000–100,000	8,533	3,454	40.48	5,079	59.52
100,000 and over	244,907	54,866	22.40	190,041	77.60
Total	11,477	3,070	26.75	8,407	73.25

a. See note to table 8-3.

The bottom panel also reports the unused contributions carried over to 1991. The average amount carried over is $330,000, roughly twice the size of the annual deduction. Adding the amount carried over to 1991 to the deductions claimed during 1987–90 and to the contributions made during 1991–96 yields cumulative contributions of $3.1 million on average, as shown in the last column of the bottom panel; about $55 million for the richest group. The average contribution over the ten-year period is about twice as large as the claimed deduction, or $3.1 million versus $1.6 million. Overall, these wealth holders are twice as generous as the deduction figures suggest.

The patterns of lifetime giving and bequests are contrasted in tables 8-7 and 8-8. Table 8-7 shows that the individuals in the sample gave about $11.5 million to charity on average; $3.1 million during life, as also shown in table 8-6, and $8.4 million in charitable bequests. About 27 percent of these transfers were made during life and the remaining 73 percent at death. Interestingly, the fraction of transfers made during life declines with wealth; it drops from a high of 100 percent for the least wealthy to about 22 percent for estates in excess of $100 million where the average bequest is about $190 million. Stated differently, and to allow for comparisons with past studies, contributions by those with wealth in excess of $10 million are roughly equal to 30 percent of bequests. This figure compares to 3 percent using one-year data on contributions in Joulfaian. Panel data seem to provide a better picture of the importance of lifetime giving.[18]

18. Joulfaian (1998, table 14).

Table 8-8. *Distribution of Contributions and Bequests, by Estate Size*

Wealth[a] (thousands of dollars)	Number of observations	With contributions		With bequests	
		Number	Percent	Number	Percent
Under 1,000	126	108	85.71	7	5.56
1,000–2,500	205	193	94.15	18	8.78
2,500–5,000	148	142	95.95	17	11.49
5,000–10,000	131	126	96.18	36	27.48
10,000–20,000	111	108	97.30	28	25.23
20,000–50,000	80	80	100.00	27	33.75
50,000–100,000	45	44	97.78	21	46.67
100,000 and over	36	36	100.00	29	80.56
Total	882	837	94.90	183	20.75

a. See note to table 8-3.

Charitable bequests represent the lion's share of transfers, but individuals are more likely to give during life. As shown in the bottom panel of table 8-8, about 95 percent of the observations in the sample report charitable contributions at least once over the ten-year period. In contrast, about 20 percent provide for charitable bequests; far more individuals give to charity during life than at death. In addition, little variation occurs in the relative frequency of contributions, as it ranges between 86 and 100 percent. Few of the least wealthy, however, some 5 percent, provide for charitable bequests; the fraction rises to about 81 percent for the wealthiest group.

The pattern of giving reported in tables 8-7 and 8-8 has interesting implications. The very rich seem to prefer charitable bequests, while the less wealthy favor charitable contributions. This pattern also suggests that the wealthy are unwilling to part with their wealth during life but become generous and philanthropic at death.

Table 8-9 provides more information on the pattern of charitable bequests. The first column repeats the figures on charitable bequests reported in table 8-7. The second column reports bequests to private foundations. The reported pattern reveals that much of the bequests of the very rich are channeled to benefit such foundations. It seems that the wealthy are not only unwilling to part with their wealth during life but get to take it with them as they immortalize themselves in the foundations they form or support.[19]

19. Note that this sample is not designed to be representative of decedents in a given year and does not reflect giving to diverse causes. To obtain a broader view of how the wealthy allocate their bequests among the various charities, see Joulfaian (2000a).

Table 8-9. *Mean Charitable Bequests by Estate Size*[a]

Thousands of dollars, except as indicated

		Bequests to foundations	
Wealth	*All bequests*	*Amount*	*Percent*
Less than 1,000	0	0	0.00
1,000–2,500	26	7	26.92
2,500–5,000	31	7	22.58
5,000–10,000	192	33	17.19
10,000–20,000	535	340	63.55
20,000–50,000	3,124	1,902	60.88
50,000–100,000	5,079	4,762	93.76
100,000 and over	190,041	182,871	96.23
Total	8,407	7,930	94.33

a. See note to table 8-3.

Multivariate Analysis

As the above tabulations show it is clear that the wealthy prefer to make their transfers to charity at death. To further clarify the pattern of giving and to empirically explore the determinants of the timing of transfers, I resort to multivariate analysis, considering the effects of taxes, wealth, business ownership, marital status, and age.

Two variables are of key interest: the cumulative sum of transfers to charity and their allocation between lifetime contributions and bequests. I focus on the determinants of all donations and their allocation between lifetime gifts and transfers at death. Charitable bequests and lifetime contributions are valued at 1997 levels. Because actual contributions, unlike the claimed deductions, are not observed in every year in the panel, I employ the cumulative measure of lifetime contributions as in table 8-7.

The tax price of bequests is defined as the reciprocal of one minus the marginal estate tax rate, or $1/(1 - e)$. The estate tax rate is computed by adding $10,000 to charitable bequests and reflects both federal and state taxes.[20] While spousal bequests, including transfers to QTIP spousal trusts, are tax

20. State estate tax rates are obtained for 1992 from the Advisory Commission on Intergovernmental Relations (1992) and incorporated in the measurement of the tax price consistent with Joulfaian (2000a). Because there was little variation in state taxes over time, the reported estimates are invariant to employing tax rates in effect in other years (1987 and post-1992).

deductible,[21] I do not treat the latter as deductible (QTIP = 0) as they are likely to be taxed at the death of the surviving spouse.[22] Because the tax price measure is likely to be endogenous to lifetime giving and charitable bequests, I compute a first-dollar tax price, which sets charitable bequests and lifetime contributions to zero.

The income tax price is defined as one minus the marginal tax rate. For individuals making noncash gifts, a further adjustment is made to capture the capital gains tax avoided on contributions of appreciated property. The price of contributions of appreciated property is $1 - t_o - t_c(\alpha G/V)$, where t_o and t_c are the ordinary and capital gains tax rates, respectively, G is the accrued gain on the asset, V is the market value of the asset, and α reflects a discounting factor for the expected holding period if the asset were not donated and the possibility that the asset might escape taxation entirely if the asset is held until death. Following Martin Feldstein and Charles Clotfelter, $\alpha G/V$ is set equal to 0.5.[23] The overall price is thus measured as a weighted average of the price of giving cash and the price of giving appreciated property with the weights determined by the average share of noncash gifts. The actual cash share varies from nearly 80 percent for the less wealthy to 26 percent for the wealthiest group. To generate an income tax price independent of wealth, a cash share of 50 percent is employed. The tax liability is calculated by setting contributions equal to the sample mean of 17 percent of AGI. The tax rate is computed by increasing contributions by $1,000. Realizations are increased by the same increment, and the capital gains tax rate is computed over this range.

Wealth is defined as the gross estate at death less debts and estate expenses, plus lifetime contributions and inter vivos or lifetime noncharitable gifts, and less the tax liability computed in the absence of contributions and bequests to charity. Income is defined as the ten-year mean after-tax AGI, computed in the absence of contributions. Marital status is determined at death and so is age. Business ownership is measured as the share of business assets in the estate at death. These include closely held corporate stock, farm, and noncorporate business assets. Ideally, and had data been available, this share should reflect lifetime gifts as well.

Given the progressive nature of the estate tax, the tax price is likely to be endogenous to the amount transferred to charity in life as well as at death. Those

---

21. A QTIP, or qualified terminable interest property, is property that passes from the decedent in which the surviving spouse has a lifetime interest; she receives all the income of the trust during her life. A number of restrictions apply to the spouse's access to the property, and remaining assets pass to the children at the spouse's death. IRC sec. 2642 b4.

22. I employ the price faced by the decedent, which may deviate from the future price the QTIP assets may face.

23. Feldstein and Clotfelter (1976, pp. 52–55).

who give to charity have smaller taxable estates and face lower marginal tax rates. Hence I estimate an equation for cumulative transfers using 2SLS, where the first-dollar price and pretax wealth are employed as instruments. The results are reported in the first panel of table 8-10, where the dependent variable is defined as the natural logarithm of cumulative donations.

The reported estimates for cumulative gifts in column one show that giving increases with the bequest tax price. The higher the estate tax rate, the costlier it is to make transfers to heirs, as the price is $1/(1 - e)$. The estimated price elasticity is 1.5 with a standard error of 0.4. Giving also rises with wealth, with an estimated elasticity of 1.1 (se = 0.1). Combined, these two coefficients suggest that charitable giving may decline by some 13 percent in the absence of the estate tax.

It also rises with income, albeit modestly. Giving seems to decline with the income tax price; the higher the tax rate the greater the giving. The estimated price elasticity is −2.8 (se = 1).[24] Business ownership, gender, marital status, and age have imprecise effects on giving.

The above estimates are replicated using Tobit FIML instead of 2SLS. Here transfers and the price of bequests, $1/(1 - e)$, are estimated simultaneously; the price equation employs the first-dollar price and pretax wealth. Given that some 96 percent of the observations report positive transfers, a priori FIML estimates should be similar to 2SLS estimates. As expected, the new estimates, reported in the middle panel of table 8-10, are fairly similar to those reported earlier.[25] The implied bequest price and wealth elasticities are 1.7 and 0.99, which suggest that charitable giving may decline by some 31 percent in the absence of the estate tax.

Next, I focus on the share of these transfers made during life. OLS estimates of the determinants of the lifetime contributions share of giving are reported in the last panel of table 8-10. These estimates show that the lifetime contribution share declines with wealth, consistent with the evidence reported in tables 8-7 and 8-8; the estimated coefficient is −0.06 (se = 0.01). Similarly, the share also rises with income and declines with the income tax price. Business ownership seems to depress lifetime giving. Individuals with greater business concentration in their portfolios prefer to provide for char-

---

24. Given its construction, we should be careful in interpreting this coefficient.

25. If the estimates were provided for married and not-married individuals separately, then for the former ($n = 615$), the coefficients on price become 1.51 (se = 0.43) for 2SLS and 1.69 (se = 0.45) for Tobit, and for wealth 0.72 (se = 0.1) and 0.64 (se = 0.1) respectively. For not-married individuals ($n = 267$), the price coefficients become 5.44 (1.5) and 6.13 (se = 1.91), and 1.34 (se = 0.18) and 1.33 (se = 0.31) for wealth respectively.

Table 8-10. *Determinants of Charitable Giving*

| | | ln Contributions and bequests | | | | Contribution share – OLS | |
| | | 2SLS | | FIML Tobit | | | |
Variable	Mean	Coefficient	Standard error	Coefficient	Standard error	Coefficient	Standard error
Constant		-9.8192	1.2132	-9.0967	1.1542	1.3305	0.11297
ln Bequest price[a]	1.6987	1.4524	0.4227	1.7062	0.4650	...	...
ln After-tax wealth	16.0858	1.0721	0.0885	0.9878	0.0822	-0.0574	0.0076
ln Income	1.2415	0.2777	0.0369	0.3017	0.0343	0.0209	0.0038
ln Income tax price	0.6809	-2.7626	0.9594	-2.9575	0.9724	-0.2225	0.0987
Business share	0.0999	-0.2328	0.4620	-0.1622	0.5071	-0.1149	0.0477
Widowed	0.2551	-0.4366	0.2370	-0.4899	0.2597	-0.1336	0.0236
Divorced	0.0476	0.2618	0.4364	0.2098	0.6100	-0.1044	0.0440
Age < 55	0.0465	0.2006	0.4827	0.2399	0.5786	0.1333	0.0492
55 ≤ age < 65	0.1168	-0.3280	0.3412	-0.2927	0.4467	0.1767	0.0347
65 ≤ age < 75	0.2800	-0.2481	0.2667	-0.2407	0.2898	0.1297	0.0273
75 ≤ age < 85	0.3061	-0.2538	0.2470	-0.2572	0.2589	0.1249	0.0255
σ				2.6839	0.0493		
2ψ[b]				-5.3613	1.4345		
Log likelihood		-2,106		442		-103	
N		882		882		882	

a. Bequest price = $[1/(1 - e)]$.

b. $\psi = \sigma_{12} / \sigma_2^2$, where 1 and 2 refer to the donations and bequest tax price equations, respectively. Based on the significance of the estimate, the null hypothesis that the error terms are not correlated is rejected.

Table 8-11. *Determinants of Charitable Giving by Type of Transfer*

Variable	ln *Donations* (2SLS)		ln *Bequests* (FIML Tobit)	
	Coefficient	*Standard error*	*Coefficient*	*Standard error*
Constant	−7.9518	1.1723	−86.9640	20.2490
ln Bequest price	1.5961	0.4085	13.3480	5.4146
ln After-tax wealth	0.8868	0.0856	4.3903	1.1833
ln Income	0.3174	0.0356	0.2212	0.3252
ln Income tax price	−2.7901	0.9271	0.2961	7.8176
Business share	−0.7529	0.4464	1.6566	3.3339
Widowed	−0.9216	0.2290	5.8808	2.2769
Divorced	−0.0931	0.4217	12.0120	4.4576
Age < 55	0.5486	0.4664	−12.5290	5.4451
55 ≤ age < 65	0.1150	0.3297	−12.5640	4.0867
65 ≤ age < 75	0.1137	0.2577	−8.1609	2.8816
75 ≤ age < 85	0.1180	0.2386	−5.7402	2.2318
2[a]			−20.4700	9.5637
σ			14.1040	2.4956
F(z)[b]			0.1660	
Log likelihood	−2,166		973	
N	882		882	

a. $\psi = \sigma_{12} / \sigma_2^2$, where 1 and 2 refer to the donations and estate tax price equations, respectively. Based on the significance of the estimate, the null hypothesis that the error terms are not correlated is rejected.

b. Probability of having a positive observation.

ity at death. In contrast, married individuals give more during life. Virtually identical estimates are obtained when two-limit Tobit is employed (not reported).

The estimates in table 8-10 combine giving in life and at death. As an alternative, table 8-11 presents separate estimates for each mode of giving. The equations for lifetime contribution are estimated using 2SLS, where the first-dollar tax price and pretax wealth are employed as instruments. These gifts seem to rise with the price of bequests, wealth, and income and decline with the income tax price. The estimated elasticities are very close to those reported in the first panel of table 8-10. Unlike the earlier estimates, however, widowed individuals give the least. Similar estimates (not reported) are obtained when the equation is estimated using FIML Tobit.

The second panel of table 8-11 reports FIML estimates for charitable bequests. As with the estimates for contributions, the coefficient on the tax price of bequests is positive. It is estimated at 13.3 (se = 5.4), for an implied elasticity of 2.3. Bequests rise with wealth, but in contrast to the earlier estimates, they are invariant to income and income tax price. They also rise with age and are smallest for married individuals, in sharp contrast to the estimates on contributions.

An implicit assumption in all the estimates so far is that the size of transfers and their allocation are determined independently. As a test of the exogeneity of the size of donations to the share transferred during life in table 8-10, I employ Wu's test and generalize it to the limited dependent variable case, which leads to the rejection of the null hypothesis of exogeneity.[26] This suggests that donations and their allocation over time are perhaps jointly determined. Consequently, the amount of donations and the share transferred during life are estimated as a system of equations. Table 8-12 presents three SLS estimates that also include the price of bequests. The first panel reports the estimates for the donations equations, followed by that of the contributions share, and the price equation. The instruments consist of the regressors employed earlier, including the first-dollar price and pretax wealth. In general, the estimated coefficients are similar to those estimated earlier.

The estimated elasticity for the bequest price in the first panel of table 8-12 is 1.2 (se = 0.4). The estimated wealth elasticity is 1.1 (se = 0.1). Combined, these two coefficients imply that charitable giving by the individuals in the panel may change very little in the absence of the estate tax. The estimates in table 8-12 continue to confirm the earlier findings that the income tax stimulates lifetime transfers, and that business owners and widowed individuals prefer to delay their transfers until death.

Conclusions

This chapter examined the pattern of charitable gifts during life and at death. It employed a ten-year panel of income tax returns for 1987 through 1996. This panel was expanded to incorporate the estate tax returns as well. Income tax data provide information on lifetime contributions and income, while estate tax returns provide information on charitable bequests and wealth.

26. Wu (1973); Rivers and Vuong (1988). Specifically, total giving is regressed on all the exogenous variables and the residual kept. Then the share equation is re-estimated including the residual. The null hypothesis of exogeneity is rejected ($\chi^2 = 82$ in case of OLS, $\chi^2 = 50$ in case of Tobit). A similar test was extended to the tax price of bequests, and the null hypothesis of exogeneity was not rejected ($\chi^2 = 0.2$ in case of OLS, $\chi^2 = 1$ in case of Tobit).

Table 8-12. *Determinants of Charitable Giving, 3SLS*[a]

Variable	In Donations		Contribution share		In Bequest price	
	Coefficient	Standard error	Coefficient	Standard error	Coefficient	Standard error
Constant	−10.1690	1.2048	1.3655	0.1131	−0.2303	0.0558
ln Bequest price	1.1605	0.4057	...	...	0.9871	0.0228
ln After-tax wealth	1.1054	0.0875	−0.0599	0.0076	0.0140	0.0041
ln Income	0.2772	0.0369	0.0212	0.0038	−0.0024	0.0019
ln Income tax price	−2.8187	0.9592	−0.2233	0.0981	−0.0175	0.0491
Business share	−0.2372	0.4620	−0.1110	0.0474	−0.0532	0.0237
Widowed	−0.3947	0.2364	−0.1336	0.0235	0.0368	0.0119
Divorced	0.3248	0.4357	−0.1052	0.0438	0.0409	0.0221
Age < 55	0.1468	0.4822	0.1321	0.0489	−0.0484	0.0246
55 ≤ age < 65	−0.3671	0.3408	0.1759	0.0345	−0.0256	0.0174
65 ≤ age < 75	−0.2728	0.2665	0.1286	0.0271	−0.0163	0.0136
75 ≤ age < 85	−0.2589	0.2469	0.1247	0.0253	−0.0063	0.0127
Log likelihood	−2103.07		−97.9877		514.7468	

a. Reported coefficients are estimates for the first dollar tax price and pretax wealth.

Both lifetime contributions and charitable bequests are found to be influenced by the tax price of bequests. Basis statistics and multivariate analysis suggest that the least wealthy make much of their transfers to charity during life; bequests seem to be the mode of transfers preferred by the very wealthy. Lifetime contributions also seem to be the preferred mode of transfers for those married. Widowed individuals and those with large business interests in their estates provide more for charity at death.

The above findings are subject to several caveats. Combining lifetime contributions into a single variable is likely to result in aggregation bias. Income tax regimes and, to a much lesser extent, estate tax regimes, have changed over the years. Certainly, marital status has changed as more married individuals have become widowed. Although data limitations on reported contributions make it difficult to examine annual data, we need to be cognizant of the potential aggregation bias. Indeed, the estimated coefficients on wealth and income are very sensitive to alternative measures of the income tax price. This weakness makes it rather difficult to pin down an accurate estimate of the effects of estate and income taxes.

Another important limitation of this chapter is that it focuses exclusively on how taxes may affect giving and overlooks the potential effects on income and wealth accumulation. If the estate tax affects wealth accumulation or lifetime income, for instance, then the chapter presents an incomplete picture of the effects of estate taxation.[27]

27. Joulfaian (1998, figure 3) and Joulfaian (2000b, 2000c) demonstrate how the wealthy alter their inter vivos gifts in response to estate taxation, and Wojciech Kopczuk and Joel Slemrod in this volume make the general case for how wealth accumulation is affected by the estate tax. This issue also extends to the effects of estate as well as income taxation on reported income. Auten and Carroll (1999); Feldstein (1995).

COMMENT BY
James R. Hines Jr.

Much of the literature analyzing the determinants of charitable bequests treats estate planning as though it were strictly a deathbed activity. The prospective decedent, in this view, is faced with the choice between leaving all of an estate (after taxes) to living heirs, or leaving most of the estate to living heirs with the remainder going to charity. The government influences this choice with an estate tax that extracts from heirs up to 55 percent of an estate's value.

Although this picture is certainly an accurate description of the choices confronting some individuals late in life, it misses the very attractive giving opportunities that are available in earlier years. As a general matter, charitable donations during lifetime are tax preferred to charitable donations at death, for the simple reason that both are deductible against the estate tax base while only gifts during lifetime are also deductible against ordinary income for the purpose of calculating the personal income tax.

David Joulfaian's study provides a much-needed perspective on estate planning and charitable giving by considering the range of giving options over a lifetime as well as at death. The contribution of this approach is that it permits a test of whether, and to what extent, tax incentives encourage taxpayers to make their charitable contributions early in life. At the same time, his careful examination of the data identifies several striking patterns.

The evidence indicates that estate size and permanent income are strongly correlated. Although this is hardly surprising, it is nonetheless reassuring to see the evidence presented in the chapter. Undoubtedly several forces are at work, and it is worth identifying what they are since they bear on the interpretation of some of the results in the chapter. The first and most obvious effect is that bequests are normal goods; individuals of greater means choose to accumulate larger estates than do individuals of lesser means. The second effect, which is very difficult to distinguish from the first, is that the kind of individual who earns higher income tends (in a cross section) also to be the kind of individual who wants to save to leave a bequest. The third effect is somewhat different: that individuals who decide to save in order to leave bequests also tend to have greater income, for the simple reason that their savings generate capital income. Thus, income and bequests are correlated not only because higher incomes lead to a greater desire to leave bequests, and because higher incomes and larger bequests are correlated owing to unobservables but also because the desire to leave bequests itself generates higher capital income.

The vast majority of the sample (95 percent) contributes to charity, and of this figure, 20 percent does so with charitable bequests. Among lifetime donors, there is an enormous amount of unused charitable deduction because contributions exceed the annual limit of 50 percent of adjusted gross income (AGI). This suggests that taxpayers fail to engage in sufficient tax planning or that they are frequently overcome with philanthropic desire to an extent that exceeds the AGI limit. In spite of their lower frequency, charitable bequests represent much more total charitable giving than does the sum of lifetime contributions. A rather small number of individuals are responsible for most charitable bequests, and of these, almost all gifts go to foundations.

The focus of the chapter is on its estimates of the impact of income and estate tax rates on charitable giving. The results are reassuring to those who have long suspected that the tax treatment of charitable giving influences its magnitude, since higher estate tax rates are associated with greater charitable bequests, while higher income tax rates are associated with greater lifetime contributions. As seems always to be true in the world of tax planning, however, matters are not that straightforward.

Two main issues arise in evaluating the regression estimates. The first one is how to interpret a set of estimated coefficients that includes not only the tax price of giving but also a taxpayer's AGI and the size of the estate. In this setting, the AGI serves not only as an indicator of lifetime income but also as a proxy for the income tax rate, a measure of the limit to annual deductibility, and a reflection of unobserved taxpayer attributes. Its ultimate contribution to the regression, then, is difficult to interpret, and may interact with tax rate variables with which it is correlated.

A second set of issues concerns the source of variation in the estate tax rate. Since all taxpayers face the same estate tax rate schedule, marginal tax rates differ primarily because of the progressivity of the rate schedule, with larger estates subject to higher estate tax rates. The well-known difficulty with using this source of tax rate variation is its endogeneity to the size of an estate, as a result of which ordinary least squares estimates of the impact of tax rates on charitable giving are biased downward. The chapter is sensitive to the econometric issues that this raises, using instrumental variables (as in the results reported in table 8-7) to estimate the impact of tax rates on charitable giving. The instruments in this specification include pre-tax income and the estate tax rate against which the first dollar of charitable bequests is deductible. This specification uses the nonlinearity of the estate tax rate schedule to identify the impact of tax rates on giving, since after-tax wealth is also included as an independent explanatory variable. Given the nature of the sample, there are few realistic alternatives to such a procedure, though it has the unfortunate aspect of identifying the tax effect by way of the assumed form of the contribution function rather than from exclusion restrictions. Put differently, the unrestricted inclusion of several additional powers of wealth on the right side of these regressions would surely change the estimated tax effects, and it is difficult, on the paucity of prior information, to exclude additional powers.

There are two other methods by which tax rate effects are identified in these regressions. The first stems from the location of taxpayers, since decedents live in different places, and American states differ in their taxation of estates. This effect is typically very small, however, since state tax rates are low and are generally absorbed by the adjustment of federal estate tax liabilities. The second source of identification comes from bequests to living spouses. Since interspousal transfers are excluded from taxable estates, it follows that the taxable portion of an estate left mostly to a spouse is taxed at a lower rate than is an equal-sized estate left entirely to heirs other than a spouse. Certain taxpayers fail to take full advantage of the favorable treatment of interspousal transfers, either because they do not have a living spouse or because they prefer their estates to be received by someone other than a spouse. It is then possible to use the variation in interspousal transfers between decedents of the same wealth to identify the effect of tax rates on charitable giving, since greater interspousal gifts generally lead to lower tax rates on the taxable portions of estates. The difficulty with such a procedure, of course, is that it takes interspousal gifts to be exogenously determined. In the plausible case that interspousal transfers and charitable gifts compete for the same funds, greater interspousal transfers are associated with lower estate tax rates and with reduced charitable giving. This association therefore induces an apparent (positive) effect of estate tax rates on charitable giving that is instead simply a reflection of the progressive nature of the estate tax rate schedule.

The chapter reports that charitable bequests are left almost exclusively by the wealthy. As long as wealth is measured as of the time of death, this association is almost automatic, whether or not the underlying behavior is volitional. A decision to bequeath wealth to charity is a decision to accumulate wealth for this purpose and therefore leads to a correlation between wealth and charitable bequests. Wisely invested, this wealth generates annual income and thereby also induces a correlation between income and charitable bequests. Unintended assets at the end of life—which might, for example, reflect excessive frugality or early demise—likewise induce associations between wealth and charitable bequests, since those with many means and few needs find there are many uses for their wealth, charity among them. Although total charitable contributions and bequests no doubt reflect the combined impact of many motivations and circumstances, it is worth at least considering the possibility that what appears to be rational tax planning reflects instead the unintended product of happenstance.

The chapter's concluding comment raises important issues that receive fuller treatment elsewhere. Estate and gift taxation can have a first-order impact on wealth accumulation in the absence of philanthropic motivation, even though accumulated wealth is subsequently given or bequeathed to charity. Understanding the way in which estate and gift taxation influences the generation of income, the accumulation of wealth, and the transmission of wealth across generations is of great importance in determining the ultimate impact of taxation on charitable giving.

References

Advisory Commission on Intergovernmental Relations. *Significant Features of Fiscal Federalism.* Vol. 1. 1992. Washington.

Auten, Gerald, and Robert Carroll. 1999. "The Effect of Income Taxes on Household Income." *Review of Economics and Statistics* 81 (November): 681–93.

Auten, Gerald, and David Joulfaian. 1996. "Charitable Contributions and Intergenerational Transfers." *Journal of Public Economics* 59 (January): 55–68.

Auten, Gerald, Charles Clotfelter, and Holger Sieg. 1999. "Charitable Giving and Income Taxation in a Life-Cycle Model: An Analysis of Panel Data." Working Paper 99-03. Duke University.

Bakjia, Jon. 1999. "Consistent Estimation of Transitory and Permanent Price and Income Elasticities: The Case of Charitable Giving." Williams College. Mimeo.

Barthold, Thomas, and Robert Plotnick. 1984. "Estate Taxation and Other Determinants of Charitable Bequests." *National Tax Journal* 37 (June): 225–37.

Boskin, Michael J. 1976. "Estate Taxation and Charitable Bequests." *Journal of Public Economics* 5 (January-February): 27–56.

Carnegie, Andrew. 1962. "The Advantages of Poverty." In *The Gospel of Wealth and Other Timely Essays*, edited by Edward C. Kirkland, 50–78 (Belknap Press of Harvard University Press).

Carroll, Christopher D. 1997. "Why Do the Rich Save So Much?" OTPR Working Paper 98-12. University of Michigan (December).

Clotfelter, Charles T. 1985. *Federal Tax Policy and Charitable Giving* (University of Chicago Press).

Commerce Clearinghouse. 2000. *U.S. Master Tax Guide*. Chicago.

Feldstein, Martin. 1995. "The Effect of Marginal Tax Rates on Taxable Income: A Panel Study of the 1986 Tax Reform Act." *Journal of Political Economy* 103 (June): 551–72.

Feldstein, Martin, and Charles T. Clotfelter. 1976. "Tax Incentives and Charitable Contributions in the United States." *Journal of Public Economics* 5 (January–February): 1–26.

Giving USA. 1999. *AAFRC Trust for Philanthropy*.

Joulfaian, David. 1991. "Charitable Bequests and Estate Taxes." *National Tax Journal* 44 (June): 169–80.

————. 1998. "The Federal Estate and Gift Tax: Description, Taxpayer Profile, and Economic Consequences." OTA Paper 80. Department of the Treasury.

————. 1999. "The Pattern of Charitable Bequests and the Influence of Estate Taxation." *Proceedings of the 1999 Annual Meeting of the National Tax Association.* Atlanta.

————. 2000a. "Estate Taxes and Charitable Bequests by the Wealthy." Working Paper 7663. Cambridge, Mass.: National Bureau of Economic Research (April).

————. 2000b. "A Quarter Century of Estate Tax Reforms." *National Tax Journal* (September): 743–63.

————. 2000c. "Choosing between Gifts and Bequests: How Taxes Affect the Timing of Wealth Transfers." OTA Paper 86. Department of the Treasury (May).

McNees, Stephen. 1973. "Deductibility of Charitable Bequests." *National Tax Journal* 26 (March): 79–98.

Randolph, William C. 1995. "Dynamic Income, Progressive Taxes, and the Timing of Charitable Contributions." *Journal of Political Economy* 103 (August): 709–38.

Rivers, Douglas, and Quang Vuong. 1988. "Limited Information Estimators and Exogeneity Tests for Simultaneous Probit Models." *Journal of Econometrics* 39 (November): 347–66.

Steuerle, Eugene. 1985. "Wealth, Realized Income, and the Measure of Well-Being." In *Horizontal Equity, Uncertainty, and Economic Well-Being,* edited by Martin David and Timothy Smeeding, 91–117. University of Chicago Press.

————. 1987. "Charitable Giving Patterns of the Wealthy." In *America's Wealthy and the Future of Foundations,* edited by Teresa Odendahl, 203–22. New York: Foundation Center.

U.S. Congress. 1997. 1998. *General Explanation of Tax Legislation Enacted.* Government Printing Office.

Wu, De-Min. 1973. "Alternative Tests of Independence between Stochastic Regressors and Disturbances." *Econometrica* 41 (July): 733–50.

MARTHA BRITTON ELLER
BRIAN ERARD
CHIH-CHIN HO

9 | *Noncompliance with the Federal Estate Tax*

T HE FEDERAL ESTATE tax is levied on the fortunes of America's wealthiest decedents. With average tax burdens in the hundreds of thousands of dollars and marginal rates as high as 60 percent, the tax creates powerful incentives for legal avoidance and evasion. In this chapter, we provide an empirical analysis of the magnitude and determinants of noncompliance with the federal estate tax.[1]

Unique Features of Estate Taxation

Most of the literature on tax compliance is based on the income tax.[2] The estate tax, however, has several unique features that potentially affect compliance and enforcement. First and foremost, the individual who may have known the most about the estate (the decedent) is not available to assist with

We are grateful to Jim Poterba and Edward Wolff for discussing details of their SCF simulations with us. We also thank Barry Johnson for many useful comments.

1. Our analysis is focused on federal estate tax noncompliance. For an analysis of noncompliance with the federal gift tax, refer to Feinstein and Ho (1999). Although the maximum statutory rate is 55 percent, the effective marginal rate can reach 60 percent as a result of a phase-out of the unified estate and gift tax credit for large estates.

2. See Andreoni, Erard, and Feinstein (1997) for a review of this literature.

the return's preparation. Second, the tax is narrowly focused on a small number of very wealthy estates, which are potentially subject to very high marginal rates. Third, valuation of assets is much more important in estate taxation than in income taxation, and many assets in an estate can be difficult to properly value. Fourth, while a substantial portion of the income tax base is subject to information reporting, withholding, and document matching, relatively little of the estate tax base is covered by these forms of independent verification.[3] Together, these features of the estate tax will magnify compliance and enforcement problems. It is important to recognize, however, that legal strategies for the avoidance of the estate tax abound, providing an alternative to outright evasion. Thus one might expect legitimate tax planning activities to reduce tax compliance problems.[4] Finally, the estate tax return is financially relevant to a potentially large number of beneficiaries. Noncompliance may therefore require some collusion among several individuals.[5] Similar strategic interactions may be present in other compliance settings. For example, married couples may negotiate over what to report on their joint income tax return.[6] Similarly, evasion of the value-added tax may require collusion among a chain of buyers and sellers. In our empirical analysis, we investigate whether the number of beneficiaries is related to the frequency and magnitude of audit assessments.

Simulations of Overall Estate Tax Noncompliance

As part of his commentary on an estate taxation article by another author, Edward N. Wolff reports on a simulation of estate tax liability he performed using the 1992 Survey of Consumer Finance (SCF).[7] His results indicate a very large gap between simulated estate tax collections ($44.5 billion) and actual 1993 collections ($10.3 billion), which he interprets as evidence of substantial

---

3. Also observe that unlike income taxes, which are filed annually in the United States, estate tax returns are filed only upon the death of an individual, so the IRS has relatively little history about the characteristics of the decedent's estate (although it may have some information about decedents who outlived their spouses.) However, the probate process may help verify wealth.

4. Of course, there are many gray areas in estate taxation that some tax planning strategies may attempt to exploit. In some cases, such strategies might exacerbate rather than lessen compliance problems.

5. We thank Joel Slemrod for raising this point.

6. Indeed, it is plausible that some married couples file separate returns precisely because they cannot agree on what to report.

7. Wolff (1996).

noncompliance. James Poterba performs a different set of simulations using the 1995 SCF, obtaining a much closer correspondence between simulated and actual collections. Using his preferred simulation based on the annuitant life table, he reports estimated collections of $15.7 billion.[8] This is within 10 percent of the $14.3 billion in taxes reported on returns for 1995 decedents.[9] In the following pages, we attempt to reconcile these conflicting results and assess the likely extent of aggregate estate tax noncompliance.

Simulation Methodologies

The simulation methodologies employed by the two authors are similar. Each begins by assigning mortality probabilities to individuals in the SCF on the basis of age, gender, and (in Wolff) race. The estate tax that would be due (if any) in the event of an individual's death is then computed by applying the appropriate tax rate schedule to a measure of the taxable estate. For each individual, the computed estate tax liability is weighted by the mortality probability, and the results are aggregated to simulate expected total estate tax receipts.

Although Wolff and Poterba employ similar approaches, the details of the simulations carried out differ in several important respects. First, Wolff relies on a mortality table for the general population.[10] One difficulty with this table is that mortality rates are not provided for ages above 80, between 66 and 69, between 71 and 74, and between 76 and 79. To fill in probabilities for these ages, he performs a straight line interpolation (extrapolation for ages above 80), using the probabilities for the nearest available ages. In his preferred approach, Poterba employs a very different mortality table (the annuitant life table), which is designed for individuals who purchase single-premium annuities from life insurance companies.[11] Since such individuals tend to be quite wealthy, Poterba argues that the annuitant life table may provide a more appropriate set of mortality rates for households with high net worth. The mortality rates for wealthy individuals are uniformly lower than the corresponding rates for the general population; therefore, the use of the annuitant life table will tend to generate lower estimates

---

8. Poterba (1997).

9. The figures in this chapter for 1995 decedents are from Johnson and Mikow (1999).

10. The table is provided in Bureau of the Census (1995).

11. This table is described in Mitchell, Poterba, and Warshawsky (1997). We thank Jim Poterba for giving us copies of the 1983 and 2000 versions of the table, from which we interpolated mortality probabilities for 1995.

of the number of taxable estates and expected estate tax receipts than an ordinary life table. Poterba also performs an alternative simulation using the population life table produced by the Social Security Administration Office of the Actuary. This latter table is similar to the one employed by Wolff and has the advantage that separate mortality probabilities are available for all ages.

A second difference between the simulations of Wolff and Poterba concerns the treatment of married individuals. Wolff applies separate mortality probabilities for each spouse and computes the tax that would be due in the event of either spouse's death on the basis of household wealth. In computing the tax, he allows a deduction equal to the average spousal bequest reported on estate returns for the household's total gross estate class. Poterba employs an alternative treatment of married individuals that results in fewer taxable returns and less aggregate tax liability. Effectively, he assumes that a married decedent would leave a sufficient bequest to his or her spouse to eliminate any estate tax liability. Thus, he only applies an estate tax in his simulations in the relatively unusual case that both spouses die in the same year. In that event, tax liability is computed on the basis of household wealth, with no adjustment for a spousal bequest.

The authors also apply somewhat different deductions and credits in their calculation of tax. Wolff allows a deduction for charitable bequests, based on the average donation on returns in the decedent's total gross estate class. Poterba allows a similar deduction; however, he also makes certain other allowances that further reduce aggregate tax liability. In particular, he accounts for a state death tax credit and a deduction for funeral expenses, in both cases relying on average return values for the decedent's total gross estate class.

Finally, the authors rely on surveys from different years: 1992 for Wolff and 1995 for Poterba.

Replication Exercises

We begin by attempting to replicate the results of the two authors. Table 9-1 compares the results of our replication exercise for the Wolff study with Wolff's original results. We obtain a fairly similar number of taxable returns but a much lower aggregate tax liability. We believe the major reason for the tax liability discrepancy is that Wolff employed a reweighted version of the SCF, whereas we employed the standard public-use version; Poterba observes that the weights employed by Wolff produce a larger wealth stock than the public-use weights, particularly among households

Table 9-1. *Replication of Wolff's Simulation of Taxable Estate Tax Returns and Aggregate Liability*

	Number of taxable returns (thousands)		Total estate collections (billions of dollars)	
Size of gross estate	Wolff	Replication	Wolff	Replication
$600,000–$999,999	13.0	9.3	0.6	0.5
$1,000,000–$2,499,999	24.9	26.0	5.3	4.7
$2,500,000–$4,999,999	12.5	9.4	15.3	5.7
$5,000,000–$9,999,999	3.5	2.9	7.9	3.1
$10,000,000–$19,999,999	1.7	1.0	8.5	2.7
$20,000,000 and over	0.6	0.2	6.9	4.6
Total	56.2	48.7	44.5	21.4

Source: Authors' calculations based on Wolff (1996). Underlying data are from the 1992 Survey of Consumer Finances (SCF).

with high net worth.[12] Nonetheless, our simulated aggregate tax liability ($21.4 billion) is still more than twice as large as the amount reported on estate tax returns in 1993 ($10.3 billion), and the simulated number of taxable returns is about 50 percent larger than the number of taxable returns filed in 1993.

In table 9-2, we compare the results of our replication exercise for the Poterba study with Poterba's original results. Our simulation using the annuitant life table produces an estimate of $16.9 billion in aggregate estate taxes, which is fairly close to Poterba's original estimate of $15.7 billion.[13] Our estimates also show a consistent distribution of estate tax liabilities by age category. Estate tax returns filed for 1995 decedents voluntarily reported $14.3 billion in taxes, which is within 10 percent of the amount originally estimated by Poterba. This seems to indicate that compliance problems with the estate tax are relatively modest.

12. The difference also may partly reflect somewhat different approaches to carrying out the necessary extrapolation of mortality probabilities beyond age 80 from the mortality table; however, we have found that raising the mortality probabilities for the upper age groups tends to increase estimated aggregate tax liability primarily by dramatically increasing the estimated number of taxable returns. Poterba (1997, p. 19).

13. The generation of 1995 mortality probabilities requires an interpolation of the 1983 and 2000 versions of the annuitant life table. We suspect that our interpolation methodology may have differed slightly from the one employed by Poterba. We also observe that we worked with a more recent version of the 1995 SCF in our analysis and that the sample weights have been updated from those originally used by Poterba.

Table 9-2. *Replication of Poterba's Simulations*
Billions of dollars

| | Total estate collections | | | |
| | Annuitant mortality table | | Population life table | |
Age of decedent	Poterba	Replication	Poterba	Replication
Less than 50	0.2	0.3	0.4	0.6
50–59	0.5	0.8	0.9	1.2
60–69	1.5	1.6	2.8	2.8
70–79	3.3	3.4	5.1	5.0
80 and over	10.2	10.8	13.8	14.1
Total	15.7	16.9	23.0	23.8

Source: Authors' calculations based on Poterba (1997). Underlying data are from the 1995 SCF.

Table 9-2 also compares the results of our simulation based on the 1995 SCF using the population life table with Poterba's original simulation. In this case, our results show an even closer match with his earlier estimates ($23.8 billion in aggregate estate tax liability compared with Poterba's original estimate of $23 billion). Based on these results, the problem with estate tax compliance seems much more severe. As first observed by Poterba, the choice of mortality table has a profound effect on the magnitude of simulated estate tax liability.

Looking Behind the Simulations

Although the choice of mortality table partly explains the divergence between Wolff's simulation results and those of Poterba, it is not the entire story. Observe that our simulation based on Poterba's methodology with the population life table yields an estimated aggregate tax liability of $23.8 billion for 1995 decedents, which is approximately 66 percent larger than actual voluntary estate tax collections for that year's decedents. In contrast, our application of Wolff's methodology to the 1992 SCF yields an estimated aggregate tax liability of $21.4 billion, which is more than twice as large as actual voluntary estate tax collections in 1993. Given that the life table used by Wolff is rather similar to the population life table, what causes the much more substantial gap between simulated and actual tax collections under Wolff's methodology? The divergence in results is largely because of differing treatments of married individuals by the two authors. Since Poterba imposes a tax on married households in his simulations only in the event that both spouses die within the same year, relatively few married decedents' estates are found taxable. The total simulated tax liability for married decedents is only $1.1 billion, or less than half the reported liability of $2.5 billion on estate returns for married 1995 decedents. When the annuitant mortality table is employed, taxes for married decedents are even more greatly understated. Our replication of Poterba's analysis using this table yields an aggregate tax liability for married decedents of only $550 million. The assumption that no estate tax liability is incurred when a decedent is survived by his spouse would be appropriate if married decedents always passed the vast majority of their estate on to their spouses as a marital bequest. In fact, however, several reasons why such a practice might not be followed come to mind. First, from the perspective of tax planning, it may make good sense to spread some of the estate tax liability to the first decedent's estate rather than to have all of the household's wealth subject to taxation when his or her spouse passes on. Given the graduated rate structure, such a strategy might result in a significant reduction in total estate tax liability, depending on the longevity of the decedent's spouse. Second, an individual may be concerned that his or her spouse may not share the same wishes for how the estate should be divided upon the spouse's subsequent death. Finally, if the spouse is not the decedent's first husband or wife, (s)he may prefer to bequeath a substantial portion of the estate to members of his or her first family.

As discussed previously, Wolff employs a different approach to simulating estate tax liability for married individuals. He applies the estate tax to the household's entire estate (less an allowance for a spousal bequest) whenever either spouse dies. He therefore obtains a much larger number of taxable estates for married decedents and simulates a much higher aggregate tax liability for them. In our replication of Wolff's simulation analysis, married decedents account for 60 percent of all taxable returns and 47 percent of aggregate total tax liability. Among estate tax returns filed in 1992, however, married decedents accounted only for 16 percent of all taxable returns and 23 percent of aggregate total tax liability.

Thus, while Poterba's methodology tends to understate the estate tax bill for married decedents, Wolff's methodology tends to substantially overstate it. It is very difficult to properly simulate potential estate tax liability for married decedents, because it is not clear what proportion of total household net worth should be assigned to the estate in the event that one of the spouses dies. It therefore seems reasonable to focus simulation efforts on unmarried individuals, whose estate tax situation is somewhat more straightforward to model.

On the surface, at least, it seems appealing to apply the annuitant mortality table to unmarried individuals in the SCF, because this table is designed to account for the mortality risk of wealthy individuals. However, our simulation based on Poterba's methodology with this table yields only 23,638 taxable estates for unmarried decedents. In contrast, 31,383 taxable returns were actually filed for unmarried 1995 decedents, or about one-third more than the simulations predicted. Moreover, this substantial understatement problem would be greatly exacerbated if we were to account for the fact that unmarried decedents within any given gross estate class tend to have much larger charitable bequests and state death tax credits than their married counterparts. In contrast, our simulation based on Poterba's methodology using the population life table (rather than the annuitant mortality table) seems more reasonable. It yields 33,655 taxable returns for unmarried decedents, or about 7 percent more than the actual number filed.

The above findings raise an important question. If the annuitant mortality table better reflects the mortality risk for wealthy individuals, why does its use result in such a dramatic understatement of the number of taxable returns even among unmarried decedents? A major part of the answer is found by considering the interaction between marital status and mortality. Although it is true that wealthy individuals tend to have a lower mortality risk than others in a given age group, it is equally true that unmarried individuals tend to have a higher mortality risk than married individuals of the same age. For example, Donna L. Hoyert, Kenneth D. Kochanek, and Sherry L. Murphy report that married individuals 75 and over have an annual mortality rate of 6,165 deaths per 100,000, compared with the much higher rates of 8,653, 9,497, and 10,685 per 100,000 for divorced, widowed, and never-married individuals in this age group, respectively.[14] This same pattern of significantly lower death rates among married individuals is observed across age, gender, and racial groups. Thus, the effects of wealth and marital status on mortality rates appear to be offsetting for unmarried individuals, raising the possibility that the population life table is better suited for simulating estate tax liabilities—at least among the unmarried population.[15] This same reasoning may help to explain why our simulation based on Wolff's methodology yields far too many taxable estates for married decedents. We suspect that the life table used by Wolff assigns too high a mortality probability to married individuals in the SCF, because it accounts neither for marital

14. Hoyert, Kochanek, and Murphy (1999, p. 78, table 22).
15. Ideally, one would want to employ a mortality table that accounted for wealth, marital status, and age. See Feinstein and Ho (2000) for an empirical analysis of mortality probabilities for individuals over 70 years of age that accounts for both marital status and wealth.

Table 9-3. *Simulation for Unmarried Individuals Based on Population Life Table*

Size of gross estate	Number of taxable returns (thousands)		Total estate collections (billions of dollars)	
	Simulation	Actual	Simulation	Actual
$600,000–$999,999	12.0	15.0	0.5	0.8
$1,000,000–$2,499,999	6.4	12.6	1.6	3.1
$2,500,000–$4,999,999	2.6	2.6	3.0	2.6
$5,000,000–$9,999,999	1.5	0.79	3.5	1.8
$10,000,000–$19,999,999	0.56	0.27	3.6	1.2
$20,000,000 and over	0.06	0.15	1.2	2.3
Total	23.3	31.3	13.4	11.8

Source: Authors' calculations based on the methodology of Poterba (1997) and using data from the 1995 SCF. See text for details.

status nor wealth, which both work to reduce the mortality risk for married individuals.[16]

In table 9-3, we attempt to simulate the number of taxable returns and aggregate tax liability for unmarried decedents by applying the population life table to the 1995 SCF. In this simulation, we employ Poterba's methodology, except that we allow charitable bequest deductions and state death tax credits based on the much larger average figures for unmarried decedents within the individual's total gross estate class. Our simulation rather substantially understates the number of taxable returns with gross estate values under $2.5 million, apparently because of the assignment of average deduction (and credit) figures to all unmarried households. Particularly among the lower gross estate categories, deductions for charitable bequests are highly concentrated among a relatively small number of returns. For example, only 23.8 percent of returns for unmarried 1995 decedents in the $600,000 to $1 million class claimed a charitable bequest deduction. Given the $600,000 threshold for the application of the estate tax in 1995 and the graduated rate structure of the tax, the methodology for assigning deductions and credits is crucial in the analysis.[17]

16. A second reason for the overestimate of the number of taxable married decedents is his apparent assignment of all household wealth to the estate of a married decedent with a surviving spouse. Often, a nontrivial share of the household assets are not attributable to the decedent's estate.

17. The unified credit in 1995 completely offset the tax that would be due on a taxable estate valued at $600,000 or less.

Table 9-4. *Simulation for Unmarried Individuals Based on
Population Life Table: Alternative Treatment of Charitable Deductions*

Size of gross estate	Number of taxable returns (thousands)		Total estate collections (billions of dollars)	
	Simulation	Actual	Simulation	Actual
$600,000–$999,999	15.3	15.0	0.8	0.8
$1,000,000–$2,499,999	9.4	12.6	2.4	3.1
$2,500,000–$4,999,999	3.7	2.6	4.8	2.6
$5,000,000–$9,999,999	2.2	0.79	5.0	1.8
$10,000,000–$19,999,999	0.86	0.27	3.8	1.2
$20,000,000 and over	0.16	0.15	2.6	2.3
Total	31.6	31.3	20.1	11.8

Source: See table 9-3.

As an illustration, we repeat our simulation with an alternative assign-ment scheme for charitable bequest deductions. We begin by computing the average deduction among unmarried 1995 decedent returns actually claim-ing a charitable bequest deduction within each gross estate category. We then randomly assign the average deduction to a subset of all unmarried in-dividuals within the relevant gross estate category of the 1995 SCF. The probability that a given return within a gross estate category will receive the deduction is set equal to the percentage of 1995 unmarried decedent returns within that category that actually claimed a charitable bequest deduction. Thus, whereas our original simulation assigned the same deduction to all in-dividuals within a gross estate category, our new simulation assigns some in-dividuals no deduction and others a very large deduction. The results of our new simulation are presented in table 9-4. The estimated number of taxable returns in the lower gross estate classes is now much higher, and the esti-mated overall number of taxable returns is now slightly larger than the num-ber of taxable returns actually filed for unmarried 1995 decedents. However, the gap between the simulated and actual aggregate tax liability has increased from 13.6 percent under the previous simulation to more than 70 percent under the current simulation.

It is clear from the above analysis that the results of SCF simulations, even for unmarried individuals, are sensitive to the method one employs to assign key deductions and credits. At a minimum, it seems that a very careful set of imputations would need to be performed before one attempts to draw any firm conclusions about estate tax compliance from the SCF.

Evidence from the Estate Postaudit Study

Given the difficulties associated with measuring aggregate estate tax under-reporting using the SCF, is there an alternative way to address this question? One approach is to rely on operational estate tax audit data. Brian Erard performed an analysis of estate tax underreporting based on a preliminary version of the data we use in our current study of the determinants of estate tax noncompliance. His model is similar in structure to the specification laid out later in this chapter.[18] The model accounts for the likelihood of an audit as well as the probability and magnitude of an audit assessment. In contrast to our current study, however, all regressors are based on the information originally reported on the estate tax return, not the corrected amount determined during examination.[19] The parameter estimates of the model are used to predict for each unaudited return the expected magnitude of noncompliance; for audited returns, the actual audit assessment measures noncompliance. Aggregating over all returns, Erard estimates that the reporting tax gap—the difference between estate taxes owed and estate taxes voluntarily reported—is $1.5 billion dollars (or approximately 13 percent of aggregate estate tax liability) on calendar year 1992 returns.[20] This figure likely understates the true tax gap, both because the audit assessment figures reflect the amount actually assessed the taxpayer after any appeals or litigation and because the estimates do not account for any noncompliance that the IRS examiner was unable to detect. To put this figure into perspective, the estimated underreporting gap by the IRS for tax year 1992 individual income tax returns amounted to approximately $72 billion dollars, or about the same percentage of true tax liability (13 percent) found for estate tax returns. However, the latter estimate is based on the examiner-recommended assessments from very comprehensive audits (not the potentially smaller amount the case was settled for after any appeals or litigation), and it incorporates a rather substantial adjustment for undetected noncompliance. Thus, it seems likely that estate tax noncompliance is at least somewhat larger in percentage terms than individual income tax noncompliance.

---

18. See Erard (1999). The main difference is that a measure of the likelihood of an audit does not enter as a regressor in the equations describing noncompliance.

19. Since the postaudit corrected figures used in the current analysis are only available for examined returns, regressors based on such figures could not be used to simulate noncompliance on unaudited returns.

20. Erard (1999, p. 1).

Data Description

The data used in our econometric analysis were derived from the 1992 Estate Post-Audit Study conducted by the Statistics of Income (SOI) division of the IRS. The SOI initiated this study to examine the extent to which accounting for audit revaluations modifies preaudit estimates of the characteristics of the population filing federal estate tax returns. The federal estate tax returns included in the study represent a stratified random sample from the overall population of returns filed in 1992. Among other objectives, the strata were designed to heavily oversample returns that were likely to have been audited. The SOI has developed sample weights that make the sample of approximately 4,200 returns broadly representative of the overall 1992 population submitting federal estate tax returns.[21] The sample includes detailed line item information from the return. An indicator is included with the data that identifies whether a return was audited. Supplementary information is available for audited returns on the overall magnitude of the eventual audit assessment as well as specific line item changes that resulted from the examination. The assessment amount represents the final value of the assessment after the case was closed, subsequent to any appeals or litigation.[22] Tax examinations entail a complex and sometimes lengthy negotiation between the IRS tax examiner and the estate, as represented by a fiduciary, usually an attorney. The audit assessment data employed in our analysis therefore represent the outcome of a negotiation between two parties, each with his own agenda and legal constraints. Even after a tentative agreement is reached between the parties, the appellate court system may be called upon by the estate to impose a final decision. We employ the audit assessment as a measure of "noncompliance." However, it is perhaps better thought of as an imperfect indicator of the degree of noncompliance with the estate tax laws rather than a precise dollar estimate. For the subsample of returns in our data file with total gross estates exceeding $5 million, we have matched information on the number of beneficiaries listed on the estate tax return. As discussed later, we perform a separate analysis on this subsample of returns that includes dummies for the number of beneficiaries as additional regressors in the audit and compliance equations of our model.

Below, we describe some of the most salient characteristics of estate tax auditing and compliance using summary tables and figures based on our data.

21. For a more detailed description of the estate postaudit study, refer to Eller and Johnson (2000).

22. In a very few cases, the assessment figures were based on figures generated before the appeals process was completed.

Table 9-5. *Returns Audited, by Size of Total Gross Estate, 1992*

Total gross estate	Returns filed	Returns audited	Percent audited
Under $1 million	31,376	3,475	11.1
$1 million up to $5 million	25,542	6,760	26.5
$5 million or more	2,260	1,098	48.6
Total	59,178	11,338	19.2

Source: This and all subsequent tables report authors' calculations based on data from the 1992 Estate Post-Audit Study of the Internal Revenue Service's Statistics of Income Division. See text for details. See Eller and Johnson (2000, figure 2).

The sample weights are employed to make the results broadly representative of the overall 1992 population filing estate tax returns. Table 9-5 summarizes estate tax auditing by size of total gross estate. The IRS estate tax examiners audited an estimated 11,338 federal estate tax returns filed in 1992, representing 19.2 percent of the 59,178 returns filed in that year. However, the audit rate for returns varied substantially by size of the reported gross estate. As one might expect, returns filed for very large gross estates had a relatively high rate of audit coverage. In fact, nearly half of all returns with gross assets exceeding $5 million were examined, compared with only 11 percent of returns with assets under $1 million.

As a whole, audits have only a fairly minor impact on total estate tax revenue. Aggregate net estate tax liability for filing year 1992 increased by $560 million (see table 9-6) as a result of examinations, or by about 5.5 percent. The preaudit value of total gross estate, $100.0 billion, increased by only 1.2 percent, creating a postaudit value of total gross estate that just exceeded $101.2 billion. And, in a somewhat unexpected result, total allowable deductions, available against gross estate, also increased as a result of operational audits. The preaudit value of total allowable deductions, $43.5 billion, increased by 0.2 percent, or $117.0 million, to $43.6 billion.

While the overall net estate tax liability for filing year 1992 increased as a result of audit, and while the majority of audits were closed with additional tax owed, a nontrivial share of examinations closed with a reduction in net estate tax liability. A surprisingly low percentage of returns, only 60.1 percent, were closed with additional tax assessed, while 21.0 percent were closed with a tax reduction, and 18.9 percent were closed with no change in original net estate tax (figure 9-1).[23]

23. Eller and Johnson (2000, p. 3).

Table 9-6. *Change in Value of Total Gross Estate, Allowable Deductions, and Net Tax as a Result of Audit, 1992*

Millions of dollars, except as indicated

Item	Total gross estate	Total allowable deductions	Net estate tax
Preaudit value	100,017	43,530	10,199
Audit revaluation	1,222	117	560
Percent change due to audit	1.2	0.2	5.5
Postaudit value	101,239	43,647	10,759

Source: Based on Eller and Johnson (2000, figure 3), available at http//www.irs.gov/tax_stats/soi/est_etr.html (December 2000).

Figure 9-1. *Change in Assessment for Audited Estate Tax Returns, 1992*

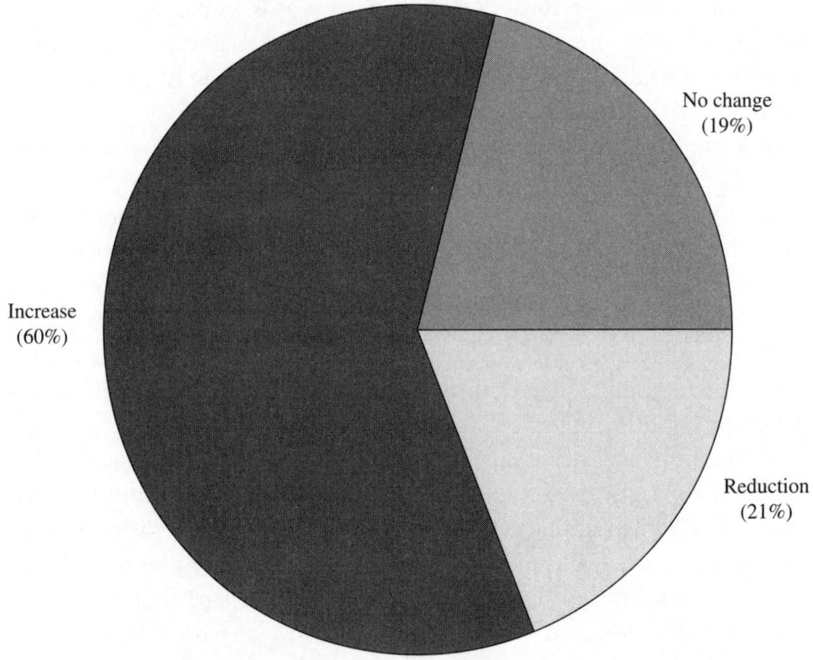

No change (19%)

Increase (60%)

Reduction (21%)

Source: This and all subsequent figures represent authors' calculations based on data from the 1992 Estate Post-Audit Study of the Internal Revenue Service's Statistics of Income Division. See text for details. See Eller and Johnson (2000, figure 4), available at http://www.irs.gov/tax_stats/soi/est_etr.html (December 2000).

Table 9-7. *Amount of Additional Tax Owed and Tax Reductions,*
by Assessment Change and Total Gross Estate, 1992

Dollars, except as indicated

Assessment change and total gross estate	Number of audited returns	Aggregate additional tax (reduction)	Average additional tax (reduction)
All			
All	11,338	559,774,617	49,372
Under $1 million	3,475	45,974,200	13,230
$1 million up to $5 million	6,760	250,667,364	37,081
$5 million or more	1,098	263,133,054	239,648
Additional tax			
All	6,807	676,564,145	99,392
Under $1 million	2,172	50,436,806	23,221
$1 million up to $5 million	3,985	311,026,677	78,049
$5 million or more	650	315,100,662	484,770
Tax reduction			
All	2,384	(116,789,520)	(48,989)
Under $1 million	439	(4,462,600)	(10,165)
$1 million up to $5 million	1,722	(60,359,312)	(35,052)
$5 million or more	224	(51,967,608)	(231,998)

Table 9-7 shows that estates with a positive audit assessment were charged $676.6 million in additional taxes, or $99,392 on average per return. Estates with a negative audit assessment received an aggregate rebate of more than $116.8 million, or $48,989 on average per return.

Estate tax attorneys nationwide, interviewed by SOI economists in response to postaudit findings, suggest that the surprisingly high percentage of returns closed with a reduction in tax liability may be explained by several factors. For instance, during the course of the audit, a property included in gross estate may be sold at a price less than its original, reported value. The possibility of an overstated basis points to an inherent difficulty in asset valuation. In some cases, the examination process generates a reduction in estate tax liability. This can occur, for example, because the fees charged by executors and attorneys to deal with an audit are deductible against the estate. Also, sometimes when an examination is initiated, an estate's fiduciary will elect to shift certain deductible expenses from the federal income tax return for trusts and estates to the federal estate tax return, because the marginal rates are

Figure 9-2. *Filing and Audited Populations for Estate Tax Returns,*
by Sex, 1992

Percent

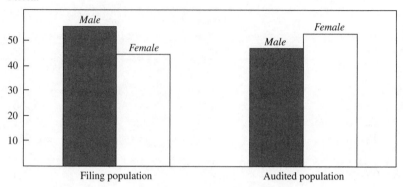

Filing population   Audited population

higher on the latter. Such a shift increases the value of total allowable deductions on the estate return, thereby reducing the value of the taxable estate.

Although estate tax examiners suggest that the size of gross estate does not
necessarily indicate a return's potential for additional tax, estate postaudit data
reveal that, on average, returns with total gross estate in excess of $5 million
yield about $240,000 in additional tax per return. Returns with smaller gross
estates yield, on average, far less in additional net tax revenue. Estates with
less than $1 million in gross estate owed an average of $13,230 in additional
tax, while estates between $1 million and $5 million owed an average of
$37,081 (table 9-7).

The gender composition of the 1992 audited population differs markedly
from the composition of the 1992 estate tax filing population as a whole.
Although the filing population is composed of 55.5 percent male decedents
and 44.5 percent female decedents, the audited population is characterized
by a female majority, with 52.9 percent female decedents and only 47.1 percent male decedents (figure 9-2). The overriding presence of widowed decedents, most often female, in the audited population explains the prevalence
of females and is a result of an audit selection process that favors nonmarried
decedents.[24]

Married decedents constitute the largest percentage of returns in the filing
population, with 46.6 percent of all decedents married at death, while the second largest marital status category is widowed decedents, with 40.6 percent

24. Eller and Johnson (2000, figure 4).

Figure 9-3. *Filing and Audited Populations for Estate Tax Returns, by Marital Status, 1992*

Percent

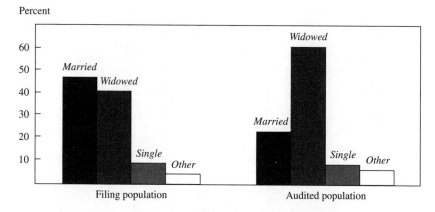

of all decedents widowed at death (figure 9-3). However, the audited population is overwhelmingly composed of widowed decedents. An estimated 61.2 percent of all decedents in the audited population are widowed, while only 23.1 percent are married.[25]

These figures reflect an intended bias in the audit selection process. For much of the recent past, according to IRS estate tax attorneys, examiners were discouraged from auditing the estates of married decedents, since those estates could use the marital deduction to transfer unlimited properties to the surviving spouses. The potential for additional tax on first estates was considered negligible, and, further, the estates of both spouses could be examined following the death of the second spouse. However, the evidence suggests that the estates of decedents with surviving spouses may very well owe additional net estate tax as a result of an audit, despite the availability of a marital deduction that can be used to "soak-up" any increase in total gross assets. About half of all such estates in the audited population were assessed additional tax (figure 9-4). While estates for decedents with no surviving spouse were certainly more likely to receive an additional tax assessment (about 63.0 percent of returns in this category were assessed more taxes), the difference between the two groups is less than what might be expected.

Several explanations are possible for the relatively large percentage of married decedents whose estates owed additional tax, according to IRS attorneys. First, as noted previously, some wealthy married couples arrange their

25. Eller and Johnson (2000, figure 5).

Figure 9-4. *Change in Assessment for Audited Estate Tax Returns, by Marital Status, 1992*

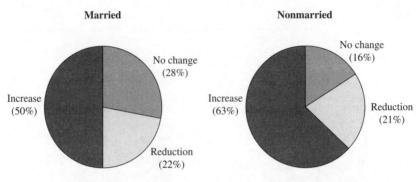

wills so that taxes are paid on both spouses' estates, thereby achieving potentially lower marginal rates. Second, the attorneys point to the increasing occurrence of second marriages. Because individuals may not leave their entire estates to second spouses and second families, it is likely that the spousal bequest in such cases will not be fully utilized to offset additional taxable wealth discovered during an audit. Finally, the marital deduction or the value of qualified terminable interest property for which the marital deduction is available, is sometimes incorrectly calculated on returns as originally filed. Such a miscalculation also can lead to additional estate tax liability.

Examination results vary by asset category. Table 9-8 indicates that real estate other than a personal residence, closely held stock, and cash are the most frequently revalued assets during an audit; the rate of adjustment for each is well in excess of 30 percent. The lowest adjustment rates are observed for annuities (6 percent), insurance (8.5 percent), unclassified mutual funds (10.4 percent), and bonds (11.6 percent). Table 9-8 also displays the average change per revalued return for different assets (computed as the average change in the asset value among returns receiving a revaluation of that asset). By this measure, mortgages and notes ($500,796), closely held stock ($387,034), depletables and intangibles ($193,577), and farm assets ($191,611) had the largest adjustments. At the other end of the spectrum, unclassified mutual funds were actually revalued downward on average. When revaluations are measured as a percentage of the amount originally reported on revalued returns, mortgages and notes (170.2 percent) and insurance (116.9 percent) show by far the largest percent changes. The mortgages and notes category includes proceeds from lawsuits, which, according to estate tax attorneys, are often understated on the original estate tax return.

Table 9-8. *Asset Revaluations for Audited Returns, by Asset Type, 1992*

	Audited returns			Change in asset value		
Asset type	Number	Aggregate value (dollars)	Percent with asset revaluation	Aggregate (dollars)	Average per revalued return (dollars)	Percent of revalued assets
Personal residence	6,251	1,717,199,287	15.9	13,720,129	13,789	4.5
Other real estate	7,611	4,335,051,498	38.0	140,142,057	48,509	9.4
Closely held stock	2,234	4,155,033,484	37.0	319,689,764	387,034	28.8
Other stock	8,879	8,687,221,836	21.8	113,406,228	58,487	5.4
Bonds	8,295	6,301,791,305	11.6	28,991,250	30,168	17.2
Unclassified mutual funds	2,242	301,332,782	10.4	-4,362,642	-18,724	-3.6
Cash	11,234	3,717,282,372	34.0	77,693,621	20,371	26.9
Insurance	5,569	568,572,557	8.5	41,170,651	86,675	116.9
Farm assets	1,042	102,287,640	22.9	45,794,993	191,611	39.5
Limited partnerships	1,498	520,072,214	14.0	19,733,013	94,416	33.0
Other noncorporate business assets	1,943	696,284,538	16.7	48,536,881	149,344	44.5
Mortgages and notes	4,219	931,794,868	12.7	268,927,346	500,796	170.2
Annuities	3,421	773,034,691	6.0	3,241,130	15,810	6.6
Depletables or intangibles	1,160	156,666,051	14.1	31,746,604	193,577	49.0
Art	425	663,691,995	23.3	1,464,218	14,790	3.3

Source: Information based on Eller and Johnson (2000, figure 7).

Several types of life insurance transfers must be reported in the decedent's gross estate, including revocable transfers and transfers with retained life interests. Estate tax attorneys indicate that these items are sometimes erroneously excluded from reported estate values.[26]

Econometric Methodology

In this section, we develop an econometric model for analyzing the determinants of estate tax noncompliance with ordinary operational audit data. Although one typically expects an examination to result in an additional tax assessment or no additional assessment, a nontrivial percentage of estate tax examinations lead to a reduction in assessed tax liability. We therefore develop a framework that allows for all three possible outcomes. Further, since audits are targeted toward returns deemed likely to have compliance problems, it is important to control for the role of audit selection in observed compliance outcomes. We therefore model audit selection jointly with compliance behavior.

Our econometric framework consists of four equations. The first is a (reduced form) probit specification of the decision whether to audit a given return:

$$(1) \qquad A^* = \beta'_A X_A + \epsilon_A.$$

The term A^* represents an index of the likelihood that a return with observed characteristics X_A will be audited. The term ϵ_A represents a standard normal random disturbance, and β_A is a vector of coefficients to be estimated. From the data, we can deduce whether A^* is greater than zero (indicated by whether an audit has been performed).

The second equation is also a probit specification. However, rather than describing the likelihood that a return will be audited, it concerns the likelihood that the assessment (of additional net wealth) would be positive should an audit take place. The equation is specified as follows:

$$(2) \qquad P^* = \beta'_P X_P + \gamma_P \Phi(\beta'_A X_A) + \epsilon_P,$$

where P^* is an index of the likelihood that the assessment would be positive, X_P is a vector of explanatory variables, β_P is a vector of coefficients to be esti-

---

26. Eller and Johnson (2000, figure 7).

mated, and ϵ_P is a standard normal random disturbance. From the data, we can deduce whether P^* is greater than zero (indicated by whether the audit assessment is positive). Observe that the probability of an audit—$\Phi(B_A' X_A)$—is included as a regressor. (The symbol $\Phi(\cdot)$ refers to the cumulative standard normal distribution.) We hypothesize that the risk of audit serves as a deterrent to noncompliance, in which case the sign of γ_P should be negative.

Should the audit assessment turn out to be positive (indicating that net wealth has been understated), it is necessary to describe the magnitude of the additional assessment. As is typical of audit results, estate tax assessments tend to be very skewed, with a few audited returns receiving extremely large assessments. To account for this feature of the assessment distribution, a log-normal specification is employed:

$$(3) \qquad \ln(R) = \beta_R' X_R + \gamma_R \Phi(\beta_A' X_A) + \epsilon_R,$$

where $\ln(R)$ represents the natural log of the audit assessment, X_R is a vector of explanatory variables, β_R is a vector of coefficients to be estimated, and ϵ_R is a normally distributed random disturbance. Again, we include the probability of an audit as a regressor, hypothesizing that the extent of noncompliance is negatively associated with the audit risk (that is, that γ_R is negative).

Should the audit assessment turn out to be nonpositive, a specification that accounts for whether the assessment is negative (indicating an overstatement of net wealth) or zero (indicating that net wealth was properly reported) is in order. For this purpose, we employ the following equation:

$$(4) \qquad \ln(M^* + D) = \beta_M' X_M + \epsilon_M,$$

where M^* is an index of the likelihood that the assessment is negative, X_M is a vector of explanatory variables, β_M is a vector of coefficients to be estimated, and ϵ_M is a random normal disturbance term. The term D (also estimated) is the displacement parameter, which indicates how far the lower bound of the log-normal distribution is shifted below zero. We observe an overstatement in the amount of M^* only if M^* is greater than zero. When M^* falls between $-D$ and zero, the assessment equals zero. Thus, our specification is similar to a Tobit structure, except that we employ the displaced log normal distribution in place of the normal to better account for the inherent skewness of the data. Observe that we do not include a measure of the risk of audit as a regressor in this equation. We assume that overstatements of wealth are largely unintentional and are therefore not responsive to the likelihood of an audit.

We allow free correlations (ρ_{AP}, ρ_{AR}, and ρ_{PR}) in our framework among the disturbances ϵ_A, ϵ_P, and ϵ_R.[27] These correlations admit the possibilities that unobserved factors that influence one equation may also affect another equation. For example, if IRS classifiers base their decision to examine a return partly on information beyond what is reported on the estate tax return, we may expect that ρ_{AP} is greater than zero. (In particular, the nonreturn information that leads to an examination tends to be positively correlated with noncompliance.) Similarly, it would not be surprising if returns that have a high probability of requiring an adjustment also tend to have large assessments when an adjustment is required. This might be indicated by a positive value for ρ_{PR}.

We estimate our model using the method of maximum likelihood. The likelihood function is presented in appendix A to this chapter.

Estimation Results

This section shows the results of our econometric analysis. We begin by describing the regressors employed in our analysis and then present and interpret our findings.

Variable Specification

The measure of noncompliance used in our econometric analysis is the difference between the assessed value of the adjusted taxable estate and the reported value. We define the adjusted taxable estate as the value of the total gross estate less allowable deductions plus adjusted taxable gifts. However, we exclude administrative expenses from our definition of allowable deductions. We do this because an examination typically results in additional administrative expenses that are deductible against the estate. Thus, examinations frequently result in the assessment of additional administrative expenses even when administrative expenses were properly reported on the original return. As a normalization, our noncompliance measure is specified in hundreds of thousands of dollars.

Our econometric framework includes three noncompliance equations—equations 2, 3, and 4—and an audit selection equation (equation 1). The noncompliance equations specify the probability that an assessment is positive, the magnitude of the assessment if it is positive, and the magnitude of the assessment if it is nonpositive, respectively. The regressors X_P, X_R, and X_M in

---

27. To keep the model tractable, we assume that the disturbance ϵ_M of equation 4 is independent of the other disturbances of the model.

these equations are identically specified in our analysis. They include a set of demographic control variables, a measure of gross wealth, and the marginal tax rate. In addition, dummies for the presence of certain types of assets and the share of gross wealth accounted for by various assets are included to investigate whether noncompliance tends to be concentrated among assets that are difficult to value (for example, closely held stock). Dummy variables are specified for certain variables that may signify tax planning, such as the presence of a will, the payment of attorney's fees or executor's expenses, the presence of adjusted taxable gifts or transfers during the decedent's life, a deduction for charitable bequests, and the presence of QTIP property. We define most of our regressors using the postaudit figures for the underlying estate tax return line items rather than the amounts originally reported on the return. We believe that the postaudit figures are likely to represent a closer approximation of the true estate characteristics than the originally reported amounts. However, we base the dummy variables for the presence of attorney's fees and executor's fees on the per return values, as we are interested in identifying whether an attorney or an executor was paid for work on the original return (see appendix B for description of variables).

The weighted mean values of the above regressors are presented in table 9-9, along with the average value of the change in the adjusted taxable estate. For returns in our data file with gross estates exceeding $5 million, we have been able to match information on the number of beneficiaries reported on the estate tax return. We have repeated our analysis on this subsample, including dummies for the number of beneficiaries as additional regressors. However, a likelihood ratio test indicates that the dummies are jointly insignificant. In future research it would be useful to explore alternative specifications involving the number of beneficiaries with a more complete sample of data.

A similar set of regressors is specified for the audit equation (X_A in equation 1), although dummy variables for the presence of an asset are used in place of the ratio of the value of the asset to the value of the total gross estate. Since the audit equation is estimated using both examined and unexamined returns, it is necessary for the regressors in this equation to be based on the values originally reported for the relevant line items of the estate tax return. We have elected not to employ asset ratio variables, because they are potentially endogenous.[28] We anticipate that a simple dummy variable for the presence of any reported closely held stock is less likely to be endoge-

28. For example, individuals might tend to report closely held stock more accurately if the likelihood of audit were to rise. If so, the ratio of reported closely held stock to reported total gross estate might also rise.

Table 9-9. *Mean Values of Variables*

Variable[a]	All audited returns	Positive assessments	Nonpositive assessments
Change in adjusted taxable estate (dollars)	142,080	232,800	(88,886)
Male	0.4704	0.4248	0.5863
Single	0.0913	0.0807	0.1184
Separated or divorced	0.0608	0.0612	0.0598
Widowed	0.6140	0.6387	0.5511
Will present	0.9122	0.9219	0.8876
1990 or earlier decedent	0.0976	0.0756	0.1535
1992 decedent	0.1522	0.1766	0.0901
Age	0.7925	0.7950	0.7862
Marginal tax rate	0.3892	0.3862	0.3967
Natural log of TGE[b]	14.3228	14.3108	14.3534
Personal residence/TGE	0.0803	0.0812	0.0778
Other real estate/TGE	0.1682	0.1788	0.1410
Bonds/TGE	0.1563	0.1552	0.1591
Closely held stock/TGE	0.0579	0.0600	0.0527
Other corporate stock/TGE	0.1617	0.1643	0.1552
Mutual funds/TGE	0.0133	0.0127	0.0151
Cash assets/TGE	0.1240	0.1126	0.1529
Noncorp. business assets/TGE	0.0155	0.0157	0.0149
Mortgages and notes/TGE	0.0251	0.0234	0.0294
Annuities/TGE	0.0290	0.0265	0.0353
Farm assets dummy	0.0960	0.1097	0.0612
Limited partnership assets dummy	0.1347	0.1198	0.1728
Art assets dummy	0.0421	0.0382	0.0522
Depletable/intangible assets dummy	0.1105	0.1077	0.1175
Other noncorp. assets dummy	0.1756	0.1612	0.2123
Closely held stock dummy	0.2235	0.2363	0.1910
Community property dummy	0.0414	0.0325	0.0641
Attorney's fees dummy	0.8728	0.8945	0.8174
Executor's fees dummy	0.6270	0.6434	0.5853
Charitable bequest dummy	0.2814	0.2974	0.2405
Power of attorney dummy	0.0486	0.0532	0.0370
Schedule G dummy	0.3291	0.3455	0.2875
Adjusted taxable gifts dummy	0.3184	0.3589	0.2154
State death tax credit dummy	0.9545	0.9675	0.9212
QTIP dummy[c]	0.0342	0.0327	0.0379
Weighted number of returns	10,215	7,334	952
Unweighted number of returns	1,206	866	340

a. See appendix B for explanation of all variables.

b. TGE = total gross estate.

c. QTIP = qualified terminable interest property.

nous. For the same reason, we replace the natural log of TGE with dummy variables for the reported value of TGE falling into the ranges $5 million–$10 million, $10 million–$25 million, and greater than $25 million. Our audit equation also includes three additional regressors:

1. *Audit coverage rate for TGE class:* The actual audit coverage rate (that is the ratio of the number of returns examined to the number of returns filed) for the estate's TGE class (TGE < $1M, $1M < = TGE < $5M, and TGE > = $5M).
2. *State audit coverage rate:* The actual audit coverage rate for the decedent's state of residence.
3. *Audit coverage rate interaction:* Interaction between the above two audit coverage rates.

Our reasoning is that the likelihood that an individual return will be audited depends in part on the fraction of returns that are audited in the estate's TGE class and in the decedent's state of residence. For example, if the decedent resided in a state in which the audit coverage rate was low, his estate's chance of audit may very well be lower than an estate filing a similar return in a state with a high audit coverage rate. By providing a source of independent variation in the audit equation, these variables aid in the identification of the parameters of the noncompliance equations.

Parameter Estimates

As a matter of policy, audit selection criteria are not publicly disclosed by the IRS. Indeed, in specifying our model, we had no detailed knowledge of the return variables or procedures used to select estate tax returns for examination. To maintain the confidentiality of estate tax audit selection criteria, we suppress the portion of our estimation results pertaining to our audit selection equation. The parameter estimates for the remaining equations are presented below.

Probability of a Positive Assessment

Table 9-10 presents the parameter estimates for equation 2, which describes the probability of a positive audit assessment. The results indicate that the estates of male decedents are relatively less likely to have a positive assessment, controlling for other factors. However, no significant difference is observed across different marital statuses or ages of decedents. The year of death is a significant factor, with a trend toward a greater likelihood of a positive assessment

Table 9-10. *Parameter Estimates for Probability of Positive Assessment Equation*

Variable[a]	Parameter	t statistic
Constant	−3.346	−3.17
Male	−0.348	−3.61
Single	−0.046	−0.27
Separated or divorced	−0.020	−0.12
Widowed	0.009	0.06
Will present	0.067	0.43
1990 or earlier decedent	−0.381	−2.79
1992 decedent	0.274	2.31
Age	−0.203	−0.58
Marginal tax rate	−2.482	−3.43
Natural log of TGE	0.150	2.65
Personal residence/TGE	−0.209	−0.60
Other real estate/TGE	0.314	1.40
Bonds/TGE	−0.007	−0.03
Closely held stock/TGE	−0.589	−2.00
Other corporate stock/TGE	−0.174	−0.88
Mutual funds/TGE	−0.583	−1.00
Cash assets/TGE	−0.986	−2.85
Noncorp. business assets/TGE	0.150	0.28
Mortgages and notes/TGE	−0.134	−0.18
Annuities/TGE	−0.823	−1.82
Farm assets dummy	0.467	2.84
Limited partnership assets dummy	−0.217	−2.15
Art assets dummy	−0.348	−2.64
Depletable/intangible assets dummy	−0.072	−0.57
Other noncorp. assets dummy	−0.107	−1.00
Closely held stock dummy	0.489	3.82
Community property dummy	−0.003	−0.01
Attorney's fees dummy	0.450	3.25
Executor's fees dummy	0.108	1.10
Charitable bequest dummy	0.283	2.84
Power of attorney dummy	0.052	0.32
Schedule G dummy	0.081	0.92
Adjusted taxable gifts dummy	0.534	5.59
State death tax credit dummy	1.790	5.80
QTIP dummy	−0.252	−1.18
Probability of audit	0.673	4.05
ρ_{AP}	0.203	0.36

a. See notes to table 9-9.

for more recent decedents. The probability of noncompliance is found to be increasing in gross wealth but decreasing in terms of the marginal tax rate.[29]

The results indicate that the probability of a positive assessment depends on the kinds and relative amounts of different assets in the estate. The probability of a positive assessment is lower the greater the shares of cash assets and annuities in the total gross estate. Estates with limited partnership assets and art assets are also relatively less likely to have a positive assessment. Depletable and intangible assets have no significant relationship to the incidence of positive assessments. The results for art assets and for depletable and intangible assets are somewhat surprising, given that one might expect valuation to be a problem for such assets. In this regard, the findings for estates with farm assets and closely held stock are more in line with expectations. The presence of either type of asset makes a positive assessment relatively more likely. Although the presence of closely held stock is associated with a greater incidence of positive assessments, the effect declines with the share of assets in the total gross estate.

Estates that make adjusted taxable gifts or that have deductions for attorney's fees or charitable bequests are relatively more likely to have a positive assessment, all else equal. This may be an indication that tax planning activities are associated with a higher incidence of noncompliance.

Perhaps most surprisingly, the results indicate that estates are relatively more likely to understate taxes the *greater* the probability of an audit. One interpretation of this finding is that estates tend to take relatively aggressive positions if the fiduciary believes an audit is likely, perhaps in an effort to create bargaining room.[30]

The correlation between the error term of the equation describing the likelihood of a positive assessment with the error term of the audit equation is positive but statistically insignificant.

Magnitude of a Positive Assessment

When the audit assessment is positive, equation 3 describes its magnitude. The parameter estimates for equation 3 are presented in table 9-11. The

29. Although the marginal tax rate depends in part of the level of wealth, a regression of the marginal rate on the natural log of TGE and the other regressors indicates that a fair amount of independent variation occurs in the marginal tax rate. This is so even when additional terms involving TGE are included as regressors. A potential problem with our measure of the marginal rate is that it will tend to vary with the level of noncompliance, which could bias the sign of the marginal rate coefficient in the negative direction.

30. Slemrod, Blumenthal, and Christian (forthcoming) obtain a similar result and come to this same interpretation in the context of income tax noncompliance.

Table 9-11. *Parameter Estimates for Magnitude of Positive Assessment Equation*

Variable[a]	Parameter	t *statistic*
Constant	−17.234	−7.19
Male	−0.220	−0.94
Single	−0.300	−1.02
Separated or divorced	−0.385	−1.29
Widowed	−0.522	−2.14
Will present	−0.361	−1.20
1990 or earlier decedent	0.229	0.81
1992 decedent	−0.122	−0.62
Age	0.091	0.16
Marginal tax rate	−1.165	−0.79
Natural log of TGE	1.110	12.36
Personal residence/TGE	0.354	0.52
Other real estate/TGE	0.988	2.41
Bonds/TGE	−1.039	−2.85
Closely held stock/TGE	0.984	2.14
Other corporate stock/TGE	−0.669	−2.24
Mutual funds/TGE	0.276	0.15
Cash assets/TGE	0.856	1.07
Noncorp. business assets/TGE	0.111	0.14
Mortgages and notes/TGE	−0.316	−0.41
Annuities/TGE	−0.507	−0.46
Farm assets dummy	−0.596	−1.91
Limited partnership assets dummy	0.102	0.54
Art assets dummy	−0.371	−1.38
Depletable/intangible assets dummy	0.311	1.55
Other noncorp. assets dummy	0.176	1.02
Closely held stock dummy	0.326	1.09
Community property dummy	−0.991	−2.50
Attorney's fees dummy	0.059	0.17
Executor's fees dummy	0.289	1.90
Charitable bequest dummy	0.060	0.29
Power of attorney dummy	0.544	2.38
Schedule G dummy	−0.035	−0.25
Adjusted taxable gifts dummy	0.859	2.98
State death tax credit dummy	0.601	0.62
QTIP dummy	−0.201	−0.50
Probability of audit	−0.589	−1.36
σ_R	1.733	14.70
ρ_{PR}	0.346	1.77
ρ_{AR}	0.345	2.07

a. See notes to table 9-9.

results for the magnitude of a positive assessment are somewhat different than those for the likelihood of a positive assessment. Previously, we found that estates of male decedents were relatively less likely to have a positive assessment, but that marital status was an insignificant factor. However, our results for the magnitude of the assessment indicate that gender is an insignificant factor, while marital status matters. The magnitude of the audit assessment for widowed decedents' estates is lower than the magnitude of the assessment for married decedents' estates. This is an important finding, given the past tendency for the IRS to devote a disproportionate share of its audit resources to the estates of unmarried decedents.

Both the probability and magnitude of a positive assessment are positively associated with the natural log of TGE, but the marginal tax rate is not significantly related to the magnitude of the assessment. Estates with a large share of wealth in the form of bonds or other corporate stock tend to have relatively small audit assessments, while estates with large shares of closely held stock or real estate other than a personal residence tend to have relatively large assessments. Estates containing assets over which the decedent had a power of appointment also tend to have relatively large assessments. Somewhat surprisingly, although estates with farm assets tend to have a greater likelihood of a positive assessment, the magnitude of the assessment tends to be relatively small. Estates with a deduction for executor's fees and those reporting adjusted taxable gifts tend to have relatively large audit assessments.

The probability of audit is of the expected sign (negative), but it is statistically insignificant. However, the correlation between the errors of the magnitude of positive assessment equation and the audit equation is positive and significant, indicating that unobservable factors that result in an audit tend to be associated with relatively large positive assessments. The correlation between the errors of the equations describing the probability and the magnitude of a positive assessment is also positive, suggesting that the incidence and magnitude of assessments are positively associated.

Magnitude of a Nonpositive Assessment

As noted previously, a nontrivial fraction of estates are found to have overstated their adjusted taxable wealth during examination. Table 9-12 presents the results from estimating equation 4, which describes the magnitude of nonpositive assessments. All else equal, the magnitude of the overstatement tends to be smaller for the estates of single and widowed decedents than for those of married decedents. Estates of decedents who had wills also tend to be associated with smaller overstatements. It seems plausible that the presence of a will

Table 9-12. *Parameter Estimates for Magnitude of Nonpositive Assessment Equation*

Variable[a]	Parameter	t *statistic*
Constant	2.735	1.45
Male	−0.077	−0.39
Single	−1.304	−3.35
Separated or divorced	−0.121	−0.34
Widowed	−1.043	−3.48
Will present	−0.861	−2.66
1990 or earlier decedent	0.557	2.31
1992 decedent	−0.480	−1.79
Age	0.838	1.13
Marginal tax rate	7.825	5.58
Natural log of TGE	−0.304	−2.44
Personal residence/TGE	−0.416	−0.57
Other real estate/TGE	0.608	1.73
Bonds/TGE	−1.273	−2.52
Closely held stock/TGE	−0.829	−1.27
Other corporate stock/TGE	−0.785	−1.87
Mutual funds/TGE	1.549	0.75
Cash assets/TGE	−1.757	−2.67
Noncorp. business assets/TGE	−2.843	−2.03
Mortgages and notes/TGE	−2.344	−1.66
Annuities/TGE	0.766	0.56
Farm assets dummy	−0.375	−1.04
Limited partnership assets dummy	−0.365	−1.72
Art assets dummy	0.527	1.89
Depletable/intangible assets dummy	−0.483	−1.78
Other noncorp. assets dummy	0.441	2.00
Closely held stock dummy	0.109	0.38
Community property dummy	0.893	1.40
Attorney's fees dummy	−0.611	−2.04
Executor's fees dummy	0.556	2.51
Charitable bequest dummy	−0.154	−0.66
Power of attorney dummy	0.283	0.75
Schedule G dummy	0.204	1.08
Adjusted taxable gifts dummy	−0.162	−0.81
State death tax credit dummy	−1.623	−2.42
QTIP dummy	−0.294	−0.67
D	0.086	4.25
σ_M	1.544	12.85

a. See notes to table 9-9.

is an indication that the decedent's affairs are in good order relative to those of a decedent with no will. The magnitude of overstatements is also associated with the year of death, with more recent decedents' estates having relatively smaller reassessments. Overstatements are negatively associated with the natural log of TGE, perhaps indicating that tax returns for wealthier estates are more carefully prepared. Somewhat surprisingly, though, the magnitude of the overstatement is positively associated with the marginal tax rate.[31]

The size of overstatements also depends on the asset composition of the estate. Estates with a high share of wealth in the form of cash assets, bonds, mortgages and notes, or other corporate stock tend to make relatively small overstatements. However, estates with art assets or other noncorporate assets tend to make relatively large overstatements. The magnitude of overstatements tends to be relatively low for estates with depletable or intangible assets and those with limited partnership assets.

Estates with a deduction for attorney's fees tend to have relatively small overstatements, consistent with the notion that expert assistance can help to reduce errors. Estates subject to state death taxes also tend to overstate wealth by less.

Conclusion

The federal estate tax represents an interesting case study in noncompliance. The base for the tax is concentrated among a small number of very wealthy estates, with marginal tax rates reaching as high as 60 percent. Furthermore, the base is inherently difficult to measure, requiring complex valuations of a variety of different types of assets. From the perspective of enforcement, the scope for third-party information reporting and document matching is rather limited, making examinations one of the few effective tools for enforcing compliance. Consequently, audit rates tend to be substantial, reaching 50 percent for the highest wealth class.

In this chapter, we have attempted to assess the magnitude and determinants of estate tax noncompliance. We have found that it is difficult to measure the overall magnitude of noncompliance using SCF data. The results appear very sensitive to the treatment of married individuals, the choice of mortality probabilities, and the allocation of deductions and credits among individuals. Nor is it obvious which choices are the most appropriate in many circumstances. Estimates based on a preliminary version of the audit

---

31. Again, this finding may be the result of our computation of the marginal tax rate based on the reported level of adjusted taxable wealth.

and tax return data used in this chapter suggest that the estate tax underreporting gap may be around 13 percent. However, this figure may substantially understate the true magnitude of the gap, because it is based on the final closing examination assessment following any appeals or litigation, and because it does not account for any noncompliance that might have escaped detection during the examination.

Our econometric analysis of the determinants of estate tax noncompliance indicates that somewhat different factors are associated with the probability of a positive audit assessment and the magnitude of the assessment. Farm assets and closely held stock are associated with a relatively high probability of a positive assessment. This may be a reflection of the difficulty in properly valuing such assets. Indeed, cash assets and annuities, which tend to be less difficult to value, are associated with a relatively low probability of a positive assessment. However, art assets (which can be difficult to value) also are associated with a reduced chance of a positive assessment. Not surprisingly, the likelihood of a positive assessment tends to increase with wealth. Like the probability, the magnitude of a positive assessment also increases with wealth, and it tends to be relatively large when there is closely held stock in the estate's portfolio. However, while the probability of a positive assessment tends to be higher when the estate contains farm assets, the magnitude of the assessment tends to be lower. The magnitude of an assessment also tends to be reduced when bonds and other corporate stocks form a substantial portion of the estate's portfolio. Finally, the likelihood of a positive assessment, but not the magnitude, tends to increase with the probability of audit.

Our econometric analysis also investigates the determinants of wealth overreporting. Unlike understatements, overstatements of the taxable estate tend to decrease with wealth. They also are smaller when the decedent has left a will, and when cash, bonds, corporate stock, and certain other assets form an important part of the estate's portfolio. Estates with substantial noncorporate assets and those with art assets tend to have relatively high overstatements.

A question left unanswered in our analysis is who is responsible for estate tax noncompliance. If noncompliance is a collusive decision among beneficiaries, we might expect to find that noncompliance is most pervasive in settings of relatively few beneficiaries. However, our preliminary analysis did not uncover such a relationship. We did find that noncompliance is relatively more likely when an attorney has been employed to assist in the preparation of the return; however, presumably attorneys would not take aggressive tax positions if their clients did not express a demand for such positions. Of course, significant overstatements of tax liability suggest that some forms of noncompliance reflect unintentional behavior rather than deliberate reporting strategies.

In the past, estate tax examiners have focused most of their audit efforts on the estates of widowed and other unmarried decedents. This decision stemmed at least partly from a belief that examinations of married decedents' estates would be unproductive. In this regard, an important finding of our analysis is that the estates of married decedents have a similar likelihood of a positive assessment, and a larger relative magnitude of assessment, than the estates of widowed decedents after controlling for wealth and other factors.

Appendix A: Likelihood Function

We estimate our model using the method of maximum likelihood. We incorporate the sample weights in estimation to make the results broadly representative of the overall population of estate tax returns filed in 1992. The observations in our sample can be constructively divided into five categories, according to whether an audit took place and the outcome of the audit. We specify the likelihood value associated with each case below.

Case 1: No Audit

The first category contains those returns that were not subjected to an audit. For a return in this category, only the audit equation applies, and the likelihood value (L_1) simply represents the probability that the return would not be audited:

(A1) $$L_1 = 1 - \Phi(\beta'_A X_A).$$

Case 2: Audit, Negative Assessment

The second category contains audited returns that received a negative assessment. For a return in this category, the likelihood value (L_2) is computed as the probability density function (pdf) for the observed tax overstatement (M) times the joint probability of the return being audited and the assessment being nonpositive:

$$L_2 = \frac{1}{(M + D)\sigma_M} \phi\left(\frac{\ln(M + D) - \beta'_M X_M}{\sigma_M}\right)$$

(A2) $$BN[-\beta'_P XP - \gamma_P \Phi(\beta'_A X_A), \beta'_A X_A, (-)\rho_{AP}],$$

where $\phi(\cdot)$ represents the standard normal pdf, and $BN[\cdot, \cdot, \rho]$ represents the standard bivariate normal cdf for correlation ρ.

Case 3: Audit, No Assessment

The third category contains audited returns that received no additional tax assessment. For a return in this category, the likelihood value (L_3) represents the probability of no assessment times the joint probability of the return being audited and the assessment being nonpositive:

$$L_3 = \Phi\left(\frac{\ln(D) - \beta'_M X_M}{\sigma_M}\right)$$

(A3)
$$BN\left[-\beta'_P X_P - \gamma_P \Phi(\beta'_A X_A), \beta'_A X_A, (-)\rho_{AP}\right].$$

Case 4: Audit, Positive Assessment

The fourth category contains audited returns that received a positive assessment. For a return in this category, the likelihood value (L_4) represents the pdf for the observed tax understatement times the conditional joint probability of the return being audited and the assessment being positive given the observed understatement:

$$L_4 = \frac{1}{R\sigma_R}\phi\left(\frac{\ln(R) - \beta'_R X_R - \gamma_R \Phi(\beta'_A X_A)}{\sigma_R}\right)$$

$$BN\left[\frac{\beta'_A X_A + \rho_{AR}\left(\dfrac{\ln(R) - \beta'_R X_R - \gamma_R \Phi(\beta'_A X_A)}{\sigma_R}\right)}{\sqrt{\left(1 - \rho^2_{AR}\right)}}, \right.$$

(A4)
$$\frac{\beta'_P X_P + \gamma_P \Phi(\beta'_A X_A) + \rho_{PR}\left(\dfrac{\ln(R) - \beta'_R X_R - \gamma_R \Phi(\beta'_A X_A)}{\sigma_R}\right)}{\sqrt{\left(1 - \rho^2_{PR}\right)}},$$

$$\left. \frac{\rho_{AP} - \rho_{AR}\rho_{PR}}{\sqrt{\left(1 - \rho^2_{AR}\right)}\sqrt{\left(1 - \rho^2_{PR}\right)}} \right].$$

Case 5: Audit, No Assessment Information

No assessment information is available for a small number of the audited returns in the sample. Although these returns consequently provide no useful information concerning the distribution of audit assessments, they do contain valuable information concerning the likelihood of an audit. Therefore, these returns have been included within the fifth and final category. The likelihood value (L_5) for a return in this category is simply the probability of the return being audited:

(A5) $$L_5 = \Phi(\beta'_A X_A).$$

Appendix B: List of Variables

1. *Constant:* Unit vector for estimating the constant term.
2. *Male:* Dummy equal to 1 if the decedent is male; 0 otherwise.
3. *Single:* Dummy equal to 1 if the decedent was single; 0 otherwise.
4. *Separated or divorced:* Dummy variable equal to 1 if the decedent was separated or divorced; 0 otherwise.
5. *Widowed:* Dummy variable equal to 1 if the decedent was widowed.
6. *Will present:* Dummy variable equal to 1 for the presence of a will; 0 otherwise.
7. *1990 or earlier decedent:* Dummy variable equal to 1 if the decedent's year of death was 1990 or earlier; 0 otherwise.
8. *1992 decedent:* Dummy variable equal to 1 if the decedent's year of death was 1992.
9. *Age:* Age of decedent divided by 100.
10. *Marginal tax rate:* Federal marginal tax rate at the reported value of the adjusted taxable estate.
11. *Natural log of TGE:* Natural log of total gross estate.
12. *Personal residence/TGE:* Ratio of value of personal residence to TGE.
13. *Other real estate/TGE:* Ratio of value of other real estate to TGE.
14. *Bonds/TGE:* Ratio of value of bonds to TGE.
15. *Closely held stock/TGE:* Ratio of value of closely held stock to TGE.
16. *Other corporate stock/TGE:* Ratio of value of other corporate stock to TGE.
17. *Mutual funds/TGE:* Ratio of value of mutual funds to TGE.
18. *Cash assets/TGE:* Ratio of value of cash assets to TGE.

19. *Noncorporate business assets/TGE:* Ratio of value of noncorporate business assets to TGE.

20. *Mortgages and notes/TGE:* Ratio of value of mortgages and notes to TGE.

21. *Annuities/TGE:* Ratio of annuities to TGE.

22. *Farm assets dummy:* Dummy variable equal to 1 if any farm assets were owned by the estate; 0 otherwise.

23. *Limited partnerships dummy:* Dummy variable equal to 1 if the estate owned any limited partnerships; 0 otherwise.

24. *Art assets dummy:* Dummy variable equal to 1 if the estate owned any art assets; 0 otherwise.

25. *Depletable/intangible dummy:* Dummy variable equal to 1 if the estate owned any depletable or intangible assets.

26. *Closely held stock dummy:* Dummy variable equal to 1 if the estate owned any noncorporate assets; 0 otherwise.

27. *Other noncorporate assets dummy:* Dummy variable equal to 1 if the estate owned any noncorporate assets; 0 otherwise.

28. *Closely held stock dummy:* Dummy variable equal to 1 if the estate owned any closely held stock; 0 otherwise.

29. *Community property dummy:* Dummy variable equal to 1 if the decedent owned community property with his/her spouse; 0 otherwise.

30. *Attorney's fees dummy:* Dummy variable equal to 1 if any attorney's fees were deducted against the estate; 0 otherwise.

31. *Executor's fees dummy:* Dummy variable equal to 1 if any executor's fees were deducted against the estate; 0 otherwise.

32. *Charitable bequest dummy:* Dummy variable equal to 1 if any charitable bequests were deducted against the estate; 0 otherwise.

33. *Power of appointment dummy:* Dummy variable equal to 1 if the decedent had the power of appointment over any property (reportable on Schedule H); 0 otherwise.

34. *Schedule G dummy:* Dummy variable equal to 1 if the decedent's estate was required to complete Schedule G ("Transfers during Decedent's Life").

35. *QTIP property dummy:* Dummy variable equal to 1 if the decedent's estate includes any QTIP property (qualified terminable interest property); 0 otherwise. This is property that the decedent transferred to trust for the income benefit of the surviving spouse; the surviving spouse has no power to appoint beneficiaries at his or her death. The decedent's estate may claim the marital deduction for such property.

COMMENT BY
Kathleen McGarry

Typically, a paper starts with the authors trying to establish why the work is useful and much needed in spite of the work that has gone before. Martha Britton Eller, Brian Erard, and Chih-Chin Ho do not just say their work is important, they show us exactly why.

They start out with the small amount of evidence that is available on the extent of noncompliance with the estate tax. This evidence consists of two sets of estimates, one from James M. Poterba and one from Edward Wolff, both of which use the Survey of Consumer Finances (SCF).[32] The papers each simulate expected estate tax revenue using the current wealth holdings of survey respondents and assigning mortality probabilities to each observation. The studies then compare these expected values with the actual tax revenues collected by the Internal Revenue Service (IRS). The difference between expected and actual payments is used as a measure of noncompliance. Despite using similar techniques, Poterba and Wolff find very different degrees of noncompliance. Poterba predicts expected estate taxes using the 1995 SCF of $15.7 billion, compared with actual taxes collected of $14.3 billion; these numbers are very close to each other and suggest noncompliance is not a problem. In contrast, Wolff calculates an expected tax bill based on the 1992 SCF of $44.5 billion, compared with actual collections of just $10.3 billion, a strikingly large shortfall.

Eller, Erard, and Ho replicate these simulations and then demonstrate how the estimates depend on the various assumptions made by each of the previous authors. Important differences arise from the choice of life tables: because wealthy people live longer on average than the less wealthy, a life table based on a sample of wealthier individuals predicts fewer deaths and a lower estate tax bill than a population life table. Similarly, married people live longer than single people, so using one life table for both groups likely yields too high a mortality rate for those who are married and too low for those who are single. The assumptions made about bequests to a surviving spouse and about giving to charitable organizations also greatly affect the estimates of the expected tax owed.

Several other factors also likely to affect the accuracy of the predicted tax bill are not mentioned in the chapter. These include the treatment of life

---

32. Poterba (1997); Wolff (1996).

insurance holdings, assumptions about the types of trust the donor has established, and assumptions about expenses involved in the settling of the estate and those incurred during the decedent's final illness. Although assumptions about the measurement of these variables may be less important than the assumptions about life expectancy, in many instances they could yield sizable differences in the value of an estate. Life insurance owned by the decedent is included as part of the estate, whereas policies on his life held by others (heirs or a trust) are not included. In survey data the actual owner of the policy may be difficult to discern.[33] Because policies typically carry large face values, their inclusion or exclusion could significantly alter the size of the estate and therefore the predicted estate tax. Similarly, it may be difficult to verify whether the trusts held by an individual are of a type that allows them to be excluded from the estate or whether their purpose is simply to avoid probate or to provide for particular methods of distribution of the decedent's wealth. Finally, it is well known that medical expenses during the last few months of life, including both hospital and nursing home stays (which are unlikely to be covered by Medicare or medi-gap plans), are large.

It is also worth considering the degree to which the SCF population is representative of those who are soon to die and therefore whether their asset holdings are representative of the decedents in that year. If the very ill are in nursing homes or hospitals, they may not be included in the sample, or they may be included through proxy interviews. Proxy interviews may lead to underreporting of assets if the respondents are unaware of the entire portfolio or its current value, a significant possibility for those extensive holdings.

Regardless of these other factors, the large changes in tax liability that Eller, Erard, and Ho find when they vary assumptions about life expectancy and the division of assets between spouses provide an important contribution to the literature. The high degree of sensitivity noted in their work should serve as a warning to researchers who are attempting to draw strong conclusions from the evidence presented thus far. Furthermore, the variation in compliance rates from 50 to 90 percent, depending on which set of assumptions is used, is likely to discourage future attempts at measuring estate tax noncompliance with simulations based on survey data. The authors have therefore done a thorough job of convincing the reader that a new study of noncompliance is needed, and that it needs to be based on a different type of data if it is to be credible. This study is taken up in the second part of the chapter.

After demonstrating the need for better data on compliance, the authors draw on a fascinating new data set of audits of estate tax returns. The data

---

33. Conversations with tax attorneys suggest that life insurance policies are often held "incorrectly," increasing the tax burden on the estate.

set provides information from the IRS on asset valuations and deductions before and after an audit. These administrative data therefore give us the best possible hope of a definitive result on noncompliance.

As is noted in the chapter, the measure of noncompliance obtained from these data is actually a lower bound of what the IRS would consider noncompliance because the tax liabilities reported are the end result of a series of negotiations and perhaps court rulings. They therefore likely represent compromises between the IRS and the estate. In some cases it may be that even after lengthy discussions the IRS believes that additional tax is due but chooses to settle for a lower amount; in this case noncompliance as measured in the data is lower than what the IRS would call noncompliance. Even if both parties are completely honest, it is possible that their estimates of the value of an asset will differ. For example, how does one value a piece of artwork if it is not being sold? Similarly for family businesses. How much goodwill is lost by the death of the owner?

At issue is just how large a discrepancy there might be between the IRS initial estimate of the tax liability and the eventual settlement. The authors cite statistics from a study of income tax noncompliance showing a rate of 13 percent relative to actual liability. This 13 percent is determined before settlement and compromise, so the eventual amount would likely be smaller. In contrast, the statistics calculated in the paper indicate a noncompliance rate for the estate tax of 13 percent *after* compromise, pointing to a much higher level of actual noncompliance. It would be helpful for understanding the difference between compliance for income and estate tax if a "net noncompliance" rate could be cited for income taxes as well. Although it is likely that the distance between the IRS calculations and the eventual tax bill differ for the two taxes, such a comparison would at least provide a better match than is possible with the current set of numbers.

The SCF estimates of the expected estate tax owed differ from the actual revenues for three reasons: tax avoidance behavior, legitimate errors, and tax evasion. The audit study discussed in this chapter captures the latter two sources of difference but does not measure how much tax is legally avoided through the use of trusts, the valuation of limited partnerships, and so on. (See Schmalbeck in this volume for a discussion of legal means of reducing estate taxes.) Avoidance strategies can be pursued prior to the estate holder's death and afterward as well. A large difference between revenues and predicted tax liability could therefore be due in part to aggressive, but legal, techniques.

On the noncompliance found in the audit study two main points should be kept in mind. First, it is important to distinguish intentional underpayments from those that are unintentional. A high fraction of unintentional errors or simple mistakes suggests that the IRS might attempt to lower the error rate through such tools as filing extensions that allow executors time to either sell assets or otherwise obtain more accurate estimates of their value; decreases in the cost of filing an amended return if it later turns out that an asset was incorrectly valued; and simplification of the laws so that fewer errors are made in the establishment of trusts and so forth.

Conversely, if *intentional* tax evasion is a significant problem, then increased monitoring and penalties may be more effective tools. In this case it would be helpful to know who is responsible for the evasion. Is the behavior the wishes of the decedent? The choice of the beneficiaries who gain financially from the lower tax bill? Or is it the decision of an independent executor who chooses to engage in aggressive avoidance behavior believing that he is better serving his clients?

Empirical Patterns

The simple cross-tabulations in tables 9-5 through 9-8 are probably some of the most valuable evidence on noncompliance available to date and provide several intriguing results. We learn several things: first, the probability of being audited is relatively small, especially for smaller estates. Only 11 percent of tax-filing estates with gross value of less than $1 million were audited. This low figure may yield a positive expected gain from noncompliance for estate holders. Second, a surprisingly large number of audited estates have overpaid and have their tax liability reduced as a result of the audit. Because one would expect at least as many honest mistakes to result in an underpayment of taxes as in an overpayment, it is likely that a large fraction (perhaps one-third) of the 60 percent that had additional taxes assessed were not behaving fraudulently but simply made errors on the tax form. The large number of errors is consistent with the expected difficulty of valuing a portfolio of assets for another individual in which many components are unlikely to have a clearly determined market value. As noted, errors of this type suggest different remedies from intentional misrepresentations.

A third notable result is that the additional amount collected from audits is small relative to the gross value of estates and increases tax liability by just over 5 percent. It would be interesting to know how this gain compares with the cost of audits. Is the IRS losing money through the process?[34]

34. Note that auditing expenses greater than the increase in revenue would not indicate that the IRS should cease to audit estate tax returns since audits likely also deter tax.

Specification

Given these patterns, the authors are then interested in examining more closely which characteristics are associated with noncompliance and the amount of underpayment. To do so, they estimate four separate equations in what amounts to a bit of a cumbersome strategy. The four equations are:

—A probit specification for the probability of an audit

$$A^* = \beta_A X_A + \epsilon_A.$$

—A probit for the probability of owing a positive amount conditional on an audit

$$P^* = \beta_P X_P + \gamma_P \Phi(\beta_A X_A) + \epsilon_P.$$

—OLS for the amount owed, conditional on it being positive

$$\ln(R) = \beta_R X_R + \gamma_P \Phi(\beta_A X_A) + \epsilon_R.$$

—Tobit for the amount owed, conditional on it being nonpositive

$$\ln(M^* + D) = \beta_M X_M + \epsilon_M.$$

Before discussing the results and what we learn from them, I offer a few comments on the specification. While the observed correlations are interesting and worthwhile, and I think we learn a lot from them, there may be other specifications that merit consideration.

Consider what policy questions these data could be used to address. It is likely that the most useful results would include an estimate of the total noncompliance in the population and information about what characteristics predict the existence and magnitude of noncompliance. The available data provide us with these measures for all estates that were audited. In principle we could sum this noncompliance and weight the observations to inflate the figure to the population total. The problem, obviously, is that audits are not random. If the IRS accurately targets audits, so that those who are audited are more likely to owe money and to owe more on average, then summing the total assessments for these estates will yield an overestimate of the amount of noncompliance. It is therefore necessary to estimate the *unconditional* relationship between observable variables and the amount of noncompliance. In this way noncompliance rates can be estimated even for those who are not audited.

The authors currently estimate an equation of the probability of being audited. These estimates can be used to construct the standard Heckman correction to estimate unconditional rates of noncompliance in a second stage. Obviously this procedure is not as straightforward as it first sounds. One needs to worry about identifying assumptions or to rely solely on functional form identification. But once obtained, the resulting estimates would give us the ability to predict how noncompliance varies with characteristics such as marital status and the composition of assets for the entire population and not just the audited subsample. This information could help better target future audits.

Along the lines of predicting population noncompliance, it should be noted that the variables currently used in the equation for the amount of noncompliance are "postaudit" measures. If one wishes to use the results of the study to predict the noncompliance of those who are *not audited,* then the empirical model needs to be based on the value of variables preaudit, so that the regressors are available for all estates filing returns. Changing the timing of the measurement of the relevant variables would therefore improve the usefulness of the results.

An additional complication is dealing with both positive and nonpositive assessments. In the chapter the two outcomes are estimated as separate equations, and the probability of an audit is assumed to affect the amount of underpayment but not the amount of overpayment. This difference stems from the assumption that the authors are implicitly making that underpayments can be due to true errors or to intentional tax evasion, whereas one would never intentionally overpay. Thus, there are two different processes and the probability of getting "caught" or audited will not affect overpayments. However, because the aggressiveness with which an individual chooses to value an estate depends on the audit probabilities, even overpayments could be correlated with the probability of an audit. Despite the theoretical prediction, the estimated equations indicate that the probability of an audit itself is not a significant predictor of behavior, but differences in coefficient estimates across equations do confirm that over- and underpayments result from different underlying processes. For instance, the size of the estate is positively correlated with the amount of a positive assessment but negatively correlated with the probability of a nonpositive assessment. Closely held stocks are also positively correlated with a positive assessment and negatively correlated with a nonpositive assessment. Thus the two equations are preferable to forcing the coefficients to be identical across outcomes. However, a fully interacted model might provide a more parsimonious specification and would allow for straightforward testing of any differences.

Including the predicted audit probability in the equation for the amount of noncompliance assumes that the individuals (the executors, the heirs, or the decedent—whoever is responsible for the decision) know that probability. The lack of significance on this coefficient may indicate that individuals do not know the audit probabilities, and their decisions are therefore not correlated with the true underlying probability. In fact, as the authors point out, the variables used to trigger an audit are not publicly known, and in the interest of preserving this confidentiality, the authors even suppress their estimates of the probability.

The issue of endogeneity could also be important in obtaining unbiased estimates. One would imagine that the unobservables in the equations, ϵ_P and ϵ_R, might be correlated with the regressors. For example, ϵ_P and ϵ_R could represent aggressive financial behavior that would be correlated with the probability of an audit and the amount owed, and which would also be correlated with the wealth, or more precisely, the value of the estate.

A final difficulty in estimating the correlates of noncompliance is less crucial to a theoretical understanding of behavior and more of a statistical issue, and that is the distribution of the amount of over- or underpayment. Many audited estates (20 percent) have no change in liability. Thus the distribution of noncompliance amounts has a mass point at zero, as well as both positive and negative amounts. There are also many more positive than negative assessments. Controlling for these factors with distributional assumptions is something that will complicate any econometric analysis.

The list of potential problems presented should not negate the importance of the results or of the chapter itself. Rather I mention them as appropriate topics to be tackled in future analyses. Of primary interest would be estimates of the unconditional amount of noncompliance, and I am sure it is something the authors are already addressing.

Results

The first set of estimates in the chapter is for the equation predicting the probability of owing additional taxes, specified as a probit model; estimates for the amount of noncompliance follow. It is useful to focus on the probit equation for owing taxes because we expect that the increase in liability modeled subsequently does not represent the true amount of noncompliance but rather a negotiated settlement and may thus contain a large amount of nonrandom error. However, while the amount might be subject to error, it is unlikely that the IRS would completely dismiss a case in which taxes were owed. The 0/1 indicator of noncompliance ought to be less subject to measurement error than the amount.

The first notable effect is that the returns of male decedents are significantly less likely to owe money than those of female decedents. Approximating the derivative, I find that the difference is about 8 percentage points on an average probability of owing a positive amount of 60 percent. It would be particularly interesting to know who is making the decisions. Is it the deceased male who structured his will or assets to comply with the tax laws, or is it the surviving spouse who makes the decision to comply, or perhaps an outside executor deciding independently? This question is particularly interesting when considering the role of sex in the equation. One might suppose that males are more likely than females to have consulted experts, planning ahead for the eventual estate taxes, and may therefore have taken advantage of the legal options for avoidance so illegal ones are not necessary. Alternatively, it could be that females as the surviving spouse are less likely than male survivors to pursue aggressive deductions.

There is also a strong time trend in the probability of a positive assessment. It would be interesting to note how time affects the underlying probability of an audit. If the number of audits is decreasing over time, then one would expect the audits that are conducted to be increasingly targeted to the most likely offenders. If this scenario were true, the probability of a positive assessment would be expected to increase over time, as in fact, it does.

Both the marginal tax rate and the log of the gross estate are included in the equation and have opposite effects. Consider how these variables interact. Holding the gross estate constant, a high marginal tax rate implies a less aggressive use of deductions. And one sees that in the estimates, a higher marginal rate is negatively related to the probability of owing additional taxes. Thus the estimates agree with our intuition when they are considered simultaneously.

The variables indicating types and relative amounts of the holdings of various assets are difficult to interpret. Certainly the composition of the portfolio will affect audit probabilities. Asset types that are difficult to evaluate may lead the IRS to audit with greater likelihood but may also make it more difficult for the IRS to dispute successfully the appraised value. For example, art work lowers the probability of a positive assessment. Although the IRS might be suspicious of the value attributed to works of art on a tax return, it may be unable to discredit the values determined by appraisers hired by the estate. As such, the holding of artwork lowers the probability of a positive assessment and in table 9-11, lowers the amount, conditional on a positive assessment.

Attorney's fees are positively correlated with the probability of a positive assessment. This result is almost tautological. If the IRS is auditing an estate, it seems likely that the estate would incur legal fees to fight any assessment or penalties.

One variable that could be particularly interesting is indicating the payment of fees to an executor. If the executor of the estate is a child or spouse of the decedent, that person may be less likely to collect the fees to which he or she is entitled (unless the tax implications make it worthwhile) than a professional. Thus this variable could proxy a professional practitioner. If it is a valid proxy, its estimated effect could potentially indicate whether professionals or heirs were responsible for pursuing the more aggressive tax avoidance strategy. Alternatively, nonprofessionals who are serving as executors may be less competent in correctly filing estate tax returns or in taking advantage of legal deductions. This variable is not significant in the equation for the probability of a positive assessment.

In comparing conditional amounts, one wants to compare the effects of variables in the two equations shown in tables 9-11 and 9-12. In some cases, one would expect opposite effects. For example, widowed individuals have a significantly lower positive assessment. One might therefore assume that they are less aggressive in pursuing deductions and may therefore also have overpaid by a larger amount. However, they in fact have a lower expected overpayment. Combining the two results, one concludes that widows are more accurate on average (conditional on being audited). The variables for all nonmarried individuals are negative; married people are assessed larger underpayments but also make larger overpayments. Perhaps surviving spouses who file estate tax returns for married decedents are less good at filing estate tax returns than children or professionals who handle such returns for singles.

The marginal tax rate and the value of the gross estate again have opposite effects. Holding marginal tax rate constant, a higher gross estate signals more deductions and is correlated with a greater positive assessment. Similarly, marginal tax rate held constant, a higher gross estate is correlated with a lower overpayment.

Attorney's fees, which were associated with a lower probability of a positive assessment, have no effect on the amount, conditional on such an assessment being made. They do, however, lower the amount of overpayment. This result seems surprising. One would imagine that additional attorney's fees associated with an audit would increase allowable deductions and actually increase the overpayment.

In both equations, an executor's fees are associated with greater over- or underpayment. If one agrees with the hypothesis that those accepting such fees are less likely to be family members, this result indicates that returns filed by professionals, conditional on being in error, have larger errors than returns filed by family members.

Conclusions

The two questions underlying much of the discussion are first, how much of the observed noncompliance is true tax evasion, and how much is mistaken reporting? And second, who is responsible for the observed tax evasion? The existence of such a large number of estates with overpayment of taxes indicates that a large fraction of the underpayments are likely to be simple errors as well. If these errors are symmetric, then approximately 40 percent of audited estates made an error, 40 percent intentionally underrepresented the value of the estate, and 20 percent filed correct returns. These fractions indicate that a number of filers have legitimate difficulties in correctly approximating the value of an estate.

As for the second question, although it is difficult to tease out an effect, there is some evidence that it may be the decedent himself who chooses how aggressive to be in evaluating the estate tax. The payment of an executor has no effect on compliance, indicating that a professional practitioner is not dictating behavior. In contrast, tax planning decisions made by the decedent such as the making of charitable bequests and previous inter vivos gifts are positively related to positive assessments. I would view this as very weak evidence but highlight this question as topic that deserves further investigation.

Finally, it would also be useful to be able to use the results from the study to assess how effectively the IRS targets its audits. For example, the authors point to the unexpectedly high rate of positive assessments on married couples as evidence that the IRS is erring when it assumes that the unlimited marital deduction will make assessments against the estates of married individuals unlikely. However, if the criteria the IRS uses to select returns for audit are well known (as is assumed by including the probability of an audit in the equation for the amount of the assessment), then individuals will have already responded to these criteria. In the case of married couples, if the probability of an audit is known to be low, then these individuals have a greater incentive to engage in tax evasion and will evade more often than singles, all else constant.

The figures in this chapter provide our first reliable estimates of the degree of noncompliance with estate taxes. They dispel a number of misconceptions. In particular, they show substantial overpayment of estate taxes, a relatively low audit rate, and some unexpected patterns in the types of estates most likely to owe additional assessments. The data used are likely to be the source for numerous important studies of tax compliance, and the authors have provided a valuable resource in presenting these first estimates.

References

Andreoni, James, Brian Erard, and Jonathan S. Feinstein. 1998. "Tax Compliance." *Journal of Economic Literature* 36 (June): 818–60.

Bureau of the Census. 1995. *Statistical Abstract of the United States.*

Eller, Martha B., and Barry W. Johnson. 2000. "Using a Sample of Federal Estate Tax Returns to Examine the Effects of Audit Revaluation on Pre-Audit Estimates." 1999 Proceedings of the American Statistical Association, Section on Government Statistics. Alexandria, Va.: American Statistical Association.

Erard, Brian. 1999. "Estate Tax Underreporting Gap Study: A Report Prepared for the Internal Revenue Service Economic Analysis and Modeling Group." Order number TIRNO-98-P-00406. Internal Revenue Service.

Feinstein, Jonathan, and Chih-Chin Ho. 1999. "Predicting Estate Tax Filings and Taxable Gifts." *IRS Research Bulletin, 1999 Update,* 39–45. Government Printing Office.

———. 2000. "Wealth, Mortality, and Estate Tax Filings: Evidence from the AHEAD Panel Data." Paper presented at the Population Association of America annual conference, Los Angeles.

Hoyert, Donna L., Kenneth D. Kochanek, and Sherry L. Murphy. 1999. "Deaths: Final Data for 1997." *National Vital Statistics Reports* 47(19): 1–108. Hyattsville, Md.: National Center for Health Statistics.

Johnson, Barry W., and Jacob M. Mikow. 1999. "Federal Estate Tax Returns, 1995–1997." *Statistics of Income Bulletin* (Summer): 69–129. Internal Revenue Service.,

Mitchell, Olivia S., James M. Poterba, and Mark J. Warshawsky. 1997. "New Evidence on the Money's Worth of Individual Annuities." Working Paper 6002. Cambridge, Mass.: National Bureau of Economic Research.

Poterba, James. 1997. "The Estate Tax and After-Tax Investment Returns." Working Paper 98–11. University of Michigan, Office of Tax Policy Research.

Slemrod, Joel, Marsha Blumenthal, and Charles Christian. Forthcoming. "Taxpayer Response to an Increased Probability of Audit: Evidence from a Controlled Experiment in Minnesota." *Journal of Public Economics.*

Wolff, Edward N. 1996. "Commentary on Douglas Holtz-Eakin. 'The Uneasy Case for Abolishing the Estate Tax.'" *Tax Law Review* 51(3): 517–21.

JAMES M. POTERBA
SCOTT WEISBENNER

10 | The Distributional Burden of Taxing Estates and Unrealized Capital Gains at Death

"BASIS STEP-UP at death," an important provision of the current income tax law, affects the total tax burden on some types of capital income. If an individual holds appreciated capital assets at the time of her death, those who inherit these assets receive them with a tax basis equal to their market value at the time of the decedent's death. Such basis step-up extinguishes capital gains tax liability for gains that occurred during the decedent's lifetime. No precise estimates exist of the fraction of capital gains that are held until death and consequently qualify for basis step-up under the income tax. Researchers have long suspected that this fraction is substantial. Martin Bailey suggested that the basis step-up provision could render the effective tax rate on capital gains only half the statutory rate on realizations.[1] Revenue estimates by the Joint Committee on Taxation, reported by the Congressional Budget Office, suggest that eliminating basis step-up at death and taxing unrealized capital gains at death would raise federal personal income tax liabilities by $10.5 billion in 2002.[2]

We are grateful to Jeffrey Brown for providing us with data on mortality rates, Barry Johnson and Jacob Mikow for data on 1998 estate tax returns, Thomas Barthold, Len Burman, David Joulfaian, Alan MacNaughton, Janet McCubbin, and Larry Ozanne for helpful discussions, and the National Science Foundation (Poterba) for research support.

1. Bailey (1969, p.38).
2. Reported in Congressional Budget Office (2000).

The recent debate on "death taxes" has sometimes focused on the combined effect of the estate and income taxes. James Poterba and others explain that individuals with high net worth face a trade-off between estate and income taxation if they hold appreciated assets.[3] If they hold their assets until death, they will avoid capital gains tax liability, at a maximum federal marginal tax rate of 20 percent, but they will face estate taxation. However, if individuals with high net worth sell their assets and realize gains before they die, then they will be liable for income taxes, but they may be able to pursue estate-planning strategies that reduce their taxable estate. Since the marginal estate tax rate peaks at 60 percent, sometimes it may pay to realize gains before death and to reduce estate taxes. The interaction between income and estate taxes is evident in some proposals that call for reducing estate tax rates, or for eliminating the estate tax, in tandem with eliminating the provisions in the federal income tax for basis step-up at death.

These reforms are sometimes paired to reduce the revenue cost of eliminating the estate tax. The revenue generated by taxing capital gains at death is very unlikely to fully offset the revenue loss from estate tax elimination. Estate tax rates are higher than tax rates on long-term capital gains, and the unrealized gains on assets held by decedents are only a fraction of their total wealth. Taxing unrealized capital gains at death would, however, raise revenue from some taxpayers who do not currently pay estate tax: decedents whose net worth falls below the estate tax threshold but who have appreciated capital assets when they die.

In this chapter, we use data from the 1998 Survey of Consumer Finances (SCF) to analyze the distributional effects of reducing estate taxes and taxing unrealized capital gains on assets held until death. We summarize the tax collected from current estate tax payers and the tax that might be paid by decedents who do not currently face the estate tax. We also explore the patterns in tax burdens that would arise if expanded capital gains taxation wholly or partially replaced estate taxation.

The Current U.S. Estate Tax and the Tax Treatment of Capital Gains at Death

There have been recent changes in both the estate tax and the income tax treatment of capital gains. The Taxpayer Relief Act of 1997 (TRA97) raised the threshold on the value of an estate that a decedent could leave without

3. See, for example, Poterba (2001).

facing estate taxation, and it also reduced the tax rate on long-term capital gains. This legislation also began the phase-in of various tax rate changes that will not be fully effective until 2006. These changes further affect the estate tax rules and the income tax treatment of long-term capital gains. This section summarizes current tax rules with emphasis on the rules in place in 1998, when the survey data that we analyze were collected.

Current Estate Tax Rules

The United States currently has a unified estate and gift tax, which means that a tax is levied on the value of assets transferred at the taxpayer's death, plus the value of taxable gifts made during the decedent's lifetime. These rules do not apply to interspousal gifts and bequests; such transfers are exempt from estate taxation. In practice, this means that when one spouse in a married couple dies, relatively little estate tax is due, but when the surviving spouse dies, often a substantial tax burden ensues.

The estate tax is highly progressive. Table 10-1 shows the set of tax rates that applied to decedents who died in 1998. Each individual receives a credit against lifetime estate and gift taxes. Between 1986 and 1997, each taxpayer received a credit of $192,800, which was precisely the estate tax liability on an estate of $600,000. TRA97 enacted changes in the estate and gift tax credit that will raise the size of estates that are exempt from tax to $1 million beginning in 2006. Table 10-2 shows the time path of the effective estate tax threshold for the 1997–2006 period.[4] TRA97 also included a special provision for estates that include family-owned businesses. Up to $675,000 of the value of a family-owned business became exempt from estate taxation effective January 1, 1998.

Although table 10-1 shows tax rates for 1998 estates valued at less than $625,000, decedents whose estates and cumulated lifetime taxable gifts are valued at less than this amount do not pay any estate tax. The value of the unified estate and gift tax credit exceeds their estate tax liability. For decedents whose taxable estates were valued at more than $625,000, the marginal estate tax rate on the 625,001st dollar of taxable estate is 37 percent. The highest statutory marginal estate tax rate is 55 percent. As a result of a surcharge that phases out the inframarginal estate tax rates of less than 55 percent, however, the highest effective marginal estate tax rate is 60 percent on estates valued at $10 million to $17.184 million.

---

4. See Joulfaian (1998) for a longer time span.

Table 10-1. *Federal Unified Estate and Gift Tax Rates, 1998*

Taxable transfer (thousands of dollars)	Marginal tax rate (percent)
0–10	18
10–20	20
20–40	22
40–60	24
60–80	26
80–100	28
100–150	30
150–250	32
250–500	34
500–750	37
750–1,000	39
1,000–1,250	41
1,250–1,500	43
1,500–2,000	45
2,000–2,500	49
2,500–3,000	53
3,000–10,000	55
10,000–17,184	60[a]
17,184 and above	55

a. The 60 percent marginal rate on estates valued at between $10 million and $17.184 million is a result of the phase-out of inframarginal tax rates of below 55 percent for estates in this valuation range. Thus for estates with taxable transfers greater than $17.184 million, the entire transfer is effectively taxed at the 55 percent rate.

Table 10-2. *Transfers Exempted from Estate and Gift Tax under Taxpayer Relief Act of 1997*[a]

Year	Estate tax threshold (dollars)
1997	600,000
1998	625,000
1999	650,000
2000–2001	675,000
2002–2003	700,000
2004	850,000
2005	950,000
2006 onward	1,000,000

a. Qualified family-owned businesses receive separate treatment under the estate tax. A deduction is provided for the value of such assets, so that the sum of this deduction and the unified credit is $1.3 million each year.

Individuals with high net worth can reduce the effective burden of the estate tax in various ways. People whose wealth is great enough to expose them to estate taxation, but not much greater than the estate tax threshold, can make tax-free gifts. Each individual may make a tax-free gift of $10,000 a year per recipient. This means that a married couple can transfer $20,000 a year to each child, grandchild, or other beneficiary. The $10,000 annual exemption has been indexed for inflation since 1999. More complex estate planning strategies might be used by households with higher net worth. Trusts that shelter assets from estate taxation, the creative use of financial products such as life insurance, and the use of multitiered transfers for family property such as businesses that permits use of "minority discounts" in valuing the assets being transferred are possibilities. George Cooper provided a classic summary of various strategies for estate tax avoidance; more recently, Christopher Drew and David Johnston have described some popular techniques. Richard Schmalbeck presents an overview of current estate-planning strategies in this volume.[5]

This book focuses exclusively on federal estate taxes, although many states tax inheritances, gifts, and estates. These taxes together raise about one-third of the revenue raised by the federal estate tax. In most cases state death taxes are creditable against federal estate tax liability for those taxpayers with federal estate tax liability, although not all decedents whose estates pay state death taxes pay federal estate taxes. One question that might arise if the federal estate tax were reduced or eliminated, but which we do not consider, is how states would modify their death taxes and how this would affect the total burden of estate taxation.

Current Tax Rules on Long-Term Capital Gains

Since 1997, long-term capital gains have been taxed at a maximum statutory tax rate of 20 percent. Long-term gains are defined as gains on assets that have been held for more than twelve months. (During 1998, the year when the Survey of Consumer Finances was carried out, long-term gains were defined as gains on assets held more than eighteen months. There was an "intermediate gains" category for gains on assets held between twelve and eighteen months.) Under current law, the marginal rate on long-term gains will decline to 18 percent, effective in 2005, for assets that have been held for at least

---

5. Cooper (1979); Christopher Drew and David Cay Johnston, "For Wealthy Americans, Death Is More Certain Than Taxes," *New York Times*, December 22, 1996, financial sec., p. 1.

five years. Basis step-up at death has been a long-standing feature of the income tax rules that apply to capital gains. Congress approved a provision that would carry over the decedent's basis in assets in the Tax Reform Act of 1976, but the provision was repealed before it could take effect.

One important class of capital gains, gains on principal residences, receives special treatment under the current capital gains tax. Homeowners may exclude $250,000 of gains, or $500,000 on joint returns, from capital gains tax calculations. This provision eliminates capital gains tax liability for many taxpayers whose only appreciated asset is their home.

Using the Survey of Consumer Finances to Estimate Estate Tax Burdens

Our empirical analysis uses information reported in the 1998 Survey of Consumer Finances, along with assumptions about the prospective mortality of each survey household. The Survey of Consumer Finances, a stratified random sample of U.S. households, is described in detail by Arthur Kennickell, Martha Starr-McCluer, and Brian Surette.[6] The survey includes a random population sample, as well as a sample that is drawn from information on tax returns and that oversamples households with high levels of capital income. The SCF is generally regarded as the best data available on the asset and liability positions of U.S. households. It also provides the best information on the segment of the population with high net worth, the segment most affected by estate tax reform.

The SCF sampled 4,305 households in its 1998 survey. Table 10-3 presents the net worth distribution of the survey respondents. One-fourth of the households have net worth of more than a million dollars, and 245 households have net worth in excess of $20 million. The wealthiest households are typically married couples. The maximum net worth in the sample is $501 million, which corresponds to the net worth threshold that a household needed to be included in the Forbes 400 richest Americans in 1998. Although data on the upper tail of the distribution of net worth are sparse, the SCF provides at least some coverage of all but the highest of households with high net worth.

Since the SCF is a survey of individuals who are alive, and the estate tax applies to individuals when they die, it is necessary to combine data on mortality rates with information on wealth holdings to estimate estate tax liability. Poterba elsewhere explains that two sets of mortality rates could be used for

6. Kennickell, Starr-McCluer, and Surette (2000).

Table 10-3. *Number of Households in 1998 Survey of Consumer Finances (SCF), by Net Worth and Marital Status of Head*[a]

Net worth (thousands of dollars)	Married[b]	Single[c]	All
Less than 500	1,640	1,287	2,927
500 up to 1,000	247	50	297
1,000 up to 5,000	442	87	529
5,000 up to 10,000	135	26	161
10,000 up to 20,000	136	10	146
20,000 up to 50,000	114	17	131
50,000 up to 100,000	58	6	64
100,000 up to 500,000	39	10	49
500,000 and over	1	0	1
All	2,812	1,493	4,305

Source: Authors' tabulation using 1998 Survey of Consumer Finance (SCF) and methods described in the text.

a. The net worth threshold to be included in the 1998 *Forbes* 400 was $500 million.

b. The five highest net worth households headed by a married couple in the Survey of Consumer Finances sample have net worth of $501 million, $452 million, $452 million, $434 million, and $404 million.

c. The highest net worth households headed by a single person in the sample have net worth of $356 million, $312 million, $223 million, $176 million, and $163 million.

this purpose.[7] The first is the population life table, reported by the Social Security Administration Office of the Actuary. This life table applies to individuals chosen randomly from the population at large. Various researchers, most recently Orazio Attanasio and Hilary Hoynes, suggest that households with high income and high net worth have lower mortality rates than their lower-income counterparts, so the population mortality table may not accurately describe the mortality rates of those who are subject to the estate tax.[8]

An alternative mortality table that may describe the mortality rates facing the high-net-worth households better than the population mortality table is the individual annuitant life table, which is described by Olivia Mitchell and others.[9] It describes the mortality experience of individuals who purchase single-premium annuities from life insurance companies. These individuals typically have sufficient accumulated resources to purchase policies with initial premiums of between $50,000 and $100,000, so they are from the upper tail of the wealth distribution. They may also have some private information

7. Poterba (2000).
8. Attanasio and Hoynes (2000).
9. Mitchell and others (1999).

suggesting longer-than-average longevity prospects, although as Amy Finkelstein and Poterba explain, it is difficult to measure the adverse selection.[10] Age-specific mortality rates in the individual annuitant table are 25 to 35 percent lower than those in the population life table.

One counterargument to the use of the annuitant mortality table recognizes that most estate tax paying decedents are single. Single individuals have higher mortality rates than married individuals, so the annuitant mortality table may understate death rates for potential estate taxpayers. Martha Eller, Brian Erard, and Chih-Chin Ho in this volume note that assumptions about the mortality rate of potential estate tax decedents have first-order effects on revenue estimates.[11] Further work is needed to calibrate the mortality table for wealthy individuals who may face estate tax liability.

We consider two different algorithms in analyzing estate tax revenues. The first assumes that estate tax liability for married couples is triggered only when the second spouse dies, while the second assumes that even the first to die may leave a taxable estate. To illustrate our procedures, we first describe our "second-to-die" algorithm. We use the annuitant mortality table to estimate the individual's probability that each household dies in a given year. The mortality probability for the household is q_h. For households with only one member, q_h is just the individual's probability of dying during the year: it depends on the age and sex of the individual. For married couples, in the second-to-die algorithm, we assume that when the first spouse dies, all assets are bequeathed to the spouse, and that there is correspondingly no estate tax liability. In this case, for married couples the relevant mortality rate for triggering estate tax liability (q_h) is the probability that both spouses die within the year. We calculate this probability assuming that the mortality rates of the two members of the married couple are independent; there is weak evidence of a positive correlation in the mortality experience of couples. The expected estate tax burden for each household is

$$(1) \qquad E\left(\text{Estate Tax}\right) = q_h{}^* \tau_e \left(NW_h\right),$$

where NW_h denotes the net worth of household h, including the face value of any life insurance policies, and $\tau_e(\ )$ denotes the estate tax function, which determines estate tax liability as a function of household net worth.

---

10. Adverse selection refers to the fact that individuals who choose to purchase annuities in private markets tend to be healthier, and to live longer, than those who do not buy annuities. From the standpoint of an insurance company that writes annuity policies, selection in favor of longer-lived individuals is "adverse" because it raises the expected cost of annuity policies. Finkelstein and Poterba (2000).

11. Eller, Erard, and Ho, chap. 11, in this volume.

Although many married couples appear to use estate plans that defer all estate taxes until the death of the second spouse, this is not necessarily the best strategy for minimizing estate taxes. Schmalbeck, in this volume, notes that this approach does not take advantage of the progressivity of the estate tax rate schedule. If a couple splits ownership of all assets, and the first-to-die bequeaths none of his or her assets to the surviving spouse, then the couple will be able to utilize two $625,000 exemptions and will also pass more of their wealth through the lower rate brackets of the estate tax. The possibility that some couples follow this strategy motivates our second algorithm for estimating the estate taxes of married couples. It assumes that assets are divided equally between spouses when one spouse dies. Thus, half of the married couple's assets will be subject to the estate tax when the first spouse dies. In this case, our estimate of estate tax liability for married couples is approximately equal to the sum of the mortality probabilities for the two members of the couple, times the estate tax due on half of their household net worth. We also add the (smaller) probability that both spouses die, times the estate tax due on their entire net worth.

Our measure of net worth, the base to which the estate tax applies, includes the face value of life insurance policies. Including insurance proceeds in the estate tax base brings a number of younger households in the SCF into the set of potential estate taxpayers. These households typically have very low probabilities of dying, so their expected estate tax is quite low. In codifying the estate tax function in equation 1, we recognize a number of detailed features of the estate tax, such as the $675,000 exemption for business assets.

One potential limitation is our use of the reported value of assets in the SCF, rather than a measure that allows for any undervaluation of assets for the purposes of estate taxation. The practice of invoking "minority discounts" in valuing some types of assets, which is discussed by Schmalbeck, is likely to result in our estimates *overstating* the estate tax that would be collected for particular assets. It is also possible that another set of biases operates in the opposite direction. If some SCF respondents omit assets when they respond to the survey, or if they use asset valuations that are potentially out of date, this may result in undervaluation of gross estates relative to their actual value.

We use an approach similar to that in equation 1 to estimate the expected capital gains tax liability that would be associated with taxing each household's unrealized capital gains at the time of death. In this case, in place of net worth for household h, we focus on our estimate of the stock of unrealized capital gains (UG_h) held by household h. We then calculate

(2) $E(\text{Tax on Capital Gains at Death}) = q_h{}^* \tau_{cg}(UG_h),$

where $\tau_{cg}(\ )$ denotes the capital gains tax schedule. Under current tax law, the tax rate on long-term capital gains at death is 20 percent. For each household in the SCF, our estimate of the ratio of the expected estate tax and the expected capital gains tax if unrealized gains were taxed at death is unaffected by the mortality rate. In calculating the revenue from taxing capital gains at death, we assume that when one spouse in a married couple dies, all assets pass to the surviving spouse and that there is no capital gains tax liability. The surviving spouse receives these assets with a stepped-up basis. One could alternatively, although we do not, assume a more complicated pattern of gain recognition associated with death of the first spouse.

The SCF provides data on the composition of a household's net worth. Survey respondents are asked the value of their holdings across many asset types such as real estate, stocks, bonds, and business interests. Households also provide the purchase price or basis for certain assets. For assets that are inherited from someone other than a spouse, the respondent reports the market value of the asset when it was received as the basis. The respondent is asked how much his nonpension plan holdings of publicly traded stock and mutual funds have gained in value since they were obtained. The SCF also records the net worth of the household's share of a business as well as the cost basis for tax purposes for all businesses in which the household has an active or nonactive management role. Finally, each survey respondent is asked the current value and what he originally paid for his primary residence as well as all other real estate holdings.

We can use this information to directly calculate a household's unrealized capital gains held in publicly traded stock, mutual funds, real estate, and businesses. Assets such as savings accounts and certificates of deposit do not generate capital gains. The purchase price or basis is not reported for such assets as bonds, vehicles, and collectibles that may have undergone a capital gain or loss. Throughout this chapter, we assume that these assets have no accrued capital gains. This group of assets constitutes less than one-tenth of aggregate net worth and only 6 percent of total estate value. We exclude assets held in retirement accounts such as IRAs or 401(k)s when we calculate unrealized capital gains, since the payouts from those accounts are taxed as ordinary income.

Federal Estate Tax Liability for Different Tax Thresholds

Barry W. Johnson, Jacob M. Mikow, and Martha Britton Eller report, in this volume, that estate tax returns filed in 1998 generated $20.3 billion in

Table 10-4. *Estimated Estate Tax Revenue from Single and Married Households, 1998*[a]

		Married households[b]			
		Bequeath all to surviving spouse		Bequeath none of estate to surviving spouse	
Item	Single households	One spouse dies	Both spouses die	One spouse dies	Both spouses die
Total estate tax (billions of dollars)	15.98	0	0.64	26.07	0.51
Number of taxable returns (thousands)	25.15	0	1.51	35.81	0.52

Source: Authors' calculations based on 1998 SCF and data supplied by Barry Johnson and Jacob Mikow.

a. Estimated estate tax is calculated using the average funeral expense, executor's commission, lawyer's fee, charitable deduction, and state death tax credit for taxable returns for each gross estate class for 1998 filers.

b. It is assumed that assets are divided equally among spouses.

revenue. Actual federal receipts from the estate tax for fiscal year 1999, primarily from 1998 decedents, were approximately $28 billion. Table 10-4 reports our estimates of estate tax revenue from 1998 decedents using the SCF and the mortality assumptions discussed earlier. Our estimates assume that each estate claims the average value, for 1998 taxable estate tax returns in its gross estate class, of funeral expenses, executor's commissions, lawyer's fees, and charitable deductions. This leads to an estimate of gross federal estate tax liability for each estate, which is then reduced by the average level of state death tax credits for taxable estates in the decedent's gross estate valuation class.

Calculating the estate tax revenue from single households is straightforward, and we estimate that the federal estate tax collected $16.0 billion from these households in 1998. Estate taxes on returns filed in 1998 by single decedents totaled $16.7 billion; this is primarily from 1997 decedents. The estimated distribution of the tax across broad estate groups matches fairly well that of single decedents who filed estate tax returns in 1998. Data from the Internal Revenue Service show that single decedents who filed 1998 returns with gross estates valued at $600,000 to $1 million paid $0.88 billion, those with $1 to 5 million paid $7.86 billion, $5–10 million paid $2.84 billion, and

Table 10-5. *Estate Tax Returns Filed in 1998, by Gross Estate and Marital Status*

	Married			Non-Married		
Returns (millions of dollars)	Fraction of returns that pay any tax (percent)	Gross estate value (billions of dollars)	Net estate tax paid (billions of dollars)	Fraction of returns that pay any tax (percent)	Gross estate value (billions of dollars)	Net estate tax paid (billions of dollars)
All returns	13.3	83.8	3.7	75.9	90.0	16.7
0.6 up to 1	5.3	15.1	0.0	62.8	23.2	0.9
1 up to 2.5	14.2	25.9	0.5	91.7	27.5	4.4
2.5 up to 5	30.5	13.6	0.7	92.4	12.7	3.5
5 up to 10	42.3	8.9	0.6	94.9	9.2	2.8
10 up to 20	53.2	6.6	0.5	93.5	6.3	2.0
20 and over	74.9	13.6	1.3	93.5	11.0	3.1

Source: Authors' calculations based on data supplied by Barry Johnson and Jacob Mikow.

estates exceeding $10 million paid $5.11 billion. Our 1998 SCF-based estimates suggest that single estate tax filers with estates of $600,000 to $1 million paid $0.24 billion in estate tax, those with estates of $1 to $5 million paid $8.22 billion, those with $5–10 million paid $3.16 billion, and those with gross estates greater than $10 million paid $4.36 billion.

We now consider our two alternative approaches to estimating the estate tax liability of married couples. The first, which assumes that the first-to-die spouse bequeaths everything to the surviving spouse, implies that there will be no estate tax liability until the surviving spouse dies. The first two columns of table 10-4 show that under this assumption, we estimate that only $0.6 billion of estate tax would have been collected from deaths of married couples during 1998. This figure reflects the small probability that both spouses die in the same year.

The last two columns of table 10-4 present estimates of estate tax revenue from married households under the alternative assumption that the first spouse to die leaves half of the couple's assets as an estate. Estimated tax revenue from deaths in married couples now rises to more than $26 billion. These divergent estimates underscore the importance of determining how deaths in married couples translate into taxable estates.

Table 10-5 sheds some light on the estate tax planning of married couples. On estate tax returns filed in 1998, only 13 percent of married decedents with gross estates valued in excess of $600,000 paid any estate tax, whereas more than 75 percent of single decedents with gross estates valued in excess of $600,000 did so. Slightly more than half of married decedents with estates valued between $10 and $20 million paid any estate tax. Further, while the gross estate value of married decedents is roughly the same as that for single decedents, married decedents accounted for only 18 percent of total estate tax revenue in 1998. Johnson and Mikow report similar results when examining the returns of 1995 decedents.[12] Thus, it seems that most couples do not employ simple tax avoidance techniques, such as having the first-to-die spouse pay some estate tax, which could reduce the couple's total estate tax. This finding parallels Poterba's results on the limited use of tax-free gifts as a strategy for reducing estate tax liability.[13]

To use the data in table 10-5 to sharpen our estimates of the estate taxes due when one member of a married couple dies, we make an important simplifying assumption. We assume either that married couples pass all of their assets to the surviving spouse, as our first algorithm assumes, or that they follow the principle of dividing their assets equally between spouses, with each spouse bequeathing half of the couple's net worth at the time of death. The latter assumption corresponds to our second algorithm. We then assume that the fraction of returns in each gross estate class that pay *any* estate tax, as in table 10-5, equals the fraction of married couples in that net worth category that follows the equal division rule. Thus, we assume that 74.9 percent of all married couples with more than $20 million in household net worth follow the equal division strategy. Using this assumption, we estimate total 1998 estate tax revenue of $27.4 billion. This figure equals taxes from single decedents, plus the weighted average of the two estimates for married couples presented in table 10-4. We also considered modeling the probability that a married decedent bequeaths nothing to his or her spouse as a function of the ratio of the average tax rate on estates of married decedents and on single decedents. This approach yields an estimate of total estate tax revenue of $22.3 billion.

The foregoing estimates describe the potential estate tax liability of households in the 1998 Survey of Consumer Finances. This survey, however, does not include the highest net worth households in the U.S. economy. By excluding the wealthiest segment of the population from its sampling, largely because they might be identified based on other publicly available information, the SCF in effect enables us to estimate the estate tax burden on the population with wealth below the level of the *Forbes* 400.

12. Johnson and Mikow (1999).
13. Poterba (2001).

Table 10-6. *Net Worth of Members of* Forbes *400 Decedents, 1995–98*[a]

| | All decedents | | Single decedents | |
Year	Number	Net worth (billions of dollars)	Number	Net worth (billions of dollars)
1998	7	16.3	1	4.0
1997	5	4.2	2	1.7
1996	6	5.3	2	1.3
1995	10	8.0	4	5.0

Source: *Forbes* magazine, various issues.

a. Total net worth for the *Forbes* 400 rose from $357 billion in 1995 to $738 billion in 1998.

Since the *Forbes* 400 members are publicly identified, we can augment the SCF data with information on the wealth holdings, and deaths, of this group. Table 10-6 summarizes the number of members of the *Forbes* 400 who died in recent years, along with the net worth of these decedents. In the average year between 1995 and 1998, seven members of the *Forbes* 400 died. The net worth of these decedents varied substantially, from $5.9 billion in 1997 to $20.3 billion in 1998. To translate the wealth of the *Forbes* 400 decedents into estate taxes, we consider the ratio of estate taxes to the gross estate value for married and single 1998 decedents with estates valued at $20 million or more. This ratio is 0.285 for single decedents and 0.094 for married decedents. Applying these ratios to the net worth of the 1998 *Forbes* 400 decedents would imply an additional $2.3 billion in estate taxes, while applying it to the 1997 decedents would generate $0.7 billion in additional taxes. These values suggest that the divergence between actual estate tax revenue as reported by the IRS, and our estimate of estate tax liability, can be attributed in part to the absence of households with very high net worth in the Survey of Consumer Finances.

Our SCF-based estimate of estate tax liability in table 10-4 corresponds fairly closely to the actual estate tax liability in recent years, particularly once we recognize the additional contribution of the highest net worth households. The net federal estate tax paid by 1998 filers was $20.4 billion, and receipts during fiscal year 1999 were about $23 billion. Our estimates suggest estate tax revenue of $16 billion from single households in 1998, and between $6 and $11 billion from married households. Adding *Forbes* 400 decedents boosts the estimated tax collection to a total between $23 and $30 billion.

The similarity of our estimate of total estate tax liability, and actual aggregate revenues, stands in contrast to Edward Wolff's related analysis.[14] He argues that an algorithm similar to ours yields a projected estate tax liability based on the 1992 SCF of $44 billion, compared with $10.5 billion in actual estate tax collections from 1992 decedents. Martin Sullivan reports calculations in a similar vein based on the 1998 Survey of Consumer Finances.[15]

The divergence between our results and those in other studies has several potential explanations. One is that Wolff uses the population mortality table, which yields a higher estimate of intergenerational transfers and estate tax liability than the annuitant mortality table that we use. A second is that Wolff relies on a re-weighted version of the 1992 Survey of Consumer Finances, with weights that generate a larger total wealth stock (hence larger bequests) than the public use weights, particularly among households with high net worth.

When we apply the algorithm described by equation 1 to the 1995 SCF, we find the expected estate tax liability for the year is $14.4 billion, while actual estate tax revenues for 1995 decedents were $14.3 billion ($11.8 billion for nonmarried decedents). The very close similarity of the estimate and actual revenue is probably coincidence. For 1992, our SCF-based estimate of estate tax liability is $7.9 billion, while actual taxes for 1992 decedents were $10.5 billion ($8.6 billion for nonmarried decedents). For both years, it seems that the expected tax generated by our algorithm is similar, to a first order, to actual estate tax revenue. Further analysis of the source of differences across years is left to future research.

Given the rough success of our algorithm in tracking federal estate tax revenues under current and recent estate tax rules, we used it to consider the impact of several counterfactual assumptions about estate and gift tax credits. Table 10-7 reports our calculations for different exemptions. The estimates in the top panel are based on a weighted average of our two approaches to treating married couples. The middle and bottom panels present results first under the assumption that married decedents leave everything to their surviving spouse, and then under the assumption that married couples follow an equal division of estates with no bequest to the surviving spouse. We assume that the fraction of married decedents that follows the strategy in the bottom panel corresponds to the fraction of returns by married decedents in each gross estate class that pays any tax (presented in table 10-5). The fraction of married decedents that leaves everything to the surviving spouse, as the middle panel in

14. Wolff (1996).
15. Martin A. Sullivan, "For Richest Americans, Two-Thirds of Wealth Escapes Estate Tax," *Tax Notes*, April 17, 2000, pp. 328–33.

Table 10-7. *Estimated Estate Tax Revenue under Various Estate and Gift Tax Credits and Exemptions*[a]
Billions of 1998 dollars

	Exemption		
Assumption	*$625,000*	*$1 million*	*$3 million*
Weighted average algorithm for calculating estate tax from married decedents[b]			
Deductions under current tax law	27.43	23.66	12.84
Allowed to deduct $1 million in principal residence	23.77	20.72	11.47
Allowed to deduct both $1 million in principal residence and $3 million in business	21.27	18.37	10.28
Married decedent leaves all to spouse			
Deductions under current tax law	16.62	13.75	6.67
Allowed to deduct $1 million in principal residence	13.95	11.72	5.78
Allowed to deduct both $1 million in principal residence and $3 million in business	12.84	10.67	5.29
Assets divided evenly; married decedent leaves nothing to spouse			
Deductions under current tax law	42.56	35.68	17.06
Allowed to deduct $1 million in principal residence	36.20	30.62	15.12
Allowed to deduct both $1 million in principal residence and $3 million in business	31.36	26.26	13.21

Source: Authors' calculations based on 1998 SCF and data supplied by Barry Johnson and Jacob Mikow.

a. Estimated estate tax is calculated using the average funeral expense, executor's commission, lawyer's fee, charitable deduction, and state death tax credit for taxable returns for each gross estate class for 1998 filers.

b. Weighted average of the bottom two panels. See text for details.

table 10-7 assumes, is understood to be the fraction of returns in each gross estate class that pays no tax.

The first column in table 10-7 presents revenue estimates under the actual 1998 law, namely, assuming a $625,000 exemption. We estimate a total federal estate tax collection of $27.4 billion. This value does not include any revenue that might be collected from the *Forbes* 400 decedents, which could yield an additional $2.3 billion based on our estimate above.

To illustrate the effect of changing exemption levels, we focus on the weighted average case. If the exemption had been $1 million in 1998, our estimate of revenues would have fallen from $27.4 billion to $23.7 billion. Revenues would drop to $12.8 billion if the exemption level was raised further to $3 million. Exempting the value of the principal residence (up to $1 million) from the estate tax would reduce estimated tax receipts by about an eighth. Expanding the deduction for an actively managed business would have a slightly more modest effect on estate tax revenue. The middle and bottom panels of table 10-7 show that total revenues are lower (higher) when we assume that married decedents leave everything (nothing) to the surviving spouse, but the direction of the effects are similar.

Taxing Capital Gains at Death versus Taxing Estates

We now consider the comparative distributional burdens of the current estate tax and a capital gains tax levied on all unrealized gains at the time of death. We begin by summarizing information on the importance of unrealized capital gains in the portfolios of decedents, and we then compare the tax payments of decedents under different tax rules. Throughout this section, we assume that the estate tax and the tax on unrealized capital gains for married couples are triggered only when the second spouse dies. In other words, we assume that transferring assets to a spouse does not generate a capital gains tax liability but that carry-over basis rules apply to such transactions. Since our tabulations are based on the SCF, they once again only apply to households with net worth below the level of the *Forbes* 400.

The type of policy change that we consider below is similar to one enacted in Canada nearly three decades ago. The 1971 Income Tax Act eliminated the Canadian federal estate tax, and at the same time a capital gains tax was adopted for gains on assets transferred at death. John Bossons presents a detailed description of the Canadian reforms and the contemporaneous estimates of the revenue effects of this policy change.[16]

---

16. Bossons (1972, 1974).

Unrealized Capital Gains as a Share of Net Worth

The Survey of Consumer Finances data enable us to estimate the unrealized capital gains in household portfolios and to compare this information with our estimate of household net worth. Table 10-8 presents summary information. The first row shows the total value of expected estates for households in different net worth categories, while the second row shows the corresponding expected unrealized capital gains for households in different categories. For all households, expected unrealized capital gains at death total $42.8 billion, or 36 percent of the total expected value of estates. There is only a weak association between the ratio of unrealized gains to estate value and estate size. The values of this ratio are close to one-third for most categories of net worth. At the highest level, for those with estates worth at least $10 million, unrealized gains represent 56 percent of the value of estates.

Table 10-8 also shows the distribution of asset holdings across different net worth categories. It demonstrates the dramatically different importance of owner-occupied real estate for those at low levels of net worth and those at higher levels. For households with net worth of less than $250,000, primary residences account for nearly 60 percent of total assets, while for those with net worth of more than $10 million, this percentage drops to only 3 percent. The decline in the importance of primary residences is matched by a sharp wealth-related increase in the importance of businesses in which the decedent was an active participant. Such businesses account for nearly half of the assets of those with net worth of at least $10 million, while they account for less than 1 percent of the assets of those with net worth of less than $1 million. The composition of capital gains across asset types matters for estate tax liabilities, since capital gains on owner-occupied housing are often taxed at a lower rate than other capital gains.

Within the stock of unrealized capital gains, significant differences occur in composition across categories of net worth. Primary residences account for more than nine-tenths of the unrealized capital gains of households with net worth of less than $500,000, while they account for less than 4 percent of unrealized gains for those with net worth of $10 million and above. Similarly, unrealized capital gains on active businesses account for more than 70 percent of the unrealized gains of households in the highest net worth category, while they account for only a negligible fraction of the unrealized gains for those in lower net worth strata. The ratio of unrealized capital gains on stock and mutual fund holdings to total gains is also much higher for the wealthy.

Table 10-9 presents more direct evidence on the importance of unrealized gains relative to estate value. The table shows the fraction of decedent

Table 10-8. *Unrealized Capital Gains in Net Worth of Expected Decedents, 1998*[a]
Billions of 1998 dollars

Item	All	Insurance-augmented net worth (thousands of dollars)					
		Up to $250	$250 up to $500	$500 up to $1,000	$1,000 up to $5,000	$5,000 up to $10,000	$10,000 and over
Value of estate (billions of dollars)	118	32.6	18.7	9.7	36.1	9.6	11.7
Unrealized capital gain (billions of dollars)	42.8	11.8	6.3	3.3	12.5	2.3	6.6
Share of total assets (percent)							
Primary residence	29.7	59.4	37.9	25.1	15.4	4.6	3.1
Other real estate	10.0	2.2	17.2	14.8	13.3	9.3	6.9
Business and farm[b]	7.2	0.4	0.7	1.0	5.1	5.2	49.4
Other business	1.0	0.0	0.2	0.7	1.7	0.6	3.0
Public stock and mutual funds[c]	19.1	3.9	10.4	19.8	30.0	41.2	22.4
Share of total unrealized capital gain (percent)							
Primary residence	54.7	100.1	83.1	46.0	35.2	10.2	3.6
Other real estate	13.1	2.8	11.3	31.9	19.8	26.0	6.9
Business and farm[b]	15.9	0.6	1.4	1.7	11.4	17.2	72.3
Other business	2.1	0.0	0.4	1.9	3.8	2.2	4.1
Public stock and mutual funds[c]	14.1	-3.5	3.8	18.4	29.9	44.4	13.1

Source: Authors' calculations based on data from 1998 SCF.

a. Estate value includes face value of life insurance. Basis and unrealized capital gain are reported for directly held stock, mutual funds, business holdings, and real estate. Bonds, vehicles, and collectibles are assumed to have no accrued capital gains. The expected value of estates and unrealized capital gains is calculated by applying 1998 annuitant mortality rates, as described in the text, to the sample of households in the 1998 SCF (appropriately weighted to reflect the population). It is assumed a decedent transfers his/her full estate to a surviving spouse. Such interspousal transfers are not included in the estate totals reported above.

b. Active business.

c. Directly held public stock.

Table 10-9. *Estate Value and Unrealized Capital Gains of Expected Decedent Households, 1998*
Percent

Unrealized gains as a share of estate	All	Insurance-augmented net worth (thousands of dollars)					
		Up to $250	$250 up to $500	$500 up to $1,000	$1,000 up to $5,000	$5,000 up to $10,000	$10,000 and over
Less than 25	49	51	34	52	48	76	21
25–50	22	21	32	11	18	14	24
50–75	16	15	18	18	31	8	36
75 or greater	13	13	16	19	3	2	18

Source: Authors' tabulations from 1998 Survey of Consumer Finances.

households, by net worth category, with unrealized capital gains of less than 25 percent, 25 to 50 percent, 50 to 75 percent, and more than 75 percent of their net worth. Half of all "expected" decedents report unrealized capital gains of less than one-quarter of their net worth. Only three-tenths report unrealized capital gains of at least half the value of their net worth, and 13 percent report unrealized gains that equal at least three-quarters of their net worth. Households with more than three-quarters of their net worth in the form of unrealized gains are concentrated in the less than $1 million and more than $10 million net worth categories.

Table 10-9 shows some of the dispersion in income tax liabilities that would result from taxing unrealized capital gains at death. There is wide dispersion in unrealized gains as a share of net worth. Since net worth is to a first approximation the basis for estate taxation, substantial differences are likely to occur across households with similar net worth in the tax payments under an income tax that taxes unrealized gains at death. The composition of unrealized capital gains across asset holdings will also be a key determinant of tax burdens, since some types of capital gains are taxed more lightly than others.

Revenue Effects of Alternative "Death Tax" Policies

Table 10-10 presents our estimates of the total taxes collected under various tax regimes, assuming that the tax changes did not affect the stocks of wealth that households reported in the 1998 Survey of Consumer Finances. (We discuss this unrealistic assumption below.) The first row shows our estimates of the taxes collected by the current (as of 1998) estate tax, with a $625,000 estate and gift tax credit, under the weighted average algorithm that we used in the top panel of table 10-7. The second row shows our estate tax estimate assuming that the first-to-die spouse in married couples leaves all assets to the surviving spouse. (This is also our assumption when we estimate capital gains tax revenue.) In the first case, we estimate estate tax revenues of $27.4 billion. In the second case, shown in the second row, we estimate aggregate revenue of $16.6 billion from the current tax, with roughly half of that amount coming from estates with values between $1 and $5 million. Our calculations using the weighted-average algorithm suggest that estates of more than $10 million generate 45 percent of current estate tax revenue. This drops to 28 percent when we assume that the first to die leaves all assets to the surviving spouse.

The third row of table 10-10 shows our estimates of the revenue from including unrealized capital gains in the income tax base for decedents. Fol-

Table 10-10. *Distribution of Various Capital Income Taxes by Net Worth, 1998*[a]

Billions of 1998 dollars

Tax	All	Insurance-augmented net worth (thousands of dollars)						
		Up to $250	$250 up to $500	$500 up to $1,000	$1,000 up to $5,000	$5,000 up to $10,000	$10,000 and over
Current estate tax (weighted average algorithm)	27.43	0.00	0.00	0.27	9.33	5.38	12.46
Current estate tax	16.62	0.00	0.00	0.27	8.50	3.22	4.63
Tax capital gains at death (no exemption)	4.53	0.09	0.25	0.42	2.02	0.43	1.32
Tax capital gains at death ($100,000 exemption)	3.75	0.00	0.05	0.26	1.74	0.39	1.31
Tax capital gains at death ($500,000 exemption)	2.54	0.00	0.00	0.02	0.95	0.28	1.29

Source: Authors' tabulations using data from 1998 SCF.

a. Calculations of net worth (estate size) include decedent's net worth plus face value of life insurance. The expected value of estates and unrealized capital gains is calculated by applying 1998 mortality numbers (interpolation of 1983 and 2000 annuitant life tables) to the sample of households in the 1998 SCF, appropriately weighted to reflect the population. The probability of death across spouses is assumed to be independent. All calculations except those in the first row assume that a decedent transfers his or her full estate to the surviving spouse, so there is no capital gains tax at death and no estate tax liability if there is a surviving spouse. Calculations in the first row follow the "weighted average algorithm" described in the text. Estates are assumed to be able to exempt up to $250,000 in capital gains from the principal residence when calculating taxable capital gains at death.

lowing current tax law, gains of up to $250,000 on principal residences are excluded from tax. We do not allow for interactions between the capital gains tax and the estate tax but rather consider them as alternative policies. If basis step-up at death were eliminated without modifying the estate tax, then a decedent's final income tax payment would include payment for capital gains tax. This tax payment would reduce the decedent's estate and correspondingly reduce estate tax liability.

We estimate that the revenue yield from eliminating basis step-up at death would have been about $4.5 billion a year in 1998. This estimate is somewhat smaller than the annual revenue estimates developed by the Joint Committee on Taxation for 2001–10, as reported by the Congressional Budget Office.[17] One possible explanation for this divergence is our use of the annuitant mortality table rather than the population mortality table, which reduces our estimated flow of taxable gains by more than one-third. Furthermore, the committee estimates may not assume that married decedents leave all of their appreciated assets to their surviving spouse, as we do.

Table 10-10 also shows the distribution of revenues across estates of various sizes. The fraction of the capital gains tax that would be collected from decedents with estates of more than $10 million is 29 percent, similar to the share of estate taxes collected from this group.

The last two rows in table 10-10 explore the effect of allowing for various exemptions, besides the housing exemption, that would reduce capital gains tax liability at death. The third row shows the impact of allowing for a $100,000 exemption from capital gains tax liability, and the fourth row shows the effect of a $500,000 exemption. We estimate that a $100,000 exemption would reduce revenues by $0.8 billion per year, while a $500,000 exemption would reduce them by $2.0 billion per year. These exemptions raise the concentration of tax liability among decedents with the highest net worth. With the $500,000 exemption, for example, 51 percent of the capital gains tax liability at death is paid by decedents with net worth of $10 million or more. The $100,000 exemption has a more modest effect. In this case, 35 percent of the capital gains taxes fall on this group with the highest net worth.

Stratifying households by net worth, as in table 10-10, is one way of assessing the distributional effects of different tax policies. It is not, however, the usual approach to constructing distribution tables for tax policy analysis. Annual income, rather than net worth, is typically used to stratify households. Table 10-11 presents information on the distribution of the same four tax policies that are analyzed in table 10-10, but households are now strati-

17. Congressional Budget Office (2000).

Table 10-11. *Distribution of Taxes on Capital Assets at Time of Death, by Income Class, 1998*[a]
Billions of 1998 dollars

		Income (thousands of dollars)					
Tax	All	Up to $250	$250 up to $500	$500 up to $1,000	$1,000 up to $5,000	$5,000 up to $10,000	$10,000 and over
By adjusted gross income							
Current estate tax							
(weighted average algorithm)	27.43	5.40	4.25	5.16	4.21	2.61	5.81
Current estate tax	16.62	5.15	3.66	3.51	2.41	0.78	1.10
Tax capital gains at death (no exemption)	4.53	1.45	0.97	0.94	0.80	0.11	0.26
Tax capital gains at death ($100,000 exemption)	3.75	0.95	0.79	0.86	0.79	0.10	0.26
Tax capital gains at death ($500,000 exemption)	2.54	0.42	0.42	0.61	0.75	0.09	0.25
By imputed income[b]							
Current estate tax							
(weighted average algorithm)	27.43	0.64	0.94	5.54	6.29	2.42	11.61
Current estate tax	16.62	0.40	0.94	5.18	5.17	0.42	4.51
Tax capital gains at death (no exemption)	4.53	0.42	0.60	0.95	1.15	0.11	1.29
Tax capital gains at death ($100,000 exemption)	3.75	0.13	0.38	0.77	1.08	0.11	1.28
Tax capital gains at death ($500,000 exemption)	2.54	0.01	0.06	0.32	0.81	0.09	1.25

Source: Authors' tabulations using 1998 SCF.
a. See note to table 10-10 for details of calculation and underlying assumptions.
b. Imputed income adds noncapital income to an imputed income stream from assets (0.075 multiplied by the stock of assets).

fied according to adjusted gross income (AGI) rather than net worth. The upper panel in table 10-11 shows households categorized by "traditional" AGI, while the lower panel shows households stratified by an imputed income measure that tries to avoid the problems raised by different income-to-value ratios for different types of capital assets. The income measure that we use to stratify households in this case is AGI less all capital income, plus 0.075 times the value of all capital assets. This procedure imputes a 7.5 percent rate of return to all assets. The Joint Committee on Taxation's report discusses several issues that bear on procedures like this imputation.[18]

The distribution of tax burdens across income categories in table 10-11 provides somewhat different insights than the distribution by net worth categories (table 10-10). Substantial differences between the results in the two panels of table 10-11, corresponding to differences between actual and imputed AGI, are shown. Since the income measure in the lower panel of table 10-11 includes a component that is proportional to net worth, a strong correlation is shown between the results in table 10-10 and those in the lower panel of table 10-11.

To highlight the results, first consider the results on the distribution of estate tax burdens in the first two rows of the upper panel in table 10-11. Under the weighted average algorithm, shown in the first row, 21 percent of estate taxes are paid by households with AGI of $1 million or more, while more than one-third (35 percent) are paid by households with AGI of less than $100,000. Assuming that the first-to-die spouse in married couples leaves all assets to the surviving spouse, as in second the row, suggests that roughly 7 percent of estate taxes are paid by decedents with AGI of $1 million or more, while more than half (53 percent) are paid by decedents with AGI of less than $100,000. These tabulations show that a substantial pool of assets that are taxed under the estate tax are held by households whose current income does not place them at the very top of the income distribution. The pattern is similar for capital gains taxes at death when there is no exemption. Households with incomes of more than $1 million pay roughly 6 percent of these taxes, and households with incomes below $100,000 account for 53 percent of these taxes. When we introduce substantial exemptions for appreciated assets, the concentration of capital gains taxes increases. In the case of the $500,000 exemption, households with incomes of less than $100,000 pay a third of the capital gains taxes, and those with incomes of more than $1 million pay a tenth of the taxes.

The concentration of tax liability is quite different when we use the imputed income measure that underlies the distribution table in the lower panel. In this

18. U.S. Congress, Joint Committee on Taxation (1993).

case, assuming that the first to die leaves all assets to the surviving spouse, more than one-quarter of the estate tax is assigned to households with annual imputed income of at least $1 million, and only 8 percent is assigned to households with incomes of less than $100,000. This changes substantially when we follow the weighted average algorithm; 42 percent of estate taxes are paid by households with at least $1 million in imputed annual income. The divergence between these results and those in the upper panel of table 10-11 highlight the importance of assets with low income flows, but substantial value, in the portfolios of households with high net worth. If we used a lower imputed income rate to translate capital assets into income flows, the results in the bottom panel of table 10-11 would look more like those in the upper panel.

Tables 10-10 and 10-11 provide some data on the patterns of estate tax liability and tax liability if gains are taxed at death, but they do not provide direct information on the relative tax burdens on different households under these policies. If one views the current estate tax as an *alternative* to taxing capital gains at death, then it makes sense to ask how many decedents face larger tax burdens under one tax regime or the other. Recall that the total revenue associated with the current estate tax is far greater than that associated with the taxation of capital gains at death. The particular policy that we consider is one that taxes all capital gains at death but allows for a $250,000 exemption for gains on a principal residence.

For all 1998 decedents who had no estate tax liability, we estimate that the probability of paying at least $1,000 in capital gains tax at death is 9 percent. The average capital gains tax liability is $11,000 for those who pay at least $1,000. The chance of facing a capital gains tax bill of $10,000 is 3 percent for those who currently do not pay estate tax. For those who currently pay the estate tax, the probability of facing a capital gains tax bill greater than the current estate tax bill is 17 percent. When we stratify estate-tax-paying decedents by the value of their estate, however, we find that taxing capital gains at death yields tax burdens similar to the current estate tax for decedents with net worth of less than $1 million. For this group, conditional on paying estate tax under the current law, 49 percent face a capital gains tax burden that exceeds their current estate tax liability. For those with a capital gains tax bill that is greater than their estate tax bill, the average increase in their tax burden is $50,100. The average tax saving for the 51 percent of current estate tax payers with net worth of less than $1 million who face higher tax bills under the estate tax than under a capital gains tax is $43,100.

Decedents with net worth of more than $1 million typically would face smaller tax liabilities if capital gains were taxed at death than they do under the current estate tax. Only 5 percent of this group would face a tax increase if the current estate tax were replaced with an income tax regime that taxed capital gains at death. For the 95 percent that would face a smaller tax burden under the capital gains tax regime, the average tax saving would be $672,700.

Carry-Over Basis versus Constructive Realization of Gains at Death

The foregoing analysis considers the case of a capital gains tax on the unrealized gains that are held by decedents at their time of death. An alternative policy that is sometimes discussed in place of taxing capital gains at death ("constructive realization") is requiring that the basis of capital assets held by the decedent "carry over" to the taxpayers who inherit these assets. Leaving aside issues about the behavioral response of taxpayers, the tax revenue associated with such a carry-over basis policy would be smaller than the revenue from taxing capital gains at death. This is because gains on assets held by the decedent will be realized at a later date under the carry-over basis policy than under the taxation of gains at death. Modeling the behavioral response to such changes in capital gains tax rules is a topic left for further research.

Conclusions and Future Directions

This chapter presents estimates of the revenue effect, and of the distributional patterns, connected with repealing basis step-up at death. The analysis assumes that the pattern of unrealized capital gains and net worth that we observe in the 1998 Survey of Consumer Finances would not be affected by legislative changes. Clearly this assumption is inappropriate, since it is well established that capital gains realizations are sensitive to the capital gains tax rates. Some evidence, such as that of Gerald Auten and David Joulfaian, even shows that estate tax rates affect capital gains realizations by older taxpayers. Wojciech Kopczuk and Joel Slemrod, in this volume, more generally explore the impact of estate tax rules on patterns of wealth accumulation.[19] The key difficulty is deciding what assumptions to make about the sensitivity of capital gains behavior and estate values to potential modifications in the tax code.

Consider the possible effects of reducing the estate tax and replacing part of the forgone revenue with a tax on unrealized capital gains. Such a tax reform would reduce the lock-in effect that discourages taxpayers from realizing gains at advanced ages, so it would presumably raise revenue from capital gains realizations in years *prior* to the death of taxpayers. Joulfaian and

---

19. Auten and Joulfaian (forthcoming); Kopczuk and Slemrod, chap. 7.

Kathleen McGarry, in this volume, explore the potential effect of raising tax rates on behavior, with particular attention to charitable giving at death and to the use of inter vivos giving.[20]

Reducing the estate tax would reduce the incentive for taxpayers to make inter vivos gifts to avoid the estate tax, so it might increase the total wealth held by decedents. This result could increase the revenue yield of the estate tax and the capital gains tax at death. As Douglas Bernheim's analysis suggests, the estate tax rate can affect not just estate tax revenue but income tax revenue as well.[21]

A related behavioral response concerns portfolio choice. At present, investors are strongly influenced to hold assets that generate capital gains rather than dividends or interest income, because the gains on these assets may ultimately escape taxation when the taxpayer dies. If unrealized gains were taxed at death, or if basis were carried forward so that those who inherited the assets would face prospective capital gains tax liability, the incentive for equity investments would be reduced. This could also affect the aggregate pool of unrealized gains that would be subject to taxation at death.

The choice of mortality table for revenue estimation is another broad issue. We have used the mortality rates for annuitants throughout our calculations. These mortality rates are lower than the mortality rates for the population at large by as much as 30 percent. This can translate into substantial differences in the estimated revenue effects of changes in the estate tax or in the potential revenues generated by taxing capital gains at the time of death.

Our discussion has focused exclusively on the relative distribution of accrued capital gains and net worth among the decedent population. We have not considered many of the detailed practical issues that arise in implementing constructive realization at death, or in structuring the tax rules for taxing gains with a carry-over basis provision. These issues include the valuation of gains on assets for which it may be difficult to determine the purchase price and the potential need for some taxpayers to sell assets to raise the capital that is needed to pay capital gains taxes.[22] These substantive issues must be addressed before the nation makes a substantial change in the tax system.

20. Joulfaian (1991, 2000); McGarry (2000).
21. Bernheim (1987).
22. See Gravelle (1994); Burman (1999); Congressional Budget Office (2000).

COMMENT BY
Leonard Burman

Janet McCubbin gave me a great deal of help on these comments and corrected many of my errors.

This chapter is creative, important, and timely. It looks at revenue and distributional issues related to the trade-off between the estate tax and taxing capital gains at death. The timeliness of this analysis is evident from the fact that weeks after this paper was delivered in May 2000, Congress passed a plan to replace the estate tax with a measure to enact carry-over basis for capital gains (although one with giant exemptions that would allow all but the largest estates to avoid any additional tax liability).[23] Since that plan is unlikely to become law this year, the Poterba and Weisbenner analysis will continue to inform the debate that is likely to linger into the next administration and Congress.

The chapter makes several important contributions. It uses the best available source of detailed data on wealth—the Survey of Consumer Finances (SCF)—plus a careful treatment of mortality probabilities to estimate taxable estates and capital gains at death. Based on those estimated data, the authors can simulate the effect of alternative policy regimes on tax receipts and the distribution of income. At this point, the model is completely static, but the authors plan to model behavioral responses in the future, which would be an exciting and useful development.

Replacing the Estate Tax with a Tax on Capital Gains at Death

One rationale for the estate tax is that it is a stopgap measure for the defects in the income tax. A notable gap, although far from the only one, is that capital gains on assets held until death escape taxation. This provision, which Michael Kinsley has dubbed the "angel-of-death loophole," creates or exacerbates a host of problems.[24] It is a major factor underlying the lock-in effect—that is, the incentive to hold assets to defer or avoid entirely capital gains tax liability. Deferral, which amounts to an interest-free loan from the government, is valuable, but total forgiveness of capital gains tax liability, which occurs at death under current law, is the big prize. Without that re-

---

23. H.R. 8, title 1, sec.103. (Death Tax Elimination Act of 2000).
24. Michael Kinsley, "Angel-of-Death Loophole," *New Republic*, July 13, 1997, p. 4.

ward, investors would have much smaller tax incentive to hold appreciated assets.[25]

The angel-of-death loophole fuels costly schemes that wealthy investors use to effectively divest themselves of the risk and return of an asset in exchange for cash without technically realizing a gain for tax purposes.[26] It also makes the tax system less fair because high-income people are much more likely to be able to arrange their affairs to defer realization of gain until death, as well as much more likely to have taxable capital gains rather than other forms of wealth.

Closing that loophole, however, would be politically difficult. As the authors point out, the United States tried and failed to implement a limited form of terminal capital gains reconciliation—so-called carry-over basis, in which heirs inherit the basis of assets so that the full amount of the gain would eventually be recognized when the heirs sell them. Carry-over basis was enacted in 1976, but it was first delayed and eventually repealed before it ever could take effect.[27] Taxing gains at death would be even more controversial—forcing estates to pay tax on gains even if the asset were not sold. Many estates would face liquidity problems that might force them to sell appreciated assets; highly leveraged estates might not have sufficient net worth to cover the tax liability.[28]

Conceivably, the public might support some form of taxation of capital gains held until death in exchange for repeal of the estate tax if it raised a similar amount of revenue from the same people, but Poterba and Weisbenner show that neither of these conditions is likely to hold, at least in a static model.

That result is not surprising for several reasons. First, the base for the estate tax includes much more than capital gains. It includes assets such as pensions

25. The empirical importance of the lock-in effect is hotly debated and unresolved. See Burman (1999) for a discussion.

26. Diana B. Henriques and Floyd Norris. "Wealthy, Helped by Wall St., Find New Ways to Escape Tax on Profits," *New York Times*, December 1, 1996, p. A1.

27. Halperin (1997).

28. This liquidity problem could also occur under carry-over basis, as the estate might have to sell appreciated assets to repay creditors, but that sale would trigger capital gains tax liability. Any estate where accrued capital gains tax liability (after any exemption) exceeded net worth minus probate costs and transaction costs would be potentially insolvent under either taxation of capital gains at death or carry-over basis. The Death Tax Elimination Act of 2000 would have avoided this problem by reducing the fair market value of "carry-over basis property" by the amount of any debt secured by those assets. This solution, however, would have created an enormous loophole. Under this regime, individuals would have an incentive to borrow enough against their appreciated assets to reduce the amount of adjusted gain below the exemption amount.

and life insurance, which escape income taxation during life and arguably should be taxed at death. Estate tax rates are also higher than income tax rates. Thus taxing capital gains at death could not fully replace the estate tax as a revenue source unless there is a huge amount of estate tax avoidance relative to the expected amount of capital gains tax avoidance.

As documented in Richard Schmalbeck's chapter in this volume and elsewhere, there are many opportunities for estate tax avoidance. But taxing capital gains at death would create similar incentives for avoidance. For example, if capital gains were taxed at death, there would be a strong incentive to discount asset values. There would be a great deal of pressure to allow exclusions for small amounts of capital gains, special preferences for small businesses and farms, and deductions for charitable contributions, as they apply under the estate tax. The vetoed Death Tax Elimination Act of 2000 would have established very large asset exemptions from carry-over basis: $1.3 million per estate plus a $3 million exemption on spousal transfers. Thus couples could avoid any tax on up to $5.6 million in appreciated property. The high exemptions were designed to avoid increasing tax on those who are currently exempt from or lightly taxed by the estate tax. But it would have accomplished that end by effectively exempting all but the largest estates from tax—and that tax liability could have been indefinitely deferred until the inherited assets were sold (possibly several generations hence).

Importantly, ending the estate tax would not end the need for estate planning, which has to be done for probate purposes and would be done to try to shelter capital gains from tax. Moreover, as the authors point out, substantial planning would be necessary if states kept their estate taxes.

Finally, if taxation of capital gains on gifts remained the same as under present law (that is, carry-over basis), people would have a greater incentive to give appreciated property to their children before they die. Taxing gains on gifts could be complex if some amount of gains are excluded from tax at death—that is, there might have to be a unified estate and gift capital gains provision, similar to the unified estate and gift tax.

The bottom line is that, in the real world, taxing capital gains at death is not likely to be the panacea that it might seem to be in the abstract.

Methodology and Data

The basic model infers estate and capital gains tax liability at death from the wealth of living people. This is a very creative way to use the best available data on wealth, the SCF, to measure *expected* estate tax liability. With a large enough sample, and a good measure of the relationship between taxable estates and wealth, that procedure could produce very accurate measures of estate tax liability and allow for simulation of policy alternatives.

A fundamental problem, though, is that data on wealth—even excellent data—do not tell one much about the value of taxable estates. As already mentioned, estates have a strong incentive and ability to reduce asset values, especially for closely held businesses and farms. Equally problematic, but essential to this model, is the treatment of couples. Under the assumption that the first spouse to die takes full advantage of the deduction for transfers to a spouse, the expected estate tax liability depends on the probability that both spouses in a married couple die in the sample year—a number that must be vanishingly small for all but the very oldest couples (the computations assume that the death of each spouse is independent, which means that the probability of both dying is the product of two very small numbers). That is reflected by the tiny estimated estate tax liability attributable to couples under that assumption, as shown in table 10-4 of the chapter.

But, as the authors note, simply passing all wealth to a spouse is poor estate planning for large estates (because the first spouse to die would not benefit from the unified credit or graduated rates). The chapter provides evidence that people are aware of that fact in table 10-5, which shows that the likelihood of a married decedent paying some tax increases sharply with estate size. The question then is how the first spouse would determine the amount of estate to give to heirs other than the surviving spouse. The chapter assumes that estates are split equally for taxable estates. That is clearly an improvement over the alternative assumption that the first spouse to die pays no tax, but suboptimal for very large estates because of the surtax that phases out the benefit of lower estate tax rates for estates between $10 million and $17.184 million.[29] A better strategy for married decedents whose combined estate is likely to exceed $20 million would limit the size of the first estate to $10 million.

Treating spouses carefully improves the accuracy of this model and increases the power of the relatively small data set. However, the results of this model, especially for simulations involving very large estates, are likely to be imprecise. Only about a quarter of the sample of 4,305 members of the SCF have net worth greater than $1 million and many of those estates will avoid tax because of credits, deductions, and valuation discounts. Married couples have much of the wealth, but only a fraction of them are likely to pay any estate tax (table 10-5). Taking all of these factors into account, the unweighted sample represents a relatively small number of taxable estates.

29. See Richard Schmalbeck, chap.3, in this volume.

Nonetheless, the authors report that their model replicates fairly closely the level of estate tax liability reported on estate tax returns after an adjustment is made for the exclusion of the missing *Forbes* 400 from the dataset. They also report that the distribution of estimated tax liability for single decedents matches very closely the distribution of estate liability reported on tax returns. The chapter does not report how well the model predicts estate tax liability for married decedents, which raises the suspicion that the problems discussed above might have a material effect on the distribution of their tax liability.

Other issues with the measurement of capital gains tax liability arise. The chapter points out that its estimate of the value of step-up in basis on capital gains at death is significantly smaller than tax expenditure estimates by the Joint Committee on Taxation (JCT) and speculates that the reason might be different assumptions about mortality. That explanation would only apply if the JCT used a similar methodology, but it is likely that the committee uses information from estate tax returns and other sources to estimate capital gains on assets held at death. The differences might instead be due to complications in the tax treatment of depreciable property, and the fact that actual tax liability attributable to gains at death is inherently uncertain since gains have never been taxed at death.

The simulations of the effects of changing from estate tax to taxing capital gains at death raise further questions. First, if there were an exemption for some amount of capital gains, the first spouse to die would have an incentive to give some appreciated property to heirs other than a spouse. That behavior probably should be modeled, just as a similar incentive is modeled for the estate tax.

The estimates of the effects of replacing the estate tax with tax on capital gains at death should also account for the repeal of the gift tax. Repealing both the estate and gift taxes together would raise the cost by approximately 25 percent. (Repealing the estate tax without the gift tax would create an immense disincentive for inter vivos gifts, which is probably not a policy objective.)

Behavioral Responses to Repeal of the Estate Tax

Although this chapter makes a valuable contribution in showing how estimates of estate tax liability and capital gains at death can be created from the SCF, it also hints at an important line of future research—that is, modeling the behavioral responses of individuals to changes in the tax rules at death. That research, however, faces some serious challenges. In my view, the most realistic policy alternatives probably involve carry-over basis for capital gains, rather than taxation at death, which is not modeled here. A further issue is that there would almost surely have to be a sizable exemption for bequeathed assets, which could complicate the taxation of inter vivos gifts as just discussed.

The chapter speculates that repealing or reducing the estate tax could reduce the incentive to make inter vivos gifts, and thus increase both the size of estates and the amount of capital gains at death. However, if gains are taxed at death while gifts remain subject to carry-over basis, people could have a greater incentive to give appreciated assets to their heirs—especially assets that they expect or hope to be held for a long time. Giving the asset to a child would allow him or her to defer the tax, whereas it would be taxed immediately at death if held. Similarly, depending on the rules, people could have a greater incentive to donate appreciated assets to charity during life than they do currently.

Another question is the effect of repealing or significantly reducing the estate tax on taxable capital gains realizations. By itself, that would discourage realizing capital gains. As pointed out by Auten and Joulfaian, the estate tax reduces the relative cost of realizing capital gains.[30] For example, paying $100 in capital gain tax would reduce the size of the taxable estate by that amount. Someone who expects to be in the 55 percent estate tax bracket would thus save $55 in estate taxes, so the net cost of realizing the capital gains would be reduced by more than half. Without the estate tax, there would be a much stronger incentive to hold appreciated assets until death.

Taxing capital gains at death would more than offset this incentive, and carry-over basis would have a smaller effect in the same direction, but enacting either alternative with large exclusions and new loopholes could actually discourage realization of capital gains—costing individual income tax revenue as well as estate taxes. The net effect of a policy change such as the recently passed (and vetoed) Death Tax Elimination Act of 2000 is thus not evident and could benefit from the careful modeling that I hope these authors will pursue.

References

Attanasio, Orazio, and Hilary Hoynes. 2000. "Differential Mortality and Wealth Accumulation." *Journal of Human Resources* 35 (Winter): 1–29.

Auten, Gerald, and David Joulfaian. Forthcoming. "Bequest Taxes and Capital Gains Realizations." *Journal of Public Economics.*

Bailey, Martin J. 1969. "Capital Gains and Income Taxation." In *The Taxation of Income from Capital,* edited by Arnold Harberger and Martin Bailey,11–49. Brookings.

Bernheim, B. Douglas. 1987. "Does the Estate Tax Raise Revenue." In *Tax Policy and the Economy,* edited by Lawrence Summers, 1, 113–38. National Bureau of Economic Research and MIT Press.

30. Auten and Joulfaian (forthcoming).

Bossons, John. 1972. "An Economic Overview of the Tax Reforms." In *Proceedings of the Twenty-Third Tax Conference,* 45–67. Toronto: Canadian Tax Foundation.

———. 1974. "The Effect of Income Tax Reform on Estate Taxes in Canada." In *Proceedings of the Sixty-Sixth Annual Conference on Taxation, National Tax Association–Tax Institute of America,* 148–94. Columbus, Ohio: National Tax Association.

Burman, Leonard E. 1999. *The Labyrinth of Capital Gains Tax Policy.* Brookings.

Congressional Budget Office. 1997. *Perspectives on the Ownership of Capital Assets and the Realization of Capital Gains.* Washington (March).

———. 2000. *Budget Options.* Washington.

Cooper, George. 1979. *A Voluntary Tax? New Perspectives on Sophisticated Tax Avoidance.* Brookings.

Eller, Martha Britton. 1996–97. "Federal Taxation of Wealth Transfers, 1992–1995." *Statistics of Income Bulletin* 16 (Winter): 8–63.

Finkelstein, Amy, and James Poterba. 2000. "Adverse Selection in Insurance Markets: Policyholder Evidence from the UK Annuity Market." Working Paper 8045. Cambridge, Mass.: National Bureau of Economic Research.

Gravelle, Jane. 1994. *The Economic Effects of Taxing Capital Income.* MIT Press.

Halperin, Daniel. 1997. "Saving the Income Tax: An Agenda for Research." *Tax Notes* 77 (November): 967–77.

Johnson, Barry W., and Jacob Mikow. 1999. "Federal Estate Tax Returns, 1995–1997." *Statistics of Income Bulletin* 19 (Summer): 69–129.

Joulfaian, David. 1991. "Charitable Bequests and Estate Taxes." *National Tax Journal* 44, 169–80.

———. 1998. "The Federal Estate and Gift Tax: Description, Profile of Taxpayers, and Economic Consequences." OTA Paper 80. Washington: Office of Tax Analysis, U.S. Treasury Department.

———. 2000. "Estate Taxes and Charitable Bequest by the Wealthy." *National Tax Journal* 53 (September): 743–63.

Kennickell, Arthur B., Martha Starr-McCluer, and Brian Surette. 2000. "Changes in U.S. Family Finances at the End of the 1990s: Results from the 1998 Survey of Consumer Finances." *Federal Reserve Bulletin* (January).

McGarry, Kathleen, 2000. "Inter Vivos Transfers or Bequests? Estate Taxes and the Timing of Parental Giving." In *Tax Policy and the Economy* 14, edited by James Poterba, 93–121. MIT Press.

Mitchell, Olivia S., and others. 1999. "New Evidence on the Money's Worth of Individual Annuities." *American Economic Review* 89 (December): 1299–1318.

Poterba, James. 2000. "The Estate Tax and After-Tax Investment Returns." In J. Slemrod, ed., *Does Atlas Shrug: The Economic Consequences of Taxing the Rich,* 333–53. Harvard University Press.

———. 2001. "Estate and Gift Taxes and Incentives for *Inter Vivos* Giving in the United States." *Journal of Public Economics* 79 (January): 237–64.

U.S. Congress, Joint Committee on Taxation. 1993. *Methodology and Issues in Measuring Changes in the Distribution of Tax Burdens.* Government Printing Office.

———. 1997. *Description and Analysis of Tax Proposals Relating to Savings and Investment (Capital Gains, IRAs, and Estate and Gift Tax).* Government Printing Office.

Wolff, Edward N. 1996. "Commentary." *Tax Law Review* 51 (Spring): 517–22.

JONATHAN S. FEINSTEIN
CHIH-CHIN HO

11 | *Elderly Asset Management and Health*

I N THE UNITED STATES approximately one-half of all household assets are owned by households in which the head is 62 years old or above.[1] That much of the nation's assets are owned by older individuals is important because older people are likely to manage their assets differently than younger people. Thus, the factors influencing saving by the elderly are likely to be different than the factors influencing saving by younger people—health is likely to be more important for the elderly, labor earnings for the young. The pattern of asset allocation may also be quite different for the old than for the young—for example, older people may hold a higher percentage of their assets in housing and a lower percentage in the stock market. Further, older people are concerned about transferring their assets to their heirs, an issue that does not arise for the young, and they can manage the transfer of their assets more or less actively—for example, they can choose to transfer some of their assets while they are still alive by giving them away as gifts. Understanding how older people manage their assets is crucial for designing estate tax policy and Social Security; and because they own such a large fraction of all assets it is also important for understanding

We thank Jonathan Skinner for his detailed comments on our paper. Many other conference participants also provided valuable remarks.

1. We made this calculation using data from the most recent Survey of Consumer Finances.

overall patterns of savings and asset allocation, patterns that have broad ramifications for investment and growth.

Many factors can be expected to influence decisionmaking by older persons about their assets. Some of these factors are identified in the standard life-cycle theory of household economic behavior. Thus the standard theory predicts that toward the end of their lives individuals should decumulate assets and plan for the transfer of their assets to their heirs, from which it follows that across a cohort of persons all of the same age, those in better health who expect to live longer should on average maintain higher savings than those in poor health. Further, the theory suggests a precautionary motive for savings—older people should maintain higher savings the more uncertain they believe their life expectancy to be and the more they are worried about incurring unexpected expenses, such as medical expenses. The theory also implies that individuals who care about their children should consider their children's well-being in estate planning, influencing both gift giving and the nature of intended bequests; indeed from the perspective of estate tax planning, older individuals with assets above the estate tax threshold should make substantial gifts each year to their heirs, because gifts below a threshold size are not taxed, so giving gifts is a way to reduce total expected tax.[2]

But although life-cycle theory and issues of tax planning are helpful for understanding how the elderly may manage their assets, these theories have significant limitations. Perhaps most important, they do not take into account—or take into account in only a very limited way—the interrelationship of economics and health. An elderly person who falls into poor health may find that her preferences about asset allocation and her feelings about how much wealth feels "safe" have changed, which in turn may influence her decisions about saving, spending, and gift giving. Further, those in ill health or falling into ill health may feel vulnerable, which may influence their interaction with their children, including that related to estate planning and gift giving. In the opposite direction, economic status influences health outcomes—it is well known that individuals of higher wealth have a significantly longer life expectancy in the United States and most countries around the world.[3] Like the causal link running from health to economics, the link running from economic status to health has not been well integrated into standard economic theories.

In this chapter we present a preliminary analysis of asset management by the elderly and elderly health, considering the interrelationship of assets, asset

2. See Poterba (1998) for a detailed discussion.
3. For a review, see Feinstein (1993).

management decisions, health, and the evolution of health. We focus on modeling a few key aspects of asset management, and we consider the influence of health on these processes and the influence of economic status on the evolution of health. Our models are not based on the life-cycle theory—they are not derived from an explicit model of utility maximization and do not explicitly include expectations. But they allow for a rich set of interrelationships between economics and health and are meant to provide a flexible framework for analyzing certain aspects of asset and health dynamics. We have estimated our models using data from waves 1 and 2 of the Asset and Health Dynamics among the Oldest Old (AHEAD) data set, which provides comprehensive data about U.S. households in which the head was 70 years old or above in 1992. We discuss the AHEAD data and present and interpret results from our estimation later in this chapter.

We view our work not as a finished product but as the first step toward developing a better understanding of how health and economic factors interact and jointly evolve among the old. We hope to develop a richer and more realistic framework that can be used to predict the dynamics of assets owned by the elderly, including the transfer by the elderly of assets to their heirs, incorporating health and a model of the evolution of health. We envision using this framework to predict estate tax revenues and to investigate the effects of Social Security and alternative Social Security Policies.

We present models for three processes—saving and the utilization of assets, gift giving, and the evolution of health. Our model of saving and asset utilization involves three basic outcomes in each period—saving money, spending down assets to meet household needs, or neither saving nor spending down to any significant extent. We analyze which of these three states a household falls into, as well as the magnitude of savings and asset spend down. Our analysis focuses on total household wealth—we do not analyze specific asset types and do not analyze patterns of asset allocation, leaving that for future work. We also do not analyze the return on specific assets, leaving that for future work as well.[4] We specify a simple model of gift giving, focusing on the total value of all gifts reported to have been made by a household in the preceding year. To capture the important influences of health on economic decisions we include variables measuring health states and changes in health in both our model of saving and asset utilization and our model of gift giving. Finally, we define three distinct health states—good

---

4. Because we restrict our analysis to actions and events that occur within a period that affect a household's assets and do not analyze asset returns, we do not perform a full analysis of changes in asset value from one period to the next; again, we hope to address this issue more fully in future work.

health, poor health, and death, and we model health outcomes as depending on both health in the preceding period and a host of demographic and socioeconomic variables.

Modeling saving, utilization of assets, and gift giving jointly allows us to capture some basic features of the economics of aging that have not previously been investigated in much detail. Intuitively, there is likely to be a relationship within a period between a household's level of savings or utilization of assets for its own use and its level of gift giving—after all, money that the household members spend on their own household is not available for gifts, and conversely, households that suddenly find themselves with a lot of "free cash" may be more likely to save and to give gifts. Our framework allows us to explore these issues. Understanding the link between savings and gift giving and whether or not older people face a trade-off between giving gifts and using assets to meet immediate needs is crucial for modeling the transfer of assets across generations and for predicting the behavioral effects induced by estate and gift tax policies.

Surprisingly, little previous work has jointly analyzed saving, utilization of assets, and gift giving. In the literature on gifts, gift giving is generally not considered in relation to either household saving or the spend down of assets by household members to meet their own needs.[5] In the voluminous literature on savings over the life cycle, including studies of the importance of savings for the elderly, gift giving is only occasionally mentioned and is not prominent.[6] Implicitly, it seems that in this literature it is assumed that gift giving is relatively insignificant compared with saving and dissaving to meet the immediate needs of a household.

But although this assumption may be correct for younger persons, it is not true for older persons. In the AHEAD data approximately 20 percent of households report savings, and the average value of savings among those who do save is $19,000; approximately 20 percent report spending out of assets, and the average value of spend down is $9,000; for gifts, a slightly larger percentage, 24 percent, report making gifts, and the average total value of all gifts made is $8,500.[7] Thus gifts are slightly more common than either savings or

---

5. For example, in their interesting work on the factors that influence gift giving Altonji, Hayashi, and Kotlikoff (1997) do not consider savings behavior. McGarry also does not consider savings and spend down in her interesting recent work on gift giving by older persons. McGarry (1998).

6. Two of the most interesting recent contributions are Deaton, Gourinchas, and Paxson (1999), and Hubbard, Skinner, and Zeldes (1995); gifts are not discussed in either. For recent work, in which again gifts are not discussed, see Dyson, Skinner, and Zeldes (2000).

7. All of these figures represent weighted values and therefore should be representative of elderly households in the United States.

spend down and on average are of about equal size as spend down. And for elderly with children gifts are even more important. That gift giving, savings, and spend down are all of comparable frequency and magnitude suggests that to understand and predict patterns of asset dynamics among the elderly requires modeling the three processes jointly.

The central variables for our analysis are measures of health and economic status. Our principal variable measuring health status is based on individuals' self-assessment of their own health. Each respondent in AHEAD reports his or her health as excellent, very good, good, fair, or poor, and based on these reports we divide households into two broad groups, good health and poor health.[8] Our principal economic variables are saving, utilization of assets, gifts, wealth, and income. Wealth is an especially important variable for our work—not only is it the basis for estate value, but it is also the crucial determinant of the economic well-being of the elderly. We have done extensive work cleaning the AHEAD wealth data—which we found noisy and in some cases not likely to be a reliable measure of wealth—to construct as accurate a measure of household wealth as possible; we discuss how we cleaned the data later in the chapter.

We are especially concerned to model interrelationships between health and economic status. In our models of saving, utilization, and gift giving we include dummy variables referring to summary measures of the health status of the head and his partner, thereby allowing for the estimation of different average levels for these variables across health groups. Further, in each model we also show how wealth and income interact with health, thereby allowing the marginal effects of income and wealth on savings, utilization, and gift-giving to vary with health. As far as we know, specifying these kinds of interactions between wealth and health is new—our specification is thus an example of how interactions between health and economics can be incorporated into econometric models. The hypothesis that marginal effects of income and wealth vary according to health status is intuitive; for example, the elderly who are relatively wealthy and fall into poor health may follow a very differ-

8. Later we describe exactly how we aggregate responses in households in which there is both a head and a partner present. In extensions of our basic specification we have drawn upon the rich health information recorded in AHEAD to construct more detailed measures of health. In particular, we have supplemented the basic information about whether a person's health is poor or not poor with information about whether health has worsened and about limitations of daily activities (ADLs) and instrumental daily activities (IADLs) and used this information to divide households into five groups; see Feinstein and Ho (1999) for more information about this. We have also explored the impact of specific health conditions, such as heart disease, on asset dynamics and gift giving. We do not discuss any of our findings using these richer measures of health in this chapter.

ent strategy for gift giving than the elderly who remain healthy, or the elderly who fall into poor health but are relatively poor.

We also model the influence of economic status on the evolution of health. Recognizing that the impact of wealth on health may be different for lower than for higher values of wealth, we include wealth splines in our model of health outcomes, so that the marginal effect of wealth on health is allowed to be different for those living in households of low wealth than for those living in households with higher wealth.

We discuss the results from estimating our models in detail later, but the main results can be summarized as follows. First, the results for gift giving indicate that the estate tax does indeed influence gift-giving behavior: households for which assets are above the estate tax threshold have a significantly greater propensity to give gifts (there is a jump at this point in the wealth distribution), and the average value of gifts given by these households is approximately $5,000 more than the average value of gifts given by other households. Not surprisingly, estate planning and transfer is linked to trust funds—controlling for the effect of wealth on gift giving, we find that households that have established trust funds have a significantly greater propensity to give gifts.

Second, our results indicate that allowing for interactions between wealth and health is important—the pattern of wealth effects for households whose members are in good health is different from the pattern for households whose members are in poor health. Perhaps the most interesting finding is that the average propensity to give gifts is lower for those in poor health, but the marginal effect of wealth is more than twice as great. We offer the following interpretation of this finding. The elderly who are in poor health and relatively poor are unwilling to part with assets—perhaps because they are worrying about future medical costs and have a strong precautionary motive to safeguard their assets, perhaps because they feel especially vulnerable, making them even more risk averse. In contrast, the elderly in poor health who are relatively wealthy feel less vulnerable and worried about spending down their assets, and become even more concerned about estate transfer than wealthy elderly who remain in good health. Similar results hold for saving, and we interpret them similarly.

Third, income is a very important determinant of saving and spend down. It is not surprising that income is linked with saving, and indeed we find that older persons, especially those in good health, save a relatively large fraction of marginal income—between 20 and 50 percent. The link between income and spend down is less obvious, and we offer a number of possible interpretations: some older persons may lead more active lives than others, and for these active persons the flow of resources in and out of the household may well be relatively high; alternatively, older persons with high income may expect their high income to continue and therefore be more willing to utilize existing assets.

Fourth, other things equal, households that save are also more likely to make gifts. Further, among those who save, increased saving is associated with increased gift giving, and similarly among those who spend down assets, increased spend down is associated with increased gift giving.

Fifth, sudden changes in family structure and health seem to be associated with utilization of assets. Especially, we find that being recently widowed is associated with a rapid depletion of assets, both to meet own needs and as gifts, dramatic enough to suggest that widowhood is an important factor to consider in models of estate planning and estate tax projections. We also find that a deterioration in health is associated with a significant increase in the likelihood of spending out of assets.

Sixth, variables related to children have less effect on gift giving than we expected. Number of children is not associated with a significant increase in the propensity to give gifts, and lower average income of children is associated with a decrease in gift giving—though the effect is not significant—contradicting simple theories of parental altruism. Indeed, the only child variable that has a significant effect on gift giving is a variable measuring the number of children for which the parents are unable to provide information about income—the more children for which information is missing, the less is the propensity to give gifts, suggesting that the closeness of relationship between parents and children is an important factor influencing parental gifts.

Finally, our results for our models of health outcomes indicate that health in the recent past is the most important factor determining health outcomes over the next two years for this population of elderly. Educational attainment is also a significant factor, with those who have earned a college degree more likely to survive and be in good health. Income and wealth, although known to be important determinants of health over the life span, are not important for explaining health outcomes in the immediate future, controlling for education and health.

We hope that our results will contribute to a shift in conventional wisdom about the link between economics and health. The importance of socioeconomic status for health has come to be widely appreciated during the past few decades. Although we believe this effect to be important over the long course of life, our results suggest that, at least for the elderly, in the immediate short-term last period health is a far more important determinant of health outcome than income or wealth. In contrast, the importance of health for understanding economic and financial decisionmaking, especially of older people, has not been as widely recognized; but our results show that it is an important influence. We hope our work will contribute to increasing appreciation for the importance of incorporating health variables into economic models of the household and will help policymakers understand how important it is to model the evolution of health and economic status jointly for the elderly.

In recent years several other researcher have also used the AHEAD data set to study elderly health and the economics of aging. In a series of papers Kathleen McGarry has investigated gift-giving patterns in AHEAD and has found that parents are more likely to make transfers to children whose current income is low and that they often make transfers only to one child in a year, or they make unequal-sized transfers.[9] However, she does not consider the link between gift giving and savings behavior and does not report any information about the influence of health on gift giving.[10] Michael Hurd, Daniel McFadden, and Angel Merrill have investigated mortality in AHEAD between waves 1 and 2.[11] They divide households into income and wealth quartiles and estimate logistic regressions for mortality risk that include as independent variables these measures as well as an extensive battery of health conditions. They report that after controlling for health conditions only one of their economic variables has a significant relationship with mortality, being in the highest-income quartile, which is associated with a significant reduction in mortality risk. They also investigate saving, defined as net change in wealth (we defining saving differently), and find that saving is significantly associated with income, as we do, but little effect of a variety of health conditions on saving. They do not investigate asset utilization or gift giving and do not interact wealth and income with health conditions as we do.[12] Neither set of researchers has tried to link changes in health, savings and spend down, and gift giving in an integrated framework.

There have also been several recent papers that study household transfer of assets through gifts as a means of reducing estate tax liability at death. Of particular interest, James Poterba has argued that individuals and couples for

9. See, in particular, McGarry (1998).

10. Kathleen has also investigated intended bequests reported by participants in AHEAD and found that most intend for their estate to be divided equally among their children, a finding that is consistent with the common wisdom about bequests.

11. See Hurd, McFadden, and Merrill (1998).

12. Hurd, McFadden, and Merrill also investigate a variety of other health outcomes. In a separate paper they have investigated the link between AHEAD respondents' estimates of their subjective probability of survival and subsequent health outcomes; see Hurd, McFadden, and Merrill (1999).

whom household assets exceed the estate tax filing threshold should give away assets to their heirs toward the end of their lives, in order to reduce expected estate tax liability.[13] His analysis of data collected in the Survey of Consumer Finances indicates that most are not giving away their assets to the extent that simple tax calculations suggest they should be.[14]

The remainder of our chapter is organized as follows. In the next section we present our models of asset dynamics, gift giving, and health outcomes and discuss issues related to our specification. Then we discuss the AHEAD data we use, describing some of the strengths and weaknesses of the data and the work we have done cleaning the data. Later we present our results and interpret them, offer a brief conclusion, and in an appendix outline an extension of our basic model that allows us to address the possibility that labor income is endogenous.

Models

In this section we present our models of saving, asset utilization, gift giving, and health outcomes. Our models allow for effects of health on household financial decisions and outcomes and for the impact of economic variables on health outcomes.

In our model of financial decisions and outcomes we measure the health status of a household by combining information about the health of the head of household and his or her partner (if he has a partner), dividing households into two groups, good and poor health. We include in our specifications a dummy variable for health status in each period and for changes in health status over time. We also include interactions between health status and wealth and income, thereby allowing for the possibility that the marginal effects of wealth and income on financial decisions and outcomes are different for households in good health than for households in poor health.

We estimate separate models of health outcomes for males and females, specifying a simple model in which a person who is alive in one period is

---

13. See Poterba (1998).

14. A separate but related issue is that many gifts may not be being reported and recorded in available data. We have also researched this issue, finding a large discrepancy between taxable gifts reported in both AHEAD and the Health and Retirement Survey and taxable gifts reported to the Internal Revenue Service (gifts to another person or household are taxable if the total of such gifts in a given year are above the gift tax filing threshold, which has for many years been $10,000 for a single person and $20,000 for a married couple). See Feinstein (1997).

either in good health or poor health or dead in the next period. We allow for the effects of wealth and income on health to be different for individuals in different conditions of health in the preceding period. We also model the effects of wealth and income using a spline model, so that, within each health category, the marginal effects of increasing wealth and income on health are allowed to be different for those of high wealth or high income than for those of low wealth or low income.

By combining estimates from our economic model with those from our health outcomes model we should be able ultimately to predict health and asset dynamics jointly. In the conclusion we briefly describe how this can be done and mention important limitations of the models as currently specified.

Saving, Asset Utilization, and Gift Giving

The evolution of household assets is governed by three basic processes. First is the accumulation or decumulation of assets by the household in relation to its own expenses—in any period it can save, use assets to meet current needs, or have expenditures approximately equal to current income. Second, the household gives assets away as gifts; note that gift giving is separate from the use of assets to meet needs. Third, the household makes choices about the allocation of its wealth across different kinds of assets, and these decisions affect future returns and therefore future wealth.

In this chapter we study the first two processes: we model saving, asset utilization, and gift giving as a system of four equations. Our model of saving and spend down has three equations. The first is an ordered probit with three outcomes: spend down of assets; neither spend down nor savings; and savings. The remaining two equations are conditioned on the outcome for the first equation: conditional on spend down, we specify a regression model for the magnitude of spend down; and conditional on saving, we specify a regression model for the magnitude of saving. Our model of gift giving is a standard Tobit model. We do not study household asset allocation, but we note that the AHEAD data provide a reasonably detailed breakdown of assets by type, and we hope to investigate asset allocation in future work.

As of the publication of this book, only two waves of data from AHEAD are currently available for public use. Our strategy is to use information about assets and health in wave 1 to establish a baseline condition for each household and then examine saving, spend down of assets, and gift giving reported for the household in wave 2. Unfortunately, given the lack of data from a third wave we are unable to estimate a panel model; again, we hope to develop such a model once wave 3 data become available.

Following are our notation and the four expressions that define our model of saving, asset utilization, and gift giving. The first expression classifies a household into one of three categories—spend down, no addition or subtraction from assets, or saving.

(1A) $$Y_1^* = X_1\beta_1 + \epsilon_1.$$

In this expression Y_1^* is a latent variable, X_1 is a vector of independent variables expected to affect household spend down and savings, β_1 is a parameter vector, and ϵ_1 is a stochastic disturbance. We define a threshold value λ and then define Y_1 to indicate which category applies for the household.

(1B) $$Y_1 = -1(spend\ down)\ if\ Y_1^* \leq 0$$

$$Y_1 = 0(no\ significant\ spend\ down\ or\ savings)\ if\ 0 < Y_1^* \leq \lambda$$

$$Y_1 = 1(savings)\ if\ Y_1^* > \lambda.$$

Conditional on $Y_1 = -1$ we define the asset utilization equation,

(2) $$Y_2 = X_2\beta_2 + \epsilon_2,$$

where Y_2 is the amount of assets the household reports having used in the current period, X_2 is a vector of independent variables, β_2 is a vector of parameters, and ϵ_2 is a stochastic disturbance. Conditional on $Y_1 = 1$ we define the savings equation,

(3) $$Y_3 = X_3\beta_3 + \epsilon_3,$$

where Y_3 is the amount of current income the household reports having contributed to savings in the current period, X_3 is a vector of independent variables, β_3 is a vector of parameters, and ϵ_3 is a stochastic disturbance.

The last expression in our model is for gift giving.

(4) $$Y_4^* = X_4\beta_4 + \epsilon_4$$

$$Y_4 = 0(no\ gifts)\ if\ Y_4^* \leq 0$$

$$Y_4 = Y_4^*\left(gifts\ in\ amount\ Y_4^*\right)\ if\ Y_4^* > 0.$$

In expression (4) Y_4 is the total value of all gifts the household reports having made in the current period, Y_4^* is a latent variable, X_4 is a vector of independent variables, β_4 is a parameter vector to be estimated, and ϵ_4 is a stochastic disturbance.

We assume that the four stochastic disturbances ϵ_1, ϵ_2, ϵ_3, and ϵ_4 are jointly normally distributed, with variances 1 (the variance of ϵ_1 is normalized to this value) σ_2^2, σ_3^2, and σ_4^2. Since a household never saves at the same time that it spends down its assets, at most one of expressions 2 and 3 can apply in each case, and therefore it is not possible to estimate a correlation between ϵ_2 and ϵ_3. But the other five correlations are in principle identifiable.

In our specification the correlation ρ_{14} is of special interest, for it provides one measure of the general nature of the relationship between a household's management of its assets for its own internal use and its use of assets for the purposes of giving gifts. Since gift giving has not normally been modeled jointly with saving and spend down of assets, this correlation has not previously been investigated as far as we are aware. Intuitively, a positive value for ρ_{14} indicates that households that are unusually likely to save compared with other comparable households (households with similar values for observable variables) are also more likely to give gifts. Conversely, a negative value indicates that households that are unusually likely to save are less likely to give gifts, perhaps reflecting a substitution effect in which own saving crowds out gift giving.

The remaining correlations also have reasonable interpretations. The correlation ρ_{12} controls for selection among the subset of households that spend down. If, for example, this correlation is positive, that indicates that a household that has an unusually high likelihood of spending down assets is also likely to spend down more than the amount spent down by comparable households. Similarly, the correlation ρ_{13} controls for selection among the subset of households that save.

The correlation ρ_{24} measures the correlation between spend down of assets and gift giving, among households that spend down. A positive value for this correlation indicates that households that spend down an unusually large amount relative to comparable households that also spend down also tend to give more in gifts than these comparable households. In turn this would indicate that some elderly are exhausting their wealth at a faster rate than others. What might cause this? Some elderly may be pursuing a more aggressive estate planning strategy or be unusually pessimistic about their health and their expected longevity. A negative value for ρ_{24} indicates that households that spend down an unusually large amount relative to comparable households that also spend down tend to give less in gifts, which would suggest a substitution effect, that households that are forced to spend an unusually large amount of their wealth on their own needs give less in gifts.

Lastly, the correlation ρ_{34} measures the correlation between savings and gift giving among households that save. A positive value for this correlation indicates that households that are able to save an unusually large amount relative to comparable households also tend to give more in gifts. This is a kind of complementarity that might arise if some elderly have unusually low expenditures or simply "feel wealthy." A negative value indicates that the elderly who save a lot relative to others of comparable economic status tend to give less in gifts—they may be miserly or simply working hard to build up assets.

As we mentioned in the introduction, our model is not a structural model derived from an explicit model of life-cycle behavior and the maximization of the expectation of current and future utility. In particular, we do not include any explicit measures of expectations, beyond the assessment of own health status, and do not attempt to fit a utility function, for example, over total household consumption. However, because we control carefully for baseline health and economic variables, we hope the model can provide reasonable estimates of how the management of assets is influenced by such factors as wealth, current income, and health. Our goal is not to recover a specific form of utility function but simply to explore the interrelationships among health and economic variables that determine the economic well-being of the household.

Households fall into six cases: (1) neither spend down nor saving and no gift giving, $Y_1 = 0$ and $Y_4 = 0$; (2) neither spend down nor saving, but gift giving, $Y_1 = 0$ and $Y_4 > 0$; (3) spend down and no gift giving, $Y_1 = -1$ and $Y_4 = 0$; (4) saving and no gift giving, $Y_1 = 1$ and $Y_4 = 0$; (5) spend down and gift giving, $Y_1 = -1$ and $Y_4 > 0$; and (6) saving and gift giving, $Y_1 = 1$ and $Y_4 > 0$. In the appendix we present the likelihood function associated with each case.

Extensions

We discuss two kinds of extensions of the basic model. First, we allow savings and spend down to enter directly into the expression for gift giving, so that expression 4 becomes

$$(5) \qquad Y_4^* = X_4\beta_4 + Y_2\gamma_2 + Y_3\gamma_3 + \epsilon_4.$$

Our model is then a recursive system with a likelihood function essentially similar to the one outlined above.[15] It is for this augmented model that we report results.

---

15. Because the model is recursive the Jacobian of transformation from the stochastic disturbances to the dependent variables is one, so the likelihood form is essentially unchanged.

Second, we consider the possibility that certain kinds of income may be endogenous, determined in part by choices that are influenced by household income or expectations about income. There are two main sources of income that might be endogenous, labor market income and capital gains income, and we discuss each in turn.[16]

Labor income might be endogenous for two reasons. Approximately 20 percent of the households in AHEAD report working and presumably the decision about whether or not to work may be influenced by current health status, wealth, other sources of income, and the desire to earn income to give as gifts, to save, or to spend. If the labor supply decision is primarily motivated by considerations of saving, expenditures, or gift giving, then labor income may be endogenous, which would make total income endogenous. We can address this issue by constructing an equation for labor income and estimating labor income jointly with the remaining four expressions in our model. The resulting likelihood has twelve cases instead of six—labor income can be zero or positive—and is slightly more complicated than the likelihood for our basic model. Since the fraction of households that report working is relatively small, and labor income is a relatively small percentage of total income for most households that do report working, we do not expect the endogeneity of labor income to be a large issue for the AHEAD population, and we do not model labor income in this chapter.

Capital gains income also might be endogenous, if household decisions to liquidate assets are influenced by the desire to save or give gifts, or anticipated expenditures. The AHEAD data do not report much information about capital gains; thus it would be difficult to address the endogeneity of capital gains income empirically in our work. The only kind of asset for which capital gains information is reported is primary residence. The data indicate that 4.6 percent of households in wave 2 report having sold a primary residence in the past two years, and that two-thirds realized a capital gain, with the average gain slightly more than $50,000. This is a substantial dollar value but applies to a relatively small percentage of households and is unlikely to have a large influence on our results.

For other assets, for example, stocks, there is some information about inflows and outflows, but not enough information about specific transactions to calculate capital gains. In principle, the endogeneity of capital gains can be addressed using a very similar approach to that used to correct for endogeneity of labor income. Thus, for example, it would be possible to estimate a

16. We thank Joel Slemrod for pointing out that capital gains income might be endogenous.

model of sale of primary residence jointly with savings, spend down, and gift giving; but we do not pursue this in the present work.

There is an additional potential source of endogeneity in income, arising from the pattern of allocation of assets. Placing a larger share of household wealth in assets that are high risk and high return should on average increase household income. If the asset allocation decision is influenced by likely expenditures or the desire to make gifts, asset returns are likely to be endogenous. This is a very interesting issue that we hope to address in future work.

Model of Health Outcomes

The second part of our model concerns the health outcomes of the head of household and partner (if present). We are interested not only in mortality but also in the distinction between being in good health as opposed to poor health, because we believe that economic decisionmaking and outcomes regarding assets, for example, the propensities to spend down assets and to give gifts, are likely to be different for households in which members are generally healthy compared with households whose members are in poor health. We estimate health outcomes with a pair of ordered probit models, one for males and one for females, estimated through maximum likelihood. As an example, the model for males is as follows (the model for females is identical).

$$(6) \qquad Y_M^* = X_M \beta_M + \epsilon_M$$

$$Y_M = 0 \, (death) \, if \, Y_M^* \leq 0$$

$$Y_M = 1 \, (poor \;\; health) \, if \, 0 < Y_M^* \leq \mu_M$$

$$Y_M = 2 \, (good \;\; health) \, if \, Y_M^* > \mu_M.$$

In this expression μ_M is a threshold that determines the value of the latent variable Y_M^* for which health shifts from poor to good, X_M are independent variables that are expected to influence health, and β_M is a vector of parameters. The stochastic disturbance ϵ_M is assumed to be distributed standard normal.

We include as independent variables in our health outcome models age, marital status, a set of demographic characteristics, several measures of health in the preceding period (baseline health), and a measure of household wealth and income in the preceding period.[17] We interact wealth with age, marital

17. For married couples we divide household wealth by 1.5 to make a simple correction for their need to spread their wealth between two individuals.

status, and baseline health status, and in each case we model the interaction using a spline, thereby allowing the slope of the relationship to be different for those of relatively low wealth than for those of high wealth, fixing the knot at $200,000. Thus, for example, we distinguish the effect of wealth on mortality for those who were in poor health in the preceding period from the effect of wealth on health outcomes for those who were in good health, and for each health group we allow the marginal effect of increasing wealth on health outcome to be different for wealth below $200,000 than for wealth values above this value.

We are assuming that there is no correlation between the stochastic disturbances affecting health outcomes of a male and female who live together in a common household. This means we are assuming that to the extent a couple is more likely to share a common health outcome than a random pair of individuals, the effect is entirely because of observable variables we are including in our model, like household wealth or similarity of age. Clearly this assumption is imperfect: for example, couples who travel together risk dying together in an accident, suggesting that the probability of both dying is larger than the simple multiplication of the probability of one dying times the probability of the other dying. It is a simple matter to address this issue by estimating our models jointly for males and females, and we intend to explore this issue in future work.

For now, our health outcomes model is independent of our model of saving, asset utilization, and gift giving. In particular, the stochastic disturbances in each model are assumed to be independent of all disturbances included in the other model, although of course the two models share almost all of their independent variables in common, including baseline wealth and health status.

In previous work we estimated a model linking gift giving in one year with mortality in the following two years and found a significant correlation between the disturbances in the gift-giving model and the mortality model, suggesting that a household might have information about its future health outcome beyond what is captured in the explanatory variables about health we have access to in the AHEAD data set.[18] In the present work our model is specified slightly differently, since we are estimating saving, asset utilization, and gift giving together with health outcomes in the same period, not future health outcomes, conditioning on baseline health and economic conditions. Nonetheless, the earlier finding suggests we should consider correlations between the disturbances included in the different models. We have not done

18. See Feinstein and Ho (1999).

so mainly because of the computational burden associated with estimating such a large model.

Data

The data we use to estimate our models are drawn from waves 1 and 2 of the AHEAD data set. The AHEAD study collects information about a stratified random sample of households for which the head of the household was 70 or above in 1993.[19] AHEAD is a longitudinal study, which began in 1993 and is interviewing members of participating households every second year. The study collects extensive information about family composition and structure, living arrangements, economic status of the household and extended family, including information about household assets and work history, and information about many different aspects of health of the head of the household and his partner.[20]

We include in our analysis only households that participated in the survey in both waves, including households that exited the survey because of death (it was a single household and the head died, or a couple and both died) but for which surviving relatives answered the exit survey. There are approximately 5,640 households that meet these criteria, containing approximately 7,700 respondents—heads and their partners—of which approximately 750 died between waves 1 and 2. We excluded from our analysis 156 households for which basic sex and age information is missing for either the head or partner, and an additional 180 households for which basic information about savings, income, and health is missing for wave 2. As described below, we also deleted approximately 420 households for which asset data were deemed too poor to be useful. After all deletions, we are left with approximately 4,880 households. For estimation of our model of saving, asset utilization, and gift giving, for which the dependent variables are wave 2 values, we omitted 356 households that exited the survey because of death, leaving us with 4,515 households. Of these households, 3,875 report having at least one child, and we estimate our models for this subset of households as well as for the full 4,515.

In our empirical estimation we use wealth, demographic, and health information from wave 1, and combine it with information about income, gift giving, savings, spend down, and changes in health (including death) reported in

---

19. Information is collected only about households for which the head is not institutionalized.
20. See Soldo and others (1997) for details about the construction of the sample and design of the survey.

wave 2. Thus our approach is to establish a baseline condition for each household using wave 1 data and then examine household decisionmaking and changes in household circumstances between waves 1 and 2, as a function of the baseline conditions. Many of our variables are drawn directly from the AHEAD data set, but others are constructed.

The AHEAD data we have worked with most extensively are the asset data. The AHEAD survey asks respondents about a variety of assets, including stocks, bonds, IRAs, business assets, house value, other real estate, checking and CD accounts, trusts, tangible assets (including cars and jewelry), and other assets. We have found the asset data not as reliable as we had hoped and have worked intensively to correct data in cases for which we have been able to make corrections. In our initial work we discovered a possible error in the way in which trust assets were calculated for wave 1, owing to a question that was asked that is worded ambiguously, which we believe respondents and the AHEAD staff interpreted differently.[21] In the face of this difficulty, we developed a method for imputing trust assets that we believe is consistent with the most plausible interpretation of respondents' answers.[22]

Many AHEAD respondents do not provide exact answers about specific assets, and their holdings of these assets are imputed either based on answers they give to a series of bracket questions or, if they refuse to or cannot answer the bracket questions, a "hot-deck" procedure is used.[23] In our more recent

21. The ambiguous question is v1779, in which the respondent was asked whether he had included trust assets in his previous answers; we believe that a yes to this question simply meant the respondent had listed all trust assets in his answer to the previous question, v1778, which asks about trust assets, whereas the AHEAD staff appears to have interpreted a yes as meaning that the assets reported in v1778 had been included in earlier asset figures provided in response to slightly earlier questions in the series.

22. Our method is as follows. If the respondent answered no to v1779 we use the AHEAD total asset measure. If the respondent answered yes we apply the following algorithm. First we compute the difference between the answer to v1778, which asks specifically about trust assets, and the AHEAD total asset measure. If this difference is negative, trust assets cannot have been included in the earlier figures and we then add the number reported in v1778 to the total asset measure. If the difference is positive we compute the ratio of the number reported in v1778 to the AHEAD total asset measure. If the ratio is greater than .75, indicating trust assets are a very large proportion of the total assets, we assume trust assets were not included in the total asset number and add the number reported in v1778 to the AHEAD measure of total assets. Conversely, if the ratio is less than .50 we assume trust assets were included and do not modify the AHEAD total asset measure. If the ratio is between .5 and .75 we linearly interpolate, adding to the AHEAD total asset measure a fraction of the number reported in v1778, with the fraction being zero at .5 and one at .75.

23. A hot deck procedure involves pairing an observation for which asset information is missing with an observation for which the asset information is present. The matching observation is drawn randomly from a pool consisting of all observations with asset information present for which the values for a set of observable characteristics are identical to those for the observation missing asset information. Unfortunately, the exact hot deck procedure used in AHEAD is not described in any of the written documentation we have had access to.

work, constructing the data set for this chapter, we have scrutinized the imputed asset data with care. For households for which significant asset holdings in wave 1 are based on imputed values, we compared the assets reported in wave 1 to what is reported for the same household in wave 2. We found large discrepancies in many cases. We deleted approximately 280 households for which essentially all asset data are imputed in both waves, believing the data were simply too unreliable to be used. We also deleted approximately 140 households for which wave 1 asset data were deemed too poor to be useful. For approximately 350 households, we used actual asset values from wave 2 to adjust imputed values in wave 1, by adjusting an imputed value— which normally is placed at the midpoint of a bracket interval—to the upper or lower admissible bound of the interval.[24] Lastly, for approximately twenty households, we believe wave 2 asset data to be far more reliable than the wave 1 data and projected the wave 2 asset values back to wave 1, typically multiplying the wave 2 values by 0.8 or 0.9 (depending on the type of asset).[25] In total, we deleted or made corrections to asset data for approximately 770 households, approximately 20 percent of the total number of households reporting asset holdings. Even so, there remain many more households for which we have serious concerns about the quality of the reported data. One problem we wish especially to note is that for many assets the bracket intervals are simply too large to be useful for evaluating asset holdings, and especially for modeling asset dynamics—an example of this problem that recurs for several of the asset types is a bracket between $250,000 and $500,000. Our main asset variable is WEALTH, equal to the total value of all assets in wave 1 (except assets in trust funds) minus total reported debts.

In contrast to the asset data, we find the data on gift giving and the saving or use of assets to be relatively clean—the numbers seem reasonable,

24. For example, if a respondent answers a series of questions indicating his household's holdings of a particular asset are bounded between $250,000 and $750,000, the normal procedure is to impute a value of $500,000 for that asset. If, however, an actual value of holdings of that asset is reported for the household in wave 2, we use it to adjust the imputed value in wave 1. If, for example, the actual holdings in wave 2 are reported as zero, we adjust the imputed value in wave 1 down to $250,000. We make an adjustment only if there is no evidence for shifts in assets between the two waves that might explain why the wave 2 value for a particular asset is very different from the wave 1 imputed value. Overall, our adjustment is a conservative one, in that we do not contradict any answers respondents gave in wave 1, even though in an example like the one we have given it is certainly very possible that the respondent in wave 1 was simply in error and the household does not hold the asset in question.

25. We used this more radical adjustment only when many different kinds of assets were reported in wave 2, all of which were missing in wave 1. In this situation it seems very unlikely that the discrepancy is because of inheritance or a sudden windfall, since in that case it is unlikely the household would so quickly have diversified its assets into many different categories. Far more likely the respondent in wave 1 simply did not recall the household's assets.

and most households provide actual values, though of course we cannot vouch for their accuracy. Respondents are asked about gifts made to children and others in the preceding year; we sum up the total value of gifts they report, and we use the value reported in wave 2, defining this to be the value of the variable GIFT. Respondents are asked about saving. And they are asked separately about use of assets, specifically excluding gifts—the exact wording of the question is, "[In the past two years] did you (and your husband/and your wife/and your partner/) use any of your investments or savings to pay for expenses, not counting any money or assets that you have given away to (children or) others?" If the respondent reports saving money, he is asked how much the household saved, and if he reports having spent out of assets he is asked how much the household utilized. We denote the amount of savings by SAVING (zero or positive) and the value of spend down by SPEND-DOWN (zero or positive). We use the values for these variables reported in wave 2 and place the household in one of three categories for that wave: savings, spend down of assets, or no significant saving or spending down of assets.

The AHEAD survey collects information about a rich array of health indicators. Respondents are asked to rate their current health as excellent, very good, good, fair, or poor, and we focus on these self-reports of overall health to construct measures of health status. Respondents are also asked whether during the past year or two their health has improved, remained about the same, or worsened, and we use information from their answers to this question as well.[26] Because we are interested in investigating the effects of ill health on asset dynamics and gift giving, we focus on creating a separate category for households whose members are overall not in good health. For each household we define the variable POORHEALTH to be equal to zero (good health) or one (poor health). If the head of household does not have a partner, POORHEALTH equals one if the head reports being in poor health; if he has a partner, POORHEALTH equals one if both the head and partner report being in poor health or if one reports being in poor health and the other reports being in fair health. We also define the variable HEALTH-CHANGE for wave 2, equal to zero (health the same) or one (health worse). If the head does not have a partner HEALTH-CHANGE equals one if the head reports being in worse health; if he has a partner, HEALTH-CHANGE

---

26. In his comments to us Bill Gale suggested that another variable that might be useful for measuring the relationship between health and decisionmaking about assets, including gifts, is the individual's assessment of the likelihood she will enter a nursing home in the foreseeable future. We agree but do not explore the matter here.

equals one if both the head and partner report being in worse health or if one reports being in worse health and the other reports that his or her health has remained about the same; if neither of these conditions holds, HEALTH-CHANGE equals one if the household has POORHEALTH equal to zero in wave 1 and one in wave 2. In extensions of our basic models we have constructed more detailed measures of health using information provided in AHEAD about functional limitations—ADLs and IADLs—and specific diseases. We define two dummy variables, HIGH-ADL and HIGH-IADL— HIGH-ADL is equal to one if a respondent is reported to have more than one ADL limitation, and HIGH-IADL is equal to one if he is reported to have more than one IADL limitation.[27] We also explored the impact of illness on economic decisionmaking, defining the variable ILLNESS to be a dummy variable equal to one if either head or partner reports having heart disease or cancer.[28]

Besides the variables defined above, we include several additional economic and demographic variables in our models. We include household income— we define INCOME to be total household income, as recorded in the

27. In work beyond what is reported in this chapter we have developed a methodology for dividing households into five distinct health groups in each wave. We define HIGH-ADL and HIGH-IADL for a household (if the head does not have a partner we used these variables as set for the head; if the head does have a partner, we set HIGH-ADL for the household equal to one if either the head or partner has ADLH equal to one, and also set HIGH-IADL for the household equal to one if either the head or partner has HIGH-IADL equal to one). We also define a variable WORSEHEALTH in wave 1— if the head has no partner WORSEHEALTH equals one, if the head reports being in worse health. If he has a partner WORSEHEALTH equals one, if both head and partner report being in worse health or one reports being in worse health and the other reports no change in health. Combining the four health indicators POORHEALTH, WORSEHEALTH, HIGH-ADL, and HIGH-IADL generates sixteen distinct health cells—each household falls in one of these cells. There are too few observations in certain cells to estimate reliably coefficients for each cell separately. Thus we group certain cells together, creating five distinct groups. The first group includes households for which all four dummies are zero— the majority of households (both of married and not married households) fall in this group. The second group includes households for which just the WORSEHEALTH variable equals one—the members of the household are not in poor health and have no limitations, but apparently feel a sense of deteriorating health. The third group includes households for which POORHEALTH is zero but at least one of ADLH or IADLH is equal to one—the respondents in these households have made relatively optimistic reports about their health but suffer from some limitations in daily living. The fourth group includes households for which POORHEALTH is one and both ADLH and IADLH are zero— the members of the household feel in poor health but do not have limitations in daily living. Lastly, the fifth group includes the remaining households, for which POORHEALTH is one and at least one of ADLH or IADLH is also one. In wave 1, about 10 percent of households fall in group two, 18 percent in group three, 5 percent in group four, and 10 percent in group five. Our simpler specification just using POORHEALTH combines groups one, two, and three in the category POORHEALTH equal zero and groups four and five in POORHEALTH equal one.

28. We have also explored the importance of cognitive limitations in economic outcomes, finding only modest effects, which we do not report.

AHEAD data set, and we use wave 2 income in our specification.[29] We include age of the head and partner, defining MALE-AGE for a male respondent to be the maximum of zero and his age minus 64, and FEMALE-AGE for a female respondent to be the maximum of zero and her age minus 64. We define MARRIED to be a dummy variable set to one if the household is a married couple in wave 1, WIDOW to be a dummy variable set to one if the head is a widow or widower in wave 1, and NEWWIDOW to be a dummy variable set equal to one if one member of a couple dies between waves 1 and 2. We define NON-WHITE to be a dummy variable set to one if either the head of household or his partner is nonwhite. We define SOUTH to be a dummy variable set to one if the household place of residence is a southern state, and URBAN to be a dummy variable set to one if the household place of residence is an urban area. We define two variables related to household finances: TRUST, a dummy variable set to one if the household owns a trust fund; and ESTATE-FILING, a dummy variable set to one if the household's total assets exceed the estate tax filing threshold, assumed to be $600,000 for single and divorced, and $1.2 million for married and widowed.[30]

Finally, we define a set of variables related to children that we expect to be important factors influencing gift giving. Our variables related to children are defined using the extensive information about family composition and living arrangements collected in wave 1. The AHEAD survey divides children into those who are coresident with their parents and those who live elsewhere. We define CORESIDENT CHILDREN to be the children who live with the head and partner, and NONRESIDENT CHILDREN to be the number of nonresident children; we include biological children and stepchildren of the head and partner, possibly from previous marriages, and we define NOCHILDREN to be a dummy variable equal to one if both CORESIDENT CHILDREN and NONRESIDENT CHILDREN are zero. As discussed earlier, for much of our analysis we restrict attention to households for which NUMCHILDREN is greater than zero, which are 3,875 of the 4,515 households in our data set. We define GRANDCHILDREN to be the total number of grandchildren. We define CHILDREN-AVERAGE-INC to be the average income of children for whom income is reported. We recognize that when a child's income is not reported, it may indicate either that the parents feel not

29. We made imputations for this variable based on the coded answers to a series of bracket questions recorded in the wave 2 data set—at the present time the imputations themselves, including hot deck, have not been done for wave 2 by the AHEAD staff.

30. Thus we assume that when one spouse dies, she or he leaves all assets to the other spouse, so that the filing threshold for widows and widowers is $1.2 million. We initially included a variable for homeownership but found it was not significant in any of our models and so omit it.

as close to the child or the child is doing poorly; to control for such effects, we define CHILDREN-NO-INC-INFO to be equal to the number of children for whom income data are missing.

Definitions and summary statistics of the variables included in our models are presented in appendix A to this chapter. Table 11A-1 provides information about numbers of zero and nonzero cases and the mean for nonzero cases for our variables; we include separate panels for the entire sample and for the sample of households having at least one child, and provide information both for the unweighted sample and the sample weighted to reflect the U.S. population. Table 11A-2 provides a more detailed breakdown of the quantile distribution of wealth, weighted and unweighted, both for the entire sample and the sample having children. In general, summary statistics are similar for the unweighted and weighted samples as well as for the entire sample and the sample of households with children.

Empirical Results and Discussion

In this section we present our results from estimating our models. We present and discuss first results for our economic model of saving, asset utilization, and gift giving, which is the model we focus on; at the end we present and briefly discuss results for our model of health outcomes.

The specification of our economic model for which we present results is the recursive model estimated for households that have children. Results are quite similar for two other specifications that we have estimated but do not present results for: the base model for all households, and the recursive model for households with children. In estimating these models we discovered that neither ρ_{24}, the correlation between the magnitude of saving and gift giving, nor ρ_{34}, the correlation between the magnitude of spend down and gift-giving, were significantly different from zero. We also found that it was difficult to identify ρ_{12}, the correlation between overall savings—spend down and the magnitude of saving, and ρ_{13}, the correlation between the overall savings—spend down and the magnitude of spend down, and we therefore set these correlations to zero.[31] With these four correlations set to zero, expressions 2 and 3 can each be estimated by ordinary least squares, separately from the remainder of the model, and that is how we estimated them. We then estimated expressions 1 and 4 jointly, allowing correlation ρ_{14} between the disturbances

---

31. We believe the reason is that we included essentially the same set of variables in expression 1 as in expressions 2 and 3.

in these two models. In all of our models ρ_{14} is positive and significant, although small in magnitude, indicating that, other things being equal, households that are more likely to save are also more likely to give gifts.

Results for the recursive model estimated for households with children are presented in table 11-1. We discuss results for each part of the model separately. Consider first household saving or spend down of assets, presented in panel A of the table. The results indicate that shocks to the household dramatically increase the likelihood of spend down: the coefficients associated with NEWWIDOW and HEALTH-CHANGE are both negative and highly significant. Not surprisingly, higher income is associated with a greater likelihood of saving, but only for those in good health and those who are married, and not for those in poor health. Wealth does not have a significant relationship with saving or spend down. Age of male is associated with an increased likelihood of saving, which somewhat contradicts the standard life-cycle theory; age of female has no significant effect. The only demographic variable that has a significant impact is living in an urban area, which is associated with a significantly greater likelihood of spend down.

Next consider results for the magnitude of spend down (asset utilization) among households that spend down assets, presented in panel B. There is a significant positive association between the amount of spend down and both age of male and age of female, which is consistent with the standard life-cycle theory. The relationship between wealth and the magnitude of spend down is positive and significant, but only for households in good health—for households in poor health there is no significant relationship. This finding suggests that households in poor health have expenditure needs that must be met and are relatively insensitive to wealth considerations, compared with households in good health that may be spending down more for luxury goods—for things that they desire, but that they do not perceive to be necessities. Finally, there is a significant positive relationship between income and the amount of spend down, for both those in good health and those in poor health. This finding is not intuitively obvious; perhaps those earning more income expect to earn more income in the future and therefore are more willing to spend assets, or perhaps they are more active and therefore have more ways to spend money for their own enjoyment.[32]

---

32. It is possible that those with greater spending needs arrange their financial concerns so as to generate more income, perhaps by investing in riskier assets, an issue we hope to investigate in future work; it is also possible that they earn income by working, an issue we will address in the next draft of this work.

Table 11-1. *Saving, Asset Utilization, and Gift-Giving Estimates for Households with at Least One Child*[a]

Variable	Parameter estimate	Absolute value of t statistic
Saving and asset utilization decision		
Constant	0.8831 (0.1125)	7.848
Married	−0.0589 (0.1016)	0.579
Widowed	−0.0697 (0.0900)	0.774
Non-white	0.0020 (0.0743)	0.027
Health-change	−0.1826 (0.0443)	4.122
South	0.0635 (0.0429)	1.480
Urban	−0.1046 (0.0493)	2.122
Male-age	0.0086 (0.0037)	2.358
Female-age	0.0024 (0.0031)	0.771
Poorhealth	−0.0738 (0.0950)	0.776
Wealth*goodhealth	0.000039 (0.0001)	0.593
Wealth*poorhealth	−0.0005 (0.0005)	0.991
Poorhealth-wave2	−0.0259 (0.1103)	0.235
Income*goodhealth	0.0044 (0.0012)	3.628
Income*poorhealth	0.0037 (0.0038)	0.950
Income*married	0.0031 (0.0012)	2.611
Newwidow	−0.2635 (0.0838)	3.145
Nonresident children	−0.0147 (0.0110)	1.339
Coresident children	−0.0229 (0.0464)	0.494
λ threshold value	1.7316 (0.0304)	57.03
Magnitude of asset utilization		
Constant	−1.1992 (3.0865)	0.389
Married	1.0776 (2.8102)	0.383
Widowed	2.5249 (2.6479)	0.954
Non-white	−1.5580 (2.5715)	0.606
Health-change	−0.2107 (1.2045)	0.175
South	−0.5050 (1.3020)	0.388
Urban	0.8755 (1.3169)	0.665
Male-age	0.2521 (0.1114)	2.263
Female-age	0.2183 (0.0854)	2.555
Poorhealth	1.0257 (2.2557)	0.455
Wealth*goodhealth	0.0128 (0.0030)	4.167
Wealth*poorhealth	0.0054 (0.0095)	0.572
Poorhealth-wave2	1.2460 (2.8939)	0.431
Income*goodhealth	0.0869 (0.0233)	3.727
Income*poorhealth	0.2718 (0.1059)	2.566
Nonresident children	−0.2623 (0.2995)	0.876

(*continued*)

Table 11-1. (*continued*)

Variable	Parameter estimate	Absolute value of t statistic
Coresident children	1.1191 (1.2331)	0.908
σ	8.6626 (0.0384)	225.2
Magnitude of saving		
Constant	−10.9227 (8.2314)	1.327
Married	1.2532 (7.4830)	0.167
Widowed	1.0740 (7.0573)	0.152
Non-white	−0.5365 (8.5633)	0.063
Health-change	2.1448 (3.1364)	0.684
South	−4.3352 (3.0844)	1.406
Urban	1.1274 (3.1824)	0.352
Male-age	0.2205 (0.2500)	0.882
Female-age	0.4454 (0.2322)	1.918
Poorhealth	−5.6421 (8.8246)	0.639
Wealth*goodhealth	0.0286 (0.0108)	2.636
Wealth*poorhealth	0.0631 (0.0290)	2.174
Poorhealth-wave2	9.1150 (7.1519)	1.274
Income*goodhealth	0.5104 (0.0511)	9.975
Income*poorhealth	0.1826 (0.0658)	2.774
Wealth*married	0.0098 (0.0121)	0.809
Income*married	−0.3184 (0.0736)	4.322
Nonresident children	0.5402 (0.8117)	0.666
Coresident children	−2.4670 (3.6112)	0.663
σ	14.0460 (0.0639)	219.8
Gift giving		
Constant	−14.1587 (1.7081)	8.289
Married	1.3562 (1.4439)	0.939
Widowed	2.2195 (1.2034)	1.844
Non-white	−2.4755 (1.1774)	2.102
Health-change	0.8198 (0.7317)	1.120
South	−0.2600 (0.6654)	0.391
Urban	1.3654 (0.7600)	1.797
Male-age	0.0718 (0.0533)	1.349
Female-age	−0.1594 (0.0523)	3.046
Poorhealth	−3.7562 (1.4438)	2.602
Wealth*goodhealth	0.0015 (0.0005)	2.891
Wealth*poorhealth	0.0223 (0.0048)	4.633
Poorhealth-wave2	−0.2413 (1.3874)	0.174
Income*goodhealth	0.1435 (0.0061)	23.54
Income*poorhealth	0.1406 (0.0242)	5.804

(*continued*)

Table 11-1. (*continued*)

Variable	Parameter estimate	Absolute value of t statistic
Income*married	−0.1033 (0.0145)	7.145
Newwidow	4.3895 (1.3347)	3.289
Nonresident children	0.2125 (0.2903)	0.732
Coresident children	−0.8992 (0.8378)	1.073
Grandchildren	−0.1872 (0.0948)	1.698
Children-average-inc	0.0259 (0.0152)	1.975
Children-no-inc-info	−1.1920 (0.3246)	3.672
Trust	3.0871 (0.9312)	3.315
Estate-filing	6.1970 (1.4974)	4.139
Spend-down	0.1024 (0.0287)	3.567
Saving	0.0279 (0.0065)	4.313
σ	13.781 (0.1502)	91.78
ρ_{14}	0.0671 (0.0256)	2.622
Number of observations	3,814	
Mean log-likelihood	−2.44319	

a. Standard errors are in parentheses.

Consider next the results for the amount of saving, presented in panel C. The coefficient associated with being in poor health in wave 1 is large and negative, while the coefficient for being in poor health in wave 2 is very large and positive, but neither is significant, most likely because there are not many in poor health who save.[33] The marginal effect on saving associated with increased levels of wealth is large, positive, and significant, both for those in good health and those in poor health; but the magnitude is more than twice as large for those in poor health. The fact that saving rises with baseline wealth is not surprising—it very likely reflects the fact that certain individuals and couples have a greater propensity to save throughout life, a propensity that persists into old age. Income has a significant positive relationship with saving, as expected; its effect is especially large for those in good health, substantially smaller for those in poor health. But note that the coefficient associated with the interaction between being a married household and income is negative and significant. Combining estimates for the interactions of income

33. Jonathan Skinner has suggested that some of our results might be sensitive to outliers, and the estimates for these coefficients are an example. But we note that this equation is estimated by ordinary least squares, not maximum likelihood, and therefore the results are not driven by functional form assumptions concerning the error term.

with health and marital status, single elders in good health are predicted to save a very large fraction of income—approximately one-half, married in good health and singles in poor health are each predicted to save approximately 20 percent of income, and married in poor health are predicted to save an amount that is essentially independent of income. No other variables have a statistically significant effect; the only other variable that is close to having a significant effect is age of female, which has a coefficient that is positive and marginally significant.

Consider lastly results for our model of gift giving. In general, our results for gift giving support the view that tax planning is an important consideration for some elderly and that health status influences the effects of wealth and income on gift giving.

Clear evidence in support of estate tax planning is that the dummy variable ESTATE-FILING for having wealth above the estate tax filing threshold is large and positive and very significant; having wealth above the threshold increases the likelihood of gift giving by nearly one-half of a standard deviation and increases the average size of gifts by more than $5,000. The dummy variable TRUST is also positive and significant, with a value of approximately 3, indicating that households that plan for estate transfer by establishing trusts are also more actively transferring their assets by gifts.

The results indicate that the marginal propensity to give gifts rises with wealth. But it rises much more rapidly for households in poor health than for households in good health—the coefficients are .0015 and .022, or a difference of more than one order of magnitude; the results imply that among the households whose members are in poor health and who give gifts a $100,000 increase in wealth increases the average value of gifts by approximately $2,200. In addition, the average propensity to give gifts is lower for households in poor health—the coefficients associated with the dummy variable POORHEALTH are negative and significant and rather large at 3.76. Thus among households of low wealth those in poor health have a lower propensity to give gifts than those in good health, but the opposite is the case among households of high wealth—for these households, those in poor health have a greater propensity to give gifts. Indeed, there is a crossover, and at the wealth level of approximately $180,000 the propensity to give gifts is estimated to be the same for the two health groups. We note that we found a similar pattern when we investigated gift giving reported in wave 1.[34] The pattern we have discovered is interesting and shows how important interactions between

---

34. See Feinstein and Ho (1999).

health and economic variables can be in understanding and ultimately in predicting household decisionmaking and outcomes.

How are we to interpret our findings about the influence on gift giving of wealth interacted with health? The elderly in poor health presumably feel vulnerable and are very sensitive to the need to maintain at least a minimum level "nest-egg" for their own uncertain future, which may involve high medical costs and also be somewhat frightening and depressing to contemplate, which makes them less willing to give when they have less wealth. Those elderly in poor health with greater resources recognize that they are not likely to exhaust their resources, even if the future does turn out to involve high costs and so reduce giving less markedly—wealth offers protection, real and psychological, against vulnerability. Indeed for wealthier individuals who fall into poor health an opposite motivation may become paramount—to give away assets in preparation for their own death. In general, these arguments are consistent with the idea that the elderly in poor health become more risk averse, wishing to hold precautionary savings, and that the degree to which their risk aversion increases declines with increasing wealth.

Returning to our model estimates, income has a significant positive effect on the propensity to give gifts for both households in good health and households in poor health, even after taking into account the fact that the coefficient associated with the variable interacting marital status with income is negative. The marginal effect of income on gift giving is similar for households in poor health and for those in good health.

One of the strongest effects on gift giving is being a new widow or widower—new widows and widowers who give gifts on average give about $4,400 more than others of comparable status. This finding is especially important in light of our finding that new widows and widowers are also significantly more likely to spend down assets for their own use. Together, the two findings depict new widows and widowers rapidly depleting assets, suggesting that new widowhood is an important factor to consider in modeling estate dynamics, including estate tax issues.[35]

Interestingly, total number of children does not have a significant effect on gift giving. The coefficient associated with the average earnings of children

---

35. During our presentation at the conference we received several valuable comments related to this issue. Practitioners in the audience mentioned that it is common to observe that new widows and widowers do in fact consciously embark on a program to give away assets as gifts—this was described as a usual part of estate planning. It was also mentioned that new widows or widowers may be suddenly more aware of their own mortality, which may make them decide to deplete assets quickly; indeed their mortality may objectively rise—results for some mortality models indicate that the probability of death rises for an individual for a few years after becoming a widow or widower.

is positive and marginally significant, which goes against the argument that parents give gifts to children who are experiencing "hard times"; apparently this motivation for gift giving is not relevant for this population, for whom most children are presumably middle-aged and fully established in life.[36] Interestingly, the variable referring to the status of children and grandchildren that has the most significant coefficient is the variable CHILDREN-NO-INC-INFO measuring the number of children for whom average earnings are not known by the parents—the larger this number, the lower the gifts. This finding suggests that parents are more likely to make gifts to children they remain in touch with and feel close to than to children with whom they have a more distant relationship.

Several of the demographic variables included in our gift model are also significant. The propensity for giving gifts is larger for married households than for other households and for those living in urban areas, and smaller for nonwhite. Age of females, whether head or partner, has a significant negative relationship with the propensity to give gifts—younger women have a higher propensity to give gifts; we have not included age of children in our specification, and it is possible that in some cases households with younger women are second marriages with younger children.

Finally, both the magnitude of spend down and the magnitude of saving are positively and significantly associated with gift giving, with the coefficient for spend down especially large. The result for saving is intuitive and suggests that saving and gift giving are linked, which is consistent with the finding that ρ_{14} is positive. One interpretation is that some of the elderly are more concerned about the future—both their own and their children's—than others. The result for spend down is less clear—apparently some households, when they do spend, spend freely; as more waves of AHEAD become available it would be interesting to try to determine whether this is a transitory phenomenon—so that a household might make many gifts and spend down assets a lot in one year but not in subsequent years—or one that persists over time for certain households, perhaps again linked to health and life expectancies.

We conclude our discussion of the economic model by mentioning some differences between results from estimating the model only for households with children and results estimating the model for all households. For all households, the model of saving and spend down now shows greater wealth associated with a significantly greater likelihood of saving for those in good

---

36. Altonji, Hayashi, and Kotlikoff (1997) argue that parents give more readily to children who are having economic difficulties.

health; this model also shows income associated with a significantly greater likelihood of saving for all households, but the interaction of marital status with income is negative and significant, so that the overall effect of income is reduced for those in good health who are married, increased for those in poor health who are not married. In the model of gift giving we include the variable NOCHILDREN but omit the other more detailed variables related to children, and we find that NOCHILDREN has a very large significant negative coefficient, indicating that individuals with no children have a re-duced propensity to give gifts, a finding that is intuitive and consistent with the life-cycle model.

The results for our model of health outcomes is presented in table 11-2. In estimating the model for men we found that we could not identify the coefficients associated with negative wealth and negative wealth interacted with age, so we omitted these variables from the specification for men.

Our main finding is that health in wave 1 is the most important factor affecting health outcomes in wave 2. Among men, educational attainment is also a significant factor associated with improved outcomes; but among women, although educational attainment is associated with improved out-comes, the effects are not significant. For men there are not other signifi-cant effects. For women, being married is associated with a significantly im-proved outcome, and so is increasing wealth, both by itself and interacted with age.

It is commonly thought that marital status benefits men more than women in regard to health, but our findings are the opposite. It is also thought that the beneficial effect of wealth on health is most important among those of lower economic status—that the marginal effect of wealth on health dimin-ishes with rising wealth; but we find that among women, the group for which there is a significant effect of wealth, the marginal effect of wealth on health is essentially constant over the entire wealth range.

Practically, our finding that health is the most important determinant of health outcomes is important, because it indicates that trajectories of health outcomes for the elderly can be predicted mainly by focusing on health vari-ables, at least in the short run, with the exception that for women wealth and marital status also matter.

Conclusion

In this chapter we have presented the results of an initial attempt to estimate integrated models of asset dynamics, gift giving, and health outcomes among

Table 11-2. *Health Status and Mortality Risk, by Gender*[a]

	Males		Females	
Variable	Parameter estimate	Absolute value of t statistic	Parameter estimate	Absolute value of t statistic
Constant	1.9816 (0.5670)	3.495	2.8487 (0.2583)	11.027
Age	−0.0176 (0.0766)	0.230	−0.0574 (0.0300)	1.914
Agesquare	0.0006 (0.0025)	0.217	0.0017 (0.0008)	1.948
Lowwealth	−0.0003 (0.0023)	0.131	0.0025 (0.0015)	1.701
Highwealth	−0.0001 (0.0010)	0.079	0.0022 (0.0012)	1.896
Negativewealth			0.1402 (0.4191)	0.334
Age*lowwealth	−0.0001 (0.0001)	1.037	−0.0001 (0.0001)	0.507
Age*highwealth	0.0001 (0.0001)	0.356	−0.0001 (0.0001)	2.556
Age*negativewealth			−0.0048 (0.0298)	0.159
Non-white	0.0017 (0.1797)	0.009	−0.0380 (0.0945)	0.402
Poorhealth	−0.7739 (0.0999)	7.746	−0.6492 (0.0796)	8.160
Worsehealth	−0.2487 (0.0840)	2.959	−0.3015 (0.0652)	4.623
Illness	−0.0341 (0.0822)	0.415	−0.1608 (0.0686)	2.344

High-adl	-0.4387 (0.2955)	1.484	-0.4328 (0.0952)	4.548
High-iadl	0.1767 (0.4565)	0.387	-0.1321 (0.1085)	1.218
Married	-0.0126 (0.5813)	0.022	-0.5389 (0.2663)	2.023
Married*age	0.0043 (0.0805)	0.054	0.0322 (0.0363)	0.886
Married*agesquare	-0.0014 (0.0027)	0.506	-0.0004 (0.0013)	0.289
Married*lowwealth	0.0007 (0.0022)	0.334	-0.0006 (0.0013)	0.415
Married*highwealth	-0.0004 (0.0009)	0.378	-0.0002 (0.0008)	0.196
Married*high-adl	0.0812 (0.3164)	0.257	0.2970 (0.1577)	1.883
Married*high-iadl	-0.4651 (0.4691)	0.991	-0.4504 (0.1746)	2.579
High school diploma	0.2345 (0.0883)	2.656	0.1088 (0.0670)	1.623
College	0.3238 (0.1173)	2.760	0.1352 (0.0910)	1.486
College degree	0.2832 (0.1699)	1.667	0.0944 (0.1303)	0.724
Post-graduate work	0.0151 (0.1191)	0.127	0.2461 (0.1630)	1.510
λ threshold value	0.3274 (0.0352)	9.303	1.0309 (0.0505)	20.400
Number of observations	2,274		3,966	
Mean log-likelihood	-0.383514		-0.375964	

a. Standard errors are in parentheses.

the elderly. Most of our results are intuitive, and we view our efforts as successful, but we recognize that more work must be done to develop models and obtain results useful for prediction and policy analysis.

Our results have several implications for the debate about the estate tax. First, the results suggest that at least some elderly are cognizant of the tax and that it influences their financial decisionmaking. There is a jump in gift giving at the wealth level associated with the estate filing threshold—elderly with assets above the threshold give more in gifts than those with assets below the threshold, controlling for many other factors. In addition, many wealthy elderly establish trust funds, and those with trust funds give more in gifts. Also, recent widows and widowers seem to alter their behavior, spending down their assets and increasing their gift giving. Since it influences behavior, the estate tax undoubtedly distorts allocations from what they would be without the tax; for example, the elderly may be giving away more of their assets sooner than they would if there were no tax. Such distortions are not necessarily bad but must be evaluated in a welfare economics framework.

Second, our results indicate that health is an important factor in elderly financial decisionmaking and therefore suggest that health influences estate planning and preferences. The fact that the marginal propensity to give gifts rises much faster with wealth for those in ill health suggests that, among the wealthy, the elderly in poor health may especially feel pressure to give away more assets than they would in the absence of the estate tax, whereas those in good health may be less affected. If this is true, it is an effect of the tax that is probably not desired by most Americans. If the estate tax is to remain in existence, perhaps the elderly need to be educated about estate planning issues earlier and made aware of the possibility that their attitudes about estate planning and gifts may change once they become sick or are widowed.

Lastly, the fact that the elderly may rush to engage in estate planning and accelerate gift giving toward the end of life, often when sick, suggests that estate tax policy should be connected with health care policy for the elderly. It seems likely that an elderly person who becomes sick will make different financial decisions concerning her estate depending on whether or not she expects to bear large medical costs or expects the government to bear those costs.

Over the next year we plan to study asset allocation patterns in the AHEAD data. Integrating asset allocation and asset returns with our current model should provide a reasonably complete framework for analyzing elderly health and economic outcomes. We also hope to compare asset allocations reported by AHEAD respondents with allocations reported by respondents in the Health and Retirement Survey, a cohort of persons approximately twenty years younger than the individuals in AHEAD.

Ultimately, for prediction and policy analysis we believe we must estimate our model using at least three waves of data from AHEAD. In particular, since we are using data in wave 1 to establish baseline economic and health conditions, we cannot estimate a true panel model with only two waves of data. With three waves we can estimate panel models, the great advantage being that we can then investigate correlations over time in household patterns of asset dynamics and gift giving. Thus, with panel estimation we should be able to distinguish households that are "savers" (saving year after year) from others that are "spenders" and determine more accurately how many of the elderly are actively managing their estates, including spend down and the transfer of assets to their heirs.[37]

Appendix A: Data

Definitions of the variables used in our models are presented below. Summary statistics are reported in tables 11A-1 and 11A-2.

Dependent variables

GIFT	Gift given reported in wave 2 (dollars)
SPEND-DOWN	Assets utilized reported in wave 2 (dollars)
SAVING	Saving reported in wave 2 (dollars)
ASSET-CHANGE	1 = save; 0 = no change; −1 = spend down in wave 2
HEALTH	2 = good health; 1 = poor health; 0 = death in wave 2

Independent variables

WEALTH	Net wealth based on assets reported in wave 1 (dollars)
INCOME	Income reported in wave 2 (dollars)
MARRIED	Married as reported in wave 1
WIDOWED	Widow or widower as reported in wave 1

37. Of course we could explore the correlation in gift giving and saving between waves 1 and 2, but we cannot do that and also establish a baseline for each household, which we believe is important for estimation.

NEWWIDOW	Married in wave 1 and widowed in wave 2
SOUTH	Household located in the South as reported in wave 1
NOCHILDREN	Neither head nor partner has children as reported in wave 1
NON-WHITE	Either head or partner is nonwhite as reported in wave 1
POORHEALTH	Household defined to be in poor health as of wave 1 (see text for definition)
GOODHEALTH	Household defined to be in good health as of wave 1 (see text for definition)
WORSEHEALTH	Household defined to be in worse health in wave 1 than in wave 2
POORHEALTH-WAVE2	Household defined to be in poor health as of wave 2
GOODHEALTH-WAVE2	Household defined to be in good health as of wave 2
HEALTH-CHANGE	Household defined to be in worse health in wave 2 than in wave 1 (see text for definition)
TRUST	Household has established trust funds as reported in wave 1
ESTATE-FILING	Household wealth exceeds estate tax filing threshold
NONRESIDENT CHILDREN	Number of children who do not live in the household as reported in wave 1
CORESIDENT CHILDREN	Number of children who live in the household as reported in wave 1
GRANDCHILDREN	Number of grandchildren as reported in wave 1
CHILDREN-NO-INC-INFO	Number of children for whom earnings information is not available as reported in wave 2
CHILDREN-AVERAGE-INC	Average earning for children whose earning information is available as reported in wave 2
MALE-AGE	Max [age of male minus 64, 0] as reported in wave 1
FEMALE-AGE	Max [age of female minus 64, 0] as reported in wave 1

NEGATIVEWEALTH	Wealth is negative
LOWWEALTH	Wealth is less than or equal to $200,000
HIGHWEALTH	Wealth is greater than $200,000
HIGH SCHOOL DIPLOMA	Respondent earned a high school diploma
COLLEGE	Respondent attended college
COLLEGE DEGREE	Respondent earned a college degree
POST-GRADUATE WORK	Respondent enrolled in a graduate program
ILLNESS	Respondent had heart disease or cancer in wave 1
HIGH-ADL	Respondent had multiple ADLs in wave 1
HIGH-IADL	Respondent had multiple IADLs in wave 1

Appendix B: Mathematical Likelihood Expressions

Following is the likelihood function associated with our model. There are six separate cases.

Case 1:

$$L_1 = CDFBVN\left[\lambda - X_1\beta_1, \frac{-X_4\beta_4}{\sigma_4}, \rho_{14}\right],$$

where CDFBVN is the bivariate normal cumulative distribution function.

Case 2: Define

$$\mu_1' = \frac{\rho_{14}}{\sigma_4}\left(Y_4 - X_4\beta_4\right).$$

Then,

$$L_2 = \frac{1}{\sigma_4}\phi\left(\frac{Y_4 - X_4\beta_4}{\sigma_4}\right)\left\{\Phi\left[\frac{\lambda - X_1\beta_1 - \mu_1'}{\sqrt{1 - \rho_{14}^2}}\right] - \Phi\left[\frac{-X_1\beta_1 - \mu_1'}{\sqrt{1 - \rho_{14}^2}}\right]\right\},$$

where ϕ and Φ are the standard normal density and cumulative distribution functions respectively.

Case 3: Define

$$\sigma_1' = \sqrt{1 - \rho_{12}^2} \qquad \sigma_4' = \sigma_4\sqrt{1 - \rho_{24}^2}$$

$$\rho_{14}' = \frac{\rho_{14} - \rho_{12}\rho_{24}}{\sqrt{1 - \rho_{12}^2}\sqrt{1 - \rho_{24}^2}}$$

$$\mu_1' = \frac{\rho_{12}}{\sigma_2}\left(Y_2 - X_2\beta_2\right) \qquad \mu_4' = \frac{\rho_{24}\sigma_4}{\sigma_2}\left(Y_2 - X_2\beta_2\right).$$

Then,

$$L_3 = \frac{1}{\sigma_2}\,\phi\left(\frac{Y_2 - X_2\beta_2}{\sigma_2}\right)CDFBVN\left[\frac{-X_1\beta_1 - \mu_1'}{\sigma_1'}, \frac{-X_4\beta_4 - \mu_4'}{\sigma_4'}, \rho_{14}'\right].$$

Case 4: Define

$$\sigma_1' = \sqrt{1 - \rho_{13}^2} \qquad \sigma_4' = \sigma_4\sqrt{1 - \rho_{34}^2}$$

$$\rho_{14}' = \frac{\rho_{14} - \rho_{13}\rho_{34}}{\sqrt{1 - \rho_{13}^2}\sqrt{1 - \rho_{34}^2}}$$

$$\mu_1' = \frac{\rho_{13}}{\sigma_3}\left(Y_3 - X_3\beta_3\right) \qquad \mu_4' = \frac{\rho_{34}\sigma_4}{\sigma_2}\left(Y_3 - X_3\beta_3\right).$$

Then,

$$L_4 = \frac{1}{\sigma_3}\,\phi\left(\frac{Y_3 - X_3\beta_3}{\sigma_3}\right)CDFBVN$$

$$\left[\frac{-\lambda + X_1\beta_1 - \mu_1'}{\sigma_1'}, \frac{-X_4\beta_4 - \mu_4'}{\sigma_4'}, -\rho_{14}'\right].$$

Case 5: Define

$$\sigma_1' = \sqrt{1 - \rho_{12}^2} \qquad \sigma_4' = \sigma_4\sqrt{1 - \rho_{24}^2}$$

$$\rho_{14}' = \frac{\rho_{14} - \rho_{12}\rho_{24}}{\sqrt{1 - \rho_{12}^2}\sqrt{1 - \rho_{24}^2}}$$

$$\mu_1' = \frac{\rho_{12}}{\sigma_2}\left(Y_2 - X_2\beta_2\right) \qquad \mu_4' = \frac{\rho_{24}\sigma_4}{\sigma_2}\left(Y_2 - X_2\beta_2\right)$$

$$\mu_1'' = \frac{\rho_{14}'\sigma_1'}{\sigma_4'}\left(Y_4 - X_4\beta_4 - \mu_4'\right) + \mu_1'$$

$$\sigma_1'' = \sigma_1'\sqrt{1 - \rho_{14}'^2}.$$

Then,

$$L_5 = \frac{1}{\sigma_2}\phi\left(\frac{Y_2 - X_2\beta_2}{\sigma_2}\right)\frac{1}{\sigma_4'}\phi\left(\frac{Y_4 + X_4\beta_4 - \mu_4'}{\sigma_4'}\right)\Phi\left[\frac{-X_1\beta_1 - \mu_1''}{\sigma_1''}\right].$$

Case 6: Define

$$\sigma_1' = \sqrt{1 - \rho_{13}^2} \qquad \sigma_4' = \sigma_4\sqrt{1 - \rho_{34}^2}$$

$$\rho_{14}' = \frac{\rho_{14} - \rho_{13}\rho_{34}}{\sqrt{1 - \rho_{13}^2}\sqrt{1 - \rho_{34}^2}}$$

$$\mu_1' = \frac{\rho_{13}}{\sigma_3}\left(Y_3 - X_3\beta_3\right) \qquad \mu_4' = \frac{\rho_{34}\sigma_4}{\sigma_3}\left(Y_3 - X_3\beta_3\right)$$

$$\mu_1'' = \frac{\rho_{14}'\sigma_1'}{\sigma_4'}\left(Y_4 - X_4\beta_4 - \mu_4'\right) + \mu_1'$$

$$\sigma_1'' = \sigma_1'\sqrt{1 - \rho_{14}'^2}.$$

Then,

$$L_6 = \frac{1}{\sigma_3}\phi\left(\frac{Y_3 - X_3\beta_3}{\sigma_3}\right)\frac{1}{\sigma_4'}\phi\left(\frac{Y_4 + X_4\beta_4 - \mu_4'}{\sigma_4'}\right)\Phi\left[\frac{-\lambda + X_1\beta_1 - \mu_1''}{\sigma_1''}\right].$$

Table 11A-1. *Summary Statistics*

	Zero			Nonzero			
Variable	*Number of households*	*Unweighted percentage*	*Weighted percentage*	*Number of households*	*Unweighted percentage*	*Weighted percentage*	*Weighted mean*[a]
All households							
Gift	3,497	77.5	76.2	1,018	22.5	23.8	8,465
Spend-down	3,644	80.7	79.4	871	19.3	20.6	9,083
Saving	3,714	82.3	80.2	801	17.7	19.8	19,203
Hold	1,672	63.0	59.6	2,843	37.0	40.4	...
Wealth	...	...	...	4,515	100.0	100.0	177,416
Income	...	...	...	4,515	100.0	100.0	26,095
Married	2,272	61.4	58.9	1,743	38.6	41.4	...
Widowed	2,233	49.5	51.1	2,282	50.5	48.9	...
Newwidow	4,254	94.2	94.5	261	5.8	5.5	...
South	2,768	61.3	69.1	1,747	38.7	30.9	...
Nochildren	3,814	84.5	84.7	701	15.5	15.3	...
Non-white	3,780	83.7	91.1	735	16.3	8.9	...
Poorhealth	3,916	86.7	88.4	599	13.3	11.6	...
Poorhealth-wave2	3,888	86.1	87.4	627	13.9	12.6	...
Health-change	2,752	61.0	61.5	1,763	39.0	38.5	...
Male-age	...	...	...	4,515	100.0	100.0	75.82
Female-age	...	...	...	4,515	100.0	100.0	76.21

Households with at least one child

Gift	2,814	73.8	72.4	1,000	26.2	27.6	8,139
Spend-down	3,080	80.8	79.5	734	19.2	20.5	8,992
Saving	3,146	82.5	80.5	668	17.5	19.5	17,796
Hold	1,402	63.2	60.1	2,412	36.8	39.9	...
Wealth	...	...	...	3,814	100.0	100.0	179,734
Income	...	...	...	3,814	100.0	100.0	26,477
Married	2,208	57.9	55.1	1,606	42.1	44.9	...
Widowed	1,882	49.3	50.8	1,932	50.7	49.2	...
Newwidow	3,570	93.6	93.9	261	6.4	6.1	...
South	2,342	61.4	69.3	1,472	38.6	30.7	...
Nonwhite	3,244	85.1	91.9	570	14.9	8.1	...
Poorhealth	3,302	86.6	88.4	512	13.4	11.6	...
Poorhealth-wave2	3,307	80.7	88.0	507	13.3	12.0	...
Health-change	2,312	60.6	61.9	1,502	39.4	38.9	...
Trust	3,502	91.8	90.8	312	8.2	9.2	...
Estate-filing	3,737	98.0	97.8	77	2.0	2.2	...
Nonresident children	118	3.1	2.7	3,696	96.9	97.3	...
Coresident children	3,120	81.8	83.0	694	18.2	17.0	...
Grandchildren	260	6.8	6.8	3,554	93.2	93.2	...
No-earnings-info	2,459	64.5	66.3	1,355	35.5	33.7	...
Average-earnings	509	13.3	12.4	3,305	86.7	87.6	41,650
Male-age	...	...	...	3,814	100.0	100.0	75.71
Female-age	...	...	...	3,814	100.0	100.0	75.88

a. Weighted means of variables specified in dollars are reported in dollars, and of age variables in years.

Table 11A-2. *Household Wealth Quantile Distribution*

Dollars

Wealth distribution percentile	Unweighted	Weighted
All households		
1	–1,000	–700
5	0	0
10	35	600
20	6,000	12,000
30	29,000	39,600
40	50,200	64,400
50	76,500	90,000
60	104,000	122,500
70	149,500	170,126
80	213,250	243,000
90	365,000	404,700
95	580,500	632,400
99	1,238,000	1,256,000
Households with at least one child		
1	–1,250	–800
5	0	0
10	125	1,000
20	7,515	15,000
30	31,000	40,700
40	52,000	66,000
50	79,102	92,000
60	108,000	125,100
70	154,200	175,000
80	220,250	244,500
90	367,000	406,700
95	595,000	632,400
99	1,240,000	1,261,000

COMMENT BY

Jonathan Skinner

The chapter by Jonathan S. Feinstein and Chih-Chin Ho contributes to our understanding of a much neglected but important topic of research: the determinants of wealth accumulation and deaccumulation for the "old-old" near the end of the life cycle. Previous research has focused on causes for asset accumulation for younger samples of households, but information has tended to be much scarcer for those a few decades past retirement.[38]

Why should this topic be important? One reason is that there appear to be quite large changes in wealth holdings surrounding a death or serious illness. Michael Hurd and David A. Wise, for example, examined the Longitudinal Retirement History and found that among couples who were initially married in 1977 and where neither died between 1977 and 1979, median wealth declined from $332,014 to $309,686, a drop of $22,328, all figures expressed in 1999 dollars.[39] By contrast, among households in which the husband died between 1977 and 1979, median wealth fell from $304,793 to just $201,659 in those two years, a decline of $103,134, or 34 percent. If these declines in wealth surrounding a spouse's death are the consequence of, for example, health-related costs, then the appropriate model for thinking about the motivation for saving at younger ages is not entirely one that focuses on bequests but instead one that includes precautionary saving against future contingencies.[40]

The Feinstein and Ho chapter improves our understanding of the dynamics of asset accumulation among the elderly along two dimensions: by allowing a generalized covariance structure between health and asset accumulation, and by highlighting the importance of gifts made to children or other relatives. The authors present intriguing evidence of how different health status affects saving and wealth accumulation—as well as intriguing evidence on the reverse effect of economic status and mortality.

---

38. See, for example, Venti and Wise (1998) and Lusardi (1999) on asset accumulation for younger samples of households.

39. See Hurd and Wise (1989). The secular decline was likely because of inflation-related losses in assets; currently the median household appears to be gaining from stock market and other wealth holdings, for example, Hurd (1999).

40. There is some contradictory evidence on the importance of out-of-pocket expenditures following serious illness; see Smith (1999); Covinsky and others (1994); and Hurd and Smith (1999); this may be because respondents may include just medical costs in their "out-of-pocket" expenditures and not more general costs for nursing or assisted living expenditures.

The authors also provide important insights about the importance of gift giving late in the life cycle. As they note, the magnitude of gift giving is quite large and similar on average to the degree of spend down (or dissaving) among the elderly. Gifts could therefore provide, in part, one piece of the puzzle for why assets decline so rapidly near death; households may be transferring resources to their children or other relatives. Gifts are of particular interest since they reflect purely unconstrained intergenerational transfers; the donors are making the choice between handing money over to recipients or keeping the money in the form of wealth or consumption. By contrast, bequests transferred at death may well represent accidental bequests in the sense that the money was held for future life cycle or precautionary purposes.

Gift behavior is also of interest because it can represent "spend-down" behavior, an attempt to avoid asset-based means testing of programs such as Medicaid.[41] For example, the fact that Feinstein and Ho find evidence that wealthier households in poor health are more likely to transfer resources is certainly suggestive of classic spend-down behavior; those in poor health are the ones most likely to enter a nursing home and hence the ones most desirous of passing along their wealth to children or other family members.

But how does this chapter relate to estate taxation? The authors devote much of their space to establishing the important regularities in the data, which is space well spent. They also suggest several applications of their results to the estate taxation debate; for example, that estate taxes appear to encourage greater levels of gift giving, presumably as a way of escaping the estate tax. While this result seems plausible, it may also be simply an artifact of the model's structure. Wealth and saving are typically nonlinear functions of income; both the wealth to income ratio and the saving rate rise with permanent income.[42] Gift giving is also likely to be a nonlinear (and elastic) function of both income and wealth. When the econometric model is one in which income and wealth enter linearly, as in Feinstein and Ho, it could be that the remaining nonlinearities will be picked up by indicator values for high wealth (and presumably high income) households—those with trust funds and with wealth above the estate tax limit.

I think the greatest value of this chapter is not in specific measures of, for example, the elasticity of gifts with respect to the estate tax but instead with moving us toward a better understanding of motives for wealth accumulation. The standard life-cycle model without any kind of bequest motive tends to predict a simplistic deaccumulation of wealth at retirement. That

---

41. See Norton (2000).
42. Dynan, Skinner, and Zeldes (2000) and citations therein.

Feinstein and Ho estimate that, for some households, the marginal propensity to save is between 20 and 50 percent casts substantial doubt on this simple model; other studies have suggested problems with the simple life-cycle model as well.[43]

A more general model of wealth accumulation beyond the life-cycle approach is one that includes a bequest motive.[44] Certainly, the desire to leave bequests is both strong and present across income groups. Half of all households believe that leaving a bequest is either important or very important; interestingly, this ratio is nearly identical by education groups.[45] Thus there appears to be at least a strong interest in leaving bequests in the population.

A different perspective on the importance of bequests comes from other survey evidence on why people save. In the 1983–89 Survey of Consumer Finances, among those who consider themselves retired, 43 percent replied that they saved for "reserves in case of illness or emergency," with fewer than 5 percent answering that they saved "for children."[46] These results are supportive of a precautionary motive for saving against the risk of poor health rather than a bequest motive. The Feinstein and Ho estimates support the importance of considering wealth and health simultaneously, since health status is a crucial determiner of both wealth accumulation and gift behavior.

How should we reconcile the bequest model of saving with the precautionary saving model? It appears that people would like, in theory, to leave bequests, but in practice they are focusing on saving enough for precautionary purposes. Wealth serves a dual purpose; in the "bad" state of the world, it is used to provide for out-of-pocket health care (and related) purposes, and in the "good" state where the risk of chronic and costly care is low, the accumulated wealth is used for bequests or, as Feinstein and Ho emphasize, a combination of inter vivos gifts and bequests.[47] This view of bequests also includes as a lagniappe the resolution of the Samaritan's Dilemma: that the prospect of an inheritance will make their children lazy. In this revised view, children can not risk spending down their future inheritance, because they know there is a small probability that their parents will need to use up all the family assets, leaving the children without any bequest.

43. For example, Bernheim, Skinner, and Weinberg (2000).
44. See, for example, chapters by Gale and Perozek, by Laitner, and by Kaplow in this volume.
45. The result obtains by splitting the sample into three groups, those who had not graduated from high school, high school graduates, and college graduates; these education groups are used as a proxy for lifetime income. These are from the Survey of Consumer Finances (1995), courtesy of Karen Dynan (personal communication).
46. See Dynan, Skinner, and Zeldes (2000).
47. See also Dynan, Skinner, and Zeldes (2000).

Assuming this general view of asset accumulation holds, what does it imply for the design of an optimal estate tax? At first glance, it suggests that wealth accumulation should not strongly respond to the magnitude of estate taxes when the precautionary motive is of primary importance. Of course, households with very large levels of assets are not likely to be as concerned with the precautionary motive, since even the interest from a $50 million estate will be enough to provide for nursing home care with round-the-clock private nurses. These larger estates may, therefore, be more responsive to estate taxation. But among those estates of less than $5 million or so, I would expect that the most important purpose for wealth accumulation is to guard against unforeseen circumstances, implying that the tax on inheritances should not exert a strong influence on the aggregate level of wealth, although it may still affect the use of trusts, charitable contributions, and (as Feinstein and Ho have suggested) the pattern of inter vivos gifts. More directly, the possible importance of health-related spending raises a question of fairness, in the sense that elderly households incur capital gains on assets sold for the purpose of financing out-of-pocket or health-related expenditures for end-of-life care but essentially escape capital gains taxation should they die with their assets intact. In sum, the Feinstein and Ho study provides a first look at what should be a central concern of policymakers seeking to improve the estate tax, which is better understanding the financial pressures and motives for saving of elderly households at older ages.

References

Altonji, Joseph G., Fumio Hayashi, and Laurence J. Kotlikoff. 1997. "Parental Altruism and Inter Vivos Transfers: Theory and Evidence." *Journal of Political Economy* 105: 1121–66.

Bernheim, B. Douglas, Jonathan Skinner, and Stephen Weinberg. Forthcoming. "What Accounts for the Variation in Retirement Saving among U.S. Households?" *American Economic Review*.

Covinsky, Kenneth E., and others.1994. "The Impact of Serious Illness on Patients' Families." *Journal of the American Medical Association* 272 (23): 1839–44.

Deaton, Angus, Pierre-Olivier Gourinchas, and Christina Paxson. 1999. "Social Security and Inequality over the Life Cycle." Working Paper 7570. Cambridge, Mass.: National Bureau of Economic Research.

Dynan, Karen, Jonathan Skinner, and Stephen Zeldes. 2000. "Do the Rich Save More?" Working Paper 7906. Cambridge, Mass.: National Bureau of Economic Research (September).

Feinstein, Jonathan S. 1997. "Strategies for Estimating the Estate and Gift Tax Gap: A Report Prepared for the Internal Revenue Service Economic Analysis and Modeling Group." Final Report. Internal Revenue Service (September).

Feinstein, Jonathan S., and Chih-Chin Ho. 1999. "An Empirical Analysis of Gift-Giving in Later Life." Mimeo.

Hubbard, R. Glenn, Jonathan Skinner, and Stephen P. Zeldes. 1995. "Precautionary Saving and Social Insurance." *Journal of Political Economy* 103: 360–99.

Hurd, Michael, and James P. Smith. 1999. "Anticipated and Actual Bequests." Working Paper 7380. Cambridge, Mass.: National Bureau of Economic Research.

Hurd, Michael, and David A. Wise. 1989. "The Wealth and Poverty of Widows: Assets before and after the Husband's Death." In *The Economics of Aging,* edited by David A. Wise, 177–99. University of Chicago Press and National Bureau of Economic Research.

Hurd, Michael D., Daniel McFadden, and Angela Merrill. 1998. "Healthy, Wealthy, and Wise? Socioeconomic Status, Morbidity, and Mortality among the Elderly." Contributed Papers 1887. Econometric Society World Congress, Evanston, Ill.

———. 1999. "Predictors of Mortality among the Elderly." Mimeo.

Lusardi, Annamaria. 1999. "Information, Expectations, and Savings for Retirement." In *Behavioral Dimensions of Retirement Economics,* edited by Henry Aaron, 81–115. Brookings and Russell Sage Foundation.

McGarry, Kathleen. 1998. "Inter Vivos Transfers and Intended Bequests." Unpublished. UCLA.

Norton, Edward. 2000. "Long-Term Care." In *Handbook of Health Economics,* edited by Anthony Culyer and Joseph Newhouse, 955–94. New York: Elsevier.

Poterba, James. 1998. "Estate and Gift Taxes and Incentives for Inter Vivos Giving in the United States." Working Paper 6842. Cambridge, Mass.: National Bureau of Economic Research (December).

Smith, James P. 1999. "Healthy Bodies and Thick Wallets: The Dual Relationship between Health and Economic Status." *Journal of Economic Perspectives* 13 (Spring): 145–66.

Soldo, Beth J., and others. 1997. "Asset and Health Dynamics among the Oldest Old: An Overview of the AHEAD Study." *Journals of Gerontology* 52B, series B (Special Is1–20.

Venti, Steven F., and David A. Wise. 1998. "The Cause of Wealth Dispersion at Retirement: Choice versus Chance?" *American Economic Review* 88 (May): 185–91.

Contributors

Alan J. Auerbach
University of California, Berkeley

Leonard Burman
The Urban Institute and
  Georgetown Public Policy Institute

Martha Britton Eller
Internal Revenue Service

Brian Erard
B. Erard & Associates

Jonathan S. Feinstein
Yale University School of
  Management

William G. Gale
Brookings Institution

Roger H. Gordon
University of California,
  San Diego

Jane Gravelle
Congressional Research Service

James R. Hines Jr.
University of Michigan

Chih-Chin Ho
Internal Revenue Service

Douglas Holtz-Eakin
Syracuse University

Barry W. Johnson
Internal Revenue Service

505

David Joulfaian
U.S. Treasury Department

Louis Kaplow
Harvard Law School

Wojciech Kopczuk
University of Michigan

John Laitner
University of Michigan

Kathleen McGarry
University of California, Los Angeles

Jacob M. Mikow
Internal Revenue Service

Maria G. Perozek
*Board of Governors of the Federal
Reserve System*

Pierre Pestieau
University of Liège

James M. Poterba
Massachusetts Institute of Technology

Richard Schmalbeck
Duke University Law School

Jonathan Skinner
Dartmouth College

Joel Slemrod
University of Michigan

C. Eugene Steuerle
The Urban Institute

Scott Weisbenner
*Board of Governors of the Federal
Reserve System*

Index

Abolition of estate tax, 55, 56, 164
Adjusted taxable estate, 5, 74
Administrative issues, 37–43
    costs, 37, 41, 155, 189–90
    tax avoidance, 154–55
Age distribution of taxpayers, 79-80
    wealth accumulation and tax avoidance, 332–37, 343
Annuities, 34, 93, 138
Art works, 142, 406
Asset and Health Dynamics among the Oldest Old (AHEAD)
    health considerations for elderly asset management, 459, 473–79
    income level of children and gift making, 464
    savings and level of gift making, 464
Asset protection trusts, 139
Audit study of estate tax returns, 385–94, 411–21
Avoidance. See Tax avoidance

Bank accounts, 89
Bentham, Jeremy, 221

Bequests vs. inter vivos gifts, 196–97, 210–11. See also Charitable bequests
Bonds, 86

Canada, 438
Capital gains
    constructive realization at death, 447–48
    and elderly asset management, 470
    family businesses and estate tax liability, 48
    inter vivos gifts, 54
    preferential tax treatment, 29
    unrealized as share of net worth, 439–42
    See also Unrealized capital gains taxed at death
Capital gains tax
    angel-of-death loophole, 450–52
    basis step-up at death, 422–23
    carry-over basis, 56, 447, 450, 455
    Death Tax Elimination Act of 2000, 450, 455
    exemption of unrealized capital gains, 106
    long-term gains, 426–27

Taxpayer Relief Act of *1997,* 424–26
See also Unrealized capital gains taxed at
        death
Capital income tax, 211
Charitable bequests, 354
    effect of estate and income tax, 350
    determinants of level and timing, 352–54
    vs. lifetime giving, 360, 362–73
    share of total bequests, 350
Charitable contribution deduction,
    unlimited, 5, 98, 102–06
    dynastic accumulation of wealth and,
        110
    foundations established by donor, 127
    incentives to charitable giving, 102
    and income tax, 53
    optimal tax framework analysis of trans-
        fer taxes, 199–201
    tax avoidance, 54, 115–17, 123–27, 150
Charitable institutions, 105
Charitable lead trusts (CLTs)
    abuse, 126
    advantages over simple split gifts, 126
    tax avoidance, 125
    unavailability of income during term of
        trust, 145
Charitable lifetime giving, 356
    vs. charitable bequests, 360, 362–73
    Deficit Reduction Act of *1984,* 352
    effect of estate tax and income tax on,
        350
    determinants of level and timing,
        352–54
    tax avoidance, 123–27
    tax on unrealized capital gains at death,
        455
    Tax Reform Act of *1986,* 352
Charitable remainder annuity trusts
    (CRATs), 124
Charitable remainder unitrusts (CRUTs),
    124
Church v. *United States,* 133
Community property, 91
Compliance costs, 37, 153
    and efficiency, 41
    optimal tax framework analysis, 189–90
    tax avoidance, 151–54

Congressional Budget Office (CBO), 12,
    56
Conservation easements, 15, 72
Consumption, lifetime
    effect of estate tax on, 308
    increased as tax avoidance technique, 139
    wealth accumulation and tax avoidance,
        309
Credit shelter trusts, 129
Credits. *See* Tax credits
Crummey trusts, 122, 131

Death Tax Elimination Act of *2000,* 450,
    455
Deductions, 98–101
    debts of decedent, 74, 98
    estate administration costs, 74, 98
    family businesses, 47, 74, 162
    farms, 47, 162
    funeral expenses, 74
    mortgages, 98
    Revenue Act of *1916,* 67
    statistical analysis of *1998* estate tax
        deductions, 9
    tax avoidance, 115, 162
    tax basis of capital assets, proposal, 56
    See also Charitable contribution
        deduction, unlimited;
    Marital deduction, unlimited, Qualified
        terminable interest property
Deficit Reduction Act of *1984,* 72, 352
Dividends, 448
Dynasty trusts, 139

Economic Recovery and Tax Act of *1981,*
    15, 71, 72
Elderly asset management, 479–92,
    499–502
    Asset and Health Dynamics among the
        Oldest Old, 459, 473–79
    capital gains income, 470
    changes in family structure, 463
    estate tax effects, 462, 465–73, 500, 502
    health changes and lifetime consumption,
        485
    income effects, 462, 487
    income level of children, 464

inter vivos gifts, 465–73
labor income, 470
lifetime consumption and gift making,
    468, 489
number of children, 463, 488, 490
savings and gift making, 463, 468, 469,
    482, 489
Survey of Consumer Finances, 501
See also Health considerations
Equity, 23–32
    burden of payment on donor, 23
    burden of payment on recipient, 28
    vs. efficiency, 33
    estate tax, 2, 3
    family businesses, 48
    horizontal equity, 30
    optimal taxation, 33
    parental rights regarding inheritance, 31
    redistribution of wealth, 181–86
    societal rights regarding inheritance, 31
    taxation at death, 32
    tax avoidance and evasion, 40, 206
    unmarried persons and marital
        deduction, 31
Estate planning
    compliance costs, 38
    post mortem, 140–42
Estate tax, generally
    arguments against, 1, 65, 106, 299
    arguments for, 2, 65, 106, 107, 299
    as property tax, 109
    as limiting dynastic accumulation of
        wealth, 108–11
    tax-exclusive nature, 7
Evasion. See Tax evasion
Exclusions
    conservation easements, 15
    family businesses, 15, 72
    Tax Reform Act of 1976, 71
    Taxpayer Relief Act of 1997, 72
    See also Inter vivos gifts, annual tax
        exclusion
Exemptions, 14, 106
Exemption, effective
    Economic Recovery and Tax Act of
        1981, 15
    historical development, 16

projections under current law, 12
proposals to raise, 57, 158
Tax Reform Act of 1976, 15
Taxpayer Relief Act of 1997, 15, 72, 423

Family businesses, 45–47
    asset valuation methods, 47, 93, 94
    community property, 91
    deductions, 47, 74, 162
    estate tax noncompliance, 406
    exclusions, 15, 72
    installment payments, 48, 77
    jointly owned property, 89
    share of taxable estates, 49
    special treatment under estate tax, 47
    tax avoidance, 162
    Taxpayer Relief Act of 1997, 72
Family limited liability companies
    valuation discounts, 97
Family limited partnerships
    annual gift exclusion, 132–36
    tax avoidance techniques, 132–36, 151
    timing of transfers, 134
    valuation discounts, 97
Farms, 45–47
    assets of estates, 88
    asset valuation methods, 47, 94
    community property, 91
    deductions, 47, 162
    estate tax noncompliance, 406
    installment payments, 48, 77
    jointly owned property, 89
    share of taxable estates, 49
    tax avoidance, 162
Foreign countries
    asset protection trusts, 139
    estate taxes, 75
    inheritance taxes, 164, 205
    tax evasion, 205
    transfer taxes, 12, 18, 19, 66
Foundations, 127
Funeral expenses, 74

Gender composition of taxpayers, 79–81
    estate tax audit study, 390, 418
    wealth accumulation and tax avoidance,
        332–36

Generation-skipping transfer tax, 7, 77
  tax avoidance considerations, 118–20
  Tax Reform Act of *1976,* 71
  Tax Reform Act of *1986,* 15
Geographic distribution of taxpayers,
  79–80
Gifts. *See* Bequests; Charitable lifetime
  giving; Inter vivos gifts; Split gifts
Grantor retained trusts (GRTs)
  death of grantor during term of trust,
    137
  grantor retained annuity trusts (GRATs),
    136
  grantor retained income trusts (GRITs),
    136
  grantor retained unitrusts (GRUTs),
    136
  intentionally defective grantor trusts
    (IDGTs), 138
  qualified personal residence trusts
    (QPRTs), 137
  tax avoidance techniques, 136–38
Great Britain, 311
Gross estate, 4, 9, 73, 85, 218
  jointly owned property, 89
  life insurance, 161
  QTIP, 74
  Revenue Act of *1916,* 67

Health and Retirement Study, 51
Health considerations, 480–94
  analytical model, 465–73, 499–502
  Asset and Health Dynamics among the
    Oldest Old, 459, 473–79
  elderly asset management, 459–96
  estate tax, 500, 502
  gift making, 487
  health changes and consumption levels,
    485
  recent health history as determinant of
    future asset management, 463, 492
Historical development of transfer taxes,
  12, 66-67
  Deficit Reduction Act of *1984,* 72
  Economic Recovery and Tax Act of
    1981, 15, 71

effective exemption, 16
  estate tax, 14
  foreign countries, 12, 66
  gift tax, 14
  inheritance taxes, 14, 66
  marginal tax rates, 16
  Omnibus Budget Reconciliation Act of
    1993, 15
  Revenue Acts (*1916–87*), 67, 70, 72
  revenues, historical trends, 17
  share of taxable estates, 17
  Taxpayer Relief Act of *1997,* 15, 72
  Tax Reform Act of *1976,* 14, 70
  Tax Reform Act of *1986,* 15
  United States, 14, 66–72
Human capital, 194–96

Income tax
  applicability to estates ruled unconstitu-
    tional, 14
  and charitable bequests, 350
  and charitable lifetime giving, 350
  charitable remainder annuity trusts, 124
  charitable remainder unitrusts, 124
  combined impact with transfer taxes, 165
  estate tax as backstop of, 106, 189
  progressivity compared with estate tax,
    24
  Sixteenth Amendment, 14
  Tax Reform Act of *1986,* 57
  treating transfers as income, 190–91
  See also Capital gains tax
Inequality, 279–81
  effect of eliminating transfer taxes,
    261–66, 293–96
  intertemporal elasticity of substitution
    and altruism, 271–77, 288–92
  lifetime consumption and altruism,
    268–70
Inheritance taxes
  continental compared with Anglo-Saxon
    estate tax model, 209
  estate tax distinguished, 57
  flexibility of estate tax compared, 207
  foreign countries, 164, 205
  historical development, 14, 66
  replacing estate tax with, 57

Insurance trusts, 130–31
Intergenerational transfers, 19–23, 175–77
    mixed motives, 208
    motives and estate tax effect on savings,
        217, 218–23, 235
    nonrational reasons for, 201
Intergenerational transfers, accidental
    bequest model, 19
    effect of estate tax on savings, 218–19,
        224–25, 236, 239–41
    optimal tax framework analysis of trans-
        fer taxes, 180–81
Intergenerational transfers, altruistic
    model, 21
    effect of eliminating estate tax on
        inequality and wealth accumulation,
        258–61
    effect of estate tax on savings, 219–22,
        227–35, 237, 243–47
    and efficiency, 35
    optimal tax framework analysis of trans-
        fer taxes, 177–78
Intergenerational transfers, exchange
    model, 22
    effect of estate tax on savings, 220,
        225–27, 236, 241–43
    optimal tax framework analysis of trans-
        fer taxes, 179–80
Intergenerational transfers, giving per se
    model, 22
    effect of estate tax on savings, 220
    optimal tax framework analysis of trans-
        fer taxes, 178–79
Intergenerational transfers, Samaritan's
    Dilemma model, 35
    effect of estate tax on savings, 237
Internal Revenue Service, Statistics of
    Income Division, 73, 386
Inter vivos gifts, 51
    capital gains realization to reduce tax
        liability, 54
    compared with bequests, 50, 196–97,
        210–11
    intrafamily division of wealth, 52
    and labor supply, 196
    step-up of basis as tax disincentive, 7

taxable at same rate as gifts at death
    proposed, 160, 196
tax on unrealized capital gains at death,
    448, 452–54, 455
timing, 51
unlimited marital deduction, 52
See also Charitable lifetime giving
Inter vivos gifts, annual tax exclusion, 4,
    120–23, 426
    Crummey trusts, 122
    Economic Recovery and Tax Act of
        1981, 72
    effectiveness of planning, 143
    family limited partnerships, 132–36, 135
    insurance trusts, 131
    minors, gifts to, 122
    underutilization, 121, 201
    use-it-or-lose-it nature, 50

Joint Committee on Taxation (JCT), 12,
    454
Joint tenancy, 89

Labor supply
    effect of estate tax, 45
    elderly asset management and labor
        income, 470
    inter vivos gifts, 196
    literature review, 310–13
    wealth accumulation and tax avoidance,
        309
Life insurance
    assets of estates, 86
    distortion of choice in tax avoidance
        techniques, 150
    inclusion in gross estate, 161
    insurance trusts, 130–31
Loopholes, 57, 158

Marital deduction, unlimited, 5, 14, 74,
    98–99
    credit shelter trusts, 129
    disadvantages to children, 159
    and dynastic accumulation of wealth,
        110
    Economic Recovery and Tax Act of
        1981, 71

equity issues, 31
inter vivos gifts, 52
post mortem estate planning, 140–42
Revenue Act of *1948,* 70
tax avoidance, 115–17, 128–30, 149
See also Qualified terminable interest
property
Marital status, 81
equity issues, 31
estate tax audit study, 390
estate tax noncompliance, 382
estate tax revenues, 432–34
wealth accumulation and tax avoidance,
321, 333–36, 343
Mill, John Stuart, 221
Minors, gifts to, 122
Mortality tables, 311, 428

Net estate, 5
Net worth, 315, 340, 342
New York Trust Company v. *Eisner,* 67
Noncompliance with estate tax
compared with intentional tax evasion,
420
family businesses, 406
farms, 406
responsibility for, 406
simulation analysis, 311, 376–85,
417–21, 436
unique features of estate tax, 375–76
See also Audit study of estate tax returns

Occupational distribution of taxpayers,
81–85
Omnibus Budget Reconciliation Act of
1993, 15
Organization for Economic Cooperation
and Development (OECD), 18, 19

Parental rights regarding inheritance, 31
Pension plans, 111
Post mortem estate planning, 140–42
Previously paid gift taxes, 5, 75
Progressivity of estate tax, 14, 29, 34,
424–25
burden of payment on donor, 23
burden of payment on recipient, 28

compared with income tax, 24
optimal tax framework analysis of transfer taxes, 181
tax avoidance and evasion, 40

Qualified personal residence trusts (QPRTs)
tax avoidance, 137
Qualified terminable interest property
(QTIP)
deductions, 71, 101–02
in gross estate, 74
trusts, 129

Real estate, 86, 89, 91, 93, 142
Reform of transfer taxes, 55–57, 157
closing loopholes, 57, 158
fire-sale valuation elimination, 161
inheritance tax replacing estate tax, 57
inter vivos gifts taxable at same rate as
gifts at death, 160
life insurance in gross estate, 161
minority discounts elimination, 161
raising effective exemption, 57, 158
reducing tax rates, 57, 158
scaling back, 56
tax avoidance, 55
Tax Reform Act of *1986,* 57
See also Abolition of estate tax
Retirement benefits, 86
Revenue Act of *1916,* 67
Revenue Act of *1924,* 70
Revenue Act of *1926,* 70
Revenue Act of *1932,* 70
Revenue Act of *1935,* 70
Revenue Act of *1948,* 70
Revenue Act of *1987,* 72
Revenues, 12, 17, 42
alternative death taxes, 442–48
marital status, effect, 432–34
optimal tax framework analysis of rais-
ing revenues through transfer taxes,
186–88
Ricardo, David, 221

Savings, 43-45, 218–23, 235–37, 248–53
accidental bequest model, 218–19,
224–25, 236, 239–41

altruistic model, 219–22, 227–35, 237, 243–47
donors' savings, 249–50
and efficiency, 248
exchange model, 220, 225–27, 236, 241–43
literature review, 310–13
misconceptions, 216, 248
motive of donor, 217, 218–23, 235
optimal tax framework analysis of effect of transfer taxes, 188–89
recipients' savings, 44, 250–52
Samaritan's Dilemma model, 237
Savings bonds, 91
Securities, 93
Size of estate, 431–38
Smith, Adam, 221
Soak-up taxes, 5
Social Security, 272, 330
Social welfare considerations of transfer taxes
accidental bequest model, 180–81
administrative costs, 189–90
altruistic model, 177–78
charitable transfers, 199–201
compliance costs, 189–90
donor-donee relationships, 197–99
donors' utility maximization, 168–69
exchange model, 179–80
giving per se model, 178–79
human capital, 194–96
inter vivos gifts taxable at same rate as gifts at death, 196
maximization, 169
optimal tax framework analysis, 167–204
progressivity of estate tax, 181
raising revenues, 186–88
redistribution of wealth, 181–86
reducing wealth accumulation, 191–93
and savings, 188–89
transfers vs. ordinary consumption, 170–72
Special use valuation of assets, 4, 94–95
Split gifts, 70, 125
State estate and gift taxes, 5, 75, 321
Stocks, 86, 318, 319, 330

Survey of Consumer Finances, 51, 311, 376–94, 423, 452–54, 501

Tangible property, 93
Tax avoidance, 40, 113–14, 159–63, 307–10, 321–22, 337–40, 344–47
annuities, 138
asset protection trusts, 139
charitable contribution deductions, 54, 115–17
charitable lifetime giving, 123–27
charitable trusts, 124, 125
costs, 38, 149–55
credit shelter trusts, 129
dilution of asset value through discounts, 97
distortion of choice in tax avoidance techniques, 149
dynasty trusts, 139
effectiveness of planning, 142
and efficiency,
and equity, 41
estate tax, 114–16
with falling asset valuation, 144
foundations established by donor, 127
generation-skipping transfer tax, 118–20
gift tax, 14, 116–18
gifts to minors, 122
grantor retained trusts, 136
Great Britain, 311
inconsistent with dispositive wishes, 129, 149
increased lifetime consumption, 139
insurance trusts, 130–31
intentionally defective grantor trusts, 138
literature review, 310–13
marginal tax rates, 331
marital deductions, 115–17, 128–30
marital status, 321, 333–36, 343
misconceptions, 113, 144, 156
QTIP trusts, 129
QPRTs, 137
reform of estate tax, 43
and revenues, 42

tax return data, 322–37, 340–43
trusts, 118
unavailability of income, 145
unlimited charitable contribution
    deduction, 54, 115–17
unlimited marital deduction, 115–17,
    128–30
valuation discounts, 48, 97
See also Inter vivos gifts, annual tax
    exclusion; Noncompliance with
    estate tax
Tax credits, 5, 71, 72, 75, 218
Tax evasion, 40, 41
    foreign countries, problems in, 205
    reform of estate tax, 43
    transfer taxes as means of eliminating,
    187
    vs. unintentional noncompliance, 420
    See also Noncompliance with estate tax
Tax liens on deferred payments, 78
Tax rates, 5, 42, 336–37
    Deficit Reduction Act of *1984,* 72
    Economic Recovery and Tax Act of
    1981, 72
    long-term capital gains tax, 426–27
    marginal, 6, 16, 42, 324–27, 331
    reduction proposed, 57, 158
    Revenue Act of *1987,* 72
    unified rate structure, 15, 70, 116
Tax Reform Act of *1976*
    effective exemption, 15
    generation-skipping transfer tax, 71
    gift tax rates, 18
    unified rate structure, 15, 70, 116
Tax Reform Act of *1986*
    charitable gifts beyond original donor
    basis, 352
    estate tax revenue projections, 12
    generation-skipping transfer tax, 15
    income tax vs. estate tax reforms, 57
Taxpayer Relief Act of *1997*
    capital gains tax, 424–26
    effective exemption, 15, 72, 423–24
    family businesses, 72
    special use valuation, 95
    unified credit, 72, 218

Tenancies by the entirety, 89
Transfer taxes, generally, 4–19, 57–58, 58
    equal opportunity as justification, 184
    extension proposed, 164
    incidence, 23
    as penalty on success, 193
    See also Historical development of trans-
    fer taxes
Trusts, 118. *See also specific trusts by name*

Uniform Transfers to Minors Act, 122
Unrealized capital gains taxed at death,
    448–49, 454–55
    Canada, 438
    distributional burdens compared,
    438–48
    liquidity problems, 451
    and revenues, effect on, 442–48, 451
    share of net worth, 439–42
U.S. Joint Economic Committee, 299

Valuation of assets
    annuities, 93
    art works, 142
    blockage discounts, 97, 141
    dilution of value, 97
    discounts in valuation, 48, 95–98
    estate tax audit study, 392
    fair market value, 4, 93
    family businesses, 47, 93, 94
    family limited liability companies, 97
    family limited partnerships, 97, 132
    farms, 47, 94
    fire-sale valuation, 142, 161
    key man discounts, 97
    lack of marketability discounts, 96
    minority discounts, 95, 161
    noncompliance with estate tax, 406
    real estate, 93, 142
    Revenue Act of *1935,* 70
    securities, 93
    stocks, 330
    tangible property, 93
    See also Special use valuation of assets
Vulture trusts
    abuse of charitable lead trusts by use of,
    126

Wealth accumulation, 259–61, 321–22,
    279-81, 315–21, 328–30, 337–40
  age of donor, 308
  analytical models, 293–96, 300–37,
    344–47
  decrease in reported net assets, 315,
    337, 345
  intertemporal elasticity of substitution
    and degree of altruism, 271–77,
    288–92
  labor supply response, 309
  lifetime consumption and, 268, 309
  literature review, 310–13
  marginal tax rates, 324, 326–27, 331
  marital status, 321, 333–36, 343
  tax return data, 322–37, 340–43
Wealth tax
  proposed as alternative to transfer taxes,
    211
Welfare considerations. *See* Social welfare
    considerations of transfer taxes
Widows and widowers, 390, 419, 488, 493